ENGLISH RECUSANT LITERATURE
1558–1640

Selected and Edited by
D. M. ROGERS

Volume 332

JOHN RASTELL
The Third Booke
1566

JOHN RASTELL
The Third Booke
1566

The Scolar Press
1977

ISBN 0 85967 348 0

Published and printed in Great Britain by
The Scolar Press Limited, 59-61 East Parade,
Ilkley, Yorkshire and
39 Great Russell Street,
London WC1

NOTE

Reproduced (original size) from a copy in the library of Downside Abbey, by permission of the Abbot and Community. In this copy the following pages are damaged, and are reproduced in the facsimile from a copy in the British Library, by permission of the Board: title-page, aii^r, aiii^{r-v}, aiv^r, bi^v, bii^r, xi^{r-v}, xii^{r-v}, xiii^{r-v}.

Reference: Allison and Rogers 708; not in STC.

THE THIRD

BOOKE, DECLARING BY

Examples out of Auncient Councels, Fathers, and Later writers, that it is time to

BEWARE OF

M: IEWEL.

By Iohn Raftel Mafter of Art and
Student of Diuinitie.

Math.7.

Beware of falfe Prophets, which come vnto
you in the cotes of sheepe, but inwardly are Ra-
uening wolues, &c.

COELI · ET · PVLOS · CORVORVM · RESPICITE VOLATILIA

I F

ANTVERPIAE,
Ex officina Ioannis Fouleri.
M. D. LXVI.

TO the Indifferent Reader.

I PERFOVRME now vnto thee (Indifferent Reader) that which I Promised in my laſt booke, which was, to geue thee other Argumentes, then preſently at that time I did proſecute, for which thou ſhouldeſt B E V V A R E of M. Iewel: The Arguments côſiſt in theſe pointes, that M. Iewel

1   Hath made an vnreaſonable Ac= *Fol. 1.* compt vpon the firſt ſix hundꝛed yeares.

2   That him ſelfe vſeth the Teſtimo= *Fol. 22.* nies of what ſo euer Age.

3   That he wil not ſtand to the Te= *Fol. 40.* ſtimonies of the firſt ſix hundꝛed yeares.

4   That he vſeth the ſelfe ſame Teſti= *Fol. 83.* monies of the firſt ſix hundꝛed yeares, a= gainſt which he bꝛingeth Exceptions.

5   That he alleageth ſuch Authoꝛities *Fol. 95.* of Fathers, as do plainely confound the Pꝛoceedinges.

6   That he alleageth foꝛ him ſelfe the *Fol. 104.*

A ij   woꝛdes

woordes and deedes of Old condemned
Heretiques.

These be the Argumentes, made to
perswade thee, to *BEVVARE* of M. Ie=
wel, And these I haue confirmed and de=
clared, by their propre and peculiar Ex=
amples. what remaineth then? Any
other thing, than that such a destroyer &
spoiler

spoiler of Soules, should be brought to
his Answer? This in deede should be
done with the first, if there were that
care in men, of their Soules, as should
be in them, that acknowledge any Im=
mortalitie of the Soule.

But I may wel compare, the seeing
and suffering of false and blind Teachers
that now take cure of Soules, to the per=
mitting & honouring of Mountebanks,
that goe abroad with diuerse thinges for
mens Bodies.

These Mountebanks, are a free kind
of wanderers, Pedlars, Surgeans,   *Mounte-
Physitians, Historiographers, Poetes,   banks for
or what so euer name besides you wil   the Body.*
geue vnto them, men altogeather for the
penie, which is the cause that they pro=
fesse so many thinges. They take vp
their standing in Market places, or void
roomes meete for the cōcourse of people,
there they set a stoole to stand vpon, or
make a litle scaffold for the purpose, from
which they play their part.

Their Greatest Grace is in the
Countenance & Tongue, through which,
they looke so Saddely, and speake so

eloquent=

eloquētly, that a man would sweare vpō
a booke for them, that they thinke as they
speake, & speak nomore, than they wil do.

what so euer thing they haue to sel,
as Newes out of India, Or The Original
of the Turkishe Empire , Or Mery Tales,
Or Songes and Ballets, Or a Pouder to kil
wormes , Or A Preseruatiue againste the
Plague , Or A Water to make the skynne
faire and white, Or Pinnes, Pointes, Laces,
whistles, & other such ware, whatsoeuer it
be , they commend it and praise it before .
But they doe it with such a Grace , with
such a Constancie, with such Copie of
words, with such mouing of Affections,
that it is wonderful . As

If it be a water, a Pouder, an Oynt=
mente , a Confection not worth twentie
pence, he wil make such a doe about it, as
though it could scarse be bought for halfe
a Kinges raunsome . And standing first
vp like a worshipful man , Arayed in his
silkes and veluettes , And al to be rayed
with braslettes & bowed peeces of golde,
And chained about the neck with a great
thing (of copper and gylt, as many iudge,
but) of pure and fine gold, as farre as the

cye

eye seeth, he wil tel his Audience : That
he is come vnto them for good wils sake,
moued in him by the Fame and worthi=
nes of them and theyr Citie or Toune :
He will tell them, that he can not tarie
long, & that, before he depart, he would
faine bestow vpon them some token of
his good affection : Then wil he bring
furth that water or pouder, or conceipt,
which he would vtter, and say, That it
was brought from beyonde Calecut, or
the Red Sea: and then wil he point with
his finger towardes Calecut, and make a
like digressiō, to declare how far that is
of, from their Countrie, as M. Iewel
doth to praise (after his maner) ye Popes
of Rome: after this, he wil shew the ver=
tue and strength of his Pouder : And
further declare, how much thereof hath
been bought in greate Cities, and of
noble Personages which he wil name :
and further yet, he wil make them think,
that it is al that he hath leaft, that which
he offereth to be bought of them : He wil
also disgrace other Mountebankes that
goe abroad the Countrie, and say, That
their wares are but counterfeit, but that

A iiij   his

his are fine, and pure, and fresh. For why
he seeketh not after gaines, as the coue=
tous and beggarly knaues doe, but as it
becommeth a good Gentleman, he tra=
uaileth farre and wide vpon his owne
Charges to get such geare, as may bring
Commodities to whole Countries. In
Coclusion, when he hath spoken as much
as he can, then he prouoketh the hearers
againe and againe to bye. And if it be
a water which he commended, he putteth
in Glasses, made for the purpose, halfe a
skore or a skore of droppes thereof : If
it be a pouder, he putteth as much as he
can hold betwen his Thombe and Fore=
finger, in seueral papers, and beginneth
to make merchandise. And that which
as it should seeme by his tale, should be
wel worth a Croune a droppe, he wil sel,
with good gaines, for a myte or two, of
which, twelue do make but a penie.

Such maner of Fellowes be the
Mountebankes. But what say the
Lordes and Signiours of the Townes
vnto them? They contemne them vn=
doubtedly in their Iudgement, & thinke
it not al worth the taking vp, which they
so

fo highly commend . Yet they laugh at
them, and fay that fo good and eloquent
an Oration, as they make to the people,
doth them a farthingworth of good, at $\bar{y}$
leaft, in relieuing their fpirits, and mouing their Affections . So that there
is no greate harme done , although it be
nothing worth, that which they vtter .
Efpecially wheras fome of the Mountebankes, do either by Singing, or plaieng
vpon Inftrumentes, fo hold the people
in the meane tyme, whiles they looke
for their merchantes, that for their fitte
of mirth onely, they are worthy of fomewhat. And befides this, al is not counterfeit, that they put furth to fale , and
though they make it more in words, than
it is worth, yet if they fhould hold their
peace altogeather, it is not nothing that
which they fel. And in Conclufion,
whiles they hurt not the State and the
Common welth, let the people and them
cope togeather, what is that to great af-
faires?

A Montebank then, may crake, and
lie, and outface his Aduerfarie, and make
fomewhat of nothing, and mingle fporte

with sadnesse, and play what part he wil in the sight of the people, and hundreds wil gase vpon him, but none wil reproue him.

Mountebankes for ye Soule.

Like vnto these, in an other kinde, there be other Mountebankes, men so free, that they be lawlesse, So ful of faire promises, that they sel, for one comming vnto them, euerlasting life, So louing & kind harted, that they forsake their owne Countrie, and without asking of licence, or directly against commaundment, bye and sel within other mens Jurisdiction.

Yet, in Faith, they doe it somewhat manerly, they rush not into Cities and Townes at the first, but, without the Towne walles, they choose out a place in the open fielde, or in some wodde, and xx. or xxx. turues being cut & set one vpõ the other, there straitewaies is a place for the Preacher, and there straitwaies doth the Mountebanke beginne to open.

But what stuffe it is, that he there openeth, it can not be declared in a short time and Preface. the Sõme yet is this: That he commeth vnto them with comfortable wares: That he commeth from farre

farre Countries : That except they wil
be thankeful and receiue the Grace that
he bringeth, he wil depart againe : That
he wil aske nothing for his labor : That
he deliuereth them quite, from feare of
Purgatorie, and Hel also (for Purgato=
torie there is none at al, and to hel he wil
warrant them neuer to come) That thei
shal haue no more bonde of fasting, wat=
ching, praying, performing of lawfull
vowes, &c : That they shal haue no more
Signe of Crosse, or Christ, or our Lady,
or any Sainct in their eye, nor any me=
morie of them in their hart, & ý they shal
haue al peace & cõfort, if they wil bye but
one dram of the doctrine ý he bringeth .

And then he instructeth them in the
Doctrine of Caluin, Or (if the Mounte=
banke be a Lutheran) in the Doctrine of
Luther, Or (if he be an Anabaptist) in
the Doctrine of Rotman .   For the
Mountebankes be of sundry sectes, and
euery one praiseth his own wares most,
and contemneth his felowes packe .

The people then, hearing of so great
treasures to be sold so good cheape, And
being wery of the discipline and grauitie

The effect
of the
Mounte
bankes
of wisdom...

of th' Auncient Religiō, they quickly take that is taught them, and within very few daies after, they were rauished with such a Contemplation of the worlde to come, that they vtterly forgotte, al honesty, and Iustice of this world. And whiles they were in that pangue and *extasis*, like men cleane besides them selues, they runne about the Cities and Countries, And of al places desired to be in Churches & Religious houses. For the Mounte-bankes alwaies lightly, doe commend Obedience vnto the Superior powers, & exhort their Audience most earnestly, to keepe their handes from doing of wrong to the Cōmenaltie.

Therefore, whether it were for Deuotion to the Church and houses of Religion, or for reuerence of their Preacher which had counselled them to be Iniurious to no man, they did not meddle with priuate mens houses, nor put them at al, directly, in any Feare. But in the Churches, their Sprite worked, and inflamed them, and fretted them, and rauished them.

In heate and force of which Sprite, they

they plucke downe Images, breake Aul= **Churches spoiled.**
ters, Spoile the vestrie of Copes, Chali=
ces, Ornamentes, Treasures, take the
very Seates and Seeling of the Chur=
ches away : Tread the Sacrament vn=
der their feete , and in their hartes, sang
al that while, praises (I trow) vnto the
Lord .

    That done , to shew their Charitie
towardes their neighbour also, as they
had by these former Signes , testified it
clearly before God , They brake open ye̸ **Poore Friers & Nonnes robbed.**
poore Celles of Friers & Nonnes, they
take violently from them, their Books,
their Clothing, their Bedding, & (which
was exceeding Charitie) they did not
kil them .   But that in deede was exce=
ding Charitie, for now thei are sory of it,
and they wil study to bring that Charity
into Order , and kil whom they take of
the Cloister, the next time that ye̸ Sprite
moueth them .

    But to make an end, after the Church
and Cloister spoiled, thei go into the Li= **Libraries burned.**
braries, and of one whole one, in ye̸ Graie
Friers at Antwerpe (which was ful of
many and goodly bookes) they left not

one vnburned . In other places, they did cut onely the Bookes , Oz sel them, oz cary them away .

Prouisiō of meat cast away. And by this time they were thirsty, I trow. For as for meat, many in these Coū tries care not much, as appeareth by the casting away of the barreled bief, & other promisiō, as y Graie Friers had gathered of almes, for this whole yere remaining.

To the good wine therefore and Beere, they make more hast , and when they had their heades ful thereof, for the *Wastlinesse.* nonce they pul out the spiket, and let the rest runne abroad in the Floore . And in the Abbey of S. Michels in Antwerp, they dranke so much, that they laie down in y celler not able to stand oz go away, oz lye waking. and they let out so much beere and wine, setting al tappes open, that they had ben drowned in it, if other more sober had not come thither, & pulled them out.

Verely this is a sowsing Gospel, which so embrueth the mindes of the folowers of it: And these are perfite and excellent Mountebanks, which can geue such preseruatiues, against al Godlines, and

and Obedience, and Honestie. If there
had ben any Feare of God or Man, remaining in these mens hartes, woulde
they haue spoiled Innocentes, Or without lawful Authoritie, haue enterprised
feates so desperate? Crake not of these
Proceedinges, O ye feruent and hote
spirited Merchantes of this worlde, and
send no letters of praise to the Lorde for
this victorie, which consisted in oppressing
of Innocentes, and in plaine robbing of
Churches. Came our Sauiour into
the worlde with such terrour? Did the
Apostles conuert the worlde, by violent
and felonious entring into any places?
Did they deny lawful Obedience vnto
the Magistrates, and the Princes & Rulers of any Countrie? The Proceedings
of these daies, are no more like the prea-
chinges of the Apostles, or the Primitiue
Church, than a Diuel is like an Angel.
And yet the Mowntebankes continue
stil, Lutherans against Caluinistes, Caluinistes against Lutherans, both they
against Anabaptistes, and Anabaptistes
against them both.

But what speake I of other? Is M.
Iewel

M. Iew,
a Mounte=
banke. Iewel him self any better than a Mounte=
banke? Consider by that only which
I haue proued against him, how faire
spoken he is, how much corrupt stuffe he
hath, how highly he setteth by it, how
loudely he craketh of it, how singularly
he auaunceth him self by it. For when
he prouoketh al the learned men that be a-
liue, And asketh for no more than One
sufficient sentence, And requireth to haue
that brought out of any Olde Catholique
Doctour or Father, or any Olde General
Councel, &c: what other thing is this,
but a Mountebankes Preface, to com=
mend his wares vnto the Audience?
As if he should say in plainer woordes
vnto them:

Deerely beloued in the Lorde, you
may take me perchaunce for a Bench=
whistler, or a man of litle knowledge and
practise, and altogeather vnhable to re=
proue the General and Catholique Do=
ctrine of the whole world, and to draw
you from those Maisters and Teachers
which alwaies hitherto, ye haue ben ru=
led by. But I shal tel you (deere bre=
thren) I haue seene and readen as much
as

as any man, yea as all the learned men a-
liue: I haue trauailed vnto the very Primitiue Church it selfe: I haue bene conuersant with Old Catholike Doctors, and
Fathers, and old General Councels. As
for these Priests, Cardinals and Popes,
whom you folowe, they bring nothing,
but Conclusions of Scholemen, and deuises of Later Doctours, and Ceremonies of their owne making, &c. But I
will bring you no other thing, but that
which is Auncient. I wil bring you back
to the Institution of Christ himself. You
wal haue al things ministred vnto you,
as they were in the time of the Apostles.
You shal heare God himself speake vnto
you. The Priestes shall robbe you no
more of halfe the Sacrament. You shall
knowe, what you heare readden in the
Church. Ye shal haue no Supremacie of
Pope, no Real Presence of Christs body
in the Sacrament. Ye shal be brought to
Old Customes, which ý Councel of Nice
would haue to preuaile: And Tertullian
shal teach you, how that is true, that was
first ordeined. And, as I saied before, so
say I now againe, If any man aliue be

＊　i　　　hable

hable to reproue me, I will become his obedient Scholer. But I know, there is not one that is able to doe it, and becaufe I know it, therefore I fpeake it. So beginneth, the Mountebanke.

But in further proceffe he is proued to be fo vaine in Craking, So crafty in Shifting, So demure in Counterfeiting, So falfe in Affirming, So defperate in Abufing of his Aduerfarie, of old Councels, and Doctours, yea and of new alfo, that it is perceiued wel inough, euen of them that fay, *God faue you my Lorde,* vnto him, that al is not fo as he faith. Neuertheleffe they haue a good fporte, to fee the prety Shiftes, and Defenfes, and Scapes, that the Mountebanke canne make, And though it be euident that he lieth, yet they thinke not, thefe maters to be fo great or neceffary, but men may fuffer them wel inough to be mainteined how fo euer it be, as long, as neyther Trade of Merchaundife, nor Study of Temporal Law, nor Paftime abrode, nor Pleafure at home, is hindered by it.

For, like as we may vnderftand by the market folkes, how the market goeth

goeth, So, when it is in sight , that in
Countries and Cities of greatest policy,
priuate mens goodes are not without
punishment touched, but the Common
Churches of the whole Countrie , are
openly spoyled: And when Papistes are
neither suffred to speak, nor to go abrode,
but Caluinistes, Lutherans, and Anabaptistes, are not only suffred to speake,
but to speake one against the other, And
in one Citie or Countrie, to set furth and
maintaine contrary Doctrines : it is easy
to perceiue, that, *The wisedome of God , is
but folly among men*. And that al is for Policie, and nothing for Religion, and that
men haue so forsaken the old Faith, that
they are not settled in any new, And that
Faith in deede is almost extinguished, by
to much folowing of Carnal Reason, and
that Reason in thousandes , is vtterly
blinded, because thei haue put from them
the Obedience vnto Faith .

  Yet this Corruption notwithstanding , I haue taken some paines in
perswading with thee (Indifferent reader) to *BEVVARE* of M. Jewel: Fearing in deede, least to many be so in In-

   * ij

To the Indifferent Reader.

different, that they paſſe not whether he
ſay true oʒ falſe: And pʒaying to God
that they may haue A deſire to know the
Trueth, which as yet, care not foʒ it, and
that other may haue a conſtancie to confeſſe the Truth when they know it,
And that the reſt, condemne
not the the Truth, befoʒe
they know it.

Farevyel.   From Leuane.

Quandoquidem liber hic tertius contra M. Ievvellum à viris Linguæ Anglicanæ & Sacræ Theologiæ eruditißimis probatus est, iudico eum tutô posse distrahi & euulgari.

Ità testor Cunerus Petri, Pastor S. Petri. Louanij. 3. Nouemb. 1566

❡ Faultes escaped in the Printing.

Folio.	Page.	Line.	Fault.	Correction.
6.	2.	1.	Latines	Latenesse
40.	2.	12	ye	he
47.	1.	6.	Degrees	Decrees
63.	1.	13.	Dionysi.	of Dionysius
63.	2.	19.	them	then
80.	2.	2.	tel lyes	to tel lies
118.	2.	14.	Cōstātin.	Constantius
141.	2.	4.	ỹ visible	that a visible
142.	2.	15.	he cōclu.	he were conclu.
160.	2.	3.	primitiue	Primate
☞ Spe=181.	2.	16.	☞the cōmu	the Lordes pray
cially to be			niō praier	(er
amended. 191.	1.	3.	peple vn.	peple might vn.
195.	1.	7.	of old Fa.	of the old Fa.
197.	1.	14.	Valétians	Valentinians
206.	1.	18.	Suprem.	Preeminence
216.	2.	27.	ỹ it were	that if it were
217.	2.	4.	at bound	are not bound
Ibid.		24.	How say	How sayed
221.	2.	10.	yet if	yet it
225.	2.	11.	can say	can truly say
230.	2.	8.	gather	easily gather
234.	2.	16.	Trick oʒ	Tricke oʒ Toy
			(two	

In the Margent.

172.	1.		foʒ is	foʒ there is
228.	1.		Iew. 21.	Ioan. 21.
Ibid.			taken out of.	taken of

The Third Booke of
BEWARE OF
M. Iewel.

IT may seeme by my Two former Bookes, ꝑ I haue detected as great Sophistrie, Brauerie, & Insinceritie of M. Iewels, as any man lightly, that hath but worldly regarde of his Trueth and Honestie, may coulourably venter to practise. But in comparison of that which I haue further to obiect, the forsaid behauiours, may seme to be perdonable.

For D. Harding is but one man, and the same not knowen to the whole worlde, and much lesse honoured of the whole. He is also his Aduersary, and M. Iewel taketh him selfe, to be in no point perchaunse, of lesse worthinesse: And if in some one or two, D. Harding farre passeth him, yet in many moe on the other side, he thinketh him selfe to be better. And therefore, when he doth handle him at his pleasure, & belye him,

Contemne him, Mocke him, and Tosse him, without doubting or blusshing: although it be very il done, yet it is not exceeding il.

But to despise men (without al doubt) worthy & notable, To set light by them, whom the whole world hath reuerèced, To interprete Lawes and Canons after his own liking, To disanul general coūcels, To corrupt Auncient Fathers, To set them vp, to pul them doune againe, To bring them in, to thrust them againe out, To binde men to the Authoritie of the first six hundred yeares, To appeale to the Primitiue Church only in his own cause, and to drawe his Aduersarie vnto any State of Churche within these last fistene hundred yeares, and for a vantage to make the practise thereof, a Definitiue sentence: This is exceding presūptuous, and exceding Iniurious, and this is that, which I shal now laie to M. Iewels Charge.

¶Of M. Iewels exact accompting vpon the vj. C. yeres next after Christ.

YOur Appeale (M. Iewel) most instantly, to the witnesses of the next six hundred yeres after Christ, by which you geaue vs to vnderstand, that either your giltie Cōscience feareth, to be tried by God and the Countrie : either that your simple vnderstanding conceiueth, to helpe your cause by remouing of it . Of which two , there is nere a good, neither Conscience alreaby condemning you, by the verdite of ix. C. yeres together : Neither lacke of wit and Consideration mouing you , of xv. vniforme witnesses ix. put aside, to Imagine that the lesser number of vj. only remaining , could be so vsed, as that they should appeere , either contrary to the nine, Or of more credite and worthinesse

tt i

then the nine. Both which thinges (either that the Church of Christe should be contrary to it selfe , or in some one part of her Age more worthy of credite than in some other) are plainly and vtterly impossible, bothe by Faith and by Reason.

For , like as we are assured by right Faith, that there is but *One God, One Iesus Christ God and man, One Spirite diuiding vnto eche as he will, One Bodie, One Doue, One Louier, One Bevvtiful and One Catholik Church:* so is it impossible by Naturall Reason, that of Vnitie , A Diuision might be made, And that one Part might be found contrary to the other, or One Part worthier than the other, where there is no Partes making at all , and therefore no Parts taking at al, to cause any Discord.

Is Christ (sayeth the Apostle) *diuided? Is it yea and naie vvith him?* Yea, doth not he himself say: *Euery kingdom diuided vvithin it selfe shall be left vvaste and desolate?* And doe not both Testamentes, new and old, plainely teache, *that his kingdome is euerlasting?* How then should his Church be contrary vnto it self, and thereby cumming

l Tim.2.
1.Cor.12.
Eph.4.
Cant 6.

2.Cor.1.

Luc.11.
Da.7.
Luc.1.
The church is one by Faith.

ming to Diuision, ende afterwardes in Diſſolution?

Againe, **The** Spirite of Truthe **was pꝛo-miſed vnto her,** which should teach her all Truthe, and tary alſo vvith her for euer. **There be alſo pꝛouided foꝛ her, meete Gouer-nours and Officers, to continue with her and ſerue her, to the** perſiting of the holy, vntill all doe meete togeather, in Vnitie of Faith, and knovvledge of the Sonne of God: **ſo that, becauſe of the Authoꝛitie of the Chiefe Maſter, whome it is Jmpoſſible to lie, And the continuall ſucceſſion of Vſhers vnder him, whome he maketh to teach as he Inſpireth: the Leſſons which at this day are readen in the Church, ought to be in deede of as greate Credite emong vs, as any of the Pꝛimitiue Churches leſſons. Except perchaunce the Spꝛite be ſo blinde oꝛ blaſphemous in any per-ſon, as to deny his Almightineſſe in ma-king of ſuch as dwel in his houſe, of One minde and Accoꝛde, Of whoſe Pꝛomiſe, Pꝛouiſion and Charitie towardes hys church, we haue ſo infallible teſtimonies.**

Therefoꝛe, as the Scriptures per-ſwade our vnderſtanding to beleue, that

B ij   the

the Church is One, That it shall Continue for ever, That it shall never Erre in Doctrine: so Reason concludeth by this gift and light of Faith, that because it is O N E, it must either be N O N E at all, or continue ONE. And because I T CONTINVETH FOR EVER, it can not therefore be NONE. Remaining then ONE, it is to be credited without all doubt, because it hath the Sprite of Truthe with her and can not erre: And as well to be credited now, as it was xv̄ .hūdꝛed yeres sense, because it is O N E, and the selfe same nowe, as it was then, concerning Assistance of the Holy ghost, Priuileges of Honour, Infalliblenesse of Truthe, Or any other like, parteining to the very Substance and nature (as I may say) of the Church of Chꝛist.

The church is alwaies one and true, by reason.

Like as, in your self (M. Jewel,) Or in any of vs, the same Reasonable Soule and Sensitiue life, that we receyued of God and our Parents at our beginning, continueth yet stil to vs the Self same in substance, Notwithstanding many thousand Alterations, in Affections of minde, and Disposition of body, which haue in

the

the meane time chaunced vnto vs, And chainged vs, in the chaunce: so, notwithstanding many Alterations, which haue bene in the Church of Chrift. these xv.C. yeres, concerning external Gouernment thereof, and Ecclefiafticall Ozders, The life yet, Soule and Sense therof. is of the same making and wozthineffe, in all Times and Circumftancies.

In the Opinion and Imagination, of fainte harted and weake Chziftians, it appeareth (I graunt) to be of moze Authozitie, If Chziff, in his owne perfon speaketh, than if S.Paule his Apoftle, by his will and commaundement speake it. And, no doubt, they haue a good Zeale therein often times and Deuotion, but they haue not alwaies good knowledge and Underftãding. The Maries bzought tidinges vnto the Apoftles, of the Refurrection of our Sauiour, and though they were but women, yet they were deuout, wise and bleffed women, And their sayinges agreed with the woozdes of Chziff himfelfe spoken vnto them befoze his Paffion, so that they might well, and (hould haue bene credited: Neuerthe-

lesse, their wordes seemed vnto the Apostles no better than A Doting and vaine tale, And S. Peter ranne to the Sepulchre, to see perchaunce whether he coulde finde a better Argument or Testimonye of the Resurrection , than the Maries had brought, vnto him and his fellowes. which Argument, when it was the selfe same daie, made after the best maner vnto them, that is, by Christes owne presence and wordes: yet S. Thomas being at that time absent, and hearing at his Returne, of the sight and ioye which his fellowes had : *Except I see* (quod he) *the print of the nailes, and put my hand into his side, I will not beleue.* As who should say, that he alone could see more in such a matter, than ten other, Or that if he once tried it and beleued it him self, then it were to be bidden by: but, if he lerned and receiued it of other mens Report and knowledge, then loe, it was not clear, and out of question. Yet the Truthe is alwaies One. And as faithfully it was to haue bene beleued , y̆, which the Maries or Apostles saw and heard , As that which S. Thomas not only saw or hard, but fealt also.
                                                        Now,

Margin notes:

Luc. 24.

Let vs not be vn=beleuing, but faith=full.

Ioan, 20.

Now, in these foꝛesaied Persons and Examples, the inward and harty deuotion, did somewhat extenuate the Carnalitie of the Affection. Mary in other Cases, it is grosser and viler. As, when A Noble and Honoꝛable man speaketh A wise woꝛde, it is regarded and remembꝛed : but when a pooꝛe and Simple Soule, doth speake the like, it lacketh the same Grace and strength, with the hearers. Yet, the Trueth and wisedome of the saying being on both sides all O N E in goodnesse, it might well become all men to honoꝛ it, without Respect of persons. ∙Carnall iudgment.∙

when our Sauiour vpon a time, pꝛeached in the Synagoge of the Iewes, so singularly well, that all men wondꝛed at his Doctrine : *Hovv cummeth this felovve,* Marci.6. (sayed they) *by all this lerning ? Is not this he, that is the Carpenter, the sonne of Mary, the brother of Iames and Ioseph ? Are not his sisters also here dvvelling vvith vs ?* As who should say, we know his bꝛinging vp well inough, And therefoꝛe he is not so greatly to be wondered at . Such is the Iudgment of carnall men, euen vnto

B iiij this

this day. They measure Truthes, by their Imaginations, And set a great Price on thinges, that are farther out of their reach, Contemning as good or better than those thinges are, when they are easy to be found or alwaies present.

1. Which thing, If it come of the Misery of our Nature, it is to be lamented, and the Remedie is to be sought for of hym, which therefore toke our whole Nature (synne excepted) vpon him, that by partaking thereof, we might be purged of

2. our sinne and Corruption. If it come of the Foly of any deintines, it is (in some parsons) to be reproued with fauor, like as Children and women are much to be borne withall in respect of their weake-

3. nesse and frailtie. If it come of lacke of better Instruction, Or dulnesse of vnderstanding (as in the Rude and Simple of the Countrie) they are to be warned, as well as we may, and for the rest to be

4. praied for and tolerated. If it come of some Pride, Spite or Contention, it is to be condemned and hated, what so euer the person be.

But in M.Iewel, whereof may I thinke,

thinke, that this Affection doth come, of
which I speake? For you also, in defi-
ning of euerlasting Trueth, by Terme of
yeares, doe seeme to haue a spice of their
disease, which contemne the good things
that are nigh vnto them.

Shall I Impute this fault, vnto the
generall Miserie of our nature , which
was corrupted in our first Parentes?
God sende you then Grace to resist euill
motions , And for this which you haue
already done, Repent and be sory.

Repent

But came it of a certaine wantones or
nicenes in you , that as Childerne craue
Dis peece or Dat peece of one and the self
same meat or bread, Or women loue far-
set and deere bought thinges, so you will
not be serued, but with the Testimonies
and Authorities of the firste six hundred
yeres of our Lord? Truely, if it be so,
you can not loke for the Fauor, that childerne and women haue in their Infir-
mities.

Or play no more the wan-ton

Will you haue it then, to be attributed
vnto lacke of Lerning , Or plaine Dulnesse, that you are so blinde and blunt, as
to set at naught the Practise and Eui-
den-

Or lerne more wit.

dencies of the Catholike Church for nine hundred yeres togeather? It seemeth so, because the Opinion undoubtedlye, which your predecessours of late, had of their owne Judgment, Knowledge and wittinesse, moued them especially, to refuse the Generall and Approued Faith of the world. And so I beleue they lacked no wit, but only Grace, and they were to wise to be Obedient and Faithful.

How now then? was it any Sprite of Malice or Contention, that caused you to rest vpon the first six hundred yeres only, that the further you went out of sight, you might the more boldly shewe foule play, Maintaine the quarell, Make the victory vncertaine, And trouble the lookers on? If it be not so, we shal easely beleue you, if you shew any good Cause or Reason, wherefore you haue appealed vnto the first six hundred yeres: And so appealed vnto them, not, as the best time to finde witnesses in: but as the only time: neither as Preferring those Daies, but as Condemning ours.

But, let vs first see the Examples, by which your fact and behanioure herein may

Or Answer the Obiection

may be Euident, And then after, we shal
the better consider it, whether you haue
any reason or no, to make for you, And
what (by likelihode) was the cause which
moued you.

Leontius Bishop of Nicopolis, The first D. Har. Example.
wrot the life of *Ioannes Eleemosinari*[o]
an holy man of the first six hundred yeres
after Christ . why should I not beleue
Leontius?

Mary, he wrote (say you) A great while Ie. pa.75
after that.

And what of that? Is S. Bedes Hi- R.
story, of the cumming of S. Augustine the
Monke into England, to be discredited,
because S. Bede began to wryte, a great
while after S. Augustine was departed
this world ? Or, because the next six
hundred after Christ, were much passed
when he wrote it ? Are the bokes of
Genesis, in any poynt, to be doubted of,
because they declare the beginning of the
world, and Actes Dated two thousand
yeres, before Moyses the wryter of them
was borne ? Yet sayeth M. Iewel a-
gainst *Leontius*, This one Circumstance

(of

(of his Latines) anſweareth the matter
wholy. And in the margine he geaueth a
ſpeciall note : M. Harding rangeth without the cumpaſſe of ſix hundred yeres.

Ie.fo.75.

Vrbanus Regius, a Doctoꝛ of Lu-
thers Schoole confeſſeth in his boke De
locis Communibus, that in the firſt Councel of Epheſus , an Oꝛder was taken foꝛ
Communion vnder one kinde : which,
he being a Lutherane, would neuer haue
wꝛyten, if he had not found it , in ſome
Auncient Recoꝛd and woꝛthy of credite.

The ij.
D. Hard.
Fol.36.

Iew.112.

But Vrbanus Regius (ſay you) departed this life, not aboue .xx. yeres a goe, and
therefore, is a very yong witneſſe to teſtify
a thing done ſo long time before.

Ra.

In decde to teſtifye it as of certaine
ſight oꝛ knowledge , it were hard foꝛ ſo
young a witneſſe : but to teſtify it , as of
good Hiſtoꝛie and Authoꝛitie, it is poſſy-
ble inough foꝛ them , which are .xx. yeres
younger.

The iij.

What ſhall we thinke of S. Bernard:
A man, not only in his own time of moſt
woꝛthy Eſtimation and Authoꝛitie, but,
in all the Church euer ſence, of ſingular
Credite and woꝛthineſſe ? If he were
now

now aliue emong vs, And might be seen and heard sensibly, would there be found in all the world any man of Honestie or Discretion, which considering his Holinesse, wisedome and Grauitie would thinke him A witnesse of litle weight and worthinesse? Yet, Father Iewel sayeth, as though he had bene a Reader of Diuinitie, when S. Bernard was yet but A Nouice in the Faith:

S. Bernard, calleth the washing of feete a Sacrament. I graunt. But S. Bernard was a Doctour but of late yeres, and therefore his Authoritie must herein weigh the lesser. **Iew.116.**

Was he of so late yeres, as Luther, Zuinglius, Caluine, Peter Martir, and other Greate Anceters of your new Religion? why dothe not the latenesse of these felowes, offend you? why think you, the th.C. yeres after Christ, to be so farre and wide from his Trueth, that no certaintie thereof maye be taken in them? And Conclude, Determine, Protest and Defend, that, to be Sure and Autentike, which riseth xv.C. and some odde yeres after Christ? **Ra.**

Of

Of the like kinde of Imaginacion and
Answer it is, where you say: Lyra and
Teutonicus Lyued, at the least, thirtene
hundred yeres after Christe, wherefore
their Authoritie in this Case must Needes
seeme the lesse. No remedy: M. Iewel
hath so appointed.

Again. Bessarions Authoritie in this
case can not seeme greate, bothe for other
sundry causes, (which you leaue) And Also, (which must needes be a good cause
and not forgotten) for that he liued at the
least fourtene hundred yeres after Christ.

And again. Pope Nicolas, was the second Bishop in Rome after Pope Iohane
the Woman. (Note here that Other
men recken, from S. Peter downeward,
this man compteth from Pope Iohane,
An English woman, as the reporter of
the tale sayth, borne at Magunce in Germany.) Which was almost nine hundred
yeres after Christ. Wherfore his Authoritie might well haue bene spared.

Thus we see then, by manifest Examples, the exact Accompt that you make of
the first six hundred yeres after Christ,
As though the whole Truthe of A mater
were

The iiij.
Iew.140

The v.
Iew.217.

The vj.
Iew.:89

Rʒ.

were loſt, if it come to knowledge, any
long time after the thing was done.

Let vs conſider now, whether any
honeſt Cauſe and Reaſon may be alleaged for your ſo doing, Or whether you
did it without cauſe, Or els were ſtur-
red vp with ſome vnlawfull Affection
and Reproueable Cauſe. And here
now, take no ſkorne M. Iewel if I ap-
poſe you in a few Queſtions. For,
either you be hable to Anſwer them, and
that ſhall be to your worſhip: either not
Anſwering them, you ſhall occaſyon
Trueth therby to be knowen. And that
ſhall be to Gods glorie and the Cumfort
of the doubtfull. Surely, if it were to
my ſelfe, and if ſo much might be obtained, that I ſhould be Anſwered in ſome
One thing thorougly, and be bid to
chooſe, out of all that which I haue to
demaunde, that One thing which ſeemeth ſtrongeſt agaynſt my Aduerſary,
and ſureſt to the Catholikes: I would
be glad of the Occaſion, and all other
maters quite and cleane put to Silence,
I would ſpeake of theſe fewe poyntes
which folow, And either wythout more
wordes,

One place for all: let M. Iew. or any other Anſwer it.

wordes, holde my peace, If in them I
were satisfied : Or require, that our Aduersaries neuer trouble their hearers or
Readers any further with other conclusions, before these fewe questions were
Answered. Therefore, I pray the (Indifferent Reader) to consider thys place
which foloweth, though thou Reade no
more of all the Booke.

The firste question. Faith, or no Faith? First, I aske of you (M Iewel) whether you haue any Faith at all, or no?

If you haue none, what meddle you,
with any Religion: except it be for Ciuil
Policie sake? For which to doe as you
doe, though it would proue you lesse mad
or vnreasonable, yet should you be (for
lacke of Faith) as deade in soule and as
Godlesse, as any Infidel in al the world.

Faithe. If ye haue any, how came you by it? for
we are not borne Christians, but Rege-
nerate : neither doe we receiue faith by
Nature, but by Teaching. And, *faith is*
Rom. 10. *by hearing,* sayeth the Apostle.

The ij. question: Lerned you it, of $ quicke or the deade? Of whome then haue you heard and
lerned your Faith? Of them that liued
and died before you were borne? Or of
such as preached and taught in the world
sens

sens your selfe were of remembrance?

If you lerned of the first, how could they teache, without A tongue? Or how could you heare without an eare? For they were now deade in body, and cleane dissolued, and you were not yet made of body and soule, nor had any instruments of senses.

If you lerned of the Quicke and Liuing, your self also quicke and liuing, were those your Teachers of such Authoritie with you, that you submitted your senses and vnderstanding, to theyr iudgment? Or examined you, by your selfe, their Doctrine and Sayinges? Of the Quicke. The ii. Question. Folowed you their Authority or no?

If you the Scholer did iudge of the Matter, you were without all doubt, a Malapert and Folishe Scholer. Malapert, because you would breake order, and proudly goe before him, whome you ought meekly to haue folowed: And Folishe, because in maters of Faith, (of which we now speake) all wit and Reason of man, is altogeather vnworthy and vnable, to Iudge of that which is Proponed.

If you then folowed their Authoritie, The iii. Question.

C i   and

and submitted your vnderstanding and will vnto their Doctrine, without Mouing or Mistrusting any doubt about it: *VVhat were they in all the world, vnto whome you gaue such credite?*

what are they?

I aske you not this question, for the time of your Childhode, in which, though true Faith be Habitually in them that are Baptised: yet there is not that Discretion or Consideration, by which they may returne their mindes vpon theyr owne actes, Or put a difference betwene their Grãdmothers tale of Bloudy bone, Raw head, Bloudelesse and ware woulf, and the Churches Doctrine of Hell and the Deuill. But I speake now, as to one that hath Vnderstanding and knowledge of his owne state, And Experience of many thinges, And Lerning inough for the purpose, And such a one, whose part and profession it is, to be able to geaue a good Cause and Reason, for the Faith and Religion which he foloweth. Of you therefore I aske, what Authority that was, Or is, which moued you to be, and continue A Christian?

Here, you must not say vnto me, that you

you considered the wrytinges of the Fa=
thers of the first six hundred yeres . And
that you gaue your minde to Reading
of the Scriptures. &c. For what so euer
such tale you tell me, it will alwaies re=
maine to be Answered of you, what Instruction or Authoritie that was, which
either Taught you, Or Moued you, to
esteeme those Auncient Doctors of the
Christian Religion, Or these Scriptures
of which you make your self so certaine?
For by your selfe , you could no more
know, the difference betwene wꝛiters
and wꝛiters, or true Scriptures and ly=
ing Fables, than A Blinde man cã iudge
of Colours , Or a Stranger know the
right way in A wildernesse, or he Rede,
that knoweth no letter on the booke.

Here let
al the here
tikes in ꝩ
woꝛld ioin
wyth the
Papiſs if
they can.

You are not (I am sure) wiſer thã S.
Augu. Neither haue you better thought
vpõ theſe maters, than he did. He ſaith of
himſelf, ꝩ concerning the Faith which he
had in Chꝛiſt. *He ſaw himſelfe, to haue bele-*
ued none, but the eſtabliſhed opinion of Peoples &
Nations , and the very Common and renoumed
Fame of him. Than which cauſe, if you can
gene any better, it is time ꝩ you ſhew it.

Auguſt. ad
Honoratũ
cap. 14. de
vtilitate
credendi.

　　　　L ij　　　　And

As for vs, neither we finde any like, And we neede not be ashamed to be perswaded by it, which moued S. Augustine him selfe, to come vnto Christ.

And I think verely, that neither you, studying neuer so much for it, can bring any so perswasible a Reason, why you beleued Christ, as this is: that, *So many Nations and peoples of the world doe beare witnesse to him.* For this is so Great and so Stronge to induce vs into Faith, that we should not now be desirous of visible Miracles for Prouing Or Confirming of it, S. Augustine moste wisely and Reasonably warning vs: *Quisquis adhuc prodigia, vt credat, inquirit: magnum est ipse prodigium, Qui MVNDO CREDENTE non credit. VVho so euer doth yet seeke after Straunge and vvonderfull thinges, to make him beleue: he is himselfe a straunge felovv or Greate vvonder, vvhich beleueth not, vvhen the vvorld beleueth.*

This Conclusion then standyng so sure, (that the Voice of the worlde, so Great, so Generall, so Certaine and so Famous, hath made wise men to come vnto

An euident Demonstration to perswade vs to beleue.

De ciuit. Dei lib. 22. Cap. 8.

vnto Chꝛist) I will, in like soꝛt, dispute with you (M. Iewel,) as S. Augustine did against the Manichees. And as he sayed against them vpon the foꝛesayde Truthe: *Cur non igitur apud eos potißimum, diligentißimè requiram, quid Christus præcepe-rit, quorum authoritate commotus, Christum a-liquid Vtile præcepiße credidi? Tune mihi melius expositurus es quid ille dixerit? Quem fuiße, aut eße, non putarem, si abs te mihi hoc commenda-retur eße credendum. Hoc ergo credidi (vt dixi) famæ, celebritate, consensione, Vetustate roboratæ. Vos autèm & tam pauci & tam turbulenti & tam noui, nemini dubium est quin nihil dignum authoritate præferatis.* Seeing I haue be=leued the constant Fame and Repoꝛte of Nations in Cummyng to Chꝛiste, *why should not I then, most diligent-ly seeke what Christ commaunded, emong them most chiefly, by whose Authoritie I haue bene moued to be-leue that Christ commaunded things profitable? VVilt thou better ex-pound vnto me what he sayd? whome*

De Vilit. cred. Cap. 14.

C iij   I

I would not beleue to haue ben, Or to be, if from thee, this were Commended vnto me to be beleued. For I *haue beleued it,* (as J ſayed) *becauſe of the fame eſtabliſhed and ſtrēghtned by Renoune, Conſent, Auncientnes : But you, both ſo Fewe, and ſo Trobleſome, and ſo New, there is no man doubteth, but that ye can ſhow nothing worthy of Authoritie.*

Thus S. Auguſtine.

Manich.

The Manichees would anſwer as heretikes doe now . What? you muſt make no queſtion of it, whether Chriſt is to be beleued or no.

Auguſt.

S. Auguſtine Replieth, and ſo do we.

Quæ igitur iſta tanta dementia eſt ? Illis crede. Chriſto eſſe credēdum, & a nobis diſce quid dixerit? Cur obſecro te? Nam ſi illi. &c.

VVhat exceding madneſſe then is this? Beleue them (the Catholikes) *that thou muſt beleue Chriſt, and*

lerne

*lerne of vs what he saied. By what
reason I pray the? For, if they should
faile, and could not teache me any
thiug, I would much more easely per=
swade my selfe, that Christ is not to
be beleued: than, that I should lerne
any thing concerning him, but of
them, through whome I had beleued
him. O what a greate Boldnesse is
this, or rather what a greate Fo=
lishnesse?*

I wil teache you (ſayeth the Deretike) what Chriſt commaunded, whome you beleue. To whome S.Auguſtine. Manich.

*VVhat if I did not beleue him?
Couldeſt thou teache me any thing of
him?* Auguſt.

Nay there is no remedy (ſayth the Ma= nichee) you muſt beleue. Sainct Augu= ſtine anſwereth: Manich.

*VVhether by your Commending
of him?* Auguſt.

Manich. No (fayeth he) For we leade them by Reafon, that beleue him.

Auguft. *For what Reafon then (fayeth S. Auguftine) muft I beleue him?*

Manich. Becaufe there is A grounded and eftablifhed Fame.

Auguft. *VVas it grounded by you or by other?*

Manich. By other fayeth he.

Auguft. *Ergo fhal I beleue them, that you maye teache me ? Perchaunce I fhould, except they had efpeciallye warned me hereof, that I fhould not at al, come vnto thee.*

Manich. Thou wilt Anfwer, They Lie.

Auguft. *How then fhall I beleue them cõcerning Chriſt, whome they haue not feene, and fhall not beleue them concerning the, whome they will not fee?*

Manich. Beleue (fayeth he) the Scriptures.

Auguft. *But what fo euer Scripture it be,*

if

if it be brought furth new and vn-
heard of before, the credite is geuen,
not vnto it, but vnto thē that bring
it furth. VVherefore, the Scriptures
themselues, if you so few and vn-
knowen do bring furth, I haue no list
to beleue them.

Here againe (saieth S. Augustine to
the Manichee) thou wilt cal m: backe vnto the multitude and the same.

And so doe our Protestantes nowe.
What (say they) will you doubte of the
Scriptures? Nay then fare well. There is
no talke with you, we perceiue. Why there
is no man that denieth them. We see how
generally they are alowed and receiued of
all men. Either we must beleue nothing,
or beleue them: whome by so many mens
Report and Consent, we finde to be agreed
vpon.

*C*ōs{er and
consider
whether the
vpstart he
retikes be
not like
the old.

To whom we answer as S. Augustin
did vnto the Manichee, which would
haue the Fame and Uoice of the world,
to be an euident and sure Argumente,
wherefore we should make no doubt of
the

of the Scriptures, And yet, would not be ruled by the Uoice and Consent of that Multitude in the rest of the Christian & Catholike Faith:

Auguſt.

Cohibe tandem pertinaciam et iſtam neſcio quam indomitam propagandi nominis libidinem, et mone potius vt huius multitudinis Primates, quæram diligentiſſime ac laborioſiſſime; vt ab his potius de his literis aliquid diſcam.&c.

Staie now at lenght your egerneſſe and contention, and this, I can not tell what, Vnruly deſire and Luſt of getting and ſtretching furth a name. And Counſel me rather to ſeeke out the Primates and Chiefe of this mul‐*titude, and to ſeeke them out moſte diligently and erneſtly, that of them rather, I may lerne ſumwhat of theſe letters.(the Scriptures.) VVhich mē if they were not, I ſhould not at all knowe it, that I had any thing to lerne. As for the (that arte the Heretike)*

returne

rèturne into THY LVRKING HOLES
AND CORNERS AGAINE.&c.

Thus far S. Augustine.

By which his Discourse against the
Manichees , and our folowing of it a=
gainst the Protestants, how Vncertaine,
Vnsensible , and Contentious must it
be , to Appeale to the vj.C. yeres only
after Christ, as though there were none,
at this preset, in the world, which might
and ought to be fully obeyed ? For, if
the Scriptures themselues are now be=
leued , not because they were belened in
the vj.C. after Christ, (for what can we
iudge by any sence of thinges paste and
gone A thousand yeres sens?) But be=
cause they which now line, and whome
we may iustly beleue, doe reporte so vn=
to vs , that they haue bene commended
vnto the world by them that saw Christ,
and heard him, and touched him: And
that they haue continued , these xv.C.
and odde yeres emong Christians , all=
waies of full Authoritie , (be it the six
hundred or ten hundred , or xv.C. after
Christe , that you will coumpt vpon.)

JF

If, I say, the Scriptures themselues are belened of vs, because of the present commendacion of this Age which we be in, and Authoritie which is in *the primates of this multitude of Christians :*

Howe can we goe in any mater of the Faith, from the Iudgement of this present Age, And refuse euery thing that is brought vnto vs, except it be out of the first sir hundred yeres after Christ?

For suppose it, that no man aliue NOW, had openly held with Christ: would M. Iewel cleaue vnto y Creedes of the first sir hundred yeres? And by his owne self, would he chuse to folow the Christian faith of those daies, if there had ben in the world, for these last yeares, no Praise or Speaking of Christ at all?

How is it credible? For being but a man, how should he not, by all likelihoode, folow the common course of men? And if he would needes be Singular, how could he discerne betwene the true and the false Opinions of the first sir hundred yeres, whereas he should finde Examples and wrytings of both? Or not able

ble to difcerne betwene them, how could
he faften his minde and beleife vpon any
one of them bothe, except he wereA Singular one in deede ? For wifemen, doe
not lightly take that way , in which they
fee not, either the Towne plainely before
them, or fome Cawfey, Pathes, or Steps
of feete to direct them: Neither doe they
vfe (when they goe in the right way, and
come at lenght to fome turning or duble
waie) to go forward, I can not tell how,
without loking backe if any folow , Or
loking about if any be within fight : but
either reft themfelues, vntill they fpie of
whome to afke , Or goe fo doubtefully
forward in that which leeketh them, that
if better Counfell and teaching come vnto thē,they wil be returned and ordered.

And if it be fo in A corporall and vifible way , ought it not to be much more
fo,in folowing the right way vnto truth
of vnderftanding and knowledge? And,
when the whole world taketh one waie,
Or diuerfe cumpanies in the world folow diuerfe waies , would any man of
Difcretion be fo Bolde or Foolifhe,as to
goe peaking alone by himfelfe in fuch an
Opi-

who hath commē̄ded Chrift vn to M. Iew. but the report of this age in which himfelfe hath liued.

Opinion o² Imagination , as no man
byſide himſelfe aloweth? And ſo directly go in it, that to liue and die, he would
not be brought from it? If therefore
theſe fortie yeres laſt paſt (o² what ſo e-
uer it be more that M. Iewel hath liued in the world) no² Chriſt had bene
Preached , no² the Primitiue Churche
commended: he could not vndoubtedly
by any good Occaſion o² Reaſon , haue
eſtemed the Chriſtian wryters of a thouſand yeres ſens , O² geauen any Faith
vnto Chriſt . Except we ſhould thinke
(otherwiſe than ẙ Apoſtle hath taught
vs) ẙ faith commeth without hearing, O²
that no man ſent fo² him , yet by ſome
Miracle perchaunce he was brought vnto Chriſt. Of which two, both are out
of courſe: And without ſome Extraordinary way of making them likely vnto
vs, both are Vnreaſonable, both are Incredible.

The preſent Fame then, Renoume, &
Teſtimonie of this Age, drawing men of
this Age vnto Chriſt, yet doth M. Iewel
ſo litle ſet by it , as though it were wo²-
thy of litle credite, o² rather none, And he
ſo

so cleaueth vnto those vj. C. yeres, past
A thousãd. yeres, almost, sens: as though
he could be sure of the Catholike & true
Faith that was then, wout the Testimonies of the Catholike Church now, Or
as though some secrete Mistery or Secu-
ritie were in them, to further him in vn-
reueled Conclusions, And exempt him
from all Iurisdiction. In so much, that
although in xv. C. yeres rekening, which
the Church hath continued in (as it shall
to the worldes end) viij. yeres can not
greatly hurt the Accompt, Yet, so true an
Audite of thẽ, is kept by M. Iewel, that
he wil not receiue the Testimonies of the
viij. yeres next after the first vj. C. but
noteth in his Booke their cumming to
late, though they came very nigh. His
wordes be these.

M. Harding knoweth wel, that this graút Iew. 242
(to be called The Head of al Churches,) Sticking
was made vnto Bonifacius the third, which vpon viij.
was Bishope of Rome in the vere of our yeres.
Lord vj. C. and viij. Euen at the same very
time, that Mahomete first began to plant his
Doctrine in Arabia. And therfore maketh
nothing to this purpose, as being without
the cumpasse of six hundred yeres.

As

Did he, think you, perſwade wyth the Emperoꝛ, to geaue ꝑ Title, Oꝛ with the Pope to receiue it? Oꝛ how bꝛing you Arabia & Rome here to=geather?

As who ſhould thinke , that withi̇n thoſe viij. yeres on this ſide the ſix hun=dꝛed, The Pope, and Emperour, with the whole woꝛld, were Sodaẏnely and Straungely , conuerted from the faith and Oꝛder which they were of viij. yeres befoꝛe, And (no Hiſtoꝛie mentioning it) were made of Pure Pꝛoteſtants , Groſſe Papiſts.

Yea, not only of viij. yeres aboue the vj. C. he maketh a ſad rekoning towards his Uantage , but of the vj. C. yere it ſelf (if he can bꝛing D. Hardings teſtimonie ſo low) he ſo vaunteth and bꝛaggeth, as though either himſelf had the Uictoꝛie, Oꝛ els , nothing ſhould be won oꝛ loſt. Foꝛ, whereas D. Harding, foꝛ pꝛofe of ꝑ Church Seruice in a Straung Tongue, and vnknowen to the Uulgare people, and that alſo within the firſt vj. C. yeres, alleaged the cumming of S. Auguſtine the Monke and our Apoſtle into Eng=land, (which was by his accompt the 14. yere of Mauritius Emperoꝛ, & the 596. of our Loꝛd.) Maſter Iewel in anſwe=ring it ſayeth.

Iew. 192. Of the 600. yeres after Chriſt, whervp-
on

on I ioyne wish him issue, Liberally, and of
his owne accord, he geueth me backe fiue
hundred, foure scoare and sixtene, And of
so greate a number (as 600. are) reserueth
vnto himself foure PO O R E Y E R E S,
and yet, is not very certaine of the same.
And then it foloweth. But if Marianus
Scotus accompt be true , that Augustine
came into this Realme not the fourtienth
of the Emperour Mauritius, but four yeres
after , which was iust the six hundred yere
afterChrist: then he reserueth not one yere
to himselfe, but yeldeth me backe altogeather.

wretched
craking.

Loe what a wise contention here is:
And how sadly M. Iewel foloweth it?
Did he thinke with himselfe, that none,
but Children or Idiotes, would Reade
his Replie? And if he prouided to make
it so, as not only wisemen should consi=
der it, but the Aduersarie also might be
answered by it: how could he for shame
of the world, so Trifle, and wrangle, and
Set furth himselfe so much , vpon so litle
occasion? For, if the vj. C. yeres shall
trie the mater, he that cometh four yeres
before they be ended , commeth time i=
nough to confute M. Iewel. And his

Ra.

Cause therefore being lost, Or his Brag-
ging at least confounded, if, in any time
before the vj.C.yeres expired, the contrarie, to this Assertion, may be proued:
why should he call them foure Poore
yeres, or set them at naught, which making to the number of the first 600.yeres
are part of the yeres vpon which he ioyned Issue, and are (by his apointement)
of greate Authoritie.

The crake herein is, like as if one
should say, In all S. Augustines workes,
you shal not finde this worde Missa, and
thervpon I wil ioyne with you: (as though
a great point of Diuinitie consisted herein.) An other answeareth, *yeas Mary,
I finde the worde in such, and such
Sermons.* Then Replieth the Challenger:

*Ser.137.
de temp:*

Of so great a number of Tomes, as S. Augustine hath writen, of so many bokes in
euery Tome.&c. (as far as his Rhetorike permitteth) you geaue me backe, Liberally, And of your owne accord, al the
sort of them almost, and reserue vnto your
selfe two POORE SERMONS: and yet
are you not very certaine of them, whether
they

they be S.Auguſtines or noe. As if he
ſhould ſay, I layed hard to his charge, and
there was but two poore places betweene
me and the victorie, which, although he
hath ouer me, yet, it ſhal not be ſaied that
I loſt it eaſely, and he ſhal not crake or triumph, that he came lightly by it.

Confer now this Example with M.
Iewels forſaied wordes . The place is
before thee , and being ſo plaine as it is,
it greueth me to ſpend time in Repeting
and Applying it.

But M. Iewel goeth further , he will
not leaue ſo much as one yeres vantage
to D. Harding. For,

If Marianus Scotus accompt be true: Ieꝛw.192.
(Note here that you know not your ſelfe
what to anſwer abſolutely) then M.Har-
ding reſerueth not one yere to himſelf, but
yeldeth me backe altogeather.

Goe to (M. Iewel) be it ſo. Let D. Ra.
Harding geaue ouer all other vantage,
and let it be ſuppoſed (which yet is moſt
falſe)that he had brought nothing for the
profe of the Publike Seruice in the Uulgare Tonge , biſide this Hiſtorye, of S.

D ij   Augu-

Auguſtines planting the Chriſtian Religion in England : Thus much only then is concluded, $\tilde{y}$ iuſt in the vj. C. yere after Chriſt (what ſo euer it was before) *The Publike Seruice was in ſome place in ſuch a tongue, as the vulgare people did not vnderſtande.*

And what now ſhall we ſay to it? where is the Uictorye ? On your ſide, or D. Harding? But firſt it would be knowen whether you, at the beginning, did take the vj. C. yeres, Excluſiue or Incluſiue? And whether you meant, that if to the laſt day of the ſix hundred yere, any thing ſhould be founde againſt you, you would ſubſcribe: Or els, that if your Aduerſaries Reaſon were not of an higher Date than the firſt day of the laſt yere of the vj. hundred, you would vtterly refuſe it.

well, how ſo euer it be, it ſeemeth now that it is but a deade victorie, Or a Stale and that he which will checke M. Jewel, muſt begin againe , If Marianus Scotus accompt be true. &c. As, on the other ſide, if it be falſe, then is he ouercummed by four pore yeres yet, as he termeth thē. But

Nothing wonne or loſt.

But consider now (Indifferent Reader) whether this be manly Dealing or no? To refuse the Authoritie that is at this present in the world? To set light by the Practise and Iudgement of the Church for ix. hundred yeres space. To pare euery thing so precisely by the firste six hundred yeres, that, If it be but a daie longer, it must be cut awaie: And if it be a few yeres shorter, it must be the lesse estemed: And if it answer iustly with the yere it self, it weigheth in no side. What Reason hath M. Iewel, or what Example and Scripture for him?

1.
2.
Absurdi-
ties.

3.

4

5.

Is the Truthe of God bound to the first six hundred yeres? And must it not passe that cumpasse which M. Iewel hath apointed vnto it. Is God a God of six hundred yeres only, and not of all time and all worldes? Was the Holyghost promised to tary with vs, til vj. C. yeres were come and gone, and not to the end of the world? The kingdome of Christ, which should be euerlasting, and his power which should not be také awai: must it be interpreted now, to haue theyr full terme out, in vj. C. yeres only?

M. Iew.
putteth
Truthe
within a
Circle of
yeres.

D iij   What

what Grace haue the first vj.C, Or what curse of God haue these last.ix.C. yeres? How know you also, when the first vj.C.ended,Or what trust haue you in them, which number the yeres vnto you? Some Historiographers recken one way, Other recken an other way. what certaintie then can you haue of thē? Again,those writers whome you folow, either do at this present liue, Or be commended vnto you by them that now liue. And how dare you trust,either those that nowe liue and write of thinges so long sens past: Or those, that a greate while sens are deade, your selfe not then borne to liue with them, and examine their doinges?

Consider also,how many haue wryten within the space of these last nine hūdred yeres: how perfite in life,how Excellent in knowledge, how Painfull in studies, how worthy in their owne dayes, How Famous with the Posteritie, How mete witnesses in the cause of God , and triall of a Pure and holy Religion? Abbates, Monkes, Friers, are in these new Gospelling dayes , termes of great shame and

and Ignominie: yet what sayeth any honest Protestant, against S. Bernard, Rupertus, Thomas Aquinas, Bonauenture, Dionysius the Carthusian, and other such? Can M. Iewel finde any fault in theyr life, by any Report of brute or Fame? Or any Irreligiousnes in their bookes and wrytinges, which are extant, for hym to consider? Let him say his worst, Let him leaue poring in Gloses of no Authoritie, to finde some mad thing or other, against the wisedome of the Church, And let him confer his leisure to Reading or Examining rather of these witnesses (accordyng to the State he taketh vpon him) whose sayinges, he knoweth, we esteeme as we ought to doe.

O, sayeth he, these were of late daies. I graunt. And not only that, but also, and you will, that they were in euyll and corrupt daies. But were they corrupted in them? Did they not write against corrupt liuing? Did they suffer new Preachers and Apostolikes, to goe out of the Church or come against ẙ church by their euil Doctrine? Or did they communicate with Pope, Cardinals, Bishops, Abbots

D iiij   or

oz any other of all the wozld in their li=
uing? Seing they neither feared hatred
noz curred fauour, why should not their
Testimonie be receiued, no other excep=
tion being bzought againt them, but
that they liued in so late daies, oz such A
wozld?

All is Ungodly, All is Unreafonable,
All is Uainegloзious, to appeale to the
times so long paft, As though that God,
at this pzefent, had not his Church in the
wozld: Oz, as though ye could well fo=
low any other, but such as you heare
with your owne eares: Oz, as though
the good and Lerned men of thefe Later
yeres, departed this wozld hundзed of
yeres fens, were not as nigh to the firft
fix hundзed yeres as ye are, and as ready
to folow the beft waie as ye: Oz, as
though it were A Joly mater and a com=
pendious waie to the Gofpell, to con=
tempne all Chзiftendome that now is,
and holde with that Chзiftendome that
was almofte a thoufand yeres fens, not
knowing yet, what Chзiftianitie mea=
neth, Noz Daring to truft it if ye knew
it, were it not foз the Authoзitie which is

at

at this present in Christendome , the Greatnesse of which hath moued you to beleue, what so euer you beleue vpon any good ground.

Here therfore M.Iewel, defend your doinges, And shew vs the cause, wherefore you doe, or should refuse the Testimonie of the last ix. hundred yeres which are against you . If it be not for Childeshnesse, or wantonesse , or Vnsensiblenesse , that you will none of so many and so graue witnesses: yet except you alleage some honest cause and reason , It will remayne, I beleue, that you doe it vpon a very blinde Stomake and contention . My questions are short, and easy to be answered , if you haue any Faith or Conscience at all . As in Example.

Was there not a Church of God , in the world, when you were borne?

Did not the Greatnes , Granitie and Authoritie of Nations which were of it, moue you to beleue?

Did the Inuisible and litle Congregation worke that effect in you?

If ye trusted the Catholike Church of
your

Here let any Protestant geaue a Reason of his faith?

your time , in commending Chziſt vnto
you , and without her Commendatyon
would not haue credited him : can you,
with a ſafe conſciéce , contemne the voice
of the ſame Church, And, to colour your
defection and fleeing from it, take holde
faſt of the firſt ſix hundzed yeres only, As
though you could with all your witte,
iudge better what the Pzimitiue Church
thought and beleued , than the pzeſent
Church which is of one Spirite wyth
the Pzimitiue . ⸪c.

But there is no Remedie, vpon the
firſt ſix hundzed yeres M. Jewel ioyneth
with vs , And if any thing be longer
than that meaſure, he will none of it: he
hath ſayed it.

¶ *How M.Iewel himselfe dothe vse
the Teſtimonies of what ſo euer
Age and wryter, though he bind
other to the firſt ſixe hundred
yeres only.*

TO the firſt ſix hundꝛed yeres cum=
paſſe then, we muſt be bound, al a=
gainſt Reaſon and Conſcience, but
what ſhall we doe, when the ſtan=
ding in our right againſt the Aduerſarie,
and the Refuſing to encountre with him
vpon his conditions, ſhallbe thought of
ſome Judges to be A Pꝛeiudice vnto our
cauſe, and A greate Argument that our
hartes faile vs?

Diſpute (ſayeth the Heretike) wyth
me, vpon theſe queſtions, whether the
Publike Seruice in an vnknowen tongue,
Or Receiuing vnder one kinde, Or Re=
ſeruing of the Sacrament in A Pix wyth
A Canopie ouer it. &c. was euer vſed
in the Pꝛimitiue Church. No Mary
(ſhould

How the
heretikes
do apointe
1. queſtiõs
2. Oꝛder
of diſpu=
ting 3. Ma=
ner of Au=
thoꝛities,
4. Age of
the wit=
neſſes : all
at pleaſure
but no=
thing, af=
ter right
and reſon?

(would J faie, if it were to me only), J will not Dispute with thee vpon theese poyntes. But, if thy Hart and Learning ferue thee, make few wordes and Anfwer me, from whence thou cumeft? who fent thee? what are their Names? where are their Sees? what is their Succeffion? what is their Authoritie? Jn which pointes if thou fatiffie me, not only then, in thefe few Articles which thou demaundeft, but in euery point and part of the Religion, which thy Church aloweth, J will be Faithfull and Obedient.

Reafonable Demaundes.

2. Dispute (fayeth he againe vnto me) on Munday come feuennight. And before that Day cummeth, he chaingeth his minde foure or fiue times with me.

First he will Dispute in Latine: Then he will wryte his minde, and fpeake nothing: After that, he wil haue the mater Reafoned in Englifhe, and wife men fhalbe Judges: And, after that againe, he will haue it done in the hearing of the people, not by quicke Difputation, but by Reading only the Argumentes out of a Booke.

Jf

If the Catholike Disagree in anye poynt, and stand vpon it: either stubburnesse, either Mistrust of his Cause, either some fault or other, shalbe layed vnto him . And so were many greate and heighnous maters Obiected against S.Ambrose, because he refused to haue the cause betwene himselfe and the Heretike Auxentius,to be tried in the Consistorie of the Emperour, before Seculer Judges . And his Exception,against the Place only and Audience , was accompted an high and intolerable Treason.

Ambr. *lib.5.* *Ep.33.*

In like maner : You shall Dispute with me (sayeth the Heretike,) and nothing shall serue you, except it be in expresse Scripture . If the Catholike refuse that Condition , and allege an hundred Reasons and Authorities , that we must beleue the vnwriten veritie, as wel as the writen, And, that the word and will of God is allwaies to be obeied, whether it be deliuered vnto vs by Tradition, or left vnto vs in wryting : Yet except he yeld at length,all England shal ring of it, That the Papistes will not be

tried

3.

tried by the liuely worde of God, That they flee the light, That they dare not commit their cause to the Scriptures.

4 To be short, when M. Iewel now, more Reasonably in deede than Some of his Masters or Felowes, which will admit nothing but Scripture: Yet heretically and stately inough, prouoketh vs to ioine with him, And chooseth his questions, and excludeth all our Answers vnto them, except they be taken iust out of the vj. C. yeres after Christ: although it be very vniustly required of him, and A Catholike should neuer come into such bondage, Or not alwaies condescend in these lesser pointes vnto A Protestant: Yet, if he striue long with him about it, and stand in the Defence of the last nine hundred yeres, alleaging many and them good causes, wherefore the Testimonie and consent of so long time should be alowed, the longer he striueth, the worse shall he be esteemed for it, and the ernest mainteining of euery Truth on his side, shall goe in Print abrode for an Argument, that in dede he hath no good right.

Be

Be it so then, The Catholike must let goe the vantage of ix. C. yeres, he must fight within that time and cumpasse that the Heretike prescribeth: And although that naturally, al men are more fauorable, to them that are called in to the law, than the suers and troblers of them, and suffer the defendant, whome worldly frindship cleane forsaketh, to haue as much right as his cause will geaue him: Yet, let all thinges be forgoten, which may commend the Catholikes, and as M. Iewel hath appointed, so, let the first six hundred yeres only be considered and alowed.

But here now let me aske one Question. Is it not Reason, like as our aduersarie prescribeth vnto vs, the number and Terme of yeres, out of which we must gather our Argumentes: that so likewise he, shuld not come against vs with any Testimony or Authority, which were out of those apointed Limites and boundes of yeres? If a Challenger shall say to the Partye whome he Prouoketh, come, let vs straite waies trie the matter

be=

A most reasonable condition.

betwene our selues in the plaine Fielde,
and bring thou thy Sword and Buckler
as I will mine : when they are agreed,
vpon the Time, Place, and kind of wea∫
pon, if the Challenger would, againſt the
others ſingle ſworde, come with ſword,
dager, horſe, ſpere, Dagge, and what ſo
euer defence or helpe he could get byſide,
ſhould he not be compted A wretched and
Contentious , and A glorious Iacke
Bragger ? He that biddeth the combat,
ſeemeth to take himſelf for the better mã,
and to like his owne cauſe and quarell
very wel: how Ignominious then and
Shamefull muſt it be vnto him , not to
fight vpon equall conditions with hys
Aduerſarie ?

Reaſon you againſt me (ſayeth M.
Iewel) out of the firſt ſix hundred yeres
only: but I for all that, will be at my li∫
bertie to vſe any Teſtimonie out of the
rv. C. and odde yeres ſens Chriſt. which
in very deede is as much to ſay, as knele
you here vpon one knee, and Fight not
out of this Circle which I make to you,
As for my ſelfe I will goe or run at my
plea∫

pleasure about you, and take my vantage
where I can finde it, sometimes within,
sometimes without the Circle, somtimes
stãding nigh, sometimes coursing about
the field.

Mary Sir, if such Priuileges might
be graunted to warriers, it were an ea=
sie mater to prolong the Battell, and to
winne the praise of much manlinesse, by
spurring out hither and thither, and no
mater how. For, he taketh no care
hereof, how truly he alleage, the Testi=
monies of these last nine hundred yeres,
Or how worthie and approued Authors
they be, whom he alleageth, but without
exception he taketh all that he findeth,
and from the highest to the lowest, from
the Text to the Glose, and emong Glo=
ses from the best to the worst of them, he
Taketh, and Draweth, and Heapeth a=
gainst vs, Al that may seeme to helpe his
Assertions.

Tel vs therefore (I pray you M. Ie=
wel) what Equitie or Conscience you fo=
low? will you binde the Catholikes, to
the first six hundred yeres, And wil your
selfe argue out of cumpasse? May not

E i   we

we vſe the worthie Authoritie of Bonifacius, becauſe he was Biſhop of Rome
in the yere of our Lord 680, and will you
admit the ſayinges and doinges of Luther, Zwinglius and Caluine, all condemned Perſons, through the Catholike
Church, and liuing xv.C. yeres after
Chriſt?

S. Bernard (you ſay) was A man of
late yeres. So was Dioniſius the Car-
thuſian, So were others, whom I haue
rekened vp, in the chapiter before: And
therefore, by your accompt, of leſſe Authoritie. And why then doe you alleage
not only S. Bernard, but Durand, Gerſon, Alexander, Lynwod, Camotenſis,
Hugo Cardinalis, Eckius, Æneas Syluius, Eraſmus, and other? I report me
to the very margine of your boke, by that
it will appeere, whether you do not ſtuffe
your boke, with Canons, Conſtitutions,
Gloſes, Hiſtories, Interpretations of
ſcripture, Teſtimonies of Fathers, Opinions of Scholemen. &c. ſuch as altogether you ſcrape out of theſe laſt nine C.
yeres. For which your ſo doing, if you
　　　　　　　　　　　　　　　　　　can

can bring any Reason, or shew any Spe=
tiall Pryuilege graunted to you, against
the law of Nature, that you might do a=
gainst an other, that, which you would
not haue done to your selfe: either, of this
vnreasonable fauor and Licence, you
must geaue some cause, or els you must
suffer vs to complaine of it, that you dele
not with vs Indifferently.

But it will be thought, perchaunse, of
others, that you alleage not ỹ later wry=
ters, of any time these nine C. yeres, for
the Estimation or Credite, which you
haue them in, but only, because your Ad=
uersary maketh great Price of them.

Suppose it were so: yet you doe him
greate wronge, to put him to Answe=
ring of more witnesses, than he should
doe by right : And to fill your Replie
with those mennes sayinges, whose Au=
thoritees though he doe not contemne,
yet he would not haue them to possesse,
& occupie ỹ place, which more Auncient
and worthier Persons should haue. And
although we think as it becometh vs, of
s. Bernard, s. Bonaueture, S. Denyse. &c.

E ij   Yet

Yet, if you would needes haue vs in
Reasoning with you , not to passe the
Boundes and Terme of vj.C.yeres,you
shoulde not,though we alowed the Per=
sons neuer so much, bring any of A low=
er degree and later age against vs, either
to stand in the place which S.Hierome,
S.Ambrose, S.Augustine, or S.Chry=
sostome should occupie, either to com=
mend that place the better by their Pre=
sence,which the Auncient Fathers of the
Primitiue Church, doe furnishe aboun=
dantly by themselues : and which also
they only should furnishe , by your ap=
pointement. And further I say, that if
you will not suffer me to take any van=
tage against you,by the testimony of any
good Man or wryter of the nine hundred
yeres last past , it is no equalitie, that,
whether I will or no, you should make
me to Answer the sayinges , which you
bring against me,out of those yeres whi=
che you passe not vpon. And whereas
it shall doe me no good,though I proue,
that S.Bernard (for Example) in that
place which you wil alleage, doth not on
ly not hinder,but allso further my cause:

to what purpose should I spend anye
time at all, in hearing or examining hys
wordes, which, although I declare to
make for me, may not be lawfully vsed
of me?

And therefore, notwithstanding you
iudge truly of vs herein and better of vs
than of your self, that we, the Catholikes,
doe not refuse the Authoritie of later Fa=
thers and Doctours, whom the Church
yet neuer condemned or despised: Yet,
this our credite which we haue them in,
must not serue you for any cause or ex=
cuse, why ye should bring them furth a=
gainst vs, except we may doe the like a=
gainst you. For, as you haue appealed
to the first vi. C. yeres, thereby to let vs
of our Libertie, so we doe require you al=
so, not to passe that nūber or cumpasse of
those yeres, thereby to cut away your su=
perfluitie. And in thus doing, we are
not weary of the later Doctours of Chri=
stendome, nor afraid of their Iudgmentes
but we are offended with your vainglo=
rious , and very wretched behauioure,
which will not keepe the law yourselfe,
that you prescribe vnto other.

Ther is, I graunt, A kind of Argumēt ad hominem, non ad rem, to the man not to the mater. As, to some of our Countrie men, at this present, and them of the most Perfite and exquisite Trade, in folowing of the Gospel, if A Catholike doe saye, that Father Caluine himself, (whose Iudgment is much praised in the Congregation,) was of this mind, and was also Zelous in it., that they did very ill, which gaue to king Harry the viii. that he should be head of the Church: this argument so taken of his Authoritie, that was a Proude, and Folishe, And Lousie Heretike, although it be nothing worth in deede, and in that respect not to be vsed of A Catholike, Yet, to him that accompteth of Caluine, as if he had bene one of ý lights of the world, ý Catholike may right wel vse it, & driue him by force of the Consequence, either to deny Caluines Authority (which he wil not) Or ý kings supremacy (which he dareth not.) So ý against him, that is addicted to any one Opinion of his own, or of other whō he buildeth vpon, to bring an Argumene grounded vpō his own Opinion & iudgmene

In Com:
Sup, Amos

ment, & thereby to make him forsake his
own opinion, or kepe stil in his memory
the Contradiction which inwardly pin-
cheth him : It is A kind of Reasoning,
good and profitable.

And, in this respect, if any Catholike
were so blinde & singular, as to set more
by the Glose vpon *Vnã Sanctã, Extr. de Ma-*
ior & Obed: than the Commentaries of S.
Hierome, and S. Chrisostome : Or by
Durand, Gerson, Lynwod. &c. than any
of the most Aunrient Fathers: M. Iewel
then, might be suffered to argue *ad homi-*
nem, that is, to alleage Gloses, Schole
men and later Doctours, to him that hath
A speciall fansie vnto those, more than a-
ny of the Primitiue Church. But now, se
y̆ Inequality & ods. For neither D. Har.
nor his Inferiors, are so ignorãt of y̆ sẽse
& strength of this word Catholike, y̆ they
shuld be addicted to any one, two, or thre
mens priuate sayings of what degree or
time so euer they haue ben, (without the
consent or warrant of the Church) neither shuld M. Iewel alleage vnto them,
any Testimony of the last nine hundred
yeres, himself referring the triall of the
       E iiij   whole

the whole mater to the first vj. C. only.
And hauing such Aduersaries, as are very well content, to be ordered by the sentence and Judgment of that first age, and
that Primitiue Church.

Yet go to for a while, let M. Jewel be
suffered : And let it be his excuse, that he
hath argued alwaies ad hominem , to the
man, when he hath vsed the Testimonies
of later times , thereby to impugne D.
Harding. Let him say (J meane) that
he hath recited in his Replye, Durand,
Gerson, Biel, Denyse, Hugo Cardinall,
Thomas Duns. &c. not, because himself
aloweth them, but, because they are estemed of ŷ party against whō he wryteth.

But is this true? And hath not he vsed
their Testimonies in respect also of hys
owne opinion, ꝙ confirmed himself in it,
because of their Testimonies ? when he
reasoneth Substantially , and Directly,
and Plainly to his Purpose , and ad rem
to the mater, and out of his owne Principles (as it were) and Authorities, doth
he not alleage the forsayde Doctours, although they were , all the sort of them,
farre vnder the first six hundred yeres,

es

to whiche onely he would haue the Deci=
sion of the controuersies referred? whe=
ther this be so or no, let Examples try it.

M. Iewel is of the Opinion that no **Iew.195.**
Christian Churches wer built in the Apostles tyme : And muche lesse then Aulters
(if his Logicke be good.) For may wee
thinke (sayth he) that Aulters were built
before the Churche? Of whiche Lye, we **In the**
shall speake in an other place. But to my **Chapiter**
purpose. It foloweth in him: **of Lyes.**

Neuther afterward, when Aulters were **Iew.**
first vsed, and so named, were they straite
waye built of Stone, as Durandus and such
others saie, they must needes be, and that,
Quia petra erat Christus, *Becauſe Chriſt vvas*
the Stone,

whereof then were they built, accor= **Ra.**
ding to your Opinion? And what Cause
or Authoritie haue you for it ? It fo=
loweth.

For Gerson saith, that Siluester Bishop **Iew.**
of Rome, first caused Stone Aultars to be
made. &c.

Is Gerson then, of Authoritie with **Ra**
you? And a man of so late yeares, and
little fame and Estimation, in compa=
rison

rison of many Fathers and Doctours of
the ix. C. yeares last past, all which you
refuse, is hee nowe a witnesse for you?
Here it is plaine that you bring in this
late writer, to serue directly your owne
Opinion, and, that he standeth you
in suche steede, that without him, you
proue not that whiche you saide.

You depende not therefore vppon
your Aduersaries allowing of Gerson.
as who shoulde saye: if he admit the Testimonie of him, then doe I confirme my
Assertion, and if he doe not, yet haue I
other Authorities to proue my sayinges
true: but, you doe so absolutely and proprely for your owne Opinion vse him,
that without him, you leaue your matters vnproued . But let vs see another Example.

It is required of M . Jewell, that
forasmuche as the Catholikes coulde neuer yet finde, that the Publike Seruice
in the Primitiue Churche, was in any
other than Greeke or Latine, and hee
yet is sure of the Contrarye, that it was
euery where in a tongue knowen to the
vulgare

Uulgare People: he shew therefore his Proses and Authorities, suche by all likelyhode, as himselfe is perswaded withall, before he woulde haue other to allowe theim. Marke then what hee sayth,

And, to auoyde multitude of woordes, the case beeing plaine, Eckius sayth, the Indians had their Seruice, in the Indian tongue, Durandus saith, The Iewes, that were Christened, had their Seruice in the Hebrew tongue.

Iew. 175.
Eckius in locis Com.
Durand. lib. 4. ca. 1.

Nycolas Lyra, and Thomas de Aquine, saye, The Common Seruice in the Primitiue Churche was in the Common vulgare tongue.

Nicolaus Lyra. Thomas in. 1. ad Cor. 14.

And in the next leafe folowing, he aleageth Aeneas Syluius and an Extrauagant de Officio Iudicis Ordinarij. and Iohn Billet in Summa de Diuinis officijs.

177.

But what are all these? were they not writers of very late yeares? were they not Popisshe Doctours, or Popysshe Proctours, not woorthe the naming

Ra.

naming (by M. Iewels Accompt) and
much lesse worth the Crediting? why then
doth he alleage them? will he saye, he
condescended herein to D. Hardinges
Infirmitie? And, that he vseth his owne
Doctours for the better contentation of
his mind? No verely he must not say so.
For he was required to bring his owne
groundes and witnesses, and not such,
as are alowed only per accidens, that is,
because it so happeneth, that an other mã
liketh them. He was content allso to
shew his profes, and to yeld to the foresaid Request, both for the goodnesse and
pregnancie of the cause, and also specially,
Good Christian Reader, (sayeth he,) for
the better Contentation of thy mind.

Iew. 175.

If the cause then be good and pregnãt,
why vse you so ill and baren Testimonies, as all theirs are (if your accompt
be true) which come furth, after the first
six hundred yeres? And, if you seeke after the Contentation of your Readers
mind, you signifie thereby, that the Authorities, which you alleage, are worthy and alowable. Not, because Doctor
Har-

Harding will make no Exception, per=
chaunce, against them, but becaufe your=
felfe like them and esteeme them.

Otherwife, what Contentation of the
Readers mind, call you this, to Reafon
vpon their Authozities, whom yourfelf
would haue to be contemned? Oz, to
establish any opinion vpō such groundes
vpon which you can build nothing, ex=
cept vnto him, which holdeth them foz
fure and good? Of which fozt of men,
you make not (I trust) euery your good
Christian Reader to be. Especially, ma=
ny of them, by your oft Appealing to the
first fix hundzed yeres, being occafioned,
to fet litle by anye Testimonie of lower
time and degree.

Thus we fee againe, that M. Iewel
hath vfed the late wzyters Testimonie
Eckius, Durand, Thomas Aquinas,
and John Biller, not, becaufe of D.
Hardinges opinion oz regard of them
(which how greate oz litle it is, he doth
not know) but, becaufe of his owne li=
king of them.

Neither doth he pecke (as it were) an
occa=

occasion to vse them, out of his Aduer=
saries estimation of them, but whether
D. Harding aloweth them oz no, M.
Iewell flatly vseth them, noz is asha=
med of the latenes of them. A thing,
at other times so materiall with hym,
that on paine of fozfaiting all a mans la=
bour, none must be bzought in foz wit=
nesses, but suche as are, within little, a
thowsand yeare olde.

See one place moze and with that, we
shall ende this Chapiter . It is a que=
stion betweene the Catholikes and the
Heretikes , whether the woozdes of
Chzifte, in the sixt of S. John, are to
be vnderstanded, onely of the spirituall
eating of his body, Oz of the Spirituall
and Sacramentall bothe . The firste
is the newe Maisters, the seconde is the
Olde Fathers. . To pzoue the firste,
that the woozdes of our Sauiour in that
Chapiter, are taken and meant of spiri=
tuall eating onely, Thus sayth Mai=
ster Iewell.

Iew.104   For to leaue S. Augustine, Origine, and
others of that age : Nicolas Lyra, a man of
later yeres saith, The said words of Christ,
                                    must

muſt needes be taken Spiritually, and none otherwiſe.

Lykewiſe, one Michael Væhe, one of late yeares, a man of M. Hardings owne ſyde, touching the ſame matter, wryteth thus (againſt 𝕷uther.) This ſaith he, is a weake reaſon, for, the woordes, that be ſpoken of Spirituall eating, He Applieth to the Sacramentall eating. Here may M. Harding ſee, beſydes S. Auguſtine, Origine, and other olde Catholike Fathers, whoſe Woordes I haue not a-leaged, what men he hathe called Newe Maiſters. Nicolas Lyra, was an Engliſhe man, and liued two hundred yeares before Luther. Michaell Væhe, was of late yeares; and wrote namelye againſt Luther.

𝕳eere 𝕴 trowe, it is perceaued that 𝕸. 𝕴ewell vſeth late writers 𝕿eſtimonies, in defence of his ſyde. 𝕿he queſtion is, whether the ſirt of 𝕾. 𝕵ohn, be vnderſtanded of 𝕾pirituall eatinge onely or no. 𝕴f it be, let vs ſee your 𝕬uthorities (𝕸. 𝕴ewell) and reaſons.

𝕿he new maſters (as 𝕯. 𝕳ard. tearmeth them) expound it ſo. Thei are not all new maſters (ſay you) that haue ſo take the

𝕳owe

How proue you that? For Nicolas Lyra (You Aunswere) saith it. and one Michael Væhe one of late yeares. They saye it not, that it is to be vnderstanded onely of Spirituall eating, but of Spirituall eating without ONELY. Suppose yet they saide it, what were that to purge the new Maisters of the fault of Singularitie, or to perswade your Reader that it must be so taken? I doe not displayse neither Nicolas Lyra, neither Michaell Vehe, but I can not but mislike it greatly in you, to aleage their Names in your defense, whose Authorities are neyther Excellent, nor Yeares Auncient. Especially, whereas you would seeme to haue S. Augustine, Origine, and others of that age, to stande with you in this matter. But you leaue them and come to Nicolas Lyra.

what doe you M. Iewel? Is there any man, in all the Catholike Churche, whiche will giue you leaue, to answere him rather by Nicolas Lyra, then S. Augustine? And dothe it become your Manheade and Corage, (whiche is so great, that you will haue Controuersies exami-

M. Iew. beleeth his witnesses.

M. Iew. leaueth S. Augustine &c. & foloweth Nicolas Lyra.

examined by no later writers, then those
of the first six hundred yeares,) thus to
leaue, S. Augustine (whose Authoritye
is worthelye regarded of all wise men)
and cleaue to Nicolas Lyra, whose testimony any man (except it be of contempt)
may lawfully let alone with out vsing or
alowing of it? You commend hym to vs
in two poyntes, He was (you saye) An
English man, and lived two hundred yeres
before Luther. I haue reade the contrarye, that he was a Iew, borne at Liere:
neuerthelesse if you for Countrye sake (as
borne perchaunce in the old or new Iury
in Londō) or for Age sake, as liuing two
hundred yeres before Luther, doe thynke
that he is a worthy witnesse to Englishe
men of this age, I will not reproue your
kindnesse of hart towardes your Coun-
trymen, nor affection to the time later by
seuen hundred yeres than the Primityue
church vnto which you apeale so precisely: But this, who can abyde? To consider M. Iuell, so great a Contemner of
later Dyuines and Scholemen, to leaue
S. Augustine, Origen and others, and to   Absurde.
defend hys felowes, by Nycolas Lyra and
       F j   Michael

Michaell Væhe? And not onely that, but to crake (as it were) that S.Augustin is also with him,and yet not so muche as to name the place where it might bee sought and sounde . For consider his wordes.

104

Here maye M. Hardinge see besydes S. Augustine , Origene, and other olde Catholike Fathers, whose wordes I haue not allegaed,what men he hath called New Maisters.

M. Iew. belieth himselfe.

In deede, hee may see that you haue brought furth, Nycolas Lyra, and one Michael Væhe: but ŷ he may se them,by-sydes S. Augustine, Origene, and other Olde Catholike Fathers, Howe is it possible ? For your selfe confesse,that,you haue not alleaged their wordes. And how then shoulde he see them ? If M. Harding doe no more, but quote onely the places of the Doctours, in whiche his sayengs be verefied, And leaue the writing out of their whole Sentences : all this (you wil say)is but a Camissado,these be but visardes : They be no faces : They are brought in, like Mummers,for a shew, and say nothing. And what pretie Counterfaiting

R4.

Iew.6.

terfeiting may we call this, to alleage a later writers saying fully , and not so much as quote the place of the olde Fathers: And yet, to make an Oftentation with, here may M. Harding fee, befides S. Augustine, Origen, and other old Catholike Fathers whofe wordes I haue not alleged, what men he hath called new masters? Verely, this is befide all reafon, to tel me that befides S. Augustine. &c. I may See what Nycolas Lyra testifieth, wher no one Sentence or Halfe sentence of S. Augustines is to be Seen, Heard, or Understanded, in the place on which I am bid to looke.

But, I haue not alleged their wordes, fayeth M. Iewel. And why did you not, I pray you, Sir? were you in such haft to come to Nycolas Lyra and Michael Væhe, that you could not tary with S. Augustin, Origene, and other old Catholike Fathers? Is it your maner of writing, to spare the Alleging of old Fathers? Or, was their word, not worth the hearing? Or, must we needes beleue your Affertion, without further euidence? The Truthe is, neither Saint Augustine, nor Origen,

This is worfethan mumery.

F ij nor

noz any other old Catholike Fathers did pzecifely fay, that the firth of S. Jhon, must be vnderstanded only of the Spiritual eating of Chzistes fleshe. And you, although you could not haue their voyces, yet you were fo bold as to vfe their Names: And pzetending, as thoughe it were eafie to fee, that they did teftifie foz you, fo, you leaue them quite and cleane, and bzing in, Nycolas Lyra an Englishe-man, and Michael Vvehe of late yeres, to fpeake fomewhat foz you.

Confider now (Jndifferent Reader) whether M. Jewel vfeth the later wzy-ters, as Neceffary witneffes in his owne caufe, oz no? And whether he bzingeth them in, as Men whom D. Harding is well content withall, Oz as Perfons, without whom, his fayinges, could haue no Pzobalitie at all? Foz, if he had alle-ged, firft S. Auguftine, Ozigen, and other old Catholike Fathers, and afterwardes, had reherfed the Opinions and Judg-mentes of later wziters: he might haue ben thought to haue done it foz A Sur-pluffage, and to haue fought thereby, to perfwade rather his Aduerfarie, than to

Con=

Confirme his owne Affertion. But on the other fide now, to leaue S. Augustine, Origen and other Fathers, and to ftay on-ly vpon Lyra and Vaæbe , what other thing is it, than to Proteft that by their Teftimonies his caufe is Sufficientlye proued? And , to take vantage of their fayinges, which liued out of the fix hun-dred, next after Chrift? And, this is that which deferueth iuft Indignation , that any man, bearing the Perfon and Face, of one that had difcretion or Confcience, fhould bind an other to a certaine com-paffe of Time and Yeres, which, in no cafe, he fhould paffe, in Debating of any controuerfie : And yet , would in the meane Time himfelfe, Argue, Reafon, and Conclude, out of any Time, and re-quire to haue it ftand, for profe good and fufficient, of his owne Affertions: And to vfe that kind of Libertie or Prerogatiue, not only when he fpeaketh ad hominem, that is, to the Meaning, Senfe, Opini-on, or Fancie of the man , with whom he hath to doe, but alfo, ad rem, that is, ac-cording to his owne Meaning & Iudg-ment, in which, he taketh the teftimonies

F iij   by

by himselfe alleaged, to perteine, Direct=
ly, and in deede, to Confirmation of the
cause, which he susteineth.

Yet (as I saied before) let M. Iewels
excuse be, that he hath vsed Late wryters
Testimonies, not for any stay of his own
Opinions (the contrary whereof I haue
shewed) but to stop only D. Hardinges
mouthe, and to set one Papist against an
other, Let him so saie, and let vs so take
it: yet, is this no indifferent dealing.
For, if he wil bind vs to the first six hun=
dred yeres, and himselfe yet, will presse
vs with Authorities of later age, either
he mindeth that we shall Answer him in
them, or holde our peace and be still.

If we shall answer: why apointed he
the Lymites of six hundred yeres to be
kept of vs? For, when he prouoketh vs,
with mater collected out of the cumpasse
of them, we must needes come also out of
them, and ioyne with him, thereypon.

And, if he minded that we should not
at all Answer him, and that himselfe yet,
would Obiect suche Testimonies vnto
vs: why did he then Obiect them? Ex=
cept we shall Iudge of him, that he is so
Folishe,

Foliſhe, as to apoint it, oʒ ſo Pʒonde and Stately, as to conceiue it, that it maye be lawfull foʒ him, in fighting againſt his Aduerſarie, to haue certaine Places open vnto his Deſperate Foynes, and that no warding of the Daunger, and no Buck= ler ſhould be vſed.   And therefoʒe,

It is not to be graunted vnto you M. Iewel, to Bind vs to the firſt ſix hun= dʒed yeres, And to be Looſe yourſelfe, concerning any witneſſe oʒ Authoʒitie, of the nine hundʒed folowinge: To ſet vs within a Circle, and yourſelfe to Diſ= courſe out of Oʒder and Cumpaſſe: To foʒbid vs, the Alleaging of S. Bernard, and yet to charge vs with the Opinion of Michael Vehe, oʒ any ſuch other. No Sir: to the firſt ſix hundʒed you haue Appealed, to the firſt ſix hundʒed only, you ſhall ſtand.

If you wil Replie, they be our owne Doctoures, and therefoʒe we maye not Refuſe them: we Anſwer ſhoʒtly vnto you, that whereas in your Singulare Iudgement they be no Doctoures at all, And whereas you will not Suffer them to be Oures, Oʒ that we maie
          F iiij   alleage

alleage them and recite thē as our own:
we therefore in this Case and State of
Reasoning with you, doe not take them
for our owne. Yea, they must be so comp=
ted vpon and so set aside, as if they wer
no mens witnesses at all, Because you, in
Drawing the mater to the first six hun=
dred yeres only, doe Import and Con=
clude thereby, that, of al later Times and
writers, you would haue A sad Silence
to be agreed vpon, and kept.

But, where will M. Jewels Glozie
be then? And, if he himselfe shall vse no
Testimonie vnder the first vj. C. yeres:
how litle wil his Replie be? How vncer=
taine must his Answers be? How greate
Blindnes and Silence must he come vn=
to? Take away from M. Jewel, and his
felowes the last nine hundred yeres, and
you take away from them the Flowers
of their Diuinitie. Out of those yeres,
they Rake all the euill that is spoken, of
Popes, Cardinals, Priestes. &c. that by
reueling other mennes Turpitude, they
may commend their owne bare Hone=
sties. Out of those, come many Canons
of Councels, Constitutions of Empe=
rours,

The flow ers of the new Gos= pell.

rours , Uarieties of Hiſtoriographers,
Concluſions and Diſtinctions of Schole
men, in the number of which, it is eaſy to
find ſomewhat, alwaies, that ſhalt ſound
againſt the Catholikes. Either, becauſe
all thinges , are not to be taken as they
lie, but neede an Interpretation : either
becauſe , when many write of one Fact,
Dr intreate of one mater, they do not alwaies ſo throughly agree, in euery point
of the Hiſtorie or Queſtion , but that he,
whome it Pleaſeth to ſtriue thereupon
with an other, may ſone find A doubt Dr
Argument to ſerue his humor of Contradiction . Dut of thoſe, many Gloſes
are peeked, ſo Obſcure or Triſling, that
were it not , for the Diligence of Heretikes, which haue brought them furth in
to light, They would as litle haue ben
ſought for of the Catholikes, As they are
now litle eſteine d of them, when they are
Found out and ſhewed to them by the
Heretikes.

Take therefore, the writinges of the
laſt nine hundred yeres , awaye from the
Proteſtantes, and there muſt needes folow , ſuch lacke of mater , to make vp
               their

their Tales, that they will sone be at an
end, both in writing and in Preachinge.
And, not only concerning their ill Purposes:(As, to bring either the Departed
into hatred, by opening their faultes, Or
them that at this Present liue, into In-
famie, by charging them with the faultes
of their Forefathers(but, concerning also good and holsome Lawes, Decrees,
Definitions, Orders of Gouernement,
Customes, Ceremonies, which haue ben
in these last nine hundred yeres, wisely
apointed, and Profitablie continued, If
nothing, that is testified by the writings
and Practise of them, shall stand in any
steede to make a Sentence or Argumēt:
what Confusion, Contention, Destruction, Blindnesse, Desperatnesse, will be
caused in both States, Spirituall and
Temporall, It is easy to be perceaued.

what Church shall keepe her Priuileges? what Clergie continue in any Order of Seruing God? what King or Emperour, mainteine the Crowne vpon
his heade? what state of Common wealth
in all Christendome maye be defended?
If, the Recordes, wrytinges, Answers,
De-

Decrees, Actes, Dispenſations, Conclu=
ſions, and Lawes of the laſt nine hun=
dꝛed yeres, muſt be, all, either vtterly re=
fuſed, Oꝛ better Examined befoꝛe they
be receiued?

For in theſe later yeres, Countries
haue ben conuerted: Religion hath ben
Planted: Hereſies, by the Authoꝛitie of
Councels, haue ben condemned: The
Empire, hath ben tranſlated: Our owne
Realme of England hath ben conquered,
And, in all theſe ſo greate pointes, the
Iudgmente and Sentence of the Pope
hath alwaies ben regarded. And that,
which at this day is holden foꝛ Truth,
in A thouſand caſes both Spirituall and
Tempoꝛall, dependeth in deede vpon the
Decree and Oꝛder, which the Gouernoꝛs
of the Church foꝛ that time, made foꝛ it
and apointed, when the caſe was firſt mo=
ned, Oꝛ exhibited.

If therefoꝛe, no Authoꝛitie oꝛ Teſti=
monie of theſe later nine hundꝛed yeres,
muſt be admitted, let M. Iewel with all
his owne wit, And Policy of his frendes
byſide, ſee how he can begin the woꝛld
a freſhe.

And,

And, the foundation of six hundred yeres standing on sure grounde, let him pull downe all, that hath beene builded, and shew vs some fyne peece of worke of his owne, suche I trowe as shall in all Proportion agree with the Primitiue Churche and ryse in a moste goodly Order of euery Hundred yeare since, one aboue another, vntill he come vnto this very time, in whiche he liueth, and geue men to see moste plainly and euidently, that his Churche now, is of the same makinge, without any Imperfection, Or gaping of the worke that may be espied . Let him I say make an Vniforme and Apte worke.

For if he will beginne at the ende of the six Hundred yeares, and immediately, ioyne thereto, the state of His Congregation at this Present : either it will be a Miraculous worke to see foundacious with metely high wals, and a Roufe a great waye from them , without any Stone, Timber, Staye or workemanshippe betweene : Either will it be a very Euilfauoured matter, to see one peece hanging so farre from the other, as Germanes

mans o2 Heretikes lippes doe hange to=
geather. If therefoze your building be
Sure and True, Ioine yeres to yeres,
and without all gappes o2 holes, make
the whole, perfite, Close, and One.

But ye are as wel able to doe it, and
knit o2 ioine your Church to the Primi=
tiue, as ye are to builde vp againe, Al the
Abbeies in England, O2 proue vnto vs
that the Stones of them, which lie now
b2oken in high waies, o2 were caried out
of the waie, to building of Gentelmens
places, doe answer rightly in the fozme
which they haue at this p2esent, to the
foundations and Pillers, remainyng,
yet, vnto some Religious houses, from
whence they haue ben taken. Especial=
ly this P2inciple of your Artificiousnes
standing, that the Testimonie of these
last nine hund2ed yeres, is not to be Al=
leaged o2 Alowed.

Which being so Uninst and Unreaso=
nable, as I haue declared, Either, let M.
Iewel vtterly put out of his Replye,
what so euer he hath gathered and sc2a=
ped, out of Canons, Gloses, Schole men,
Here=

Heretikes, Historiographers, and other wryters whatsoeuer of later yeres, And from henseforth, fill no more Papers with such kind of stuffe: Either els, let him be ashamed, to bind vs to the first six hundred only, himselfe not able to Conteine himselfe, Or Maintaine hys cause, within that cumpasse.

But, I know, I aske his losse. For, If he may not pecke out of all times such Signes of Defence for his cause, as maie seeme to serue for it, he will be quickly vndone in the best Limme he hath, And, without all doubt will be Tongtied. As, on the other side, If he will let vs haue right, and suffer vs to proue our cause by godly and Lerned witnesses, of what so euer Age they be, so that he can make no lawfull Exception against them, then is he vtterly vndone in his owne Conscience: knowing that the Catholike Church, doth expressely and by name, condemne his Maisters Heresies. So that it is not otherwise likely, but he will haue vs to stand fast bound to the first six hundred yeres, and will reserue
vnto

vnto himselfe, that special Priuilege, to
Take and Make his vantage , where,
and when so euer he may.

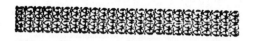

1 *That M. Iewel refuseth to be tried*
  by the Sentence or Testimony of
  the first six hundred yeres , to
  which only he appealeth.

WHat Remedie then? If M.
Iewel shall prouoke manful-
ly, and wretchedly apoint vs
a bound, which we may not go
beyond in cõming against him: If he may
vse vb.C.yeres and odd, and we not vj.
C.and one day ouer: If he shal fetch nede
lesse vagaries , and we be restrained of
our lawfull libertie : what Remaineth?
                         Verely,

Werelye to haue pacience, vntill it shall please Almighty God either to conuerte his heart to repentaunce, either to moue the mindes of other, to haue a better consideration of these Matters whiche pertaine to their Saluation, either to come himselfe in Judgemente, and make an rnde of all Proceedings . Yet this in the meane time, thou maist consider (indifferent Reader) that we are two manner of wayes abused, by M. Jewell. First, that ye wil prescribe vnto vs from whence we shall take our Argumentes against him . Secondly, that himselfe will not be content with those Condicions, whiche he prescribeth vnto vs.

But is this all the wrong that Maister Jewell doth vnto Us ? No, it is not all . For now, I shall declare vnto thee, how Himselfe will not admitte the witnesses of the very first six hundred yeares, vnto whiche he straightly byndeth vs . And what can bee more vnreasonable ? For in seperating the last nine Hundred from the first six, and in alowing the Firste, and condemning the Latter, what dothe he but note vnto vs
the

the Incorruption and Puritie of Faith in those daies, and not warrant the Testimonies to be good, if it be taken out of the first six hundred yeres after Christ. Of the first he saieth, If ani learned mã. &c **Iew. a.1** be able to bring any one Sufficient Sentence. &c. that the thinges vpon which he Chalengeth vs, were vsed or alowed in the Primitiue Churche, for the space of six hundred yeres after Christ, I am content to yeld and subscribe. Of the Later yeres he saieth. S. Bernard is a Doctour **116.** but of late yeres, therefore his Authoritie must weigh the Lighter.

If therefore there be no Excellencie or Prerogatiue in the first six hundred, why diuided he them, so Precisely and Diligently from the later nine? And, If there be so Great, as he seemeth to make, why will not he himselfe stand vnto the Iudgment of that Primitiue Churche, And that first age so chast and vndefiled? Choose one of these two (M: Iewel,) which you will: And let vs see an Example and token, either of your wisdome and Prudencie, in Separating, for some iust cause, the Beginninges of the One,

B i and

and whole Summe of rv. C. yeres, from the latter endes of it: either of your Justice and Indifferencie, in regarding the witnesses of the First six hundred yeres, which you require to be exactly folowed of others.

Iew.140. For as you say, Lyra and Teutonicus, liued at the least, Thirtene C. yeares after Christ: Therefore their Authoritie must needes seeme the lesse: why saye ye not also, S. Leo, and S. Gregorie, liued fiue hundred yeares after Christe, Therefore their Authoritie must nedes seme the lesse? Or why put you A Difference, betwene the Former and the later yeres of the rv. C. in which Christ hath ruled his church? And, if your wisedome saw good causes, wherefore you should sort y yeres which haue passed sence Christes Incarnation after a rare maner, & cul out (as it were) the best from the worst: with what Conscience then and Equitie, can you refuse to be ordered by the Testimonie of the better sort of them?

For, if against the later nine hundred yeres which you take from vs, this Excepa ception of yours is inough to discredite them, that they were Late: It foloweth consequently, that to the first six hundred yeres, this alone is Commendacion inough, that yourselfe make no Exception against them, but permit vs to take all the vantage we can out of them. As if you should haue expressely said vnto vs: for as much as I will admit no Late Catholike Doctour, Father, or Councel, but Catholike, Old and Auncient, And, for as much as I take the last nine hundred and odde yeres sens Christ, to be but late, and out of the cumpasse, which I will alow vnto you in reasoning against me: Therefore, if you looke, that I shall make no Exception against the Authoritie and Witnesses which you will bringe, Prouide by time, that they be taken out of the vj.C. yeres, next after Christ,

M. Iew. speciall Exception against the last ir.C. yeres, vzoueth that he would be ozdered by the vj.C.ɏ went befoze.

This Trueth therefoze so standyng, that, In refusing the witnesses of Later yeres, you must be vnderstanded to alow vnto vs the Catholyke wzyters of Auncient time, and this Auncient tyme, being defined vnto vs by you, ɏ it

B ij con-

conſiſteth iuſt in ᵽ vj. C. next after Chꝛiſt, ſo that if it be founde later but by one yere, you wil not take it to be old inough: Let vs ſee now, in what Maner and Faſhion, you confoꝛme yourſelf to the iudgment of that very Time, which you toke yourſelfe vnto, So Pꝛeciſely, as if it ſhould make altogeather foꝛ you.

Firſte of all, you dooe not allowe, Clemens de Conſti Apoſt. Neither Abdias: noꝛ Hypolitus Martyr. And Athanaſius Epiſtle is to you a Scar crow ſtuft vp in ſtraw, and Iulius Epiſtle ſeemeth to fauoure of ſome corruption: And at one woꝛde, the Decrees and Epiſtles decretal depraue the Scriptures, Maintaine the kingdome of the Pope, Publiſhe a multitude of Vaine Ceremonies, and I can not tell what. Foꝛ how woꝛſhipfull and woꝛthy cauſes, you make Exceptions againſt them, you ſhall better vnderſtand that by him, whiche alleaged them.

But concerning my Obiectiō, I haue moꝛe plaine and ſenſible Demonſtrations, to declare, how you refuſe Auncient Fathers, and witneſſes, that I nede not to reaſon at all with you, about your

Igno=

Marginal notes:
Iew. 7. 8. 9. 12. 233. 264. 66. and. 223.

Auncient Authoꝛities denied by M. Iewel.

Ignominious and Iniurious Extenua=
tions of the forsaid Authorities. And, if
by these Examples which I shall nowe
bring, it be not made Open and manifest,
that in deede you litle regard Antiquitie,
then will nothing euer make it playne:
And, if this which I shall declare, doe
proue so much to the Indifferēt Reader,
Inough is as Much, as he can require.

Here then, it would be remembred or
considered, that, which D. Harding brin=
geth, out of the Ecclesiastical Historie, for *Hiſt. Eccl.*
A token and argument of Communion *li.8.ca.5.*
vnder one kind: The Storie is, of A
noble woman an Heretike, which, being
driuen thereto, by feare of leesing her
husband, promised him to Receiue with
him. And, at the time of the Misteries,
hauyng the Sacrament deliuered into
her handes, she Receiued it not, but toke
of her Maied that stode by, A peece of
Breade, that she had caused to be brought
for the purpose, from her owne house.
which, as she would haue biten, it har=
dened in to a Stone. Hereof D. Harding
gathereth, that.

If

Harding.
Fol.45

If both kindes had then ben mi-
nistred , she would haue practised
some other shift , for the auoiding of
the Cup, which, had not ben so easie.
what sayeth M. Iewel herebnto?

Iew.136.
Flatering
lp.

I maie not disgrace the credite of this
Storie, albeit, in Sozomenus and Nicephorus, of bothe whome, the same is recorded,
there be sundrie thinges , that may well be
Filed.

R4.

You signifie then , that you might doe
moze, than you will . And, were it not
foz A certaine quiet Affection, that is so=
dainly come ouer your mind, we see, that,
becaufe Sozonemus and Nicephozus
haue fundzic thinges, that may wel be filed, Undoubtedly, this Stozye should
be one of them, If it were, at this pzefent
your Pleafure. But, becaufe you feare no
Inconuenience, If you should graunt it,
therfoze you make no Exception againft
it. And yet, leaft by this letting of the
Stozie to paffe fo quietly , you shoulde
feeme to geaue Occafion to some hereafter, of taking bantage againft you there=
by:

by: you geaue your Reader a watche worde, that you doe not alowe the Storye absolutely, but that you doe not Disgrace it, And that this selfesame not Disgracing of it, cummeth rather of your free will and Humanitie, than of any bounden Dutie. For, In Sozomenus and Nicephorus bothe, Sundrye thinges (you saye) may well be Filed. But perchaunce ye neede not in this Storye, to shew how finely you can file it. For it foloweth.

But I see no cause yet, wherfore M.Harding should blow the Triumph. *Iew.*

As who should saie: If there were any losse cumming vnto you, by this Storie, then loe, you would File it. But there is no feare of any. And why so? For, *Ra.*

Why might she not take the Cup, and faine that she dranke: and yet, Drinke nothing. *Iew.*

Shee might haue done so in deede by the nature of Absolute Possibilitie, but we speake nowe, what is likely to haue been done, by the course of the Storie. *Ra.*

B iiij   And

And whereas in bowing downe, after shee had taken the Sacramente into her handes, and making resemblaunce to Praye, shee might haue so handled the matter, that shee should haue seemed to haue put somwhat in her mouth. &c. And yet did not so, but prouided betweene her selfe and her maide, to bring Breade from her owne house and to eate that in steede of the Sacrament : And yet practised no shift to auoide the Cuppe, It is very Likelye and Probable, that there was no receauing of the Cuppe, at that Present : for which, because there is (as you wil not deny) a sleight in a womans witte, shee shoulde haue rather prouided, as beinge more harde to bringe to passe.

For in deede, to put the Cuppe vnto her mouth, and faine that shee dranke, It was an Easy matter: And more easy it was, when shee bowed downe her selfe, (after the taking of ỹ Sacrament into her hands), like one that would praie, to put her hand only vnto her mouth, And, either faine that she Receiued, or conueigh the mater so closely, that it should not be
                                                    Percea-

Perceaued : But, the Circumstance of the Storie geaueth it, that she coulde not escape so : (For then vndoubtedly she had ben a very Naturall, to trouble her Maied and her selfe, with care, to coueigh the houshold breade vnto her, and care to receiue it. &c.) Ergo, neither by putting the Cuppe only to her mouth, (if any then had ben vsed) she could haue satisfied her husband Or the common expectation of the lookers on, or her owne feare.

Now, whereas no Cuppe was at that present receiued, she was deliuered of the care, to find A shift to auoide it, And the Precise and Singular prouiding to receiue householde breade, vnder colour of the Sacrament, proueth, that she was not trobled with any feare of receiuing the Cuppe, or care of auoiding it. And this Reason or Argument, is problablye gathered out of the Storie it selfe. But let vs heare M. Jewels Deuise and Imagination.

Touching the Trueth of this whole mater, if a man list only to goe by Gheasse, as M.Harding doeth, why may he not thus Imagine Jew.137.

1.

Imagine with hymſelfe : If this Woman would thus diſſemble in a Caſe ſo daunge-rous, what needed her to take the Bread at her Maides handes, And ſpecially at that

2.

Time, in that Place, And in the ſight of the whole people? Or, how could ſhe ſo o-

3.

penly Receiue it without Suſpition ? Or why might ſhe not haue brought it in A

4.
5.
6.

napkin, ſecreetly aboute herſelf? The bur-then was not greate: Her faining and hipo-criſie had ben the eaſier.

R2.

Thus (ſayeth M̃. Jewel) Why maye not A man Imagine with himſelfe, it he liſt. But, wil ye know why not ? J will tell you. No man ought to make ſuch A Gloſe, as ſhall marre the Texte. Nor J-magine that, whiche goeth Directlye againſte the Literall Senſe of an Hi-ſtorye ? For, the Hiſtorye , the cre-dite whereof you maie not diſgrace, (you

Conſider M. Jew. liſting and imagining againſt ỹ Storie.

ſayed befoze) maketh expreſſe mention, of bzeade taken at her Maides handes, And of the ſame receyued by the Mae-ſtres in the open Church , And of her

whiche he promiſſed not to diſ-grace.

faining and Hypocriſy, how it was con-founded. And this now , is done and paſt aboue A thouſand yeres ſens, And how

how it was done it remaineth in wryting. But you, neuerthelesse, come in
with your Listing and Imagining. Not
to find out that, by probable Coniectures
which lieth hid in the Storie , but by
cleane Contrarie and froward Fancye,
destroying the very Literall state and
Description thereof.

And to this effect, as thoughe that the
Sleight of a womans wit were litle worth,
you adde of your owne inuention A further fetch. which, perchaunse, the woman would haue folowed , if she had
knowen it in tyme: but now, after all is
done, to aske, what neede she had to take
the Breade at her maides handes. Or to
wonder, how she could so openly Receiue
it without Suspition. Or to teache her,
that she might haue brought it in a napkin
Or to perswade with her , that the bur-
then was not greate, as thoughe the gentelwoman had bene so tender and fine,
ẏ she could not haue caried ẏ weight of
A Singing cake more then her Ordinarie , Or to Conclude with her,
that her Faining woulde be the Easyer:
                                        thus,

thus, I saie when all is past remedie, to feede your owne Fancie, or fill your Readers eares, with so long and so vaine A tale, It is to simple for any womans wit.

For Imagine you, as much as ye list, that she neded not to take the bread at her maides handes: The Storie so plainely testifying, that she toke it, what must folow? No other thing surely, but that the Storie is vnlikely. And so of euery other of the Circumstancies, which your man that hath A list to Imagine, gathereth of that which hymselfe thinketh meete to haue ben done, what other thing foloweth, but that the Storie, which reporteth the Contrary to haue ben done, is very vnlikely and Incredible.

Such a Fauorer you be of Antiquitie, and promising at the beginning of your Answer, not to disgrace the credite of this Storie, you fall afterwarde, into such A path of your accustomed Rhetorike, that by A Figure of listing and Imagining, and by certaine howes and whyes, ye destroye A plaine fact and confessed. who maye trust you in Obscure or Long maters, which

Such is M. Jew. when him listeth.

which is an Euident and Short historie, doe so boldly argue against it? No wonder if you perswade your Felowes or folowers, to Discredite Clemens, Abdias, Hippolitus, Martialis, Athanasius, and all the whole Boke of Degrees and Decretals, which haue the Grace and Feate, to let an Historie stand for true: and yet so rightly to Gheasse at it, that, If the gesse be True, the historie must be False.

The Historie saith, the Gentelwoman toke the Breade at her maides hand: M. Jewels, or his Gheasse that (by hys graunt) listeth, is, What neede she, how could she without Suspition? Why might she not haue brought it in a napkin. &c.

Now whether D. Hardinges Gheasse, (as M. Jewel termeth it,) concerning the Receauing in this place vnder one kind only, be as vnhable to stand wyth the historie, as the Imaginations which M. Jewel hath here rekened vp for greater, than the Sleight of a womans wit did atteine vnto, let the Indifferent Reader conferre and iudge. My proper intent and purpose was, to shew by this Example, how M. Jewel, can speake, so fauorarablie, of the Auncient Histories of the first vj. C. yeres, as though he would not Discredite them: And yet how in deede, he practiseth with suche Libertie or Licentiousnesse rather against them, as thoughe what him listeth to Imagine, might be better alowed and liked, than the fact it selfe, which the Historye wytnesseth.

But let vs trie M. Jewels fidelity, in an other Example. what say you, to the Liturgie of S. James? I trust you will not make exception against it, that it was found very lately in the Ile of Candie, Or, sought out, and found, and set abroade of very late yeres, Or, that it is a very little boke of smal price lateli set abrode in print about vij. yeres past: (which are so greate maters in your Judgment, that for these causes, you will repell an Authoritye,) I trust, that you haue no such thing, to laye against S. James Masse. For, by the testimonye of an auncient Councel, we vnderstand, that S. James wrote a Liturgie or forme of a Masse. what saye you then vnto it? It may be doubted of, you say. And why so? For,

S. Iames Liturgie hathe a speciall praier
for

for them that liue in Monasteries. And yet
it was very rathe to haue Monasteries built
in al S. Iames time.

You meane, I thinke, ÿ there were no
suche Monasteries then built, as of late
haue ben pulled downe in Englãd, large
& fair, & Cõmodious places for holy pur=
poses, w̄ Church, Cloister, Capiter house
Refectory, Dormitorie, Infirmatorie, bi-
sides Reuenues & lãdes for euer, left ther
by Deuont, Noble, and worthy Men &
woimen, to that end; that God might be
serued of men and women accordingly, &
the religious hauing all things prouided
vnto their hãds, might serue him quietli.

But, what thẽ? The forme & accidentes
of an house, do not make a Monastery, no
more then ÿ maner of aparel doth make a
Monke. And although, in the Apostles
time, no suche peace or glory was in the
church, ÿ by great buildings or têporal=
ties, it was known & esteemed in ÿ world:
yet (without all doubt) the Ordres and
Rules emong some Christians of that
time so rathe (as you call it) were so re=
ligious and well appointed, that S.
Iames might well praye for suche as li-

ued

ued in a singular manner and fashion of a Monasticall and Spirituall life.

I will not trouble you with many witnesses in a mater so plaine and euident. I referre you to Eusebius, and He wil direct you to Philo Iudeus, which liued in the time of the Apostles, and wrote suche things, as himselfe knewe to be practized of Christians, before the name of Christians was well knowen abroade.

Euseb.Ecc.
hist.lib.2.
ca.17.et 17

First, he testifieth of them, that they renounced all their goods, that they went out of the Citie, and liued together, lyke with lyke, in their small grounds and gardens abroade.

He declareth also, that they had certaine speciall houses appointed for Prayer, which they called σεμνεῖα or Μοναστήρια.

He testifieth of their Exercisies, that from Morning to Night, they were occupied in the studieng vpon Scriptures.

He telleth, howe they leied Chastitie, and Continencie, as it were a Foundacion in their Heartes, and that the Women aud Virgins liued by them selues and the men by them selues.

He sheweth, that none of them did eate

or

or Drinke, before Sunne set, and that they neither did eate Fleshe nor drinke Wine.

He Testifieth of their Watchinges all night long, and fastinges togeather with it, at some times especially, as at Ester. **And,** of their order in Singing of Psalmes.

To conclude. He sheweth how the priestes and Ministers did then their Duties, and how the Bishopes See was aboue All.

This doth Philo testifie, as done, at the very beginning, vnder the Apostles, in whose time himselfe also liued. And how far is this of, from A Monasticall life? Yet, saieth M. Iewel.

It was verye rathe, to haue Monasteries built in al S. Iames time.

But was it very rathe, **to haue Men and women liue in A Monasticall kind of life by Sequestring themselues from resort, and haunt of Townes, by wilfull Pouertie, Obedience, Chastitie, and Spirituall exercises of Fasting, watching, and Praying? You here what Philo testifieth, and howe can you then for shame either denie it, or doubt of it?**

If therefore there were that so lyued, they liued in some Places I trowe. In

H i **Caues**

Canes vnder the ground, o₂ vnder trees,
o₂ vnder Rockes at the leaſt, if you will
alowe them no better rome. And yet, of
their ſpeciall place of P₂aier, where they
met together , Philo maketh an ex-
p₂eſſe mention , calling them μοναϛκρια
monaſteries. And who, but wilful & wild
Aduerſaries, will thinke, that they liued
here and there, out of o₂der, in the open
Fieldes and Aire, without any defence o₂
couer, againſt wind and weather, O₂ a-
ny diſtinction and cloſeneſſe of dwelling,
which both, are ſo much deſired, and are
ſo neceſſary, fo₂ the religious in deede?
Now, if they had places to p₂ay, to cõfer
to Eat, to Slepe, & to do other things in,
which our Infirmity requireth to be occupied o₂ ſuſteined by , what let is there,
but ỹ S. James might p₂ay fo₂ them that
liued in Monaſteries? O₂, what Repug-
nance o₂ Impoſſibility is there in ỹ mater, that, becauſe ſuch Monaſticall houſes
were not then builded, as are now extãt,
therefo₂e the Monaſtical and Religious
perſons which then were extant to the
p₂aiſ: of Ch₂iſtianitye , and Glo₂y of our
Sauiour, might not be commended vnto
                                           God

God in S. James Praier?

But cōsider in this place, how M. Ie=
wel carieth the Readers mind away, frō
the mater: And turneth it, frō the persons
to the places: from the edifying of soules,
to building of houses: from setting of mē
in an order of perfite life together, to ioy=
ning of Stones and framing of Timber:
from that which no man will deny, (As,
that in the Primitiue Church, there were
found, which for the loue of God contem=
ning the world, did liue solitarily and or=
derly & cōtemplatiuely) to that which no
man will say (As, that monasteries were
built in the Apostles time) vnderstādīg
by Monasteries, such places as cōmonly
now in this Age, goe vnder that name.

But what should he win by it, so to
chainge frō the persons to y̆ places? mary
thus much at the least: that, wheras euery
man, without further Examining of the
mater, wil reasonably gather, that the po=
uerty and Paucitye, of the Christians in
the Primitiue Church, could not well
stretch to the Building of any such rich &
great houses for the seruice of god, as are
now called, by the name of Monasteries:

it ſhould therfoꝛe be ſuſpected, that there
could be no Monkes at al in thoſe daies.
Foꝛ although wiſe and Lerned men, may
eaſely conſider it , that the thing it ſelfe
muſt go befoꝛe the name, and the Monke
befoꝛe the Monaſtery, and the Subſtance
befoꝛe the Accidentes, yet, thꝛough the
Deſperateneſſe of Heretikes, which care
not what they ſpeake oꝛ faine againſt the
Catholike Faithe, the Simple oꝛ Common ſoꝛt is made to beleue, that the Papiſtes doe put ſo greate A Religion and
Excellencie in externall thinges , that it
muſt folow , there were no Monkes in
the Apoſtles time, if it be graunted there
were no Monaſteries.   And Monaſteries, they can not conceiue, what they
were, oꝛ will not beleue that any were,
except we ſhould pꝛoue, that they were
of like making with theſe which they remember, to haue ſtoode very faire once,
in England, oꝛ yet to ſtand and remaine
beyond the Seas.

    It was therefoꝛe nothing els , but A
very Craftineſſe of M. Jewels, to argue
againſt the Religious, foꝛ whome Saint
James pꝛaieth , becauſe there was no
                                    buil-

building of Monasteries, in S.Iames
time. Or,if it was not Craftines, it was
plaine vnsensiblenes.

For what can he answer? S.Iames Liturgie (sayeth he) hath an expresse praier
for them that liue in Monasteries.Be it so.
But what call you them in one worde?
for A name, I am sure they haue. Surely
what so euer name you geaue them,your
Argument must be this: there were no
Monasteries built in S.Iames time, Ergo,
there were no μοναχοι,κοινοβίται ἀσκηται:
that is to saie, there were no Religious
men, so rathe in the world,neither liuing
alone in solitarines, neither in felowship
with al thinges Common emong thē.&c.
As though S.Ihon the Baptist, or before him,Delizeus,andDelias,could not
in their life time be Commended vnto
God,in a Speciall Prayer for Monkes,
Heremites, or Religious persons, because it was very rathe to haueMonaste-
ries or Religious houses built,so long
before the Gospel of Christ.

Not to espie therefore, the rudenes of
this Argument, it was very grosse and
vnsensible, and vnlike, perchaunse, to be
         H iij   found

found in M. Jewel: But, to remoue the Intention of the Reader, from the Persons to their houses: and to draw the question vnto this Common place, not whether Monkes or Religious Persons were extant in the Apostles time, But, whether Monasteries were built so rath, (In which question, taking the word Monasterie Grammatically, he should be easely confuted, but taking it Commonly, as it is now vsed of the people, he might probably mainteine his Assertion, and also, vnder the Ambiguitie of the worde, goe from one Sense to an other, and make A shew of a good cause and plentifull, because in some sense his wordes be true.) This in deede proceedeth of M. Jewels wit. Of whom that thou maist the better Beware, Remember how he seemeth to alowe and esteeme the Testimonies of the first six hundred yeres, and Consider vpon how light and vaine Occasions, he taketh Authority away, from the Liturgie of S. Iames the Apostle.

Of the like Reuerence to Antiquitye, and wisedome in making of Arguments, that also cummeth, which you gather, a-
gayust

gainſt S. Chriſoſtomes Maſſe: ſaying.

Iew. 10.
S. Chri-
ſoſtomes
Liturgie
denied.

Chriſoſtomes Liturgie praieth for pope
Nicolas. &c. And likewiſe in the ſame Liturgie, there is A Praier for the Empire,
and victorie of the Emperour Alexius. &c.
Now it were very much, for M. Harding
to ſai, Chriſoſtome praied for mē by name,
ſcuen hundred yeares before they were
borne. I trow that were propheſiyng, and
not Praying.

R4.

Your troweing is Reaſonable: And if
S. Chriſoſtome ſhould be affirmed vnto
me, to haue praicd for A Pope and an
Emperour, borne fiue or ſix hundred
yeres after him, I could not but ſuſpect
the mater. But will you examine and
conſider it no better? Or will you geaue
ſentence againſt a Boke, before you haue
ſeen the Copy of it?

M. Iew.
haſty in
his iudge-
ment.

Why, you will Anſwer me, that you
read in the printed Liturgies which are
now extant, and attributed to S. Chriſoſtome, the names of Nicolas & Alexius.
Yea but where read you, that S. Chriſoſtome vſed thoſe Names, when he came
to his Memento in his Maſſe? Why
ſay you, did not he ſpeake euery worde,

H iiij   as

as it is now expressed vnto vs in Print, that he did speake: No forsothe, concerning the names. For, in setting out the forme of A Masse, the most of the thinges that should be folowed, he might so appoint, that they should neuer neede to be chainged. As, the maner, of cumming to the aultare, Of standing & tarying there, Of Bringing thither þ bread that should be consecrated, Of putting wine and water togeather, Of Praying alowde, Of Praying Secretly, Of Drawing the curtaines, Of shewing the Sacrament, Of receauing the Sacrament and so furth: the maner (I say) of these thinges, might so be Inuented or Deliuered at the first, that they might (if it pleased the Posteritie) wel continue for euer after.

But, whereas in certaine places of his Liturgie, he would haue special mention made of the holy Sainctes in heauen, or some singular Persons on earth: could he put presentli al their names in, whom he would haue to be remembred in those places? In deede, that required A gift of Prophesying, which in this place neeðed not. For, in all Formes and Paternes

All these things are found in S. Chrisostomes Liturgie: whether are they also in þ new Comuniō bokes, in which the forme of al Antiquity (they say) is expressed?

ternes not only of Publike Seruice, but
also of Common and temporall matters,
(as, the Stiles of Princes, the Tenours
of Indentures and Obligations, The
maner of Inditements. &c.) the rest of
the wordes are expressed, as they shall
continue, only, when the place commeth,
where the Persons name must be specified, to whom the cause perteineth, there
is no certaine name Defined, but A great
N. set, to keepe the roome, and to signify, that when you put that forme of write
in Practise, you shall place the partyes
Name, where that letter standeth.

So was it in S. Chrisostomes Liturgie. The Forme wherof being wel liked,
and therefore copied out that it mighte
goe abrode and continue, was not chainged in any point, concerning the maner
of Celebrating and Praying, which presently then might be defined. But, where
as he maketh, in Distinct places of hys
Masse, speciall mention of the Sainte,
whose feast shall happen to be celebrated
that daie, and of the Patriarche and Emperour, which should be aliue when hys
Masse would be saied, he could not presently

sently put in their Names.

What remained then but that he shuld put in such a phrase (as ὅσις ἂν ἦ, ὁ δ Ἄνος) by which it should be declared, ᵱ what so euer Sainct, Patriarch or Emperour he were, there his name shuld be reherced where ᵱ ὅσις ἂν ἦ, was found to stand.

Yet, this notwithstanding who can let, but he that would, might in copying out the Liturgie, apply it to his owne time, & name the Emperour then liuing. But when ᵱ Emperor shal afterward depart, his name must be scraped out, to geaue place to an other, except priestes shuld al waies do so much without boke, as to pray for the Emperor ᵱ liueth, though ᵱ name of the dead Emperor continue in ᵱ Masse boke. Of the name therfore, of either Patriarche or Emperour, which is specified in some Liturgie, no Argument can be made ᵱ the forme therof was not extant, before the Persons therin expressed were borne, but only, that when they liued and Ruled in those quarters, they were praied for in the Publike Masse.

But of this mater, how some Copies haue the name of *Nycolas vniuersall Patriarch*, and of the Emperour, *Alexius*: And,

the Greeke Liturgies printed at Uenys
and Parys, haue no expresse mention of
any, though speciall Praier be made in
them, both for the Patriarch and Empe=
rour: Also, by what occasion Nycolas and
Alexius names, came in: Againe, how the
Nycolas, whom you speake of, was not
ỹ Pope of Rome, which liued 200. yeres
before Alexius, but the Patriarch of Con=
stantinople which liued at one time with
him: And in conclusion how euidentlye
it may be perceiued, that this Liturgie,
which is said to be Chrysostomes, was
in very deede, that blessed Doctours ma=
king, of all this, Master Pointz in his
Testimonies for the Real Presence, M. Pointz
hath spoken truly & aboūdantly. There ca, 7.
may he, ỹ will see, find how absurdly and
Ignorantly M. Iewel hath argued. For
me it is inough to declare, that he make
light of the Authors within ỹ first vj. C
yeres. And, ỹ he hath no other shift, but
to deny thē. And, ỹ his reasō, vpon which
he groūdeth his opiniō in refusing some
of thē, is so feble & vain, ỹ, as it cōfirmeth
his purpose nothing at al, so it declareth,
ỹ he hath a very light head of his owne,
                                                    and

and a very Presumptuous mind, which vpon small Occasion, yea rather againſt all Occasion, was ſo ready to take authoritie away from that Liturgie, which, both the Greeke Church vſeth, And the Latin aloweth, for Chriſoſtomes owne.

But thou ſeeſt not yet (Indifferent Reader) the worſt of M. Iewel, As in ſome examples more I will make plaine vnto thee, and ſo end this Chapiter. Of Dioniſius Ariopagita, in whom expreſſe and reuerend Signes or Examples of the Catholike Religion or Popiſhe, is to be ſeen, thus he ſaieth.

Iew.10.

Dioniſius althoughe he be an Auncient writer, as it maie many waies well appeare, yet, it is iudged by Eraſmus, Iohn Colet, and other many graue and Learned men, that it can not be Ariopagita S. Paules Diſciple that is mentioned in the Actes.

Ra,
M. Iew.
anſwered
by M.
Iewel.

I will Anſwer you with your owne wiſe Reaſon, which you make Agaynſt *S. Bernard, Lyra, Teutonicus, and Beſſarion:* and in your Termes I ſaye vnto you: *Eraſmus and Iohn Colet liued at the leaſt, xv. C. yeres after Chriſt, wherfore*

fore their *Authoritie muste needes
seeme the lesse.*

Here, If you like your owne Reason,
you be Answered: If you mislike it, I am
glad that you are wiser, than you were
wont to be.

Yet, I doe not refuse Erasmus, or D.
Colets iudgment, because, they were of
late yeres, but I preferre the Grauitie,
Learning, and Number of their betters,
and their elders. Those I meane, which
liued and florished A thousand yere together, before Erasmus was borne, and of
whome, you can find no one, which hath
denied the Dionisius of whom we speake
to be S. Paules scholer: And I can name
some vnto you which haue not only beleued it, but for reuerence and worthines
of him, haue geuen light to his bokes by
their Commentaries.

But consider you (M. Iewel) in this
place, whether it be not most true in you,
that you seeke alwaies, how to Destroye
or Diminishe all thinges, as much as ye
can? For, if there be no false Doctrine in
these bokes, nor any thing contrarye to
goo<u>d</u>

*Dionysius
Alexandr.
Maximus.
Pachyme-
res,
Dionysius
Carthus.*

The spite of the new Gospell is a spoiler. good maners, what should it hurt you or your cause, to haue men beleue, that they be the workes of that Dyonisius, which was S. Paules scholar? And because you shall see my meaning in an other Example, as also haue it noted vnto you, that Erasmus, whom, in disgracing of S. Denyse, you bring in, as A graue and lerned man, is better interteined of you than he deserueth, I say:

Erasmus iustly reprehended. Before Erasmus (more bold, surely, than wise in that poynt) before he began to play the Censor, and by once reading of A Boke ouer, to gather A priuate councel within his owne heade, and geaue A Definitiue sentence, against auncient fathers workes, or els for them, before (I say) he toke so much vpon him, and exequuted it not alwaies discreetly, the boke *In Cēsura* *ad Quirinum*, was embraced as S. Cypri- *de libris* ans. Erasmus yet putteth the mater in *ad Quiri-* question, and after great argumēts made *num.* *Pro et Con,* win himself, his finall answer is, that, probabilius videtur non esse Cypriani, it seemeth more probable that it is not S. Cyprians.

Wel M. Doctor and Censor, S. Hieronimo

rome is witnesse that it is, and vseth A
Chapiter thereof as an Authorityc of S.
Cyprians, wherefore you may perceaue,
that either you haue not seen al thinges,
either haue not remembred them, Or els
that your iudgment is not all of the best.

But let this passe, that S. Hierome is
directly against you, was there any thing
in the Boke ad Quirinum, hurtful either
to Faith or good Maners? No verely,
you find no such fault in the boke. why
Disputed you then, whether it were S.
Cyprians or no? And, if for your exercise sake, yon would needes moue the
doubt, you should better haue inuented
an Answer against the Obiection which
did hinder the Estimation of it, than by
needlesse making of it, minister any Occasion vnto your Reader to set lesse by
such a worke, as by much crediting of
which, he could take no harme.

For suppose it so, that being not S.
Cyprians in deede, I so loue and Reade
the boke, as if it were his: what daunger
hereby is cumming vnto me: the Boke
being Sound and good, whyche I doe
Reade?

But

But now on the other side, the Boke being tried to be S. Cyprias, or if it should not be so tried, yet, in trueth, being hys: yourselfe first, doe hurt your owne Fame and Estimation, in geauing so rashe a sentence, And you cause me to haue lesse mind vnto a good boke, and to Suspect that, which should not be distrusted. So that in letting the titles of Bokes alone, as we found them, though they shoulde (by putting the case so) bear false names, there is no Iniury done or taken, if the booke be alowable: but in Changing or Disgracing them, when it needeth not, (for any harme which is to be feared in Reading of the boke,) it lacketh not a peece of vaine Glorie, Or of angry Foly.

As in our case now (M. Iewel) of the Boke *de Ecelesiastica Hierarchia,* you tell vs that it is Iudged (of such men, as neyther you nor we, make greate accompt vpon) that it can not be the boke of Ariopagita, S. Paules disciple, that is mentioned in the Actes. But to what end tell you me so? Is the boke to be Credited or no, tell me that? Is there any Heresy in it? Is there any Irreligion? Is there any Folie?

Is

Is there any thing that you can con=
temne? Or forbid to be readen? I can not
so thinke of you, whereas yourselfe con=
fesse it, that the Author of the forsaid boke
was, An Auncient writer, as it may, many **Iew.10**
waies well appeare.

To what purpose then is it that you
teach vs, that he can not be Ariopagita S.
Paules disciple. For, If he be an Aunci=
ent and worthy writer, though he should
not be so old, as an Apostles Scholer,
what is that to vs, which seke after aun=
cientnes in writers, such as may suppres
with graue countenaunce, the lusty and
high lokes of youthful Scriblers, and not
such, as must be so old, that there may
not wel be A Superior? And if, by your
owne confession, the Author be Aunc:et,
though his name be not Dionisius Ariopagita, what is that to the disprofe of the
mater which we defend by him?

Did you thinke (M. Iewel) by wry=
ring your mind in this fashion, not to
hinder, in any respect, the credite of the
forsaide boke, but only to shew a point of
your knowledge, And how that you wer
not Ignorant, what Erasmus, Iohn Colet
          I j   and

and others (J cã not tel, who) thought in this mater? Uanitie (M. Jewel) vanitie: to make your own Fame the end of your doinges, wout any profit to your reader.

Uanitie.

But, said you so much as you haue don, that the boke might be disgraced, & that some Scruple might be cast in the Reaters way, to trouble him only, ẙ he shuld not quietly assent, vnto ẙ contents therof? And how can you thē excuse yourself, of blind Foly and Contentiousnesse?

Conten- tion.

For, whereas S. Denyse the Ariopagite, is not he alone, that must be credited, but euery Auncient writer (whome you doe alowe for auncient) may well stãd for a witnesse: what wiseman would euer enterprise, to diminish the Estimation of A Substantiall witnesse, by casting in against him (of his owne or other mennes Suspition,) that in some Corners he hath an other name, than generally he is taken by? And, whereas it helpeth your cause nothing at all, though *Dyonisius Ariopagita* were not Author of the boke *de Eccles. Hierarch:* so ẙ you deny him not to be an Auncient and credible witnesse, who but Unquiet and Con-

Contentious, would labour to make A question about it?

Surely (M. Iewel) if you were not more desirous, of marring than making, and of contrarying your aduersary, than agreeing with Reason : you should all-waies folowe, the more Peaceable and Harmelesse Opinion. And whereas you might know , that for One *Erasmus and Iohn Colet*, there haue ben in these laste thousand yeres, a thousand Lerned men, which haue taken S. Denyse the Ariopa-gite, for the Author of the foresaid Boke, what Quiet and Good nature would in-cline to the worse of the two, and thynk, that more probable, which tendeth to the Disgracing (so much as it is) of a Diuine & Excellent peece of worke? But (if there be no Remedy) kepe yourself in your Trade of mistrusting, Denying, & Spoi-ling the Monumentes of the Catholike and True Religion, and let me holde my peace, and permit vnto you, that the Au-thor (of whom we speake) was not *Dio-aysius Ariopagita*. What was he then?

An Auncient writer, as it may, many Iew.10. waies, wel appeere.

I ij we

We Require you then, to stand to his Testimony. For no doubt, he is within the first six hundred yeres, whome you vouchesafe to call Auncient And what so euer his Name be, so that he be A writer whom you admit, al is One to vs, which seeke only, to declare A Trueth, and not to Prolong A Talke. After which sort, if you also be disposed, let vs not striue vpon it, whether he be Ariopagita, or no, but spend the time better, in considering what he telleth of the Churches Orders in his daies. And then, comparing it with the Popishe Religion, and the Protestantes Reformation, let vs see, which of the two, is more like vnto it.

M. Jew. requires to stãd on-to Junciet witnesses.

First you shall finde in his *Ecclesiastica Hierarchia*, that, the *Apostles deliuered heauenly thinges vnder sensibles signes. &c.* partly by *vvrite, partly vnvvriten Institutions and Traditions.* And this is directly against them, to whome there are no Verities but vnwriten. After this.

Unwritẽ Verities.

In the ministration of the Sacrament of Baptisme, you finde plaine mention made, Of *Hymnes:* Of *Kissing the holy Table:* Of *God Father:* Of *turning the partie vvhich is*

Godfather

to

to be Baptized, *tovvardes the Vveast* : *Of bid-*
ding him to Blovve and Puffe out the Diuell thre
times, And thrise to pronounce solemne vvordes,
of Abrenuntiation and Defiance against him: Of Abrenun-
Turning him againe tovvardes the East: Of Bles- tiation.
sing him, and putting of handes vpon him : Of
Stripping him: Of making the Signe of the Crosse Signe of
vpon him three times, before he be Anointed ouer the Crosse.
the vvhole Body: Of Sanctifiing the vvater,vvith Oile.
thrise pouring in, of Oyle thereto, in forme of A halovving
Crosse: *Of Dipping him thrise into the vvater,* of the vva-
vvith naming of the three Persons in Trinitie: Of ter.
putting A nevv Cote vpon him,Of Anointing him Chrisome.
againe : Of Pronouncing him ready for the Sa- Confirma-
crament of the Aultare. tion.

These Ceremonies and holy Signes,
in which the Apostles couered the Secrete Misteries, (which were not to be
told all men,) how vnreuerently you e-
steeme of, your Grinning, and Railing
at them, and Abrogating or Abbrigging
of them,doth proue abundantly. But let
vs goe further.

Concerning the reuerent administration, of the Communion , you shall find
expressely declared. *Hovv the Bishop begin-*
ning at the Aultare,goeth censing about the holy Incensing.
I iij *Place.*

Place. Hovv, after his returne thither made, he
Singing of *beginneth to sing psalmes : Then, hovv the Lessons*
Psalmes. *be reade in order . Hovv the Cathecumini*
Readmg of (which were **Nouices** yet in the **faith**
Lessons. & **Lerners** of it) *And Energumini* (which
Putting were **possessed and trobled with euil spi**-
out of the **rites**) *And Pœnitentes,* (which had not ful-
vnvvorthy ly **done their Penance**) *vvere, all, put out of*
the Church : hovv the Ministers are diuided in
Orders of *their Officies, Some standing at the Dores, some*
Officies. *bringing farth Breade and vvine, some doing o-*
Hymnes. *ther thinges: hovv they Praise God : hovv they*
VVashing *they Salute one an Other : Hovv the Byshop*
of handes. *vvasheth his handes, and standeth at the middest*
of the Aultare : hovv the Priestes vvashe their
handes, and stand aboute hym, vvith the Select
Ministers only . Hovv the Bishope, ea quæ di-
Consecra- *uinissima sunt, rite perficit, doth vvorke and per-*
tion. *site dulie , those thinges that are most Diuyne:*
Shevving *hovv he shevveth the Giftes Diuinely vvrought:*
of the Sa- *Hovv he receiueth himselfe , and inuiteth other*
crament. *thereto . Hovv he endeth vviiv Thankes gea-*
Cōmunion *uing.*

Now, with how **Reuerent behauiour**
of body, with how **conuenient Gestures,**
with how **solemne wordes, Signes and**
Lete-

Cerimonies, with how singular Prepa=
ration, Attention, Deuotion, Adoration,
on, all those things were done, it is easy
to gather, of these fewe pointes whiche
are noted heere vnto vs, whiche coulde
not bee so quickelye done, as theye are
shortly spoken, and of whiche, as short=
ly as they be spoken, the Author maketh
Diuine and high Mysteries.

For Incensing, Singing, Shutting
of dores, washing of handes, stan-
ding alone, persiting of the Giftes,
(which are ye bread and wine proponed)
Shewinge of the Sacrament, Recea-
uing , And Thankes geauing,
These things are sone told, but if a man
hadde beene Present, to see, with what
Countenaunce, Gate, Action, Circum=
staunce, Order and Reuerence, euery
one of them was exequuted, I doubt not
but it woulde haue seemed vnto him , a
more Popisshe and Superstitious Ser=
uice (as the Heretikes nowe call it,)
than that which is now done euery Sō=
daie, at S. Michels in Antwerpe. To

I iiij.   which

Are these
signes and
tokens of
a Cōmuni
on , after ye
last maner
of the Eng
lish church
Or of A
Popishe
Masse.

whiche Churche, I referre my selfe, because the Deacon and Subdeacon, dooe
Ordinarily, there, Cõmunicate on suche
Dayes with the Priest, so that M. Iewels olde shift, shall not serue, in making his Reader beleue, that our Masse
is such a thing as is Distincted from a
Communion. And true it is in deede, Of
an Englishe Communion, but not of a
Catholike and Christian Communion.

But here is not all, that is to be marked, out of the forsaid Author. For, *he de-*
halovving   clareth also how *Oyle vvas halovved. Fi∫t the*
of Oyle.   *vnvvorthy vvere put out. Then folovved incensing,*
Singing, Reading of Le∫sons, putting of the Oyle
vpon the Aultare couered before, vvith xij. vvhin-
ges: Praying ouer it, and halovving it vvith ho-
Re∫erua-   *ly Ceremonies, and keeping of it, to serue in all*
tion.   *Bishoply Office.*

He declareth further, *hovv Bishops, hovv*
Priestes, hovv Ministers are Consecrated, Some
Geuing of   *kneeling on both knees, some vpon one, some by*
Orders.   *Impo∫ition of handes, other vvith the Bible al∫o*
holden ouer their heade. But, all, haue the Signe
of the Cro∫se made vpon them.

Monkes.   He declareth also howe Monkes are
Consecrated, *They ∫tand only behind the Priest,*
vvhich

which hauing ended his misticall Praier for them Professio
asketh vvhether they Renounce all Secular and
distracted kind of Life, Then, *doth he make the*
Signe of the Crosse vpon them, and sheare them, Signe of
in the name of the Trinitie, And *putting them* the Crosse.
out of their former Apparell, he doth other on Shearing.
them, Saluteth them, and Ministreth the Sa- Inuesting.
crament vnto them.

He declareth, last of all, the maner of
Burying. *If he that is departed vvere A Priest,*
he is laied before the Aultare, if he be of the Distinctiõ
Laietie, or A Monke, he is laied before the holy of places
Place vvhere the Priestes goe in. But who so in burying
euer he be: *Solemne Praiers and Thankes, are* Solemni-
made and geauen vnto God. Promises of the ties in Fu-
Resurrection are rehersed, Psalmes are Songe, nerals.
Cathecumeni are put out of the Churche, The
Good men departed are praised and blessed, The Praying
Liuing and present are exhorted to praye for a for the
good end. And then *Cummeth the Bishope to* Soules de-
the departed: Praieth for him: Saluteth him, parted.
and after him, all that be present: Poureth Oyle Pouring of
vpon him: And Laieth his body in an honorable Oyle.
place, vvith others of the same Order.

Thus haue I, sumwhat largely, gathered out of the forsaied Author, these
Pait

Particulars: that, by the more open fight of thefe maters, it might the better be confidered, which of the two, the Church or the Congregation, the Papiftes or the Proteftantes, the Old men or the New, are liker in their doinges, to the Primitiue Church. And here now let vs ioyne with M. Jewel.

Iudge now, who foeuer wil

Sir, Alow you thefe doinges of the Primitiue Church, or do ye not? If you doe: why are they not extant then, in your Congregation? Or, if yourfelfe will be more Spirituall and Deiforme, than to vfe External & Senfible meanes, to conduct you vnto that, which is One, Single, Pure, and Inuifible: why haue you not fuffered others, which haue not the lyke Eleuation and Abftraction of mind, to vfe thefe vifible and holy fignes, of Incenfing, Wafhing, Croffing, Anoynting, Confecrating, Shearing, and other which I haue mentioned?

The ioyning of the iffue with M. Jew.

If you doe not: how looke you like one, that would follow Autentike and Graue Examples, teftified by Aunciene and fad writers? And, wherefore doe you make the world beleue, that you, good

good men, would haue all thinges re=
formed, according vnto the Paterne of
the Primitiue Church, whose Procee=
dinges are found to be so contrarie, vn=
to the Ecclesiastical Orders of that time?

Be plaine (M. Jewel) in that which
you intend, and *Quod facis fac citius.*

If you esteeme Antiquitie, let neither
Baptisme lacke Abrenuntiation. &c: nei=
ther Confirmation, Oile: neither the Sa=
crament of the Aultare, singular demon=
stration of it, & Reuerence: neither Prie=
stes their due Consecration: Nor the Li=
uing, Occasions to bring them by out=
ward Signes to Deuotion: nor the dead,
Praiers: And that Sign, which hath ben
vsed in all holy Functions, and which, of
old, they made in the Foreheade, to testify
that they were not ashamed of Christ, the
signe I meane of his *C R O S S E,* which
is not only now A Foly to Panimes, or
Offence to Iewes, but an Ignomynie
to the Gospell, and Apishnes in the Ca=
tholikes, as some worse than Iewes
or Painimes doe Blaspheme, thys
Signe of the Crosse (Maylter Iew=
el) restore againe vnto the Churches,
and

and suffer not them to be in Honours, which thinke it a shame to haue a Token of our Redemption, before their Eyes: If you esteeme Antiquitie.

And if ye regarde it not, why make ye vs beleeue, that you woulde be ruled by yt? Or why feede you the common sort with sweete hope of hauing a Sincere and Pure Religion restored vnto them, according to the Exaumple and Orders of the Auncient and holy Church, wheras you haue, either blindely abandoned them, before you knew them, either desperately doe contemne them, after ye be aduertised of them.

O, say you, He, that wrot those bokes De Ecclesiastica Hierarchia, was not S. Denyse the Ariopagite. As who should say, that if it were he, you woulde in no wise contrary him. But how shall I beleeue you? whereas you pretende, that you will be content with the Auncient Fathers testimonies, and yet cry out against that forme of Administringe the Sacraments, whiche euery man seeth to haue been vsed in the Catholike auncient worlde, by reporte of this writer.

whome

whome your selfe confesse to be Auncient
and that it may so appeere many wayes.

And nowe, after it is euidente, that
whosoeuer he be, he maketh against you
would you Chaunge you Opinion (M.
Iewell) and Repente your selfe of all
former Lightnes, If in deede a more
Learned and Graue man, than Eras=
mus, Iohn Collet, or any other that you
can tell of, shoulde testifie, that it is S.
Denyse the Apariopagitas worke? We=
rely S. Gregorie the Greate, maketh *greg.ho.34*
mention Dionysius Ariopagita, which is
vnto him, Antiquus & Venerabilis, Pa=
ter an Auncient and venerable father, whō
he saith, by reporte of other, to haue wri=
ten of the nyne Orders of Aungels. Of
whiche bookes this that wee speake of,
De Ecclesiastica Hierarchia, is the fellow:
Origene also maketh an expresse menti= *Orig.Ho.t*
on of him, alleaginge a text out of these *in Ioan*
Bookes whiche you mistrust.

But woulde this make you Chaunge
you Opinion? No: you woulde haue
xx.questions vnto me, and escape from
me by xx.waies, rather than I should
holde you so fast, by this Argument out
of

out of S. Gregorie or Origine, that you
should not but confesse vnto vs, that you
are deceaued in your Judgment, concerning this Boke *de Ecclesiastica Hierarchia.*
And, if to proue me to be suspitious, you
would, in deede, incline to that side, that
not only some Auncient Father, but A-
riopagita himselfe, were Author of this
boke: Reform then yourself, and stop the
mouthes of the Railing and Ignorant,
vnto whoe, Crossing, Incensing, Anointing, & Signifying of Spiritual thinges
by Corporall and Externall Formes and
Imagies, seemeth to be, altogeather Pa-
pistrie.

 Yet it is no mater to me, in this obiecting against you, what the name of that
Author was. You côfesse him to be auncient: I infer them, that he is worthy of
Short and clear. credite. You wil not be ruled by his Testimonie, I gather then, that you Regard
not the Auncient. And that I proue by
an other Example. The Supremacie
of the Bishop of Rome, of how greate
force and strength it is, the Catholikes &
Heretikes bothe, doe see. And as we doe
proue it by true Experience, that nothing
         is

is moze needfull to be perswaded vnto
such as loue to haue a sure Staye in all
maters of Controuersies : so, our aduersaries doe set against nothing so Ernest-
ly and Outragiously, as the Pzerogatiue
of that See . Herevpon starteth a Cha-
lenger vp : Shew me (sayeth he) that the
Pope was euer Called Heade of the
Church. The Catholike Answereth, He
was, in deede, Head of the Church, as appeereth many waies, though he were not
called in his Ozdinarie Stile of wzityng,
Head thereof.

Nay, sayeth the Challenger, shewe me   Iew.306.
the name it selfe, That, is the very thing
that we deny. But ye can not.

Sir, how oft must I bzing furth y̆ name?   Ra.

Mary, If any learned mā of our aduersa-   Iew.1.
ries, or if all the learned men that be aliue,
be hable to bring any one sufficient sétence
&c. I am content to yelde and subscribe.
And again. As I saied at the beginning, one
good sentence were proufe sufficient.

Very wel Sir : One you shall haue, if   Ra.
that can perswade you to Subscribe.
Eugenius Bishop of *Carthage* answered to
Obadus, requiring A Councell to be kept
in

in Aphrica, wherein, The Arrians might dispute with the Catholikes, concerning Religion and Faith: that, he would write to his brethren, that his felow Bishops might come. *Et precipue, Ecclesia Romana que Caput est omnium Ecclesiarum, and the Church of Rome especially, vvhich is the head of all Churches.*

Here now, of this Story and Text, I gather, that the Bishop of Rome, is *H E A D* of all Bishops, & so much ought the Aduersarye to graunt vnto me, if he loued not, by force of consequence, to be driuen vnto the confession of Truth, but, of his owne accord, to yeld vnto reason. For, when Eugenius the Bishop answered, that he would write, that the Church of *R*ome (most chiefly,) should come to ye Councel, what meant he thereby? Dyd he meane that any message should be sent, to the marble Pillars, Foundations, Rowses, walles of Stone, or any such vnsensible thing, perteining to the Materiall Church of Rome? Truly, then, for hys wit, who so euer should thinke so, might be President of that Councell, where Postes and Pillers should meete togeather

ther, and heare the cause of our Religion
debated.

But did he meane by the Church of
Rome al the Christians of Rome? who
then should keepe the Citie whiles they
were from home? Or how was al Carthage, able to receiue them? Or what
hath the Laitie to do in Councels? Yf
then, neither the walles &c. of Rome,
neither al the Christen people of it, be
rightly vnderstanded by the Churche of
Rome, which B. Eugenius would haue
to come to the Councel at Carthage, what
other thing may be meant thereby?

You wil say, perhaps, the Clergie
thereof. Whether al, or some? Yf al,
do you thinke Eugenius to be so simple
as to require, that al Priestes, Deacons,
Subdeacons, Lectours, Exorcistes, Sex-
tines, Clerkes, bel ringers, and Quie-
resters, might come to the Councel?
Yf some: what should they be? Exempted from the Iurisdiction and Gouernement of the Pope, Or subiect vnto him?
Yf Exempted: who should they be in al
Rome, with whom the B. of Rome,
should haue nothing to do? If subiect:
how

B. j

how could they come without his leaue and licence? Or how should not he that sendeth them, be much more higher and worthier, then those which must aske leaue to goe?

what so euer you Answere, If the *Church of Rome be heade of al Churches*, because of some parte of the Clergie therof: must it not much more *be heade of al Churches* because of the Bishop there, which is head ouer that Clergie?

For, if the lesser thing, be in Estimation and Authoritie, much more the greater in the same kinde must be in Authoritie. As, if an Angel naturally doth passe in degree of worthines, euery man, much more he, that by the giftes of nature doth excel among Angels, must consequently be farre aboue man.

we neede not vse so many wordes, in opening this Argument, if we had to do with Quiet and Reasonable men: but M. Iewel wil needes be Ignorant, or Contentious. For (saith he) Victor which reporteth the forsaid Aunswere of Iew. 310. Eugenius the Bishope, Doth not cal the Bishop of Rome the Head of the vniuersal Church.

Church, only he faith, Rome is the Chiefe, or Head Church of al other.

No, he faith not *Rome, but y̆ Churche of Rome*. And if you wil defend your self, that by *Rome* the *Church of Rome* is meant in common fpeache, I pray you Syr, can you not alfo remember, that in naming the *Church of Rome*, the *Bishop of Rome* is vnderftanded to be fpoken of? And, if in other places it might be fomtimes otherwife, yet in this teftimonie of Victor, it can not but be meant of the Bifhoppe of Rome efpecially.

For confider, I pray thee (Indifferent Reader) the Circumftancies of the Storie.

Obadus the Capitaine required a Councel to be kept in Aphrica. In which, it is for Bifhoppes, not onely to fitte, when it is called, but firft to determine whether it fhalbe called or no.

He required it alfo, of the Bifhope Eugenius. For although Hunerycke his Maifter, King of the Vandales was in thofe partes a Conqueror, yet there were not at that time fuch Flatterers or Gofpellers as might tel his Grace, that him

K ij　　　felfe

selfe was Supreame head of the Church, and that he needed not to care, what the Popishe Bishopes would thinke in any mater.

Thirdly Eugenius answered, that he would write to his Bretherne, that his felowbishopes might come. By which it is cleare, that he wiished, not, either for the material Church of beyonde the seas, or al the Ministers and officers of those Churches, but only for Bishopes.

Fynally and Chiefly, he would write (he answered) that the *Church of Rome the head Church of al Churches*, might come. And howe can this otherwyse be vnderstanded, but according to $\hat{y}$ nature of the Mater, and Persons which he spake of before? For, whereas A Councel requireth Bishopes to be present, And hymselfe expressly declareth it, that he would haue his Felowbishopes come: In saying, immediatly after, that aboue all other he would the Churche of Rome to come, he must so take these wordes, *the Churche of Rome*. as they maie serue for A Councel, and for the meeting together of Catholike Bishoppes, But to suche A

pur-

purpose, it was neither possible, to bring the externall Churche of Tymber and Stone, neither was it conuenient, profitable, or cuſtomable, to haue ẏ whole Clergie of euery countrie, to be preſent at Councels : Ergo he meant it of the Biſhoppe of Rome, hymſelfe.

Then whereas he would, the Church of Rome moſt Chiefely to come, *becauſe it is heade of all Churches*, he ſignifieth thereby, that his mynde and deſire was, to haue other Churches to come al-ſo. For els he would haue ſaied, I beſeech the Churche of Rome, only to come, and not Chiefely. Becauſe the word (Chiefely) hath A Relation to other that ſhould come alſo, though not ſo principally and agreablie to his intent and purpoſe.

Nowe in expreſſing this his mynde, that he would haue other Churches, of beyonde the Seas, to come, what words vſeth he ? Doth he not cal ſtraitewaies for his felowbyſhopes? And in reſpecte of them, doth he not require, that *moſt Chiefely the Church of Rome ſhould come?*

K   iij   And

And what other sense can that haue, by any reaso, but that the Bishop of Rome should come? For, if he had said thus, *I vvil vvrite to my Brethren, that the Churches of beyond the Seas may come, and most chiefly to the Church of Rome,* then had the setence gone forwarde in like termes. And in this case, who but Rude and Igno-rant, would deny, that by *Churches* he meaneth the Bishops them selues, Or by theyr appointment some to represent or fil their place? But he changed the Termes, and in one parte speaking of *Bishops,* in the other he nameth not the Bishope, but the *Church of Rome.*

Yet what of this? Shal this chan-ging of Termes alter his meaning? And wishing in the former parte of his sentence, that Bishoppes should come, but especially the *Churche of Rome,* what can he rightly meane by the *church of Rome* but the Bishoppe of Rome, yf one part of the sentence hangeth with the other? For this were al together out of reason, that, naming first Bishops, and then a thing more requisite in the same kinde of purpose, then Bishops: he should meane by by that thing which he preferreth, a lesse in effect and Authoritie, then they were whom he had lesse compted vpon.

This place then making so plainly, for the Authoritie of ÿ Bishop or Church of Rome (for al is in effect one, to them that vnderstand the common phrases of Speach) what wil M. Iewel do? Subscribe to antiquitie, Or maintain stil his Heresie? No, he loueth him selfe, and his owne vaine glory so much, that rather then he wil seme to take a foyle, and to haue spoken more, then he is hable to assure, he wil not lacke his Exceptions, against the witnesses of the First six hundred yeares. For thus he openeth him selfe more and more, saying:

Touching Victor that wrote the story of the Vandales, he is neither Scripture:

For Scripture he was not alleaged. And this also is against sincere and honest dealing, to promise or rather protest that you would be tried by any Doctor, Father, Councel, or Example of the Primitiue Churche: and now so desperately to come in with this exceptiõ, that Victor is no Scripture. It foloweth.

Iew.310. Consider by this that foloweth how willing M. Iew. is to admitte Antiquitie, & how profoundly he reasoneth.

B iiij Nor

Iewel.

Nor Councel.

Remember your selfe M. Iewel. There are, emong your Fauorers, some discrete, Sadde, and Iust men. whome, your Inuention in this place, wil litle please. And your much seeking to extenuate Victors Authoritie, wil be an Argument vnto them, that you fall to Copie of wordes, and shiftes of Rhetorike(meete for Childerne)when Copie of Sense, and certaintie of good Answer, doth not serue your greate Stomacke.

151.

You saied wel once, that one good sentence were Proufe sufficient, and are you so much chainged, so sodainely, that you dare set light by an Aunctient and graue wytnesse, because he is no Councel? You neede surely some good counsel, least by extreme folowing with al your wit, the defense of your mad Challenge, you chaunce to fall bysides your wittes, and haue no sense at al of your doinges. It foloweth.

Iewel.

Nor Doctour.

How define you then, A Doctour? For in deede, whome you wil alowe to beare that name, I can not tel. And, such Libertie you haue take now vnto your selfe, self, of binding vs to your meaning, that if you wil vnderstand by a Doctour none other, but either S. Ambrose, S. Hierome, S. Augustine, or S. Gregorie, which are called the foure Doctours of the Church, Or some such, as hath been solemly Created and made Doctour in some Vniuersitie: we must be content with your sense, and let you haue your owne minde and meaning.

But if you wil be ordered by reason, you wil not deny (I suppose) that Victor might wel be A Doctour, which being a Bishop of no smal Citie in Aphrica; had by al likelyhoode the knowledge of Scriptures, and grace of expounding them, and diligence in executing his office. Except that M. Iewel wil be so Iniurious to the first six hundred yeares after Christ, in which Victor lined, that he wil Iudge any one to haue ben made Bishoppe in those daies, which was vnworthy to be a Doctour.

Againe if he were no Doctour, was he therfore no Father? And your self promising, to admit any sufficient testimonie
of

of any Father, how wisely make ye now, an Exception against Victor, becaule he was no Doctor. It foloweth.

Iewel.

Nor writeth the Order or Practise of the Primitiue Church.

O worthy Exception. Doth S. Augustine in his bookes of Confession, write the Order or Practise of the Primitiue Church? Nothing lesse. For altogether they are compiled, of his owne Actes, Lyfe, Chaunces, Cogitations, and Interrogations. But what then? Might not one, for al this, bring a good testimonie out of those bokes, for proufe of any mater that is in controuersie?

Confeß. lib. 9.

And when the Heretike denieth prayers for the Dead, should not the example of S. Augustine (whose prayer for his Mothers soule, is extant in his Confessions) quite and cleane stoppe his Proceedinges, and make his very Impudencie, ashamed?

What new found reason then, is this of M. Iewels, to contemne an Annciet writer, if he write not of those Maters, and write also, in such Order, of them, as he requireth?

when

When we alleage Clemens, de Consti-
tutionibus Apostolicis, S. Denyse de Cælesti & Ecclesiastica Hierarchia, S. Iames Liturgie, S. Chrysostomes Liturgie, Sozomenus, Nicephorus, Or,
the Decrees and Decretales : straitwaies you
either deny them, either suspect them, either wil fyle them better, before you beleue them . Yet, there are not, in whom
you may see more expressely, the printes
and the formes, of the order or practise of
the Primitiue Church . For where shal
one better finde, what the Religion was
in euery Age, than, in the Histories of
those times, and in Decrees, Answeres,
and forme of publike Seruice, that in e-
uery of them was vsed?

You therefore which , so litle set by
those writers, by whom we may vnderstand most plainly, what the particulars
were, of the cause and state of our Religion in the Primitiue Churche : now,
when Victor is brought against you, so-
dainly you be so chaunged, as though it
might be an exception against a witnes,
that he writeth not the Order or Practise
of the Primitiue Church.

And yet, this Exception of yours,
commeth

commeth not so luckely against Victor,
which although he take not into his storie, the Actes of the Apostles, or the succession of Bishoppes, after them, or al the
persecutions throughout Christendome,
or the Martyrs of al Countries, Or the
perfection and rule of those holy Monks
that liued in wildernesses, Or the Decrees of al Councels, Or euery other
such mater as might be spoken of, by a
General Historiographer : yet, what
state the Church was in, vnder the Uandales, he describeth sufficiently.   And
by his telling this much we vnderstande
of the Order and Practise, (yf not of the
Primitiue Church, yet) of that Church,
which was within the six hundred yeres
after Christe, the which time you haue
allowed vs, that in a mater concerning
Faith, and in a Councel to be gathered,
it was thought meete then, to make o-
ther Bishoppes besydes them of Aphrica priny thereof: and especially to haue
the presence of the Bishoppes of Rome,
because *The Church of Rome is head of al churches*.   Which Euidence, because it is so
plaine

plaine againſt you, therefoze hauing no=
thing to ſaie reaſonably againſt the ſen=
tence, you haue ſtretched your wittes
to finde Exceptions againſt the Repoz=
ter of it, And you ſaie farther againſt
him.

Nor is it wel knowen, either of what   Iewel.
credite he was, or when he liued,

Concerning his Credite, he was
Biſhoppe of Vtica, and by likelyhoode
therefoze, of good Eſtimation among
the Catholiques, and A Man wozthy to
be beleued. For in al kindes and Con=
trarieties of Religion, ſuch as are high
Pzieſtes, Biſhops, oz Superintendents,
it ſeemeth that they are of the better ſozt,
of the Familie, Churche, oz Congrega=
tion: out of which they are taken do doe
that Office. And further, whoſe bookes
were compted then wozthy the copieng
out, and were ſo kept then, that they re=
maine yet vnto vs. And are ſo accepted
at this pzeſent, that they be tranſlated in=
to French: His credite needeth not to be
miſtruſted, oz called without cauſe into
queſtion. He wzote alſo vnto Hunericus
King of Vandales an accōpt of his faith
                                          being

being driuen thereto by the Commaunde-ment of ye King. By which you may per-ceiue that great accōpt was made of him.

Concerning then his age, he liued not long after the time of S. Augu-stine: farre within the first six hundred yeares, out of which, any Testimonie is sufficient against you. For when the Uandales were in Aphrica, and were busy in furthering the Procedinges of the Arrians, then liued Uictor, as may appeere by his Answer to Hunericus, & by diuerse places of his historie, in which he speaketh of him selfe as one present at ye doing of things. For in this very place which is alleged out of him for ye Supre-macie of the Church of Rome, he saith, that when Hunericus had required by his Edict and Commaundement, that the Catholike Bishops, should by a day, meete at Carthage, there to haue theyr faith examined and tried:

Cognoscentibus igitur qui aderamus si-mul, &c. We then that were togeather kne-wing of this Decree, did tremble at the hart, especially because of those wordes of the Edict, In Prouincijs nostris à Deo nobis concessis, scan-

dalum

dalum esse nolumus, quasi id diceret, in Prouincijs nostris, Catholicos esse nolumus : Vve vvil, that in the Prouinces graunted by God to vs, there be no scandalum or offense, as though he should say. vve vvil not that any Catholiques be in our Prouincies. Him self therfoze being then pzesent when Hunericus Edict came to the Bithops of Aphzica, and that perfequution of the Uandales beginning about the yeare of our Lozd. 435. no man should reafonablie doubt, of the age in which Uictoz liued.

But thefe thinges you say, are not wel knowen. If they be knowen, it is inough : As foz the wel knowing of them you are either fo fufpitious oz malicious ŷ. (I feare) it wil neuer be wel knowen, ŷ which commeth directly againft your Pzocedinges. Foz how eafy a mater is it to deny, and doubt, and obiect, and finde faulte, and make fomwhat alwaies lacking?

You finde the Boke extant, and that befoze this age in which your Herefies haue upftarted, and the Catholikes haue fought to fuppzeffe them : You fee it alleaged ; You fee it allowed ; You bzing
nothing

nothing againste it, neither that it was found of late, neither that the phrases of Speach are vncongrue and barbarouse, neither that he hath any fault in his storie, neither that graue and learned men haue doubted of him, nor ani other exception which maie take Credite away from it. And what reason then, is there in it, that you should make strife and contention, where none was before, and rather folow your owne Negatiue, without any cause or probabilitie, than the Catholikes Affirmatyue, which bring furth the Euidence of the booke it selfe, for them?

Maie we thinke you to haue any regard to the first six hundred yeres, Or any Reuerence towardes Auncient writers, which are so loth to admit the bokes that come furth in their names, and so Ready to make all the Exceptions, that ye possibly can, Or Suspitions against them?

It is not wel knowen (say you) of what Credite he was, or when he lyued. Is it not well knowen? If he made in any point, for the Lutherans or Sacramentaries opinion, you would not only haue knowen hym wel, but also praised him exceedingly

cedingly, but now, because he confirmeth
the Catholike Faith, and declareth such
cruell practises of the Barbarous Uandales then, against the Catholike Priestes and Bishopes, as are most lyke the
merciful Procedings of the Gentle Gospellers of these tymes, againste the
Catholikes: And because he preferreth
the Church of Rome, before all other
Churches, And praieth to the Sainctes,
And sheweth hymselfe most Euidently
to be A Papist: you knowe hym not, and
you regard hym not. So that you be
ruled by Affections and not by Reasons,
and you passe no more vpon Antiquitie,
sauing for ý fasshion that al lerned and
wise men doe make accompte of it, than
you doe vpon your rochet, gowne, typet,
fower cornerd Cap, and other such thinges, that goe cleane againste the Conscience, sauing that you condescend therin vnto the weaklings, as yet, in your
faith, least you should make them wery
of you, altogether.

Yet, although you be very wyse
hypocrites, out breaketh for al that sometymes, the Iesting and Scoffing inward
L j Sprite

Spirit, that in open Sermons and printed Bokes, speaketh of the holy and old Fathers, ful Reuerently, As shal by most manifeste examples appeere.

S. Benet, how Uertuous, wyse, holy, Contemplatiue, and Diuine a Father he was, if the world that hath bene euer sens, would or could saie nothing, S. Gregorie alone hath saied inough. which being now Pope, and to good a man, to mynd vnprofitable tales, and to muche occupied, to intend it, in writing fower bookes of notable and worthie men and maters, the Second he bestoweth vppon S. Benet alone: Declaring suche thinges in it, as he had heard of most Reuerende Fathers, and S. Benets owne Scholars, Constantius, Valentinianus, Simplicius, and Honoratus: by reading of whiche, the Faithful coulde not but be moued, to beleue that God is *Wonderfull in his holy ones*, and that his frindes are exceding honored. In tellinge then many thinges of S. Benet, he cummeth at length vnto this.

VVhen a certaine younge Monke of S.Benets

ial.lib.
.in præf.

Ps.67.
Psal.138.

Greg.lib.
.dial.ca.
.4.

ueis , had vppon a tyme gone out of the Monaste-
rie, vvithout his blessinge , home to his Father &
Mothers house , vvhich he loued more then he
shoulde haue done , the selfe same daie , as sone
as he vvas come vnto them he dyed. And after he
had ben novve buried, his bodie the next daie vvas
founde caste vp , vvhiche they prouided to burie
againe . But they founde it the nexte daie cast
vp againe , and vnburied as before . Then loe
they ranne vvith speede vnto Father Benets
feete , and vvith muche vveepinge desyred hym,
to be so good as to graunt hys fauour ænd mer-
tie vnto hym . To vvhome , the Man of God
gaue straite vvaye vvith his ovvne handes the
Communion of our Lordes bodie , saieng . Goe
ye , and put ye this bodie of our Lord vppon his
breaste , and so burie hym . Vvhich as sone as
it vvas done , the earth toke and kepte his bodie,
and cast it vp no more.

𝕿𝖍𝖚𝖘 𝖋𝖆𝖗 𝕾. 𝕲𝖗𝖊𝖌𝖔𝖗𝖎𝖊. 𝕭𝖚𝖙 𝖜𝖍𝖆𝖊
𝖘𝖆𝖎𝖊𝖙𝖍 𝕸. 𝕴𝖊𝖜𝖊𝖑 𝖙𝖔 𝖙𝖍𝖊 𝖒𝖆𝖙𝖊𝖗? 𝕱𝖔𝖗𝖘𝖔𝖙𝖍
𝖍𝖎𝖘 𝖘𝖊𝖓𝖙𝖊𝖓𝖈𝖊 𝖎𝖘 𝖙𝖍𝖎𝖘.

It was but fondly done by S. Benet, Iewio 44
as Gregorie reporteth of hym, to cause the Impu-
Sacrament to be laied vpon a dead mans dentlp.
breast.

𝖂𝖆𝖘 𝖎𝖙 𝖇𝖚𝖙 fondly 𝖉𝖔𝖓𝖓𝖊?   𝕳𝖔𝖜𝖊 Ra:
      𝕷 ij   𝖉𝖆𝖗𝖊

dare you so interpzete the fact of an Auncient and holy Father ?   How dare you
diſſent from the Opinion that S. Gregorie and other elder Fathers whom he
folowed, had of it ?   Are you he, that regardeth Antiquitie? Are you he, whom
one ſufficient ſentence of any Catholike
Father oz Doctoz ſhal make to yeld?

The fact you doe not denie: Againſt
the wozker of it you bzing no exception:
S. Gregozie the Repozter of it , lyued
within the firſt ſix hundzed yeres, And he
repozteth it to the Pzaiſe of S. Benet,
And the effect whiche God gaue, declareth that it was not miſlyked : and how
dare you ſay, it was but fondly done?

But this is it that I ſay. Though
you looke demurely vpon Reuerend and
old Fathers, and ſpeake, as though you
regarded their wozdes and deedes : yet
ſometymes your Spzite is ſo moued in
you, that from the pytte of your harte, it
cummeth vp to the typ of your tongue,
and boldly geaueth ſentence againſt thoſe
perſons, whom the whole wozld, foz age,
Holynes, Lerning and Judgement, doth
wozthely eſteeme, and whom yourſelfe
dare

A Lur-
king ſpzite
and wat-
ching foz
moze oppoz-
tunitie to
bzeake o-
penly out.

dare not dishonour but couertly. Where=
fore, that this fowle Spirite of Contempt
of Old Fathers whiche lurketh in the
breast of M. Jewel, may be the better ex=
amined and espied what it is, whiles it
waggeth now his tongue: we shal not
neede to haue an Exorcist for the mater,
but any reasonable and Indifferent man,
shal be hable, to conuince hym, by these
short questions.

For first of al, how know you (M.
Jewel) that it was fondly done of S. Benet
to cause the Sacrament to be laied vpon a
dead mans breast? Dyd S. Benet hym=
selfe, thinke it to be fondly done? Then
would neither he euer haue done it, or
they whiche sought Remedie of hym a=
gainst ỹ terrible chaunce, you may be af=
sured, nor they so willingly haue obeyed.

Dyd S. Gregorie find any such fault in
it? He would neuer haue rehersed it then,
to ỹ disgracing of hym, whom he intended
to honor. And byfides this, the *Epiphonema*
or sententious conclusion whiche he in=
ferreth immediatly vppon the forsayed
example or fact, doth proue that he high=
ly estemed it, For, vnto Peter his

L iij Dea=

S. benet
defended,

Deacon, with whom he talketh in those Dialogues :

Perpendis Petre & c. Thou seest Peter (saieth he) *Vvhat merite and vvorthines, this man vvas of, before Iesus Christ our Lord, that the earth dyd cast farth his bodie, vvhich had not the Fauor and blesfing of S. Benet.*

Dyd God hymselfe misfyke with it? The euent doth proue otherwyse. For, as the castinge vp of the Childes bodye againe and againe, after it was buried, doth fignifie that al was not wel about it, where such extraozdnarie effect folowed: so the resting of it in the earth after the body of our Lozd was put vpon it, doth declare that he was now pleased, which before was offended. If then none of al these can be perceaued to haue misfyked S. Benets precept oz Counsel: by what Authozitie faieth M. Jewel, it was fondly done by him?

Againe, what thinketh M. Jewel of S. Benet? It seemeth, that he contemneth hym not vtterly, because of the (S.) which he putteth before his name. Except he would haue it vnderstanded, that the (S.) in this place must goe not foz

Sainct

Sainct Benet, but for Syr Benet. He lyued also within the first six hundred yeares, and was for al vertue and holynes, A very miracle in the world. It seemeth then, that his docinges are to be Iudged of, with Reuerence. Furth then to S. Gregorie.

what opinion hath M. Iewel of him? I should thinke very good. For he was an holy and lerned Father, and lyued also within the first six hundred yeares. And (which is more worth than al this) A Late writer in deede, but as he would be thought, a greate Frind and Patrone of Antiquitie, One M. Iewel hath these wordes of hym: Verely S. Gregories Authoritie in this case were very good, if he Pa.188. would saie the worde. If therefore, so greate Authoritie make for this fact of whiche we speake, and if the spirite of God were in those two Fathers S. Benet and S. Gregorie: what knowledge is that in M. Iewell, by whiche he is hable to saie, It was but fondly done by S. Benet, &c?

If y like case should happen vnto him, that any of his brethernes bodyes in

Z iiij the

the Congregation of Sarum, should be cast vp againe after it were once buryed, what would his polytike wisedome doe? Commaunde it he would perchaunse, to be buryed againe. So might he in dede.

But if it were cast vp againe after the second burieing, and if further yet, as oft as it should be put vnder the earth ouer night, it were found vpon the ground in the mornyng : what then would his holynes or wisedome doe ? would he byd the Brothers or Systers, cast that (with al care after it)out of the waie, and suffer that to rotte aboue ground, which wyll not lie stil vnder ground, when it was wel inough buried? For his wysedome and deuotion he might do it wel inough.

But if God, which suffered the forsaied castinges vp againe, of the deade bodie, to signifie thereby a displeasure iustly conceiued, if he now would by other waies declare the same, euen vpon this bodie which M. Iewel should leaue vnburied, were he hable to abyde the terror of it? And wonld he not seeke for some Remedie against an extraordinarie and straunge effect of Gods indignation?

And

And what remedie would that be?
I can not tel verely, there is so litle po=
wer oz none rather at al, in any thinge
that they can doe. Yet (foz crample
sake) if it were put in his minde to make
a Crosse vpon the bzeast of the deade bo=
dy, oz to put a Relique of some holy man
vpon it, Oz the Gospel of S. Iohn, Oz
a peece of holy bzeade, Oz (if these things
would not like him) if he should venter
to put vpon it a leafe of Caluines Insti=
tutions, Oz of the Communion bookes,
Oz a peece of Latimers staffe, Oz Cran=
mers gowne, oz Hoopers bones, Oz any
other thing that he estemeth : If that af=
ter any of these thinges were put on the
Body, it should be quiet & lie stil where
it were cast oz buried : were it a likely
mater that it should be fondely done, to
haue applied that to the deade Bodie, of
which a merueilouse and comfoztable
effect should be seen to folow?

Surely, if by your Cōmunion booke,
oz any bone of your false Martyzs, a Mi=
racle should seme to be wzought, I woid
neuer thinke, that you did fondly to vse
the meanes of those things that are pze=
tious

cious emonge you, to the bzinging of some purposes to passe: but this I would certainely Judge, that your selues are very fond men to esteeme those thinges that you doe, and that the Diuel had power to illude you. Now if you dare saie, that S. Benet did not wel, to haue so excellent and great opinion of the Sacrament as he had, Oz that it was the wozke of the diuel of hel and not of God, that the Monkes bodie remained vnder the earth, after the Bodie of Chzistewas laied vpon it: then loe, I perceiue that you haue spoken very fauozablie of S. Benet in saying, that it was but fondly done by him, and that in deede, you Judge it to haue been wickedly and shamefully done of him. And you must iudge, not of him onely, so, but of Constantius, Valentinianus, Simplicius (S. Benets successours) And of S. Gregozie a most excellēt father, And of al other at ȳ tyme, vnto whom, these mens authozities were singular, of al these, you must iudge, ȳ they were blind, fond, grosse, superstitious, wicked, deceiued by illusiōs of diuels, & void of ȳ Grace of ȳ Gospel.

Put

Put of your vysard (M. Iewel) and
shew your selfe in your owne likenesse.
Put of your apparel of a sadde and discrete persō, which knoweth his nurture,
and can tel how to geue place vnto Re=
uerend and holy Fathers: & come furth
in your owne solemne Robes, with iags
& tassels inough about it, that your cote
may declare what you are. For in dede
were you not desperate, you would more
quietly haue iudged of S. Benets fact,
than you haue done, and not so quickely
haue condemned it as but fondly done:
and were you not your selfe very fonde,
you would neuer haue contemned that,
which was done and regestred and com=
mended within the first six hundred after
Chrift, your selfe so appealing vnto those
yeres, as though you would be reformed
by the Example and Testimonie of any
Catholike Father within those yeares.

Yet if you continue stil in your
Hypocrisie, the Indifferent Reader wil
(I trust) perceiue wel inough, that
you are but a Counterfaict, and that
you beare no hartie good wil and reue=
rence, towards old and blessed Fathers.
For

For what would not he not doe, if feare of the Magiſtrates and ſhame of the worlde (as yet) did not let him, which is ſo foliſhe hardy, as to put in one caſe oʒ degree the tales of Heathen Poetes, & the Recoʒdes of Chʒiſtian Hiſtoʒiographers: the Fancies of Idle men, and the Diſpenſatiõs of almighty God : the Cõceptes that moue ſenſualitie, and the Examples that pʒocure deuotion? He bʒingeth it in, by occaſion of S. Baſils viſion which Amphilochius ſpeaketh of: and ſo much the moʒe vttereth his cankred Stomake, by how much he had the leſſe occaſion to folow it ! His wooʒdes be theſe.

Iew.83.
Shame
to thee.

We may now the better beleue that Iupiter with his Goddes went downe ſometimes for his pleaſure to banket in Aethiopia, Or that an Angel euermore miniſtred the Sacramente vnto Marcus that Holy Monke: Or. &c.

As who ſhould ſay, the one is as likely as the other, Oʒ, the one as vaine as ŷ other. But what man of honeſty would euer ſay ſo ? Yf ſome bʒutiſhe and vnſenſible Heretike ſhould plainely, at the beginning

ginning, proteſt, that he would no bet=
ter eſteeme what ſo euer Fathers Teſtimonie, than Chriſtian men doe regarde
Homers Poetrie, although for his blūt=
nes he might be condemned, yet for his
plaineſſe he ſhould not be blamed. Mary
if an other man, who knoweth the price
of ſundry bookes though thei be not ſcri=
pture, and moſt diſtinctly ſignifieth it,
that he wil admit any Catholike writer,
of the firſt ſix hundred after Chriſte, if he
ſodainly wil liken any Auncient wri=
ters narration, to Homer the Father of
al Poetes Imagination, he ſhameth vt=
terly his owne ſtudie, doinges, promiſe,
and honeſtie.

Are the comming of Iuppiter downe
to a banket in *Aethiopia*, and the Angels
comming to Marcus an holy Monke to
geaue him the Sacrament, are theſe two
ſo like, that M. Iewel could thinke it
reaſonable, to put them in one ſentence,
and in one kinde of caſe togeather? As
for Iuppiters Godhead and his banket-
ting in *Aethiopia*, not onely al Chriſtians
doe take for a wretched and vaine fable,
but the Painimes alſo themſelues, ſuch
as

Aug. de ci-
ui. Dei. lib.
4. cap. 27,
& 31.

as were of the more learned sorte, did neuer so accompt of him: as in outward wordes they seemed to doe. But Marcus the Monkes holines, and the Seruice that the Angel did vnder God, vnto him, none surely but Infidels wil iudge to be fained. For to a good and faithful minde, what is there in this storie that doth sound absurdely?

To haue a Monke holy, should that seeme incredible? He doth very il him selfe when he is alone, that Iudgeth so wickedly of the Solitarie lyfe. And this Reproche or Sclaunder, doth not touch onely Marcus, Hilarion, Antonius, Moyses and other of whom Ecclesistical Stories make mention, but Helias also and Helizens, and S. Iohn the Baptist him selfe.

The storie
of the holy
Monke
Marcus,
defended.

But is it like to be fained, when the Sacrament is saied to be geauen vnto some persons by the ministerie of an Angel? what shal we thinke then, of the Angel that caried the Prophete Abacuc by an heare of his heade, from Iudea to Babylon? Or, of the Angel Raphael that went like a goodly yong man, **with**

·in. 24.
·bie. 5.

with Tobie the yonger, and did eate
drinke, talke, make mery with him, and
instructed him in al thinges, in like ma=
ner as deere and hartie friendes and fe=
lowes behaue them selues towardes their
friendes and companions? Uerely,
whereas almightie God him selfe hath
so debased him selfe, that he is become
man, and geaueth him selfe wholy vnto
man, to be eaten of him, that man might
be vnited vnto God and liue by his life:
it were no wonder at al, in comparison, if
ẏ Diuine foode should be alwaies mini=
stred to man, by the visible seruice of An=
gels. For neither can the Angels dis=
daine at it, to serue that Creature, the
nature of whiche he seeth to be exal=
ted aboue al Principates, Potestates,
Dominations, Cherubines, and Se=
raphins: And when Gods infinite ma=
iestie wil be meate, he can not be loth to
carie the Dishe.

wherefore then, doth M. Iewel
ioyne so wickedly togeather: An Angel ministring the Sacramente, and Iuppiter going to banket in AEthiopia?

was Sozomenus that reporteth it
A

A fabler onely, as Homer was, so much the more at libertie tel lyes, because he wrote in prose, and not in verse? He liued within the first six hundred yeres, he was A Christian, he wrote an Ecclesiastical Historie, and not Poetical Fables, his writinges are allowed and receiued, and this, which he reporteth, of the Angels ministring the Sacrament to Marcus an holy Monke, he confirmeth by the Testimonie of Macarius an Auncient and Famous Priest. Which not onely said it, but for the Truth and certaintie thereof assured it, that at the time of receiuing, an Angel did alwaies geue marcus the Sacrament, and not he. And that he saw alwayes an hand only, as far as vnto the wreast of it, at which Marcus tooke the Sacrament. In testimonie vndoubtedly of the cleane and singular good soule that was in Marcus. For he was euen from his youth merueilous expert in the Scriptures, and Gentle, and Chaste, and Deuoute, and at that present, one of the most notable in al the worlde.

What findeth M. Iewel in this story, that

Sozeme-nus lib. 6. cap. 29.

that he maie contemne? Or why refuseth
he the iudgement of Sozomenus and of
Macarius? Of whom, the one reporteth
it, the other confirmeth it: And the one
in reporting it, signifieth it to be credible,
the other in seeing it, assureth it to be no=
table.

If it were altogether fayned in deede,
and if other yet should be perswaded to
accept it as Trueth, what harme could
come to them by it? For al, that maie be
gathered thereof, is, that Marcus was
a merueylous holy, and angelical man.
And that God euen in this world, doth
excedingly comfort his seruants by more
waies than one: And that the Seruice
and attendance of the Angels vpon men
is singular: And that, if the vncleanes of
our wretched lyfe did not let it, we should
find the Angels more present and comfor=
table, then they are perceiued to be. And
is there any harme in this, to iudge wel,
of man, Angel, and God? If M. Iewel
can find no greater faultes or hinderan=
cies to good lyfe and true Faith, in the
going of Iuppiter to bankette with his
yonger Goddes in Aethiopia, I would

M j   neuer

neuer sticke to beleue it, or at the leaste waies, to permit it. But the oddes is so greate and euident, that he which hath put Iuppiter and the Angel in one case, may iustly seme to be vnsensible.

Hold that fast that you haue, you that haue any faith remayning yet vnto you: And you that haue no faith, And mynde (God knoweth when) but for all that, mynd to take it, take it by tyme, whiles the Heretikes them selues wil not, in some pointes, speake against it. For now,

Take time while tyme is. ꝑ world is not yet at the worst.

not to beleue the Canonical Scriptures who dareth? And how greate cause hath A fainte and weake harte to assent vnto them, whiles the enemies of the Catholike faith, doe not openly denie them? But, when hereafter, Iniquitie and Impudencie shall so abounde, that faith shal be measured by Reason and not by Authoritie, and when by litle and litle men shalbe accustomed to contemne & mocke the Apparitions made vnto holy persons by Angels, Saintes, the Mother of God, or Christ hymselfe, and lyken them to fables and Illusions of the vaine Poetes and wicked Sprites that raigned emong the

the Panymes: what credite wil be geaue
shortly after to the Scriptures themselues?

wil not the Commyng of the three
Angels to Abraham, and the Feast which   *Gene.17.*
they toke at his handes, wil not the wra-
stling of the Angel with Iacob a whole   *32.*
night longe together, wyl not the Angels that appeered to Agaz, Iosue, Ba-
lam, Manue, Dauid, Elias, wil not the   *Gen.21.*
fiery Chariots that Elizeus saw, wil not   *Iosu.5.*
the Terrible horse with one in golden   *Num.22.*
armour sitting vpon him, and two good-   *Iud.13.*
ly and glorious yong men in bewtifull   *1.Paral.28*
apparel, which scourged Heliodorus that *3.Re.19.*
would haue spoyled the Orphanes, and   *4.Re.6.*
wydowes, and other, of their goodes   *Mach.2.*
that laie in safe keepinge in the Temple
of Hierusalem: wil not the Angels ap-
peering to the Maries, and the Apostles, *Mar.16.*
al in white, and the Angel that byd S.   *Acto.1. &*
Peter aryse, and put on his hose and   *12.*
shewes, wil not al these thinges be quikly and desperately resembled to the con-
uersations which Homers Goddes and
Goddesses had with such as they fauored?

Nothing is so easie as to cal thinges

into doubt, & to disgrace a true and holy Storie, by objecting a lyke vnto it, of the telling of Jdolatours, or the making of Poetes. Jn which kind of Confounding, Marring, and Spoyling of thinges, M. Jewel hath a Folish Grace: and if he had any Reuerence to Old and Approued Stories, he woulde neuer haue ioyned Sozomenus, and Homer together.

He therefore that hath Faith, let hym thanke God for it, and praic for the increase: he that hath none, but is negligente or Judifferent, let hym thinke aduysedly vpon the sauing, of both soule and bodye, and make speede to beleue the Scriptures themselues, whiles so litle contradiction is, against them. For other writers then afterwardes, let hym consider, whether it will stand with saluation to beleue none, or whether it be of necessitie, to admit al: Or whether it can agree with any reason and constancie, to contemne them, whome he hath, for good cause, once alowed.

Jn beleuing nothing but Scripture there is present daunger. For by that Reason, Scripture it selfe can not be

cc.

credited, because it is not written in all
Scripture.

In beleuinge euery thing there is
absurditie, because of so many Contradictions and Contrarieties as are found
emong Writers.

In beleuing of certaine bookes not
yet as Scripture, but as the bookes of
Lerned, Auncient, and Generally receiued Authors, and sayinges as worthie to
be credited and esteemed as our owne
opinions, there is wisedome and discretion.

But, if (as M. Iewel hath geauen
most shameful Examples) any man wil
contemne the selfesame, whome he would
seeme to allowe, that is such a point, not
only of Hypocrisie, but of Iniurie also, that, as he should B E W A R E
OF M. IEWEL for it, so should
he take heed to hym selfe
least he fal in it.

*How M. Iewel vseth the selfesame
testimonies, of the first six hun=
dred yeares, against whiche he
bringeth Exceptions, when his
Aduersarie allegeth them.*

Thus far then we are come against
M. Iewel, y̌ I haue proued him,
to bind y̌ Catholikes vnto y̌ first
six hundred yeres, bysides al rea=
son and equitie, And that hymselfe allea=
geth Authorities of later yeres, with all
boldnes and libertie: Thirdly, that he
wil not stand, to the witnesses of the first
six hundred yeres, vnto which he appea=
led so precisely.

And what is there now, that maie
be added vnto his Chiualrie? For in
deede, this maie be well called his Chi=
ualrie, to pronoke, as it were al the
world, and, to make conditions such as
please hym, and when the battel increa=
seth, to chainge his armour, to put on a
Brasen face, to denie that he alowed, to
                                            alowe

alow that he denied. In which, as he
hath shewed hymselfe (lyke as I, by Ex=
amples, haue declared) A man: so, what
he maie or hath added therunto, it would
be considered. And I find that his noble
Courage and tried Magnanimitie is so
greate, that, the selfe same Authorities,
against which he fought toothe and naile,
in the Chappiter before, he hymselfe, in
his owne proper person, aloweth in
other places of his Replie, and vseth for
substantiall and good Argumentes.

This, to proue at large, were very
easie, but in recompense of the last Chap=
piter before, which hath ben longer than
my opinion, I wil make this preset one,
shorter than my first determination. And
shortnes also maie wel be taken whē the
mater is in sight that is to be proued. I
saie therefore.

Against S. Chrysostomes Masse,
M. Iewel doth argue in the 10. page of
his Replie, And not only reasoneth sim=
plie, that it can not be his, but taunteth
also them pretily, that would haue it to
be S. Chrysostomes. But, how much he
is deceaued in his Argument, and how
P iiij lide

litle cauſe he hath to dalie as though he had the victorie, it is ſufficiently declared alreadie fo. 53. of this booke.

The ſame M. Jewel in the 89. and 90. page of the Replie where the place of S. Chryſoſtome (There is none to Com-municate) is layed againſt hym, there, I ſaie, he vſeth the teſtimonie of this Li-turgie, & confeſſeth it to be S. Chryſoſto-mes. For theſe be his wordes.

Iew.89.

90.

Chryſoſtome himſelfe in his Liturgie ſaith thus. Againe. But what needeth much proufe, in a Caſe that is ſo plaine? Chryſo-ſtome hymſelfe in his Liturgie that Com-monly beareth his name, foloweth the ſame order. Againe, This was the order of S. Chryſoſtomes Maſſe, touching the Clergie, and that by the wytneſſe of S. Chryſoſtom himſelfe.

Ra.

Iew. p.10

Note the wordes (Indifferent Rea-der) and ſee what proportion is in M. Iewels doeings. That Liturgie, which, before, could not be S. Chryſoſtomes, becauſe it praieth for Pope Nicolas: and becauſe, A praier is there, for the Empire and Victorie of the Emperour Alexius: and becauſe, I trowe it were propheſieing and not praieing, that Chryſoſtome praied for

men

men by name, seuen hundred yeres before
they were borne : that same nowe is S.
Chrysostomes, by M. Iewels owne
confession. And not only S. Chrysostomes, but Chrysostomes hymselfe.

For herein also is a greate strength:
that ỷ place, which was obiected against
hym, beinge taken out of S. Chrysostome, he thought to adde a Grace vnto
his Answere by continuinge in the testimonies of the selfe same Doctour, and
by making S. Chrysostome to agree
with S. Chrysostom. And so he repea-
teth oftentymes, Chrysostome hymselfe,
sayinge: Chrysostome HYMSELFE
in his Liturgie. Chrysostom HIMSELF
in the Liturgie. The very order of Chrysostomes Masse, by the witnesse of Chrysostome HYMSELFE. As though
that nothing were so much to be feared,
as that some lyke hymself, would deme
it to be S. Chrysostomes Liturgie, and
then should he leese a good Argument.
Therefore he setteth the Booke furth
very wel, and nameth it the Liturgie
of Chrysostome hymselfe, and maketh
so muche of it, that he signifieth it, to
haue in it self Authoritie inough to proue

Chryso-
stoms Li-
turgie con
fessed by
M. Iew,

all

an assertion, without any more wordes. For thus saith M. Iewel.

But what needeth much proufe, in a case that is so plain? Chrysostome him self. &c.

As if he should saie: That the Clergie receiued in olde time, with the Priest that celebrated, I haue proued it, by the Canons of the Apostles, by Pope Anacletus Decree, by the Councel of Nice, Cartige, Laodicea, and of Toledo. But what needeth much proufe in a case that is so plaine? I could allege more witnesses, Antiquitie is ful of Examples, The case is cleare and euident. But to be short, I wil bring one Testimone for al.

And what is that? Mary, Chrysostome him selfe: where I pray you? In the Liturgie. why did Chrysostome euer make any? where should one find it? By what note might one know it? In the Liturgie (saith M. Iewel) that comonly beareth his name. Speake you that to the discommendacion or praise of it? If to the discommendacion, as though it were not S. Chrysostomes in deede, but bare only his name, how agreeth it, that Chry-

Chrysostom him selfe, should witnesse any
thing by this Liturgie? For if you should
haue said no more but this, Chrysostome
in the Liturgie that comonly beareth his
name &c, you might haue ben thought to
haue called it S. Chrysostomes Liturr-
gie, because other so name it, and no certaintie might be gathered therby, of your
owne opinion and iudgement. But now
in saying Chrysostom him self &c, you declare by y addition of the Pronoune him
selfe, that your opinion is, S. Chrysostom,
euen he that made the 61. Homelie ad po-
pulum Antiochen. to be the very Author
of this Liturgie. If therefore you cast not
in these wordes that comonly beareth his
name, to the dispraise or discredite of the
Liturgie, then haue you not only confessed, that Chrysostome him selfe should be
maker of it, but farder also, you teach vs
to find out that Liturgie by the title of y
booke and name of S. Chrysostom, which
it commonly beareth, either you make a
good Argumēt against singular and precise Heretiques, which wil needes haue
thinges otherwise to be taken, then commonly they are called.

Now

Now, if you dyd put in, the forsaied words (that commonly beareth his name) neither to the praise nor displaise of the Liturgie, but as it came to your mynde so you lette it fall out into the Paper, that which might wel inough haue ben spared: let so take it then. And what remaineth, but that Chrysostome himselfe muste be the vndoubted Author of this Liturgie, by your conclusion? Otherwise you haue not proued by Chrysostom himself, that the Priestes and Deacons (whiche no man denieth) receiued with the Bishop or Chiefe Exequutor at the Aultare, if the Liturgie, by which you proue it, be not S. Chrysostomes owne.

Ergo, say I now, whereas M. Iewel in the 10. page of his Replie, disproueth the Liturgie of S. Chrysostome: And, in the 89. and 90. of the same Replie, affirmeth S. Chrysostome hymselfe, to saie that, whiche in the Liturgie is affirmed: It is most plaine and euident, that the selfesame Authorities of the first six hundred yeres, which he wil destroie and denie rather, than his Aduersarie should vse them, he yet hymselfe will occupie

occupie at his pleasure, and make a great shew and countenance, that he is a folo=wer of Antiquitie.

　　In like maner in the. 66. page of his Replie, he argueth against a Decree of Soter Bishop of Rome, and in the. 76 page folowing, he applieth the selfe same Decree to his purpose. Read and con=sider yͤ places them selues, you to whom M. Iewels sayinges are pretious, I wil note only the brief some of the whole mater.

Soter Bishope of Rome (saith D. Harding) *made this statute or decree, That no Priest should presume to celebrate the solemnitie of the Masse, except there were two present and answere him, so as he him selfe be the third. For whereas he saith,* Dominus vobiscum, *Our Lord be vvith yon, and like=wise in the* Secretes, Orate pro me, *Pray for me: it semeth euidently couenient, that answere be made to his Saluta=tion accordingly.*

Hard.
De Conf.
dist. 1. can.
Hoc quo-
que.

Now of this Decree he gathereth, that al the people were not present of necessitie at the Seruice, and much more, $\tilde{y}$ al did not receiue with the Priest when so euer he celebrated. For it had ben vnreasonable so earnestly to prouide by a solemne Decree, that without the presence of twe more besides him selfe, no Priest should be so bolde as to celebrate, if the general & necessarie practise of that time, had so defined it that al the parish should communicate, or that without a number of Communicantes, there shoulde be no Masse said at al. This Decree therefore, which so euidently destroyeth the position of M. Iewel, see how he laboreth to disgrace.

First he setteth men togeather by the eares (as it were) with Som saie, this decree was made by Pope Anacletus, Some others saie by Soter. And so whiles some say one thing some an other, he thinketh that the quiet Reader which loueth concord and peace, wil folow his resolution, which is to follow none of the both, but to haue an opinion of his owne, that it is neither Soter nor Anacletus his decree.

After

Iew. 66.
Note the
processe of
M. Iew.

After this he falleth into a common place, that It was euermore the common practise of Deceiuers, to blase their doings by the names of such, as thei knew to be in estimation in the world. And in this place to let passe Homer, Hesiode, Cicero, Plautus, he allegeth S. Paul. 2. Thess. 2 And counterfeite Gospels and workes, in the name of Peter, Thomas, and other the Apostles, Concluding, that we ought the lesse to merueil, if the like haue happened vnto Anacletus, Euaristus, Soter. &c. So that y̍ Coclusion is brought to an If.

Thirdly, he speaketh finally a-gainst the Decretal Epistles, Alleaging Gratian, that thei haue been doubted of among Learned men, and D. Smith, although his aucthoritie be not greate, that thei can not possiblie be theirs, whose names thei beare.

Soters Decree refused by M. Iew. Dist. 19.

Fourthly, he confirmeth D. Smithes sayinges by certaine reasons not of D. Smiths, but of his owne: as, These De-cretal Epistles, manifestlie depraue and a-buse the Scriptures. Thei maintaine no-thing so much as the kingdom of the Pope. Thei publish a multitude of vaine and su-perstitious Ceremonies, Thei proclaime such

1.

2.

3.
4.

such thinges as M. Harding knoweth to be open and knowen lyes, & this later pointe is proued by certaine coniectures.

But al this hitherto, is nothing to the disprouing of the foresaid Decree, either that it is not Soters, either that it is not to be credited, if as others say, it were Anacletus. He busieth him selfe in general and Indefinite propositions, to no purpose, or conclusion, but to breed Suspitions and Doubtes. Much like as if in reasoning against some heretike, I would not, nor could not proue that he were a Diuel, but yet would tel a long tale and proue it very substantially, that the Diuel hath oftentimes gone abroad and ben conuersant with men, and spoken very manerly of Religion, so like an honest and true man, as any may seme to be in al the worlde.

Fiftly then, after all Preludes or Preambles ended, he toucheth specially the decree it selfe, vpon which the Argument of D. Hardings was grounded. And his reasons against it, are shortly these. S. Austin, & S. Hierom who liued. 250. yeres after Soter, Haue recorded that the people

ple of Rome vſed to take the Communion
togeather euerie daie, *ergo that practiſe
wil hardly ſtand with Soters decree. As
who ſhould ſaie, that al the people might
not receaue at one prieſtes handes if any
other prieſt, when they were departed,
ſhould goe to the Aultare, and haue no
moe but two to anſwere hym.*

Item, this word Solennia ſeemeth to
imporre a ſolemne companie or reſorte of
people. *Yea but* Miſſarum ſolennia *doth
import, not by ſeeming, but by plaine
conſtruing, neither cumpanie of maſſes,
neither of people, but the Apointed and
Reuerend & Catholike maner of exequu-
ting the Myſteries.*

Item, It maie wel be doubted, whether Dominus vobiſcu, and, Orate prome
fratres *(which woordes are in the decree)*
were any part of the Liturgie of Rome in
Soters tyme. *what harme I praie you
is in thoſe woordes, that it might be well
douted, whether they were vſed ſo tyme-
ly in the Church?* In Dominus vobiſ-
cum, *our Lord be with you, the Prieſt ſa-
luteth the pople Charitabiy and Godly,
And in* Orate pro me, *praie for me, he con-*

N i *ſeueth*

fesseth hymselfe a synner, and requireth
their helpe, both deuoutly and humbly.
But because the selfe same wordes are
now in the Masse, M. Iewell can not
brooke them, as he can neither the worde
Masse it selfe, for which in this place (sul-
sinely forsoth) he vseth the terme of Liturgie of Rome and not of Masse of Rome.
And so he that can not abyde to haue S.
Chrysostomes Liturgie called A Masse
(which is our English worde, to signifie that Seruice of the Church, that answereth the Liturgie of the Grecians)
he nowe lyke a mery Greeke, speaking
of that Seruice of Rome which was euer
called emong the Latinistes Missa, and
emong ỹ English, Masse: termeth it very
trymly in English, the Liturgie of Rome.
But let vs go forward.

After all these foresaid Inuentions
to moue an Altercation and busynes a-
bout the decree of Soter, he would make
the Catholikes afraied, as if he should
say: If you wil hold with Soters decree,
I will dryue you to an Inconuenience,
and therefore you were beste to let goe
your holdfast. But what is that Inconuenience?

Fine M. Iewel.

Iew.12.

nenience? Mary saieth he, in that So=
ter requireth, that the two (of whom he
speaketh)make answer vnto the Prieste,
therein is included both nearnesse of place,
for the people to stand in,and to heare,and
also a Common knowen tongue. Which
both are Contrarie to M. Hardinges Masse.

But he standeth nigh inough , I
trowe, that standeth by the Altrace,and
he answereth in a Common knowē tonᵹ=
gue, that answereth in ẏ Latine tongue.
And both these thinges are done , by the
simple Parisshe Clerke , or litle boie that
serueth the Priest at Masse . And there=
fore the decree of Soter hyndereth the
Catholikes, nothing at al. And if you
haue no more to obiect againſt it , than
these foresaid trifles,you maie either holb
your peace , or bring some other fresser
Argumentes .

But other Argumentes you haue
none: Only you take it for a good sporte,
to note the questions whiche are moued
by ths Canonistes about this Decree.
As, whether the two whose presence is required , ought to be two Clerkes or two
laie men;or one Clerke and one laie mā ,or
N ij one

one man and one woman. The Resolution whereof is, that they muste be two
Clerkes. Yet you declare out of Summa
Angelica, that in Priuate Masse one is sufficient. And to this you alleage Gersons
Opinion, that the Priest maie wel saie,
Dominus vobiscū, our Lord be with you,
though but one be present, because he
speaketh vnto the whole Churche of the
faithful, and not to that one only, that
standeth by hym. Or (as Innocentius
saieth) because it maie be thought, there be
Angels there, to supplie the mens Rome.

Thus you make some sport to your
selfe by rekenyng vp of the Canonistes
opinions, but what sad conclusion you
can pecke out thereof, againste Soters
Decree, it is not perceaued. Except you
wil reason after this sort, that, because the
Late Doctours or Rulers of the Church,
haue either expounded accordyng to Charitie the wordes of that Decree, Or haue
loosed accordyng to their Authoritie, the
bond which was put vpon the Priestes
by the Positiue Law thereof; therefore
Soter was neuer author of it.

The last quarel that M. Iewel hath
to

to Soters Decre, is that it maketh mention of Secreta the Secretes of the Masse, which to haue ben in the tyme of Soter, it were very hard for D. Harding to proue. For the Euery peece of the Masse was spoken alowde. But, how proue you that? For concernyng D. Harding, he maie speake vpon some Authoritie, because he alleageth the plaine wordes of Soters Decree for it.

But it is not my purpose, exactly to refel M. Iewels Argumentes made against Soter: Only this I praie thee now to consider (Indifferent Reader) how many fetches and deuises he hath in this place had, against that Decree of his. Anacletus(quod he)as some saie,made it: Then,Counterfeite Bookes haue bene set abrode. Furthermore Decretal Epistles haue ben doubted of. And more specially to the mater, The practise (saieth he)of S.Augustine and S.Hieromes tyme can hardly stande with that is here imagined. Againe, Solennia seemeth to import, a resorte of people. Againe, it maie be wel doubted whether Dominus vobiscū were any part of the Liturgie of Rome in Soters tyme. Againe, That any Secreta were in

A bundle of shiftes.

the

N iij

the tyme of Soter, it were very hard for M.
Harding to proue. **Then adde vnto this.**
That queſtion is moued by the Canoniſtes
what thoſe two ought to be, whoſe preſéce
is required, at the Prieſtes Maſſe. **And firſt,**
the Reſolution is this, **Straitwaies**, The
mater is otherwyſe determined. **Then,**
Gerſon ſaieth this. **Yet,** Pope Innocentius
hath an other fetche.

**How thinke we now, hath this fe⸗
low lefte any corner vnſearched, out of
which he might ſcrape any Gheaſſe, con⸗
iecture, or Suſpition, to Diminiſſhe the
Authoritie of this decree of Soter? From
Generals which proued nothing, cum⸗
mieth he not to bare coniectures againſte
the Specialties of the decree? when he
could ſaie no more againſt p̃ decree itſelfe,
ſought he not to bring it into contempte
by queſtions, Reſolutions, & variations
of the Canoniſtes about it? wel, M. Ie⸗
wel, you ſhall haue your aſking. Let not
this be Pope Soters decree, whiche D.
Harding hath brought againſt you. And
that, which you, with ſo greate bending
of witte and turning of Bookes, haue
ſought to conquer vs in, let vs (in triall
of a farther concluſion) yelde voluntary⸗
lp**

ly vnto you. And so it remaineth, that it be not vsed of any of vs, as an Auncient Decree of Sater.

Tel me then, wherefore doe you al-lege it? This very Decree (Indifferent Reader) about Discrediting and disgra-cing of whiche, M. Iewel bestowed a whole leafe together in his Replie, this selfesame he vseth, not sir leaues after, in the selfesame Replie. But consider with what Constancie he doeth it, & with how greate Reuerence towardes Aunciēt De-crees. His purpose was to disproue the Priuate Masse, whiche Ioannes Eleemo-sinarius an Auncient and holy Bishope is reported to haue saied. His wordes be these. M. Hardinges Leontius saieth, Iohn the Almonar saied Masse in his Oratorie at home, being sure of no more companie but of one of his owne household seruāts alone.

Soters decree al-leaged by M. Iew.

Iew.76.

Here is a dubble lie. For neither Leontius saieth so muche, neither D. Harding gathereth it. For by Leontius, it appeareth that he sent for A certaine noble man to come vnto hym, as though it had ben aboute some mater of the com-mon weale: And so, was the noble man

Ra

A iiij alse

also present, at the priuate Masse with the Bishopes seruant. And D. Harding gathereth not that he was sure, of no more cumpanie, but of one of his owne household Seruantes alone, but rather, that he was sure neither of the noble man, neither of his seruant, that they could or would receiue with hym. But of their companie concerninge presence in the place, though not in participation of the Mysteries, he was so sure as one may be of that whiche he presently seeth before his eies, because both were with hym at Masse and Answered hym. But this lye of M. Iewel must be dissembled, if you wil see how earnestly he allegeth the decree of Soter. Suppose it then to be so, (against both Leontius, and D. Hardinges plaine saicinges) that the Bishoppe was sure of no more but one, to be present at his Masse. what can you laie against him for it?

Iew. 76. Let vs consider (saie you) how safely he might so doe by the order of holy Canons.

Ra. why Syr, in breaking of them, what daunger is there? Mary,

Iew To breake them, Damasus saieth, is
blas-

blasphemie against the holy Ghost.

Shew then, against what order of holy Canōs, Ioannes Eleemosinarius hath done in saying Masse, none but his seruaunt (according to your sense) being present?

Pope Soter as it is before alleged by M. Iew. Harding straightly commaundeth, that no Priest presume to celebrate the Sacrament without the cumpanie of two togeather.

What say you M. Iewel? that very Ra. Decree of Pope Soter against which not fiue leaues before you were so vehement, is it compted now among the holy Canons? That Decree, against which that you might haue the more vantage, you entered into a Cōmon place of bringing the whole Booke of Decrees and Decrecretals into discredite or contempt, (so greate was your Stomake against Soter) the same now do ye allege so formally, and with so greate Charge commend ye it vnto vs? For to breake the order of holy Canōs (you say out of Damasus) that it is blasphemy against the holy ghost.

And where then was your modestie (for Gods sake) when of the Decretal

Epistles

Iew. 67.

Epistles, you vtter a Copie onely of that, which lieth in your Store against them, affirming that they manifestly depraue & abuse the Scriptures, Mainteine the kingdome of the Pope, Publish a multitude of vaine and superstious Ceremonies, Proclaime open Lies? For if to breake the order of holy Canons, it be blasphemie against the holy Ghoste: How farre of are you from the Sinne against the holy Ghoste, which plainely doe contemne Auncient Canons (as this of Soters) & yet allege the selfesame afterward, which you contemned before? For, if in speaking against it, you folowed your Conscience, could the same Conscience also permitte you to hold with it? And if, on the other side, your conscience gaue you, that it was Soters Decree (as in this place you allege it for no lesse) was it not of plaine malice, and directly against your owne knowledge, that you busied your selfe so much, as I haue declared, with seeking & cumpassing to deface it?

Consider then (indifferent Reader) and see by this which I haue declared, whether M. Iewel vse not for his owne poore vantage, the selfsame Testimonies

of

of ý first six hundred yeres, which he striueth most extremely to discredite, when ý Catholikes doe allege them. Concerning which poynt, if thow couet to haue moe examples, remember what he saith against Dionysius, Sozomenus, The Decrees and Epistles Decretal, and then do no more but looke in the quotacions onely of his Replie, whether thou findest them not alleged of him. And if thou find them not, neuer trust me hereafter: but if ý shalt perceiue, Dionysius, Sozomenus & others to be brought in of him, as occasion somtimes serueth, but ý Decrees & Decretal Epistles to be so thickly set in his Reply, as though he were some great Canonist & Papist, & not the exact folower of fine Diuinitie, thē haue I proued my Obiection. And now what is he worthy to haue, which so abuseth ý world in setting vp & pulling downe of Auncient & approued witnesses? For whereas by writing & reasoning we seke alwayes to come nerer and nerer to some Conclusion, by this libertie of Replieng which M. Iew. foloweth, we shal be alwaies ý further of from ý ending of cōtrouersies.

For

Iew. 9. 136. 66. 223.

For if he would haue plainely sayed, you
shal bring forth no witnesse, except he liued within the first six hundred yeares,
and of those very yeares I wil not allow
al witnesses, and especially the Decrees
and Decretals I refuse vtterly : then
would his Replie haue ben shorter by.xx
partes, & with more spede it should haue
ben answered, and with more facilitie it
would haue ben perceiued . But now,
when he is so vncertaine, that he can not
readily tel, what to allow or refuse, and
is so mutable , that he alloweth in some
one place the same which he disproued in
an other, how should it not be both cumberous and iniurious? Cumberous,
because of the heaping of many Authorities and Testimonies, such as him selfe
knoweth and maketh to be vncertaine &
doubtful : Iniurious, because of taking
away from an other, the free vse of those
writings, which himself with al boldnes
auoucheth. So y when D. Harding allegeth Pope Soters Decree, al the decrees
and Decretals should heare the worse for
it : And when M. Iewel allegeth the self
same Decree, straitwaies it is blasphemie
against

againſt the holy ghoſt, to bꝛeake any of the holy Canons.

Such Hypocrits and wꝛanglers, and bꝛaggers, & Goſpellers, by whoſe meanes new Contentions and troubles are reiſed and cōtinued in ẙ woꝛld, it is pitie (to ſpeake the leaſt) ẙ euer they were admitted befoꝛe thei were examined, oꝛ that now ſtil they ſhoulde be credited, aᷤter that they be detected.

How M. Iewel allegeth, to ſmal purpoſes, ſuch Authorities of Fathers, as do plainly cōfound ẙ procedings.

BUt what ſhal we ſay? we are not Maſters of other mens wils? neither do we beleue that this creature (man) whom God hath made after his owne Image, ſhould lacke that power of his ſoule, and gift of God, which conſiſteth in free wil. If therfoꝛe men wil not Beware, whē they may, what ſhould we do? I haue already declared in ſpecial chapiters, ſuch mater againſt M. Iewel, that of al men that euer yet wꝛote, there

there was neuer any of lesse Grauitie, Sinceritie, or Cõscience in his writing. To him that hath a wil to saue his soule, so much is sufficient to make him seke after better Instructiõ: To him that thinketh onely of Ciuile Policie, or of Temporal life and liuing, and wil not trouble his head with the euerlastingnes of the Soule, and a worlde to come, no Argumentes against M. Iewel can be sufficient. But concerning them which would in sad earnest saue one, and are not fully resolued that M. Iewel behaueth himself vnreasonablie & wickedly, may it please them to consider, how he shal be yet better taken in his Hypocrisie.

To Antiquitie he appealeth: And (because he would be seene to deale plainly) he apointeth out the first six hundred after Christ, for trial of the mater. Now when some witnesses of that time come against him, he wil not yet allow them. And yet when he hath taken them away from his Aduersarie, him selfe for al that wil afterwards allege them. And of these pointes we haue spokē already: but what may be added more, to the discouering of

his

his behauiour? Mary this much I can
say & proue more, that such testimonies of
Holy Fathers & Councels, as he bringeth
in against the Catholiques, do in the self
same sentence ỹ he allegeth, geue a great
wound to his Religiõ. So greedy he is
of troubling ỹ Catholikes peace, that to
make some of them shrinke, as if in deede
a blowe were cõming, he is content him
selfe to bring his owne cause into ỹ dau-
ger, that he ỹ wil take the aduãtage may
quikly so strike it, ỹ it wil neuer be good
after. And not only so, but so litle fauored
he is of Antiquitie, ỹ in veri mani places
he cannot vtter the ful sentẽce, but it shal
straitwaies be perceiued, that ỹ late procedings do impugne directly the orders,
practise, and Religion that were vsed in
the Primitiue Church. As in Example.

M. Iewel, thinking to destroy therby, the Sole Receiuing of the Priest,
proueth it, that in the Primitiue Church,
they which would not Communicate,
were bidde to auoide. For, *It is Decreed* The 13.
(saith he) *by the Canons of the Apostles,* Example
*that al faithful that enter into the Churche, and
heare the Scriptures, and do not continue out the*
prayers,

Can. Apoſt
Can.9.
Ievvel.
pag.39.
Chryſoſt.
ad popul.
Antiochē.
Hom.61.
Ievvel.
pag.23.
Ra.

prayers, nor receiue the Cōmuɴion, ſhould be ex-
cōmunicate, as men vvoorking the trouble aɴd
diſorder of the Church. Againe : If thou be not
vvorthy to receiue the Commuɴion, then artɇ
thou not vvorthy to be preſent at the prayers .
Therfore M. Harding ſhould driue his vnworthy people from the Churche, and not
ſuffer them to heare his Maſſe .

Let me aſke you then one queſtion
M. Iewel . why do you conſtraine, by
feare of high diſpleaſure, Loſſe of goodes
and impriſonment , ſuch as neuer were
yet of your Religion, to come into your
Cōgregations, & to receiue alſo tō you?
You woulde haue D. Harding to driue
them out which are vnworthy by the au-

Compel-
ling of
catholikes
to come to
the Con-
gregation.

thoritie of this ſaying of S. Chryſoſtom:
Should not you by the ſame reaſon, ceaſe
to drawe them into your Congregation,
which are no brothers of your Religion?
D. Hard. gathering it of your Sermon,
that you ſhould be of the mind, to haue al
the people to Receiue, Or them y̔ would
not, to be driuen out of the Church, you

Fol. 79,

cry out and ſay : O M. Harding, how long
wil you thus wilfully peruert the waies of
the Lord? You know, this is neither the
Doctrine,

doctrine neither the practise of the Church.
Howebeit the Auncient Doctours haue
both taught so, and also practised the same.
Anacletus de Conf. dist. 1. Episcopus Ca-
lixtus de conf. dist. 2. Peracta.

But O M. Iewel why say you so?
Doe you confesse that auncient Fathers
haue vsed it, and yet dare you Protesse,
that your Church hath no such practise?
where is your Reuerence now, to the
first six hundred after Christ? where is
your bringing al thinges, to the first Paterne? I perceaue by this, what your answere wilbe to my question out of S.
Chrysostome. You wil plainely say, that
your Church foloweth him not. And
wherefore then doe you make out of him,
Rules to the present Churche, whome
your selfe wil not solowe, in the selfsame
sentence, which you lay against vs? O
M. Iewell, how long wil you Impe-
rially alow and refuse the Authoritie of
auncient Doctors, al at wil and pleasure? The secōd

Lykewise to proue that which no man Example.
denieth, that in the primitiue Church the
people dyd communicate with the priest,
M. Iewell declareth the maner of their

D i assem-

assemblies, saying out of Justinus Martyr: *Before the end of our praiers, vve kisse eche of vs one an other. Then is ther brought vnto him, that is the chief of the bretherne, bread and a cup of Vvine and vvater mingled together: Vvhich, hauing receiued, he praiseth God and geaueth thankes a good space. And that done, the vvhole people confirmeth this praier saieing, Amen. After that, they that among vs be called Deacons geue vnto euery of thē that be present, part of the bread and likevvyse of the vvine and vvater that are consecrate, vvith thankes geuing, and cary the same home vnto them, that happen to be absent.*

Againe speakinge of the effect of the Sacrament, by vvhich vve are made al one in Christ, and all one emong our selues, he allegeth S. Chrysostome. *Propterea in mysterijs & c. For that cause in the tyme of the mysteries vve embrace one an other, that being many vve may become one.*

Againe, speaking of the people receiuing of the Sacrament in their owne handes, vvhich is also a mater indifferent in it selfe, he saieth to proue it: *I speake of him, vvhose cosse of peace ye receiued at the ministration, and at vvhose handes ye layed the Sacrament.*

The

Jew. 11. Justinus Martyr. in 2. Apol.

Jewel fol. 27. Chrysost. ad po. An. Hom. 61.

Jew. fol. 48. August. contra. lit. Petil. lib. 2 cap. 23.

The Testimonies are of your owne *Ra.*
bringing, and therefore, I would thinke
of your owne alowing. Where then is
your mingling of wine and water together, water
in your Mysteries? Where is the embra- and wine
cing of one an other, and the Cosse, so mingled to-
much vsed in the primitiue Church? The gether.
Church sence that tyme, hath chaunged Geauing
the maner of kissing, and kepte the signi- of a cosse.
fication whiche was in it, by geauing of
the pax or peace.

But this peace (say you) was not a litle *Iew.153.*
table of syluer or somwhat els, as hath bene
vsed (yea and is still vsed) in the Churche
of Rome: but a very cosse in deede in token
of perfit peace and vnitie in faith and religion. So Iustinus Martyr saieth speaking of
the tyme of the holy Mysteries: we salute
one an other with a cosse, So likewyse
Chrysostome and others.

Trne it is M. Iewel, and knowing *Re.*
so much of the practise in the Primitiue
Church, why doe ye not vse this so Auncient and holy a Ceremonie? If you will
not haue the Pax of syluer, either for spa-
ringe of charges, Or feare of Commis-
sioners vpon Church goodes, Or in despite of the Church of Rome: vse then in

O.ij. your

your mysteries a very cosse in deede, according to the Paterne of the Primitiue Church. And if neither old nor newe Ceremonies can please you, why crake you, in contemning the Later, that yet you regarde stil, the Auncient and Approued Orders? Or with what face doe you allege these approued Fathers testimonies, by whose sayings you wil not be ruled?

The third Example.

M. Iewel is alwaies busie in prouing, that the people in the Primitiue Churche dyd Communicate with the Priest. As though the concluding of that were a cleane ouerthrowe to the Catholike Religion: yet no Catholike did euer denie it, and at this tyme also when Charitie is exceding cold, yet doe the people often in the yere receiue with the Priest. Now by occasion of prouing this, which (I must againe saie) no man denieth, he saieth in diuerse places of his Replie. *The Deacons receiue the Communion, afterward the Mysteries be caried vnto a place, where the people must Communicate*

It is lavvful only for the Priestes of the Church, to enter into the place, where the Aultare standeth, and there to Communicate.

Ieb.pa.
11.

Chrysost.
in Litur.

Iew.pa.
90.
Concil.
Laod, ca.
19.

Let

Let the Priestes and Deacons Communicate
before the aultare, the Clerkes in the quiere, and
the people vvithout the quiere.

Howe like you these diſtinctions of
places and perſons, M. Iewel? Yea rather why lyke you them not? Haue not
you pulled downe Channcell, Taken a-
way partitions, made the pauement tho-
roughout leuell, Set the Communion
table in the myddle, Set formes for the
Laitie to ſit about it? And haue not your
ſelfe geauen ſtrange orders, as it were to
al the people, noting it by your owne wit
(as appeereth) out of Fabian the Pope:
that men and women made the ſacrifice of
the aultare, and of bread and wine, and
therefore after the order of Melchiſedech?
But, if the people could not ſo much as
come nigh the Aultare where the prieſt
ſtode, or receyue, at the moſt, in the quier:
how far of were they, at thoſe daies, from
ẏ irreuerẽcie ẏ now is vſed? And how far
wide are you, frõ ẏ towardnes to reforme
al things, by the parerne of the primitiue
Church? Yet are you not afraied nor
Aſhamed, to allege thoſe Councels and
Authorities, which condemne your pro-

            D iij   cedinges

The
fourth
Example.
*Basil. exe.
ad piet.
serm.4.*
Iew.
pag.3.

cedinges vtterly.

S. Basile (saieth M. Iewel, thinking still all thinges to helpe hym that proue a cōmunicating of moe together) reporteth an ecclesiasticall decree or Canō, that at the receiuing of the holy Communion which he calleth Mysticum pasca, ther ought to be twelue persons at the least, and neuer vnder.

Ra.

And you, to proue your selues folowers of Antiquitie, and Restorers of ecclesiasticall Canons, haue decreed, that thrée shall make vp a Communion, and for A neede, the Prieste and the sicke person alone.

The fifth
Example.
*Chrysost.
in opere
imper.
Hom.11.*

Si hæc vasa & c. If the mater be so daungerous, to put these sanctified vessels vnto Priuate vses, wherein is conteined, not the very body of Christ, but the mysterie or Sacrament of Christes body, & c.

Ra.

You iudge, I perceiue, the Author of that booke to be S. Chrysostome, and this place to be true and godly. Therefore that you maie consider it the better, and, by your commendacion, other Protestantes: I wil englishe the whole sentence vnto them. The Author of that booke, whosoeuer he were, persuading
with

with the people, to vſe wel their tongue, leaſt vncleane ſpirites doe enter thereby into their bodies : *If it be ſynne and daunger (ſaieth he) to put haloued veſſels, vnto priuate vſes: as Balthaſar teacheth vs, vvhich, becauſe he dranke in halovved cuppes, vvas put byſide his kingdome and his life : If then it be ſo daunge-rous a mater to put theſe ſanctified veſſels vnto priuate vſes, in vvhich the true bodie of Chriſt is not, but the myſterie of his bodie is conteined:hovv much more behoueth it vs, concerning the veſſels of our bodie, vhich God hath prepared for himſelfe to dvvel in, not to geaue the deuil place to doe in them vvhat he vvil?*

A ſtronge argument ſurely and per-ſuaſible. For, if deade metal, which by it ſelfe is not apte to receiue holineſſe, be had yet in Reuerence, becauſe of the ſpe-ciall vſe which it ſerueth for, in the tem-ple of God: how ſhould not our bodies, the lyuely veſſels of our reaſonable Sou-les be kepte ſtill pure and Inuiolated? If, for the veſſels which Balthaſar pro-phaned, which ſerued in the Figures of the old law, which had not ye very body of Chriſt in them, but A ſigne and Myſterie only thereof: If for theſe, God plagueth and ſtriketh, how ſhal they eſcape, which receiue into their bodies, the very true Body of Chriſt, and haue God corporally dwelling in them, through the Myſterie of his Incarnation and vertue of his Conſecration: And yet dare turne themſelues, vnto prophane & vncleane vſes? This is the true ſenſe of that place.

But when begyn you (M. Iewel) to tell openly the daunger which they incurre before god (though y world alow it) which, Either after vow made of Chaſtitie, haue turned them ſelues, firſt out of their Monaſteries, and ſhortly after, haue ouerturned themſelues into Inceſtuous Carnalitie: Either ſpoiling the Churches of God, of the halowed and conſecrated veſſels, haue conuerted them into prophane vſes, and drinke in Chalices at their Tables? No doubt, by the example of Balthaſar, but that they are in ſore daunger, which ſerue themſelues and their priuate Affections, with the peculiar, and proper veſſels appointed for God. And if it be ſo in corruptible and baſe maters, are not the polluted weddinges of Nonnes, Monkes, harlottes

Church gooues.

lottes , and Renegates , much moze accurfed and execrable? But when wil you
pzoteft this much M. Iewel? And if
you like not this confequence, why refufe
you your owne witneffe?

This place alfo that foloweth, is made
to ferue foz pzonfe, that there were that
Communicated with the Pzieft .

The. 6.
Example.
Iew, 74.

They that haue fallen into Herefie and do
penance for the same, vvhen the Nouices that be
not yet Chriftened be commaunded to depart out
of the Church, let them depart alfo . Ergo they
that remained, did Communicate togeather.

wel to let go ƥ Argumēt, the grañ-
ting of which pzoueth nothing againft
vs : what place is that in al your Communion, where Nouices oz Penitentes
muft go out? Oz how agreeth this with
the compelling of men into your Cõgre-
gation againft their willes?

Ra.

The people rife before day and hie them to
the house of prayer.

The, 7,
Example.
Iew. 174

You bzing in this vpon occafion of
Pzaying in a knowen tongue, which the
Greeke and Latine both are . Of which
I haue fpoken of, in the third Article of
my firft booke . But how like you this
rifing befoze day?

Ra.
Bafil. in
epift. ad
Clericos
Neocef.
Nem

The.8.
Example.
Chrysost.
in Mat.
Hom 2.
Jew. 208

Ra.

Non sum, inquis, Monachus. &c. Thou vvilt say, I am no Monke, I haue vvife and children and charge of household. This is it, that as it vvere vvith a Pestilence, infecteth altogether, that ye thinke the reading of the holy Scriptures belongeth only vnto Monkes.

This is spoken of M. Iewel, to exhort the people to ye getting of knowlege which may be wel spoken to them, and sone goten of them, if Curiositie doth not let it. But what were these Monkes, so distincted by the studie of Scriptures, from the rest of the people? And what like Profession or Example haue you, in al your Reformations?

The.9.
Example.
Concil.
Chalced.
actione
prima.
Jew 245
Ra.

Decernimus eum extraneum esse. &c. Vve decree that he shal be remoued from his office of Priesthoode, and from our Communion, and from the Primacie of his Abbie.

This is alleaged of M. Iewel, to proue a confessed Truth, that Primatus is taken for any preferrement before others. But let him consider it: were Abbies then within the. 600. yeres after Christ? And in such reputacio, that a general Councel counted it, emong other thinges, for a great Ignominie and Punishment,

nithment, a Monke to be deposed from y
Primacie in them? M. Iew. hoping to
conclude therby y the B. of Rome should
not be Supreme ouer al, sheweth what
large Priuilegies Emperours haue geuen to the Clergie, which for Ciuil Actions he may do wel inough, as being in
them Suprem himself: *Omnes qui vbicuque* ___ The. 10.
sunt, &c. Al that be or hereafter shal be Priestes ___ Example.
or Clerkes of the Catholike faith, of vvhat De- ___ Cod. de E-
gree so euer they be, Monkes also, let them not in ___ pisc. &
any Ciuile Actions be dravven foorth to any fo- ___ Clericis:
ren Iudgement by the summon or commaunde- ___ Omnes.
ment of any Iudge more or lesse: neither let them ___ Iew. 267
bee driuen to come foorth of either the Pro-
uince, or the place, or the countrie vvhere they
dvvel.

Yf you see then how greately the ___ R2.
Clergie was honored in times past, and
allow the Authors of their Priuilegies:
why labour you, as much as ye can, to
to bring al the Spiritual power into sub- ___ Priuile-
iection? Or why defende you not the ___ gies grā-
right of the Clergie, like Reformers of ___ to to priestes
the Church? ___ & monkes

Priestes and Clerkes are before your
face, drawen before temporal Iudges into
their

their Courtes. Monkes, not only not
saued from the paines, to go for any mater out of the Countrie, but not suffred to
haue any place in your Countrie. Such
charitie hath ben taught by your Gospel,
and with such pure folowing of antiquitie you haue proceded.

The place appointed vnto the priest for the
holy Ministerie as it may be gathered by
S. Chrysostome, at certaine times of the
Seruice, was drawen with Curtaines.

Ra.

This proueth not, that the Aultare
was placed in the middest of the Church,
as M. Iewel would haue it, but by this
we may wel gather, that great reuerence
was vsed then aboute the Mysteries,
which you, forsooth, haue so mainteined,
that as though the Celebration of the
Mysteries was not open inough before,
you haue, in some places pulled downe
the Partition, between the body of the
Church and the Quier, And haue caused
generally, the Communion Table to be
brought downe neerer the people, least
the Curtaines, which you occupy, should
let their sight.

Ergo vt hæc possint. &c. Therefore that
these

these thinges may be vvel examined , it is vvel prouided, that euery yeare in euery Prouince, at tvvo seueral times, there be holden a Councel of Bishoppes : that they meeting together out of al partes of the Prouince may heare and determine such complaintes.

when beginne you to put this Canon in execution?

Truely Liberatus saith, The manner was in Alexandria , that who so euer was chosen Bishop there , should come to the beare, and laie his Predecessours hand vpon his head, and put on S. Markes Cloke, and then was he sufficiently confirmed Bishoppe, without any mention made of Rome.

you are a special frinde to the Bishoppe of Rome , whiche rather then he should haue to do with Consecrating of Bishoppes, you can wel fansie a deade mans blessing , and the solemne vsing of a Relique : whiche how hartely ye fauour, I am in donbt.

I proue it therefore vnto thee by these Examples (Indifferent Reader) not onely that M. Iewel is a deceitful Man,

Còc. Nic.
primum.
Can. 5.
Iew. 265

Ra.

The. 13.
Example.
Liberatus
Cap. 20.
Iew. 283

Ra.

Man, but I geue the also occasions how
to trie him, whether he be in dede an hypocrite, oz no. Foz if he thinke the foz-
said testimonies out of the holy Fathers
oz Councels to be of such foze and generalitie, that we may in no case receiue a
diuerse ozder from theirs: why are not
Monasteries standing with them? why
are not olde Ceremonies obserued? why
is not water and wine mingled together
in their Chalice, as plain Examples of y̅
Primitiue Churche, declare vnto vs, to
haue been then vsed? And, if he Answer, that the Canons, Ozders, and Fas-
shions, oz practises of old time, are not so
to be vnderstanded of vs, as though the
Ages folowing might not by lawful Authozitie & ful consent, put an other Canõ
in place of the olde: why laieth he it to y̅
Catholiks charge, that the Priestes now
say Masse, though but one alone be pzesent, which was otherwise by Pope Soters decree? Oz why telleth he vs (out of
S. Basil) of an old Canon y̅ appointed
twelue at the least to receiue together?

Here (I should thinke) he must nedes
be takē.(foz who knoweth the vttermost

gꝭ

of his Art in shifting?) but I thinke verely he coulde not escape in this place, a iust note either of high malice, in obiecting that, against his Aduersarie, which him self knoweth to be litle worth: either of deepe Hypocrisie, in pretending a Reuerence towardes Antiquitie, which in very deede he contemneth.

How M. Iewel allegeth for himself, the woordes and deedes of Olde condemned Heretiques.

BEVVARE therefore of M. Iewel, pon that seeme to haue, as it were, A Conscience, and make a Religiõ of Religion. For many there are that liue emong Christians, them selues also being Christians, which so hartely folow ȳ world & their own cõcupiscētes, ȳ neither Catholike bookes wil do them good, they are so carelesse, neither heretical do them harme, they are so desperate. But you, which are not past al feare of God, and care of Saluation: whom examples of sinne, which were to be seene

among

emong the Papistes, or were gathered
out of al Stories and Countries against
them, did make to abhorre euen the Religion it selfe, which corrupte persons
professed : whome faire Promises of
Gospellers, that they would shewe you
a ready and shorte way vnto Heauen, in
which you should haue no cariage of Ceremonie, Tradition, Lentes, Fast, Pe-
naunce, Feare of Purgatorie, &c. And
that you should haue al things ministred
vnto you, in like order and manner, as
they were vsed emong the faithful in the
Primitiue Churche : you I say, whom
these faire promises, haue made to forsake the Olde and Catholique Religion,
vpon hope to finde a more Auncient and
Receiued Religiõ which ÿ new Masters
& holy Doctors & councels would teach
you : BEWARE you of M. Iewel.

For wheras you would not haue forsaken ÿ religion in which you were baptized, & which al Christians then in al the
world professed openly, except you had beleued ÿ, as it was told you, so you should
be reduced to the perfite state of A true
Religion, euen as it was to be found

in

in the Primitiue Church: how miserably
are ye nowe deceaued, where your Ma=
sters doe not in deede regarde the Ex=
ample and practise of the same Churche,
for loue and desier of which you folowed
them, leading you quite awaie, from the
Obedience of the present Church? How
wel maie euerie one of you, whome M.
Iewel hath peruerted, saie vnto hym?

Syr, haue you put me in this hope,
that in folowing of you, I should goe in
the safe waie of the primitiue Church, of
holy Fathers, of Auncient Councels?
And my mynde geauing me, that al was
not wel in this present Church in which
you and I both were baptised, and that
the neerer one might come to the begin=
ninges of the Christian Faith, he should
find it the more surer and purer, haue
you serued my humour therein: and pro=
mising to reforme al thinges according
to the paterne of the Auncient Catholike
Church, are you proued in the end to neg
lect those selfe same orders, which were
obserued in the most best and most Aun=
cient tymes? Spake you faire vnto me,
vntil I was come vnto you, from the

P i   Cum=

Cumpanie where I lyued, and doe ye
not perforzme those thinges vnto me, for
hope of whiche I brake from my Cumpanie? A coffe, I know, oz a curtaine, Oz
A partition in the Church, are not essen-
cial, and without them we maie be saued:
But yet, if in the pure and Primitiue
Churche such thinges were alowed, you
haue not done wel, to make me contemne
the Pax, oz vestmentes, oz distinction of
places, such as were vsed in the Church,
from which I departed.

And yet: If these thinges be but
light, and Ragges, as some wil saie, of
the Romish Religion, was the building
of Monasteries a light mater in the primitiue Church? And that Rule of lyfe,
which Monkes then folowed, was it of
smal importance, by the Iudgement of
that worlde so nigh to Christ? You haue
made me beleue, that to lyue in such Ozder, should be a derogation to the merites of Christe, A trusting to our owne
workes, A Bondage of conscience, a promise of thinges impossible, A Superssi-
tious and Popishe fashion, and at one
worde, that Monkerie should be Trum-
perie

perie: And yet doth it appeare, by our owne allegations, that Monkes and Abbates were in the Primitiue Church, and that they were also in greate reputation.

what shal I saie of the most highe and dreadful Mysterie, the Sacrament of the bodie and Bloud of Christ, whereas the witnesses that you bring in for other purposes, doe testifie vnto me, that the Cuppe of the Lord was mingled with wine and water: can I take in good parte and with a quiet Conscience, that you put no water at al in the Cup of the Lord?

If you had not chalenged, if you had not prouoked, if you had not grauen most infallible tokens (as me thought) that al Antiquitie had gone sinothe with you: or, if you had refused at $\tilde{y}$ beginning al other Authoritie bysides the Expresse Scriptures, I might haue deliberated whether I would haue folowed you, or no: But now, making so large & goodly promises, that you would not take my Religion awaie from me, but that you would only reforme it, & that you would not denie the Faith, whiche the whole world professeth, but require it to be re-

P ij duced

duced vnto the order of the Primitiue Church, I yelded quickly therein vnto you, and thought, that these surely be the men of God, whiche shall purge the Church of al Superfluites, and leaue it in as good health & constitution, as euer it was in her florishing tyme. And are you not ashamed, that the very printes, and steppes of papistry, are found, euen within that age, which you warranted vnto me to be altogether for the Gospel? And that, in those selfsame testimonies, which your selfe vpon occasion, doe bring out against the Papistes? what were not they themselues lykely to shew, if they might be suffered to vtter, what diuersitie there is betwixt this Late welfauored Gospel, and the Catholike old Religion: seeing that you can not so order the mater, in reciting of Auncient Fathers & Councels, but it must be straite wayes perceaued, that your procedings are not conformable vnto the Primitiue Church.

O wretched and vile Glorie, to fill the margine of a Booke, with the Councels of Nice, Carthage, Chalcedon, Constantinople, Ephesus, &c, and with the testi-

teſtimonies of Anacletus , Felir, Soter,
Calirtus, Chzyſoſtom, Baſile, Ambzoſe,
Auguſtine,ꝛc.as though that it were not
M. Jewel that made any thing of his
owne , but as though in al that he concluded, he folowed moſt eractly , the holy
Councels and Fathers:and, befoze all be
knowen , to be conuinced moſt clcerly
and euidently, that his doeinges are not
lyke the holy Fathers Religion , what
a confuſion is it vnto that Glozie , and
what a Detriment to right meaning and
wel willing conſciencies ?

 In this ſozt might an honeſte and
graue man complaine, and ſay leſſe than
M. Jewel deſerueth. Foz now J will
ſhew vnto thee (Indifferēt Reader) that
he allegeth, and that very ſadly and ſo-
lemly , the teſtimonies of Heretikes as
though it were no mater at al,how wel it
would be admitted emong the lerned,ſo
that the common Reader be perſwaded
that M. Jewel ſpeaketh not without his
Authozities. Foz pzouſe thereof let this
be one Erample.

 The Biſhopes of the Eaſt part of the vvorlde Jew.166
being Arians, vvriting vnto Iulius the Biſhope of
    P iij *Rome,*

Sozome.
lib.3.ca.8.

Rome, tooke it greenously, that he vvould presume to ouer rule them. And shevved him, that it vvas not lavvful for him, by any sleight or colour of appeale, to vndoe that thing, that they had done.

This is one of M. Iewels testimonies, to proue against the Bishoppe of Romes Supremacie. In alleaging of which, although he lacked a point of discretion, in bringing of their sentencies furth, whom al the worlde hath condemned for starcke Heretikes: yet he hath not forgoten al conscience and charity, in that he confesseth to his Reader, that these Bishoppes of the East, whose doinges he thinketh worthie to be consydered, were Arians. Which I praie thee (Indifferent Reader) to thinke wel vpon, that it maie be perceiued, howe wel the Protestantes and Arrians agree together, in their prowde and rebellious behauyours : & how wel the testimonie of blasphemous Heretikes maie serue, to disproue any Catholike and honest conclusion. An other Example is.

Arrians
witnesse
for M.
Iewel.

Iew.27.

Donatus being condemned, by threescore & ten Bishops in Aphrica, Appealed vnto the Emperour Constantinus, and was
receiued

receiued.

But what was Donatus? A singular
prowd heretike. For profe wherof, let
Epistles and bookes, whiche S. Augustin wrote against him and his folowers,
be witnesses. Let that Boke also be witnesse, which S. Augustine wrote purposely of heresies: In which the *Donatia-
ni* or *Donatiste* haue their proper place.
For when Cecilanus, A Catholike and
good man, was made against their wils,
Bishope of Carthage, they obiected certaine crimes against vs, which being not
proued, and sentence going against them,
Donatus being their Captain they tooke
such a Stomake, that they turned their
Schisme into heresie, and helde the opinion, that al they, whatsoeuer they were
in the worlde bysides, that agreed not
with them, were infected, and excommunicated persons. And hereupon (as the
nature of heresie is to goe, deeper and
deeper still, into desperate blindnes and
presumption) they dyd baptise againe,
suche as had ben alreadie baptised in the
Catholike Churche. It appeereth also,
what an honest and Catholike man Do-

natus

Ra.

*Aug. de hæ-
resibus ad
Quodvult
deum.*

natus was, in that M. Iewel confesseth hym to haue been condemned of thzee scoze and ten Bishopes, whiche was not, I beleue, foz any humilitie, Obedience, Faith, oz Charitie of his.

Donatus then beinge an Heretike, what hath M. Iewel to doe with hym? Lyke will to lyke perchaunce, and the same Spzite y̆ inflamed Donatus, warmeth M. Iewel: otherwyse, it is not to be gathered out of the pzactises of Heretikes, what the Ozder that we ought to folowe, was in the Pzimitiue Churche: But of the Catholike and alowed Examples. And if M. Iewel, could shewe, that this Appeale of Donatus vnto the Emperour from the Bishopes that condemned hym, was good and lawful, in the Iudgement of any Father oz Doctour of that age, then might this example haue some lykelyhoode in it, to serue his purpose: otherwise him selfe doth minister the Catholike an Exception againste his owne witnesse, the Auncient and Reuerend Heretike Donatus.

But Constantinus the Emperour receaued his Appeale. what of that? Is
all

Donatus the Heretike a pzesent witnesse foz M. Iew.

al wel done, that Emperours doe? And
are not manie thinges permitted vnto
them for Ciuile Policie, and quiet sake,
which, by right folowing of Ecclesiastical orders, should not be suffered? A-
gaine, Constantinus, was a Christian,
Catholike and good Emperour: and he
receiued in deede Donatus Appeale, but
receaued he it willingly, or no? And
thought he hymselfe to doe therein lawfully, as A Supreme head and Gouernour, or els to passe the bondes of his
Imperial Authoritie, and to medle with
a Iurisdiction belonging to more excellent Officers? Vndoubtedly, he would
faine haue been rid, of the importunitie
of the Donatistes, and lyked it not in his
owne conscience, that himselfe should be
taken for the highest Iudge in maters
Ecclesiastical. How proue I this now?
Sufficiently inough: by S. Augustine.
And marke the place well (Indifferent
Reader) that thou maiest see the deuotion of that so mightie an Emperour.

First, Donatus and his felowes,
perceiuing that, although they had condemned Cecilianus ỹ Bishope of Car=
thage,

The true
store of ỹ
Dona=

tittes ap-
peale to ý
Emperor

thage, and set an other, of their owne
making in his place: Yet the rest of the
Bishopes of the world, dyd stil write and
send to Cecilianus, as the true Bishope
in deede, and such as they communicated withal: they (I saie) perceauing this,
made sute to Constantinus the Emperour, that they might haue the cause of
Cecilianus examined, before the Bishopes of beyond the seas. In which point,
S. Augustine findeth, that they had a
duble fetche and subtiltie.

The one, that if those Bishoppes,
whom the Emperour had procured to
heare the whole mater, should condemne
Cecilianus, then loe, they should haue
their lust fulfilled: The other, that if those
should absolue him, then would he with
his fellowes say, that the Iudges were
not indifferent, and so, by consequence,
appeale from them. In which case,
though (as S. Augustin saith) there remained a general Councel of the vniuersal Church, in which the cause betweene
them and their Iudges, shoulde haue
ben handeled, yet what did they? Mary,
they went to the Emperour, and accused
the

the foresaid Bishopes before him. And
how was this taken (thinke we) of the
Catholikes ? Uerely not wel, as appea=
reth by S. Augustine , which noteth the
Donatiskes of folish boldnes therein.

   Iudices enim Ecclesiasticos &c. For the *August.*
Ecclesiastical Iudges, Bishopes of so great Autho- *Epist. 162.*
ritie, by vvhose sentence and iudgement both the
Innocencie of Cecilianus, and their naughtinesse
vvas declared (these men of such worthi=
nes saith S. Augustine) they durst accuse,
not before other their felovvebishopes and Col-
legies, but vnto the Emperour, that they had not
iudged vvel.

  But now, when they had broken the
order of the Ecclesiastical Law, and were
come to the Emperour , what did he ?
Did he commende their Obedience, or
wisedome ? Did he preferre his owne
Courte and Authoritie, before the Con=
sistorie and Iudgement of Bishoppes ?
what he did , the Actes and Registers
of his owne Courte declare , as S. Au=
stine recordeth out of it. For after ŷ Do=
natistes were now condemned by ŷ Pope
of Rome & other Bishopes assistant, and
refuset

refused to stand to their sentence, requiring helpe at the Emperours handes: *Dedit ille aliud Iudicium Arelatense, aliorum scilicet Episcoporum: He gaue and appointed vnto them other Iudges at Arles, I meane other Bishoppes*

why: if the Emperour had in those daies taken the Pope for chiefe Bishope in al the worlde, would he haue further committed, vnto the Bishop of Arls, the sitting vpon that cause, which already was decided by the Bishop of Rome? It seemeth altogeather vnlikely: And therefore M. Iewel may be thought to bring in deede an inuincible Argument for the Emperours Supremacie, against the Supremacie of the Bishop of Rome.

But marke the Circumstances and Considerations which moued the Emperour, and then wil the contrary conclusion be manifestly proued, that the Emperour tooke him selfe to be the inferiour vnto Bishops, euen in that cause, which was brought vnto him after Bishopes, and which he caused to be examined againe, after it was sufficiently iudged. For thus it foloweth in S. Austin.

Dedit

Dedit ille aliud Arelatense Iudicium, non quia iam necesse erat, sed eorum peruersitatibus cedens & omnimodo cupiens tantam Impudentiam Cohibere . **That is,** *He gaue other Iudges, not because it vvas novv necessarie , but because he yelded to the frovvardnes of them (* **the Donatistes** *) and desired by al meanes, to restraine so great impudencie of them.* Neque enim ausus est Christianus Imperator, sic eorū tumultuosas & fallaces querelas suscipere, vt de iudicio Episcoporum , qui Romae sederant , ipse Iudicaret, sed alios, vt dixi, Episcopos dedit .* For the Christian Emperour* **(as who should say, other Emperours, which forgette them selues to be Christians, and in whose eares nothing standeth so much, as** *Obey the higher povvers. &, obey the King as the chief.* **which is by the interpretation of blinde Gospellers and Flatterers , that euery Prince is for his own Countrie Suprem vnder God in al maters both Ecclesiastical and Temporal, such Emperours : woulde not onely haue conteinned the sentences of Priestes in comparison of their Maiesties Iudgement , but also haue punished such as would signifie it, by neuer so smal a token, that the Emperour**

perour can not wel be Supreme Iudge in maters Ecclesiasticall , But) *the Christian Emperoure durst not receiue their* (the Donatistes) *Seditiouse and deceitful complaintes , in such sorte , as that him selfe vvould iudge of the sentence of the Bishopes that sate at Rome, but he apointed* (*as I haue said*) *other bishopes.* And that , for the causes aboue mentioned : which were,the *fro-vvardnes* and the *impudencie* of the Dona-tistes.

A quibus tamen illi ad ipsum rursum Imperatorem prouocare maluerunt. From vvhich *Bisshoppes for al that they chose to prouoke againe to the Emperour.* And what saied he vnto them ? Forsoothe , he Iudged *Cacilianum Innocentissimum , illos improbissimos, Cacilian to be most Innocent, and them most vvicked .*

Yea but, you will Replie, did not the Emperour sitte Iudge vppon the mater, when it had been , twise before referred to Bishoppes ? True it is in deede, that you saie : But consider, that they were Heretiques, which ap-pealed from Byshoppes to the Empe-rour,

tour, and that although he heard their
Cause, yet he detested their Contentiousnesse, and thought also before vpon
it, to aske pardone of the Bisshoppes,
for medling in the matter after them.
For thus it foloweth in Sainct Augustine.

Qua in re illos quemadmodum dete-
* stetur, audistis. Atque Vtinam saltem ipsiue*
Iudicio insanißimis animositatibus suis finem
posuissent . Atque vt eis ipse cessit, vt de illa
causa post Episcopos iudicaret, à Sanctis Au-
tistitibus postea veniam petiturus, dum tamen
illi, quod vlterius dicerent non haberent, se
eius sententiæ non obtemperarent, ad quem
ipsi prouocauerunt, sic & illi aliquando cede-
rent Veritati . Iu vvhich thing (that they
appealed vnto him, after they had been
with two seuerall Iudges of the Clergie)
hovv he detested them, you haue heard. And
Vvould God they had made an ende of their most
outragious stomaking of the mater, if it had ben
for no more then for his sentence sake. And as he
(the Emperour) yelded vnto them, to iudge
of that cause after the Byshopes, minding to aske
pardone aftervvarde of the holy Bishoppes, so
that

that they (the Donatiftes) fhould not haue to fay further, if they vvould not obey his fentence, vnto vvhom they appealed : So vvould God, that they once yet vvould yeelde into the truth .

Confider now indifferently with me, vpon this whole mater (gentle Reader) And this appealing of the Donatifts vnto the Emperour, and his hearing of the whole caufe, being not once or twife, but very oft alleged by M. Iew. it is worth while to be wel remembred, that which I haue already faid, & that which by occafion hereof may be further gathered, and wel be noted.

See then firft, what bufie Heretikes thefe Donatiftes were, and how ful they were of Shiftes and Quarels making : From the Emperour to Rome : From Rome they go to the Emperour againe : From him then by appointement and agreement, they goe to Arls and the Bifhops there : And frō Arls, they returne, with complaint, to the Emperour yet againe . At laft, the Emperour himfelf heareth ꝑ caufe, yet would they not ftand to the Emperours fentence, but main-
reined

reined ftil their falfe Bifhope, whom to put in the See of Carthage, they thrufte out Cecilian, and they continued ftil in their herefie, accompting al the Chriftians of þ woȝld accurfed, which were not of the fyde of Donatus.

Such is the nature and pȝactife of Heretikes, they pȝetend confcience, they commend holy and Auncient Fathers, They appeale to the Pȝimitiue Church: They craue foȝ Beneral Councels, foȝ free difputations, foȝ furceafe of Inquifition, foȝ Seruice in the vulgar tongue, foȝ Communion in both kindes, and other fuch thinges moe. If the Pȝinces & Bouernours refift them in any point, ftraite waies they make exclamations, they fturre vp angers, they complaine of fentence geauen vpon them befoȝe they be heard, of the lack of ghoftly cõfolation, which fhould come to the people by vnderftanding of Scriptures and receiuing the Sacramentes, of the penalties of lawes and Statutes. what is it fo litle, that they wil not murmur againft, if they maie not haue their ful wil? In refpect then of peace and publike tranquilitie,

R j iS

if you wil not ſtriue wt them vpõ maters indifferent, but diſpenſe with them in theyr requeſtes or demaundes, yet will they not ſuffer the Catholikes to be in reſt:And if you put them out of ſcare of the Inquiſition, they wil troble yet the whole Countrie with preaching in the open field:And if you prouide a General Councel to ſatiſfie them, they will not come at it:& if at euery maſſe there ſhould be Communicantes, they wil not alow the Sacrifice. And when the Prince is made by them the Supreme Gouernour vnder God, in any countrie, yet wil they ſtoutly diſobey ye prince in a ſmal matter of wearing a ſeemely gowne & cap. So ye al ye they doe, is but to mainteine talke, and finde alwaies ſomewhat, in whiche they maie occupie the Catholikes, vntil that at length, when theyr power is ſo greate, that they dare meete in field with their Aduerſaries, they maie boldely and deſperately, leaue al reaſoning, conferring, Applealing, demaunding, protesting, and Lawleying, and with open face come againſt the Catholikes: Pull downe Churches, Vſurpe officies:Take awaie Sacramentes, Alter the ſtate of

common weales, hang, draw and quarter
Priestes: Set Inquisition againste Catholikes: And confirme their Gospel by
terrour.

These and suche like thinges we in
our daies see by experience. Constantinus the Emperour dyd not see so much:
Yet fearing the busie nature of Schys-
matykes, and hoping by faire demeanes
to bring the Donatistes to a peace with
al Christendome, he yelded as much vnto
them as he could, and (as ye haue heard)
he receiued theyr prouoking to hym, not
because he thought that hym selfe was
the chiefest Iudge in all the world, euen
in maters Ecclesiastical, but because he
hoped, in yelding vnto the Donatistes
in al their requestes aboute apointynge
or changing of ye Iudges, to bring them
at length vnto suche a remembrance of
themselues, that they should cease, for
shame, to make any further brable about
that, in which by euery Iudge that dyd
heare the cause, they were condemned.

Now, if at those daies, either the wyse
and lerned aboute hym, or he hymselfe,
had beleued the hearing of causes Eccle-

M ij   siastical

fiaftical to belong vnto his court or con=
fiftorie, what needed hym to borowe a
point of the law, & to accompte vpon af=
kyng of pardon of the Bifhopes, for his
meddling with that caufe, which they al=
readie had ended? Can we haue any
thing more plaine and manifeft, that this
Chriftian and worthie Emperour, dyd
in confcience thinke himfelf to bafe to fit
and Iudge after Bifhopes, whereas
enforced thereunto by the importunitie
of the Donatiftes, and trufting, by that
his yelding, to pacifie the commotion
ŷ was reyfed in the catholike Church, yet
was not fure of his doeinges herein, but
determined to afke forgeauenes of the
holy Bifhopes?

As if he fhould faie: The Donatiftes
here, trouble the Church, They appeale
vnto me, as though I were chiefe. If
I wil not heare their caufe, there is no
man fhal Rule them: And if I take open
me to heare it, the Bifhops, which alrea=
haue decided it, wil be offended. wel, I
wil venter yet, And if the Donatiftes
wil ftand to my iudgement, and be quiet
for euer after, that is fo greate a benefite,
that

that to cumpaſſe it, I maie ſtretche my
conſcience. And if, for al that pretenſe, my
fact ſhal be miſliked, I wil aſke pardon
of the holy Biſhopes, which haue alreadie iudged of the mater. This is the very
trueth of the Emperours receiuing of
the Donatiſtes Appeale. He dyd it vpon
occaſion, and if it were not wel done, he
was readie to take a pardon for it. In
all thinges he ſought the beſte waie to
helpe the Church, and ſhewed his moſte
due, and humble, and Obedient affection
towardes Biſhopes.

Yet doth M. Iewel bring in this
Story, to proue that *It is vvel knovven, that* **Iew, 272**
Appeales euen in the Eccleſiaſtical cauſes, vvere
made to the Emperours and Ciuil Princes. Secon-
ly, that the Biſhope of Rome determined ſuch ca-
ſes of Appeale, by vvarrant and commiſſion from
the Emperour. Thirdly, that maters being heard
and determined by the Biſhope of Rome, haue
ben, by Appeale from him, remoued further vnto
others. Which Concluſion wil ſeeme well
inough to folowe vpon the Appeale of
the Donatiſtes vnto y̌ Emperour, and
y̌ Emperours ſending of them firſt vnto
the Biſhope of Rome, and then to the
Ꝺ iij Biſh-

Bishope of Arles, but consider the mater truely, and M. Iewels Arguments must be these.

Schismatikes *Appealed in an Ecclesiastical cause vnto the Emperour Constantinus: Ergo Catholikes, maie in like causes, appeale to Ciuile Princes.*

Againe, Constantinus *the Emperour, receiued for quietnes sake the Schismatikes appeale, and sent them to* Rome *there to be tried, and durste not him selfe iudge of that cause, vvhen the Bishope of* Rome *had determined it.* Ergo *the Bishope of Rome had a vvarrant and commission sent vnto hym, to heare and determine that mater.*

Againe, Constantinus *the Emperour yeldinge vnto the importunitie of Schismatikes, vvhen they vvould not obeie the Sentence of the Bishope of Rome, sent them to the Bishope of Arls, and vvhe they vvould not be ruled neither by that Sentence, he heard the cause hymselfe, and mynded to aske pardon of the holy Bishopes, for his sitting vpon that mater, vvhich alreadie by them vvas determined:* Ergo *Appeales maie be lavvfully made from the Bishope of Rome to other Bishopes, and the Emperour is Supreme head vnder God in earth: So that al causes must in the* **end**

end be referred vnto hym. These be the only premisses which the Storie geaueth, vnto which if he can ioine his conclusion, then shal he make contraries agree: but whereas he can not, whi maketh he conclusions without premisses? Or why maketh he Argumentes out of ý, which either Schismatikes vsed, or that which Catholikes yelded vnto, in consideration of Schismatikes? wyl M. Iewel neuer leaue his impudencie? But let vs go further.

The third Example. Iew. 289

The Councel of Antioche deposed Pope Iulius: Yet was not Iulius therfore deposed.

Ra.

This you bring in (M. Iewel) to declare, that the sentence geuen in Councels was not alwaies put in execution. To which I answer, that if the Councel be lawfull and Catholike, the decrees ought to be put in executiõ: if thei be not, it foloweth not, that the Sentence of the Councel maie be contemned, or neglected, but that they which being of Authoritie do not see the Councels wel performed, are to be amended. As for vnlawful Councels, neither their decrees, neither their examples are to be regarded,

R iij   You

You reason muche like, as if one should saie against the Obedience due vnto the priuye Councel of a Realme: The Sonnes of King Dauid, the Capitanes of the hostes, Abiathar also the high Priest, consented and agreed, saieing: Viuat Rex Adonias, God saue Adonias the King, and yet Adonias was not king, ergo the Proclamations or Determinations of lawful Authoritie maie be litle estemed. For this Councel of Antioche, was a Schismatical assemble, and wheras they deposed hym, ouer whom they had no Authoritie, there is no absurditie at al, nor fault to be laied vnto any mans charge, that wil not obey, or lyke their procedings & doings therein. But when the lawful & head Bishope of the worlde, doth define and subscribe in a Generall Counnel, though there folow no execution in acte, yet there is one to be done by right. And it can be no sufficient excuse before God, when the conscience shal be examined, to allege, that because Schismatikes decrees haue not ben executed, therfore the Obedience which is due to the Sentence of Catholikes, maie be dimi-

Co.3.ca.1.

diminished. But see yet an other Exaple.

M. Iewel wil proue that Bishops of other Countries, neuer yeelded to the Popes Supremacie. For saith he:

The Bishopes of the East, writing vnto Iulius, allege that the faith that then was in Rome, came first from them, and that their Churches, as Sozomenus writeth, ought not to be accompted inferiour to the Church of Rome: And as Socrates further reporteth, that they ought not to be ordered by the Romaine Bishope.

The. 4. Example. fcio. 178

You haue much to do M. Iewel with the Bishopes of the Easte, and no man, I thinke, that readeth your Booke wil iudge otherwise, but that they were learned and good men, such as whose opinions both your selfe allow, and commend vnto others to be regarded. And truely, if they were such men, I wil say nothing, but that he that is disposed, may esteeme their sayinges: but, if it shal be proued most manifestly, y̌ thei were rank and obstinate Arrians, then truely, the more ignominiously and cotemptuously they spak against the Bishops of Rome, the better they do declare, of what kind and

Ra.

and succeffion they are at this pzefent, which fet their whole studies against the See Apostolyke, and will not be ruled by the highest Bishop in Chzistendom.

For pzoufe of your affertion, you refer vs to Sozomenus, and Socrates, Auncient and lawful Historiographers, whome we also do admit. And, as though any man would striue with you herevpon, that the Bishopes of the East, did not so litle set by þ Bishop of Romes Authozitie, as you seme to gather, you put in the margen the greeke text it self, that he which knoweth no greeke at all may yet say to him selfe: Bir Lady M. Jewel alleageth þ expzesse Text foz him-selfe, and it apeareth by þ English ther-of, that the Bishopes of the East made no such accompt of the Pope, as at these Daies is allowed.

But what shall we say? It can not be denied, but the Bishoppes of the Easte, those of whome Sozomenus and Socrates speake, did take them selues to be as good as the Bishop of Rome, and disdayned to yelde obedience vnto him.
   But

Perians alleaged by M. Jewel ful boly:

But, were they Catholiks, oʒ Heretiks? Undoutedly Heretikes, and that of the woʒſte making. Foʒ they were Arrians. Howe pʒoue I this? Mary by Sozomenus and Socrates both, which agree in telling the Stoʒie. And that is this.

At what tyme, S. Athanaſius fled to Rome, being perſequuted of the Arrians, foʒ defending of the Conſubſtantialitie of God the Sonne with the Father, it ſo came to paſſe, that, at the ſame time, Paulus Biſſhoppe of Conſtantinople, and Marcellus Biſſhoppe of Ancyra, and Aſclepas Biſſhoppe of Gaʒa, and Lucius Biſſhop of Hadʒianople, came alſo to Rome, being al Catholike Biſſhoppes, and al dʒyuen out of their Churches and Sees, thʒough the Accuſations and Inuaſions of the Arrians.

Sozomenus lib. 3. Cap. 8. Socrates lib. 2. C4. 15.

Herevpon Iulius the Biſſhoppe of Rome, vnderſtanding what faultes were layed to their charges, And perceiuynge, that all were of one mynde concernynge the Decʒees of the Micene Councell, bethoughte it meete to com

communicate with them, as with men of
the same faith and opinion with him.
And as Sozomenus writeth διὰ τὴν ἀξίω
αν τῶ Ἰρόνȣ because of the vvorthines and dig-
niti of his See. or as Socrates saith ἅτε προ-
νομία, Τῆς ἐν ῥώμη εκκλησίας ἐχούσης, foraf-
much as the church of Rome had the Prerogatiues
& priuilegies, he restored euery one of them

to his See, And wrote freely and sharp-
ly to the Bishops of the East which had
expelled them, declaring that they had
troubled the Churche, and that they had
not iudged aright, of the forsaid Bishops
Requiring furthermore, y some of them
should appere at an appointed day before
him, and that he would not suffer it, if
they ceased not to be newfangled.

The Arrian Bishoppes, vppon the
receipt of this letter, and for indignation
that the Bishop of Rome had restored to
their lauful Sees, the catholike Bishops
Athanasius, Paulus, Marcellus, Asclepas, Lucius, whom they had vnplaced,

they called a Councel at Antioche, and
wrote againe a faire letter to Pope Iulius, ful of piety scoffes and tauntes, and
not without sharpe threatenings also.

And

And, emong other points, these that M. Iewel reckeneth are some, that, forsoth, they *ought not to be accompied inferiour to the Church of Rome*. And that they ought not to be ordered by the Romaine Bishope. Hitherto is the storie as I gather it out of Socrates and Sozomenus.

Consider now of it indifferent Reader.

Was Athanasius an holy Bishope, or no? was he a most worthy and tried defendour of the Catholike faith, or no? Did almighty God miraculously defend him against al his enemies, or no? Eusebius, Sozomenus, Socrates, Theodoritus, al ý euer wrote the storie of ý time, speak so much good of him, & declare such a prouidence of God to haue ben about him, that he must be a very blinde and wretched Arrian, which seeth not his worthines, Or ennieth at his Glory.

And whom then follow you M. Iewel? Those Bishops of the East, whom your wisdome and Religion bringeth in for substantial witnesses? They condemned Athanasius. And for what other cause so principally, as for his defending of the Catholike faith, against the blasphemies

phemies of ý Arrians? Alow yow then
his condemnaion? Vtter now your stomake and speake plainly, whether you
beleue ý Christ is of one & the selfe same
Substaunce with his Father. Shew
your selfe, as you are, in your Opinions,
and put of the name and person of an honest Superintendent, which you would
seeme to beare, and with al boldenesse,
vtter your secrete Diuinitie.

For here nowe I chalenge you, & here
I charge you. Alow you the Condemnation of Athanasius, which your Bishops
of the East concluded vpon? If you doe,
Auaunt Arrian: If you doe not, how can
you but thinke euil of such arrogant and
wicked Arrians, which not ôly put him
out of his See, but also, when he was
restored againe vnto it, by the Iudgement of the Bisshop of Rome, contemned that his Sentêce, with greater spite
and Insolencie, than they had expelled
Athanasius and others, at the first.

I say further: If Athanasius, Paulus, Marcellus, Asclepas, and Lucius, so
Reuerend Fathers, being expelled by
the Bsshopes of the Easte, thought them
selues

The Cha
lenger cha
lenged.

selues safe inough against all their Enemies, hauing the letters of the Bishop
of Rome for their lawful Returne vnto
their Sees, should not this alone, be
Argument inough to any Indifferent
Protestant in all y̆ world, that he should
not Contemne, Abandone and Accurse
the Authoritie of the See of Rome? For,
whereas the Examples of Learned and
Holy men are to be followed : And,
whereas M. Iewel the Challenger w̃
others of his vaine, doe pretend greate
Reuerence towardes Antiquitie, prouoking their Aduersaries, to bring Testimonies out of the Primitiue Church,
And exhorting their Hearers and Readers, to consider the practise of the Auncient tymes and Fathers: how should he
not haue the Bishop of Rome in greate
Admiration, whom he seeth to haue ben
so highly estemed, of the greate Bishops
or Patriarches, rather of y̆ Easte Church
Athanasius, Paulus, Marcellus &c. y̆ his
letters were of more force w̃ them, to restore them to their Sees, than their own
Power & Habilitie was, to kepe thēsel-
ues in their own places, when they had
them?

If Fa-
thers shal
be folow-
ed, here
they are.

Note

Note also, that whereas they were expelled by violence, And wer sent home again, not with an Armie, but with Letters onely, Yet those letters preuailed so much with the People also of their Cities and Countries, that straite wayes they were gladly receiued. And had it not ben for the Conuenticle and Conspiracie of the forsaid Arrian Bishops of the East, in which they not onely set al their owne Power, against the Catholike Bishops Athanasius, Paulus, &c. restored by the Pope of Rome, but accused them to the Emperour Constantinus, making him to vse Violence against them: the Catholike people of Constantinople, Alexandria, and other places, would haue honored and Obeyed them stil, as their owne true and lanful Bishopes.

Of which it is easy to gather, that, First the Blessed and Reuerend Bishops themselues Athanasius, Paulus, &c. did set very much by ye Bishop of Romes letters and sentence: And then, that the Catholik and deuout people also of those quarters, did regard and obey the same: Thirdly, that such as resisted then the Autho-

See what a monstrous testimonie M. Iew. hath sought against the B. of Rome.

Authoritie of ỹ Bishope of Rome, were
plaine Arrians. And last of al, that it was
not done by law or any order, that those
holy Bishopes, Athanasius, Paulus & c.
enioyed not the right of their own Sees,
but by false Accusations of the Arrian
Superintendentes, and Indignation,
Stomake, Edict, Violence, & Persecu-
tion, of the Emperour Constantius.

How litle then doth this Example
of the Arrian Bishoppes make for M.
Iewels purpose? Yea rather, how much
doth it make cleane against hym? For
when wicked and nawghtie mens factes
are put furth in writing, they are for this
end put furth, to be abhorred, and not to
be folowed: As Cains murdering of his
brother, or Iudas betrayinge of his
Master.

Yet, when the persons are notorious, as Cain and Iudas, Or the factes
them selues are euidently naught, as to
kyll or betray Innocentes, he should not
doe much harme, which would desperat-
ly goe about to perswade any to folowe
such Examples. But here is the mischief,
when Historiographers are brought in,

R i as

as alowing that whiche they condemne
in deede, Or when heretikes are made to
go for catholike Bishops: And when ẏ is
put furth as an Example to be folowed,
which serued rather to dehort men from
resisting Trueth and Authoritie: And
when by natural reason the mater is not
so euident, but examples of former times
in the one side or other, maie wel moue
the vnlearned to folowe them.

And in this arte M. Iewel is a doctor. For if he would haue expressely said,
The Arrians and Heretikes of the Easte
Church whéthey had wrongfully expelled
the catholikes and good Bispopes, Paulus,
Athanasius, & c. out of their sees, they contemned the Bishope of Romes letters by
which they were required to receiue them
againe, and to set aside al Iniurie and new-
fanglenes: Ergo the Bishope of Rome is
supreame head of the Church: If M. Iewel would after this open and plaine
manner haue vsed hymselfe, there is not,
I suppose, so vnsensible A Protestant,
which would not haue iudged hym, to
haue reasoned very folishly.

But now whiles he geueth them no
worse name than the Bishops of the East,

and

and kepeth frome the knowlege of his Readers, that they were Heretikes and Arrians, he maketh them to thinke, that al is wel, And that these Bishopes were men of much credite and woorthines, and that not only late Gospellers, but old Catholique Fathers also, haue denied Obedience to the Bishoppe of Rome. whiche thinges being altogether other=wise, the Readers are driuen into per=dition: And M. Iewel either seeth not that an Argument brought from the Au=thoritie of blasphemous heretikes is no=thing woorth (which is incredible in him that hath so greate insighte in the true Logyke and Diuinitie) either seinge it, he maketh no conscience of it, to bring his purposes to an end, by what meanes soeuer he maie, & this is so credible, that it agreeth very wel both with the despe=ratues of his cause and of his stomake.

BEVVARE therefore (Indifferent Rea=der) of M. Iewel, and knowe this for most certeine, that as I haue declared by a few Examples in this Chapiter that he allegeth the condemned sayinges and doings of Heretikes vnder the colour of

R ij Ca-

Catholike and approued witnesses, so in many moe places of his Replie, he doth in like maner, abuse them most shamfully. But of them thou shalt reade in other Bookes.

And what now is there more (M. Iewel) that ye wil require or vse against vs? To the first six hundred yeres only you haue appealed, your selfe yet do vse the testimonies of al ages. To the first six hundred only you haue appealed, and yet against the approued writers of that selfe tyme, you haue excepted. Besydes this as though ther were not to be found Catholike witnesses inough in the cause of the catholike Faith, you couertly bring in against vs, the accursed sayinges and doeinges of Heretikes. which one point excepted (that you shal not in question of the Catholyke Faith and Tradition, make any old Heretikes Iudges in the cause, Or witnesses) for the reste I dare graunt vnto you, to take your vantage, where you can finde it.

But hauing so large cumpasse graunted vnto you, against the expresse reason & Equitie which should be in your Chalenge,

lenge , ſhal it not become you, to vſe this priuilege diſcreetly and truly? And ſo to allege your witneſſes , as in deede they meane in their owne ſenſe , without falſe applying thereof: And as they ſpeake in their owne tongue, without adding vnto their ſayinges , oz taking awaie from them, any thing that is of the ſubſtance of their verdicte? Thus, whether you doe obſerue oz no, let it be tried.

And that it maie be tried the better, I wil briefely and plainely proue againſt you (M. Iewel) befoze any indifferent Reader: Firſt, ẙ you haue abuſed Councels , then Lawes , Canon and Ciuil: Thirdly, Fathers and Doctours , Auncient and Late: And that ye haue ſpared no kind of writer that came in your way.

How M. Iewel hath abuſed Councels.

Councels , in one ſenſe, are abuſed, when that which is ſound in them to be condemned , is brought furth by any Protestant as though it were approued

R iij   proued

proued. As in example wheras D. Harding concluded, vpon the profite which cometh of celebrating the memorie of our Lords Passion, that the Sacrifice of the Aultar, which is made in remembrance therof, shuld not be intermitted, although the people would not communicate: M. Iewel,

To adde a lytle more weighte to this seely reason, saieth further in D. Hardings behalfe

Iew, 25.   If this Sacrifice be so necessarie, as it is supposed, then is the Priest bound to Sacrifice euery daie, yea although he him selfe Receaue not.

Ra.   But howe proueth he this? it foloweth.

Iew. For the Sacrifice and the receauing are
foure reaso. sundrie thinges.

Ra.   And what of that? For although Communion bread and wine be sundrie thinges, yet you wil not permit the Receiuing of the Lords supper in one kinde only. And so although Sacrifice and Receiuing be distinct: yet doth it not folow, that a Priest maie offer and not receaue. But you wil proue it, by better Authoritie then your owne, for thus
you

you faie .

As it is alfo noted in a late Councel holden at Toledo in Spaine . Quidam Sacerdotes & cæt . Certaine Priestes there be, that euery day offer many Sacrifices, and yet in euery Sacrifice withhold themfelfe from the Communion . **Iew.**

what is your Ergo then vpon this place? your Conclusion should be, Ergo **Ra.** A priest maie Sacrifice, although he him felfe doe not Receaue . But can you ga= ther this out of the Councel? Doth it not rather make expressely to the contrarie? Doth it not repioue the priestes, which Sacrifice, & Receaue not? Let the place be considered, & then conferred with M. Ie= wels collection. The whole place is this.

Relatum est . & cæt . It is tolde vs , that **Con.Tolet.** *certaine emonge the Priestes , doe not so manie* **12.cap 5.** *tymes Receaue the grace of the holy Communi= on , as they seeme to offer Sacrificies in one daie, but if they Offer moe Sacrificies in one daie, they vvithhold themfelues in euerie offering from the Communion , and they take the grace of the holie Communion, only is the laste offering of the Sacrifice: As though that they should not, so ofte participate the true & singular Sacrifice, as oft as* the offering of the body and bloud of our Saviour Iesus Christ shal be sure to haue ben made. For behold, the *Apostle saieth, doe not they eate the Sacrificies, which are partakers of the Aultar? Certaine it is, that they which doe Sacrifice and doe not eate, are giltie of the Sacrament of our Lord. From henceforth therefore, whatsoever Priest shal come to the Diuine Aultar to offer vp Sacrifice, and withhold himselfe from the Communion, let him know, that for one yeres space he is repelled frō the grace of the Cūmuniō, of which he hath vnsemely depriued him selfe. For, what maner of sacrifice shal that be, of which no not he that doth Sacrifice, is knowven to be partaker? Therefore, by all meanes it must be obserued, that as oft as the Sacrificer doth offer and Sacrifice vpon the Aultar the bodie and bloud of our Lord Iesus Christ, so ofte he geue himselfe to be partaker of the bodie & bloud of our Lord Iesus Christ.* Hitherto the Councel of Toledo.

How thinke we then? Hath not M. Iewel properly alleged it for his purpose? could he haue brought a place, more plaine against himselfe? M. Iewel saieth that Sacrifice and Receiuing are sundrie thinges: And meaneth thereby, that the priest may do ẏ once & leaue the other, that

Is not this sham fully don?

16

is, Offer and not Receiue : the Councel defineth, that whatso euer Priest do Offer and not Receiue, he shalbe kept away from the Communion a tweluemonth togeather. And what other thing is this to say, then that Sacrifice and Communion are so sundrie, that the Priest for al that, can not put them a sunder, Or do one without the other? Thus hath M. Iewel, to put more weight to his seely reason, confirmed it by a fact condemned by the same Councel, in which it is sould reported. And this is one way of Abusing of Councels.

In an other kinde, it is an abusing of Councels, when that is Attributed vnto them which at al is not in them. As in Example.

The Intention (saith M. Iewel) of the Churche of Rome, is, to woorke the Transubstantiation of bread and wine, The Grek church had neuer that Intentió, as it is plaine by the Coúcel of Florence.

Iewel.

Flat lye.

Thus you say M. Iewel, and in the Margin you referre vs to the last session of the Councel of Florence, but in that Session there is no mention at al of Transub=

Ra.

Trāsubstantiation, Or, Intention. The
greatest and the only mater, therein Discussed and defined, was, concerning the
Proceding of God the Holyghost from
the Father and the Sonne, in which
point the Grecians then were at one wt
the Latines. It folowed then, after
a few dayes that the vnion was made,
that the Bishop of Rome sent for the
Grecians, and asked of them certaine
questions, concerning their Priestes
and Bishopes, and Anoynting of their
dead, & Praiers in their Liturgie, and
choosing of their Patriarches.

But it was neither Demaunded of
them what Intention they had in Consecrating, Neither Aunswered they any
thing to any such effect, Neither did the
Bishop open vnto them, his Faith and
beliefe therein. So that altogether it is
a very flat lye, that M. Iewel here maketh vpon that Councel. Except he
meane the Doctrine that there foloweth
grauen to the Armenians, in which Trāsubstantiation and Intention both is cō-
prehended, wherevnto the Sacred Coūcel whereof the Grecians were a parte,
                                    gaue

gaue their consent.

A third maner of Abusing Councels,
is, to allege them truely in dede as they
say, but yet to allege them to no purpose.
As in example. The fourth Councel of
Carthage decreed, that in certaine cases,
the Sacrament should be powred into
the sicke mans mouth. of which worde
(powred) being proper only to thinges
that are fluent and liquide, D. Harding
gathereth, that the Sacrament whiche
they receaued, was in the forme of wine,
and not of bread. Hereupon M. Iewel commeth against him, and he calleth
it a Gheasse, that the bread can not be
powred into a sicke mans mouth.　　But
howe proueth he it to be but a Gheasse?
Or what sayeth he to the contrarie? He
foloweth.

And yet he maie learne, by the thirde 　*Iew.140*
Councel of Carthage, and by the abridge- *Concil.*
ment of the Councel of Hippo, that the *Carth.3.*
Sacrament was then put into dead mens *C.t.5.*
mouthes.

Your Argument then is this: One　　*R2.*
(y is so foolish or superstitious) may put
the Sacrament into a dead mans mouth,
　　　　　　　　　　　　　　　　Ergo

A worthy cósequéce of M. Ie-wels.

Ergo D. Harding doth not gheasse wel, that bread can not be powred into a sicke mans mouth. But al thinges are here vnlike, both Persons, and Actes, and Termes.

First of al, dead men are distincted from Sicke men, and the dead you may order violentlie, but the sicke wil be vsed Reasonablie, except none but Enemies be about them.

Then, in the one side, the Act is vn-lauful (to put the Sacrament in a dead mans mouth) On the other, it is lauful (to power it into a sicke mans mouth).

Beside this, Putting is one thing, and Pouring is an other, and whether it be bread or wine, you may be suffered to say, that they are put into the mouth, but how bread should be poured into ones mouth, except in al haste you minded to choke him or fil him, I can not tel.

Last of al, the terme Sacrament, which is forbidden to be put in the dead mans mouth, may signifie any of the two kindes: That is, either of Bread or wine. but in naming the Bread, you are bound to that one kinde only of the Sacrament, and

and must not meane thereby, wine. So
that there is neither Rime nor Reason in
it, to tel vs ful solemlie, that the Sacrament was put in dead mens mouthes,
the Proposition, which you therby would
disproue, being onely this, that Bread
can not be poured into sicke mens mouthes.   And therefore to speake the least,
and best of it, this is a very vain and idle
Abusing of the Authorities of Councels.

But of al other it passeth, when M.   **Marke**
Iewel taketh, as much as pleaseth him,   **this trick.**
of any Canon of Councel, and maketh a
ful point before he come to the end of the
Sentence :   Mainteining his Heresie,
by that Peece which he pulleth away,
And dissembling that which remaineth,
by which his Obiection should be straitwaies refelled .   For otherwise , to re-
herse no more of a Canon , than serueth
our purpose, it is common and tolerable .
But when that point which an Heretike
leaueth out, per taineth to the qualifying
of that other Peece, which he would haue
to be vnderstand absolutely , that is such
a point of an Heretike, as may wel cause
any reasonable mā to *B E V V A R E* of him.
                                                          But

But is it poſſible, that M. Iewel maie be taken in this fault? If he be not, then wil I graunt, that he hath not, in as Ample and Shamfull maner abuſed Councels, as any of the moſt Deſperate, of all that euer wrote. And if he be, I aſke nomore, but that he may goe for ſuch as he is. The Example ſhal make this plaine.

Iew.153. In the Councel of Laodicea it is decreed like as alſo in the Councell of Carthage, that nothing be readde in the Church vnto the people, ſauing only the Canonical Scriptures.

Ra.

What anſwerye? I wonder then, what your Homelies doe in the Church, except you thinke that they be Canonical Scriptures, Or els, that you ſo preciſe folowers of Antiquitie, are not bound to the Canons of Auncient Councels. But as I doe graũt vnto you, that the Councel of Laodicea hath, that ſuch only bookes as are of the old & new Teſtamẽt ſhould be readen in the Church, ſo, that ẏ like alſo is declared (as you boldly ſay) in the Councel of Carthage, it is ſo manifeſtly vntrue, ẏ it may not be ſuffered. For theſe are the verie wordes

wordes of the Councel .

Item placuit, vt præter Scripturas Canoni-
cas nihil in Ecclesia legatur sub nomine Diuina-
rum Scripturarum . **that is , ** *Vve like it also ,*
that nothing besides the Canonical Scriptures be
readen in the Church, in the name of the Diuine
Scriptures .

The Councel therefore forbiddeth not
other things bysides the Canonical scriptures to be readen in the Church, but it
prouideth, that nothing be readen there,
as *in the name of Scripture* which is not true
Scripture in dede . And this appeereth
most euidently by other wordes , which
folowe in the selfe same Canon where it
is sayed .

Liceat etiam legi Passiones Martyrum, Cum
Anniuersarij eorū celebrantur . *Be it lauful also*
to haue the Passions of Martyrs readen , vvhen
their yerely Daies are celebrated and kept holy .

By this, it is most euident, that other
thinges bysydes the Canonicall Scriptures, as the Passions of Martyrs (such
vndoutedly as we haue, for a great part,
in the Legends of the Church) were permitted to be readen in the publike Seruice : And that M. Iewels comparison

Passions
of Mar-
tyrs readē
in Chur-
ch, & their
yeerely
Daies kept

(that

(that the Lessons then read in y̆ Church were taken out of y̆ holy Bible (ONLY as he meneth) as it is now vsed in the church of England,) hath no agreablenes and Proportion . For what one Martyr is there in al the whole booke of the Common praier of England (S. Steuen only excepted) which hath any Festiual day appointed out for him, or any storie of his Passion declared?

But like perfite Diuines , you wil no other thing, but Scripture onely reaaden in your Churches : in which pointe, you would be seene to follow the Councel of Carthage . You deceaue the people, by your glorious lying. The Councel of Carthage (as you perceiue by the wordes which I haue alleged) alloweth not onely Canonical Scriptures , but Martyrs Passions also to be Readen in the Church . Why say you then so impudentlie, that it it was there Decreed, that nothing should be read in y̆ Church vnto the People, sauing onely the Canonical Scriptures ?

I aske of you also , where the Passions of those Martyrs are, which at the begin-

An Impudent lie of M. Iewel.

beginninge had their Holidaies in the
Churche: And should to this daie haue
them if(as you doe chalenge it)you were
of the holie and Catholike Church? S.
Clement, Cornelius, Cyprian, Xistus,
Lawrence, Uincent, Sebastiane, and
other,whom the whole world honoreth:
what solemme Feastes haue you of them,
or what Lessons and Homilies are Readen in your Churches,of their Passions?
were there no Martyrs in the world,af-
ter the Apostles were once departed this
lyfe? Or know you any more excellent,
than these whome J haue named? Or
haue you no mynde or affection to any of
them? Or haue you spied a Canon in the
Councel of Carthage, that nothing but
Canonical Scriptures shal be readen in
the Church? And could you not see the
plaine Exception,which is straite waies
in the same Canon made against it, that,
notwithstanding the former wordes, *the*
passions of martyrs should be reade in the Church,
vvhen their yerelie daies are celebrated?

But of the beggarlines of this new
Religion,and how it is altogether desti-
tuted of Martyrs, Confessors. Uirgins,

S i **of**

of all kinde of Sainctes, it is to be spo=
ken at more leasure: in the meane tyme,
this I leaue most euidentlie proued, that
M. Iewel hath abused Councels.

How M. Iewel hath abused the Decrees of the Canon Lawe.

There is smal hope, that he whiche
dareth wrest, Belie, and Peruerte
Councels, wil spare to vse al Lose=
nesse and Libertie in squaring of
Decrees and Decretals to his purpose.
And manie will thinke on the other side,
that M. Iewel is so honest and good, of
nature, that he would not, no not of the
diuell himselfe (if he might) winne any
thing by lying, and muchlesse in the cause
of God & his true Religion, reporte any
thing, of any man that euer yet wrote,
otherwyse then the Trueth is, and the
wordes of the Author. Examples then
muste confirme my obiection, emonge
which this is one.

Iew. 69.
Fabianus
decree ab=
used.

Fabianus (saieth M. Iewel) Bishop
of Rome hath plainely decreed, that the
people

people should receaue the Communion
euery fondaie. His wordes be plaine. Decernimus & c. We decree that euery fon-
day the Oblation of the Aultare, be made
of al men and women, both of bread and
wine.

True it is, that ꝼabianus willed
such Oblations of bꝛead and wine to be
made, and them to this end, *Vt à peccatorū*
suorum fascibus liberentur, **that the people**
might be deliuered of the burden of their
sinnes. But offering euerie Sonday, and
Receiuing euerie Sondaie are two thin=
ges. To pꝛouide, that the people should
Offer Bꝛead and wine euerie Sondaie,
it was necessarie, because, that is the pꝛo=
per mater of which the Sacrament of the
Aultare is made, and because the Clergie
also liued then, of the offerings of the
people. But to decree, that al men and
women should Receiue euerie Sonday,
it is altogether vnreasonable, that it
should haue ben ꝼabianus mynde.

ꝼoꝛ, in the verie same place, there is
another Decree of his, that men should
Communicate thꝛise, at the least (if no
oftener) in a yere, that is *At Easter, VVittefon-*
tide, and Christmasse, except perchaunce some

R a,

Epist.g. ad.
Hilarum.

S ij   man

man be letted by anie kind of the grevous crimes.

If then he required no moze, but that the people should Receaue thzile a yere, how is it poſsible, that, by this decree, of which M. Jewel ſpeaketh, and in which there is no mention of the peoples receauing, but of their Offering only of Bzead and wine, any charge should be laied vppon al men and womens conſciencies, to Receaue euery Sondaie? Ye might as wel conclude, that in euery pariſh of England, there was ſome one oz other of the laie people, that Receaued alwaies on Sondaie, in one kinde, at the leaſte, with the Pzieſt, becauſe an holy loafe (as we cal it) was Offered euery Sondaie.

But conſider yet further (Indifferent Reader) how finely and pzoperly, M. Jewel gathereth Argumentes out of Aunctient Popes decrees. He noteth, out of the fozeſaied wozdes, not only that men and women Receaued euery Sondaie, but alſo that they Offered bzead and wine euery Sondaie, accozding to the Order of Melchiſedech. By which accompte, ſo manie Pzieſtes and Sacriſiers were in the Church, as were men

and

Abſurde.

and women that offered bread and wine.

Yea, not only men, and women that are of perfitte discreation, but all the boies and wenches of the Parishe, may, with litle charges, be quickly within orders. For, as M. Iewel compteth, there is no more in it, but to Offer bread and wine to the Aultare, and straitewaies al that doe so, are Priestes, after the Order of Melchisedech.

But if that be so, how is the order of Melchisedech more perfitte, than the Order of Aaron? Or how was there such a Religion and Reuerence aboute the order of Aaron, that none but of a certaine tribe should be made Priestes, neither they also, without vocation and consecration: if to the order of Melchisedech (at ȳ coming of which, that of Aaron is perfited and accomplished) euery woman be within the Order, by offering of bread and wine to the Aultar? You M. Iewel that haue such knowledge in the vnderstanding of the Popes decrees, are you Ignorant in the law of Moyses? Remember you not, that emong other thinges that the people Offered, Bread and

Leu. 2.
& 23.

S ij   wine

wine were in ẙ number? But what speak
I of the peoples Acte? The priests them
selues, ẙ toke such bread at their handes,
and lifted it vp before their Lord, & offe
red likewise of the wine, by powring out
of it in the sight of the Lord: were they of
the order of Melchisedech or no? No sure
ly not of Melchisedechs order, but of the
order of Aaron only . If therefore a so
lemne offering of bread & wine , euen in
persons consecrated, doth not include the
order of Melchisedech, you are much to se
king of your purpose, which note, that ẙ
men and women that offered in S. Fabi
ans time, bread and wine to the Aultar,
were offerers after the order of Melchise
dech. So absurde it is, ẙ a Pope of Rome
should haue any such meaning in his de
cree, as you do gather thereof, ẙ I beleue
the most folishe heretike in al the world,
wold not, but w much study haue peeked
it out. But let vs cõsider an other exáple.

Certainly (saieth M. Iewel) it seemeth
that S. Gregorie in his time , thought sin
ging in the Church to be a fitter thing for
the multitude of the people, thé for ẙ priest.
For he expressely forbiddeth the Priest to
sing in the Church. But I do not remember
that euer he forbadde the People.   The

The more you warrant it with your
Certainly, that S. Gregorie should be of
the mind which you imagine. y more er=
nestly I beseech thee (indifferet reader) to
mark how substātially M. Iew. buildeth
wout any foūdation. For this first is ma=
nifest, ther haue ben, frō y beginning, di=
stict orders & officers in y church of christ
as Bishops, priests, deacons, subdeacōs,
acolites, exorcists, readers, sextins, Sin=
gers. And if these distinctions were euer
kepte in the Church, without question,
they were obserued most orderly, in S.
Gregories time, whome, for his greate
diligence in setting furth of the seruice of
god, the heretikes themselues doe cal, sa=
uing their charity, Magistrū ceremoniarū,
the Master of ceremonies. He therefore
seing this faulte in the Church of Rome,
that men apointed to higher offices, wer
also chosen to serue in lower functions,
as in example, y Deacons to become sin=
gingmen, prouideth by a special decree,
to haue it reformed. The Decree is this.

In sancta Romana Ecclesia, dudum consue-
tudo est valde reprehensibilis exorta, & cat.
There is risen of late, a very il custome, in the holy
Church of Rome, that certaine, vvhich are apoin-

S iiij ted

ted to serue at the holy aultare, are chosen to be Singyng men. And that they, vvhich are placed in the degree of Deaconship, should be occupied about the svveete tuning and deliuering of their voices: vvhom it vvere more meete, to intend their office of preaching, and to be diligent in distributing of Almes. Vvhereof, for the more parte, it cummeth to passe, that vvhiles a svveete voice is sought for, at anable & agreable life is neglected: and the Minister or Deacon vvhich is A Singing man doth pricke and greeu: God vvith his manners, vvhiles he deligh: eth the people vvith his voice. Vvherfore by this present decree, I apointe it, that, in this See, the Ministers at the holy Aultare, shal not singe, (vnderstand, beneth in the quier as Singing men doe) and that they shal only doe their Office in Reading the Gospel at the Celebration of Masse. As for psalmes, and so furth lessons, I decree that they shalbe done by the Subdeacons, or (if necessitie require) by the lesser Orders.

This is the whole decree. But where is it here, that a Priest should not Singe? The caule of making this decree, was the faulte of the Deacons. And, the Singing, which was forbidden them, was of that kinde as p̃ Singing mē vsed, and no such Singing, as is vsed in Reading of a Gospel. **Te**

To speake also of the Priest, thinketh M. Iewel, that the Masse which he celebrated solemlie in S. Gregories time was of his part celebrated without note? And that in beginning of, *Gloria in excelsis*, Or in saying of, *Dominus vobiscum*, Or, *Sursum coda*, and so furth in the Preface, he sang it not out, in a certaine quiet and easy run? The contrary is so cleare, that the note which is vsed in the Church in prefaces of ý Masse and in halowing of the Font, which are done by a Priest only or Bishop, is called *Cantus Gregorianus.*

But goe to M. Iewel, proceede in your Abusing of Decrees: If singing be not fit for a Priest, for whom is it fitte? You answer that:

Certeinly, it seemeth that S. Gregorie in his time thought singing in the Church, to be a thing fitter for the multitude of the People, then for the Priest.

Iew.
How certainly he auoucheth a Lye.
Ra.

Now for shame of your selfe, dare ye put it in print, ý Certainly it semeth so? And dare ye note vnto vs the Decree *In Sancta Romana*, for proufe thereof? There

is

is no one word in the whole Decree, that
soundeth to ẏ purpose. There is no mention of the multitude. Yea the multitude
of people is excluded, as it is certainly to
be gathered, of the decree. For it appoin-
teth the Psalmes to be song of the Subdeacons, by name. But if necessity should
require, ẏ then, thei of the inferior orders
of the Church, might execute ẏ office. If
therfore, it was not Ordinarie, no not for
euery one of the Clergie, to sing ẏ Psalmes , & if when ẏ case of necessitie came,
that only case made it lauful, for ẏ inferiour Orders to sing & reade in ẏ Church:
how Absurdlie or impudentlie gather ye
out of this Decree, ẏ to sing in the church
was thought fitter for the multitude of
the people, then for the Priest?

It is to be noted further, ẏ M. Iewel
speaketh not of people Indefinitely , but
of the multitude of people, Cōfusely. For
people to be suffered to sing, may haue a
tolerable sense, when certain meet for the
purpose, should be taken therbnto (And
yet in S. Gregories time, this would not
not haue ben suffered in Rome , as appeareth by the forsaid Decree) but ẏ multitude of people to be compted fit for singing

ging in the church, it is altogether so out
of tune and Order, that they lacke both
eares and reason that can admit it .

And wheras in S. Gregories time,
none (as it appereth) but of ye Clergie did
serue in the church, And in our more loose
daies, al persons yet, without distinctiō,
are not permitted to execute the office of
Singing or Reading in the Church: M.
Iew. in speaking for the multitude, that
(by likelyhood) as a copie thereof is to
be seene, at their Sermons, so in ye churches, Men, women, boyes, wēches, soul-
diars, mariners, merchāts, beggers, tag
& rag, al should be fit persons to beare a
part: as he is therein more open & loose
than we of these dissolute daies, so, with
S. Gregorie & his time, he agreeth nothing at al. Conferre, and Iudge.

An other Example. Omnes Episcopi,
qui huius apostolicę sedes ordinationi sub-
iacét. &c. Al Bishops saith M. Iew. out of
an epistle of Anacletus) ye be boūd to haue
their orders cōfirmed bi this apostolik see,
&c. wherby it may be gathered, ye other bishops wer not subiect to ye ordināce of ye see

Iew. 183.
Neither
true inter
pretation,
nor Col-
lection.

This Decree is two waies abused: first
in englishing it, then in resoning vpō it.

R 2.

Con-

The third Booke.

Concerning the Interpretation: it is two thinges, to say, Al Bishopes that are bound to haue their orders of the Apostolike See. And, Al Bishopes that are boūd to haue their Orders confirmed by the Apostolike See: Because ỹ second is twentiy times larger then the first. Of the first Anacletus speaketh, meaning that al they, which are immediately subiect to the Bishop of Rome, and take Orders immedietlie at his hands, shal (as it soloweth in the Decree) com or send yerely about the Ides of May, to S. Peter & Paules Church in Rome. Of the Second M. Iewel speaketh, which are out of the peculiar Prouince of the Bishope of Rome, And which yet, when they are by their Clergi named & elected at home must be afterwards confirmed by the B. of Rome, and are so ordeined and consecrated in their owne Prouince: So that the Bishopes of Italie, are ordeined and confirmed both, by the B. of Rome: but the Bishoppes of Fraunce or England (when it was good) are not made by him, but confirmed, that is to say (as the woorde it selfe geueth) he ratisieth that
which

which other haue or shal doe.

The Interpretation therfore of M. Iewels is false : so is also his collection and Argument. For, although al the Bishopes that are vnder the Bishope of Rome, and boūd to receiue their orders at his handes immediatelie, although al these (I say) be within Italie onely, or nigh thereabout, as farre as his special Prouince goeth, yet doth it not follow therevpon, that the Bishope of Arls, or Caunterburie are not at al subiect vnto him. Like as in an Armie, where ꝑ King him selfe is present, when he shal diuide the battel, and appoint the gouernement of diuerse bandes to diuerse Capitaines, reseruing to him selfe one emong al of which he, by him self, wil haue ꝑ charge: Although these now that he hath chosen out, be al that he hath to sette in aray and order by him self, yet must you not infer, that he hath no Authoritie ouer the other partes of the Armie, because he doth not as immediately gouerne the whole, as his special parte? For, Immediatelie, but one part is vnder his charge, but by meanes of his Capitaines, whom he on=

ly

he hath appointed, & whom he againe by his authority mai vterly displace, or other wise dispose, he is King ouer the whole. So is it in ÿ B. of Rome. His authoritie is as large, as the name of Christians doth spread abroad, And Christe which committed vnto S. Peter his Lambes & Sheepe, charged thereby, al that would be of his flocke, to obey his Vicepastor. Now, because the faithful are so multiplied, that one man by himselfe, can not Personally come to euery place, therfore, euen from ÿ beginning, there was made distinction of Prouinces, and Iurisdictions in the Church of Christ: in so much, that the Pope himself had and hath stil, a determined portion. Not that any Archebishope in the world, should take him self for as good as his Patriarche, Or ÿ the Primates themselues shuld presume to be as Supreme as the Pope: but that ÿ charge being diuided emong many, ÿ whole might be with more spede & lesse trouble, disposed. He ruleth therfore his owne part, as if he were but a Bishope, Archbishope, or Patriarche, he ruleth ÿ whole, as the Vicare of Christ, & head of his Church vnder him. He ruleth his

owne

 own part, Proportionablie, becaufe he is a man which can not do al by himfelf: he ruleth the whole by fpecial prerogatiue of Chriftes grace & power, becaufe he is the chief Steward ouer y house of Chrift, which he hath purchafed by his moſt pretious death, the whole world. Concerning his own part, other Bifhops be his fellowes, as laboring to the perfection of that whole, in which euery of them hath alfo a part. Concerning the whole, fome are Archebifhops, & Primates, fome Patriarches, euery one of a larger Iurifdiction then other, and one alone, is Pope.

This diftinctiō then being moft plain & manifeft, that Rule and Gouernement, is put in practife, both Immediatlie by y Rulers owne Act, And Mediatlie, or by meanes of other: to take away the fecōd by affirming y firft, wheras firft & fecond do in fundry refpectes wel ſtād together, it is without reafon or confequence. As, if one would fay, The King chargeth al his Lords & Officers about him, to mete where he hath appointed, ergo it may be gathered, that no other within England befide them of y Court, are bound to appeere where he fhal appointe them.

And

And so doth M. Iewel reason, Al Bis-
shopes that are bound to take their Orders, (or as he falsifieth the text, to haue
their Orders confirmed) by the Apostolique See, must (as it soloweth in the
Law) come or send yearely to Rome:
Ergo other Bishopes that are not Immediatly, but Mediatly vnder him, are
not subiect to the ordinaunce of that See.

Note also, that whereas the Decree
of Anacletus, is concerning the yearely
comming of Bishopes to Rome, and not
of any other point of Obedience and dutie: M. Iewel might wel argue thus.
The Bishopes onely of Italie, that are
subiect to the Apostolique See, are boūd
yerely to come to Rome, &c. Ergo the
Bishoppes of other Countries, that are
further of, are not bound to come yerely
thither. But, from this one particular
for which onely the Decree was made, to
reason generally, of the Obedience and
Subiection due to the ordinaunce of that
See, it is Sophistically and Vnreasonably done.

By this I proue then sufficiently, ꝑ
he hath abused the Canon Law.

How

How M. Iewel abuseth the very Gloses of the Canon law.

BUt doth his boldnesse stretch no further, than to the Text? or doth he not corrupt also the Gloses? verely he leaueth neither them vntouched, that is to say, vncorrupted. For if M. Iewel once touche a place, it is very hard but it wil be the worse for his handling. And cause truly he hath none, why he should allege any Glose of the Canon law, at al. For whereas himselfe regardeth not, no not the Text it selfe, and the Catholiks also wil not be bound to make good the priuate sayeing of any Gloser, it is a greate vanitie, to bring in such witnesses, as him selfe may well knowe are not sufficient. Yet, though I say so, he shall not require of me, to mocke straitewayes at any Gloses, Or to bring furth vnto y knowlege of the fine wittes of y worlde, some simple deuises and disconr-

ſes that they haue made, to thentent thei
may be laughed at . For there are Degrees in euery thing, and he that wil not
be ſo good as to praiſe euery Inuention
of the Gloſe, needeth not to be ſo il, as to
ſeeke how to finde fault with it, but may
wel inough be ſuffered to hold his peace.

Now concerning M. Iewels beha-
uiour, if he hath ſuch an itche, y̋ he thinketh to rubbe vs on the gal, by alleaging
ſuch witneſſes as we may and do lauful-
ly refuſe , why doth he not allege them
truely? why doth he tel their tale after
them in ſuch ſort, as he findeth not in
their owne words? why doth he (vpon
this preiudice emong the greater number that Gloſers are but Ignorante and
trifling men) bring forth blind and vain
ſentences out of them, which in dede are
not theirs, (though it wil be eaſily ſuſ-
ſpected) but M. Iewels: whome many
compte ſo honeſt, that he wil not in any
caſe make a Lie, or miſſuſe his own witneſſes in any point?

This Obiection of mine, to Exem-
plifie or Proſequute at large, I dooe not
intend, but, in one or two examples, I
wil

wil beginne the Chapiter, that he which
herafter wil adde moze vnto it, may haue
a plaine & peculiar place where to put it.

In the Answere to D. Hardinges
Preface, it pleaseth M. Iew. to open his
mouth awide, and to auouch that the
Pope speaketh after this maner.

Iewel in
§ Answer
to D.
Hardings
Preface.
R2.

    I can do what so euer Chrift him self
can do : I am al, and aboue al : Al power is
geuen to me, as wel in Heauen as in Earth.

You are not so honeft as to be tru-
fted vpon your bare wozde, and therfoze
name vnto vs your witneffes which may
depofe foz you, that the Popes haue euer
vttered wozdes with fuch Arrogancie.
And you referre vs to the Glofe *De Ma-
ioritate & Obedientia. vnam Sanctam*. But
what faith that Glofe? Doth it tel of any
one Pope by name, Oz doth it report fo
much of the ozder and fucceffion of them,
that euery one of them, hath in his courfe
and foz his time, founded it out into al the
world, that, I can do, what so euer Chrift
him felfe can do, &c?

Iewel.

You wil Anfwer (becaufe there is
no other fhift) that the Glofer fpeaketh
fuch wozds of the Pope, not that § Pope
            T ij   him

himfelf, doth fpeak them, in his own perfon, of him felfe. why then, I Iudge you
by your own words, that you haue made
an open lye, in attributing that, vnto the
Popes owne Act, which is not his, but ye
Glofers collection vpõ the Canon law.

Then, further I fay, that many
thinges are verified in fundry Perfons,
concerning their Vocation, or Office,
which it cannot bee me the perfons thē-
felues, to appropriat to them felues. For
the Apoftles of Chrift *vvere lighte of the*
vvorlde: yet if S. Peter had begon his E-
piftles with this ftile and Title, *Peter*

the Apoſtle of Ieſus Chriſt, and one
of the lightes of the world, he could
not haue ben thought to haue folowed
the humility which was in Iefus Chrift.
Lykewife, euery man that is in the ftate
of Grace, is vndoubtedly the Sonne of
God, and Felow of Angels, and Con-
querour of Diuels, vntyl he doe forfake
that Grace: Yet if you (M. Iewell)
fhould repent yourfelfe of al your brag-
ging, diffimbling, lying, &c. and Returne
to ye Catholike Church, & be receiued into the Communion of Saintes, it would
vs

5.

Euerie
thing, that
may truly
be fpoken,
is not, for
al that, to
be fpoken.

not be liked in you, to write yourselfe
Ihon Iewel A Conqueror of y wicked
Sprites, A terrour to heretikes, A
Cōfort to Catholikes, A welbeloued
of al Virgins, Confeßours, Martyrs,
Apostles and Patriarchs, A felow w
the Angels, A Cußon of our Ladies,
A sonne of Almighty God.

And so the Conclusion being true, that
there is no Autoritie in the world compa
rable to that which Christ gaue to S. Pe=
ter & his Successors, yet doth it not agree
that the Pope should in the first person
crake or sound out of himselfe, I can doe
whatsoeuer Christ himselfe can doe.
For whereas high dignitie & Autoritie is
geuen vnto men, for others sake which
are to be gouerned, & not for their owne
which beare the Office, and whereas such
Gifts & Graces of gouernemēt make not
the receauer of them acceptable (as faith,
hope & charitie doe) there is no occasiō to
crake of that which perteineth not to any
man in respect of his Person, but only of
his Office. $\mathbf{T}$ iij Or

On the other side, wheras to cōfesse the worthinesse of an Office, may wel become a wise and worshipful man, so that he attribute nothing therof vnto himself as he is one singular person: if the Pope Concerning his Office do confesse it that the chiefe Bishoppe in the Church, must rule al Christians and be subiect to none of them al: M. Iewel must not therefore slaunder him, that he openeth his mouth a wide, and vttereth blaspemies and soundeth out these wordes into al the world: I may iudge al mē, but al the world may not Iudge me. But by such forme of speach the simple Reader, and common Protestant, cōceiueth of the Pope, that he standeth a tipp toe: And ouerlooketh al the world: And is in great loue and conceipt of him selfe : And respecteth alwayes his priuate Estimation: And forgetteth that there is a God and right Iudge, and that him selfe is a Man and a Sinner as other folkes are : and that he attributeth an Omnipotencie to his owne proper person, &c. wherevpon, he taketh an Indignation, and accompteth him to be a very Beast or Diuel and no man, that

so preferreth him selfe before other men,
And is ready to accurse, and detest, and
reuile, and speake, and iudge the worst ȳ
he can of the Pope.

And this is one of the vile and wicked kindes of Rhetorique, that is vsed
now in the worlde. For, when it is
plainely and simply said, Christ breathed
vpon the Apostles, and saied, take ye the
holy ghost, whose sinnes ye forgeue, they
be forgeuen, whose sinnes ye retaine, they
be retained, he that wil finde any faulte,
must not be angry w̄ the Apostles which
take the Grace, but with the Author and
geauer of it, Iesus Christe : But no
Christian I (thinke) and faithful man,
doth abhorre to heare these wordes spoken. Now then

The Diuel which seeth Christe his
owne person to be in much honour, and
that when wordes are considered as spoken of him, the Christians harts are sub-
dued by them: what doth he? He turneth his forme of speach, and vnderstanding wel inough the Pride and Malice
of our corrupte nature, he maketh his
Oratours and Interpretours, to bring

the selffame wordes (which in dede haue
strength of Christ only) out of the mouthes
of spiritual Persõs, Bishops or Priestes:
A 10 deuiseth, that they shal vtter them in
their owne persons: as in exãple, he ma=
keth the Pope to say: Whose synnes I forgeue they be forgeué, Whose synnes I re-
ceine thei be reteined. Which because it is
Proudly & Arrogantly spoken, it is easy
to make him contemned which taketh so
exceding much vpõ him, and to bring the
Office & Authority it self into discredite,
because it agreeth not with the nature &
infirmitie of the persons, to speak so big-
ly and to performe it accordingly.

Concerning then now the Glose of which
M. Iewel speaketh, if in dede it be there
funnd, that Al Power is geuen to the Pope,
as wel in heauen as in Earth, yet to make
the Pope speake it in his own person, Al
power is geuen to me as wel in Heauē as in
Earth, it is spitefully & wickedly turned.

But let vs see the Glose it selfe, whe=
ther it hath that Sence, which M. Iewel
gathereth thereof. For touching the forme
of words, it is manifest that they are not
to be found there, as spoken in the firste
person.   The

The question, whiche the Glose
moueth, is this. *Whether the Spirituall
power ought to Rule the Temporall.* And it
seemeth (saieth the Glose) that not: wherevpon he bringeth in certaine Argumentes, for the Temporall, against the Spiritual Iurisdiction, but afterwardes he
dissolueth euery doubt & obiection laieng
this one Argument for a foundation.

*Christ committed his Vicarshipe, vnto the
highest Bishope :*

*But all power vvas geauen to Christe in
Heauen and in Earth, Mat. 28.*

*Ergo the highest Bishop vvhich is his Vicar,
shal haue this power.*

And what is the thing nowe, that
M. Iewel in this place doth misliyke?
Or what Sense, gathereth his vnderstanding hereof? Mary sir of this place
he concludeth the Pope to saie, Al power
is geauen to me, as well in Heauen as in
Earth But the Glose (M. Iewel) concludeth not so. For according to the mater whiche is proponed, the cumpasse
of the Conclusion must be ordered. Of
the Spiritual and Temporal Gouernement here in earth, the Glose speaketh:

As

de maiori-
tate & ob-
vnam san-
ctam in
Glosa.

It speaketh also, of the gouernement, as it parteineth to one that supplieth the place of Chrift on Earth, and not as it is enlarged to heauen. That vifible man fhould be left, after the departure and aftenfion of God and man, to gouerne that vifible Church which confifteth of men: It is fo Comfortable and Reafonable, that Faith, Order, and Peace, without it,

The glofe abufed. could not wel haue ben kept. But to make any man, liuing yet on earth, A Doer and Officer, concerning the Triumphant Church in heauē, where Chrift himfelf is in his perfon fo prefent, that he vfeth not a Vicare, that is abfurde and vnlikely, and with this, M. Iewel, chargeth the Pope, that he fhould Open his mowthe awyde and faie, al power is geauen to me, as well in Heauen as in Earth. which Conclufion is not vttered nor intended in the Glofe.

Obiection No faie you, doth not the Glofe, vppon this text of the Scripture fpoken of **Math. 28.** Chrift, al power is geauen to me in Heauen and in Earth, Doth it not infer, that the high Prieft, his Vicare on earth, hath the **Anfwer.** fame? no it fpeaketh not of the fame, but, of

This

This power. And this power is meant not generally of all power that Christ hath, but of that whiche is proponed in the question, that is, the Spiritual & Temporal power here in Earth.   As if he should more plainely haue concluded: *Al powver both in Heauen and Earth, is geauen to Christ : Ergo that in Earth.* Againe, *the high-heste Bishope hath Christes place and Rome in Earth, Ergo he hath al povver in Earth: Ergo the Spirituall povver ought to Rule the Temporal.*

The weake brother in Faith and witte maie replie. If the Pope haue as much power on Earth as Christ, It wil folow that Christs power in Earth being infinite, the Pope also maie doe what he wil, as in example, Remoue hils, go dryshod ouer great riuers, turn water into wine, strike fiue thousand men downe with a word, as our Sauiour did in the Garden. *Obiection*

No my frind, the Generalitie of a proposition, is to be measured by the mater which is in question. And because the question, moued in this place by $\bar{p}$ Glose, is not of working miracles, or wha soeuer els it be, ouer which $\bar{p}$ almightines of our Sauiour hath absolute power in Earth, but of the Authority, preeminece, *Answer,*

and

and Iurisdiction, which the Spirituall ru∣lers should haue aboue the Temporall, within the Church of Christ, that is yet militant: therfore the supplieing of Chri∣stes place in earth, and the Recciuing of the same power which he had, must be ex∣tended no further, than to the ruling and Gouerning of men here, beneth in the world, or though out of the world, yet in their waie vnto heauen.

And therefore M. Iewel hath shame∣fully abused this glose, as though it made the Pope a God, and that without anie Limitation or distinction, or interpreta∣tion, he concluded to haue al power, as wel in heauen as in Earth, euen as Christ him selfe hath.

An other glose M. Iewel hath peeked out, from the decree *24. quæsti. 1.* saieing Certû est quòd Papa errare potest, certaine it is, that the Pope maie erre.

But, do not you M. Iewel, most sham∣fully erre in mistaking ƿ glose? Let vs see for what purpose it was alleged of you, & tou... we shal the better consider, whether it see neth that, for which you alleged it. D. Harding said agreeably to the catho∣like

Iew, 275

Ra.

like faith, ŷ *Although the See of Rome
hath failed sometimes in charity, yet
it neuer failed in Faith.* Against this
conclusion M. Iewel commeth in with
these wordes.

Certainely the very glose vpon the Decretals putteth this mater vtterly out of
doubt: these be the words, Certū est quod
Papaerrare potest : It is certaine that the
Pope maie erre.

Iew.175

This is
not the
mater.

As if he should say: to proue by ŷ text it
self of ŷ decretals, ŷ the church of Rome,
may erre in Faith, it is so easie a mater,
I nede not worke ŷ way. But the very
glose vpō the decretals, which alwaies is
fauorable to ŷ see of Rome, & which by
al meanes possible, mainteineth ŷ Popes
kingdom, & which is, not of ŷ making of
any auncient or lerned doctor, but of some
old mūsimus papist & barbarous master,
yet this very glose is against ŷ priuilege
of ŷ see of Rome, ŷ it can not err in faith.
But is this trū? Yea certely quod M. Ie.
it putteth this mater out of dout, & ŷ vtterli.

Ra.

How bolde
dely?

Certainely, if the glose hath so taken the
mater, it is a great argumēt, ŷ much more
ŷ text is against vs, or if the text be to the

Catho-

Catholikes, It is a simple argument of
M. Iewels, to bring a Glose against the
Text, and so to speake of the Glose, as
though the text were much more for his
purpose? For the very Glose (saieth he)
putteth the mater vtterly out of dout. Let
vs see then, first of al, what is the Text.

Lucius the Pope, writing to certaine Bishops which were trobled with
heretikes, And shewing them, whereby-
pon to staie themselues, that they might
not wauer hither and thither: willeth
them to folow the Church of Rome, in
praise of which, thus he saieth. *Hæc sancta
& Apostolica, mater omnium Ecclesiarum Chri-
sti, Ecclesia, quæ per Dei Omnipotentis gratiam,
a tramite Apostolicæ traditionis nunquam erraße
probatur.* This holy and Apostolike Church, is the
mother of all the Churches of Christ: Vvhiche
(through the Grace of almightie God) hath neuer ben proued to haue erred frō the right trade
and pathe of the Tradition of the Apostles. Thus
saieth Pope Lucius, and he maketh expressely for D. Harding, as far downeward, as Lucius owne Popedome was,
Anno Do. 258.

This conclusion then being certaine,
by

Can. 24
q. 1 ca. A
recta fide

The
Church of
Rome ne-
uer pro-
ued to
haue erred

by the expresse text of the law , what saith the Glose therevpon ? Doth it folow the text oz no? If it do not: Remember then (I praie you M. Iewel) your charitable and affectuous wozdes to D. Harding: O M. Harding, It is an old saying: Maledicta Glosa quæ corrumpit textum. Accursed be that Glosing construction, or Glose that corruppteth the text. Remēber wel this old saying , & fozget not yourselfe, which bzing furth with so great a confidence, a Glose that impugneth the text .

But doth the Glose folow the text? If it do, be ashamed man then ofyourself, which doe so Certainely warrant it, that the very Glose putteth this mater out of doubt (that the See of Rome maie erre in faith) the text it selfe making to the contrarie .

But of this , perchaunce, you haue litle regarde, how the Glose agreeth oz disagreeth with the Text . And where you find your vantage, there you are de= termined to take it , hauing a simple and plaine eye, neither loking to that which goeth befoze , noz that which foloweth, neither that which is of any side of you.

Let M. Iew. answer, oz geue ouer

Iew. 120

Simplicitie about circumspection, but not about craftines.

And

And so, the Glose saieing, that Certaine it is the Pope maie erre, that is inough for you, and that, putteth the mater vtterly out of doubt, that the Churche of Rome may erre.

You are deceaued, M. Iewel, through your Simplicitie: For if you, or your frindes about you, had ben circumspect, you woulde neuer haue broughte this Glose furth, with such confidence, as you haue done. It is two thinges, to saie, The Pope maie erre, and, the Churche of Rome maie erre. The first is graunted: That it maie possibly be, that the Pope, concerning his owne priuate mynd and opinion, maie erre in vnderstanding, as Ioānes 22. dyd, or whom soeuer els you can name vnto vs. The second is vtterly denied, that the Church of Rome can erre. For that presupposeth, ý the Pope should be geauen ouer, to decree, Sette furth or determine by his Iudicial Sentence, some thing, contrarie to the Apostolike Faith, & that it should be receiued & beleued in the Church. which absurditie (that any error should be suffered to haue credit in that Church, which is ý Mother of al Churches; & that vnder the gouer

gouernement of the holy ghost which cō-
tinueth with it, (& is the spirit of Trueth)
because it is impossible, therfore it is also
impossible y̆ the Church of Rome shonld
erre, in any point of y̆ Faith. And in such
extremities, where y̆ Pope, for his owne
person, is perswaded in a contrary cōclusion vnto our Faith, almighty God, that
his care ouer the church may be manifest,
prouideth alwaies, to take such persons
out of the way, when they might (if they
had liued) done harme, as he did, *Ioannes. 22.* and *Anastasius.*

Now that the Glose saith no more,
but, the Pope may erre, which we wil not
denie, and not that the Churche of Rome
may erre. which was D. Hardings affir-
mation: by whom shal I better proue it,
thā by y̆ glose it self, which is a litle before
in this very cause. 24. q 1. out of which M
Iew. peeked his *Certainti* y̆ out of doubt
the See of Rome mai erre. In y̆ chapiter
Quodcunque ligaueris, the Glose vpō a certaine word there gathereth an Argumēt,
*that the sentence of the vvhole Churche, is to be
preferred before the church of Rome, if thei gain-
say it, in any point.* And he cōfirmeth it by y̆
93. Distinction, Legimus. But doth the Glose

the Pope
to err and
y̆ Church
of Rome
to err, are
two sun-
dry things
euen by y̆
very glose
which M
Iew. al-
leageth.
*Cause. 24
quæst .1.
In Glosa.*

U i rth

cest there? as M. Iew. Certainly anoni-
cheth it, doth it put the mater vtterly out of
doubt that the church of Rome may erre?
Iudge of the mind of the Glosator, by y
words of y Glose. For thus it soloweth.

Sed contrariū credo but I beleue the contrary.
And for cōfirmatiō of his belief, he referreth vs to y Chap. *hec est* which soloweth
in y cause & question: *Nisi* (saith he)*erraret*

Beholde
M. Iew.
the Glose,
if ye like
not the
Text.

Romana Ecclesia,quod nō credo posse fieri, quia
Deus nō mitteret. Arg.infra ead.c.4 Recta & c.
Pudēda. Except the church of Rome should erre,
which I beleue cānot be. because God would not
suffer it. As it is proued in the Chapiters
solowing, which begin, *A Recta & Pudenda.*

Consider now (Indifferent Reader)
& iudge betwene vs both. M. Iew. saith
The Glose putteth the mater vtterly out of
doubt, that y Church of Rome may erre,
because it saith,*the Pope may err:* I answer,
y the Glose vpon y chapiter *a Recta,* assureth it, *that the Pope may Erre:* but, in the
third Chapiter before, *Quodcūque ligaueris,*
it beleueth, that *it cānot be,that the church*
of Rome should erre,because God would not per-
mit it. Wherof I gather,that the Pope to
erre, & the Church of Rome to erre, are
distinct pointes, & that if it be graunted
vnto

vied him, y the Pope in his owne priuat sense may hold an heretical opinion, yet y church of Rome for al y, cannot erre, because God wil not suffer it, y any thing should be decreed by y Pope, y is cōtrary to faith. And this is manifest, euen by y very Glose which M. Iewel trusteth so much, y he toke y mater to be vtterli out of dout, when the Glose had once spoken it.

what is abusing of testimonies if this be not? what cōscience is there, either in preferring of Gloses before y text: either in expoūding of Gloses against y Text: either in setting of one and the selfe same glose against it self(wheras being rightly interpreted, it agreeth wel inough w it self) either in obiecting y part of y glose against y Aduersarie, which being graūted hurteth nothing, & dissembling or not seing an other part of y same glose, which clearly cōfirmeth y purpose of the Aduersarie, except the Glose could speake more plainly for D.Harding, then it hath don, when it saith: *Credo non posse fieri, quia Deus non permitteret.* I beleue that it can not be(that the Church of Rome should erre) *because God would not suffer it.* Now.

1.
2.
3.
4.

24. quæst. In Glosa.

W y For

For more Examples I am not carefull, And more might be foūd, if I would take the paines to seeke. But I would wish the learned in the Law, to examine and consider right wel, M. Iewels testimonies out of the Lawe. They shal speake with more Grace, as speaking of thinges in which they are practised, and with more facilitie, they shal dif ouer M. Iewels vnskilfulnes, as knowing at the first sight, wherein and when the Lawes or Gloses are abused. And if nothing els were, the common Ennemie to al Trueth, should be conuicted by the expert in euery Facultie.

How M. Iewel abuseth the Constitutions of the Ciuile Law.

YF the Canon law be, at these daies, of so litle price emong Heretiques, that, for spite they haue to y Pope, and the Clergie, they care not how they misreporte it and disorder it : of the Cōstitutions yet of Temporal Princes, they should haue some more reguard, leaft

whiles

whiles they be manifestly proued to vse
their accustomed libertie, of alleaging or
interpreting the textes also of the Ciuile
law, thei care not with how litle truth or
honesty, they should be rightly conuinced
to haue neither Spiritual nor Temporal
law for them selues . Now , whether
M. Iewel be as bolde with Constitutions of Princes, as Decrees of Popes, I
wil bring in his owne woordes as they
lie, and conferre them with the Constitution, vpon which he groundeth them.
Thus he saith .

If onely the negligence of the People
haue enforced Priuate Masse , How then
came it into Colleges, Monasteries, Cathedral churches, yea (marke now indifferent Reader, how constantly he speaketh)
euen into the very holy church of Rome,
whereas be such numbers of Clerkes, Vicars, Monkes, Priestes, and Prebendaries,
that the Emperour Iustinian was faine to
stay the encrease of them, al Idle, al in studie and cótemplation, al void from worldly cares , al confessed, al in cleane life, al
prepared?

I trust, after so great a vomit, your
Stomak be somwhat better at ease. And

U iij   first

Iew. 17.
Au g.
Colla. t.
vt deter-
minatus
sit nume-
rus Cleri-
corum.

R2.

first cōcerning $\tilde{y}$ question it selfe, D. Har.
hath it not, $\tilde{y}$ only $\tilde{y}$ negligēce of $\tilde{y}$ peo=
ple, hath enforced priuat Masse, but
$\tilde{y}$ oft times $\tilde{y}$ Priest at Masse hath no
cōpartners to receiue $\tilde{w}$ him, it proce
deth of lak of deuotiō of $\tilde{y}$ peples part.
And so hath it somtimes come of lacke of
deuotiō, $\tilde{y}$ religious mē haue not receued
so oft as they might. And if this doth cō=
fort your hart, $\tilde{y}$ I graūt vnto you, faults
to haue ben soūd emōg religious persōs,
I cannot let you of your own wil, but I
wōder at your fansie, to feed vpō carren.

Somtimes therfore, $\tilde{y}$ Priest receiueth
alone, because none is ready to be his cō=
partener, & so is his Sole receiuing or as
M. Iew. would say, his priuat Masse, not
enforced but occasioned therby. For $\tilde{y}$ lak
of deuotiō or diligence in $\tilde{y}$ people is not
an Essential, but an Accident of, neither a
cause that goeth before, but $\tilde{y}$ soloweth after, & it doth not make $\tilde{y}$ Sole receiuing,
but is made rather therof. For, to speake
proprely & orderly, if I were asked what
is $\tilde{y}$ cause, why the Priest receiueth alone
I would answer: The Cause is, $\tilde{y}$ he is
not

M. Iew.
maketh
those Cau
ses, which
are not
Causes.

not boūd to haue company, and ꝑ he hath
a godly defire to celebrate ꝗ receiue, and ꝑ
the celebrating of ꝑ Myfteries ꝗ enioying of them, depēdeth not vpō the mutabilitie of ꝑ peoples minde, but vpon cōmiſſion, power autoritie, grace, ꝗ effects,
ꝑ Chriſte hath indued his Prieſtes ꝗ his
Sacramēts wal. And this much concerning M. Iewels Obiection, leaft any
ſhould be troubled with it.   Now to ꝑ
Cōftitution of Iuftinian. Firſt M. Iew.
would haue it conceiued ꝑ Themperour
ſhould find fault wᵗ the numbers ofClerkes, ꝗc. in his time, becauſe of ſome diforder oꝛ miſbehauiour emong them, ꝗ to
to this purpoſe, he thruſteth into his ſentence, by a certain figure of lying ꝗ mocking, Al Idle, al in ftudie & cōtemplacion,
al void from worldly cares. &c.

Faultes
which M.
Iew, maketh in alleaging
Iuftiniās
Conſtitution.

Then would he haue it to be cōceined
ꝑ either there were that wēt about to redꝛeſſe this geare ꝗ could not preuail, oꝛ ꝑ
in dede neither Pope, noꝛ Cardinal, noꝛ
Biſhop cared for it, ſo ꝑ the Emperoꝛ Iu
ſtinian was fain to ftai the encreaſe of them.
Thirdly, he ſo ſpeaketh as though Vicars
Monkes and Prebendaries were noted in
the Conſtitution,   B iiȷ   Laſt

Last of al, which is chiefly to be marked, he is so bold as to say it, that Justinian should be fain to staie the encrease of Clerkes, &c. ye euen in the holy Church of Rome, where, &c. As though the Emperour had ben so loftie, as to take vpon himselfe the office of the Pope, and in the Churches, which are specially vnder the gouernement of the B. of Rome.

Concerning therefore the first & second of these pointes, it is manifest in $\tilde{y}$ Constitution, $\tilde{y}$ the cause of staying the number of Clerkes in Constantinople, & therabout, was not for ani such misliking as heretikes haue now with the number of Priestes which are not al of $\tilde{y}$ best, but only becaule the Reuenewes of $\tilde{y}$ church in Constantinople were not able wel to find them. And therfore (how much the Spiritual Rulers did thinke of $\tilde{y}$ mater, I can tel, but) the Emperour, for the honour of the Clergie, and not for cōtempt of the Degree, wrote vnto Epiphanius, the Archebithop of Cōstantinople about this mater, & no doubt but with his aduise and cōsent, appointed $\tilde{y}$ order which should be taken. which was this, that as

many

many as alreadye, had alowance or liuing in ye great Church or other of Constantinople, should haue it still, but that from thencefurth, no more should be found of the Church, than answered the iust number of the persons, which by the foundation of the Churches had por ions and stipendes to mainteine them.

To the third point then I answer, ye Iustinian speaketh not of Vicars, Monkes and Prebendaries, and that herein M. Iewel shewed a point of an heretical Spite, to geaue such names to the persons whom the Emperour should seeme to bring vnder his lawe, as are at these daies most odious, and to moue suspicion to his Reader, that the number of Monkes were euen in Iustinians tyme abhorred. which is so false, as it is true, that in al that Constitution, there is no mention of Monke or Religious person but only of such as serued in the Cathedrall Church, and other of Constantinople, or the quarters there about.

And by this, it doth wel appeere, that it is to to impudently said (touching the fourth point) Iustinians Constitution

for

foz ſtaieing the increaſe of the number of Clerkes &c. ſhould be made, yea, euen for the very holy Church of Rome. Foz it is directed only to Epiphanius Archbiſhope of Conſtantinople, and all the conſtitution, through, he maketh mentiõ only, *Huius Regiæ Ciuitatis, of this princely Citie,* meaning Conſtantinople, and eſpecially, of the greate Churche there. Of which, he hath ſuche care, and foz which, he taketh ſuch a Special ozder, that he apointeth, how many Pzieſtes, Deacons, and Subdeacons &c. it ſhould haue, and not aboue. As *three skore Prieſies, a hundred Deacons, and Women fortie* (which were not, you may be ſure their wyues, excepte two men and an halfe ſhould haue gone to one) *Subdeacõs ſyneſie. Readers a hundred and ten, Singers fiue and twentie: ſo that al the number of the moſt Reuerende Clerkes of the moſt holy Great Church ſhal conſiſt in foure hundred twenty and ſiue, beſides end at one a hundred of them which are called Oſiarij, that is,* Pozters,

So many then, Juſtinian aloweth to the number of one Church in Conſtanti-

ſantinople, for all his ſtaie made, that
Clerkes ſhould not encreaſe. And that,
becauſe that one Church was wel hable
to find ſo manie, without borowing of
others or laying to pleage oftheir owne.
But with the Churche of Rome or with
Monks, he doth not once meddle, I
ſaie it againe M. Iewel, he doth not
meddle, ſo much as once.

With what Face then and Conſcience referre you this Conſtitution to
the Church of Rome? And in ſo greate
a mater, as the Supremacie is, wherefore abuſe you the Authoritie of the Emperour, in making your Reader conceaue, that Iuſtinian for all that the Papiſtes call the Churche of Rome, Holy,
feared not yet to make a Lawe, that it
ſhould not haue aboue a certaine number of Uicars, Monkes, and Prebendaries, of which it would folowe by likelyhood, that the Emperour tooke him
ſelfe for a worthier Head of the Church,
than the Pope.

A plainer Exaple thã this to ſhew M.
Iewels falſehod, I can not lightly haue:
but that he ſhal not ſay that this is al I

can

Ergo M.
Iew. is
very bold.

can obiect against him, for mistaking or misusing of the Ciuile Lawe, behold an other.

Feud.17:
Tipe at
the first.

The Law saith, Generaliter dictum, Generaliter est accipiendum . The thing that is spoken Generally, must be taken Generally.

Rx.

The Law saith it not, But wheras a Legacie is to be paid *parentibus & liberis, to parents and children* , no mention being made in the Testament , how farre these names should stretch, (For in the name of Parents, Father, Mother, Grandsire, and Grandmother , And in the name of Children, not only the Natural, but the Adoptiue sonnes and daughters, &c. are vnderstanded) The Prætor in this case, answereth that they may be referred vnto al that may be comprehended within the forsaid Names. Hereof the Lawiers gather a Rule, that *The thing that is spoken Generally, must be taken Generally* . But the Law it selfe saith it not .

Now these Rules of the Lawiers witte and collection are not General but indefinite , neither they in al places true, but in certaine . They are, as some call them

them, but *Burchardica*, that is, of the
making of Burchardus the B. of wormes, or (as other say) *Brocardica*, that
is to say, meete Rules for such fine felowes emonge Lawiers, as brokers are
emong the Merchants. They geue a
shew of cunning & learning, as though
he that vseth them, both knewe and
spake law: but in deede none but triflers
and pelters vse them, except they prose-
cute them in their right sense.

For, how sone maie it be Obiected,
by any man, that, if this Rule were true,
no man should be so hardie, as to kill a
lowse: because the law of God saieth, *thou
shalt not kil*, and M. Iewels lawe saieth,
that, the thing that is spokē generally, must
be také generally, vpō which obiection, if
M. Iewel would byd me staie a while,
and to vnderstand the lawe of God, according to the Rule of reason and equity,
and that the killing only of man is for-
bydden, such as procedeth without lawful Authoritie, or tendeth to the breache
of Charitie & c: I would Replie (not so
wisely in dede as it should become a reasonable man, but after as wise manner
and

Exod. 20.

M. Iew.
apposed in
his owne
Rules.

and faſhion, as M. Iewel vſeth) and
ſore, It is commonly ſaid, vbilex non di-
ſtinguit, nos diſtinguere non debemus,
where the law maketh no diſtinction, there
ought we to make no diſtinction. And
therefore awaie with this Sophiſticall
Diſtinction, of lawful and vnlawful killing, and goe to the Text it ſelfe, whiche
ſaith expreſſely: *Thou ſhalt not kil.* And ſo
by this meane which M. Iewel foloweth, an Heretike might be louſie by
Authoritie, nor only of the Law of God,
but the Rule of man: except he would be
ſo merciful as not to kil the vermyne,
but, by ſome other waie put them awaie
from hym.

Now, if M. Iewel knew not ſo much,
as that theſe Rules, which he allegeth,
are not to be vnderſtanded Generally,
although they ſounde Generally: why
would he meddle with that, which he
dyd not knowe? On the other ſide, if he
knewe wel inough, that there are manie
limitations vpon theſe rules, why would
he put that furth to be taken, of his Reader, abſolutely and Generally, which is
not true but in certaine caſes only?

Certainely, ỹ learned in law, whē they
ſpeake

Yew.172.

ſpeake of theſe very rules, they reſtrict the
many waies, which I nede not rehearſe
vnto you, being acquainted very well
with the ciuile Lawiers, or law. Otherwyſe if you were not, you ſhould do wel
to reade *Alciat de verborū ſingnſi. & Nico aus
Euerardas* in his booke intitled *Loci argu-
mentorum legales.* And becauſe one example
againſt you to ope your naughty dealing
in this point, is inough, as alſo, becauſe
the example is better perceined of the common people then the rule, I wil reherſe y
one moſt ſenſible caſe, which the lawiers
them ſelues do put to proue, that y foreſaid
rules which you haue put furth for general, muſt be limited.

*Alciatus
de ver.ſig.
lib 1
Euerard.
in loco a
rationis le
gis ſtricta.*

Suppoſe, y there is an act or law made
by the prince, y *Whoſoeuer ſtryketh A
man within his court, and maketh
him bleede, ſhal leeſe his head, or his
hand for it.* Here, the law is general, in
ſaying whoſoeuer, without exception of
perſons, & therfore (as M. Iewel would
haue it ſeme) it muſt be taken Generally.
It chaunceth then after this, y ſome of y
priuy Chāber lieth ſick of a pleuriſy. And
the

What thin
keth M.
Iew, in
this caſe.

the Phisitiō being at hand, he counseleth
ẏ party to be let bloud. And this being ẏ
most preset remedy : the Barbar cūmeth,
stretcheth the vaine, maketh the Gentle‑
man bleed, and loketh for a good reward:
I aske thē whether the Barbar shal leese
his head or his hand for his labor ? And
who seeth not, that no? Yet the law was
general that whosoeuer strecheth & c. yea
but the Rule is not general, that, the
thing that is generally spoken, must be ta‑
kē generally. For where ẏ cōmon wealth
should take hurte by it, if the lawe were
vnderstanded generally (as in the case of
the Barbar, it is not for the cōmon weal‑
thes profite, that he an Innocent shonld
leese either life or lymme) there must be
vsed necessarily one Restriction (at the
least) of the lawes Generalitie .

I dodger

    wherefore then doth M . Iewel, so
lyke a dodger, come in with such Rules,
as deceaue the simple Reader, and fil his
papers to no purpose ?   wherefore ma‑
keth he Obiections which he knoweth
to haue easie answer? Or why hath he no
care by what meanes he bringeth his
matters to passe , so that for the present,
                   he

he say somewhat to his Aduersarie.
Upon confidence of these general Rules,
which at the first seeme reasonable, he carieth the Readers away with him , into
blinde knowledge , mainteyning his
owne heresies and their errours, by the
superficial wordes of the Ciuile Law, either not atteining to the sense therof, Or
quite leauing it.   And this wil I proue
by a manifest example, so much the more
willingly, because I shal haue in the end
a further Occasion, to shew an other limitation vnto this rule which M. Iewel
would haue to be taken Generally.

D. Harding alleaged out of an Edict
of Iustinians this euident place, for the
Supremacie of the B. of Rome. *Sancimus,*
&c. VVe ordeine, according to the determinati-
ons of the Canons, that the most holy Pope of the
Elder Rome, be formost and chief of al Bishopes.
But it is worth the marking , to heare
how Iustinian bringeth in these wordes.

VVe Decree (saith he) that the holy Ec- In Authēt
clesiastical Rules, vvhich haue ben set forth and De Ecclesi-
established of the foure Councels (of Nice, Tit.
Constantinople, Ephesus, and Chalce-
done) shal stand in stede of Lavves. For vve

receiue the Decrees of the foure Synodes, as the holy Scriptures, and the Rules of them vve obserue as Lawes. And therfore vre ordeine, according to the determinations of them, that the most holy Pope of the Elder Rome, shal be formost and Chiefe of al Priestes ☞ Now vnto this so plaine an Argumēt for ẏ Supremacie, what Answereth M. Iewel? Forsothe

Iew. 141
The question of Rome, the Answer of Constantinople.
Ra.

The Emperour Iustinian had a special Inclinatiō to the Citie of Cōstantinople, for that it was now growē in welth & puissāce, &c. And for that it was as he saith, Mater pietatis nostræ, the Mother of his Maiestie.

wel, here is some cause why he should sauour the Citie of Constantinople, but what is this to Rome? It foloweth.

Iew.

For like Consideration the Emperour gaue out this special Priuilege (vpō which D. Harding groundeth his Argument) in sauour of the See of Rome.

Ra.

Let this also be graunted, that he fauoured Rome as wel as Cōstantinople. But what reason can ye shew, wherefore he should prefer it before Cōstantinople, and set Rome in the first degree & place, and Constantinople in the next? For by al likelyhod, Constantinople being the place where he kept his court & to which most

most resorte was made, concerning ma=
ters of the Empire, if the geuing of Pri=
uilegies vnto See and Bishops had de=
pēded of his fauour only, he would haue
honored first of al, the Patriarche of his
Chief and Imperial Citie.

But is it not a manifest lie, that the
Emperour gaue the Chiefdom to the B.
of Rome, vpon a special inclinatiō which
he had to ẏ Citie? Consider the wordes
of his Edict. what are they? *Vve Ordeine*
(saith the Emperour) *according to the de-*
termination of the Canōs, that the Pope of Rome
be Chief of al Priestes. He folowed then, the
Law of the first foure general Councels,
& not his own Inclinatiō. And he hono=
red ẏ See of Rome with his Edict, not
because he fauored Rome in his special af
sectiō, aboue al other Sees, but because ẏ
former Coūcels which he regarded as ẏ
Scriptures themselues, & as inuiolable
lawes, had so decreed & determined, ẏ the
B. of Rome should be *Primus, First or Chief*
of al Priestes. How impudētly then doth
M. Iew. abuse ẏ Emperors edict, by ma=
king ẏ to be ẏ chief cause therof, which in
dede was not the cause? But let him go
forward.   F ij   And

Note the Lie.

Iew.
To what purpose?

And by the way least any errour happen to grow of this woorde Papa, it behoueth thee, Good Reader, to vnderstand, that Papa in olde times, in the Greek tong, signified a Father. &c. And further in S. Augustines time, & before, the same name was geuen generally to al Bishopes, &c

Ra.

You say truely, and you proue it exceedingly, and if ye would be rather called Pope Iewel, then Bishope Iewel, be it at your owne choyse, and your friendes most wise. But returne, I pray you, againe into the way, and Aunswere the Edict of Iustinian.

Iewel.
Feare, where no cause is shewed.

But to returne to the mater, M. Harding may not of euery thing that he readeth, conclude what he listeth.

Ra.

If he doe, you can with fewer Circumstancies tel him of it. But *Primus omnium Sacerdotum*, is in English the *First and Chiefe of al Priestes*. And he which hath so much geuen vnto him, by General Councels of the Primitiue church, he is higher (I trow) then any of his Felowes. And therefore it is much looked for, that you should Answere directly to the Priuilege.

Iew.

This Priuilege graunted vnto the Bishop

shop of Rome, to be the First of al Priestes was not to beare the whole sway, and to o-uer rule al the world.

Ye speake like a man that were of-fended with tyranny, and ye speake of o-uer ruling. But we thinke not, that, as the chief emong the Brothers, when he hath gotten, Hugonotes, Guses, Loite-rers, Lutherans, Caluinistes, Anabap-tistes, and other diuine felowes inough, aboute him, then he beginneth to ouer rule and ouer run the Counttie, by spoi-ling of Churches, killing of Religions persons, rauishing of holy Uirgins, and doing of other feates of your Gospel: so the Pope may set and let, pul in, plucke out, kil and saue, and do what him listeth vpon a Furie or Brauerie: but that po-wer onely we require to be geauen him, which they acknowleged, that determi-ned him to be *First or Chiefe of al Priestes.* And we aske you, of his Power that he hath to rule ouer al the world, and not of ouer rule al the world. For although y places, to which his Iurisdiction exten-deth it selfe, are not limited, yet his po-wer to rule them is limited: and he that

X iij ouer

Ra.

ouer ruleth any one Countrie, be it neuer
so much his owne, doth more then he
ought to do, by that which is ouer mea=
sure and Rule. Leauing therfore to presse
vs w your odious & slanderous termes,
as though any Catholike were of y opi=
nion, y the Pope might or should play y
part of a Tyran, & care for no law nor rea=
son, but ouer rule al the world, and beare
the whole sway in the world, Answer to y
Authoritie of Justinians Edict, & shew
wherin was the Priuilege graunted vn
to the Bishope of Rome. It was not
(you say) to ouer rule al the world.

Jewel.

But onely in General meetinges, and
Councels to sitte in place aboue al others,
and for auoiding of Confusion, to directe
and order them in their doinges.

Ra.

How proue you this? And re=
member, that you must proue, that the
Priuilege graunted vnto the Bishope of
Rome was to sitte onely aboue others.
&c.

Jew.
**This was
not spoke
for the B.
of Rome.**

The Emperours woordes be plaine,
Prærogatiua in Episcoporú Cösilio, vel extra Conciliú ante alios residendi. A Prerogatiue in the Coúcel of bishops, or without
the

the Councel, to sit in order aboue other.

Oh Desperatenesse. The Emperours woordes (you say) be plaine.
They are so in deede plaine to the eye,
both in your Booke which is wel printed, and in the Code of Parise printe,
where they may be readen without spectacles, except a mans sight be very yll.
But dare you say, that this place perteineth to the Bishoppe of Rome? For of
the Bishoppe of Rome our question is,
whether his Priuilege to be First and
Chiefe of al Priestes, consisted onely
in sitting aboue other, in Generall
meetinges. I wil tel thee (Indifferent Reader) the Sense of these foresaid
woordes, and the Cause of making the
Decree in which thei are found, that thou
maist iudge whether M. Iewel be a fine
and vpright Lawyer.

whiles the Emperour Leo was
gone towardes the Easte, Odactus A
Tyranne, inuaded in the meane tyme
the Churches, and set foorth many Lawes and Statutes, against the Liberties and the Priuilegies of them.

Re.

X iiij   The

The Emperour hereupon made a Law, after the Countrie was diliuered of the Tyranny, that, those thinges being abrogated and taken away, which had ben done against the true Religion of God, al other concerning Churches and Martyrs Chappels should stand in the same state which they were in before his time. And further, he Decreed that it should be vtterly abrogated, what so euer had bene newly brought vp, against the Churches and the Bishopes of them, *Seu de iure Sacerdotalium creationum. seu de expulsione cuiusquam Episcopi à quolibet his temporibus facta, seu de prærogatiua in Episcoporum Concilio, vel extra Concilium ante alios residendi, Either concerning the right of making of Priestes, either the expulsio of any bishop made by any mã at this time, or the prerogatiue of sitting before other, either in the Councel of Biskopes, or vvithout it.*

Cod. de Sacrosact. Eccle. Decernimus.

Consider now (Indifferent Reader) whether the Prerogatiue, of which the Law here speaketh, was meant only of the Bishope of Rome : Or whether y *Emperours vvoo. des* here be plaine, to proue that the Bishope of Rome should sit first in General meetings, whereas there is

no

no mention at al in this place of the B.
of Rome, but only of Acatius, by name,
Patriarche of Constantinople, and of
other Bishoppes in general, which had
taken wronge vnder Odoactus the Tyranne. And whether the B. of Rome
were one of that number, it appeereth
not by any word of the Decree: so that it
is altogether boldely and nothing discreetly said, that the Prerogatiue spoken
of in this place, is plaine for the Popes
sitting aboue other, or that the Popes
Prerogatiue is no more but to sit aboue
al others. It foloweth.

This Prerogatiue in Greeke is called
προεδρία, that is, the Priuilege of the first
place.

So is the saining of a Person,
and making of that to speake, which hath
no sense or tongue, called in Greeke προσ-
ωποποιία: but we require not here of you,
to tel your Countriemen what is Greeke
for this or y thing, but what is y answer
to the Argument that is made, against
you. For let it be so, that προεδρία in
greeke signifieth the Priuilege of the first
place: you do not yet shew vnto vs, that
the

Iew.248
Greeke
for the pri-
uilege of y
first place

Ra.

the Priuilege , spoken of in this Edict of the Emperours, is so called: or that it is meant of the Bishope of Rome, to proue that his Prerogatiue is no more but A προτεία A priuilege of the first place. But you procede out of the purpose and saie,

That these phrases in that tongue be knowen, and Cōmon τὰ προτεκ ἐχει, τὰ δ ἐυτερᾱ, τὰ τριτᾱ. Like as also these in the latine tongue, obtinere primas, secūdas, Tertias, that is , to haue the Preeminence of the first, Second, and Third place.

This woulde serue well , if either we doubted , Or were ignorant of these phrases, or if the declaring of them perteined any point to the question . And yet I saie vnto you, that , Obtinere primas , or τὰ τρωτᾱ ἐχει, is , not only to haue the first place , but also, to wynne the best game , Or to haue the Chiefeste parte in any Feare or Acte , Or to beare the highest Office , and so furthe . So that, to your mater of the Place , they doe not serue necessarily . And if by Obtinere Primas, this only thinge were meant, to sitte in the First Place , yet should not this proue, that the Edicte

e

of the Emperour, in whiche you shewe not that the selfe same Phrase is vsed, doeth plainely make for it: That the Popes Prerogatiue is no greater, than to sitte first at Generall meetinges. For this is the question, and not what, Obtinere Primas, or Secundas, signifieth in good Latine. And to this we looke for your Answer.

But you saie (as though you had proued so much) in further confirmation thereof,

And that the Emperour Iustinian meant ONLY thus, and none OTHERWISE, it is manifeste euen by the selfe same place, that M. Harding hath here alleged.

Mary Syr that is worth the bearing: but marke thou (Indifferent Reader) M. Iewels wordes ONLY, and NONE OTHERWYSE. For except I be fowly deceaued, he wil not proue so much as he pretendeth. But let vs heare the Emperour, and M. Iewels Comment vpon him.

Sancimus &c. We ordeine.

Your &c. Here, first of all, hath no Place: For it putteth these wordes out

Iew. 24?
you dos it none it.

R2.

Iew.

R3.

out, which are much to the mater. And they are theſe: *Sancimus ſecundum Canonum definitiones, vꝫ ordaine according to the determinations of the Canons, that, &c.*

By which it appeereth, that Iuſtinian dyd no moꝛe but exquute the foꝛmer Decrees, and was not hymſelfe the Authour oꝛ Geauer, of the ſingular Pꝛiuilege which is due to the See of Rome. And nowe lette M. Iewel goe foꝛewarde.

We ordeine, & cæt. that the Pope (Reade Sanctisſimum, moſte holy) of the Elder Rome ſhalbe (Reade, is) the firſt of al the Prieſtes, and that the moſte holy Archebiſhope of Conſtantinople, which is named Newe Rome, haue the ſeconde place: It foloweth in the Decree. After the holy Apoſtolike See of the Elder Rome.

But what concludeth M. Iewel hertof? It foloweth.

Hereby it is plaine, that this Priuilege ſtandeth ONLY in placing the B. of Rome in the firſt Seate aboue others.

It is ſo plaine, that no man ſeeth it. Be thou Iudge, Indifferent Reader: Yea lette any Pꝛoteſtant in al the woꝛld

woulde tell Trueth and lye not. Doth
he find in the foresaied wordes of Iustinians Decree, this worde ONLY? Doth
he find, that the Prerogatiue of the B.
of Rome, is declared by the Emperour,
to stand in none other thinge, but in sitting first?

    A worthie matter in deede, for An
Emperour to see furth Seates for Bisshoppes, if he haue no further respecte,
than vnto the Seate. But first, he declareth the Bishope of Rome to be *Primum omnium Sacerdotum* that is, to be *Chief
of Priests,* and not I trow to sit only in the
best Chaire. Then, he apointeth the
Bishope of Constantinople to haue the
Second place. But wherein? Ouer Seates,
Or ouer Priestes? Verely he spake not
of Seates but of Priestes, in respect of
which, he saieth, let the Bishope of Constantinople haue τὰς δευτέρας τάξιν that
is, as M. Iewel limiteth it, The seconde
place, but as the Trueth is, ye maie englishe it, the Second Dignitie, Or wor-
shipe. For the worde τάξις signifieth,
A rome, An Order, An Office, A Dignitie, A Degree, and A place, not only to
                          sit

sitte first in, but to Goe, to Stande, to
fight to Speake, to Determine, or to
doe what so euer it be, worth the speaking.

And therefore (M. Iewel) hath in
Who saith this place, twyse togeather abused the
M. Iew. decree of Iustinian: first, restricting that,
beth not vnto sitting in a place, which was spo-
lye er ken of Prerogatiue ouer Priestes. And
then in saying, that the priuilege consisted
only in sitting in the first Seate, wheras
this terme only, or any other word to like
effecte is not at al in the Decree.

Iew. 242 But I beseech thee, Gentle Reader,
weigh wel the wordes that folowe in the
same Decree.

Ra. And I beseech thee also, Gentle Reader, to weigh them wel.

Iew. It soloweth immediatly. We ordeine
that the most holy Archebishope of Iustiniana the first whiche is in our Countrie,
shal haue for euer vnder his iurisdictiõ the
Bishops of the prouinces of Dacia, Dania,
& c. and that he, in the prouinces subiect
vnto hym, shal haue the place of the Apostolike See or Rome.

Ra. But what of this?

Here

Here we see, the Bishoppe of Iustiniana sette in as high Authoritie, and power within his own Iurisdiction, as the B. of Rome within his.

But by whome was he sette in so high Authoritie? By the Emperour? And who gaue the Emperour such power? Or was he so priuileged by the Pope? Yea surely by the Pope, if any Authoritie were lawfully taken and exercised. But so much doth not appeere by the Decree. Yes verely doth it. But M. Iewel taketh his vantage, and mangleth Decrees at his pleasure. For thus it foloweth in the same. that the Bishoppe of Iustiniana shal haue in the Prouinces subiect vnto him, ý place of the Apostolik See. *Secundum ea quæ definita sunt a Sanctissimo Papa Vigilio, according to that which hath ben determined by the most holy Pope Vigilius.*

More Typing of sentences, that is, more of M. Iewel's figure tine Ellipsis.

See then, if the Bishope of Iustiniana, for al that the Emperor honoured that Countrie so much, if he receaued so greate Authoritie from the Pope: how much was the Pope aboue him, ý gaue him ý authoritie? Could ý Pope subiect vnto a newe Bishope the Prouinces of

Da-

Dacia, Dania, Dardania, Misia, and Panno-
nia? Or exempt him from the Iurisdiction
of his Metropolitan, or primitiue, except
in dede his authoritie had ben vniuersal?
Yet such priuileges gaue the Pope vnto
the B. of Iustiniana, and the Emperour
was not the doer in it, but y Executour
only of the Popes determination.

Note also and see (M. Iewel) that
it is not in this decree, that the B. of Iustiniana, shal haue within his owne Iurisdiction, as high authoritie as the Bishop
of Rome within his, there is no such comparison made, but only that he shal haue
within his Iurisdiction, the place of the
Apostolike See of Rome. And so haue many of the Popes Legates, in the prouincies vnto which they be directed, but
none was euer yet so folish, as to gather
hereof, y the Pope therfore cā do no more
than his Legate. For as y is true, in such
cases as the Pope permitteth vnto y Legates ordinance: so absolutely it is most
false, because the Pope may when he wil
depose his Legate, or abbridge his Au-
tority, or send an other to gouern with
him, but no such thing may be exequuted against the Pope.   If

Desw ful
or t.l te
head?

If therefore the B. of Iustiniana do neuer so muche enioye the Priuilegies graunted vnto him by the B. of Rome, let him take them as Priuileges, not as Canons: Let him acknowledge himself to supplie the Place of the Bisshoppe of Rome within his owne Prouincies, and not to sit, as it were, in his owne proper and ordinarie Place: Let him gene place to the B. of Rome, if he should persostally come within his Iurisdiction, and let him not crake of it, that he hath as high Authoritie within his Iurisdiction, as the B. of Rome within his. For if he doe, Uigilius the Pope that gaue him such prerogatiue, may pull it away agayne from him, And M. Iewels argumene shalbe vtterly dasshed, that thinketh, the Priuilege of the Apostolike See, graunted to any particular Bisshoppe ouer his country, to derogate from the Authority of the Apostolike See which is in Rome, And whiche hath Iurisdiction ouer all Bisshoppes in Christendome.

Nowe one place more, and so we shall end this Chapiter. M. Iewel goeth further and sayeth.

2 I

In

The third Boke

Jew. 242

In lyke sorte, the Emperour Iustinian saieth: Ecclesia vrbis Constantinopolitanæ Romæ veteris prærogatiua lætatur. The Church of the Citie of Constantinople, enioyeth now the prerogatiue of Rome the Elder.

Ra.

Let me be answered then in one question. You said, not twenty lines before, that the prerogatiue of the Bishoppe of Rome consisted only, in sitting in the first place, at general meetings. If therefore the B. of Constantinople haue the same Prerogatiue that the B. of Rome, who shal sit first I praie you? Or shal they sit one in an others lap? Or, shal one of them stand whiles the other sitteth? Or shal the prerogatiue of the B. of Rome be interpreted, to signifie some other thing byside the sitting only in the first place?

How can it be Answered?

For, if the prerogatiue, of the Pope be to sit only first, and if the B. of Constantinople haue the like prerogatiue as the B. of Rome, he must likewise sit first: Ergo, Iustinians Constitution, that the B. of Constantinople, should sit in the secōd place, is void. Ergo M. Iewel by one law (through his blind interpretation) doth destroy an other. Surely this alone doth

doth proue sufficiétly, that you huddle vp
Constitntions one vppon an other, to
make a shew only of great learning, and
not becanse either you vnderstand the
law , Or speake after it, or seeke to make
the trueth plaine and euident .

But let vs consider the place it selfe.
The Church (you saie) of Constantinople
enioyeth the priuilege of the Elder Rome:
But what priuilege is that? To Rule the
whole world? To cal general Councels?
To Confirme them ? To disproue them?
To increase the Iurisdiction of Bishops
or Patriarches, and to diminish it againe
as it shal be profitable for the Church of
Christ ?

The B. of Rome , is hable to geaue
vnto any B, in al the world, as great prerogatiue ouer his diocese, as himself hath
ouer Italie, like as Uigilius the Pope
gaue to the B. of Iustiniana: but is any
Archebishope in al ý world hable to geue
an other , either the Prerogatiue of the
Church of Rome, either the Prerogatiue
which himselfe hath from the Church of
Rome, without asking of leaue of ý B. of
Rome ?   No surely, the Effect can not

worke vpward towardes the cause, or worke so excellently downeward, as the cause: neither the Bisshops of Constantinople or Justiniana, taking their Prerogatiues from Rome, can endue others with like Priuileges, without consent of the Bisshop of Rome.

Therefore, although the Bisshop of Constantinople hath the Prerogatiue of the Citie of Rome, it foloweth not, that the Bisshop of Rome is nothing superiour to the Bisshop of Constantinople. And if þ Lord President in Wales should haue geauen vnto him all the Prerogatiues of the Kings Court in England, it foloweth not, that the King and he are Hayle felowes wel mette for euer after. And Christ our Sauiour although he said vnto his Apostles As my father sent me so I send yow, geauing thereby vnto them as greate Prerogatiue as himselfe had, yet he meant not, that þ Apostles should think themselues as good as their head, euen in those thinges which they should doe as wel as Christ.

M. Jewel therefore doth very vnreasonably conceiue of the Law, that the

Popes

Popes Supremacie was not acknow=
ledged, because, the Communicating of
his Prerogatiue with some other Bis=
shops, is found expressed in the Law.

But it wil be replied, that *Genera-*
liter dictum generaliter est accipiendum,
The thing that is spoken generally must be
taken Generally. I answer: this Rule
fayleth, when by other expresse texte of
the Law, that which seemeth to be spo=
kē Generally in one place, is restricted &
limited in an other. For in the next title
before this of which we speak, the Empe=
rour sayth to ȳ B. of Rome. *Omnes Sacer-* De Sūma
dotes, vniuersi Orientalis tractus, & subijcere & Trinit. &
vnire Sedi vestræ Sanctitatis properauimus. *Vve* fid. Cath.
haue made speede, both to subiecte and to vnite l. Nos red-
vnto the See of your Holines, all the Priestes of dentes.
the Vvest partes. Againe in the same law,
a litle after. *Vve vvil not suffer (sayeth Iu-*
stinian) that any thing, vvhich perteineth to
the state of Churches, although that vvhich is
in controuersie be vndoubted and manifest, shall t
not also come to the knovvledge of your Holines,]
Quæ Caput est omnium Sanctarum Ecclesiarum,
Vvhich is the Head of al holy Churches.

Let the Bishope then of Constantinople enioy the Prerogatiue of the Citie of Rome, in as large and Generall sense as M. Iewel wil, yet this must be prouided for, first of al, that the Prerogatiue which the B. of Constantinople shal enioye, doe not contrary the former law, which *Subiecteth al Priestes of the vvest vnto his holynes.* And which confesseth him to be *head ouer al Churches.*

Thus haue I sufficiently and manifestly proued, that M. Iewel hath abused the Canon Law. The Lawiers themselues haue more to say vnto him for his impudencie, if he be so impudent as euer to shew his face before them.

And nowe to the Olde Fathers, and Doctoures.

How M. Iewel hath abused the Auncient Fathers.

IT is incredible, how M. Iewel hath abused the Doctours. Incredible (I meane) not, in respect of Protestantes which thinke so wel of him, that they beleue

leue no one euident vntrueth to be within all his Replye: but of Catholikes,
which knowing the cause that he defen-
deth, to be vtterly false, may iustly suspect euery witnesse, that he bringeth in
for his Doctrine, And which hauing already taken him in manifest corrupting
of witnesses, cannot but know him for
one that loketh suspitiously, whē so euer
he is about Auncient Fathers. Yet (I assure thee Indifferent Reader) the Catholikes themselues did not thinke, that
any man would so haue corrupted true
Sentences, as he hath done: Or so ofte
haue folowed such vnlawfull craftes, as
are not once to be vsed of honest men.

But these, you will say, are but
wordes: let vs therefore come, to the
thinges themselues. And first, concerning such Illations of M. Iewels, as he
vseth in geuing of the cause or proufe of
his sayinges, He applieth thereto, the
Testimonies of Auncient Fathers, so
loosely and so disagreeably, as if a man
would saie: The waters of Bath are
exceding good against the Ache in the
Ioyntes. And so the Prophete saieth:

omnes

Omnes sitientes venite ad aquas, Al ye that be a thirst, come to the waters. Yea ᛗ. Iewels Applications doe worse agree with the premisses. For his position, lightly, is heretical or erroneous, and his Authoritie for it, is no more proper vnto it, than the foresayed sentence of Esaie serueth to the commendation of the Bathes in England. For proufe hereof I wil choose but one place, in which, for establishing of his Assertion, he bringeth one vppon an other very thicke, foure Auncient Doctours togeather, Of all which there is not one that serueth his purpose.

Ihon.230
You proue it not by a 2 of the testimonis y folow.

M. Hardinges Athanasius saieth, Power to bind and loose is geauen to the holy See of Rome, And yet the old Catholike Fathers could neuer vnderstand any such speciall Priuilege.

Ra.

Marke now, Indifferent Reader, whether the places whiche ᛗ. Iewell wil allege, do proue any such thing at al.

S. Cyprian abused.

Iew.
Faultes escaped in

S Cyprian saieth: Quàmuis Dominus Apostolis omnibus &c. The Lord (read, And although our Lorde) after his Resurrection

rection gaue like power vnto his Apostles
(**Reade**, all his Apostles) yet to declare
vnitie, he disposed by his Authoritie, the
Original of vnitie (**Reade**, of the same vnitie)beginning of one: The rest of the Apostles were euen the same that Peter was,
endewed with like felowship, both of honour and of power (**here doth M. Iewel
make a full pointe , yet it foloweth in the
same very sentence**) But the Original cometh of vnitie, to declare that the Church
is one.

*ỹ trãsla-
ting of S.
Cyprian.*

**In this testimonie of S. Cyprian, those
wordes(And although)which M. Iewel
left out in the beginning of the sentence,
are first to be considered , as depending
of the sentences, which immediatly went
before, And opening the question which
now we hane in hand .　For after S.
Cypriane had declared , that the Deuil,
seeing the Idols and Temples which he
occupied before , to be forsaken and lefte
void, through ỹ increase of the Faithfull,
conuerted his craft to deuising of Schismes and Heresies , by which he might
ouerturne the Faith** , corrupte the trueth,
and cut or diuide vnitie. **After this he inferreth**

Ra.

Cypr. de Simplici= tate prae= lat.

fereth: *Hoc eò fit, fratres dilectiss. dum ad verita= tis originem non reditur, nec caput quaeritur, nec magistri coelestis doctrina Seruatur* : This moste deere brethren, (**vnderstand, that Heresies are set abroad**) doth therefore come to passe, for that vve return not vnto the original of truth And for that an Head is not fought for, nor the Doctrine of our heauenly Master is obserued.

Now becaufe euery man perceiueth not the force of this saying, and diuerse would haue it better opened and expres= fed vnto them, He addeth : *Probatio est ad fidem facilis compendio veritatis,* that is, The proufe hereof, to make thee beleue it, is eafy, be= caufe of the compendicufnes of the truth. **And how is that? It foloweth,** *Loquitur Do= minus ad Petrum, &c.* Our Lord fpeaketh to Pe= ter, I tel thee (faith he) that thou art Peter, and vpon this Peter (**or Rocke**) I vvil builde my Church, and the gates of hel shalnot ouer= come it. Vnto the vvil I geue the keyes of the kingdome of Heauens, and thofe thinges that thou shalt bind in earth, shal be boûd in the hea= uens alfo, and vvhatfoeuer thou shalt loofe vp= on earth, shal be loofed alfo in the Heauens. And vnto the fame (**Peter**) after his refurre= ction he faith: feede my sheepe.

By

By these wordes then it is mani=
feſt, what is, *Original*, *Head*, and *Doctrine*
of our heauenly Maiſter, that is, to the for=
ſaking of which, Sainct Cyprian im=
puteth the Proceedinges of the Diuel,
and of Hereſies. Verely no other, than
that, which our Sauiour by the foreſaid
expreſſe Scriptures, gaue to S. Peter.

But now, heere ariſeth a greate
doubt and queſtion, that S. Peter can
not wel be the Heade, becauſe euery one
of the Apoſtles, was as great in Power
as he. And this in deede is the Argu=
ment, that M. Jewel maketh, out of S.
Cyprian, againſt the Supremacie.
Which if Sainct Cyprian hadde not eſ=
pied and Anſwered, then ſhould M. Je=
wel eaſily be pardoned: But now, what
an intolerable kinde of foule dealing is
this, to take an Obiection out of an
Olde Father, and either for Haſt, Or
Negligence, Or Craftines, Or Deſpe=
ratnes, to let go the right anſwer vnto it?

For, concerning the Obiection,
Sainct Cyprian thus withſtandeth it,
ſaiyng: *And although he gaue after his re=*
ſurrection, lyke powrer vnto al his Apoſtles, &c.
yet

Note vn=
reaſonable
foule dea=
ling.

yet to declare vnitie, he difpofed by his Authority, the Original of the fame vnitie, begining of one .

By the Obiection then it feemeth, that no moze accompt fhould be made of S. Peter, then of the reft of the Apoftles, which feuerally was as greate in power as he : But by the Aunfwere , made with this Aduerfatiue *Tamen, Yet,* it is manifeft, that, notwithftanding the equalitie emong ẏ Apoftles, S. Peter yet was ẏ Firft and the Head among them. Foz Chzift difpofed by his Authozitie (faith S. Cypzian) *the Original not of vnitie* (as you mangle it M. Jewel) but, *of the fame vnitie* (which vndoubtedly was in the Apoftles) *beginning of one* , which is S. Peter .

Ys not this mangling of fentéces?

As in the Sentence folowing, moze manifeftly appeereth, to the further opening of S. Cypzians right meaning, and your falfe dealing . Foz the one halfe of the Sentence is this : *In deede the reft alfo of the Apoftles vvere the fame that Peter vvas : endevved vvith like fellovrfhip, honour, and povver :* This half M. Jewel you reft vpon, and build your Conclufion, that one of them had no moze Pziuilege than

am

an other . And why interpreted you no further? Is the sentence or Sense, (thinke you) at an ende, when you haue your purpose? Doth not S. Cyprian Interpret, Correct, Amend, or Determine it with an Aduersatiue *yet*, saying (least any mã should through his former words set lesse by S. Peter or his Chaire) *But yet the Original commeth from vnitie , that the Church may be shewed to be one ?* And what other thing is this to say, but that, notwithstanding it to be true, that the Apostles were endewed with like honour & power as S. Peter was , yet no manne ought to gather heereof, that there was no Order among them, Or that one Bishope now hath as large and absolute Authoritie as an other . But this rather must folowe , that because schismes and Heresies doe grow apase , *vvhere no Original or Head is sought for or regarded*, And because it should be perceiued , that the Church is One, in that it cõsisteth of one *Head*, vnto whome al the rest, were they neuer so high or felow like, must be referred : therefore Christ, *by his Authoritie, disposed the Original of that vnitie*, & endewed ed S.Peter with a singular Prerogatiue, that he shoulde be that *One* in the Church, from whom whosoeuer departed, should not be of the Church.

And note wel the Cause, why the beginning must rise of *One, vt Ecclesia vna monstretur, that the Church might be shewed to be one.* Why? Should it not be One, though in euery Diocese, through the world, euery seueral Bishop were Chief therein? No surely, by S.Cyprian, it should not be. But, in that the *Head* thereof is but *one* the vnitie of her doth folow necessarily. How doth it folow? Mary, whosoeuer holdeth not with this Head, he is not in the Church, and so must none remaine within her, but the Catholike & obedient Christians. How can they but agree then al in one Head, if they mind to continue in the Church, wheras the departure from him, is to take an other Church, besides that, whose special marke is *Vnitie* in one Head. This conclusion then standing, that S.Peter was set, by the Autoritie of Christ, in the first place, was that no special Priuilege, trow you? Or was he First, to that intent oly, that in reckening vp the Apostles, men should know where

The vnitie of the Church, is moued by the one Head thereof.

Simple conclusions

where to begin? Or, that in their mee∍
tings together, he should sitte first? Or
speake first? Or subscribe first? How
simple things are these for the wisedome
of God to think of? And how litle anai∍
lable to the preseruing of the Churche in
Vnitie, if no further Preeminence were
geuen him?

And againe, if the B. of Romes au∍
thoritie now, as S. Peters was then,
were of no more force, yet beeing of so
much, if other would sit before him, Or
speake before him in any Councel, should
they not be Offenders against the ordi∍
nance of God? How can it be otherwise,
whereas he appointed by his Authoritie
the Original of Vnitie to begin of One? Suppose
then, that some one transgresseth this or∍
der, who shal reproue him? If none,
how vnreasonable is it, to set a law, and
not to include therby an authority to pu∍
nish the transgressor of the Law? If any:
who more worthy of that Office then the
Chief Bishope? Ergo there was in S.
Peter, a proper Authoritie ioyned to
that dignitie of his first place (which M.
Ie. graunteth vnto him) by which he had
power to cotroll them, y̆ should or wold

The Pri∍
uilege of
S. Peter
must be
more then
to sitte or
be
first.

resist that Primacie of his in how smal thing so euer it consisted . And if there were such Authority, Ergo, some special Priuilege of Binding or Losing, which no other of the Apostles had . Except ye wil be so mad as to thinke, that in cōtrolling of a fault committed against any Excellent Person, his Inferiour should be Iudge in the mater, and bind or loose at his wil or discretion.

I leaue it therefore as most manifest, that notwithstanding the Apostles were equal in felowshipp of honour and power, with S. Peter, *yet the Original of Vnitie*, was appointed by our Salniour him selfe, to begin of S. Peter only, and none other. And this his preeminence (make you it as litle as you can) requiring A Proportional Authoritie to be graunted vnto him, for the defense therof against al disdaine or disobedience that might be procured or vsed against it: he had, without al doubt, some Prerogatiue of Iurisdiction aboue any other, and by Consequence some more power, then the rest of the Apostles had .

And this I speak with the least, because

cause our Aduersaries be contentious, knowing in dede, ý if J would preſſe thē further with this Teſtimonie of S. Cyprian, they could not honeſtly denie, but ſuch a wiſdome of God, and prerogatiue of S. Peter was expreſſed, in erecting one Head and beginning, as ſhould keepe the Church in vnitie, And be a ſure and certaine way for al them to take, whiche liue in danger of hereſies. which can not be ſo meane a thing, as to ſit firſt only in a place, or ſpeake only before other, without further ſuperioritie aboue other: but enough is alreadie ſaid, both to declare ý trueth of S. Cyprians words, & the falſehoode of M. Jewel in abuſing them.

Origene abuſed.

Origene ſaieth: An verò ſoli Petro & c. Iew 239. What, hath Chriſt geauen the keies of the kingedome of heauen, vnto Peter only? and ſhall no holy man els receaue them? This ſaieng, *To thee vvil I geue the keies of the kingdome of heauen*, is cōmon alſo to the reſt.

In a miſti cal ſenſe this is true, not in the literal.

To whom the reſt? Verely to euery good man, which ſhal haue it reueled vnto him, that Chriſt is the ſonne of the lyuing God. How thinke you then M.

R a.

　　　　　Z i　　Iew

Abſurdities folo-
wing vpõ
M. Iew-
els ſenſe.

I.Cor.12.

Eph.4.

Iewel, hath euery good and faithfull
Chriſtian in the world, as great & as ſpecial authoritie as S. Peter? If it be ſo:
how doth S. Paule ſay, that, *God hath a-*
pointed in his Church firſt Apoſtles, then Euan-
geliſtes, Thirdly doctours &c. How ſaith he in
an other place, that, *Chriſt hath geauen to his*
Church ſome to be Apoſtles, ſome Prophetes, other
Euangeliſtes, and other to be Paſtours and Do-
ctours. Or how is not the Subdeacon as
great in authoritie as the Prieſt, and the
Prieſt as the Archebiſhope? Yea the common laie men or women ſtedfaſtly con-
feſſing Chriſt, how haue not they, ý keies
of ý kingdome of heauen in their hands,
euen as the Apoſtles or S. Peter himſelf
had? For Origene pronounceth without
exception, that, to haue the keies of the
kingdome of heauen, is promiſed to al
that haue it reueled vnto them, *that Chriſt*
is the Sonne of the Liuing God.

If therfore this ſenſe can not ſtand, we
muſt, of neceſſitie ſeke an other. And conſider in what ſort Origen ſaith, the keies
of the kingedome of heauen to be geuen,
not only to S. Peter, but to the reſt alſo
of good & godly men. But nothing more
eaſy to be found. For Origen in ý place

as

(as his maner is) gathereth a myſtical or morall ſenſe of the literal and plaine hiſtorie: Not by denying the Hiſtorie, but by applying it to edificatiõ. Like as ſ. Paul, writing vnto the Galathians, & declaring vnto thẽ, ÿ the two ſonnes of Abraham, the one borne of Agar ÿ ſeruant, the other of Sara the free womã, ſignified the two Teſtamentes: meant not to make vs beleue, that there was not ſuch a man, as Abraham is deſcribed to haue ben, or that ſuch real and corporal promiſes were not made vnto him, as the Scriptures doe teſtifie, but out of the Literal hiſtorie, he gathereth a myſtical ſenſe, knowing that vnto the Fathers of the old law, al things chaunced in figures, the Trueth of which is reueled by Chriſt vnto his Church.

Gala. 4.

1. Cor. 10.

Now, that Origen doth ſo as I do ſay, it is plaine by his owne words. For after he had ſhortly gone ouer ÿ text, of Chriſts queſtiõ to his Apoſtles (*vvhõ do men ſay the ſonne of mã to be*) & the Apoſtles anſwering therunto: then entring, as it were, into a new mater, & leuing ÿ hiſtorie ÿ he might come to ÿ moralitie, he ſaith: *Fortaſsis autẽ quod Simõ Petrus reſpõdes dixit, tu es Chriſtus fi-*

Orig. tra. 1. in Mat.

Z ij *lius*

lius dei viui, si dixerimus ita quéadmodū dixit Pe-
trus non à carne & sanguine nobis reuelatū, sed à
luce quæ illuxit cordi noſtro, à patre qui eſt in cœ-
lis, sumus & ipsi quod fuit Petrus &c. Novv perchaunce, that vvhich Peter anſvvered and saied,
Thou art Chriſte the Sonne of the lyuing God , If
vve shal likevvyse saie as Peter did, being reueled
vnto vs not of fleshe and blud , but of the light
vvhich lighteth our hart frō the Father vvhich is
in heauē, vve also are that vvhich Peter vvas. & c.

And afterward he saieth, that if we
confesse as Peter dyd, it shall be saied
vnto vs , Thou arte Peter, and so furth as
it foloweth in the Gospel . So that the
Church is builded, vpon euery such good
man, and the keies of the Kingdome of
Heauen , are geauen vnto him, and the
gates of hel shal not preuaile againſt him.

And againe, if any man say to Chriſt:
Thou art Chriſt the sonne of the lyuing God: Non
ex carnis aut sanguinis reuelatione , sed patris
qui in cœlis eſt , consequetur ea quæ dicta sunt, vt
euangelij quidem scriptum habet , ad illum Pe-
trum , vt verò docet illius ſpiritus ad quemuis
qui talis factus fuerit, qualis erat ille Petrus. That
is, If any say to Chriſt , thou art the sonne of the
lyuing God, not by reuelation of flesh and bloud,

Origen
himselfe
putteth a
difference
betwene
the Literal
and Myſti-
cal sense of
the fore-
said place.

but

but of the father vvhich is in heauē, he shal attain vnto those things vvhich (as the vvriting of the Gospel hath it) vvere spoken of to that Peter: but as the sprite of him, or thereof, teacheth vnto vvhomsoeuer you vvil, vvhich shal be made such a one as Peter vvas. It is plaine then by these wordes of Origene, that he setteth a difference betwene the Literal sense, and the Spiritual, And, that according to the text of the Scripture, *Thou art Peter*, was spoken vnto that singular Apostle S. Peter. But according to a Mystical or Spiritual sense, it is and may be spoken, vnto any good and Faithful Christian. Yet euery one of them shal not be an Apostle, Or haue power to forgeaue sinnes or exercise Iurisdiction.

This is therefore much to be noted, and to be abhorred in M. Iewel. He taketh the wordes of A Doctour, which in the Doctours owne sense are true and godly, and draweth them to his owne Interpretation, in which they are moste false & vnreasonable. So haue rebels don hertofore, as ye rebels of Germanie, saing out of the Scriptures, *Bretherne ye be called vnto libertie*, and gathering ther vpon that

Note wherein consisteth M. Iewels abusing of Origen.

X iij the

the Nobilitie if their Countrie must not be suffered to haue them in Subiection. Yet, the Scripture spake not of the deliuery from al Homage and Seruice, due to our Lords, but of our deliuerance from Synne, Death, and the Deuill. we are called also in the Scriptures, Kinges and Priestes. And true it is in a Mysticall Sense, concerning the power and grace, geauen vnto vs to subdue our Affections, And to Offer vp Prayers and Thankes vnto God. But if any lewde Hugonotes or Buses, would so conster this true saying, that they would haue no external Priesthood nor Soueraincty of any one man in any Countrie aboue an other: who seeth not, ẏ not only pulling downe of Churches and diuiding of the goodes emong them, wil folow: but contempt also of Kings and Princes, & a general confusion & vnrulynes ouer al?

The greater is M. Jewels faulte, which knowing (except he haue vtterly lost his witte) that it is to the present daunger of the common Reader, to haue the words of any Doctour alleaged vnto him, without the plaine declaration how they

2.Petr.2. (margin)

Do so no more M. Jew, and repent for this. (margin)

they are taken: doth, for al this, suffer, yea
teach him to beleue, that Literally, which
is true only mystically or moraliy . As,
that S . Peter had no greater Priuilege
than any other , because, after a spiritual
vnderstanding , it is said vnto euery one
that confesseth Christ accordingly , Thou
art Peter. After which rate, our Ladie only, should not be the singural and natural
Mother of Christ , because whosoeuer
doth y wil of his Father, is his Mother.

S. Cyril abused.

S. Cyril saieth: Apostolis & eorum in
Ecclesijs Successoribus plenam concessit
potestatem, Christ gaue ful power vnto the
Apostles , and others that succeded them
in the Churches.

What conclude you hereby? That euery
Bishoppe in the world hath a ful power,
in al things, as the Apostles had ? It is
against al law and reason . For the Apostles , euery of them, might (I graunt)
without further askinge of any Leaue
Preach and Celebrate, in any place of the
world: but that it is so with the Bishops
that now gouerne the world, the borders
which are apointed to euery ones diocese,

I iij And

Iew. 239
He falsi-
fieth the
place, for
is no men-
tion of po-
wer.
Ra.

And the Correction, due and ready for them whiche without license obteined, meddle in an other mans Office, doe plainely proue the contrarie.

And therefore vndoubtedly, if you wil haue this place vnderstanded particular∣ly of euery Bishope, and saie, that God hath geauen eche of them, ful power: the practise not only of al Christendome, but of your owne congregation, wil confute you, In which there is difference betwen the Superintendent of Sarum and of Canterburie. But, if you wil refer the gift of ful power, vnto some singular suc∣cessours of the Apostles, then is this text nothing preiudicial, to the Supremacie of the Bishope of Rome, in whom alone, when ful power resteth, the saying of S. Cyril may be verified. For what they haue, it is true to say, that the Apostles successours haue it.

And this alone were inough to an∣swer: But now I say further, That S. Cyril hath not as you report. For in re∣peting shortly the Spiritual sense, which was to be gathered out of those two actes of Christ, the one, when he passed ouer the

the See of **Tyberias** (signifying therby, the forsaking of the **Iewes**) and wente vp againe into an hil with his disciples: The other, when he cast vp his eyes, and beholding a number of people comming toward him, fedde them to the ful, with fiue loaues and two fishes, of this mira=culous fact of our **Sauiour** he saith: *Qua-re, vetera & noua scripturæ mandata, fidelibus per Apostolos apposita intelligebamus, cuius my-sterij plenā & Apostoli & eorum in Ecclesijs suc-cessores gratiam possidebunt:* By vvhich thing (that is by **Christes** feeding of fiue thou=sand with fiue loaues and two fishes) *Vve vnderstand the Olde and Nevv Commaun-dementes of the Scripture, to be sette by the A-postles before the faithful. The full grace of vvhich ministerie, both the Apostles and their successours in the Churches shal possesse.*

Cyril in Ioan. l.3. cap. 20.

    Conferre now (**Indifferent Rea-der**) these thinges togeather. **M. Ie-wel** telleth thee (as out of **S. Cyril**) of a *ful povrer*: **S. Cyril** speaketh of no more than a *ful grace*. **M. Iewel** by this *ful povrer*, would haue thee thinke, that in the authoritie of binding and loosing, no **Bishop** is higher then an other: **S. Cyril** by

Is not this wic-kedly don of M. Ie-wel?

by his *ful grace* comprehendeth the grace of preaching only, & instructing of other. The *ful grace* which S. Cyril nameth, is so cōfessed to be in ý Apostles & their successours, ý yet he signifieth not, whether al should haue it equally, or som be therein before their fellowes, or whether the heades of the Church, should apoint the Preachers (which is nothing cōtrary to a Supremacie) or euery man vse his gift before he be licenced, which were altogether out of order: M. Iew. concludeth *of that ful povver* (which he maketh S. Cyril to speake of) not only ý such a *povver* was in the Apostles, & is in their Successors, but also that it is *ful* in euery one of their successours, & that the B. of Rome hath not ý Supremacie. For which his handeling of ý auncient Fathers, if he may yet escape ý note of a Falsifier, then go not the proceedings forward by indifferencie, but with hatred of the contrary side, & with euident iniurie. And now soloweth immediatly the abusing of an other Doctor.

Great ods betweene M. Iew. and S. Cyril.

S. Basil abused.

Iew. 239, Basilius de And S. Basil saith: Christ appointed Peter to be Pastour of his Church after him: And

And consequently gaue the same power vnto al Pastours and Doctours. A toke wherof is this, that al Pastours do equally binde
and loose as wel as he.

vita Soli-
taria.c. 23
quemada
modii ille.
Ra.

First let vs see vpon what occasion, &
to what end, these words are spoken. S,
Basiles purpose in y̆ whole Chapiter out
of which those words are take was, to exhort vnto obediēce, such as liued in solitarines & exercise of perfectiō. Hervpō he
bringeth furth y̆ authoritie of Scripture,
saying, *Let euery man be subiect vnto the hig-*
her powers. which Text, by his collection, proueth more strongly that Religious men should obey their Priors, than
Temporal men the Princes of the world.
Againe, he alleageth *Obey your Prepositours*
and be ye subiect vnto them.

Rom. 13.

Heb. 13.

After this, he commeth to the Examples of Abraham, in the Olde Testament, and the Apostles in the New: and
saith of the Apostles, that Christ did perfectly instruct them in the way of Obedience, willing them to suffer gladdely
Ieoperdies, Contumilies, Araigne-
mentes, Ignominies, Stoning to death,
han-

hanging vpon Crosses, and diuerse other
thinges. But how? For their owne
fakes onely? No, but *Vt per eos formā relin=*
queret eandē fequutur a pofteritati, that by them
he might leaue the fame Example and Paterne,
to the Pofteritie that should folovv. what

How li=
keth M.
Iewel
this Obe=
dience?

Paterne? Mary the Paterne of Obedi=
ence, that as the Apoftles folowed Chrift
through al Contradictions of the world,
and Aduerfities, and Deathes: fo should
Religious men obey their Fathers and
Superiours in al thinges. Then doth it
folow.

Bafil.c.23.
Conftit.
Monaft.

Atque hoc à Chrifto ipfo docemur, dum Pe-
trum Ecclefiæ fuæ paftorem poft fe conftituit.
And this vvè be taught of Chrift him felfe, vvhen
he appointed Peter to be the Paftor of his Church
after him. what *This,* be we taught?
whether that one Apoftle is as good as
an other, or one Bishope as high as an
other, or the Curate of as great Authori=
tie as the Person, or the Person of as
large a Iurifdiction as the Bishope?
No. But that we should be obedient
vnto our Paftours. For thus it folo=
weth in S. Bafile.

Quemadmodum igitur. &c. *Therefore*
like

lyke as Sheepe obey the Sheepeherd, and go vvhat
soeuer vvay he vvil, so they that excercise them
selues in godlines, muſt obey their Rulers, and
nothing at al ſerch their commaundementes cu-
riouſly vvhen they haue no ſinne in them, but cō-
traryvvise to accomplish them vvith moſt readi-
neſſe of minde and diligence. As if he ſhould
ſhortly haue ſaid :

Chriſt appointed Peter and other
after him in order to beSheepherds,

Ergo Chriſte appointed ſuch as
vvere vnder their Charge to be as
Sheepe.

But Sheepe obey their Shepherd
vvithout making any inquiſition vp-
on his leading and guiding of them:

Ergo vve be taught obedience by
Chriſt him ſelfe, in this alſo, that he
made Peter ẏ Paſtour of theChurch
after him .

To this ende, by theſe meanes, S.
Baſile bringeth his diſcourſe in the foreſaid Chapiter, which J haue the more at
large

large opened vnto thee, that thou maiſt
ſee (Indifferent Reader) how litle he
intended to ſpeake againſt the Popes ſu-
premacie, or for the equalitie of Prieſtes
or Biſhopes, that one of them ſhould be
as high as another.

What moued then M. Iewel, to vſe
ſ. Baſil in this place? Or what words are
they here, by which he cōfirmeth his Aſſertiō? His Aſſertiō is y, the old Catholik
Fathers could neuer vnderſtande any ſuch
ſpecial Priuilege of binding and looſing, as
M. Dardinges Athanaſius attributeth
to the See of Rome? But how proueth
he this? Chriſt (ſaith he out of S. Baſil)
appointed Peter to be Paſtor of his church
after him. Note then, that Chriſt is Firſt
and S. Peter Next. And this maketh
directly for the Supremacie. But it foloweth.

And ſo conſequently gaue the ſame povver vnto al Paſtours and Doctours.

Be it ſo. But what is conſequently? How M. Iewel taketh it, I can not
tel, but τοῖς ἐφεξῆς ποιμέσι, in greke, which
phraſe S. Baſile vſeth, ſignifieth the Paſtours that ſolow in order and row after
S. Peter

Iew. 239

S. Baſile
for the ſu-
premacie.

S. Peter. Now *Order* requireth, that although al be Pastours, yet they may not take vpon them, and rule consusely al in a clumpe togeather, but euery man in his place & degree, according vnto ꝑ proportion of his Flocke and Charge. And therfore this, hitherto proueth rather that ꝑ Pope of Rome, is the Chief after Christ, and that al other what so euer they be, go not cheeke by cheeke by him, & as worthy or Supreme as he, but euery man in his order and degree after him. But this that foloweth, is perchaunce altogeather for M. Iewel. what is that? Marie

A token vvhereof is this, that al Pastours dooe equally both binde and loose as vvel as he.

True it is M. Iewel, the most simple in al the world doth binde and loose, like as the Pope him selfe. But this is true, in such chinges, as are permitted vnto his Iurisdiction. For in some kind of Faultes, the partie must be referred vnto the Iudgement of the Bishoppe, And in cases of Heresie, Breaking of Vowes, and Robbing of Churches, the Bishop

Ra'

Bishop hath not in his hands to absolue the offender, but the whole must be reserued vnto the Pope. And therefore, although in such faultes as euery Prior or Priest may forgeue or retaine, the Iurisdiction, which he exerciseth, be as effectual, as if S. Peter himself had absolued or bound the parties: yet this is nothing against the special Priuilegies aboue al others which are graunted vnto the See of Rome. As in example of fiue hundred Capitaines in a field, Or fiue hundred Lordes in a Countrie, euery one commaundeth the Souldier of his band, or Tenant of his land, and yet this is not preiudicial vnto the worthines & excellencie of the General Capitaines and chiefe Lordes. The Angels doe al of them waite and attende vpon God, and at the later Day, al the Electe shal haue euery one his penie and reward: yet the Cherubins are of higher Authoritie than the inferiour Angels, and the Apostles shal be in greater Glorie, then Confessours. What shal we say of Christ himselfe? *As my Father* (saith he) *sent me, so send I you, And vvhen he had said this, he brea-*
                                                                        thed

Al that to one thing equally, are not of like Authoritie.

Ioan. 20.

thed vpon them, and saith vnto them: *Take ye the
holy Ghost. Whose sinnes you shal forgeaue them,
they are forgeuen them, and whose sinnes ye do
reteine, they be reteined.* Here loe, you may
see that he hath made the Apostles equal
with hym . How then? wil you conclude
that Christ is not supreme in his Church,
and that he hath not the authoritie of bin=
ding and loosing in a more high degree
than any of his Apostles ? Such yet is
your diuinitie(M . Iewel)that because al
Pastours do equally bind & loose , there=
fore the Pope hath no special Priuilege
aboue other . But you lacked the vnder=
standing , that al do equally bind & loose
in such cases and Persons , as are subie=
cted vnto them, And that, because euery
Bishop can not exercise the power of his
Orders when and where it pleaseth him,
therefore it is euident , that all are not
equal , but that the Superiours may re=
straine the Iurisdiction of the Inferi=
ours,which is inough to proue a Supre=
macie.

    Thus hath M . Iewel brought foure
seueral Auncient Fathers, al in a cum=
panie togeather,to proue that, the B . of

Rome hath no speciall Priuilege aboue others of binding and loosing. and there is not one of them al, which proueth that Cōclusion. For S. Cyprian, is plaine for one head, notwithstanding the equalitie of the Apostles in honour and power. Origen, and S. Cyril, speake not literally but mystically, And S. Basile last of all telleth such a Trueth as euery Catholike wil confesse, and is nothing contrarie to the doctrine of the Supremacie, excepte there be so vnsensible an heretike, that wil think the lowest Minister in the congregatiō, to be as high in Authoritie as the greatest Superintendent or general, because he preacheth and baptiseth, and ministreth the Lordes Supper, and burneth (if neede be) in his opinion, in lyke sorte as the Chiefest Superintendentes themselues doe.

And this vanitie and falsehood of M. Iewels, when he allegeth Auncient Fathers wordes without their Sense, is so common, that I wil be bounde to make a whole boke of his So saith S. Cyprian, and Therefore S. Hierome saieth, and other such Idle Illations: if either it were not inough lnongh, to note only what he is, Oz if my wil and leisure serued me so much, as to be occupied in so tediouse A mater. But now let vs goe fozwarde with the Doctours, and shew how shamefully he hath abused them.

Our Sauiour (saith D. Harding out of S. *Epist. 118.* Augustine) *gaue not commaüdement, in vvhat* ad Iano Order *the Sacramẽt should be receiued, meaning to reserue that mater vnto the Apostles, by vvhom he vvould direct and dispose his Church.*

Ergo, *the obseruation, of number of Communicãts, of Place, of Tyme, of Order, Maner, and Circumstance in Receiuing, dependeth of the Churches ordinaunce, and not of Christes Institution.*

S. Augstine abused.

S. Augustine speaketh not one worde Iew. 10. of any number.

He speaketh of a power left with the Apostles, to apoint in what ozder the Sacrament should be Receaued, but the Ozder and Manner of doing a thing, extendeth it self to al Circumstances: ergo

Aa ij to

to number also . And therefore it is no wrong dealing, to inferre A particular vpon the graunt of the proper vniuersal thereof .

Againe, whereas the blessed Apostle, after certaine talke had about the Sacrament, concluded saying: *Cætera cum venero ordinabo, As for the rest vvhen I come my selfe I vvil set in Order,* S. Augustine inferreth, *Vnde datur intelligi:quia multū erat,vt in epistola totū illum agendi ordinē insinuaret,quem vniuersa per orbē seruat ecclesia , ab ipso ordinatum esse quod nulla morū diuersitate variatur.*Wherof it is geauen vs to vnderstand, that it vvas ordeined of the Apostle,that vvhich is not varied by any diuersity of maner & fashion,becaus̃e it vvas, much for him to shevv in an epistle,al that order of Celebrating.and Ministring the Communion, vvhich the vvhole Church through out all the vvorld doth obserue.

As who should say: If it had not ben, that the Apostle had not place inough, in his Epistle to the Corinthians,to declare his mind at ful:In what order,and with what Ceremonies and Circumstancies, he would haue the celebrating of y mysteries to procede , he would haue left it in plaine

1.Cor.11.

To dispose and sette thinges in order concerning y mysteries it was left vnto the Apostles, and not finished by Christ.

plaine writing, how al thinges should be don: but because that was to much for an epistle, to receaue, And because the order which he would haue obserued, was not so quickly appointed, as to Reade A Chapiter or two of the Bible, and to tell the storie of Christs entring into his passion, and that done, to receiue bread and wine in remembrance thereof, and to be thankeful: therefore he promised to come hymselfe, and set thinges in order: and therefore such orders and maners, as the whole Church hath and doth throughly vse, about the celebration of the Mysteries, are to be thought to haue come from the Apostles.

Of these words then also (*As for the rest vvhen I come my selfe : I vvil dispose*) it maie, with good reason, be gathered, that the Apostle did prescribe orders and rules to be obserued concerning Persons, Time, and Place, with other Circumstances, And that the Institution of Christ, stretched no further than to Consecration, Oblation and Participation of his pretious bodie: And that one alone or manie togeather to receaue, was not, by Christ,

apointed, but left to his Apostles to be
ordered. But it foloweth in M. Iewel: that,

Iew. 2 0.

S. Augustine in this place, speaketh not
one word of any number. But, only of the
time of Receauing, whether it might seme
conuenient to minister the Communion
after Supper.

Ra.

J. Iew=
is bold=
nes

You be verie bold, either with S.
Augustine, or with your Reader. Doe ye
cal ỹ speaking only of the time, where the
question of tyme is not at al spoken of?
Reade the place who wil, and if there be
any such question intreated, as M. Iewel
reporteth, although I haue many Arguments to the contrarie, yet wil I say he
is an honest and true man.

In the fifthe chapiter of that epistle,
these questions are mentioned, whether
vpon good friday, Oblation and Sacrifice should be done twise, in the morning
first, and then after supper, Item, whether the people should, first keepe their
faste, then eate that daies meale, and last
of all haue the Oblation and Sacrifice
made. Or, first keepe their faste, and then
haue the Sacrifice made, and last of al go

to their meales meat. To which questions his anſwer is, that euery man ſhould, in theſe points, do, as ý vſe of the church is, vnto which he cummeth. Becauſe ther is nothing in them, againſt either Faith oʒ good maners.

In the next chapiter ſolowing, out of which D. Harding toke his teſtimony, the queſtion & doubt is, not, whether one might Offer oʒ Receaue in the moʒning, oʒ at euening (which perteineth to tyme) but, whether he that had eaten the ſame daie befoʒe, might afterwardes either Offer, oʒ Receaue the bodie of Chriſte, whiche is A Queſtion concerninge the ſtate of the perſons only, And not the qualitie of Tyme. Vnto which, his anſwer is, that it hath pleaſed ý holy Ghoſt, that foʒ the honour of ſo great a Sacrament, the bodie of our Loʒd ſhould firſt enter into the mouth of a Chriſtian, befoʒe external and carnal meates.

The reuerence geué to thé Sacrament.

Now becauſe the heretike might ſay (as ſome in theſe daies vphold) where is it in al the Scripture, that a man ſhould come faſting to the communion? And whi might not one (if he would) receiue after

Aa iiij Sup=

Supper, as the Apostles dyd, or in the Supper tyme, as the Corinthians dyd: S. Augustine meeteth with this obiection, alleging that sentence which M. Harding to like effect vsed, and saying: *That in vvhat order the Sacrament should be receiued, Christ gaue no præcept thereof, but left that office to his Apostles.*

Let M. Jewel now, defend hymselfe, if he can, and proue, that he hath not falsly reported of S. Augustine, in the place of the Epistle *ad Ianuarium*, saying of hym, that he speaketh not one word of the number (of Comunicantes) but only of the tyme of Receauing.

That he speaketh only of the time of Receauing, it is false. For these be his wordes: *Saluator non præcepit quo deinceps ordine sumeretur, vt Apostolis, per quos dispositurus erat, ecclesiam, seruaret hunc locum. Our Sauiour gaue no commaundemēt, in vvhat order it should be Receaued, to the intent he might leaue that mater to his Apostles, by vvhom he vvould dispose his Church.*

Hereof I gather this Argument. The apointing of Order, how thinges should be don, doth extend itself to more, than

than apointing only of the time, in which
it is to be done: But, of the Authoritie
left with the Apostles, to set an Order in
Receauing of the Sacrament, S. Augu=
stine doth speake, in his epistle *ad Ianuari-*
um, Ergo M. Iewel doth report falsly of
S. Augustine, that in that epistle he spea=
keth only of the tyme of receauing.

S. Augu-
stin belied
of M. Ie-
wel.

S. Gregorie abused.

In the communion, As the people saied
the Lordes praier altogether (as it is noted
by S. Gregorie) so they Receaued al togeather.

Iew. 76.

impudēcie

Are ye not ashamed so to say, that it
is noted so by S. Gregorie? we haue (I
thinke) his epistles in the same print as
you haue them, and $\mathring{y}$ effect of that epistle,
out of which, you haue gathered this note
vpon S. Gregorie, is, that he answereth
certaine persons, which thought it was
vnmeete, that he should goe aboute to
keepe vnder the Church of Constanti=
nople, whereas he folowed the customes
of that Church in Rome, it selfe: And S.
Gregorie answereth, that in Singing of
Alleluia, Kyrieleison, Pater noster &c. he
foloweth not Constantinople, but his
owne

Ra.

it agreeth
not here.
it is like,
was a po=
pish masse
so longe
agoe?

owne Church. And of the Pater noster he saith: *Dominica oratio apud Græcos ab omni populo dicitur , apud nos autem a solo Sacerdote. Our Lordes praier is said among the Grecians, of al the people , but vvith vs , it is saied by the Priest alone .*

Here then I appose you againe (M. Iewel) was the Masse of S. Gregozies tyme, a Communion oz Priuate Masse? (foz you make an oppositiõ betwen these two thinges). If it were a priuate masse, then must you yeld and subscribe, because it is then found by your own confession, within the first six hundzed yeres . If it were a Communion, how say you , that the people said the cõmunion praier al together, as it is noted by S. Gregorie, whereas you see him, so plainely, to testifie, that in Rome , the Priest alone dyd saie our Lozdes Praier?

I wonder what cã be answered.

Yea (say you perchaunce) but it was otherwise emonge the Greekes , and in their Communion the people saied the Lozds praier al together . Yea: but S. Gregozie noteth not any such point, and he speaketh not, of their communion, oz not Cõmunion. So that you be exceding much

Ergo M. Iew hath telled him

much to blame for abusing the names of holy Doctours so vainely, and making them to becompted to thinke that, which they doe not speake.

S. Cyprian abused.

The Catholike faith is, that the Churche is not bound by the vertue of Christes Institution, to deliuer the Sacrament, vnder forme of wine, vnto the people. The heretikes repine against it, and saie, that by Christes Institution the people should Receiue the Cup also. But how wil this be proued? By many old Fathers. But,

In steede of many, for shortnes sake, to allege but one, S. Cyprians wordes in this mater be verie plaine. Iew.106

Remember then, what the mater is. You must proue out of S. Cyprian, that the people should Receaue not in the one kinde alone of Bread, but of wine also. And if you (M. Iewel) wil not remember it, yet I praie thee (gentle Reader) to marke diligently whether he proue any such thing out of S. Cyprian. Ra.

Marke what is to be proued.

Some ther be, that in sanctifiyng the cup, and deliuering it to the people, do not that thing Iew.

Cypri. li 2
Epiſt. 3.

thing that Ieſus Chriſt our Lord and God, the Author and Teacher of this Sacrifice, both did and tawght.

Ra.

Surely, whoſoeuer he be that doth ſo, is much to blame. For Chriſtes Inſtitution is to be obſerued. But the queſtion is, whether to deliuer the Chalice to the laie people, be of ẏ neceſſitie of Chriſtes Inſtitution. But go ẏe further in S. Cypꝛian.

Iew.
Truely ſaied, but to no purpoſe.

He addeth further. If any man be in this errour, ſeing the light of the Trueth let him returne againe vnto the Roote, and vnto the Original of the Lordes Tradition.

Ra.

This alſo is wel done, ſo charitably to warne the deceaued, to returne vnto the trueth. But I thinke it is not wiſely done, to ſpeake ſo generally of errour and truth, our queſtion being ſpecially about one Article. But you haue moꝛe to ſay out of S. Cypꝛian.

Iew.
ydle talke

And after in the ſame Epiſtle, we keepe not the thing that is commaunded vs, vnleſſe we do the ſame that the Lord did.

Ra.

Here is much a do to pꝛoue, that we muſt keepe the Inſtitution of Chꝛiſte, which we do not denie: but where is it here, ẏ to geue the Cup vnto the people

is

is Christes Institution, so absolute, that
they may not be serued in one kinde?
Proue this, which we aske, out of S. Cy=
prian, and let that passe, which we no=
thing doubt of. It foloweth.

    In these few wordes, S. Cyprian saith,
the Lord both did it & taught it to be don.
He calleth it the Lordes commaundemét.

    what is this (it) of which you speake?
why name ye not the thing it selfe, that
we may know where about ye go? Say,
if ye dare, that by this terme (it)you vn=
derstand the deliucry of the Cup vnto
the people. If ye dare, how can you veri=
fie it, That the Lord did it? For Christ,
I am sure, gaue not the Cup in his last
supper to the peple. If ye dare not, what
honestie is this, to bring in so craftely in=
to your conclusion, that, which was not
proued by the premisses?

    Is this the S. Cyprian, whom in
steed of many you promised to allege? Is
this ẏ shortnes for which sake you would
allege but one Father? Cal ye these words
of S. Cyprians, verie plain, for proufe here=
of, ẏ Christes Institution chargeth vs to
deliuer the Cup also, vnto the people,
                   where=

whereas he speaketh of no such contro=
uersie at al.

Jew.

M.Harding(you say)can not here steale
awaie in the myste and saie, S. Cyprian
meant al this of the cup that the Priest cõse-
crateth for himself. For his words be plaine
to the contrarie, In calice dominico sancti-
ficando & ministrando, that is, in sãctifieng
the Lordes cup, and ministring it vnto the
People.

R2.

Steale you awaie, no more than D.
Harding doth, and it wil sone be percea=
ued who is the theefe. For in deede, you
plaie that good felows part, which being
himselfe in daunger of taking, woulde

M. Jew.
is y theefe
& byddeth
other take
heed leaste
D. Har=
ding steale
awaie.

point to another y is giltlesse, and bid the
standers by to looke that he scape not
awaie from them. As if he should say, my
masters and frendes, of al thinges I hate
stealing and iuggling. And see therefore
I praie you, diligently to that fellowe
that goeth yonder, y he cast not a myste
before your eyes, and so steale awaie.

For that which you speake, as it
were to take D. Harding, as though he
would flee from that, which you imagine
against him, that is nothing so. D. Har=
ding wil not, I warrant you, say, that
$.

S. Cyprian meant al y̆ you haue recited
out of him, of the cup that y̆ Priest conse=
crateth for himselfe. But as the Catho=
like Church leadeth hym, he confesseth,
that in y̆ primitiue Church the people re=
ceaued in both kindes. And therefore S.
Cyprian speaking of the Cup sanctified
and distributed vnto the people, can not
moue hym (which confesseth it, to be a=
greable with that tyme) to steale awaie
for the mater.

But here is the question, whether this
distributing of the Cup to the people, be
That tradition, for keeping of which, S.
Cypriane maketh, so iustly so manie
words? Do you marke this M. Iewel?
Steale not you, I praie you, awaie here
in this place. We confesse that the cup
was deliuered vnto y̆ people, in S. Cy=
prians tyme, but we aske now, whether
S. Cyprian in this foresaid epistle, saith, **Answer**
that it is the Institution of Christ that it **directly**
should be so. The fact we graunt, but of
the necessitie of it, whether vpon paine of
Gods Indignation, the people muste
haue the Cup deliuered vnto them, that
we demaund, And to that you answer,
that

that they muſt, And to that you applie theſe foreſaied teſtimonies, making your Reader, to beleue that the Lordes Tradition, and ẏ Lords commaundement of which S. Cyprian ſpeaketh ſo erneſtly, are meant of the deliuerie of the Cup vnto the people.

But, if there were no other argument to the contrarie, what yet could be ſpoken more abſurdly and idlely? For if the Tradition of our Lord, which S. Cyprian mentioneth, is to be vnderſtanded of ẏ deliuerie of the cup to the people, of which point only, our queſtion is, then loe, when he ſaieth: *Some there be, that in sanctifieng the Cup, and deliuering it vnto the people, doe not that thing, that Iesus Chriſt both did and taught:* he ſhould meane thus, that *Some there be that in ſanctifieng the Cup and deliuering it to the people, doe not deliuer it vnto the people, as our Lord both did and taught.*

Plaine contradiction after M. Iewels ſenſe vpon S. Cyprian.

And how then doth this geare hang togeather, that, in deliuering it vnto the people, they ſhould not deliuer it vnto the people? Or, that S. Cyprian ſhould reproue

reproue any man for not keeping of our
lords traditiō in deliuering of ƴ Cup to ƴ
people,wheras he plainly saith that it is
sanctified & deliuered, and yet, that our
Lords tradition is not obserued? By
which it is most euident,that the Tradition,which S. Cyprian in this place, so
grieuouslie taketh to be omitted,can not
possibly be referred to the deliuery of the
Cup to the people,which he confesseth to
be obserued.

And this much might be said with good
reason, if S. Cyprians meaning were
not to be found expressed in open words,
within ten lines of these,which M. Iew.
hath rehersed. But it is so euidēt,ƴ euen
at the very begining of ƴ Epistle, he declareth,what the cause of his writing is,
and what the fault is, which he woulde
haue amended. For the first Sentence
thereof hath this sense.

Albeit I know (most deere brother)that ma-
ny Bishops do keepe the Order and Rules of our
Lordes Tradition,yet because some in sanctifieng
the Cup and deliuering it vnto the people,do not
that thing,vvhich our Lord both did and taught,
I thought it good and necessary to vvrite letters

therof vnto you, that if any man be deceiued, he may returne, vnto the Original of our Lordes Tradition.

This is the first sentence, in which there is Generally signified a thing to be amisse, but what that is, it is not yet specially declared. And out of this one sentence, &c. Iew. pecketh an absolute Testimonie, that it is Christes Institutiō, that the people should haue the Cup deliuered vnto them, because he loueth not ƴ truth should be stolen away in a mist. The sese of the next sentence is,

And thinke not, (most deere Brother) that I vvrite this vpon myne ovvne minde and vvil, but vvhen any thing is cōmaunded by the Inspiration of God, the faithful seruaunt must obey. So that this hitherto is nothing but a preface or entrence to the mater. Then foloweth the third sentence.

Admonitos autem nos sitas &c. But ye shal vnderstand, that vve are vvarned (by special reuelacion from God) that in offering of the Chalice, the Traditio of our Lord be kept, & that no other thing be don of vs, than that vvhich our Lord did for vs, first, that the Chalice vvhich is offered in remembraunce of him , should be mixt vvith vvine.   Loe

Lo this is the state of ý whole Epistle, and the *Tradition & Commaundement of God*, which so oft & so earnestly he speaketh of, is referred to this end only, ý wine & water should be offered vp togeather in the Mysteries. And ý fault which he findeth with the celebrating ý some vsed, was, ý they toke water only into ý Chalice, like as on the cōtrary side ý Heretikes now take only wine. Both which extremes the Traditiō & Cōmaundement of God (which S. Cyprian doth proue, by ý olde and new Testament most abundantly) doth so fully & perfitely confound, that as the *Aquarij* then were disproued, so the *Vinarij* now should be ashamed.

wine and water to be ming-led togea-ther in the Chalice is ý Tra-ditiō and Cōmaun-dement of Christ.

But as concerning the deliuering of the Sacrament, in one or both kindes, he intended it not, nor determineth it. And this M. Iewel perceiued wel inough, ý S. Cyprian in that Epistle was wholy bent against *Aquarij* (were they schisma-tikes only or heretiks) and, that the fault which he laboreth to amēd in them, was, not for not geuing the cup vnto the peo-ple, but for geuing water only in it, and not wine mixt with water.

BB ij   Where

Indiscretiō vnwozthy M. Iewels fine dispofition.

where then was M. Iewels wit to let go many fathers, which he wold haue it thought, to be foz him, and, foz shortnes sake to allege only S. Cyprian, and, that S. Cyprian should speake nothing at al, of that questiō which properly is demaūded of vs, and to which we looked foz an absolute and perfite answer from him?

It is not credible but he saw wel inough, what we could Replie, and therfoze he prouided this safegard foz his eftimation. Foz thus he saith:

Iewel. See the fetch, leaft S. Cyprian should feeme to make nothing foz him, But it is a foolish one.
Ra.

If S. Cyprian might wel write thus against the Heretikes called Aquarij, which in the holy miniftratiō, would not vfe wine but in ftede thereof did Confecrate water, and Miniftred it vnto the People, much more may we fay the fame againft our Aduerfaries, which Confecrate and Minifter vnto the people, no Cup at al.

what you may faie, it is an other queftion, but we feke now, what S. Cyprian did fay. If that Learned and bleffed Father, whom you haue alleaged in ftede of many, if he fpake nothing directly of our queftion, it is no mater to vs, what you wil Applie him vnto, neither was it cunningly inough donne of you,

you, to bring him alone (whereas you had, except you belie your selfe, copie) which maketh nothing at al for you, but by a consequence of your owne deuising.

And yet this very Consequence of yours, doth nothing folow. For to consecrate in water onely, and to minister it so vnto the people (which clause of ministring it vnto the people, is in deede out of the mater which S. Cyprian discussed. But let it occupie a place, if you thinke it wil ease you) To Consecrate (I say againe) in water only, and to minister it so vnto the people, is against the Tradition, Institution, and Commaundement of our Sauiour. And this is proued at large throughout y̅ whole epistle of s. Cypriā.

But, to cōsecrate the wine & water together, & not to minister it vnto y̅ people who is against it? what Scripture, coūcel, or father? You say it is against Christes Institutiō. we deny it. You made, as though you would proue it out of S. Cyprian. But S. Cypriā speaketh not of this questiō: yet, you say, y̅ as S. Cypriā spake against y̅ *Aquarios* for cōsecrating in water only, and ministring it so vnto the

BB iij   people,

peple: so may you much more speake a-
gainst the Church, for ministring no Cup
at al vnto the peple. I haue shewed how
vnlike this comparison is.

But wil you haue a good Argument,
and like to ỹ of S. Cyprians? This it is.

S. *Cyprian iustlie founde faulte*
with the Aquarios for consecrating
in water onely, and ministring it so
vnto the peple: Ergo, he would haue
found fault with your Procedings,
which put wine only in the Cup, and
minister it so vnto the people.

For the Reason on both sides is one,
that the Tradition of our Lord, is to be
obserued, and that to. Consecrate wine
and water togeather, was his Traditiõ.

Answere this Argument with al your
cũning (Learned M. Iewel) and answer
your deere friendes expectation, which
wil thinke, that you haue not abused S.
Cyprian. The iudgement wherof, I
permit, vnto any reasonable Aduersarie.

S. Augustine abused.

S. Augustine, willing the Priestes to applie

An Inuincible Argumẽt except M. Ieb, wil denie S. Cyprians authoritie: which onely he hath bso in steede of many Fathers.

plie their studies, to correct their errours
of their Latin speach, addeth thervnto this
Reason, *Vt populus ad ia quod planè intelligit,*
dicat Amen. That the people vnto the thing, that
they plainly vnderstand, may say Amen. This
of S. Augustine seemeth to be spoken Generally of al tongues.

How can it seeme so, wheras he so expressly speketh of the Latin tongue only?

S. Augustine (you say) willing the Priestes, &c. This first of al is falsely reported. For S. Augustin in this place, went
not about to exhorte the Priestes to the
studie of þ Latine tongue, as who should
thinke that it were not to be suffered, A
Priest or Bishop to be ignorant therein:
but he shewed, how such, as come fresh &
fine from the Scholes of Grammarians,
and Rhetoricians, with knowledge and
Eloquence inough of wordes, should, in
their first entrance into þ church, there to
be instructed of þ Catholike Faith, learne
to be humble & wise in iudgement, & not
to contemne þ Scriptures, because they
be not write in so loftie & exquisit a Style
as prophane bokes, nor to set more by flo
rish of words, than substance of Sense.

BB iiij And

And further he saith :

August. de Catechis. rud. cap. 9.

Nouerint etiam nõ esse vocem ad aures dei, sed animi affectũ. ita enim nõ irridebũt, si aliquos Antistites & ministros Ecclesiæ forte animaduerterint, vel cũ barbarismis & solæcismis Deũ inuocare, vel eadẽ verba quæ pronũciant nõ intelligere, pturbatéque distinguere. **that is,** *Let them vnderstand also, that it is not the voice, that soũdeth in the eares of God, but the hartines and deuotiõ of mind. For so they shal not laugh the Bishops and ministers of the church to scorn, if perchaunce, they shal perceiue them to cal vpõ God, either vvith barbarouse and incongrue Latine: or els not to vnderstand the vvords that they speak, either to point them out of order .*

M. Iew. a crafty dissembler

To such therfore, S. Austine directeth his talke in ỳ place, & maketh no exhortatiõ at al to Priestes, to learne their latine tongue better. And why shonld M. Iew. dissemble ỳ true persons, of whom S. Augustine there speaketh ? I wil tel you : There is not a place more plainer than this, if it be considered, to proue ỳ it was not thought in S. Augustines time, so necessary a mater, that al thinges in the Churche should be donne in a knowen Tongue, as now it is auouched to be.

For

For if the Publike Seruice was euerie where executed, at that tyme, in the vulgar Tongue, or in a knowen one to the common people, although it were not their vulgar, how is it possible, that the Bishopes themselues, should be to see= king in the right pronouncing, & poin= ting, and vnderstanding of that, whiche they openly said in the Church?

The Syr Iohn Lacklatines (of which there is much speaking among the bro= thers) they haue ben such an occasion of ruine and perdition to the worldly wise, as none hath ben greater. For the euil life of Priestes, although it be A greate Argument vnto them, that the Religion is not effectual, which hath such holy ons in it: yet whiles they see in euerie kinde of Protestation or Confession, many such to be found, of whom they may wel inough be ashamed, they temper their Iudge= ment, and wil not vtterly condemne a Religion for this cause only, that some Professours thereof be wicked.

Lacke of knowledg doth more hurt i this world. thā lacke of good life.

But when they see Publike Seruice to be saied of them which vnderstand it not, and for them which are also as igno=
rant

rant, this seemeth to be so absurde, that they cannot conceaue, howe the Spirite of God should directe their doeinges, which see, and suffer, yea and defend, that Publike Seruice maie be done, in a tong which the vulgar people doe not vnderstand. And in this point, they are so much the more vehement, because they see, how all the new Gospellers solow a contrary waie, and vse no lerned Tounge at all in their Ordinary Seruice, but the vulgar and knowen Tounge of the Countrie, where they pitch. So that, the Protestantes are compted herein, to worke so sincerely, to speake so reasonably, and to chalenge so inuincibly, that thousandes of the worldly wise, whiles they stand in their owne iudgement, fal in deede into euerlasting perdition, by the iudgement of the blessed and lerned Fathers.

For, if al thinges must be don in the Church, so, as the people do vnderstand what is praied, how should that case euer be heard of in the Primitiue Churche, where some Bishoppes, vnderstode not what they praied in the open Church?

Maie we think, that any of them,

vnder￹

vnderstoode not the vulgare speache of
his coūtrie? That is verie incredible, because, vnto the high office, of Ruling and
teaching the whole people, he should
not be chosen, which could not wel be
vnderstanded of the people.

But maie we rather thinke, that the
publike Seruice, was in a lerned toung,
sometymes not persitly knowen of the
Bishope himselfe, like as vnto the vulgar people it was not knowen? Of this,
there is no doubt: Because in praieng to
God, deuotion and not eloqnution is required, and because he might haue a good
grace, of preaching in his natural tongue
vnto the people, which yet had very simple vnderstanding, of any Greeke or latine writtinges: And because, it is plaine
by S. Augustine, that some such were in
his tyme.

How then (you wil saie) is Ignorance in a Bishope to be suffered? I say
not so, neither on the other side, I thinke
that al is marred, except euery man, woman and childe maie haue the Bible in
the vulgar Tounge. Or, that no Tounge
is to be suffered in the Church of God,

but

That the Seruice was in S. Augustines tyme in y latin Tongue which was vn-knowē to y vulgare people.

but that, which is the common and knowen tounge, of the Countrie. But as
there is a difference betwene wincking
and staring, so is there a discreation and
iudgement to be vsed in this mater of
Tounges of which we speake. And S.
Augustine aloweth it not, that a Bishope
should not vnderstand the Latin tounge
in which he praieth, neither yet doth he
crie out against that lacke of theirs, requiring that al Publike Seruice should
straitwaies be in the vulgare Tounge.
For after he had told it, how some Bishopes praie in false and barbarouse Latine, and vnderstād not what they praie,
he addeth further least, you should think
hym to alowe Ignorance, and saieth:

*Aug. de
Catethi.
rud. ca. 9.*

Non quia ista minimè corrigenda sint , vt
populus ad id quod planè intelligit, dicat, Amen:
I would, that the freshe and trym Scho-
lers, comming lately from their Eloquēt
Lessons, should not laugh ꝑ Bishops to
skorne, which speake in their praiers false
Latin: *not because these thinges vvere not to be
amended* in the Bishopes , *to the entent the
people might ansvver Amen, to that vvhich they
clerelie vnderstand.* (as who should say , I
alow

elow not their lacke of knowledge: And it were wel, that they dyd so speake, as the people vnderstand them) *Sed tamen pie toleranda sunt ab eis qui didicerunt vt sono in foro, sic veto in ecclesia benedici .* but yet these lackes, are charitably to be borne vvithal, of them, vvhich haue lerned, that as thinges are vvel said in court before Iudges, by sounde (of voice) so are they vvel saied in the Church, by vovve of minde.

Of which wordes I gather, that as he would wishe it better, ỹ the Bishops & Priestes of the Church should so speak, as the people might vnderstand: yet, he would not haue the Seruice of the church vtterly chaunged from the Latine tonge not vnderstanded, to the vulgar tounge which nor Priest nor peole could be ignorant of. But, euen those wantes of some Bishopes and Priestes, in the true Reading, Pointing, and Understanding of their Publike Praiers, he would to be charitably borne and suffered, vpon this consideration, that although in the eares of men, their wordes sound not plaine and good, yet in ỹ sight of God, the good affection of their harte is alowed.

Now

The Ig=
norance of
the latine
tongue in
the Latine
praiers is
to be tole=
rated in a
Priest or
Bishop, &
not more.

Now if S. Augustine had ben of the Protestantes mind, he would not haue take the mater so quietly, but with great Stomake would haue said, awaie with this murmuring of praiers not vnderstanded: awaie with this Latine and strange tounge, which, the Priest hymselfe knoweth not, what it meaneth: Awaie with this lip labour: Let vs haue the Bible turned into the vulgar tounge, let euery man come to the Church and singe Psalmes to the Lord: let the people vnderstand what is said: let vs do as the Apostle commaundeth vs, let vs speake with tounges: and so furth, with a great tale, out of the xiiij. Chapiter of the first to the Corinthians, altogeather out of purpose.

But, as it appeereth by this place, which I haue opened, S. Augustine was of an other mind, & would haue gene such Protestantes an other lesson, that they should not mocke at poore Syr Johns, which praie in latine and yet vnderstand not latine, like as his counsel is, to eloquent and smoeth tounged Gentlemen, that come from secular Scholes, to the
Church

S. Auga. would neuer haue said so.

Church of Christ, there to be instructed.

And because the opening of so much, would haue ben a great disauantage to M. Iewel and his felowes, therefore he speaketh only of Priestes whom S. Augustine willed to correct the errours of their latine tounge, and dissimbleth the answer, which S. Augustine geueth to those ioly felowes, which would be ready to mocke at Priestes, because of their barbarouse and false praieng, in the Publike Seruice. By which we vnderstand, that the publike Seruice was then in Latine, and that it was so strainge also vnto the vulgar people, that some of the Priestes and Bishopes did not vnderstand it.

Of this also it foloweth, that the conclusion which M. Iewel pecketh out of this testimonie of S. Austine, is so grosse and vnsensible, that I wonder where his wittes were when he wrote it. Thus he saieth.

This of S. Augustin seemeth to be spoken generally of al tounges.

Seemeth it so in deede? And do not your self so vnderstãd the place in ye very begynning of your alleging thereof, that you

Iew.
False and absurde.
Ra.

you faie, S. Auguſtine willeth the Prieſtes to correct the errours of their latine tonge? If then it be the latine tounge by name, for which he reaſoneth, how doth it ſeme vnto you that he ſpeaketh generally of al Tounges?

Againe, if he ſpake generally of al tounges, ergo of the Punike tounge. I aſke you then, which of the two, it is like that the Aphꝛicanes vnderſtoode better, the Aphꝛicane and Punike tounge, Oꝛ the Latine?

If the Aphꝛicane (as being their natural and vulgar tounge) was moꝛe familiar with them, why doth S. Auguſtine wil the Pꝛieſts to ſtudie the Latine tongue, that the people might vnderſtãd them the better, wheras (by your accõpt) they ſhould haue ſpoken in their owne vulgar tongue, and ſo with leſſe labour, the people ſhould haue bin moꝛe edified?

If the Latin was moꝛe familiar, how could any Pꝛieſt oꝛ Biſhope in Aphꝛica, be ſo ignoꝛant thereof, that he ſhould not pꝛonounce his Latine pꝛaiers, and vnderſtand them? Oꝛ, how doth S. Auguſtin ſeeme to ſpeake generally of al tongues, which

Here is no eſcape oꝛ ſhiſt foꝛ M. Iew.

which extendeth out his Reason and argument, no not vnto the Punik tongue? Here againe I praie thee (Indifferent Reader) to consider, whether M. Iewel hath not clerckly alleged the Doctours.

S. Irenens abused.

S. Irenens, hath a manifest testimonie for the Supremacie of the Church of Rome. *Euerie Church* (saieth he) *must resort to this Church of Rome, because of the mightier Principalitie of the same.* And this place trobleth M. Iewel very much, as it appeereth by ye extranagants, and idle discourses, which he maketh about it. But one of his Answers is this, that,

Lib.3. Cap. 3.

The Principalitie that Ireneus meant, was the Ciuile Dominion and Temporall State of the Citie of Rome, in which God had then planted the Empire of the world, and made al nations subiect vnto it.

Iew.244

Impuden cy or blind nes.

See the impudencie or blindenes of the man. Are ye not very carnal in your Iudgement, and make ye not the like arguments, as the worldlings do ? what societie, betwene light and darknes? and what participation, betwene Christ and Belial ? what hath the euerlasting king-

Ra.

C C   i   dom

dom, to depend vpon the transitorie and temporal kingdom? And why should the wealth or dominiō of any Citie diminish or increase the Estimation of any one Church?

Consider I pray thee, Indifferēt Reader, what a wise interpretour M. Iewel is? He maketh ÿ lerned Father S. Irenæus to haue this dul & grosse sense in him.

M. Iew. a grosse interpretour

All the Churches of the world must resort vnto the Church of Rome, because the ciuile dominion and state thereof, is the greatest in the world, Or thus, Al the faithful in the world, must resort to S.Peters Successours, because the Romain Emperours, are the migthtiest Princes in the world.

By what consequence? The cause vndoubtedly, whiche should moue the Faithful to come to Rome, must haue ben spiritual and not temporal. They should haue resorted thither, to be instructed in their faith, against the Heresies that trobled their vnderstanding, and not to aske any Counsel, or secke any worldly benefite,

ise, at the handes of the Ciuilians or
Nobles of Rome: Or put vp any sup-
plication, in the Court of the Emperour.
The cause then, why ſ Christians ſhould
ſeeke vnto Rome, perteyning to the
maters of Conſcience, ſuch as al the Emperours, and Lordes, and Senatours,
and Phyloſophers of the world, could
not anſwer vnto, and ſuch yet as the Biſhops of the Church of Chriſt might wel
aſſiſte them in, why are they byd to S.
Irenens, to reſort vnto hanc Eccliſiam,
his Church of Rome?

And he anſwereth, propter potentiorem
principalitaté, because of the mightier prin
cipalitie: whereof? of the Ciuil dominion?
nay, he ſpake not of it. And the Sub-
ſtantiue, which goeth immediatly before,
is hanc eccleſiam, this Church. Aſke you,
ſ your ſelfe haue ſo ſtudied diuinitie, that
on haue forgoten your grammar, aſke
on, of M. Cooper whom I dare truſt
lſo in this mater, whether the Princi-
alitie muſt not be referred to ſ Church,
which went in the wordes next before,
nd not to the Ciuil dominion of Rome,
ſ which there is no mention at all.

Haue M.
Iewel to
his gram-
mar a-
gaine,

　　　　　C C ij　　Againe,

Cauſed
why the
Principa-
litie of
which Ire
neus ſpea-
keth, can
not be vn-
derſtáded
of the ciuil
dominion
of ý Citie
of Rome.

Againe, in this one ſentéce, S. Ireneus
doth twiſe name Eccleſiam Church. If
therefore in the firſt place, M. Iewel wil
haue the Ciuil dominion of Rome to be
vnderſtand by, hanc Eccleſiá, thisChurch:
then is it reaſon that he meane by omnem
eccleſiá euerie Church (which words folow in the ſentence) the Ciuil dominion
in euerie parte of the world. But S. Ireneus by euerie Church, vnderſtandeth as
him ſelfe expoundeth it , eos qui vndique
ſunt fideles, ý faithful that are euerie where
about: Ergo by Eccleſiam the Church, in
the former part of his ſentéce, he meaneth
the companie of the Faithful that are in
Rome , of which the Biſhop there is the
principal head.

I adde further , If the Principality
of the Ciuil dominion in Rome, did ſeme
a worthie cauſe vnto the lerned and auncient Father Ireneus , why al Faithfull
ſhould reſort chiefly thither , than which
Concluſion, he thought nothing leſſe, yei
if M. Iewel wil needes haue that con-
ſequence , how chaunced it , that , wher
Conſtantine the great , gaue place to S.
Peter , and went with his Principaliti

o

of Ciuil dominion vnto Constantinople, that al the Churches of the world did not for all that so resorte vnto the Church of Constantinople, but that the Church of Rome continued stil in her Supremacie?

As for that which you say, that prin- Iew. 244 cipalis Ecclesia is sometime vsed of old Fathers, to signifie the ciuil dominiō and principalitie of the Citie, where the Church is: (although in the Examples whiche you bring, in the first of them. 7. quest. 1. pla- Proueses nothing perteining to the proposition. cuit principalis cathedra, doth properly sig nify a spiritual office & not a worldly dominion, And in the second, inter epistolas Augustini 35. epi. although the word principalis, be referred to Alipius as Bishope) yet let me graunt so much, and consider your diuine Logike. After the alleging af the foresaid testimonies, which in dede make quite against you, you conclude saying.

Thus the principality that Iren. meaneth, Iew. stoode not in the preaching of the Gospel, but in the ciuile estate and worldly dominion, not in the Bishoppe that professed Christ, but in the Emperour that was an heathen, not in the Church, but in the persequutours and enemies of the Church.

Yea mary, becauſe the Principalitie,
of which there is mention in. 7 . queſt. 1.
placuit, And, inter epiſtolas Auguſt. ep. 35.
is takē(which is not ſo in dede)foꝛ woꝛld
ly Dominion, Ergo, Thus, the Principality that Ireneus meaneth,ſtoode not in the
preaching of the Goſpel & c. Is not this
man woꝛthie to be made A Biſhope foꝛ
his wiſedome, which ſo definitinely maketh Ireneus agree with Paulinus?
and pꝛoueth that Ireneus woꝛdes,muſt
be Ruled by their phꝛaſes , which were
boꝛne hundꝛed of yeres after him?

If you would haue ſaid,Ireneus taketh Principalitas in this ſenſe, Ergo,
Paulinus in vſing the woꝛd Principalis,
may be interpꝛeted to haue the like ſenſe:
Although this alſo were no good Argument,when the woꝛd hath moꝛe then one
oꝛ two Relations: yet in the deſcending
from the ſuperiour to the inferiour,there
might appeere a ſhew of likelyhod.But
this Logike paſſeth in dede(foꝛ it is M
Iewels) that *Paulinus whiche was
borne three hundred yeres after Ireneus , vſeth the worde principalis in
this*

this sense, Ergo Principalitas of which Ireneus speaketh stoode not in the Bishope that professed Christe, but in the Emperour that was an heathen.

Thus thou maist see (Indifferent Reader) what fowle shifts, and denises, and lyes, M. Iewel had made to turne awaie the Authoritie of Ireneus, that it should not be taken for the Principalitie of the Church of Rome. But his conclusion is notable.

To be shorte (saieth he) If the Church of Rome would nowe faithfully keepe the Traditions, and Doctrine of the Apostles, we would frākely yeld her all that honour, that Ireneus geueth her: but she hath shaken of the yoke of Christ.

O good men. It was then, by likelihod, for pure loue of God and godlines, that you are departed from the See of Rome. There were so fewe Sacramentes, and those of so litle effecte, there was so litle fasting, watching, Praying, so litle chastitie, Discipline, and Order, that you could not abyde to lyue so loosely, but

Iew.
The cause of the Su-premacie is not Des-perat. M. Iewel al-low it on condition.

Ra.

C C iij   would

Holy Hypocrites.

would needes take an yoke vpon you, to keepe your bodies low (by carying your yokefelowes about the Countries with you besides other burdens) And to keepe your spirits humble (by obeying, neither spiritual nor temporal Iurisdiction). For the Saxons in Germanie, the Hugonots in France, the Guses in Flaunders and Brabant, which of late, because the yoke was not heauie inough vpō their shoulders, haue (I can not tel for what penāce sake) made themselues great fardels and packes of Church goodes, and sweate againe with the carriage of them awaie, were not they, and are not these, Cusson germans vnto you?

But you wil do more for Christs sake than this. You wil be content, I perceaue, to go euen to Rome it selfe, vpon certaine conditions. And what are they? Forsoth, if ỹ church of Rome would keepe the Traditions & doctrine of the Apostles, then lo, you wold frankly honour it. And, is this possible? Traditions you knowe, are verities and orders not written in the Scriptures, but deliuered without writing. And is there any thing which
you

you wil frankely beare, except it be writē in expreſſe Scriptures? Surely, I can ſcarſe beleue it, yet if ye would, vpon conditions gene y̆ honour to the Church of Rome, which S. Ireneus abſolutely gaue, without any ſuch cautels, you are not ſo vnlike to be a Papiſt as I thought you were.

For let vs ſuppoſe it , that as you would wiſh, ſo al the Traditions and Doctrine of the Apoſtles, were faithfully kept in Rome, would ye frankly yeld her, al honour that Ireneus geueth her? Tel me then, if *Valentians, Cerdoniſtes, Marcioniſtes* oꝛ any other Heretikes , would deuiſe fantaſies of their owne, & trouble the Church of England with them, wold ye go to Rome foꝛ the mater, and aſke of the Ciuile Eſtate there, Oꝛ the Emperoꝛ if he were a heathen, Oꝛ of the perſequutours oꝛ Ennemies of the Church (yf ſuch felowes had dominion there) wold ye aſke of them, what ſhould be thought of the Olde Heretiques newly vpſtarted?

Yf ye would go to them that haue no Religion, to aſke counſel of them about

M. Iew. would not do as he ſaith.

bout Religion, or to make them priuy
of the state thereof, which haue a deadly
hatred against it : yf yourselfe woulde
nedes be the Legate, the veriest fooles
in al the Countrie, might be your assi=
stantes .

Yf ye would not go thither(the case
so standing as I haue put it)then would
ye not yeld her al that honour that S. Ireneus (after your interpretation) geaueth
her .For so wisely you haue expounded
that Auncient Father , that the mightier
Principalitie (for which Principalities
sake he would al the Faithful to resort to
ÿ Church of Rome)stood not in the Preaching of the Gospel, but in the worldly dominion, not, in the Bishope that professed
Christe, but in the Emperour that was an
heathen, which is as much to say , As ye
must resorte to the Church especially of
Rome, when sundry and strange fanta=
sies of heretikes, trouble your Churches
at home, because the worldly Dominion
is there, and the Emperour is an heathē,
and his Subiectes are persequutors and
enemies of the Church . So vnrea=
sonable and absurde interpretation, you
gaue

geaue to S. Ireneus woordes, which make so plainely for the Supremacie.

But I haue more to say vnto you, that your politike and holy handeling of so Reuerend a Father, may the better be remembred. To Rome you would go, there should be no staie, and that Church we should neuer desire you to honor, you would do it so frankely, if the Traditions and doctrine of th'Apostles might be faithfully kept there. But how thinke you first? could ye do it? I mean this. would ye honor it, before a Parlement were called for the mater? And in that parlemēt would you perswade, that the King (for the time) of England, is not by the plaine word of God the Supreme Head vnder God of the Church of England? And that there is a Church without ÿ Realme vnto which, for the mightier Principalitie thereof, a greater honour is to be geuen?

Let some Indifferent Protestant one or other, aske (and if it be for no more, than his owne knowledge) how M. Iewel can Aunswere my Question.

For,

For, concerning plaine heresies, we are now so accustomed to read them & heare them, that thei are not straunge vnto vs, but, when hypocrisie is ioyned with heresie, Or whē veritie is dissēbled through feare or flatterie, there we are desirous to haue the partie examined, And constreined, either plainly to confesse his heresie, Or faithfully to stand with ȳ veritie.

Shortly therfore to you M. Iewel.

Yf you would honour the Church of Rome in like sorte as S. Iræneus chargeth al the faithful to doe, how doe ye geue to the kinges of England, and that by the expresse Scriptures (as you interprete them) such Supremacie in maters ecclesiastical, as can not stand possibly with the going to Rome, in any question of faith? For by Act of Parlement, and your owne othes, and the practise of the Realme, there is no foraine power that hath to do with the Church of England. And therefore, were Rome neuer so perfite, no greater Principalitie could be attributed to the Church of Rome, than the King of England hath, whom you vphold to be supreme head vnder God in al causes.

On

You fal in a premunire M. Iewel except you refuse S. Iræneus.

On the other side, if ye wil defend ſtil that, which hitherto ye haue ſet furth, by Lawes, Othes, Sermons, Bookes, Promiſes, Threatenings, &c. What an Hypocrite are you, ſo to ſpeake as though ye would, as frankelie yeld to the Church of Rome principal honour, as Jreneus doth earneſtlie require it, that for the *mightier Principalitie therof,* al Churches ſhould for trial of true doctrine, reſorte vnto it.

Yf S. Peter and Paule them ſelues were now liuing in Rome, would ye go to them, for deciſion of a controuerſie, & would ye take them for Judges, in Religion? You could not nor ſhould not, by the law of the Realme. And by S. Peter and Paules owne words, you would proue, that no foraine power hath to doe with you. Of the which one ſaith, *obey the King as the Chiefe*, the Other, *Lette euery manne be ſubiect vnto the Superiour powers.* Which is to ſay (as the newe found Commentaries of theſe daies declare it) Chriſt is Supreame Heade in heauen and earth, and euery King, Supreame in his owne dominions, in both
Courts

1 *Pet.* 2.
Rom. 13.

Courtes, Spiritual and Temporal.

By this Example then, it appereth,
not only that M. Iewel like a blind he=
retike, misconstrueth the plaine wordes
of S. Ireneus : but also, that like a false
Hypocrite, he pretendeth Humilitie and
Obedience, where al his whole practise
is cleane to the contrary. For if in deede
he would be amended, ÿ Pope that now
liueth, is so meeke in Spirit, so diligent
in his Office, so exact in folowing of the
Apostolical Doctrine, so vpright in exe=
quuting of Iustice, so Mighty against ÿ
Diuels themselues (For of late he ex=
pelled some of them, with his Commaun=
dement and worde, without further Ce=
remonie) that he hath not to finde now
so great fault with the Pope, but he may
wel inough yeld due honour vnto him.
But, it is not his meaning so to doo,
what so euer he saith, that if the Church
of Rome would keepe the Apostles Tra=
dition and Doctrine, he woulde frankely
yelde honour vnto it. So great an Hy=
pocrite he is.

S. Hierome abused.

M. Harding to proue the Custome of
the

the peoples Receiuing at home, hath alledged S. Hierom that earneſtli reproueth that cuſtome, and would not haue them receiue at home. S. Hieromes wordes be theſe.

Vvhy dare they not go to the Temples built in the remembrance of Martyrs? Vvhy go they not to the Church? Vvhat is there one Chriſt abroad, an an other at home? If the people did wel, why doth S. Hierome reproue them? If they did il, why doth M.Har. thus allow them?

Hier. 51.
S. Hierome doth not reproue it.

S. Hierõ doth not reproue ẏ Cuſtom. No? doth he not, ſay you. S. Hieroms words be theſe. *Vvhy dare they not go to the Temples built in the remembraunce of Martyrs?* You engliſh not wel, *Ire ad Martyres.* For Churches may be built in ẏ remembrãce of Martyrs, where yet no body or bone of ẏ Martyr is, but by *Ire ad Martyres, to go to the Martyrs,* is ſignified ẏ body or ſome Relik of the Martyr to be in Toumbe, coffin, Shrine, or other like conuenient corner, within ẏ Church or Chappel, where the people made their Stations. But, leaſt it ſhold be perceiued that you agree not wel in your doings tõ the Primitiue Church, at which time, ẏ Martyrs bodies & Reliks wer had in as great reuerẽce as you

Ra.

A falſe engliſhing of Ire ad martyres for feare of cõmending of Reliques.

you of these daies haue them in cõtempt &
dishonour, therfore you speak of no more
then ÿ Temples built in their remembrãce.
And yet this very building of Temples,
in the honour of Martyrs, it seemeth not
that you like very wel, wheras vnto any
one of your so stinking a cũpany of Martyrs, we heare of no ground ÿ you haue
meatte out as yet, to laie therein ÿ fun-
dations of any Pulpit, House, or Memorie, of your Champions.

where be the memo-ries of M. Iewels martyrs?

Now to the sense of S. Hieromes
wordes. *Vvhy do they not goe to the Martyrs? Vvhy go they not to the Church?* That
is, as you (M. Iewel) vnderstand him,
why Receiue they at home, and not at
Church? But this is not S. Hieroms
meaning. For he reproueth not their
Receiuing at home, but their Receiuing
at home the next day that folowed their
nightes pleasure taking of their wines.
Marke that Circumstance, and you shal
quickly perceiue, that you are deceiued,
or haue deceiued.

S. Hierõ reproueth not Receiuing at home.

For take the whole Sentence with
you. *I know (saith S. Hierome) that
this Custome is in Rome, that the faithful do receiue*

Hier. in Apologia

aduersus Iouinianū

ceiue daily the *Body of Chriſt* . And what ſay you than to that Cuſtome? He Anſwereth . Q*uod nec reprehendo , nec probo*. which thinge I neither reproue nor alowe, for euery man abundeth in his owne ſenſe.

What ſhal we ſay then to this caſe? If a man be ſufficiently prepared , and receaue the Sacramēt in his owne houſe at home , and neuer goe to the Publike church for it, may he do it lawfully, or no? S. Hierome ſaieth nothing therevnto, for it perteyned not to the queſtion of Mariage maters, of which he there conſidereth . Yet, M. Iewel thinketh, that S . Hierome Anſwereth this foreſaied queſtion, and that he maketh a ful determination thereof, with an erneſt reproufe of the parties offending againſt it . As if S . Hierom ſhould ſay to the Romaines : what meane you to doubt in this plaine mater? Or why ſhould ye thinke that Receauing at home were lawfull? Do ye not know that the Lordes ſupper is A Communion, and muſt not be taken of one alone? Why dare ye not goe to the Temples of the Martyrs? Are ye afraied of ſprites? Why goe ye not to the Church?

M. Iewels falſe comment.

DD i Is

Is not that, the proper place, to Receaue the Communion in?

Such a Comment would M. Iewel make vpon S. Hierome, And to this effect, he draweth his ernest and sharpe Interrogations. But ye case vnto which S. Hieromes words do rightly answer, is only this. whether he, that hath had carnal knowledge of his wise the night before, do not wel to absteine the next day from going to ye Memories of Martyrs, and the Churches abroade, Or whether he may not Receaue the Sacrament at home? To which his Answer shortly is this, that he may as wel receiue at church as at home, and that he should doe wel not to receaue at al, the day solowing the night of his carnal pleasure, wt his wife.

For after he had said, that he would neither reproue nor cōmend the Custome of daily receiuing of the faithful of Rome: he cōmeth in with an aduersatiue *But, in this sort:* Sed ipsorum conscientiam conuenio, qui eodem die post coitum cōmunicant & c. Quare ad Matyres ire non audent? Quare non ingrediuntur ecclesias? But yet I appose their cōscience, vvhich cōmunicate the same day after they haue carnally

carnally knovven their Vuiues . Vvhy dare they not goe to the Martyrs Memories? Vvhy goe they not to Church? Is Chriſt one abroade ,an other at home? That , vvhich is not lavvful at Church, is not lauful at home. To God nothing is hidden, yea darkeneſſe alſo shineth before him. Let euery one examine himſelf, & ſo coine to the body of Chriſt.

To this end therefore S. Hierome bringeth his whole Argument, not, that it were simplie to be reproued to receaue at home, but, that such as had companied with their wiues the night before, ſhould not the day after Receaue at home, conſidering that they are worthily abaſhed to come before the Martyrs Reliques after such nightes, and that Chriſt is to be honoured, aboue al, and in al places, both at home and abroade . Of which concluſion it would folow, that Matrimonie is not so good as Virginitie, which was one of the hereſies of the Proteſtant Iouinian, whereas by the Acte of Matrimonie, the partie is made for a tyme vnmeete to Receaue the bleſſed Sacrament .

Iudge thou now (Indifferent Reader) whether S . Hierome doth erneſtly reproue the cuſtom of Receiuing at home,

with-

without any addition of such Circum=
stance as varieth the whole question.

S. Augustine abused.

Vho is he (saieth D. Harding out of
S. Augustine) *that knovveth not, that the
Principalitie of Apostleship, is to be preferred before any Bishoprike that is?* which words S.
Augustine speaketh , because of a compa=
rison which he made , betwene S. Peter
and S. Cyprian. For whereas the Dona=
tistes , dyd much obiect against the Ca=
tholikes , that S . Cyprian, with many
other his Felowbishopes, concluded and
determined in a Councel had emong them
selues, that such as were baptized of he=
retikes should be rebaptized againe, whē
they came to the Catholike Church , by
which Authoritie of S. Cyprians name &
other Bishops many, thei thought to bear
downe ỹ papists before them: S. Austine,
like an holy & reuerend father, contēneth
not the Authority of S. Cyprian, but pre=
ferreth ỹ authoritie of S. Peter, before it.

Now, these foresaid words making
expressly for the Principalitie of the Apostleshipe , which was in S . Peter, what
saieth M. Iewel vnto them ? Mary his
first

first Answer is , that Principatus Principality, doth not signifie an vniuersal power, Iew. 249 Of which Answer we haue already spoken, but shortly, this may be repeted, that Spoken grammatically. although *Principatus*, put alone by it self, doth not signifie alwaies an *vniuersal power* (for in euery degree of act and art the best hath the Principalitie, and yet he shall not be Pope or Emperour) yet *Principatus Apostolatus, the Principalitie of Apostleshipe,* doth declare, that in that Order itselfe of Apostles, he that hath the Principalititie is the Chiefe. And surely then , the Chiefe emong the Apostles which were heads of the world, must needes be Supreame Gouernour ouer al Christendom . And thus muche shortly concerning M. Iewels first Answer. The second Answer, or not answer properly, but Cauil and onarel, is,

That M.Harding dissimbleth the words, Iew. 250 that S . Augustine in the very same place allegeth out of S. Cyprian, very wel seruing to this purpose.

To what purpose ? To proue that Ra there is no Supremacie in the Church ?

DD iij Or

Or that S. Peter had not the *Principalitie of Apostleshipe?* Werely, if there might be found any suche sentence, any thing nigh that place, which D. Harding hath alleged for ÿ Supremacie, he could not be excused, either of dissimulation, either of rashnes. But how can you charge hym with any such fault?

Iewel.
D. Harding had no cause to dissimble them, for rightly aledged they make for his purpose.
Ra.

The wordes be these, Nec Petrus vendicauit &c. Neither did Peter challége any thing, or proudly presume of himselfe, to saie, that he had the primacie, and that therfore others, as Nouices and Vnderlinges should be Obedient vnto hym. All these thinges M. Harding dissimbleth.

Is this it, that very well serueth to the purpose? Doth the omitting of this sentence, make D. Harding a Dissimbler? In these wordes, as you allege them, I see the humilitie of S. Peter much commended, but I see not the Principality of his Apostleshipe disproued. wherefore then should D. Harding haue alleged them, or why laie you dissimulation to his charge, for omitting that, which if it had ben vttered, had nothing hindered the Principalitie of Apostleship, which he sought to declare?

But

But I praie thee (Indifferent Reader) to consider M. Iewels sinceritie in this place. In this place I saie, where he obiecteth it againe and againe, and triumpheth vpon it, that M. Harding dissimbleth, and that to fournishe out his mater, and to smoothe his Reader, he leaueth out, what he listeth.

Marke this place again and againe.

O the Trueth that is in M. Iewel. It semeth by him, that if he might winne whole kingdomes, he would not leaue out any iote of Chapiter, that should very wel serue to the purpose. But is he not deceiued in his owne opinion of himself? Is not he himselfe properly a dissimbler?

This that foloweth wil trie it.

Behold what he hath done. In this very sentence, for leaning out of which, he noteth D. Harding, hymselfe leaueth quite and cleane out those wordes, which if he had interpreted, as he did the rest of the sentence, it should easily haue ben perceaued, that D. Harding had no cause to dissimble. What meane I hereby? Mary this I mean, that this sentence, which M. Iewel would haue to be taken, as qualifieing and diminishing, the Principalitie of Apostleshipe, by whiche D.

D.D. iiij Har=

Harding did proue the Supremacie, this very Sentence, I say, doth manifestly confirme the Principalitie or Supremacie of S. Peter, if it had ben truly and wholy set furth of M. Iewel. And therefore seeing it made for the Supremacie, D. Harding could not possibly be a dissimbler, in leauing it out. For he left that out, which made to his purpose, if he would haue ben copious, and not that, which was any thing againste hym, to proue him thereby iniurious to the trueth. For these be the wordes.

Lib.2.con.
Donat.c.1.

Peter
Chiefe
and first.

Cyp.ad
Quirinū.

Nec Petrus, quem primum Dominus ele-git, & super quem ædificauit Ecclesiam suam, cum secum Paulus de Circumcisione disceptaret, postmodum vendicat sibi aliquid, & c. Neither did Peter (vvhom our Lord did choose to be first andChiefe, and vpō vvhom he builded his church) strangely chalenge any thing aftervvarde vnto himselfe, or proudly take vpon him, vvhen Paule did striue vvith him concerning Circumcision, saieing that he had the Primacie, and that the Nouices and Vnderlinges should rather obey him.

As if S. Cyprian should haue saied (for S. Cyprianes wordes they be) S. Peter had the Primacie, yet he disdained

not

not at S. Paules iudgemēt about circū=
cisiō, though S. Paul were his inferiour.
By like argument to which S. Augustin
also withstādeth the obiection of the Do=
natistes, which toke great holdfast of S.
Cyprians Authoritie concerning rebap=
tisation, and saieth thus in effect: Like as
S. Peter though he were Primate and
had the Church builded vpon hym, was
better aduised by S. Paule a later Apo=
stle than hymselfe: So although S. Cy=
prian be of excellent Authoritie and me=
rite, he must not yet refuse to haue his
opinion amended by other of lower de=
gree and worthines.

And this being the Sense of the place,
doth it not euidently make for S. Peters
Supremacie? Doth it not commend his
humilitie vnto vs, in that Supremacie?
Doth it not preferre him before S. P aule
in vocation and Authoritie? And doth it
not set furth his lowlines and charitie,
in most quiet yelding vnto S. Paul, not=
withstanding he might haue stood vpon
his principalitie? He therefore that saith,
the Principalitie of Apostleshipe to be in
S. Peter, and addeth not thereunto, that
　　　　　　　　our

S. Pe=
ters supre=
macie
proued by
that very
place
which M.
Iewel
brought
against it.

our Lord chose him to be first, and that vppon him he builded his Church, iu not
aɮding this later part, he diſſimbleth not,
noʒ hideth from the Readers knowlege,
any thing that wel ſerueth to the purpoſe.
Foʒ this later part, ſo litle coʒrecteth the
foʒmer, that it geaueth moʒe ſtrengthe
vnto it.

M. Iew.
the diſ-
ſimbler,

But wil A man ſee a diſſimbler?
You M. Iewel are he. And that in this
very place where you are buſy in finding
fault with other foʒ diſſimbling. Theſe
woʒdes, M. Iewel, touching S. Peter,
*VVhom our Lord choſe to be firſt or
Chiefe, and vpon whom he builded
his Church,* Dyd ye not ſee theſe woʒds
M. Iewel? How could ye but ſee them,
wheras they ſtand in that ſentence which
you ſo much eied, that foʒ not ſpeaking of
it, you find fault with D. Harding? The
begynning and end of which, wheras
you interpʒeted vnto the Reader, how
could ye but ſee the myddle? And there=
foʒe ſeeing the woʒdes, and yet ſkipping
them, who now is the diſſimbler, if we
may come befoʒe equal Iudges? The
woʒds

woods which you leue out, are not light, they are not impertinent to the question of ý Supremacie, they are plaine and euident, that *Our Lord chose Peter to be first or Chiefe,* and that vppon hym, *he builded his Church.* And yet you (good man) haue dealt plainely, in leauing them out altogeather.

And now, becaufe fuch diſſimulation is very wicked, and that your honeſtie (M. Iewel) may the better be noted, I wil bring one place more out of the Doctours, in which I wil shew, ý you haue abuſed them in this ſpecial point of diſſimbling, and Smoothing your Reader, and leauing out what liſteth you.

S. Ambroſe abuſed.

To proue, that S. Peters Supremacie was no greater than his felowes, you allege S. Ambroſe after this ſort. Euen ſo ſaith S. Ambroſe too, and that, in the very ſame place that M Harding hath alleged. *Inter Petrum & Paulum quis cui præponatur, incertum eſt. Of Peter and Paule vvhether ought to be preferred before other, it is not knovven.*

Doth S. Ambroſe ſpeake theſe words, as doubting which were higher in dignity

Iohn. 246 Moſt ſhãful diſſimulacion and craft.

Ra.

nity & power? It is hard to beleue it of A Catholike Doctour. Yet except we proue ꝑ contrary out of this place, M. Iewels affirmatiue shall vtterly ouercome our coniecture. Let the place then be considered. what foloweth (speake M. Iewel) what foloweth in S. Ambrose, immediatly vpon the wordes, which you haue alleged? Mary this foloweth.

Ambro.
Ser.66.

Puto enim illos æquales esse meritis, quia æquales sunt passione. Of Peter and Paule vvhether ought to be preferred before other, is it not knovvē: For I thinke them to be equal in Merites, becaule they are equal in suffering, And I thinke that they lyued in like deuotion of Faith, vvhom vve haue seen to haue come to the Glory of Martyrdome togeather.

How say you then, doth not this plainely declare, that the doubt in which S. Ambrose was, whether of the two

S.Peter & Paule equal in Merites.

ought to be preferred before the other, came not of ignorāce of that point, which concerned the Supremacie of the See and Church of Rome, but of this which perteineth to their personal deserts and merites, In which, he thinketh that the one was equal with the other?

And

And wherefore then haue you left out those wordes that folowed so immediatly, by which the true and right vnderstanding of the place might be perceiued? Is not this crafty dissimbling? wil you say that you dyd not see so much, whereas so much foloweth immediatly in S. Ambrose? Or can you say ý you thought it litle to serue to the purpose, whereas the true Answer to your Obiection, is thereby vttered and expressed? But let vs come neerer.

Not sixlynes before this place of which you would haue your Reader to geather, that S. Peter had no greater Supremacie than S. Paule, thus saieth S. Ambrose after a short discourse made vpon S. Peter and Paule. *Ambo igitur claues à Domino perceperunt, Scientiæ iste. ille potentiæ. So then both of them haue receaued keies of our Lord, S. Paule of science, S. Peter of povver.*

Consider now of this place, Indifferent Reader, was S. Ambrose in any doubt, which of the two, S. Peter or S. Paul was to be preferred? He was, and he was not. Concerning their godlines and Merites, he knew not whom to preferre

S. Peter & Paule not equal in power.

ferue before the other, but thinketh them to be equal therein. Concerning Authoritie and Office, he knew how to geaue eche of thē his owne, preferring S. Paule for his knowledge, and S. Peter for his power. It is not therefore simply true, as M. Iewel reherseth the wordes of S. Ambrose, that, whether of them ought to be preferred before the other it is not knowē. For if he would haue looked to that, which went but a litle before, he should haue readen the keies of Science geauen to S. Paule, and the keies of power to S. Peter.

what say we then to this blindnes or Craft? Is M. Iewel that felow, that doth not dissimble? Doth not he take what hym lyketh, and refuse what hym listeth? He beginneth Sentencies where hym pleaseth. He endeth senses when he is disposed. The myddle of Sentencies, he leaueth quite and cleane out, That which went before or commeth after, he looketh nothing vnto, such is his Simplicitie. To make hymselfe the lesse suspected, he findeth (without iust occasion) fault with other for leauing out I can not

not tel what. To be short, there was ne=
uer, I thinke, an Heretike so ful of wor=
des, so vntrue in wordes, so faire spoken,
so fowly intending, so muche alleging
Auncient Fathers, so litle regarding any
Authoritie, So precise in appealing to
phrases, termes, and titles, And so loose
in abusing the sense and the meaning of
his witnesses. And thus much concer=
ning the Auncient Fathers.

How M. Iewel hath abused the Later Writers.

TO speake of ᵱ Later writers, whõ
M. Iewel hath abused, I haue no
greate mynd, because if I proue,
neuer so plainely, any article of the
Catholike Faith by them: that auaileth
nothing vnto them, which vtterly refuse
al Late writers, at their pleasure. Yet
that M. Iewel may hereafter, vse more
Trueth and Sinceritie in his writings,
he shall perceaue that they are like to be
marked, how tedious so euer he shal mak
them through his heaps of allegations:
I wil

I will beginne the Chapiter vnto which, such his abusing of Late wꝛiters is to be referred, as shal be found easily in his wꝛitinges.

And first, concerning holy and Re=uerend Fathers though not so old as others, I wil bꝛing in S. Bernard as M. Iewel saieth, but as the Trueth is Guerricus: In the second place A=lexander de Hales foꝛ Scholemen: In the third Polidoꝛe Vergile, foꝛ huma=nitians, that how few kinde of wꝛiters M. Iewel spareth, it may easily be per=ceined in Examples. As thus.

Iohn. 69
Heresl.

Guerricus abused.

Men and Womē made the Sacrifice of the Aultar, and that of Bread & wine. And therefore after the order of Melchisedech. Therefore S. Bernard saieth, Non solus Sacerdos sacrificat, sed totus Conuentus Fidelium, not only the Priest Sacrificeth, but also the whole Cūpanie of the Faithful.

Ra.

Is it possible that S. Bernard might say so? An Abbote, A Saier of Masse, A notable Papist? Oꝛ is it possible that M. Iewel, hath in al his art, any shift to de=fend himselfe in this place from lying?

First

First it is most euident, that S. Bernard hath no such wordes. The Sermon which M. Iewel referreth vs vnto, is the holy Fathers Guerricus Abbat of Igniacum.

In any of these two poits M. Iew. may be apprehended.

Then, neither he saith as M. Iewel concludeth. For why? there is not in al his Sermon, any mention of Bread and wine offered at the Aulter, Or, to the Aulter, by men and women, Neither of the Order of Melchisedech.

Of the offering vp of Turtles and Doues, he speaketh, but he meaneth not of the birdes themselues, but of the vertues represented by them : as Chastitie of body and soule, Compunction of hart, Simplicitie, Patience, Charitie, & such like. wherevpon he inferreth, concerning Priestes, saying :

Such manner of men it becommeth vs to be, vvhen vye Consecrate the Body of Christ. &c. And concerning the Laietie : *Such maner of men also it behoueth you to be, vvhich receiue of our handes, the holy Sacrament, &c.*

Guerricus in Ser. de purificationes.

Now because it might be obiected, that it is for Priestes to haue the foresaid vertues, Or that it is their charge onely,

EE i   13

to prepare them selues, least they receiue the Sacrament vnworthily (as though the standers by, had litle to do with him in those maters) he answereth, We must not beleue that the forsaid vertues are necessary for the Priest only, as though he alone should Consecrate or offer the Body of Christ. He doth not sacrifice alone, he alone doth not consecrate, but al the cumpanie of the faithful (and here M. Iewel maketh a ful and a fowle point) that standeth by doth consecrate with him, doth sacrifice with him.

A point of M. Iewels art.

But how? After the order of Melchisedech, Or, by their own Act & Priesthood, as M. Iewel gathereth? Surely, except Guerricus him selfe had made it plaine, in what sense the Priest and the People do offer, no doubt, but M. Iewel in this place, would outface vs, that this Abbat meant, that men and women were Priestes after the order of Melchisedech. Notwithstanding that it is not saied, the cũpani of the faithful do cõsecrate, as though they might do it by themselues, but they consecrate with him (the Priest) signifieng the Office to be singular. And it foloweth in the Sermon.

Neither

Neither the Carpenter alone doth make a house, but one bringeth roddes, an other rafters, an other postes or beames and other things. By which Similitude, it is manifest, that the people consecrate, in this sense, that they bring sumwhat to that end. And what is that? By this that foloweth it wil be vnderstanded. For thus he concludeth.

Therefore the standers by, ought to haue of their ovvne, euen as the Priest ought? What? A Cope trow you M. Iewel, vpon their backes, or a Surplesse like Ministers, or power and Authoritie of Priesthod? No. but, a sure faith, a pure prayer, a godly deuotion. where then is the Breade and wine, or the Order of Melchisedech, which you would proue to perteine to the common people with, Therfore S. Bernard saith, or Otherwise called Guerricus.

Answer to this point.

Here is a Conclusion without Premisses, And a comparison without any likelyhoode, And A falsification without truth or honestie.

Alexander of Hales abused.

Iew. 98.

The people taking but one kind only receiueth iniurie, as M. Harding may see

EE ij   by

by Alexander de Hales, and Durandus, &
other of his owne Doctours. Alexanders
wordes be these. Licèt illa Sumptio, &c.
Although that Order of Receiuing the Sacrament, which is vnder one kinde, be sufficient, yet the other which is vnder both
kindes, is of greater merite.

Ra.

Al this, M. Iewel, is true : but this
proueth not, that the people haue any
iniury done vnto them. For to Receiue
vnder one kinde, it is sufficient by Alexanders expresse wordes : but vndoubtedly,
if any thing lacked of that which were
due, there wer not sufficiécy : Ergo, how
proue you by Alexander, that the people
are Iniuried , in receining vnder one
kinde ?

*M, Iew.
faileth of
his pur-
pose.*

You wil Replie out of him, that it is
of greater merite to receiue in both kinds,
than one. And what of that ? It is a
greater merite to Celebrate thrise a day
(as at Christmasse) then once, as Ordinarily Priestes do vse. Do ye thinke
then, that any Priestes haue Iniury don
vnto them, because the Order is otherwise, that they say but one Masse in one
daie, except one daie onely in the yeare :
Againe I say, that Alexander noteth
a greater

*It is not
alwaies
Iniurie,
when y̆ is
limited
which is
of greater
merite.*

a greater merite to be in Receiuing vnder both than one kind, not in respect of
the Sacramente , which is as persite in
one as both, and in the least part of one,
as the whole: but in respect of the Recei-
uers, because their Deuotion is encrea-
sed,and their Faith dilated by longer cō-
tinuing in th'Act of Receiuing,and their
Receiuing is more Complete as being
ministred in both kindes . And as the
causes on the behalfe of the Receiuer, do
make it, to a person so disposed, more effectual, to Receiue in both than one : So
other causes there be, which doe make ẙ
Receiuing vnder one kinde, to be to the
party so affected, more fruictful and me-
ritorious,than if he tooke both. For,he
that would say vnto him self, I wil content my selfe with the common Order of
the Church, I wil not make any Sturre
about both kindes, knowing ẙ as much
is vnder one as both : vndoubtedly such
a man should both for his Humilitie,and
for his Faith, deserue more a great deale,
then if he should Receiue in both kindes,
and find a certaine sense and tast of Deuotion .

A greater
merit:
may be in
receiuing
vnder one
kind than
both.

C C iij The

The strength therefore and efficacie which Alexander speaketh of, depending vpon the Act of the Receiuer, and not vpon the Vertue of $\tilde{y}$ Sacrament, which is al one in effect, whether it be ministred in one or both kindes: M. Iewel doth very iniuriously, to put a fault herein, $\tilde{y}$ they Receiue not vnder both, & to make Alexander of this opinion, that to minister in one kinde, were an Iniurie vnto the people.

For this I would aske further of him, whether the simple and deuout people, are not more stirred vp to remember the Death and Blond of Christe, if they should Receiue in Claret or Red wine, than in white? No doubt, but the imaginatiō would be more affected and moued, by seeing a like colour vnto $\tilde{y}$ which it would conceiue, than a contrary or diuerse colour. How then? would M. Iewel thinke it an Iniury to minister in white wine vnto the people, though thei would be desirous of Red? He should not thinke it, if he be wise. And why so? Mary, because they haue as much in the white as the Red, and to receiue in Red, han▪

A Case to M. Iew.

hangeth vpon their priuate deuotion, &
not vpon any precept of the Churche, or
doctrine of the Apostles, or Institution
of Christe, to which onely, the Priest is
bound, and which, if he obserue, he doth
his duety,

Be it so then, that many good folke
for diuerse causes, should be exceedingly
moued and edified, by drinking of the
Chalice, and contemplating of more then
is Ordinarie in their minde: should they
haue any Iniurie done vnto them, if they
receiued afterwardes, when the Priest
should iudge it expedient, vnder þ forme
of bread only? Neyther doth Alexander de Hales so say, neither any reason
doth make for it. But let vs see an o-
ther place of Alexander, which M. Iewel hath abused.

The same Alexander againe saith, Totus Christus, &c. Whole Christ is not conteined vnder ech kind by way of Sacramēt
but the fleash onely, vnder the fourme of
bread, and the bloud vnder the fourme of
wine.

Pcw.99.
Shameful-
ly abused.

Ra.

The woordes can not be denied to
be Alexanders, but what sense gathereth
M. Iewel of them?

CC iiij   Here

Iew.
Open Lie

Here M. Hardinges owne Doctours confesse, that the people Receiuing vnder one kinde, receiueth not the ful Sacramét, nor the bloud of Christe by way of Sacrament.

Ra.

You vnderstand not Alexander, or you wil not. For, whereas he saith: *Christ is not conteined vnder ech kinde Sacramentally*, he meaneth not, that the people Receiue not the *Ful Sacrament* and their owne Maker, Godde and Manne, vnder eche kinde: but by this woorde *Sacramentally*, he meaneth, that concerning the forme of woordes, by which consecration is perfited in eche kinde, and by external forme of the Signes vnder which Christ is exhibited, *the flesh only is conteined vnder the forme of Breade, and the bloud vnder the forme of Vvine*. As, when Christ said: *This is my bloud* : the woordes which we heare, doe signify no more than Bloude to be there present, And ý external Signe and liquor of wine, doth represent a presence of bloud onely. And this is that which Alexander meaneth, by the woorde *Sacramentally*, when he saith, *Vvhole Christ is not conteined vnder ech kind Sacramentally*.

For

For he speaketh of the representation on¹
ly which is made to our senses, by exter¹
nal wordes & Signes, and not of y⁹ thing
it selfe and substance of the Sacrament,
which is apprehended by Faith.

Now that Alexander was not of
this mind, which M. Iew. would make
him to be of, that whole Christ should
not be receaued vnder ech kind, though
whole Christ were not signified by the
sound of the wordes of Consecration in
ech kind, it is manifest by the next article
in him, where he concludeth, that, *Christus* q. 49.
integer Deus & homo est sub specie Panis. Vvhole Mem. 3.
ChristGod and Man is vnder the forme of Bread. art. 3.
And, both sayinges are true, that *vvhole
Christ is not vnder ech kind.* if ye consider on¹
ly the Signe of the wordes that are spo¹
ken, or the ringes that are shewed (for   Let M.
in saying, this is my bodie, no mention is   Iew. dis¹
made of bloud). And againe, that, *vvhole*   tinct thin¹
Christ God and man is vnder the forme of Bread,   ges right
if ye consider the mater Really.   ly and he
shal per¹

Alexander therfore, speaketh no other¹   ceiue quic
wise in this point, then it becummeth A   kly his
faithful and Catholike man to do. And   owne ig¹
M. Iewel doth no otherwise, than he is   norance.
wont

wont to do, but otherwise surely than becummeth an honest and lerned man, specially hauinge no neede to alleage any
Scholemen, and lesse neede to corrupt
them, when he allegeth them.

Polidorus Uergilius abused.

Cyp.lib.1,
Epist.3.

9. Cyprian calleth the Church of
Rome, *Ecclesiam principalem, vnde vnitas Sa-*
cerdotalis exorta est, the principal Church, from
vvhence the Vnitie of Priestes hath spronge. Out
of which testimonie M. Jewel gathereth
A force, as it were, of two Argumentes
that might be made, the one in that it is
called, *Ecclesia principalis, the principal or chief*
Churche : the other because it soloweth,
vnde vnitas Sacerdotalis exorta est (whiche
wordes D. Harding doth interpret thus)
from vvhence the vnitie of Priestes is spronge.
M. Jewel thus, fró whence the vnitie of
the Priesthood first began. In which his
Interpretation there is a plaine falsehod
and craftines.

For in repeting the wordes, and in
writing of them, so as if they were D.
Hardings, it becummed hym to deliuer
them furth in the same forme, as he found
them

them in D. Harding. Then, whereas it is not al one to say, the vnitie of Priesthood sprange from Rome, and the vnitie of Priesthod began first at Rome (for there may be springs two or three in one place, and although the water issue not out, first at the lowest, yet the lowest of the three maie be the chiefe head vnto al the riuers beneth) M. Iewels intent was not simple, to cast in this word (first) into the sentence, as though the question were, not whether the Chife Prieste in all the world were at Rome, but, whether the first Priest in al the world began at Rome. Betwene which two propositions, there is a great Difference.

Craft in changing and interpreting.

But what sayth M. Iewel to these wordes, Vnde vnitas Sacerdotalis exorta est, from whence the vnitie of Priesthoode first begã, as he englisheth it for a vātage?

For that these words seme for to weigh much, I thinke it good herein to heare the Iudgement of some other man, that may seeme Indifferent.

Iew.305

Why should Polidore Vergile be Indifferent? He lyued not fiftie yeres sens he was a Collectour to ꝑ Bishop of Rome, and therefore to you not Indifferent

Ra.

rent. And to vs on the other side, not
Indifferent, becauſe this very booke *de
Inuentoribus rerum*, is condemned by the
Generral Councel at Trent. But you
haue fond ſomewhat in him by likelihod,
which maketh for you, that you eſteeme
of hym ſo wel. And what is that, I praie
you? we aſke you for the Anſwer to
S. Cyprians words, you bring in Polidore to expound them. but what wil ye

conclude of Polidore? That, This commendation (of which S. Cyprian ſpeaketh)
was geauen by S. Cyprian to the Church
of Rome in reſpect of Italie, and not in reſpect of the whole world.

Whether this be ſo or no, Polidors
owne wordes ſhal trie it. In his fourth
booke the ſixth Chapiter, his purpoſe
was to ſhew, of whom firſt the Order of
Prieſthood was Inſtituted. And he proueth, that Chriſt hym ſelfe was the firſt
maker of Prieſtes. Then doth it folowe
in hym.

*At poſt Chriſtum Petrus in Sacerdotio præro-
gatiuam habuiſſe dicitur, quòd primus in Apo-
ſtolorum ordine, & eius Sacroſancti Collegij
Caput fuiſſet. Quapropter D. Cyprianus epiſt. 3. ad
Corne-*

Corneliū Cathedram Petri Principalē vocat. But after Chriſt Peter is ſaid to haue had the prero-gatiue in prieſthood , becauſe he vvas the firſt in the revv of the Apoſtles , and head of that holy College. VVherefore S. Cyprian in his third epiſtle to Cornelius, calleth the Chaire or See of S. Peter the Chiefe or principal.

Moꝛe then this, touching any woꝛds of S. Cypꝛian, if any man can there find in Polidoꝛe, I wil leeſe my right hand foꝛ it , and neuer wꝛite hereafter againſt any heretike. but the Booke is common, the place is intelligible, and my eyes and vnderſtanding ſerueth me ſo wel, that, I am ſure , Polidoꝛe in that place expoun-deth not theſe woꝛdes of S . Cypꝛian, *Vnde Vnitas Sacerdotalis exorta eſt .*

Let M. Iewel re proueme. if he can.

what Impudencie then is it in M. Iewel, forthat theſe words ſeme to weigh much , **to bꝛing furth the Iudgement of Polidoꝛe, a man** that may ſeme to be In-different, **whereas they are not at all in Polidoꝛe?** Polidorus Virgilius (ſaieth he) expoūdeth the ſame words of S. Cyprian. **Dare ye ſay he expoundeth them, where-as he hath not them ? He bꝛingeth in S. Cypꝛian , to pꝛone that the See of S.**

impudēcie

Peter

Peter was principal, but, of Vnitas Sacerdotalis, the vnitie of Priesthood, Vpon which wordes, you made haste to shewe his exposition, he maketh no mention. He saieth in his owne wordes, not in S. Cyprians, that *the order of Priesthood can not be saied to haue grovven first from the Bishope of Rome, onlesse vve vnderstand it only by Italie, for Priesthood vvas rightly instituted at Hierusalem* but that the Commendation geauen by S. Cyprian to the Church of Rome was geauen in respect only of Italy, and not in respect of the whole world, he saied it not, nor intended it.

The Order also of Priesthood, and vnitie of Priesthood are two thinges. In the Order, is considered, the Author and effect of that Sacrament: In the Vnitie is considered, the preseruation and Gouernement of that Order. Of the Order it selfe, and where Priesthood first began, Polidore doth speake. Of the vnity, and of the Relation which all Priestes should haue to their chiefe head and Gouernour, S. Cyprian doth speake, and Polidore saieth nothing. The Order began at Hierusalem and not at Rome.

The

The vnity, I wil not say begā at Rome,
but after ẏ S. Peter had by his martyrdō
there takē ful possession of that Sec, then
was it seen, where the Principal Church
in al the world was, and to what begynning al thinges should be referred, and
in what vnitie they should be preserued.

Hath not M. Iewel, then, done very sincerely, to allege Polidore, so farre
and wyde from the meaning of Polidor?
I would there were some man so indifferent, as M. Iewel taketh Polidore to
be, to Iudge betwene hym and vs, whether he hath not shamefully abused the
Later wryters.

Of M. Iewels Contra-
dictions.

Hytherto, by many Examples I
haue proued it, ẏ M. Iewel hath
not vnderstanded other men: now
wil I shew it, by a fewe Arguments, that he doth not wel vnderstand
hymselfe. And no maruel truly, if in
speaking so many words, he hath not remembred

membred euery word, Or, if in coueting
to saue his honestie for the present place,
he saie and vnsay againe, like A man that
were not sure yet what to byde by. But
because his Feindes and Felowes wil
thinke this incredible , that out of his
smooth'mouth, a doctrine squared by the
rule of the Scriptures, Fathers, & Coūcels , any thing should procede hacked &
flittered . therefore wil J geaue an occasion to the Indifferent, to Beware of the
dubble tongue and mynd, in one and the
selfe same Master Jewel .

Jew.25.

The Receiuing with Companie, is no
substantial part of Christes Institution: Ergo, we are not bounde therein, to folow the

we are
bound to ẏ
example of
Christ.

Example of Christ . First this Antecedent
is false, and if it were no part, of the substāce
of Christes Institution , Yet we are neuerthelesse bound to his Example, because he
hath commaunded vs so to doe .

Ra.

Here in this place (M. Jewel) you
are of the mynd that there is a difference,
betwene the Institution of Christ, and the
Example of Christ . Otherwise your
saying were very folishe , As by which
this only is imported , that , it were no
part of Christs Institutiō, yet are we neuer
the

thelesse bound to his Institution . **which maketh a plaine contradiction, if that by Institution and Example, you meane but one thing .** An other thing that I note here, is, that you say , we are bound to Christes Example, although the thing **which is to be done, were not of his Institution.**

what say ye then, to washing of feete, for which you haue the expresse words of our Sauiour in the Gospel? *If I (sayth* Io. 13. *he) your Lord and Master haue vvashed your feete, you also ought to vvash one the others feete. For I haue geauen an Example vnto you, that as I haue done, so likevvyse that ye also doe.* **what say you then (M. Iewel) to this example of our Sauiour? shal it be folowed, or no?** You Answer,

That this Obiection of washing of Iew.116. feete is common , and hath ben often Answered . **And in the same page.** The washing of feete, was neither Institution of we are Christ, nor any part of the Sacrament, nor not bound Specially apointed to be done by the Apo- to the exāstles, nor the breache thereof euer deemed Christ. Sacrilege .

To let passe the manifest lye, which here you make, that Christ apointed not Ra.

FF j   washing

washing of feete to be done by the Apostles, I marke this only for the present, ̄y you labour with al your wit,to proue,that ye are bound to keepe ̄y Example of Chrikt. Reconcile me then (I praie you) thefe two places, And tel vs how it may stand togeather,that we are boúd to Chrikts example, in that which is not of the Sub-stance of Chrikts Institution, And yet that you may freely(as ye do) let go washing of feete in your Congregation,becauſe it was not Chrikstes Institution?

Jew.31.

Not for
the ſicke.

In the Primitiue church,this order(of ſending the Sacramēt to them that were departing this world)was thought expe-dient not for the Sicke : For they in their health receiued daily .

Ra.

Ergo , if in health , they needed, or vſed that daily ſuſtenance, was it not pro-uided for them in their ſicknes ? Yeas,ye confeſſe ſo much, And therefore you ſay:

Jew.
For the
ſicke.
Ra.

And in their ſickneſſe, had the Sacra-ment Ordinarily ſent home vnto them.

How ſay ye then euen now,that this order (concerning the neceſſarie vitaile, the Sacrament) was not thought expe-dient for the ſicke? Except you know that a man may be in ſickneſſe , and yet not
ſicke

ficke. But goe ye forwarde, and make an
end of your tale. If the neceſſarie vitaile,
was not for ẙ ſicke, for whô was it then?

Not for the ſicke & c. but for perſons
Excômunicate, & c.

Iew.
For per-
ſons excô
municate.

Uery wel. How long wil you tarie
in this mynd? Ye amend it, within xx.
lynes folowing. For thus ye remember
your ſelfe better.

Ra.

Howbeit I confeſſe, ſometimes it was
otherwiſe vſed.

Iew.
For other
than excô=
municate.

We take your confeſſion, that you
know not wel where to ſtaie. For diuiding (as it were) al the Faithful, Into
Sicke, and Excommunicate, And ſub=
diuiding the Sicke, into them that were
either in health, either in Sicknes: You
left none but Perſons Excommunicate,
for whom the neceſſarie vitaile, called via-
ticum, ſhould ſerue. How be it, ye confeſſe
it was Sometimes otherwiſe vſed, and ſo
it muſt neceſſarely folow, that it was not
for the Excommunicate only. How theſe
thinges agree, I doe but aſke you the
queſtion.

Ra.

A pretty
Diuiſion.

If there had ben in it any ſhew of trueth,
M. Harding as he is eloquent, would haue
laied out al the circumſtancies, when this

Iew. 112

FF ij

ſtrange

ſtrange errour firſt began, where, and how longe it continued, who wrote againſt it, And by whom, and in what Councel it was condemned. Verely this greate Silence declareth ſome want.

Declarig of Circū= ces requi= red.

Ra.

See how erneſt the man is, to haue al Circumſtances declared. But, I trow, he wil not tary ſtil in this minde. For when D. Harding (as reaſon is) aſked, when the Latine Seruice began in England, and when the Engliſh ceaſed (for Heretikes ſay, ẏ in the primitiue Church, al publike praier was in the knowen and vulgare Tongue, And the Catholikes thinke, that ſome token then or Monument ſhould be extant, of ſo generall a mater) M. Iewel with open mouthe replieth:

Iew. 187 Declarig of Circū= ſtancies refuſed.

O what folie is this? Who is hable to ſhew any Boke writen in Engliſh a thowſand yeres agoe? Or if it could be ſhewed, yet who were hable to vnderſtand it?

Ra.

Loe, now it is foly to require, but ſome litle ſigne of the begynning or ceaſing of a publike and common mater, but in an other place he thinketh it wiſely ſpoken (for he ſpeaketh it hym ſelfe) to demaund particularly of diuerſe Circū=
ſtancies

ſtancies, when, where, how, who, by whō, and in what Councell, errours began or appeared.

That certeine godly perſons both men and women in time of perſequution, or of ſicknes, or of other neceſſitie receaued the Sacrament in their houſes, it is not denied. Iew.42. Receuing at home alowed.

Ergo Receauing at home is not reproueable, for which there are to be found the Examples of Godly perſons both men and women. Ra.

This maner of receauing at home was not lauful for the Laiemen. For it was aboliſhed by godly Biſhops in general Coūcel. Iew.42. Receuing at home diſalowed

You belye the Councel, vnto which you referre vs. For of Receauing at home it ſpeaketh no one word, but, *If any perſon,* ſaith it, *be proued not to haue receiued in the Church, and not to haue made an end, of the Grace of the Euchariſt. let him be accurſed for euer.* **Now this forbyddeth not, but that the Prieſt may carie the Sacramēt home to the houſes of Chriſtians, as it is, at this preſent, vſed in the catholike church, And that they may with good Conſcience receaue it. But let this be referred to the Chapiter,** *How M. Iewel hath abuſed Councels.* **In this place, I preſſe hym** Ra. Concil. Caſarauguſtanū. Cap. 3.

FF ij only

only with his contradiction: that sometymes he doth not denie, but that Godly
Perſons did receaue, Privately at home,
and, at an other tyme, he is altogeather
chaunged, and wil needes haue receiuing
at home to be an Abuse condemned by
Councels and Fathers.

The Single Cōmuniō was neuer taken for
lawful, but only in conſideration of circumſtancies, and caſes of neceſſitie.

How then is the Myſtical diſtribution
a part of the ſubſtance of Chriſtes Supper,
if, for any reſpecte it maie be altered or
omitted?

Thinketh M. Harding, that the Sacrifice, whereof neither Chriſt nor his Diſciples euer ſpake one word, is the ſubſtance
of his Supper, And that the Myſtical Diſtribution in remembraunce of his Death,
whereof he gaue vs ſuch a ſtraight Commaundement, in ſo manifeſt and ſo plaine
wordes, is no part of the Subſtance?

And thinke you, that if Diſtribution
be neceſſary, any mā may receiue by him
ſelfe alone, in any kind of Caſe or Cir-
cumſtance? For as no neceſſity can make
it lawful, to Conſecrate in Cheeſe or
Milke, becauſe Bread and Wine perteine

to

Iew. 59.
Singl:
Cōmuniō
in ſom ca-
ſes lauful.
Ra.

Iew. 61.
Diſtribu-
tion is of ý
Subſtāce
of Chriſts
Supper.
And ſo is
Single
Commu-
nion abſo-
lutely vn-
lawful.
Ra.

to the mater and Substance of the Sacrament: So, if the Single Communion be lawful, that is, if one by him selfe alone may Receiue the Sacrament, it must needes folow, that to Receiue with Cumpany, is not of the Substaunce of Chzistes Institution.

The simple people hearing Masse in a strange Language, is deafe, and heareth not at al.

Jew.70. Hearing and not Hearing. Ra.

You must expound your meaning, oz els hearing, and not hearing, wil not be wel perceiued. For, if ye referre hearing of Masse, to the hearing of ẏ wozds, the sownd doth strike the eare, though ẏ meaning come not to the mind. And if ye referre hearing of Masse, to ẏ vnderstanding of ẏ which is there done, then doth euery faithful, ẏ beleueth ẏ body of Chzist there to be offered vp vnbloudily, foz him, &c. heare the Masse as excellently, as if he could conster and parse euery wozd of the Canon. And therefoze you can not without plain iniury, make ẏ people not to heare ẏ, which thei do heare with their eares: oz not to appzehēd ẏ in their hart, which they be assured of by Faith.

FF iiij *Melanch-*

*Melanchthon and Bucer ac=
compted the receiuing in one or both
kindes a thing indifferent.* M. Iewel
answereth :

Thus farre furth their desire was, it might
be iudged free, not that thei thought Christ
had not ordeined the Sacrament to be ministred vnto the people in both kindes, or
that in itselfe it is Indifferent, but that the
Faithful of God might indifferently and
freely vse it without controlment.

Iew.110.

Not indif=
ferent.

Indifferēt

Ra.

These wordes neede A Reconci=
liation, to bring them at one togeather.
For if the receiuing in both kinds be not
in it selfe Indifferent, how may the faithful of God indifferently vse it? And if they
may Indifferently vse it, how it is not In=
different?

Note also the Crafte or blindnes of
M. Iewel. He Interpreteth Melanch=
thon and Bucer, in suche sorte, as if the
question had ben, Whether the people
might not choose, whether they would receaue in both kindes, or not receaue at all.
And he maketh them to answer, that they
wishe it to be free and Indifferent, to Re=
ceaue in both if they wil. But the que=
stion

M. Iew=
els priuat
comment
vpon Me
lancthon &
Bucer.

ſion in deede, is of Receauing in both
kinds,or in one: And they Anſwer, that it
is a thing Indifferent. And what is ẏ
to ſay? whether that it ſhould be free for
the people to Receaue in both? Yea truly
this is one part of the ſenſe. But another
is,that it ſhould be as free, for them that
would,to receaue in one alſo .

For the two pointes, betwene which
the Indifferencie goeth,are,to receaue in
one kind, Or to receaue in both , without
controlment. which being graunted to
the Proteſtants, they ſhould not inueigh
and crie out againſt the Papiſtes, for re-
ceauiug in one, but they might thinke
themſelues charitably diſpenſed withal,
for their free Receauing vnder both . So
that Melanchthon and Bucer were not
of the mynde to condemne the maner of
other Chriſtians , as M. Iewel in this
place falſely interpꝛeteth them , but lyke
wiſe Heretikes, they pꝛouided for their
owne ſafetie , wiſhing that it might be
lawful foꝛ their bꝛothers, to Receaue in
both kindes,without cótrolment, and ẏ it
ſhould not be made a mater of conſcience
and Religion , whether the people were
ſerued

serued in both oʒ one kind, the thing in it selfe being Indifferent.

Iew.119
He onely
saith it,

To minister vnto the vulgare people in both kindes was not Christes Institution, saith D. Harding. oʒ. Iewel replieth: Thus he saith, and saith it often, and only saith it. Other Authoritie than his owne he bringeth none.

Ra.

Surely we must loke foʒ no reason oʒ cause of his so saying. Yet it foloweth Immediately:

Iew.
His reasō
is this.

The Reason that moueth him, I weene is this. For that there was no Laie people at that banket with Christ, but the Apostles only.

Ra.

I weene then, he doth moʒe than onely say it, when he geaueth A Reason foʒ it.

Iew.117
The
Termes
of Cere=
monies ꝥ
Substāce
allowable
Ra.

It doth not folow, We may breake A Ceremonie: Ergo we maie breake the Substance of Christes Institution.

It foloweth not in dede. And hereby you may see, that the Termes of Ceremonies and Substance, in Chʒistes Institution, are not Unnecessarie and vaine.

Iew.60.

This difference in Termes of Substance

stance and Accidentes in Christes Institution, is newly found out, and hath no warrant, neither of the Scriptures, neither of the Olde Fathers.

You be to fine and precise, M. Iewel, for simple Catholikes, And it seemeth that yourselfe would not speake but out of Scripture or Old Father, like as some in the world more curious than diligent, will haue no one worde in all their writinges, which they can not bring out of Cicero.

But, I pray you, is not the Distinction of things about Christes Institution, into Substance and Accidents, as reasonable and as necessary, as into Substance and Ceremonies? For by Ceremonies you must needes meane a diuerse thing from Substance, and such as may be let alone or taken away, without corruption, of Subiect or Principal mater. And what other thing is that but a plain Accident?

Yf ye find then any warrāt of the Scriptures or of the old Fathers, to iustify your Termes of Substaunce and Ceremonies about Christes Institution; you may be bold bolde without further warrant, to admit the Termes of Accidentes and Substance, about the same Institution. And if that you (notwithwstãding you find not that former distinctiõ in Scriptures or old Doctors) dare boldly sai, ÿ it doth not folow, we may breake a Ceremonie, Ergo, we may breake the substance of Chrifts Institution: it foloweth then, that the Distinction is good, and ÿ we may affirme, wel inough, A reasonable Conclusiõ: And vse proper Termes and wordes to expresse it by, although we haue no warrant of the Scriptures neither of the old Fathers.

The Councel of Basile aboue one hundred and thirtie yeeres past, made no conscience to graunt the vse of both kinds vnto the kingdom of Bohemia, and this Coũcel now presently holden at Trident, vpon certaine cõditions hath graunted the same, to other kingdomes and Countries.

Of whome then speake you these wordes, in an other place of your Replie?

These men take quite awaie from the people both the Element and kind of wine, and also the wordes of Consecration.

Cal you this, takinge of the kind of wine quite awaie, the vse whereof was per=

(margin notes)
Iew. 97.

The Papistes graunt ÿ vse of both kindes.

Ra.

Iew. 115.
The Papists take quitaway the kinde of wine.
Ra.

permitteð to Bohemie, and at this ðay
is reaðy to be permitteð vnto other, if
that woulð ðeliuer them from their he-
relies? If neeðes you wil lye, you Ihoulð
ðoe it alwaies fo warely (as ye can, wel
inough, when you be ðifpofeð) that you
might not yet be côuinceð therof, through
any of your owne worðs, fpokê at other
times. But now it is paſt remeðy, except
you wil Repent, becauſe I point you to
the places, wher ye confeſſe, both that the
Papiſtes haue graunted the vſe of wine to
other kingdomes and Countries, byſiðes
Bohemie, and alſo obiect, that they haue
quite taken awaie the kinde of wine from
the people.

   Al the Eaſt ſpeaketh the Greeke Tongue Iew.162
faieth S. Hierome. *To this I Anſwer,*
(faith D. Harðing) *y̆ ſome of al Coun-*
tries of the Eaſt ſpake Greeke.   **J.**
Iewel Replieth:

   M. Harðings diſtinction of al in General, and al in Particular, that he hath here
deuiſed to Ihift of S. Hierome, ſeemeth verie homely and h ome made. For how can it
be a general, onleſſe it include euery Parti-
                 cular

It cannot
be general
ōleſſe it in
cluðe eue=
ry particu
lar.

cular ? By M. Hardinges conſtruction
we muſt take A L, for S O M E, or A L, not
for the tenth part of A L, And by this Rhetorike, leſſe then halfe, is as much as A L,
and ſo A L is not A L.

Ra.

I would ſay vnto you, ſauing that
you be a ſore fellow when you come to
quiddities, and alſo that you would aſke
for a warrant of the Scriptures or olde Fathers, to iuſtify my woordes by it, els I
would ſay, that A L that you haue now
ſpoken, is *Nothing*: and that ſhould ſeeme
more abſurd, than that A L is not A L.
But I wil not geaue you this vantage,
I wil put your owne wordes vnto you.

Iew. 164

1. Cor. 10.

Al the Iewes Generally gloried of the
Law, euen ſo, al the Greekes Generally,
gloried in their wiſedome. And S. Paule
ſayeth Generally of them both : *The Ievves*
call for Signes and Miracles, and the Ievves
call for knovvledge. And therefore one of
the Philoſophers ſayed, In old times there
were Seuen Wiſe men emong the Greks,
but nowe there are not ſo manie Fooles,
for that they all Gloried in their Wiſedome.

Ra,

what thinke you then of the Apoſtles, Or of our bleſſed Lady herſelf, and
other

other good and holy Iewes, did they cal for Signes? Yf they did, then were they reproueable, because the strength of a Christian, resteth vpon Faith, which commeth by hearing of Goddes woord, and requireth not the shewing of Merueilouse Signes . If they did not, How did al the Iewes cal for Signes, except you also wil take A L for S O M E, or A L, for not A L?

M. Iew. constreined to take A L, for not A L.

The Philosopher also , which saied very wittily, in reproche of the Grecians vaine Opinion of themselues, that there were not so manye Fooles emonge them, as of Olde time were Wise men, for that they all Gloried in theyr Wisedome : He meant, I trow, ỹ there were almost seuen fooles in Greece, nigh to the number of the Seuen wise, that were in Olde times there. And he tooke him selfe perchaunce to be one of the Seuen : So that his General Proposition included not euery Particular . But I haue yet a better Example to declare my purpose .

what say you (M. Iewel) to S. Chrysostomes woordes? No body doth Communicate? You Answer: His purpose was to

Iew. 88.

to rebuke the negligence of the people, for that in so populous a Citie, thei came to the holy Communion in so smal companies, which companies, he, in a vehemencie of speach, by an exaggeration, in respect of the whole, calleth NO BODY. The like maner of Speach, is vsed also sometimes in the Scriptures. S. Iohn saith of Christe, Testimoniū eius nemo accipit, not for that no bouy at al receiued his witnesse (for his Disciples and many other receiued it) but for that of a great multitude, very few receiued it. In like Phrase Chrysostom him selfe saith other where, Nemo diuina sapit, No Body sauoreth Godly thinges.

It may be general although it include not euery particular

Ra.

Iew. 162

These be your owne woordes, M. Iewel, & whose were those other, where you said: How can it be a General, onlesse it include euery Particular? Be not these also yours? How make you then, both to agree togeather? For NO BODY importeth an vniuersal and general Negatiue, and then by your very homly and home made Logique, it includeth euery Particular. How make ye then in this place, of NO BODY, SOME BODY, and of NO BODY not NO BODI, but Disciples of Christe, and many other?

M. Iew. beaten w his owne Bodde.

Thus

Thus you see, that by your owne wordes in one place, you be driuen from your owne Sense in an other, And by reason of your Contradictions, none more Ennemie to M. Iewell, than M. Iewel.

Notwithstanding S. Augustine (whome S. Gregorie sent into England) withdrew the English Nation from their grosse Idolatrie, wherein he had no great trauaile (for perchaunce it is an easie mater to conuert Countries) Yet it is certaine he planted not Religion in this Realme.

Iew.185 Conuer-ted from Idolatri. not turned to Religiō.

what did he then vnto them whom he withdrew from their Idolatrie? Did he leaue them without a Religion? Did he pul their olde Cote from them, and geue them no newe? He Baptised at one Christmasse, *more than ten thousand English men*, as S. Gregorie witnesseth. And before he baptised them, did he not plante Religion in theyr hartes? Otherwyse how is it credible, that euer they would haue come to Baptisme? Yet I note this place, not for the open lie, which is in it, but for the Contradiction, for that it seemeth impossible, ỹ a Nation should

R2.

Greg.lib.7 ep.30.

GG i be

be conuerted from Idolatrie, and yet not turned to Religion, whereas, the very Conuersion it selfe, doth import a forsaking of one mind and taking of an other. And no Heretikes haue power to turne Nations, and the Catholiques to whom God geaueth that Grace, do for that end tourne them from Idolatrie, that afterwardes they may become Chriftians. Which End if they be not brought vnto, who can fay that they are conuerted?

Iew.226
The title of Vniuerfal Bishop, condemned
Iew.242
The title of Vniuerfal Bishop, alleaged.
Ra.

S. Gregorie iudgeth Generally of the Name of Vniuerfal Bishop, that it is vaine and hurtful, the Corruption, the Poifon, and vtter and Vniuerfal deftruction of the Church, &c.

Verely Iuftinian him felfe writing vnto Epiphanius the Bishop of Conftantinople, calleth him the Vniuerfal Patriarke.

Whom then do you folow, the Pope or the Emperour? S. Gregorie, or Iuftinian? Ye folow both, and ye are contrary vnto your felfe, at one time defying the Title, at an other, alleaging it.

Iew.274
For the euil life fake of the preachers

Certainly Balaam, notwithftanding he were a Falfe Prophete, yet he opened his mouth and Bleffed the people of God: Cayphas, although he were a wicked Bisshop,

shop, yet he ꝓpheſied and ſpake the truth:
A Seale although it be caſt in Leade, yet it
geaueth a perfite Printe. The Scribes and
Phariſeis, although they were Hypocrites
and liued not wel, yet they inſtructed the
Congregation and ſaied wel.

By theſe Examples then it appea‑   Ra.
reth, that A Doctrine is not to be foꝛſa‑
ken, becauſe of the euil lyfe of the Pꝛea‑
cher. What faulte then is Doctour
Harding in, foꝛ ſaying, that

*Be the Biſhoppe of Romes lyfe
neuer ſo wicked, yet may we not ſe‑
uer our ſelues from the Churche of
Rome?*

Foꝛ if other cauſes be alleaged,
wherefoꝛe we ſhould do it, they are to be
Aunſwered: but this Obiection of the
euil lyfe of the Biſhoppes of Rome, is
ſufficiently confuted by theſe Examples
which M. Iewel, here hath clearely al‑
lowed. Yet (ſee the nature of the man)
when D. Hardinge had ſaied ſo much,
he could not abide it, but ſtraitewaies
commeth againſt it with this Autho‑
ritie.

Iew. 276
For y euel
life fake y
peple muſt
feuer them
felues frō
their Ru=
lers.

How be it, S. Cyprian ſaith otherwiſe,
Plebs obſequens, &c. The people obeying
Gods Commaundemēts, muſt ſeuer them
ſelues from the Wicked that ruleth ouer
them.

Ra.
Lib.1.ep.4

S. Cypꝛian ſpeaketh of Baſilides
and Martialis, Biſhops that had defiled
them ſelues with Libels, in which they
gaue their names to Jdolatrie. Foꝛ
which cauſe, they were excommunicated
of other Biſhopes, and the people were
foꝛbid to come to their Sacrifice. But
it is no mater to M. Jewel, how the caſe
ſtandeth with anie Teſtimonie, that he
bꝛingeth. So deſyꝛous he is to gaynſaie
D. Harding, that he falleth into Contra=
dictions with himſelfe alſo. ſpeaking at
one time foꝛ credite to be geuen to Pꝛie=
ſtes, notwithſtanding theyꝛ euil life, And
at an other time making it lawful, to foꝛ=
ſake the Doctrine of the Pꝛeacher oꝛ Ru=
ler, foꝛ becauſe of his euil life.

Iew. 103
The Ar=
gument
Ab Autho=
ritate ne=
gatiuè,
allowed.

When Chriſt had deliuered both kinds
vnto his Diſciples, he ſayd vnto them, this
doe ye, the ſame that you ſee I haue done.
But where did Chriſt euer ſay, Miniſter vn
to yourſelues one way, and an other wai vn
to the people? The like Argument he
maketh

maketh.pa. 119. Where did Chrift. & cæt.
As who fhould faie, Chꝛift hath not ex-
pꝛeffed it, Ergo it is not to be obferued.

Here loe we fee, that M. Iewell
aloweth the Argument called in Scholes
Ab Autoritate Negatiuè. except you wil fay
that him felfe vfeth that, which him felfe
alloweth not. But heare now what he
faith in other places of his Replie.

M. HardingGheaffeth thus · It appereth not by Beda, the Seruice was in English, Ergo the Seruice was in Latine.
What kinde of Logique haue we here?
Or how may this Reafon hold ? It concludeth Ab Autoritate negatiuè. I beleue M.
Harding him felfe wil not allow it.

The Argument in deede he wil not
allow, as you haue made it. But foꝛ
as much as Bede purpofely fpeaketh of
fuch thinges, as concerned Religion,
*It is not to be thought, that he would
haue paffed it ouer in Silence, if the
Maffe had been tranflated into the
English tongue.*

But how agree you M. Iewel, with
your felfe, that can both refufe and vfe,

Ra.

Iew.187
The Ar-
gument
Ab Autho-
ritate ne-
gatiuè,
difpꝛoued.

Ra.

one and the selfe same kind of Argumēt?
You haue, I trow, some defense for you
selfe in this mater.   For you say in an
other place :

Jew. 126   The weight of M. Hardinges Argument, is taken, as they name it in Scholes,
Ab Autoritate negatiuè, and vnlesse it be
in consideration of some other circumstāce
it is so simple, that a very Child may sone
Answere it.

Ra.   what Circumstance then is that,
which being obserued maketh the Argument *ab Authoritate negatiuè*, good? Surely that Circumstance were wel worth the
learning, that we might perceaue, both,
how to make such Arguments ourselues,
without doubt of your repcehension, and
also howe to warne you thereof, when
yourselfe goe without the Cumpasse of
your owne Circumstance. Perchaunce
you meane hereby noe more, but that
which you haue alreadie expressed in the
first Article, where D. Harding obiecteth vnto you, the Common vse of this
kind of Reasoning, which is *ab Authoritate negatiuè*.   For thus you say, and it
is (I beleue) the moste you can say, that,

Jew. 68   The Argument ab Authoritate negatiuè
is

is thought to be good, when so euer prouf
is taken of Gods word, and is vsed not only by vs, but also by S. Paule, and by many
of the Catholike Fathers. S. Paule sayeth:
*God sayed not vnto Abraham, In thy S E E D E S
al nations shal be blessed, but in thy S E E D E,
vvhich is Christ.* And thereof he thought
he made a good Argument.

The Ar=
gument
Ab Autho
ritate ne=
natiuè,
taken out
of Gods
wozde is
good.
Galat.3.
Ra.

Suffer me than to make a like Ar=
gument out of Gods woozd, and let me
haue your Answer vnto it. Christ saith to
S. Peter, *Feede my sheep,* he said not these or
them: *Ergo vvithout Exception he committed his
sheep vnto S. Peter* But you like not this
Argument. For you say, it is against the
Rules of Logique, and that it was

Iew.21.

An Errour in Bonifacius, to reason
thus, Dominus dixit Generaliter, &c.
The Lord said Generally vnto Peter feede
my Sheepe, he said not specially feed these
or them: therefore we must vnderstande,
that he committed them vnto Peter altogeather.

Iew.305
The Ar=
gument
Ab Autho
ritate ne=
gatiuè,
taken out
of Gods
woozd is
naught.
Ra.

Yet this Argument, is like to that
of S. Paules of *S E E D E S* and *S E E D E,*
which in deede is not *Ab Autoritate nega=
tiuè,* but *Affirmatiuè.* For he presseth the
woozde of the Scripture *S E E D E,* in the

GG iiii Sin=

Singular nūber, which to make the better obſerued, he biddeth it to be noted, ẏ it was not ſaid, *S E E D E S.* But how ſo euer that be, M. Iewels Art may be wel inough eſpied, which al at pleaſure affirmeth and denieth, ſaieth and vnſayeth, maketh Rules and Obſerueth them not, and is Contradictorie vnto him ſelf in very many places.

Iew.306   This very name, the H E A D E of the vniuerſal Church, is the very thing that we deny.

Ra: Then are you a very vnwiſe man, to ſett the State and Subſtance of your queſtion vpon a Name : And to contend vpon words, affirming them to be the very thinges . And there appeereth here vnto me to be a manifeſt Contradiction, that the name ſhould be the thing . For if it were ſo, that al this writing on both ſides, were no more but an Alteration of Grammarians or Rhetoricians, then in deede it might be a queſtiō, whether this woorde *H E A D E* were euer Readen in ſuch a Caſe , or ſuch an Author, or euer applied to ſuch and ſuch a perſon, & then properly the Name ſhould be the thing.

But

But now wheras al our cóflict, is about the Truth of thinges that are to be bele=ned, and we seeke not after Termes and Phrases of Speache, but sense and mea=ning of Truthes, And whereas the vn=derstanding (which both partes thinke to instructe) is not bettered by any *N A M E S*, but by the very thinges them selues : It is al togeather vnreasona=ble, to say or thinke , that the very name should be the very thing, emong the Di=uines.

Yet who so considereth diligently, M. Jewels maner & behauiour of wri=ting, shal sone perceiue, that he so han=deleth the mater, as though he were a Grammarian onely, or a Rhethorician, and not a Diuine, and as though in dede he passed not vpon the very Thinges, so that he might haue the very wordes that could serue his turne. For which cause he hath furnished himself with Testimo=nies and Phrases inough, For ỹ church, Against the Churche, For Custome, A=gainst Custome, For Fathers, Against Fathers, For Councels, Against Coun=cels, For Receiuing at home, Against re=ceiuing

ceiuing at home, For Receiuing in One
kinde, Against Receiuing in One, For
Receiuing alone, Against Receiuing a-
lone, For S. Peters Principalitie, A-
gainst S. Peters principalitie, For equalitie of Bishops, Against equalitie of Bishops, For Distinctions, against Distinctions, For Arguments taken of Authoritie, Against Argumentes taken of Authoritie, And so furth in many thinges
moe, which I haue shewed partly in the
Second Booke, partly in this Chapiter
of Contradictions, And were more to be
shewed, if time or occasion required.
But now to an other mater.

A Note Concerning M. Ie-wels Lies.

And what other mater might that
be? For I haue already discoue-
red his vnreasonablenes and fals-
hod, by so many waies, that it may
seeme, both that I am at an End, of finding any moe Obiectios, and he of ministring any moe Occasions. For as
con-

concerning his Lies, of which I eyther
intended or promised to make a special
Chapiter, there can be no worse nor plai=
ner, than I haue already declared , and
therfore let me be excused, if I satisfie not
al expectation, In prouing that, by newe
and freshe Examples, which is so abun=
dantly testified .

D. Harding doth charge him, with
225. Untruthes .

M. Stapleton (excepting the Un=
truths of the first Article, in which he can
not but meete with D. Harding) doth
charge him with. 474.

I recken not the . 218 . which D.
Sander obiecteth against him .

And of the vntruthes, which my self
haue founde in him , in talking with him
about the State of the Question in the
first foure Articles, and about his sham=
ful ordering of D. Harding, And about
his abusing of Councels, Canons, Glo=
ses, Auncient Fathers, And Later wri=
ters: the truth is, I haue kept no recke=
ning .

But this I am sure of , that al=
though 699 , Untruthes are founde in
his

A shorte
Somme of
M. Iew=
els Lies
in foure
only of his
Articles :
that at the
first rea=
ding of
them ouer

his foure firſt Articles only, yet many of them that I obiect vnto him, are none of the number of thoſe. 699. And yet I paſſe not the cūpaſſe of the ſame Articles.

More ſpecialties than theſe, if any man wil require, I am not my ſelf at leiſure, but if he thinke it expedient, he may by him ſelfe gather the Particulars into one Chapiter, by telling onely the bare Vntrueth, without further diſcourſing vpon it. And he ſhould do wel, not to recken euery one (for that would occupie a great roome) but ſuch notable and ſingular Lies, as might not only be vnderſtanded, but felt as it were and ſeene. As if this Lie ſhould be the Firſt in the Rewe.

Ieſw.13.
The Biſhop of Rome and his Cardinals, ſcarſely haue leiſure to Sacrifice once in the whole yeare.   And Againe :
15.
They do ſcarſely Cōmunicate once in the yeare.

For this is ſo notorious a Lie, and ſo palpable, that he that would report it, to another that neuer yet was at Rome, might be thought neuer to haue come to Church, whiles he taried there : And he
that

that shal haue occasion to iorney thither, shal sensibly perceiue and see, that it is a most shamful Lie.

And so furth in other of the like ma=king, the number of which, although it would be lesse, yet it should appeere most manifestly, that the plaine meaning con=sciencies, had neede to *BEVVARE of M. IEVVEL.*

How M. Iewel hath left some places altogeather vnanswered.

THus then the Chapiter of Lies, being referred to the diligence of other that would haue them sette in their Rankes, and which haue leisure to bring it to passe by themselues, Is there any more to be obiected against M. Iewel? Yea mary is there, and that to his reproch and ignominie. For pre=tending to Answere euery woorde of D. Hardings, and shewing a countenance of such Learning, that he could, and such diligence, that he would leaue nothing vndiscussed, and vnperfited: a great and iust

iuſt ſhame it is, for him, that many and euident Argumentes and Teſtimonies againſt him, he ſo paſſeth by, as though he had neuer ſeene them. As in example:

Iew.57. *Do ye reproue the Maſſe,* (ſaith D. Harding) *Or doe ye reproue the Priuate Maſſe?* And M. Iewel Annſwereth with other queſtions vnto him againe, concerning Sole Receiuing, and Single Cōmunion, Priuate Maſſe and Sole Receiuing, Sacrifice of the newTeſtament and A litle Booke of his owne, but to the queſtion it ſelfe, he Anſwereth not.

Concerning the publike Seruice of our Realme, if it had ben in Engliſh at ý

Iew.127 beginning, *Doubtleſſe* (ſaith D. Har. *ſome mētion would haue ben made of ý time and cauſes of the leauing ſuch kind of Seruice, & of ý beginning of the New Latine Seruice. As certain of S. Gregories workes turned into Engliſh by Bede himſelfe haue been kept ſo as they remaine to this day:* But M. Iewel wil not, or cānot anſwer.

Si

Si Benedixeris Spiritu, &c.   If thou make thy prayer in the Cōgregation, with thy Spirit or noise of Strange wordes, how shal the vnlerned man, thervnto say Amē? **Thus doth M. Iewel interpret ȳ place:** *But ȳ translation (saith D. Harding) authorised by King Edward and his Councel, is truer, which hath thus:* When thou blessest vvith the Spirit, hovv shal he that occupieth the roome of the vnlearned, say Amen, at thy geauing of thankes, seeing he vnderstandeth not vvhat thou saiest?   **And M. Iewel aunswereth not one worde in his owne defense, for saying,** The vnlearned, **in steede of,** He that occupieth the roome of the vnlearned .

Of the Seruice in ȳ vulgare tongue the people (saith D. Har.) wil frame lewd & peruerse meanings, of their own lewd senses. **Of ȳ Latin they cānot do so: Ergo Latine is more meet for publik seruice. M. Iew. āswereth nothing.**

S. Peter (saith Hilarius) deserued for the confession of his blessed faith, Supéreminentem Locum , A Preeminence about

Iew.246 *aboue other.* To Supereminence, or
Preeminence aboue other, which is imported by *Super, aboue,* &c. Iewel answereth nothing.

Iew.258 *How shal the Contumacie and*
Pertinacitie of mischieuous persons
be repressed, specially if the Bishops
be at dissension within themselues,
if there be not a Supreme Power,
who, towards some, may vse the rod,
towardes other some, the spirite of
Lenitie?

&c. Iewel answereth nothing.

Iew.248
Aug. de
vtilit.cre-
dend.c.17.
*Cum tantum &c. Vvhereas vve see (*fayeth
S.Augustine*)so greate helpe of God, so greate*
profite and fruite, shal vve stand in doubt, vvhe-
ther vve may hyde ourselues in the Lappe of the
Churche, vvhich (though Heretikes barke at it,
round about, condemned partly by the Iudgemēt
of the people themselues, partly by the Sadnesse of
Councels, and partly by the Maiestie of Miracles,
euen to the Confession of Mankind) from the A-
postolike See, by Successions of Bishopes, hath ob-
teined the toppe or highest degree of Autoritie?
To

To vvhich Church, if vve vvil not geue and grant the Primacie, soothly it is a pointe either of most high vvickednesse, or of headlong arrogance.

To this place M. Iewel answereth nothing, I beleue, because he had nothing. For, his diligence and Order in Answering three other places of S. Augustine, which went Immediatly before this, in his 14. Diuision of the fourth Article, doe proue, that he lacked not Occasion to Answere this also, which was so largely alleged by D. Harding, and folowed so Immediatly, in the 14. Diuision, but that, he knew not wel what to say vnto it.

After this maner, it were easie to finde moe places, and them of no small weight, which should declare M. Iewel, for al his fayre shewe of an Absolute Replie, not to haue touched yet many principall Reasons and Testimonies of D. Hardings. But I haue already proued my purpose sufficiently.

H H j   Of

The third booke.

Of a new deuised and childish Obie-ction, solemnly vsed of late, against the Catholikes, by which M. Iewel also is touched.

AND nowe to make an ende, what may any Indifferent Reader aske for more, to perswade him in this one point and Conclusion, that he ought to *BEVVARE OF M. IEVVEL?* There cannot be a greater Bragger, than he that prouoketh al the men aliue: Nor a greater Shifter, than he that wil suffer no question to stand in the state, in which he did first put it: Nor a greater wrang-ler, than he that dissimbleth the meaning of his Aduersarie, almost in euery Argu-mēt: Nor a greater Corruptour of wit-nesses, than he that wil suffer nor Texte, nor Glose, nor Canon nor Ciuil Lawe, nor Old nor Late writer, to continue in his right forme of Verdict: Nor a writer more perilous, than M. Iewel.

But in one thing, I trowe, he is faultlesse, And what is that? Mary he
hath

hath not, I warrant you, any such Testi=
monies for confirmation of his sayings,
as other haue vsed before him. why? Is
that a Fault? By whose Iudgement and
determination? Or by whose Fansie ra=
ther and Imagination?

Uerely as the Sonne & Moone are
common vnto all that wil vse them : So
are the Scriptures, So are the Fathers,
vnto al Students of Diuinitie . And he
taketh not of all other mans goodes, but
claimeth, by iust Title, his owne, whoso=
euer gathereth out of the writings of the
Apostles or Commentaries of the Fa=
thers . And though another vse the same
place with me, to a like purpose & Argu=
ment, yet neither he of me, neither I of
him, doe borrow any thing, but both of
vs take our owne, where we find it .

where then hath he learned it, he that
obiecteth it to a Catholike, for an Igno=
minie, that he vseth in his writings the
selfe same Authorities, which other haue
vsed before him? Hath he learned it in
Scholes emong the poore Boyes, or in
Courtes emong the Galant and Braue
Felowes?

A childish obiection.

DD i In

In Scholes , it is a vaine glory and pride emong ꝑ boyes , to contemne that, which is common , to affect singular and rare things,to refuse that which an other vseth , and to fal out with their felowes, that take out of their Notebokes, any of their treasures . which Affection all= though they be not beaten for, becaufe of the firſt beginnings which are nouriſhed with hope of praiſe: yet the humour is naught and corrupt, which breedeth fuch an ytch of folie , or canker of Enuie in them .

In Courtes alſo , it is a ſadde pride and glory, to haue fuch a Cutte of Appa= raile , or fuch a Tricke or two aboute it , as none els vſeth . which after it begyn to be recciued of other , the Authors are ſtraite waies wery of it , and turne them ſelues to other faſhions . Concerning whiche maters , there be greate Rules and Obſeruations , As that a man muſt not weare one Coate aboue a certayne time , Alſo that he weare his owne ⁊ not an other mans Coate , And generally, that in all his manners, he may ſeeme to ſtand by himſelfe alone, and to depend of

no

no other. In so much, that it is a greate griefe vnto some, to heare it sayed vnto them, I knowe where you had this, or wher you bought that, As though al were lost, because they can not be singular.

Now, if this Contention and Folie shall be alowed also in maters of Lear-ning, that it shal not be laulul for euerie man, freely to vse what so euer he gathe-reth out of Scripture or Doctour, but it shal be a certaine Ignominie vnto him, if the same be found alleged of other be-fore his time: And if it shal not be lawfull for Students, to aske A question of the better learned, and to Reade their bokes which haue long trauailed in any Con-trouersie: why then, let euery man holde his peace, And from hence furth let it be our Studie, to inuent new Opinions, to geue strange Interpretations, to make the world wonder at our Deuises & In-uentions, and so much to esteeme euerie thing ỹ better, the lesse it can be brought to any beginning, sauing that, which it hath in our braine and Imagination.

By these meanes then, let no man hereafter proue, either the Presence of
  D D iij Christes

Absurde.

Chzistes body in the Sacrament by, *This is my body*, Oz the Consubstantiality of the Father & the Sonne, by, *I and my Father are one*, Oz the necessitie of Faith, by, *He that beleueth not, shal be condemned*, Oz the Obedience due to Pzinces, by, *Let euery man be subiect vnto the Superiour Povvers.* Foz al these places haue already bene vsed of thousandes, that haue entreated of these matters. But he that can bzing any fresh & new Testimony neuer hard of befoze, let him only haue Audience, and lette all other be but Triflers.

Verely he may wel be called *Novel.*, which is so greate a frind to Nouelties. And if his Obiection be alowed, we shal haue shoztly either a meruelous Silece, oz very strange & wonderful Opinions. But it is altogeather Childish and Foolishe, if it were altogeather true, as he Imagineth, that one of vs did bozow of an other, and that we were not hable to take of the Fountaines themselues. And to laye any suche thing to M. Iewels charge, as a burden and shame, it is vnreasonable. Yet if any of the Bzothers make a weightie and greate matter of it,

Let

Math.26. / Io. 10. / Marci.16. / Rom.13.

Let him vnderstand brieflie, howe M.
Iewel also may be pressed with it.

S. Cyprian. *Lib. 2. Epist. 3.* For the Institution of Christe.	Alleged, in the Defense of the Trueth. Fol. 11.	Used by M. Iewel. Pag. 106.	
Tertullians place, *aduersus* Traxeam. *That is true, that was first ordeined.*	Alleged, in the Defense of the Trueth. Fol. 11.	In the Apologie of England.	Used by M. Iewel Pa. 258. 313.
The Storie of Zosimus.	Declared by Fox. Pag. 9.	Used by M. Iew. Pag. 236.	
The Glose, *Domine cur it à facis? Syr vvhy do ye so?*	Alleaged by M. Nowel. Fol. 26.	Used by M. Iewel. Pag. 258. & 313.	
That the Booke called ἀσκητικα, **is not S. Basiles.**	Labored by the *Magdeburgenses. Cent. 4. Cap. 10. Col. 946.*	Used by M. Iewel Pag. 86.	

That S. Augustine, whom S. Gregorie sent into England, was of no Apostolike Spirite, &c.
→ Set furth by Bale. *Lib. 2. de actis. Ro. Pontificum* Pag. 51. 52. 53.
→ Alleged, by the *Magdeburgenses*. *Cent. 6. ca. 10. col. 748.*
→ Used by M. Iewel. pag. 185.

The discourse vpon the first bringers in of the Faith into England.
→ Made by the *Magdeburgenses, Cent 1. lib. 2. cap. 3. col. 23. Cent. 2. cap. 1. col. 6. & 8. cent. 3. cap. 2. col. 4.*
→ Used by M. Iewel. Pag. 196.

The argumentes against the Decretal Epistles
→ ab Autoritate negatiue of { S. Hierom. Gennadius. Damisus. } → Made of the Magdeb Cent. 2. ca. 7. col. 151.

And of the sayinges of
{ Clemens. Antherus. Marcellin. Marcellus. Zepherin. Meltiades. }
→ Cent. 2. ca. 7. col. 185
Cent. 3. ca. 7. col. 189
Cet. 4. ca. 7. col. 576
Cent. ibidē. col. 578
Cēt. 3 ca. 7. col. 179
Cēt. 4. ca. 7. co 577

Argu=

Argumentes against Anacletus Epistles gathered			Alleged by the Magdebur.	Used by M. Iewel, not one argumēt left out. Pag.67. 223. & 224.
1	1	Of the Story of Tymes.	1 Cent.1.li.2. c.10.co.637.	
2	2	Of the building of S. Peters Church.	2 Centur.2. cap.7. col.142.	
3	3	Of the alleging of old Fathers Decrees.	3 Centur.2. cap 7. col.144.	
4	4	Of ý Phrases of the Epistles.	4 Cent.2.c.7 col.143.	
5	5	Of the Interlacing of the Scriptures.	5 Centur.2. cap.7. col.145.	
6	6	Of the needelesse alleging of them.	6 Cent.2.c.7 co.140.141. 142.148.	

This for an Example is inough. For if a man were so disposed, to spend long time in examining of this one Pointe, whether M. Iewels great & ful stuffed Reply, cam imediatli frō his own singular Inuētion & diligēce, or no: there

there is no dout, but he hath either none
at al, oz very few Argumentes & Autho=
rities, which are not to be founde also in
other that haue wziten befoze him. Espe=
cially if it shal be rightly confidered, how
much Peter Martyz, Caluine, and the
Magdeburgenſes onely (to lette other
ſcrapers paſſe) haue wziten againſt y Ca=
tholik Church, euen vpõ theſe very que=
ſtions which M. Iewel hath pzoponed.

Yet I thinke not, that al that he hath
gathered, hath com out of them, although
it may be founde in them also (foz why
may not an Englishe Pzoteſtant, be as
ſone taken vp, to ſerue the Diuel in ſet=
ting furth of Hereſies, and to Receiue
ſecrete Intelligence from him, what he
shal ſtudy vppon, and marke eſpecially ,
as any Heretique of beyond the Seas ?)
And if it were gathered out of them , I
would not Obiect it vnto him, as one of
the Deadly ſinnes foz which men should
B E V V A R E of him. Foz emong friends
al thinges are common, and no man that
wiſe is and honeſt, wziteth to make him
ſelfe a name in the wozld, but to help the
common cauſe, foz which him ſelfe, with
other, ſtandeth.　　　　　　　　　　**But**

But this much onely I note, that such as seke very egrely and impotently, to hurt the Catholikes estimation by it, in telling them that they are Borowers, may vnderstand, that the same Obiection (if it be any thing worth) may be easily returned backe vpon them againe.

In making of which, I thinke in dede, that the Author thereof was no borower, although there hath bene already so much inuented and imagined agaynst Catholikes, as more, by any occasion, could not be vttered. Let him therefore alone haue the praise of it, for deuising & mainteining so vnsensible an Obiection, as neither hath bene vsed of former Heretikes, though they sought all meanes how to deface vs, neither can be reproch= full vnto the Catholikes, which knowe that nothing is newe vnder the Sonne, And, that al Scriptures, and Doctours, and writers are oures, which make for the Defense or Sense of the true Faith.

Vnto your charge therefore, M. Iewel, I doe not laye it, whether you haue taken out of the Magdeburgenses, or any Notebookes of other men, that which

which you vtter, but, with your Appealing vnto the first sir hundred yeares,
and your Refusing of the Authorities
within the same yeares, And with your
Excoursing into al Ages for witnesses,
And for your Abusing of the witnesses of
al Ages, with these so principal maters,
I burthen you. which if it seeme light
vnto you, I do not care (for I make no
accompt vpon it, that your selfe should
haue leisure or respect to my smal writinges) but that other might thinke better of it, I haue prouided by special noting of such mater, in which M, Iewel
might be taken for no great Iewel when
al is knowen.

In gathering and setting furth of
which, if I seeme to haue done otherwise
than wel, I am ready either to defende
it, either to confesse it. Assured for al
that, that there is no one Protestant in
al England, that shal be able to disproue
my Obiections, and trusting, that in the
Iudgement of the Catholiques, I shal
not much neede to craue any pardon.
And now, as from y beginning through
the Booke, I haue alwaies appealed to
the

the Indifferent Reader : so now to con=
clude, I say vnto him, and desire of him,
that he neither fauour Iewel, because of
the Procedinges : nor hate Rastel, be=
cause of his Religion, but Iudge accor=
ding vnto that which is alleged & pro=
ued ,whether M. Iewel be not
that Felow, of whom the
whole coūtrie ought
to *BEVVARE.*

Commonsense Grammar and Style

Commonsense Grammar and *Style by Robert E. Morsberger*

Second Edition
Revised and Expanded

based on Commonsense Grammar
by Janet Aiken

Thomas Y. Crowell Company
New York
Established 1834

Designed by Judith Woracek Barry

Manufactured in the United States of America
by Vail-Ballou Press, Inc., Binghamton, New York

Library of Congress Catalog Card No. 72-78273

1 2 3 4 5 6 7 8 9 10   ISBN 0-690-20337-3

√ Acknowledgments

Quotations in this volume include copyright material, used with
permission from the following sources:

Lines from Robert Bolt, *A Man for All Seasons*, © Copyright, 1960,
1962, by Robert Bolt; from Truman Capote, *Breakfast at Tiffany's*,
Copyright © 1958 by Truman Capote; and from Alfred Duggan, *The
Cunning of the Dove*, © 1960 by Alfred Duggan, reprinted by permission
of Random House, Inc.

Quotations from the Edgar Rice Burroughs Tarzan stories by permission
of Edgar Rice Burroughs, Inc., Tarzana, California.

Lines by Robert Frost from *Complete Poems of Robert Frost*, Copyright
1923 by Holt, Rinehart and Winston, Inc., Copyright 1942 by Robert
Frost. Copyright renewed 1951 by Robert Frost. Reprinted by permission
of Holt, Rinehart and Winston, Inc.

Harcourt, Brace & World, Inc., for permission to quote lines from George
Orwell, "Politics and the English Language," in *Shooting an Elephant
and Other Essays;* from Vernon L. Parrington, *Main Currents in American
Thought;* from Charles Carpenter Fries, *The Structure of English;* and
from E. E. Cummings, *Poems 1923–1954.*

Lines from *To Kill a Mockingbird* by Harper Lee. Copyright © 1960 by
Harper Lee. Published by J. B. Lippincott Company.

Lines from *Sincerely, Willis Wayde* by John P. Marquand, Copyright
1954, 1955 by The Curtis Publishing Company, Copyright 1955 by John
P. Marquand, reprinted by permission of Little, Brown and Company,
Publishers.

Lines from *My Fair Lady, A Musical Play in Two Acts,* Based on *Pygmalion* by Bernard Shaw, Adaptation and Lyrics by Alan Jay Lerner, Music

My work on this book was assisted by a research grant from Michigan State University. I wish to thank Dr. Ahmed Metwalli and Mary Ellen Metwalli for constructive criticism on the linguistics material in the final chapter.

For *Grace, Wendy,* and *Robbie*

√ Foreword

This book derives from *Commonsense Grammar*, by Janet Ranken Aiken of Columbia University. First published in 1936, *Commonsense Grammar* went through five editions and seemed to answer a need of the time. At a period when much teaching of grammar was still Latinate and prescriptive, *Commonsense Grammar* was a welcome and refreshing change, dealing in a sensible and tolerant way with actual usage rather than absolute rules. Written with warmth and wit, it was a pioneering work in examining the way people use words in practical situations.

A generation later, the publisher wanted to reissue the book but found it somewhat dated. There have been many changes in both linguistic usage and attitudes since the 1930's, and a new edition would have required extensive revision.

The present book is a new work almost altogether. Its general approach is indebted to Mrs. Aiken's, but most of the text is original. Chapters 2 and 18 borrow heavily from Mrs. Aiken, and a few sentences and examples have been incorporated into Chapters 4, 7, 10, and 12. The rest of the book is entirely new.

The new *Commonsense Grammar and Style* was published in 1965. For the revised edition of 1972, I have removed some now questionable comments about the stigma attached to some usages and have added some concluding comments about the English of ethnic minorities and residents of the inner city and barrio. In addition, I have appended a brief discussion of some of the newer linguistic approaches to grammar. I have updated some of the main body of the text to provide more modern examples and to include consideration of such currently habitual idioms as "you know" and "where it's at." I have added answers to the 44 sections of exercises. The exercises and examples contain a good many allusions to old movies and comic strips that I let stand because they match the current interest in pop art and nostalgia and date less rapidly than last year's less durable fashions. *King Kong* lives.

In writing a book for the 1970's, I have tried to create a descriptive grammar on historical principles, with many illustrative examples of actual usage, from Chaucer to *Catch-22,* including contemporary literature, journalism, politics, and advertising. My approach is liberal and often uses satire to examine the relationships of style and sense, language and logic. I am happy to follow in Mrs. Aiken's footsteps, especially because she once walked down Broadway in her bare feet to protest some issue in the 1930's.

Contents

Commonsense
Grammar
and
Style

1 √ Common Sense and the Psychology of Grammar

Winston Spencer Churchill, one of the modern masters of English prose, stated, "We are divided by a common language." To a considerable extent this is true; for people classify each other by their grammar, vocabulary, and pronunciation. They feel comfortable with those who speak like themselves and look with suspicion or resentment upon those with different habits of speech. Thus, a lyric from *My Fair Lady* asserts that

An Englishman's way of speaking absolutely classifies him.
The moment he talks he makes some other Englishman despise him.[1]

To criticize a person's language, whether explicitly or implicitly through one's own different speech, is to challenge his background, his family, his social status, his intelligence, and to a very real degree his sense of personal worth. Thus, grammar is a social and psychological, even an economic and political matter; and it is no wonder that the subject arouses antagonisms.

Traditionally, teachers of grammar saw themselves as champions of a linguistic establishment, as authorities who should regulate the language and fix it in a prescribed and near-perfect form. They considered deviations from that form to be degenerate. But clearly it is impossible for any group of specialists to control the verbal habits of over 400 million English-speaking people; and linguists have proved that popular usage rather than academic elitism determines the course of a language. Elitism dies hard; when *Webster's Third New International Dictionary* was published in 1961, there was a brief but furious uproar against its practice of following usage rather than academic authority. Its descriptive lexicography was labeled "permissive" and was associated with every malaise of social and political change from Bolshevism to anarchy.

1

The trouble is that most students and some teachers have a mistaken concept of the nature of grammar and the role of the grammarian. Grammar is not an external order to be compulsorily superimposed upon the speech habits of the hapless student and citizen. It is instead a description of those habits and to some extent a classification of them. Drilled for years in "rules" of English, students may see the grammarian as a drillmaster, and grammar as a rather meaningless manual of arms that they must somehow perform if they are to graduate, an external and arbitrary discipline threatening their independence and natural expression.

In a broad sense, there is no such thing as ungrammatical English. Everyone speaking the English language must use grammar, though some uses are more unconventional than others and a few are highly idiosyncratic. It is not even so much that ungrammatical speakers are unconventional as that they follow different conventions from those approved in educated circles and that there is more individuality within the conventions they follow. This "unacceptable" grammar has its own patterns; and Mark Twain, William Faulkner, John Steinbeck, Ring Lardner, Sinclair Lewis, and a host of other authors with an ear attuned to the vernacular have created with its aid quite recognizably realistic and sometimes eloquent dialogue and first-person narrative. If it were presented as their own grammar, it would rarely receive a passing grade from an English teacher. In fact, *Huckleberry Finn* when it first appeared was banned in many communities, partly because critics complained of Huck's "uncouth" grammar, which they considered an affront to cultivated gentility. But Mark Twain observed, in "The Stolen White Elephant," that "a nation's language is a very large matter. It is not simply a matter of speech obtaining among the educated handful; the manner obtaining among the vast uneducated multitude must be considered also."

The die-hard purist is something of a reactionary. He fears that language is in constant danger of being corrupted and that about nine tenths of the people already speak a debased, ungrammatical version of English. (Noah Webster condemned "the well-nigh universal misuses of English," but if everyone misuses the language, how can there be a right use?) Since language is developed by the people rather than revealed from God on high, these are curious statistics reminiscent of the old Puritan concepts of election and depravity by which nine tenths of the human race were predestined for hell. But, if English is being corrupted, what is it being corrupted from? Probably the oldest surviving scrap of English writing is the Anglo-Saxon poem *Widsith,* which begins:

> Wīdsīð maðolade, wordhord onlēac,
> sē þe [monna] mæst mægþa ofer eorþan,
> folca geondfērde . . . .

But then about seven hundred years later than the "pure" language of *Widsith,* we find the language corrupted into the more modern (hence debased) English of Layamon:

> An preost wes on leoden, Laʒamon wes i-hoten;
> He wes Leovenaðes sone: liðe him beo Drihten!

Two hundred years later, we find English further corrupted and modernized in *The Second Shepherd's Play:*

> Lord, what these weders ar cold! and I am yll happyd;
> I am nere-hande dold, so long have I nappyd.

But all is not lost. As we go down to the year 1702 and examine the writings of Cotton Mather, we seem to have a return from the "depraved" simplicity of *The Second Shepherd's Play* to something more remote and hence more pure:

> *Reader!* I have done the part of an *Impartial Historian,* albeit not without all occasion perhaps, for the Rule which a worthy Writer, in his *Historica,* gives to every Reader, *Historici Legantur cum Moderations & venia, & cogitetur fieri non posse ut in omnibus circumstantiis sint Lyncei.* *Polybius* complains of those *Historians,* who always made either the *Carthagenians* brave, and the Romans base, or *è contra,* in all their Actions, as their Affection for their own *Party* led them.

Yet, alas, when we remove the Latin and the italics, we find that the Reverend Mr. Mather has corrupted the language by changing it yet further from the primitive purity of *Widsith.* Finally we come to the mid-twentieth century, where we encounter such debased prose as "Snoopy's out there stranded on top of his doghouse! He needs help!" [2] Certainly Widsith would find this unintelligible, and the Second Shepherd would doubtless find it difficult.

Obviously there is no "well of English undefiled." If we are no longer using precisely the language of Shakespeare and Spenser, Shakespeare and Spenser did not use the language of Chaucer, and Chaucer did not use that of *Beowulf.* What some pedants mean when they say that English is corrupted is that it is a corruption

3

from Latin. A Germanic language, English was never based on Latin, so it is hard to see how it could be a corruption of it. But from the Middle Ages (when Latin was already dead as a vernacular language) down into the nineteenth century, Latin was the language of Western scholarship. Its advocates praised the logic of its structure (forgetting that the actual Romans never spoke the pure classical Latin of Cicero and that even St. Jerome wrote in the vulgate) and insisted that it should be the model for all language. Some people have said that they never really understood English grammar until they studied Latin; but they say this in English, not in Latin, grammar. The only thing the study of Latin grammar can do is to make the student conscious that words have formal inflections and functional relationships, if he hasn't already bothered to discover this in English. Certainly both form and function are un-English, as in the Latin *Assurgentem regem resupinat* and its translation, "As the king was trying to rise, he threw him down." It is true that classical Latin has the abstract logic of mathematical equations, but a living language is not abstract; it is spoken by individual throats, tongues, and teeth in an infinite variety of specific contexts and situations. Thus it is impossible for grammarians to enforce any linguistic laws, even if such laws were logical, as often they are not. It is not the grammarian's province to police the language.

Yet there have been penalties for not using the grammar and vocabulary approved in more dominant and highly educated circles. A person's educational opportunities and future—the sort of job he could get (and therefore his standard of living and the neighborhood in which he could afford to live), the sort of close associates he would have, the person he would marry, and even the future of his children—have been to a considerable extent determined by his use of language. If his grammar and diction are considered vulgar or semiliterate, he would be so classified by the more "cultivated."

"You see this creature with her kerbstone English; the English that will keep her in the gutter to the end of her days," says Henry Higgins in Bernard Shaw's *Pygmalion*. In this play and its musical version *My Fair Lady*, Higgins, a professor of phonetics and elocution, takes a penniless flower girl and turns her into a lady by teaching her upper-class grammar, pronunciation, and manners. For grammar and pronunciation are a species of manners, a socially relative matter rather than a sign of intrinsic merit. Neither grammar nor pronunciation by itself is enough. If Eliza had precise grammar and a slum accent, she would be an anomaly indeed. As

4

it is, she learns elocution first and makes a trial appearance at a tea party where, with the most impeccable accent, she tells in guttersnipe grammar a story about her aunt's being murdered in gin row: "But it's my belief they done the old woman in." The incongruity is ludicrous, and Higgins quickly explains that Eliza is merely entertaining them with the new small talk. A young man present finds it vastly amusing; but Eliza, bewildered, demands, "If I was doing it proper, what was you laughing at?" So Eliza must proceed to learn to speak grammatically, though she complains, "I don't want to talk grammar. I want to talk like a lady."

In the sentimental and genteel American novels of the first half of the nineteenth century, social status was extremely important; rarely could anyone qualify as hero or heroine who did not come from an upper-class background and independent wealth. Thus, frontiersmen like Leatherstocking and his many imitations were ineligible because of their crudeness and particularly because of their backwoods dialect. Since an aristocrat might outwardly disguise himself as a hunter or trapper, dialect became the ultimate test of status. Historian Henry Nash Smith, who made an extensive study of such novels, observed, "The belief that no one is suitable to conduct a sentimental courtship unless he speaks a pure English is very strong."[3] Smith further noted that if a person from a lowly background became involved in a love affair, his English almost immediately became free of dialect, regardless of his earlier usage or that of his parents. However, this aristocratic speech was stilted rhetoric fossilized by literary convention and infinitely less vital than the socially unacceptable language of Huck Finn. Some of Mark Twain's contemporaries (like the "proper" element in Huck's own town of St. Petersburg) condemned Huck as worthless and immoral trash, a social outcast. Actually, Huck, though ragged around the edges, is a profoundly moral and decent person, far more so than the slaveowners in his society. As for his language, there is no such thing as correct or incorrect, good or bad English grammar in any moral sense, though these labels have been used to embarrass and to color the values of generations of schoolchildren. Language can indeed be used immorally, as a vehicle of illogical persuasion, thought control, hate-mongering, or euphemistic diction to conceal the true names of political atrocities. But a person who uses nonstandard grammar is not thereby morally inferior ("I'm a good girl, I am," Eliza keeps telling Henry Higgins), whereas Shakespeare's villains often speak an exalted rhetoric. If one grammatical usage is preferable to another, there must be some concrete reason, not simply the abstract concept of what is good and bad.

As you can see in the quotations from *Widsith* to *Peanuts*, language changes. As it does so, standard practices may become nonstandard, while other nonstandard ones may become standard. For instance, the multiple negative, now unacceptable, was customary in the time of King Alfred and was common in Chaucer. *Thou* and *thee* and their accompanying verb endings have disappeared from ordinary usage. *Right* as an adverb (*right good, right soon*), which is now frowned upon, was common in Elizabethan English. Principal parts of many verbs have changed. Even in isolated communities, language changes, though it may do so in different ways than the main stream. In one Tarzan book, the apeman discovers a lost city inhabited by descendants of the Crusaders. Their costumes, customs, and language are supposed to be unchanged from the Middle Ages. But the dialogue Edgar Rice Burroughs gives them is not early Middle English; instead it is imitative of Sir Walter Scott's medieval romances—nineteenth-century prose with a sprinkling of archaic diction and word order and a few *thees* and *thous:*

"Whence comest thou," he asked, "and what doest thou in the Valley of the Sepulcher, varlet?"

Blake, the American, mistakes the latter-day Crusader for a movie extra and asks to see the director:

"Director? Forsooth. I know not what thou meanest."
"Yes, you don't!" snapped Blake, with fine sarcasm. "But let me tell you right off the bat that no seven-fifty a day extra can pull anything like that with me!"

"Od's blud, fellow! I ken not the meaning of all the words, but I mislike thy tone."[4]

The actual English Crusaders would have spoken Norman French or else a form of English largely unintelligible in pronunciation, grammar, and vocabulary to the modern Englishman. The real Robin Hood, if there was one, did not speak like Errol Flynn; his language would have been something like "Biþinne castelwalle,/ þer i was atte ʒate;/ Nolde hi me in late./ Modi i-hote hadde/ To bure þat me hire ladde." Some misinformed people claim that pure Elizabethan is still spoken in the more isolated communities of the Southern Appalachians, but this is no more true of those living there than it

6

is of Tarzan's Crusaders. Try this for a sample of Appalachian mountain dialect and see if it is pure Elizabethan: "Hit didn't happen me that I wushed to contrary the revenoors, but hit turns my stomach over-fair to think how them thar shammuckin' revenoors has mommocked up an' well-nigh ruinated things fer the blockaders an' pore ailin' bodies."[5]

It would be outside the province of this book to discuss the detailed development of the language from Old to Modern English, but the lesson is plain that there are no absolute rules or authorities, nor any fixed, ideal standard of English grammar. Instead, there are, subject to change, certain linguistic forms and practices accepted in each generation by the majority of well-educated people. (These can, if you like, for the time being, be considered rules, though *conventions* is the more accurate word.) Language conforming with these forms is known as standard English, and departures from them are termed nonstandard or—if really illiterate—substandard.

Thus, standard English is really a sort of class dialect, and that is the reason for the prejudices, antagonisms, and resentments that grammar and diction arouse. One of Steinbeck's characters explains, "You know, Doc, men are suspicious of a man who doesn't talk their way. You can insult a man pretty badly by using a word he doesn't understand. Maybe he won't say anything, but he'll hate you for it."[6]

This reaction operates not only among Steinbeck's migrant farm workers; the "upper" levels of society also harbor resentment against the so-called lower ones. Many native-born Americans looked down upon non-British immigrants because of their dialect and broken grammar; and for several generations during the height of immigration, we had programs of compulsory Americanization. The prejudice extended to unfamiliar-sounding foreign names. In 1919, when an Armenian, Bagdasar Baghdigian, went to register at a Kansas City night school, the teacher winced at his name and said, "Oh, give that up and change your name to Smith, Jones, or some name like that and become Americanized. Give up everything you brought with you from the Old Country. You did not bring anything worthwhile anyway." Baghdigian reacted angrily, but many others did change their names, as part of their climb to so-called respectability. Nevertheless, some new immigrants, even when handicapped by a limited knowledge of English grammar, managed to be more eloquent than most native-born Americans. In

James Thurber's and Elliott Nugent's play *The Male Animal,* a bigoted trustee attacks a university professor who wants to read to his class a passage from Bartolomeo Vanzetti, the Italian fishpeddler who many believe was unjustly convicted of murder. When the trustee belligerently asks why Professor Turner can't read from some American instead—Herbert Hoover, perhaps—Turner replies that Hoover can't write as well as Vanzetti.

For several generations after the Civil War, dialect humor was much in vogue, and the source of such humor is partly a snobbish amusement towards those whose pronunciation is different and therefore felt to be inferior. The minstrel show laughed condescendingly at a stereotype of Negro dialect. For a long time, Hollywood movies offensively portrayed Negroes mostly as amiable oafs speaking a "Yassuh, sho-nuff, boss" type of dialogue, and there are still derogatory jokes told in allegedly Negro and Jewish dialects. Actually there is no specifically Jewish dialect, and many Negroes speak English undistinguishable from that of other Americans. Such dialect as there is, is regional (i.e., Brooklynese, Deep Southern), rather than religious or racial.

All Americans are immigrants, and our language as well as our population rightly reflects this inheritance. Thus, for well over a century and a quarter after the United States won its independence, many British men of letters sneered at the English used by all Americans, even that of Jefferson, John Marshall, and John Quincy Adams, terming it vulgar and uncouth. Some Anglophilic Americans agreed with them; as late as 1893, one went so far as to describe it as "an inferior dialect of the English." In 1908, a British writer in *Blackwood's Magazine* stated that America still acknowledged the sovereignty of English letters: "American is heard at the street corner. It is still English that is written in the study." Thus Alexis de Tocqueville, the French critic who examined American democracy in the 1830's, observed, "It is not then to the written but to the spoken language that attention must be paid, if we would detect the modifications which the idiom of an aristocratic people may undergo when it becomes the language of a democracy." The more class barriers a nation has, the deeper are its linguistic divisions; and Britain still contains more numerous and divergent dialects than does the entire United States. American social change enriched and vitalized the language, whereas the British status quo has made modern British literature much more linguistically conservative, except for the work of some Welsh and Irish rebels.

8

Today the younger British writers from working-class backgrounds and provincial universities, people from outside the Establishment, are producing some of the most vigorous and unorthodox poetry and prose.

The "English that is written in the study" was never that of the majority of Britons any more than of Americans; it belonged wholly to the educated literary caste. But what is the language of English literature? Does it not include the language of Thomas Hardy's peasants and of William Faulkner's sharecroppers? Robert Burns wrote far better in Scots dialect than in academic English. Many distinguished American writers (including Benjamin Franklin, Herman Melville, Abraham Lincoln, Mark Twain, Walt Whitman, Sherwood Anderson, Theodore Dreiser, Jack London, Ernest Hemingway, and William Faulkner) have had a limited formal education. James Fenimore Cooper was among the most militantly aristocratic of our authors, yet Mark Twain became a vastly superior stylist and wrote several essays satirizing and improving Cooper's prose. Though for a long time, as we mentioned earlier, Mark Twain was not considered entirely respectable in established literary circles (both because of his background and his use of the vernacular), Oxford University eventually recognized his merit and awarded him an honorary doctorate of letters. On the other hand, many "proper" writers, praised at the time, have been forgotten by all but the most specialized literary historians.

Still, language remains a sign of class distinction. The incongruous mixture of a snobbish attitude with nonstandard grammar is a reliable source of humor. Helen Hokinson's first captioned cartoon (1925) has a salesgirl tell a customer of a perfume: "It's *N'Aimez Que Moi*, madam—don't love nobody but me." And in the *Thurber Carnival* revue, a woman boasts, "So I gave him a haughty look and I said, 'Whom do you think you are, anyways?'" Her *whom* is the result of overcompensation, the nonstandard speaker being so anxious to appear superior that she rejects the natural *who* for the incorrect case. It is more pathetic than amusing when people are so distrustful of their speech that they suspect any natural expressions and believe the proper ones must be the opposite of their own usage.

Bergen Evans, a leading spokesman for the liberal linguists, says that scholars "do not believe that anyone who is a native speaker of a standard language will get into any linguistic trouble unless he is misled by snobbishness or timidity or vanity." [7] This is perhaps too utopian; *will* should be changed to *should*, for it is still possible to get into trouble. Should you speak as your neighbor speaks? This depends partly on your neighbor and partly on your own ambitions. If Lincoln had known only the frontier speech of New Salem, Illinois, he would not have been asked to run for President. On the other hand, politicians sometimes cultivate a fake folksy speech in order to win votes. In June 1962, the Salem, Indiana, *Democrat* noted, "The word 'ain't' has been declared respectable, and we candidates for office must develop something else to show that no one is more ordinary than we are." Apparently some politicians are indifferent to St. Augustine's advice that one should never smite an opponent in bad grammar. In 1952 and 1956, Adlai Stevenson spoke a clear and polished prose while Dwight Eisenhower's grammar was often garbled, yet Stevenson's speech showed so much education that many people reacted against it, while Eisenhower's occasional incoherencies apparently didn't bother the public. In fact, Eisenhower's grammar was standard but sometimes sufficiently awkward to make his style sometimes seem like a self-parody.

In a democratic society, the signs of class distinction are not always visible. Americans have always been uneasy about democracy; we claim to believe in equality, but we really feel that some are more equal than others. The newly rich may be uncultured clods, while the underpaid professor represents one sort of elite despite his dearth of conspicuous consumption. Since a goon in a three-hundred-dollar suit is still a goon, while a Barrymore in rags is obviously a gentleman, people insecure socially are particularly uneasy about their use of English. They can relax with friends, but in unfamiliar company, they may become apologetic about their pronunciation, grammar, or vocabulary. Even the well-educated are sometimes embarrassed by their educated usage.

The English teacher is too often thought of (and perhaps considers himself) a linguistic traffic cop, but this is not his function. The usual comment people make when introduced to an English teacher is, "Oh, oh! I'll have to watch my language." Apparently they think of the English teacher as a prissy, fastidious character, like the Puritan God outraged at the least offense. Actually, no English teacher with any sense goes around "correcting" the language of others. In fact, the professional student of language is likely to be far more broad-minded than the person who exclaims, "I'll have to watch my language." Far from being disturbed, he is apt to be intrigued with linguistic idiosyncrasies. For the true func-

10

tion of the linguist is to observe and describe how language is used, rather than to prescribe how it should be used. He is a historian, instead of a lawgiver, and he realizes the futility of trying to legislate language for millions and to enforce such legislation. The Italians in 1582 and the French in 1635 established an academy to stand guard over their national tongue, to purge it of any impurities, and to prevent any change (hence decay) from setting in. Some English men of letters, like Dryden and Defoe in the late seventeenth century and Swift and a host of lesser figures in the eighteenth, urged the founding of an English academy to perform a similar function. Had they succeeded, Huck Finn would have had one more reason for running away from the restrictions of "siviliza-tion."

Language should not be a rigid set of rules to be followed but a supple and flexible instrument to be used. The authoritarian uses grammar like the Articles of War; but language is a vehicle of communication, not commandment. The literary artist employs it to create the effects he wants; he is its master, not its prisoner. Thus Lionel Trilling writes of *Huckleberry Finn:* "As for the style of the book, it is not less than definitive in American literature. The prose of *Huckleberry Finn* established for written prose the virtues of American colloquial speech. This has nothing to do with pronunciation or grammar. It has something to do with ease and freedom in the use of the language. Most of all it has to do with the structure of the sentence, which is simple, direct, and fluent, maintaining the rhythm of the word-groups of speech and the intonations of the speaking voice." [8] Actually, style does have something to do with grammar, for a writer who straitjackets himself by rigidly following prescriptive and artificial rules too far removed from actual usage will not get the fluent freedom of Mark Twain.

Lionel Trilling stresses Twain's awareness of the cadences of oral speech; and it is important to remember that essentially language is spoken, not written. Only within the last two centuries has there been a wide reading public for English; and in the world at large a great majority is still illiterate. Written English is usually more careful and precise than casual speech, but it must be based upon spoken usage, or it becomes increasingly separate and ultimately dead—the written language of a particular caste or class, like classical Sanskrit. As if in recognition of this, we speak of languages as *tongues,* not as *pens, presses,* or *typewriters.* Only Tarzan learned to read and write English before he could speak it. He grew

11

up speaking the "language" of the great apes but discovered his parents' books in their cabin on the edge of the jungle; and there, sitting by his parents' skeletons, he taught himself to read and write by the "look-see" method, beginning with the pictures and words in children's primers (D-O-G matches the picture of a dog) and progressing to adult books with abstract words that he could have never learned by such a method or any other, since they then had no context or significance to him. When he did discover human speech, he learned French before he learned English. This could happen only in science fiction.

Unlike Tarzan, most people speak English better than they write it. Some who are fluent and vigorous in conversation become incoherent and atrocious stylists when they try to express themselves on paper. Despite the linguists' stress on spoken language, a person who writes English poorly is usually a poor reader and therefore reads little. We usually connect grammar and literacy. So grammar is involved in reading as well as in writing and speaking, and few people write well who do not read extensively in the work of superior authors. Business firms complain of poor writing and advertise, "Send me a man who reads." According to a survey made in the late 1950's, only about 17 percent of Americans were then reading a book, as compared to 34 percent of the Australians and 55 percent of the British. Over a century ago, Thoreau complained: "We are underbred and low-lived and illiterate; and in this respect I confess I do not make any very broad distinction between the illiterateness of my townsman who cannot read at all and the illiterateness of him who has learned to read only what is for children and feeble intellects." He went on to complain, "The best books are not read even by those who are called good readers," and observed, "Most men have learned to read to serve a paltry convenience, as they have learned to cipher in order to keep accounts and not be cheated in trade. . . ." Yet, "To read well, that is, to read true books in a true spirit, is a noble exercise, and one that will task the reader more than any exercise which the customs of the day esteem. It requires a training such as the athletes underwent. . . ." Benjamin Franklin had a much more utilitarian view of literature than Thoreau, but he related that being very ambitious to write well, he studied and imitated the best authors of his time until he developed his own workmanlike style; and towards the end of his career, he claimed that he owed much of his success to his writing ability.

12

By contrast, many a college student confesses that he never reads a book that is not assigned and cannot comprehend how anyone can read for pleasure. Just as the musically uneducated may find serious music painful, the poorly read student usually has a tin ear for language (which is, after all, a sort of music, as poets realize) and is incapable of revising his own written work or developing an effective style. Thoreau urged that the classics and other important works of the past be read, whereas there is some tendency today for high school students to be assigned easy, modern popular books or versions of the classics rewritten in simpler (and undistinguished) language with most of the intellectual content removed. (On the other hand, some high school reading lists sound like those for a master's degree.) But a badly written, though intellectually easy, book is slower and more difficult to read than a well-written one; hack writing is like poor, unoiled machinery, with a jerky rather than a forward movement and rhythm.

Thus there is grammar in a broad as well as a narrow sense, yet too often only the latter is taught. Many students and apparently some teachers do not see the connection between grammar and style and clear, perceptive thinking. Instead, they concentrate on the mere mechanics of grammar—exercises on agreement, antecedents, verb forms, and writing complete sentences, without considering whether the examples themselves have any grace, style, or wit. As a result, some students give up in frustration and boredom, while others turn out prose that is grammatically correct but hopelessly awkward. On the other hand, skilled stylists often violate "correct" grammar to achieve gracefulness or emphasis. James Thurber frequently attacked modern manglings of grammar, but he also satirized his old English composition teacher, Miss Groby, who loved to torture the life out of sentences by parsing them on the blackboard and who saw literature only as a hunting ground for figures of speech that could be picked out and labeled. Probably she would have agreed with Thomas Wentworth Higginson, who wanted to "correct" some of the grammar in Emily Dickinson's poetry. Yet Higginson confessed that "When a thought takes one's breath away, a lesson on grammar seems an impertinence."

Does teacher know best? Even if there were a definitive "best," as there is not in many cases, not all English teachers would be able to recognize it—let alone teach their students to do so. According to a bulletin published by the National Education Association, about one third of those teaching high school English did not

13

themselves major in English or in any related field while at college. Ninety percent of the teachers interviewed said they thought they were not qualified to teach reading, over half considered themselves inadequately prepared to teach composition, and about half felt they were not prepared to teach literature and language. Though elementary school teachers spend more time on English than on any other subject, fewer than 10 percent of them had majored in English; only one in three had been required to study literature; and less than one in five had been required to take more than a freshman course in composition. In the light of these statistics, the average teacher's "authority" is not too reliable. William Morris reported in the *Washington Post* that an English teacher in a highly rated Connecticut school maintained that "Have you become accustom to the noise?" was correct and "accustomed" incorrect. (Can you imagine Rex Harrison singing, "I've been accustom to her face"?) And three teachers told a student that of the sentences (1) "You are suppose to do your schoolwork" and (2) "You are supposed to do your schoolwork," only the first is acceptable. Four confused teachers are not, of course, enough to indicate a trend; and there are many others who, underpaid and overworked, do a fine job in recognizing and encouraging effective writing.

The effective teacher will be a guide, rather than a lawgiver; he will have some knowledge of the history and evolution of English, and he will recognize that usage, the only real authority, is both changing and relative. However, the principle of relativity can be carried to impractical extremes. Some liberal, descriptive grammarians bend so far over backwards to avoid anything that can be construed as a value judgment that they may end by making no judgments at all. One professor maintained that if he were teaching secondary school and had students who used the kind of grammar represented by "I knowed we was suppose to hand in our papers, but them assignments wasn't no easy ones to do," he would ask the students what they planned to do after they graduated. If they expected to work in a garage or on an assembly line, he would tell them not to worry about their language, because it would be appropriate to that environment. But if they hoped to have a white-collar job or become an executive, then they should elevate their grammar to a standard acceptable in higher social and occupational circles. This would be an adequate explanation if language were merely a matter of adjustment or adaptation. Some timid souls even suggest that you should alter your diction and

14

grammar to conform to the company in which you find yourself, so you won't be rejected as different. Thus if you are in basic training, you should adopt nonstandard grammar and employ the omnipresent obscenity of the troops. But this approach is both dishonest and unnecessary. Nobody objects to standard grammar or demands obscenities; as long as you use relaxed colloquial English and avoid snobbish affectations, you will get along anywhere. You might, as Steinbeck observed, be resented if you use a learned vocabulary beyond your listener's level of understanding; but this is a question of manners, not of grammar. Assuredly you will be resented if you lecture people on the unacceptability of their language. Lawrence of Arabia confessed, "I became . . . quite intolerable to the Staff on the Canal. I took every opportunity to rub into them their comparative ignorance and inefficiency in the department of intelligence and irritated them yet further by literary airs, correcting Shavian split infinitives and tautologies in their reports." [9] In *To Kill a Mockingbird*, the children Jem and Scout criticize their housekeeper Calpurnia for using different levels of language at home and at work. She explains, ". . . folks don't like to have somebody around knowin' more than they do. It aggravates 'em. You're not gonna change any of them by talking right, they've got to want to learn themselves, and when they don't want to learn there's nothing you can do but keep your mouth shut or talk their language." [10]

Obviously, not everyone is going to become a skilled grammarian and stylist, and it is pointless to bemoan this fact. But this does not mean that the grammarian should give up his job or that there is no advantage in standard English. Though standards change, there is a decided advantage in using grammar and diction that is clearer, more precise, more effective in expressing complex ideas and subtle distinctions of meaning. Though some moving passages in literature are written in the vernacular (e.g., much of Scott, Dickens, Hardy, Twain, Steinbeck, and J. D. Salinger), nonstandard tends to lapse into clichés (as is apparent in the work of Salinger), to be far more monotonous and limited than educated usage. Paradoxically, standard English is more flexible, and the very limitations of nonstandard tend to standardize thought. This is particularly true of the dialogue in television Western, hillbilly, and crime shows that grind out standardized nonstandard speech and thereby kill the colorful diversity of genuine regionalisms.

Of course, many regionalisms are perfectly acceptable. In a broad sense, everybody's English is the product of some sort of regionalism. Pronunciation is the most obvious regional distinction, but diction and grammar also change somewhat from area to area. As for pronunciation, no particular dialect is intrinsically superior to any other. Most Americans share a broad-gauge common pronunciation, but this does not make a Bostonian or Southern accent any less valid. If the New Englander wants to call his region *Noon Gland*, if the Missourian wants to call his state *Missourah*, and the Nevadan to flatten the *a* in the name of his, that is their privilege. Dialects are a weakness only if they are so thick and so localized as to be a barrier to broad communication. Thus the characters in the British movie *Sparrows Can't Sing* spoke such an impenetrable East End Londonese that it was necessary to provide subtitles for the American audiences—and possibly for some British ones as well. Certainly there is no need for anyone to apologize for an accent, though snobbery may try to raise social and professional barriers against people whose accents are unfashionable. Some writers use phony spelling like *sed, sez, luv, trubble, wuz, pore,* and *likker,* to suggest regional ignorance or illiteracy, though this is the way these words are properly pronounced. Actors and public speakers may find it advisable to overcome the limitations of accent, and mush-mouths and nasal twangs may not be euphonious, but there is no genuine basis for disparaging anyone's accent. This is not to say that there aren't mispronunciations; for example, it is nowhere acceptable to say *heenious* for *heinous, inviduous* for *invidious, peotry* for *poetry,* or *liberry* for *library.* Thus, *sho nuff* is accepted as a regionalism, whereas *nucular* (for *nuclear*) is nonstandard even when used by prominent politicians.

As for diction and grammar, some regionalisms are all right in their cultural context. Some words are standard in one region and not in another; the distinction is geographical, not moral, though pedants try to make it so. Henry Higgins even tells Eliza, "You will get much further with the Lord if you learn not to offend His ears." [11] Within different regionalisms, there is standard and nonstandard usage, just as there are social distinctions within regions. Nancy Mitford wrote a satiric book distinguishing between the vocabulary used by upper-class and non-upper-class Britons, whereupon social snobs became quite alarmed lest they be caught using Non-U instead of U terminology. Which is U—*sofa* or *couch*—and does it matter? George Bernard Shaw wrote in *Pygmalion* that "an honest and natural slum dialect is more tolerable than the attempt

16

of a phonetically untaught person to imitate the vulgar dialect of the golf club. . . ." In America, so-called provincial speech is not necessarily inferior to that of the urban areas. It is simply that some regionalisms are "in" and others are "out"; thus Pennsylvania Dutch is considered provincial but Bostonian is not. Why should *might could* be frowned upon as shibboleth and the ubiquitous suffix *-wise* be accepted as "sophisticated"? Merely because every little "in" group has a jargon all its own.

Carrying relativism to extremes, researchers at University College, London, wrote that when comparing the language of the King James and New English versions of the Bible, "No one has good grounds for supposing that one of these styles is necessarily better than the other; nor, for that matter, does one have evidence for thinking that either of these styles is better than the style of advertising. . . ." For the versions of the Bible, they are correct in general but perhaps wrong in particular. That is, seventeenth-century prose is not necessarily superior to that of the twentieth-century. Certainly Hemingway wrote better than Gabriel Harvey. Yet styles are not abstract; you must look at particular works, and it may well be that in many specific passages the King James translation is more eloquent and poetic than the New English Version. Freed from archaisms, the latter is undoubtedly clearer to modern readers, but clarity is not everything. *Better* has several meanings, and you must ask, "Better in what way?" The style used in advertising may be appropriate for advertising; but when applied to religion, it produces billboards demanding that you "Get Right with God!" When scholars insist that there is only one acceptable style, they produce a dead "literary" language with the stereotyped rhetoric of the old Shakespearean actor in the movies and comic strips. On the other hand, it is doubtful that the London researchers would concede that the style of *Hamlet* in *Classic Comics* is as good as that in Shakespeare's play. In speaking of style, they should amend "better" to "appropriate"; for if no style is better, then all distinctions vanish: Mickey Spillane and Edgar Guest are the equal of James Joyce and Robert Frost.

However, this does not mean that there is one "right" style. Robert Frost, T. S. Eliot, E. E. Cummings, Dylan Thomas, Wallace Stevens, and Robert Lowell are all great twentieth-century poets, yet each has his own distinctive voice. In fact, many writers have several styles for different occasions. Style, of course, is more than grammar, but it includes grammar. Usually, literary artists employ standard usage except in some dialogue, but there is considerable leeway between relaxed colloquial and highly formal grammar. Even colloquial grammar has a rather formal control in Hemingway's concise prose—including his dialogue, nonstandard though some of it is. For Hemingway's prose shows the discipline of the artist, not of the authoritarian. Literature uses the unregimented language of the imagination. Thus James Thurber, though irritated at much modern grammar, protested because too much advertising, bureaucratic, and journalistic prose is slovenly, rather than because it breaks absolute rules. Thurber's style, like Hemingway's, was disciplined, but he wanted to do his own disciplining. When editor Harold Ross of *The New Yorker* red-penciled a writer's work too rigidly, in accordance with Fowler's *Modern English Usage,* Thurber protested, "I was increasingly disturbed by Ross's insistence on super-clarity, over-punctuation, and strict rules of grammar and syntax and parsing. I knew that if McNulty became a prisoner of pattern, something warm and unique would go out of his writing." [12] For language is not a ritual incantation but a personal voice. It should be exciting rather than inhibiting. Just as the modern composer makes use of the twelve-tone scale, jazz, and hitherto unorthodox instruments, such as the saxophone or exotic percussion, so the modern creative writer should be able to exploit all the resources of the language.

This does not mean that anything goes and that standard grammar is obsolete. Nor does it mean that any nonstandard habit can be justified on grounds of widespread usage. When mangled grammar interferes with clarity and logic, when it produces prose as graceless as a spavined mule, as shabby as a sharecropper's cabin, and as precise as a politician's promises, then it certainly needs revision. The remedy is functional, rather than formal, grammar. The grammatical equivalent of five-finger exercises may help at first, but later you must be free to relax and to experiment. For, let me repeat, there is no single, abstract standard for correct or good writing. There is only effective writing. This requires contextual grammar; the question is not whether it is abstractly right, but whether it works in context. If you break grammatical conventions, you must do so effectively, not ignorantly and carelessly. There is a world of difference between E. E. Cummings's "what if a much of a which of a wind/gives the truth to summer's lie" and "Us Tareyton smokers would rather fight than switch"; between Cummings's "my father moved through dooms of love/ through sames of am through haves of give" and "We don't want none of them eggheads in politics."

In short, you should be a stylist, rather than a pedant. Much writing that is grammatically "correct" is dull and clumsy. It is relatively easy to achieve academic correctness; but really effective writing, far from practicing the idea that anything goes, requires far more sensitivity and self-discipline than the schoolmarm dreams of. Thus without being imitative, you should follow the practice of effective authors, rather than the precepts of linguistic legislators. This is a pragmatic approach in which clarity is more important than purity.

If there are laws, they must be enforced, and some critics think English teachers should have the job of policing the language. Thus Louis B. Salomon, writing in the *Bulletin of the American Association of University Professors,* insists that "If English teachers don't want to be traffic cops . . . then they might as well turn in their badges." [13] But to police traffic is dull stuff; to go on exploring expeditions is more exciting, and the teacher can be a guide. Expeditions, of course, need careful planning and the right equipment. So what of the rules of grammar? If these are merely analogous to marching in rank, then they are expendable; but if they embody some common sense, like scouting the terrain and knowing the location of waterholes, then they are invaluable. The issue should be one of common sense. If a grammar rule is merely arbitrary (like the distinction between *shall* and *will* or *like* and *as,* the use of the apostrophe, or the injunction against ending a sentence with a preposition), then it is apt to be violated and eventually discarded. But most grammar is not just a set of arbitrary edicts; it has a commonsense foundation. Clarity demands that subjects agree with their verbs, that most pronouns have antecedents and that they clearly agree with these antecedents, that modifiers not dangle or be misplaced, that parallel constructions be in the same grammatical form, in short, that the relation between sentence elements be unambiguous. Why should grammatical conventions have developed at all? The enduring ones have a built-in logic, lacking in the distinction between *shall* and *will.*

As for such formal problems as the plurals of nouns or the principal parts of verbs, language needs some stability as well as growth; despite linguistic change and relativity, we need a common core for communication. "All right," you may argue, "but nonstandard English can communicate clearly. 'Who done it?' is as clear as 'Who did it?' " True. In this case the answer is merely that discriminating usage prefers the latter. The descriptive grammarian will avoid branding someone's speech as vulgar or bad, but he should have the honesty to indicate where stigmas and shibboleths do exist (whether they should or not) and point out the perils of breaking standard conventions. When the publisher Henry Holt carefully wrote a letter in reformed, i.e., simplified, spelling to his new mother-in-law (a Beacon Hill dowager), the lady was not converted but exclaimed in dismay, "Florence has married a man who doesn't know how to spell!"

Thus usage itself acts as a powerful control against both change (let alone the idea that anything goes) and the enforcement of obsolete (and perhaps unjustifiable) rules. Try to teach a child some usage conflicting with that of his (ugh) peer group and see how far you get. Likewise, one well-read lady, aware of the proscriptions of pedants, said, "I try not to use *contact* as a verb, but I can't help it." Her worry is pointless; *contact* in its verbal sense has been established by widespread usage for at least forty years. It is perfectly legitimate and rarely meets with objections. As for more questionable practices, such as the use of *irregardless* (for *regardless*) and *where is it at?* these are undesirable not for moral or social reasons but because the *ir-* and *at* are irritating dead wood, as useless and unnecessary as a sixth toe.

The fact that grammar is an intellectual and emotional habit is not enough. Writing can be an art, and art requires consciousness and control. Even the slovenly writer watches his grammar more carefully on the page than in his speech; people who say *ain't* and *you was* are not apt to write them. Since the writer can revise, there is less excuse for the wordy, imprecise, bumbling, and grammatically dubious prose that sometimes slips by in careless conversation. But the prose used in conversation can also be an art. In Hemingway's story "In Another Country," an American soldier hospitalized in Milan tells an Italian major that he had difficulty taking an interest in Italian because it seemed too easy. " 'Ah, yes,' the major said. 'Why, then, do you not take up the use of grammar?' So we took up the use of grammar, and soon Italian was such a difficult language that I was afraid to talk to him until I had the grammar straight in my mind." [14]

On this encouraging note, let us begin.

20

2 √ Grammar down the Ages

Formal grammar has been traditionally used to impart a dead language to a living people. Our word *grammar* is derived from *grammatikē* (γραμμᾶτική), from *gramma* or "something engraved," hence a letter. In the early Christian era, grammatical studies at Alexandria and Pergamum dealt with the elucidation of texts, textual criticism, and rhetoric. Gradually the name was transferred to the study we now call grammar.* As long as language is thought of as divinely inspired, the problems involved with it are philosophical rather than philological. Did language come from the gods? Was there a supernatural sanction for certain words and a prohibition against others? Were there some words so sacred or so dreadful that they should never be uttered? Is there a necessary connection between words and the visible world? The Greeks and Hebrews were both concerned with the origin of language and the significance of names, and their approach was speculative rather than scientific.

¶ THE FIRST GRAMMARIANS

The first formal grammar antedates Christianity by about a thousand years. It developed in India and consisted of a few short stanzas to be recited or sung as an aid to memorizing and understanding the Vedas—the sacred hymns, rules, and stories of the ancient Hindu religion. Originally composed in Sanskrit, the Vedas were handed down by word of mouth (for when they were composed, there was no alphabet); and as the vernacular speech of the people altered, there was increasing danger of error being introduced into the sacred texts. So priests and scholars began to analyze

* An odd offshoot of the term is *gramarye*, a medieval word for magic; an even more surprising one is *glamour*, derived from *gramarye* in the sense of "bewitch or allure."

and systematize words, sounds, and syllables in a remarkable system designed to help both memory and comprehension. They developed the six branches of Vedic linguistic science—phonetics, meter, grammar, etymology, astronomy, and ceremonial—all necessary to the proper use and perpetuation of the Vedas.

For some centuries Vedic grammatical science grew and developed. Grammars were memorized, superseded, and forgotten. This oral transmission was a surprisingly accurate system, so that today our texts of the Vedas are better preserved than those of the Hebrews, who wrote on rolls of parchment. The first and the greatest Sanskrit grammar to survive is the work of Panini, who is to Sanskrit what Euclid is to geometry. Panini was born at Shalatura in the Punjab. Tradition says he was so wayward and stupid in his youth that his Brahman teacher expelled him. Stung by shame, Panini did so many acts of penance that he touched the heart of the god Siva, who became his guide and graciously revealed more grammar to him than was known by all his teachers. Legend says he was killed by a lion.

Panini's grammar is composed in the traditional mnemonic style, although by this time (variously estimated as from 700 to 200 B.C.) the Hindus had probably developed their alphabet and could commit their books to writing. Panini's grammar is not altogether original (he mentions some sixty-four predecessors), but it is unique in its arrangement and analysis. It consists of eight parts of four chapters each, comprising 3,996 sutras or aphorisms—brief rules in the form of stanzas to be recited. Panini's central theory was that nouns grew out of verbal ideas. He classified inflections according to the sounds composing them. Phonetic changes were his chief concern, and he largely disregarded syntax. His work is still used as the standard grammar for the study of the Vedas, the *Mahabharata,* and the *Ramayana* in the Brahmanic schools of India, but it did not become known to Western scholars until the early nineteenth century.

¶ HEBREW GRAMMAR

The early Hebrew grammar was speculative and philosophical rather than religious. For example, men asked themselves why it was that the earth held so many and such different tongues, and some one gave an answer in the story of the tower of Babel. The Hebrews were also intrigued to discover or invent the origins of proper names and developed a practice of composing etymological stories to account for them. They were not then concerned with the accurate elucidation and preservation of their sacred texts, many of which are contemporary with Homer.

¶ WHEN GREEK MEETS GREEK

The Greek approach to language centered around a question. Are words developed through a positive connection with the things or ideas they name, or are they arbitrary symbols that became conventional? The Analogists saw a necessary connection (analogy) between words and ideas; the Anomalists denied it. This may seem like a mere quibble until you examine the issue carefully. Then you realize that questions on the origins of language are related to the origin of man, religion, god, law, and the nature of authority— more urgent matters than whether or not an infinitive should be split or a sentence ended with a preposition. The problem is as old as Plato and as current as *Webster's Third New International Dictionary*. Protagoras and Socrates, two of the most famous teachers in Greece's golden age, both pursued these questions; and although they opposed each other's philosophical views, both were accused of impiety, of atheism, and of corrupting youth. Protagoras died at sea as he was fleeing into exile; Socrates was tried and executed, during a period of civil instability.

Socrates was concerned with the search for absolutes, the Platonic ideals of beauty and truth. In the *Cratylus,* he advanced the idea of language as something revealed by a divine lawgiver and also the opposite position that custom and convention play a part in the development of language. He discussed the view (still widely though erroneously held) that the language was debased from its ideal state in an original golden age or Garden of Eden, a common belief in ancient times. The concept of progress is quite recent. Socrates was not sure of his theory of linguistic origin, but neither could he accept the notion of Heraclitus that all is in a state of continual change:

Whether there is this eternal nature in things, or whether the truth is what Heraclitus and his followers and many others say, is a question hard to determine; and no man of sense will like to put himself or the education of his mind in the power of names; neither will he so far trust names or the givers of names as to be confident in any knowledge which con-

23

demns himself and other existences to an unhealthy state of unreality; he will not believe that all things leak like a pot, or that the whole external world is afflicted with rheum and catarrh.

Protagoras was more inclined to the relative view: "For he says that man is the measure of all things, and that things are to me as they appear to me, and that they are to you as they appear to you." (Plato, *Cratylus*.) In the *Protagoras*, he and Socrates debate whether virtue (in the sense of the classic virtues: wisdom, courage, temperance, justice) can be taught. The extreme relativist position can make these terms meaningless; on the other hand, Protagoras revealed the weakness of the absolutist position by this line of argument:

I know plenty of things—foods, drinks, drugs, and many others—which are harmful to men, and others which are beneficial, and others again which, so far as men are concerned, are neither, but are harmful or beneficial to horses, and others only to cattle or dogs. . . . Manure, for instance, is good for all plants when applied to their roots, but utterly destructive if put on the shoots of young branches. Or take olive oil. It is very bad for plants, and most inimical to the hair of all animals except man, whereas men find it of service both to the hair and to the rest of the body. So diverse and multiform is goodness that even with us the same thing is good when applied externally but deadly when taken internally.

One point upon which they were agreed was that "the most important part of a man's education is to become an authority on poetry." By this they meant the ability to read carefully, to organize one's thoughts, and to give a carefully reasoned opinion when called upon. Thus the relation of poetry to politics becomes more apparent. Our technical civilization has somewhat obscured the basic issue which, however, is still very much with us: What does a man need to know to govern himself? And the answers are still, in large part, connected with the use of language, basic to all communication and knowledge.

Aristotle, whose life spans approximately the same period in the fourth century B.C., as Protagoras' life does in the fifth, was interested in the detail as well as in the philosophy of grammar. Aristotle distinguished cases in the Greek noun, differentiated the parts of speech, and classified nouns as simple and compound. Scattered throughout his writings are bits of grammar which, taken together, form a fairly extensive body of knowledge. It was not until two centuries later, however, that the first formal Greek grammar was

24

written by Crates of Mallus, about 150 B.C. This Crates founded a famous school of grammar at Pergamum and made numerous written contributions to the scholarship of his time.

Greek culture and the Greek language were widespread over the civilized world. In Palestine the earliest surviving manuscripts of the New Testament were written in Greek. In Rome, about 50 B.C., Dionysius Thrax wrote a Greek grammar for Roman schoolboys that had an extraordinary longevity; it was still in use in England until the end of the eighteenth century as a textbook at Winchester. At Alexandria there was endless debate in the schools between the analogists and the anomalists; on the whole, scholarly opinion seemed inclined toward the analogist view. But besides such philosophical speculation, there was philological progress, such as the work done in the second century by Apollonius Dyscolus and his still more celebrated son Herodian, who wrote treatises on syntax and the parts of speech. Greek was then becoming the accepted language of Western scholarship, and it was necessary to establish texts. Herodian, who flourished in Alexandria and Rome, dedicated his grammar to the emperor Marcus Aurelius. He was dignified with the title *maximus auctor artis grammaticae*—the greatest shaper of the grammatical art. By this time the Romans ruled the Mediterranean.

¶ WHEN IN ROME

Just as the conquering Romans appropriated the world they conquered, so they appropriated scholarship wherever it was found. But they were far from being experts on the Greek grammar they sought to adapt as Latin grammar, and they made some curious mistranslations, some of which still confuse grammatical terminology. For example, the word *accusative* was translated into Latin as though it came from a Greek verb meaning *accuse,* whereas the Greek term meant simply "the case of object," a meaning restored in *objective,* which has replaced *accusative* in most English grammars. The Latin *genitivus* means mistakenly "the case of origin," whereas the Greek term in fact meant "the case of kind or species." Here again the term *possessive* has been substituted, though it does not entirely clear up matters because the possessive case is used for situations ("a day's work") that do not involve any actual possession.

Once again, the Latin language went through the same process as Sanskrit, from spoken to written to sacred or scholarly texts,

25

while a new vernacular developed and the former Roman Empire spoke the Romance languages—Italian, French, Spanish, Portuguese, and Rumanian—or else outlandish tongues like Slavic, Celtic, and Anglo-Saxon. By the Middle Ages, Latin had become the language of religion and of scholarship. Despite the dominance of Aristotle (read in Latin translation), Greek literature lapsed into relative obscurity, to be rediscovered in the Renaissance. Latin grammar throughout the Middle Ages was dominated by the work of two scholars. The first is Aelius Donatus, a Roman of the fourth century, who is noted as the teacher of St. Jerome. His grammatical writings are in three books, which concern respectively letters, syllables, feet, and tones; the eight parts of speech; and barbarisms and solecisms. So popular were these treatises of Donatus that in everyday speech a *donat* or *donet* came to be a term for any sort of textbook. The word is still to be found in the second edition of *Webster's New International Dictionary,* though it has been dropped from the third. Priscian, the other outstanding Latin grammarian, lived and wrote about two centuries after Donatus. The eighteen books he called *Commentariorum Grammaticorum Libri XVIII* were dedicated to the consul Julianus of Constantinople, where Prescian taught at court on a government salary. For centuries his and Donatus's books were the grammatical authority for churchmen and scholars.

¶ VENI, VIDI, VICI

Probably the first English grammarian was Alcuin of York (735–804), an early exchange professor who became adviser to Charlemagne and wrote his grammar (a Latin grammar, of course) in the form of a dialog between the emperor and himself. Later, about the year 1000, Aelfric surnamed the Grammarian wrote of Latin declensions and conjugations for the benefit of small Saxon chieftains and perhaps for the family of King Canute the Dane as well. After the Norman Conquest, French was for several centuries the language of the court; and with Latin for scholarship, the church, and the law, English became the language of the lower classes. Chaucer (like Dante with Italian) was the first major figure to write in the English vernacular; his contemporary Gower wrote three books, the first in Latin, the second in French, and only with the last dared use his native tongue. Latin grammars for English pupils continued in use. The most famous by William Lily or Lyly (grandfather of the poet and playwright) monopolized the Tudor textbook trade and continued in use for centuries.

The story of this celebrated grammar is remarkable. Its author, born in 1468, learned his Latin, Greek, and Hebrew at first hand on extensive journeys to Jerusalem, Rhodes, and Rome, after his graduation from Oxford. By 1512, he had been appointed high master of St. Paul's Cathedral School, and his biographers have ever since been busy asserting or refuting stories of his "cruel and inhuman severity" toward his pupils. His famous book first appeared some time after 1509, but only as a part of Colet's *Grammatices Rudimenta*. It was a brief statement of Latin syntax, the rules being given in English. Later, about 1513, this same syntax, with rules in Latin instead of English, was published anonymously as the *Absolutissimus de Octo Orationis Partium Constructione*. The lack of an author's name was probably due to the fact that Erasmus had a large share in the work.

About 1540, both versions were merged into one, and later a special copy on vellum was made for Edward VI. The grammar did not reach its final form until the revision of 1574, over half a century after Lily's death, when it was called in plain English *A Short Introduction of Grammar*. Bills were more than once introduced into Parliament to make it the official textbook for all schools, but it was so in fact even if it never became so by law. That Shakespeare learned Latin from it can be demonstrated by tags in *Love's Labour's Lost* and other plays.

Grammar to the Elizabethans was, of course, Latin grammar; if English had a grammar, it was thought scarcely worth study. (in fact, not until 1857 did a professor of poetry at Oxford University [Matthew Arnold] lecture in English rather than in Latin.) British scholars of the sixteenth century were concerned with two problems about the English language: the regularization of its chaotic spelling and the extent to which foreign, particularly Latin, words should be allowed to enter the native tongue. Ben Jonson (1573–1637) and John Milton (1608–1674) both wrote brief treatises on English grammar. These, as well as other early English grammars, were little more than Latin terms and classifications applied to native words. From five to seven cases were ascribed to the English noun; even though it had no dative, ablative, locative or vocative, Latin had these cases so English should have them too. In 1653 John Wallis in his *Grammatica Linguae Anglicanae* ventured to protest that English was a language different from Latin (though Wallis wrote his protest in Latin) and that it therefore required different treatment, but his argument went largely unheeded. It was not so much that scholars consciously idealized Latin language patterns as that these were so much an ingrained part of their mental equipment that English naturally took form in their image. John Dryden, in fact, confessed that he often framed his thoughts in Latin before expressing them in English.

Still the mass of Englishmen knew nothing of Latin and continued, as the mass of people always do, speaking their native tongue according to hereditary and environmental habits. English, in its oldest form, came to the British Isles about the time of the fall of the Roman Empire. Previously the Britons spoke Celtic, with a smattering of words borrowed from the Roman overlords who governed after the legions of Claudius began to subjugate the more accessible parts of the island in A.D. 43. Continued barbarian invasions and onslaughts weakened the frontiers of the empire, and in the middle of the fifth century, successive waves of Teutonic invaders (Angles, Saxons, and Jutes) ravaged the eastern coast of Britain and drove the Celts (those who survived the slaughter) into the Highland marches of Scotland, Wales, and Cornwall or over the sea to Ireland, where Celtic (Gaelic) can still be heard today. The Anglo-Saxons became the English and their language the oldest form of English. The first invaders were heathen; but by the beginning of the seventh century, missionaries from Rome and Ireland made considerable headway in restoring Christianity and with it the Latin of the church, from which the English borrowed about 450 words during the Old English period. From the middle of the eighth to the early eleventh century, the Vikings (Norse, Danish, and other Scandinavian sea rovers) harassed, plundered, and sometimes settled along the east coast. Those who stayed intermarried with the inhabitants and adopted their language but in so doing, brought about nine hundred Old Norse words into English as well as about fourteen hundred Scandinavian place names. Despite Latin and Danish borrowings, Old English grammar was Germanic, a highly inflected synthetic grammar far more difficult than ours today.

Old English remained the vernacular for about six hundred years —longer than any subsequent period in the history of the language. It was violently interrupted by the Norman Conquest of 1066. With the triumph of William the Conqueror, Norman French became the language of the ruling class. The common people continued to speak English, but their tongue began to be modified by that of their conquerors. By the time of Chaucer (1340?–1400), English was once more the paramount language of the land, but an English greatly changed by interaction with French. The basic vocabulary and grammar remained English, but many inflectional endings were leveled. Eighty-five percent of the Old English vocabulary was lost, while over ten thousand words were borrowed from French as well as more Latin vocabulary from the church and the law. The language from about 1100 to 1500 is known as Middle English, a transitional period in which the vernacular became simplified from that of Alfred the Great (now unintelligible except to translators) to a version not too difficult for the modern reader. (See *Le Morte d'Arthur*: "For this book was ended the ninth yere of the reygne of King Edward the Fourth, by Syr Thomas Maleoré, Knight, as Jesu helpe hym for Hys grete myght, as he is the servaunt of Jesu bothe day and nyght.") Modern English emerged at the beginning of the sixteenth century, without any help from grammarians, who had contempt for any speech but cloistered Latin. The great flexibility of our language, its natural gender, few inflections, reasonable and logical word order, versatile vocabulary and rich hoard of synonyms were all developed in the Old and Middle periods when English had no formalized grammar and was scorned as a vernacular for illiterates.

And then, paradoxically, just as Englishmen began to esteem their native speech and scholars to use it for treatises and dissertations, the bars began to be raised. Modern English has been conditioned by two powerfully conservative forces: the printing press and the schoolhouse. Both have tended to fix English and to lessen the rate of linguistic change, with the result that English has achieved less simplification during the four and a half centuries since 1500 than in the two centuries previous. Considering the chaotic nature of Middle English, in which grammar, dialect, and spelling were each man for himself, this stabilization has been a great gain to communication, but it can be too rigid. Where Chaucer might spell a word in a score of different ways, about the best the sixteenth century could do is illustrated by a pamphlet of Robert Greene's of 1591, where the word *cony* (meaning "dupe" or "gull") appears in nine forms: *cony, conye, conie, coni, conny, cuny, cunny, connie,* and *cunnie*. A like approach to restraint is observed in grammar.

Such "native woodnotes wild" flourished even more weakly in the first half of the seventeenth century and were pretty well clipped into regularity by the time of the Restoration (1660) and the

Latinate language of John Dryden. As early as Shakespeare's time, education was beginning to draw English into the cloister. "Free" grammar schools were found in most English villages, where children were forced to undergo the rigors of the language of culture and scholarship, namely Latin. Even though English was not taught in such schools and it was Latin verses that must be "just" or "correct," the schools were spreading the general notion of grammatical regulation. That inveterate Latinist Ben Jonson—bricklayer, swordsman, poet, playwright, and graduate of the Westminster school—charged Shakespeare with having "small Latin and less Greek"; and this was perhaps fortunate, for in Shakespeare's work we see the greatest expression of a free diction largely unbound by the shackles of rule and dogma.

What sort of English did Shakespeare use? How would his voice sound to us today? No doubt his speech was, or became, that of the cultivated people of his time; it is not probable that an actor who performed before monarch and court would fail to alter his Warwickshire argot where necessary to harmonize with more aristocratic accents.

These aristocratic accents were certainly different from ours in some aspects, such as the value given to final *s* in certain common words. *His* was *hiss* instead of *hiz*, and *was* was *wass* instead of *wuz*. Thus *is* and *this* are good rhymes for Shakespeare, also *his* and *bliss*. When Iago tells Desdemona and Emilia that they are ". . . players in your housewifery, and housewives in your beds," *house* is pronounced *huss* as in *hussy*, with the implication of that word as well.

Shakespeare, no doubt, used with fair consistency the pronunciation which is now rustic dialect in such a phrase as "Consarn ye!" The vowel before *r* plus consonant, that vowel which we spell so variously in *curt, word, bird,* and *heard,* was *ah. Servant* was *sarvent, concern* was *consarn,* and *clerk* was *clark*—the vowel sound of the latter being still so pronounced in modern British usage. Some tags and remnants of this fashion still persist in Scottish dialect and in words like *heart, hearth,* and *sergeant,* while the spelling though not the sound has come down to us in *Southwark* (pronounced *Sutherk*).

For Shakespeare, *work* rhymed with *dark,* and *word* with *guard.* As late as the 1800's, Noah Webster had to warn the users of his famous blue-backed speller not to pronounce *mercy* "marcy" or *perfect* "parfect."

But probably the most noticeable feature of Shakespeare's pronunciation would be what would sound to us like an Irish brogue. A considerable group of words, mainly those we spell with *ea* and pronounce with *ee*, such as *sea, east, leap, heat, speak,* and *steal,* were pronounced by the careful, cultivated Elizabethan with the vowel of *hay*: *say, ayst, lape, spake,* and so on. For Shakespeare, *gape* and *leap, pail* and *steal* were good rhymes.

The inflections Shakespeare used were somewhat different from ours. For one thing, he enjoyed greater freedom in his choice of third-person verb forms. Notice in Portia's celebrated mercy speech, how the *-eth* ending—*blesseth, droppeth, doth*—alternates with the *-s* ending—*gives, takes, becomes, shows.* For the poet this alteration must have been a boon, for a syllable might be added or subtracted in any verb by the simple device of changing the ending. But freedom was passing; the *-s* form, already dominant, drove out the *-eth* completely.

Like his contemporaries, Shakespeare retained the distinction between *thou* and *you* in the singular. The former was used incongruously enough to indicate either affectionate intimacy or blighting contempt; the latter, distance and respect. Most of the changes are rung in the first scene of *Othello*; where the Venetian senator Brabantio, not recognizing Roderigo, addresses him with the conventional *you*; but discerning his daughter's unsuccessful suitor and being enraged at his own rude awakening, he turns to the *thou* of scorn and contempt. At the end of the scene, overcome by the humiliation of Desdemona's elopement with a Moor, he falters, "Oh, that you had her!"

Elizabethan inflectional forms included many *-en* plurals now lost —*eyen* for *eyes, shoon* for *shoes, housen* for *houses.* On the other hand, some innovations have appeared since 1600. For instance, *its,* as the neuter possessive pronoun, is almost unknown in Shakespeare; the cultivated Elizabethan might use instead *his, the, it, thereof,* or some circumlocution.

As for syntax, probably the most sweeping change we have made since Shakespeare's time is our use of the auxiliary *do* in questions and negative statements. Rosalind says, "What talk we of fathers?" where her modern cousin would say, "Why do we talk of fathers?" Falstaff says, "I hear not of Master Brook," where "I do not hear" would be the contemporary usage. Page says, "I do invite you to breakfast," where we would omit the *do.* And Brabantio asks, "What said she to you?" instead of "What did she say to you?"

Shakespeare and his contemporaries use certain other construc-

31

tions since outlawed, such as the double comparative, the adverb lacking *-ly*, and the double negative. To Shakespeare a point could be *more higher* or *most highest*, and a thing could be *done noble*, or *noble done*. In general, however, Elizabethan syntax is not too far removed from modern syntax; the conventions have not, from then to now, altered greatly.

It is different with idioms and with word meanings, where much change has taken place, shifts often so complete as to confuse the modern reader. Shakespeare could speak of *hitting of* (i.e., "hitting on," "recalling") a man's name; he could use *censure* and *notorious* with good intent, while *companion* usually meant "low companion." To Shakespeare, *nowadays* was probably a vulgar word; he gives it only to Bottom in *A Midsummer Night's Dream,* to the gravedigger in *Hamlet,* and to a fisherman in *Pericles. Charm* to Shakespeare was always connected with magic; *bonnets* were worn by men as well as by babies. A *blue-eyed* person was not attractive but ugly, with bluish circles around sunken eyes. One's *favor* was one's face or general appearance, and *wretch* was a term of endearment.

Shakespeare's attitude toward certain words can be shown to have changed with his development as a playwright. He uses *beautify* in several of his earlier works, but later, in *Hamlet,* he permits Polonius to say, "That's a vile phrase! Beautified is a vile phrase!" and afterwards he excludes it from his vocabulary. The word *wood,* in its Middle English meaning of *insane,* he uses also in his earlier plays but not the later ones. By the year 1600 this use of *wood* was probably a provincialism.

The famous linguist Otto Jespersen gives figures which throw some light on the Shakespeare-Bacon controversy. Where Shakespeare uses *also* only twenty-two times and those nearly always in vulgar or affected speech, Bacon uses the word freely and indiscriminately. Where Bacon has both *might* and *mought,* Shakespeare prefers *might* with one solitary exceptional *mought.* Bacon uses only *amongst,* while Shakespeare frequently has *among.* Bacon confines himself to *scarce,* while Shakespeare uses both *scarce* and *scarcely.* And finally, Bacon makes fairly frequent use of *whereas,* whereas the word is entirely absent from the works of Shakespeare.

Shakespeare's vocabulary has been variously estimated at from 15,000 to 24,000 words, which is not more than are known to the average intelligent high school boy or girl of today. But to know a word and to use it are wholly separate things; few writers have actually used so great a vocabulary. Several experts estimate that one quarter of our speech is covered by just nine words—*and, be, have, it, of, the, to, will,* and *you*—and we do not usually show any great ingenuity or variety in selecting the other three quarters. To Shakespeare, disdain is "sour-eyed"; hate is "barren"; murder is "withered"; a traitor is "toad-spotted"; about to rape Lucrece, Tarquin has a "ravishing stride"; a flea sticking upon Bardolph's nose is "a black soul burning in hell-fire," and as for "mincing poetry, 'Tis like the forc'd gait of a shuffling nag." No writer ever had a greater gift for the sharp, surprising, but precise word or employed metaphor with more inventive vitality.

Curious misunderstandings have grown up around some of Shakespeare's lines, which have had their original meaning distorted by later quotation. A double instance occurs in *Hamlet,* Act I, scene 4, lines 13–16:

> But to my mind—though I am native here
> And to the manner born—it is a custom
> More honoured in the breach than the observance.

Hamlet is referring to the drunken wassail kept by the king his uncle to celebrate his marriage to Gertrude, Hamlet's mother. Hamlet admits that such revelry is a custom of the country, but adds that though he is born into this custom, or manner, he feels that it is more honorable when omitted than when observed. There is no *manor*—that is a misquotation introduced by later speakers in place of *manner*—and Hamlet does not say that this custom has actually fallen into disuse, but that it should do so.

A predominant feature of Shakespeare's diction is his reliance on functional shift. *Stranger, nose, lip, mutiny, villain, ruffian* (". . . it hath ruffian'd so upon the sea"), *paragon* (". . . he hath achieved a maid/ That paragons description and wild fame"), *weapon* ("though you do see me weapon'd"), and practically any unlikely noun can also be a verb. *Both-sides* and *flood-gate* ("my particular grief/ Is of so flood-gate and o'erbearing nature") are adjectives; *backward* can be a noun, and Antony can be *unqualitied* for shame. Normally an adjective, *soft* can be a reflexive verb ("Soft you; a word or two before you go."). This freedom to use words out of their ordinary functions contributes more than a little to the fresh and startling effect of the dialog. No barriers are put up, for instance, against using *contact* as anything but a noun. As for Shakespeare's nouns, they often have an unorthodox shape, like

33

"the importance of Cyprus to the Turk," "for every minute is expectancy of more arrivance."

And then we come to those passages in Shakespeare which would certainly be blue-penciled if found in any theme in high school or college composition. One such is in *All's Well That Ends Well*, Act I, scene 3, lines 173–174:

> Can't no other
> But I your daughter, he must be my brother?

This passage is so packed overful with its statement that the words burst and crack. To paraphrase it requires nearly twice as many words.

The infrequency of *whom* in Shakespeare has already been mentioned, if not illustrated. Rosalind says, as any modern girl might, "Who do you speak to," and Corin tells her of the shepherd, "Who you saw sitting by me on the turf." These are both ordinary usage in Shakespeare, but a choice instance is Cassio's response when Iago states, "He's married." "To who?" says Cassio. Likewise, in *Much Ado About Nothing*, Benedick says of Claudio, "He is in love. With who?"

One odd thing about Shakespeare's grammatical originalities is that they are not too easily perceived, not glaring to the casual eye. How many times, for example, one might read over *The Merchant of Venice*, Act IV, scene 1, lines 75–76, and see nothing curious:

> You may as well forbid the mountain pines
> To wag their high tops and to make no noise.

Yet if we press the dull business of analysis, we are startled to find the pines being forbidden first to move and next to be silent—which is certainly not what Shakespeare intended. Editors explain the thing on the basis of ellipsis: the real meaning is "forbid them to make noise when they walk." In the same play (Act II, scene 1, lines 32–33) we hear the Prince of Morocco saying:

> If Hercules and Lichas play at dice
> Which is the better man . . .

Here no question is intended in the second line. The sense will be plain if we put *to determine* after *dice*.

Ellipsis appears either for rhythm and meter or for conciseness. Sometimes Shakespeare was guilty of indulging in meandering word play too intricate to be followed by the audience and too tedious to move the action; perhaps there was a touch of autobiography in Polonius, who after all once acted Caesar on the stage. But when Shakespeare wanted action, he could cut out words as a cavalryman might lop off heads at a gallop. "Myself will straight abroad," says Lodovico at the end of *Othello*; had he said, "I myself will immediately go abroad," he might have missed the ship.

Any high school student desirous of emulating Shakespeare in this sort of phrasing would receive short shrift from his English instructor. He could not leave out *who*, as does Launcelot Gobbo:

> There will come a Christian by,
> Will be worth a Jewess' eye.

The Merchant of Venice is full of such passages as must fairly shriek to the consistently minded: How can a thing be wrong in the composition class and great literature in the Shakespeare class? How can students be blamed for doing what the greatest master of English commonly did? Is it possible that high school teachers would do well to encourage writing a little more along the lines Shakespeare marked out?

Here is yet another sample (from *King John*, Act II, scene 1, line 65): "With them a bastard of the king's deceased." It is safe to say that out of its context this line could never be understood, and even within its context there is nothing to show plainly whether the bastard or the king is dead. As every one in the audience knows the bastard is alive and well, why should Shakespeare labor to make clarity doubly clear? The meaning of the line is: "With them came a bastard of the deceased king."

A verbal puzzle occurs in *Pericles*, Act IV, scene 1, line 5, where the wicked Dionyza is warning her henchman Leonine not to falter in the task of killing the princess, Marina. Says Dionyza, "Let not conscience, which is but cold, inflaming thy love bosom, inflame too nicely." Editors, recognizing that something or someone—poet, transcriber, or compositor—is askew here, emend this line to "inflaming love in thy bosom." But is it conscience which inflames love? And can a cold thing inflame? The idea is, "Let neither cold conscience nor inflaming love come too near thy bosom." Here the grammar is an obstacle to understanding.

Another tangle needs untying in *Love's Labour's Lost*, Act II, scene 1, line 238, describing the King of Navarre as having, "His tongue all impatient to speak and not see" the Princess of France. For *to* read "because it could only," and you have the generally accepted solution. This is by no means writing that cannot be misunderstood, or even writing that can be readily understood. We know the general effect (of admiration) Shakespeare wanted to convey, but again the words seem to be secondary in importance. It was Shakespeare's aim ever to create an effect. He was a linguistic impressionist. So long as the whole speech did what he wanted, he cared little about the detailed means by which the effect was gained. That ancient precept, "Write not so that you can be understood, but so that you cannot be misunderstood," was not Shakespeare's guiding principle.

Many of Shakespeare's grammatical experiments can be explained by the demands of versification, but they occur in his prose as well. It is often overlooked that much of Shakespeare's finest dialogue is prose; both Falstaff and Iago customarily speak in it, and Benedick and Beatrice in *Much Ado About Nothing* wage a good deal of their duel of wits in it. In an age of intricate baroque prose, Shakespeare's seems remarkably natural and modern. Yet both poetry and prose often present elaborate conceits (prolonged metaphors) and complex cadences sometimes more majestic than immediately meaningful.

To Shakespeare the whole was more than the parts, the line than the words, the speech than the lines. If he wished to show men being incited to fury, torn by uncertainty, overcome by love, he made those emotions live in the broad sweep of language; he did not niggle and twist among single words. If he wanted to show a young girl being put to sleep by the prosy, involved recitation of long-past events, this is how he went to work (*The Tempest,* Act I, scene 2, lines 66–74):

> My brother and thy uncle, call'd Antonio—
> I pray thee, mark me—that a brother should
> Be so perfidious!—he whom next thyself,
> Of all the world I lov'd, and to him put
> The manage of my state; as at that time,
> Through all the signiories it was the first,
> And Prospero the prime duke; being so reputed
> In dignity, and for the liberal arts,
> Without a parallel . . .

The grammar may be bad, but it is masterly for the purpose; it is precisely suited to Prospero.

Ambiguity is dangerous where a single sentence is your unit. If a sentence is all you have, you had better make it clear. But clarity as a principle may apply to either larger or smaller effects, and if the large ones are clear, as they are so magnificently in Shakespeare, there is less need to worry about the small. Shakespeare might throw a word to the dogs, as he would toss a penny to a beggar; his larger reaches, the coins of his main fortune, are pure gold.

As seventeenth-century England evolved from the baroque to the neoclassic period, its literary language became increasingly formalized. It was handled not so much from the scientific as from the moralistic or regulatory angle. English was like a garden whose luxuriant growth had never been pruned. Now it must be clipped into classic patterns. English must be inventoried, stabilized, and standardized, so as to separate the good from the bad, the correct from the incorrect.

Failing to establish an official body to regulate and codify English, eighteenth-century purists published a succession of prescriptive grammars, legislating on hundreds of expressions, most of them minute and unimportant. Of these the most popular were Robert Lowth's *Short Introduction to English Grammar* (1762) in England and Noah Webster's *A Grammatical Institute of the English Language* (1784) in America. By contrast, Joseph Priestley's sensible and progressive *The Rudiments of English Grammar* (1761) was largely ignored.

While Priestley, a scientist, recognized that English must and should grow, change, and develop as any living language does, Lowth and his many successors and imitators sought not to describe but to stabilize or fix English, setting up a body of rules as final authorities to govern the language for all time to come. These rules were not determined by any great scientific knowledge of the character and history of English. Many of them were conscious or unconscious analogies from Latin; others were based on observation of actual cultivated usage; and too many others were mere matters of personal prejudice.

In 1710, Jonathan Swift had published a paper in *The Tatler* in which he vented a long series of personal antipathies to certain words, such as *sham, banter, bubble, shuffling*; against abbreviated words, such as *mob* (instead of *mobile vulgus*), *rep* (*reputation*) and *incog*; and against contractions, such as *shan't, he's, disturb'd, rebuk'd*, the last two of which he would have pronounced with three syllables (*dis-turb-ed*). None of Swift's prejudices seem to have actually succeeded in modifying the course of English,

37

but Lowth is probably responsible for the present use of *have written*, rather than *have writ* (the form used by Shakespeare) or *have wrote* (a form popular in the sixteenth century).

Lindley Murray's immensely popular textbooks typify the general temper of nineteenth-century grammar. Of Quaker stock, Lindley Murray early moved from Pennsylvania to New York. A lawyer and merchant, Murray amassed a small fortune and retired, first to Long Island and thence to Yorkshire, England. As a diversion, he occupied himself in teaching at a nearby school, for which he produced his famous *English Grammar,* followed by *English Exercises,* the *English Reader,* the *Spelling Book,* and other authoritarian and absolutist textbooks. Following down the path marked out by Lowth, Murray's was a grammar of dogmatic rules with no exceptions, of prejudices magnified into edicts. If anything could have fixed the English language, it would have been such widely used books as those of Lowth and Murray.

But a rival grammar, based on the historical and scientific study of English, as well as on the comparative study of Indo-European and other languages, beginning in the late eighteenth century and growing in the nineteenth, was eventually to undermine the authority of dogma. Scandinavian and German philologists like Rasmus Rask, Jacob Grimm, and Karl Verner demonstrated relationships between Germanic and non-Germanic branches of the Indo-European family of languages, of which English is one. The study of Old English began to flourish. In 1864, the Early English Text Society was established to edit and publish medieval texts hitherto preserved only in manuscript. Work was begun on *A New English Dictionary Based on Historical Principles,* with quotations illustrating changing usage; this finally became the great *Oxford English Dictionary,* or *OED.* Linguists like Sweet, Ellis, Max Muller, and Whitney began to study grammar from the point of view of explorer, rather than legislator. It was not until the twentieth century that this new science of linguistics began to come into actual conflict with the legislative grammarians. Today there are still conservative champions of prescriptive grammar, who become indignantly outspoken against the descriptive method used in *Webster's Third International Dictionary;* but they are fighting a rearguard action. Among students of language the principle of usage is clearly established.

3 √ You Name It

Grammars traditionally begin with an account of the parts of speech:

1. *Nouns* are names of persons ("W. C. Fields"), places ("Jamaica"), things ("crossbow"), actions ("battle," "execution"), abstract qualities ("fortitude"), collective groups ("a herd," "cattle").

2. *Pronouns* substitute for nouns ("Homer smote *his* lyre").

3. *Adjectives* describe or modify nouns and pronouns ("the *yellow* book").

4. *Verbs* convey action ("Dracula *entered* his coffin"), state ("I *feel* faint"), or being ("Gibraltar *is* a rock").

5. *Adverbs* modify verbs ("fight *fiercely*"), adjectives ("*incredibly* dull"), or other adverbs ("she sings *quite* badly").

6. *Prepositions* show the relationship between a noun or pronoun and some other element in the sentence ("fell *to* the ground," "sat *on* the table," "live *in* Albuquerque").

7. *Conjunctions* or *connectives* connect words ("Laurel *and* Hardy"), phrases ("to go *or* to stay later"), and clauses ("She won't go *because* it's raining").

8. *Interjections* are words or phrases used as an exclamation without grammatical connection (Yeech!).

¶ FORM VERSUS FUNCTION

The trouble is that a great many words cannot be confined to one part of speech but function in several capacities. *Dog,* for instance, though conventionally labeled a noun, can be used as an adjective ("dog biscuit"), an adverbial prefix ("dog-tired"), a transitive verb ("dog his footsteps"), or an interjection ("hot dog!"). Similarly, *water* can be a noun, a transitive verb ("water the grass"), an intransitive verb ("his mouth watered"), an adjective ("water buffalo"), or an adverbial prefix ("watertight"). *Wine* can be a noun or an adverbial prefix ("the wine-dark sea"); *box* can be a noun, a verb ("to *box* something in") or an adjective ("box kite"). A few prepositions can be nouns ("an *in* with the director"). "A record high" has a noun used as an adjective and an adjective used as a noun.

Dictionaries still label words as particular parts of speech, but this is only one way of examining them. Words have both form and function. Formally, nouns and pronouns have number and case; adjectives and adverbs have forms for the positive, comparative, and superlative degrees; and verbs can be conjugated. Grammar involves function as well as form, and errors can occur in both. When you give nouns and pronouns the wrong number or the wrong case, when you use a faulty comparative or superlative, when you use the wrong past tense or past participle of a verb, you have made an error in form. But equally or even more important is function. On this score, you can make errors in agreement or reference, make modification unclear, upset parallel phrasing, use dead wood and faulty diction, and write sentences mangled in structure and style.

Dictionaries contain more nouns than any other kind of word; they are the most frequent element in English expression. But *noun* is an inadequate label in that it describes only form and not function. Traditional definitions say that a noun is a naming word, but nouns have no monopoly here; verbs certainly name actions or conditions; prepositions name directions or time sequences (*over, under, behind, before, after*); adjectives name qualities (*hard, green, hot*) and in fact most nouns can double as adjectives (e.g., "*passenger* pigeon," "*disaster* area," "*sword* blade"). Furthermore, nouns can have various grammatical functions. They can be used as the subject of a verb ("*Koala bears* eat eucalyptus leaves"), as the object of a verb ("We saw the *Koala bears* eating eucalyptus leaves"), as the object of a preposition ("Give the eucalyptus leaves to the *koala bears*"), as predicate noun ("My daughter was made an honorary *koala bear*"), as appositive noun ("Those animals, *koala bears*, live in New Zealand"), as adjectival modifier ("*koala* bear," "*eucalyptus* leaves," "*giant* auk," "*symphony* orchestra"), and as adverbial modifier ("I like to loaf *weekends*," "I stayed home *yesterday*").

Thus it is often more helpful to talk about sentence relationships (subject, complement, verb, modifier, connective) than about parts of speech per se. Professor Fries would use a new terminology and distinguish words by four classes, each with several frames and by

40

groups *A* through *O*. James Sledd would use *nominal* instead of *noun*, and define nominal as "a word or larger form which occupies a position typically occupied by nouns." For subjects and complements can be participles ("I enjoy *swimming*"), phrases ("*The blade of the sword* snapped in two." "*To believe in racial superiority* is a sign of ignorance"), and clauses ("People thought *that the play was over*"). Some nominal phrases cause problems with the possessive case, so that you seem to have to put the apostrophe *-s* on a preposition or participle: "The girl he was dancing with's name was Natasha," "The dog I was feeding's tail wagged," "The man she was talking to's teeth were bad." To get around this, use the periphrastic, "The name of the girl he was dancing with was Ysolde."

In informal speech, one often hears nominal constructions like "I liked *when they put the watch in the geyser*." But *when, where,* and *because* are not acceptable as nouns; and students are corrected if they write "An example is when . . ." "An example is where Huck talks about kings," or "The reason is because . . ." These are frequent errors both in form and function. "Because some Indians were crude was no reason for the whites to treat them as animals" should be changed to "The fact that some Indians were crude was no reason . . ." "One bad thing about freedom of speech is when a citizen can't think of anything to say he says it anyway" also needs a *that* before the *when*.

You must be able to recognize the subject of a sentence if you are to avoid errors in case, number, or forming grammatically incomplete sentences. There are a number of situations where fragmentary sentences may be effective, but every complete sentence and clause must have a subject and verb. First, find the verb; then see if it has a subject. If not, or if the subject is unclear, you need to rewrite the sentence. Second-person imperative verbs (so-called commands, though they may not be very commanding) are the only ones that do not require that their subject be expressed: "*Open* the window"; "Please *pass* the salt." Once you have found the subject, make sure it is in the subjective case. Then see if the subject is singular or plural and make sure that the verb is in the same number. In nominal phrases, you have to single out the particular word that governs the number of the verb. This may prove confusing if a singular noun is followed by a plural modifier. For example, in the sentence, "A pair of swords is on the wall," the subject is *pair*, not *swords*, and so, "A pair of swords are on the wall" has an error in subject-verb agreement. Similarly, "The highwayman, together with his gang, were captured" is wrong, because the subject is the singular *highwayman,* which requires a singular verb, *was.* These matters will be treated in detail in the chapters on case, agreement, and sentence structure. Nouns used as objects pose fewer difficulties; the only problem is to put them in the proper (i.e., objective) case.

¶ TYPES OF NOUNS

But we still have not adequately defined nouns. The term comes from the Latin word *nomen* ("name"), and traditional descriptions say that a noun is the name of a person, place, thing, abstract quality, collective group, or action. Nouns have several categories: (1) Proper nouns are the names of specific persons, places, or things (*Alfred E. Neuman, Utah, Magna Charta*); the first letter of each important word is capitalized. (2) Common nouns are all that are not proper nouns. (3) Abstract nouns name qualities (*honor, courage, weight, joy, sorrow, dignity*) and include many gerunds (present participles used as nouns: *thinking, creating, dreaming*). Often these abstract terms have to be made more specific: *Happiness Is a Warm Puppy, Misery Is a Cold Hot Dog.* (4) Collective nouns are words like *congregation, team, audience, militia, navy, fleet, family.* There may be those who are uncertain as to whether *backs* and *ends* are collective nouns in the sentence, "And Navy came onto the field with orange phosphorescent helmets on their backs and ends"; but if they are not, the picture is pretty ludicrous.

¶ DECLENSION

Since, as we have seen, many nouns can also function as other parts of speech, how can we tell whether, or rather when, a given word is a noun? In context, *when* is more important than *whether;* the way a word is used, as subject, object, or modifier, is more significant than its grammatical name. If we consider words out of context, we can say that they are nouns if they can be preceded by the article *the* (not necessarily by *a* or *an;* we never encounter *a milk, a wheat, a tea, a sugar, a flour,* or similar words). Considering form rather than function, we find that nouns have the characteristics of case, number, and gender. The form of the English noun has been greatly simplified from Old to Modern English. Like Latin and German, Old English was a highly inflected language that used different

42

endings to indicate whether a noun was nominative, singular or plural; masculine, feminine, or neuter. These various endings are called a noun's declension. There were several declensions of Old English nouns, all with different inflectional endings for case, number, and gender. For example, *fugol* ("bird") was masculine and was declined as follows:

	SINGULAR	PLURAL
NOMINATIVE AND ACCUSATIVE	fugol	fuglas
GENITIVE	fugles	fugla
DATIVE AND INSTRUMENTAL	fugle	fuglum

Today, English nouns remain the same in the subjective (nominative) and objective (accusative) cases and inflect only for the possessive (genitive) case and for the plural. (For the possessive, see Chapter VII on case and the apostrophe.)

¶ **PLURALS OF NOUNS**

About ninety-five percent of all English nouns form the plural simply by adding -s or -es to the singular, but there are a number of categories in which problems arise:

1. Nouns ending in -s, -x, -z, -ch, or -sh add -es to avoid a double sibilant (*hisses, taxes, quizzes, researches, dishes*). Sometimes little children mistake an -s ending for the singular and form faulty plurals by analogy: *birdses, pigses, wormses.*

2. Nouns ending in -o preceded by a vowel add -s (*rodeos, radios*). Most nouns ending in -o preceded by a consonant add -es (*heroes, Negroes, tomatoes*); but some, mostly of Italian or Spanish origin, add -s only (*albinos, falsettos, gauchos, pianos, virtuosos*). A few words ending in -o take either -s or -es (*buffalos—buffaloes; cargos—cargoes*).

3. Nouns ending in -y preceded by a consonant change the -y to *i* and add -es (*duty—duties, navy—navies*) unless they are proper names ("Last night there were four Marys"). Nouns ending in -y preceded by a vowel retain the -y (*donkey—donkeys, joy—joys, tray—trays*).

4. Some nouns ending in -f, -fe, or -ff change the *f* to a *v* and add -es (*calf—calves, knife—knives, leaf—leaves, life—lives, shelf—shelves*). The British sometimes use *beeves* as a plural for *beef*, but

Americans no longer do so. Be careful not to make an error with a word that retains the *f*, particularly common when there is a verb ending in *-ves* in the third person singular: *belief—beliefs* (NOT *believes*).

5. A few words, keeping the Old English umlaut form, change the vowel: *foot—feet, goose—geese, louse—lice, man—men, mouse —mice, tooth—teeth, woman—women.* (Sometimes you encounter a faulty analogous plural for humorous effect: *house—hice, grouse— grice, spouse—spice,* and Jinks the cat's "I hate meeces to pieces.") *Children, brethren,* and *oxen* are also survivals from the Old English form.

6. Some nouns, usually names of animals, keep the same form in the singular and the plural: *deer, fish* (but *fishes* for more than one kind or species of fish), *sheep, swine, species.* Others have a singular meaning but appear only in the plural form: *athletics, barracks, gallows, mathematics, mumps, news, pants, trousers* (*trousers* always has a plural form as a noun, but it can be singular as an adjective "up his trouser leg").

7. The largest group of irregular plurals occurs in nouns borrowed from foreign languages. In some instances, popular usage is now giving them Anglicized plurals; and there is no reason why it should not do so, since English has done so with thousands of other borrowings. Usage is the determining factor, and some words still retain the foreign practice:

(*a*) Latin nouns ending in *-a* use *-ae* in the plural (*alumna— alumnae, lacuna—lacunae*).

(*b*) Latin nouns ending in *-us* use *-i* in the plural (*alumnus— alumni, nucleus—nuclei*).

(*c*) Latin nouns ending in *-um* use *-a* in the plural (*agendum— agenda, curriculum—curricula, medium—media*).

(*d*) Greek nouns ending in *-is* use *-es* in the plural (*crisis—crises, parenthesis—parentheses*).

(*e*) Greek nouns ending in *-on* use *-a* in the plural (*criterion— criteria, phenomenon—phenomena*).

(*f*) French nouns ending in *-eau* add *-x* for the plural (*beau— beaux, tableau—tableaux*).

Some words that occasionally appear in one of the forms above use as often or more often an Anglicized plural: *formulas, vertebras, funguses, millenniums, beaus.* In practice, some foreign borrowings appear usually or always in the plural, which is often given a singular meaning, as in *data, agenda, insignia. Media,* originally the plural of *medium,* is so often used as a singular that we have now given the word a new plural, *medias,* though this does not yet have academic approval. There are no hard and fast rules for foreign plurals; the best way to settle any doubts is to consult the dictionary. If you don't, you may commit errors like the faulty plural of *cherubim* in the sentence attributed to a "youth leader": "Cherubims aren't particularly impressive to a generation that has become used to astronauts."

8. Compound words form their plurals in several ways. Most simply use the plural of the last and most significant unit: *motorboats, raincoats, church workers, piano players.* If the most significant word comes first, it usually takes the plural: *mothers-in-law* and other in-law relatives (but *in-laws* by itself), *passers-by, attorneys at law, justices of the peace, crèpes suzette.* The significant word remains plural when preceded by *assistant* or *deputy* (assistant chiefs of staff). When both words are equally significant, both are made plural (*men students, women doctors*). A few compounds go either way: *attorney generals* or *attorneys general, court-martials* or *courts-martial, poet laureates* or *poets laureate.* Compounds ending in *-ful* as a unit of measure add *-s* to the last unit: *bucketfuls, cupfuls, spoonfuls.* If the stress is on the container rather than the measurement, then we say "two buckets full of sand."

Nonstandard American-English speech sometimes uses a singular form for a plural with numbers: "He's six foot tall," "It's three year old," "The garage is ten mile from here," "Gimme three gallon of whiskey." This practice is actually a vestigial medieval partitive genitive plural after numbers (which you can immediately forget) and is older than current standard English.

¶ GENDER

One great advantage of English grammar is that it uses a natural rather than an artificial gender. In German and Latin, nouns are ascribed to the masculine, feminine, or neuter gender; and in Romance languages they are ordained masculine or feminine by grammatical rule rather than through any actual sexual attributes. A word for the same object can be masculine in one language, feminine in another, and neuter in a third. There is no logic, and the poor student has to memorize the gender of each noun, so that he will be able to use the proper article, pronoun, and adjective endings with it. Thus French has *le crayon* ("pencil") but *la plume*

45

("pen"); "il est cassé," but "*elle* est plein*e* d'encre." Old English had grammatical gender, but it gradually disappeared during the centuries after the Norman Conquest, and good riddance. Probably no other feature is so troublesome to a language, since it involves agreement in all articles, adjectives, pronouns, past participles and even requires that these have different sets of endings. In Old English, *woman* (*wif-mann*) was masculine, but *wife* (*wif*) was neuter, as it is today in German. *Goat, goose, louse,* and *mouse* were feminine; *bird* and *horse* were masculine; *cattle* was neuter. *Hand* and *tongue* were feminine; *eye,* neuter. Medieval monks might find it appropriate that *temptation, sin,* and *hell* were feminine, but why should *coat of mail, battle,* and *tomb* be so, and why should *weapon* be neuter?

Except for a few nouns that have a different form in the masculine and the feminine (*actor—actress, czar—czarina, earl—countess, fox—vixen, hero—heroine, maharaja—maharani, marquis—marquise, master—mistress*), gender is now a problem only when pronoun reference is involved. Today some feminine words have a slightly derogatory connotation in activities shared by both sexes. We have several feminine suffixes: *-ess, -ette, -trix, -ine.* These are connotatively neutral in *countess, heiress, actress, majorette, executrix,* and *heroine.* But *-ette* can also mean diminutive (*cigarette, dinette*) or commercially even imitation or synthetic (*leatherette*). Sometimes *-ette* and *-ess* are not merely grammatical suffixes but convey status as well. *Suffragette* is still a bit derogatory, and nobody thinks of a *farmerette* as doing any real work. *Jewess* and *Negress* convey a distinct flavor of derogation and prejudice which is not present in *Jew* and *Negro.* When women do the same work as men, the feminine suffix can be condescending; *authoress, directress, mayoress, lawyeress, poetess, sculptress* are slighting and suggest dilettante or amateur standing. Why not simply *author, director, mayor, poet, sculptor?* Sometimes a distinction is necessary, as in *ballerina*; but *woman* or *lady doctor, lady author, woman scientist,* etc., seem condescending and discriminatory. One artist wrote to *Esquire,* "It was very thoughtful of you to refer to me as a 'lady painter'. . . . Due to the huge numbers of man painters named Anita running about, there might have been considerable misunderstanding—and your foresight, I'm certain, saved us the humiliation of mistaken identity." [1] Certainly *male nurse* and *male dancer* give an undesirable image, and men teaching in elementary and junior high school would hardly like to be called *male teachers.*

Sometimes gender presents amusing problems. Is the person conducting the meeting of a woman's club a chairman or a chairwoman? It seems ridiculous to speak of a girl busboy, but have you ever heard of a busgirl? What about a freshman woman? And is the plural *freshman women* or *freshmen women*? The ultimate absurdity is the scene in the movie *Mr. Roberts*: when the chief Navy nurse commands her sexy subordinates, "Carry on, men," Jack Lemmon as Ensign Pulver does a double take and repeats ironically, "Yeah, carry on . . . men."

¶ BLENDS

Hundreds of thousands of new words have entered the language in the last two centuries, most of them nouns from science and technology, with many others from politics, sociology, and psychology. Linguistic growth is healthy, but there are always some blighted growths, and some neologistic nouns are both weird and wonderful. Advertisers and journalists, as well as scientists, are particularly fond of coining blends; that is, combining parts from two or more words into one, supposedly to achieve a clever or striking result. Blends go back quite a ways, with long-established terms like *cablegram, newscast, motel,* and *urinalysis* for *cable telegram, news broadcast, motorist's hotel,* and *urine analysis*. As a form of simplification, the blend can be useful; *paratrooper* is better than *parachute trooper,* and *cortisone* is certainly preferable to *17-hydroxy 11-dehydrocorticosterone hormone*.

But merchandising blends are often no more than coy puns, like *funderwear, lapkin, broasted* ("broiled and roasted" or "baked and roasted"?), *play-jama, scardigan* ("scarf and cardigan"), *Fabricadabra!, angel-abra* (angel and candelabra), *leisurals* (leisure and casual shoes), *funderful, flexagons* ("flexible hexagons"), *sportraits,* and similar slanguage. Many blends are culinary and gastronomical, from *groceteria* to *vegamato* to raisin-bran *brunchwiches* ("breakfast-lunch sandwiches") to *fishkabob*. Macaroni is often dehydrated into *-roni* in such blends as *Beef-a-roni, Elbo-Roni, Noodle Roni, Rice-a-Roni, Saladroni, Scallop-a-Roni, Tenderoni,* and (urp!) *Twist-a-Roni*. It would be as valid to use *Mac-a-beef* or *Mac-a-noodle,* but the suffix has prevailed. Hamburgers were originally named after the German town of Hamburg, but Americans apparently think that they are made of ham, instead of beef, and so blend the suffix *-burger* with everything from fish to pizza until you encounter such toothsome morsels (crunch!) as *rampburgers*. No doubt, a *foodaholic* washes them down with *Nectaroma*; and if he fails to survive the ordeal, his ashes can be preserved as *cremains*.

¶ **ACRONYMS**

Closely related to blends are acronyms, words made up of the initial letters or first syllables of the words in a phrase. Government and science have produced so many of these that they have been called alphabet soup, but they can be useful abbreviations. *Laser,* which is an acronym of the italicized letters in "*l*ight *a*mplification by *s*timulated *e*mission of *r*adiation" is certainly handier than the original. Often organizations pick a name that will form a convenient and easily remembered acronym: SHAPE (*S*upreme *H*eadquarters *A*llied *P*owers in *E*urope), CORE (*C*ongress *o*f *R*acial *E*quality), SOAR (*S*ave *O*ur *A*merican *R*esources), SWAP (*S*easonal *W*orkers *a*t *P*arks, also *S*ummer *W*ork *A*lliance *P*rogram), MAYA (*M*exican-*A*merican *Y*outh *A*ssociation), CARE (*C*ooperative for *A*merican *R*emittances to *E*verywhere). In the latter example, the acronym is used exclusively except for some technical documents. Some acronyms have almost entirely replaced the original in common speech; e.g., ANZAC, WACS, WAVES, NATO, UNESCO, UNICEF. Some in fact, have become so universal that the original is all but forgotten: *Jeep* (*gp*—general purpose vehicle), *GI* (Government Issue), *Seabees* (*CB* —Construction Battalion). Some, like *awol* ("absent without leave") and *radar* are usually written lower-case as a word. Others like QUINK (quick-drying ink) remain merely brand names. Some remain essentially spoken slang, as *Veep* for Vice President, a term that John Adams would have scorned when he held that office. On the other hand, *VIP* is widely spoken and printed, but you rarely if ever encounter "very important person." Some acronyms are satiric, like GASP (*G*roup *A*gainst *S*mog *P*ollution), GOO (*G*et *O*il *O*ut), SPIT (*S*ociety for the *P*revention of *I*nadvertent *T*ransatlanticisms), MAD (*M*others *A*gainst *D*elinquency), MAW (*M*others for *A*dequate *W*elfare), CRAWL (*C*itizens for the *R*esurrection of the *A*merican *W*ay of *L*ife) or NUTS (*N*orthwestern *U*niversity *T*rail Society). Most are harmless, and some are helpful.

George Orwell found sinister possibilities in political acronyms and noted that the tendency to use them "was most marked in totalitarian countries and totalitarian organizations." As examples, he gave *Nazi* ("National Socialist"), *Gestapo* ("*Ge*heime *Staats-*

polizei"), Comintern ("Communist International"), *Inprecorr,* and *Agitprop* ("Ministry of Agitation and Propaganda"); and one might add the changing name of the Soviet secret police. The acronym is intentionally sinister in SPECTRE ("SPecial Executive for Counterintelligence, Terrorism, Revenge and Extortion"). Orwell wrote that "In the beginning the practice had been adopted as it were instinctively, but in Newspeak it was used with a conscious purpose. It was perceived that in thus abbreviating a name one narrowed and subtly altered its meaning, by cutting out most of the associations that would otherwise cling to it." The connotations are removed, leaving a rather abstract bureaucracy and dogma." "Agitation and propaganda" suggests violence and conspiracy, whereas *Agitprop* sounds efficient and antiseptic. "Communist International" might suggest the heretical idea of human brotherhood. "The word Comintern, on the other hand, suggests merely a closely knit organization and a well-defined body of doctrine." [2] Whereas the individual words suggest a picture and require at least a minimum of thought, the abstract acronym can be automatic, thoughtless jargon.

¶ RAMATHON RIDES AGAIN

Equally thoughtless are the proliferating words ending in *-rama, -thon,* and *-ness,* that I have elsewhere called "Ramathon and the ness monster." [3] As a Greek suffix, *-rama* (actually a clipped form of *-horama*) means "a view"; in this sense it is used legitimately in *panorama, cinerama, cyclorama,* and even in the *Futurama* of the 1939 World's Fair. *Silverama* TV may be O.K., too, but we are getting into loose territory with the British *Striperama* ("Take it off"), though it certainly gives a view. But *-rama* has spread like a mindless fungus until it has become simply advertising jargon in *Educator Crackerama,* ham-o-rama (Dogpatch hams?), *freeze-a-rama* (Brrr!), *bowlerama* (Strike!), *playorama* toys, *launderama* ("Lady, youse is usin' de wrong detergent"), *cleanorama, garagearama* (three-car family?), *trailorama, camporama, confedorama* (Hoo-hah!), *gorgarama, pearlorama, tint-o-rama* (sunglasses), *souparama, tacorama, bananarama, gagerama,* and other *pun-o-ramas.* If you try to get a close view of *spinnorama* 45 r.p.m. records, you may become bug-eyed. *Sniff-o-rama* perfume and *Scent-a-rama* (British whiskey sniffers) are as patently absurd as the short-lived *Aromarama* movie; etymologically, all three mean a view of a smell. Show biz has also provided *Wonderama* (Captain Jolly on TV), *horrorama, nervo-rama* ("2 Fiendish Features in a New Horror Show!—*Werewolf in a Girl's Dormitory* [The Ghoul in School] and *Corridors of Blood*"), and even pictures filmed in *sin-a-rama* ("I always knew I shouldn't have taken her to that hotel room"). Usually *-rama* suggests merely an indiscriminate superlative (though *slendorama* lunch shouldn't make you a living skeleton), and *rumorama* has it that *-rama* is best translated as "big deal." It becomes ghoulish in *death-a-rama* (Discount Funeral Parlor) and sacrilegious when a store in Quebec that sells religious items advertises *Christorama*.

Amputated from *marathon, -thon* seems to be losing the race with *-rama,* but it is used loosely in such blends as *saleathon, pushathon, telethon, phoneathon, laffathon,* and even *rock-a-thon* (around the clock, naturally).

The trouble with "ramathon" is that such nouns show an impoverished verbal imagination that simply plays follow-the-leader instead of finding a way to describe precise words. This is even truer of the cancerous growth of *-ness,* which is devouring other suffixes or adding superfluous ones and reducing nouns to a monotonous uniformity. As *Vogue* says, "Appetizingness is no skin off anyone's nose." [4] Thus students turn *safety* into *safeness, youth* into *youngness, waste* into *wastefulness, hunger* into *hungriness, election* (in the Calvinist sense) into *electness, treason* into *treasonness, hatred* into *hateness,* and show their *inadequateness* (inadequacy) by turning *wisdom* into *wiseness.* Is it *naïveness* or *stupidness* that creates *greatestness* as a superlative? At any rate, democracy is safe as long as we have *freeness* and *equalness.* Let freeness ring! Liberty, equalness, and fraternity!

¶ **N O W Y O U S E E I T , N O W Y O U D O N ' T**

There are many curious examples of nouns used for other parts of speech and other parts of speech pressed into service as nouns. In the Great Smoky Mountains this interchange is particularly colorful. Verbs serve as nouns in "The mountain people have a *lavish* of pride," "You can git you one more *gittin'* of wood out of that pile," "I didn't hyear no *give-out* about hit," and "Listen, all you *settin' rounders.*" Nouns double as verbs in "I didn't *fault* him for hit," "That b'ar'll *meat* me for a month," and "*Chair-bottomin'* is easy settin' down work." [5] Adjectives function as nouns in "Them Yankee soldiers stole a right *smart* of horses" and "It's a better kind of *different.*" An adverb becomes a noun in "A person has a *rather* about what he drinks." The mountain people often use redundant compound nouns like *rifle gun, tooth dentist, sulphur match, ham meat, cow critter,* and *preacher man.*

But these are tame examples compared to current journalistic and advertising practices, where we find *two for* used as a noun (i.e., two theatre tickets for the price of one) and *7-Up* used as a verb ("7-Up your thirst away"). You can also "*rainbow* your 7-Up floats." If you buy a *two for* (or *toofer*), *The New York Times* says that "Seated is how to look at Lincoln Center." You can *holiday* in Majorca and *porpoise* about in the water, or you can *splendor* at a French château. If you have a *yearn* for home, you can *garage* your car, but it's better to take to the open road, for as Texans say, American cars are "hell for *stout.*" When you go *supermarketing,* you'll find that "There's more to a ham than its *lean.*" But the best shopping is for ladies' fashions, where, as *Vogue* announces, you can buy pajamas "All sinuous *slink* to a voluminous *swell* of trousers." "Gone: the *little-girlisms.* Arrived! . . . the intriguery of fabrics with demeanor and dimension." Among Hollywood columnists, it has become semiofficial jargon to use certain nouns for verbs. Film stars never entertain anyone or give anyone a gift or have a romance; instead they *guest, gift,* or *romance* someone. It is doubtful that F. Scott Fitzgerald would have approved Sheilah Graham's diction when she wrote that "Columbia gifted Carl Foreman with an expensive 1962 limousine. . . ."

¶ A SHREWDNESS OF APES

While some new nouns seem witless and expendable, there are certain obsolete ones with sufficient character or charm that they deserve to be rescued from antiquity, notably the medieval collective nouns, or "company terms" for groups of animals and birds in farming, hunting, and falconry. Today we use *herd* and *flock* or more loosely *bunch* or *group* to cover most cases, but knights and squires were not so casual. *Flock* was appropriate for sheep and *herd* for cattle, but cattle could also be a *drove.* One spoke of a *harras* of horses, a *rag* of colts, a *pack* of hounds, a *cowardice* of curs, a *kennel* of raches, a *route* of wolves, a *skulk* of foxes, a *kindle* of kittens, a *down* of hares, a *swarm* of bees, a *bundling* of ducks, a *gaggle* of geese, a *group* of ganders, a *sord* of mallards, a *rafter* of turkeys, a *plump* of wild fowl, a *company* of widgeon, a *wisp* of snipe, a *fall* of woodcock, a *nye* of pheasants, a *covey* of partridges or quail, a *bevy* of quail, a *stand* of plovers, a *cast* of hawks, a *herd* of cranes, a *sedge* of herons, a *watch* of nightingales, a *muster* of peacocks, a *brood* of grouse, a *flight* of swallows, a *building* of rooks, a *murmuration* of starlings, a *dule* of turtledoves, an *exaltation* of larks, and a *murder* of crows. Any knight that spoke of a *wisp* of pheasants was apt to have his spurs hacked off. There were a *cete* of badgers, a *doylt* of tame swine, a *sounder* of wild swine, a *singular* of boars (an odd—or singular—choice for a collective noun), a *bevy* of roebucks, a *gang* of elk, a *pace* of asses, and a *bale* of turtles. In the water, one found a *shoal* of fish, a *hover* of trout, a *stand* of salmon, a *gam* of whales, a *trip* of seals, and a *pod* of walruses. To go farther afield, there were a *sloth* of bears, a *troop* of buffaloes, a *pride* of lions, a *leap* of leopards, a *crash* of rhinoceroses, a *troop* of monkeys, and a *shrewdness of apes.* Unfortunately, there is not much demand for these terms; but some of them vividly characterize the birds or beasts they apply to, and the language would be enriched by their return. Instead, *quail* has become a slang term for sexy wenches (cf. *Kiss Me, Kate*), and so we speak of a bevy of girls. *Life* made a new "company term" when it wrote of "an orgy of Barrymores." Who could ask for anything more?

Exercise 1: Replace the following *-ness* monster words with more precise suffixes. For instance, *braveness* should be *bravery*.

1. scholarness	. . . . . .	11. spectacularness	. . . . . .
2. beautifulness	. . . . . .	12. feminineness	. . . .
3. savageness	. . . .	13. expensiveness	. . . . . .
4. angriness	. . . .	14. suppressiveness	. . . . . .
5. futileness	. . . .	15. cowardness	. . . . . .
6. vandalness	. . . .	16. courageousness	. . . . . .
7. hostileness	. . . .	17. confusingness	. . . . .
8. curiousness	. . . .	18. miserableness	. . . . . .
9. honestness	. . . .	19. euphoniousness	. . . . . .
10. aggressiveness	. . . . . .	20. illiterateness	. . . .

52

4 √ The Perplexing Pronoun

The noun—like Lon Chaney, Alec Guinness, or Peter Sellers—can appear in many guises and perform in many roles, sometimes in one and the same sentence. Much the same characteristic is true of the pronoun. It has not one grammatical function but four. No two grammars include the same words in their lists of pronouns; and it is, as we shall see, very difficult to define a pronoun adequately. It might be simpler to drop the pronoun classification altogether, but for the fact that there are six words set apart by using special forms in the subjective and objective cases. These six words (*I, we, he, she, they,* and *who*) require some separate category. Technically, they are case survivals, but they are customarily called pronouns.

The pronoun is usually defined as a noun substitute, but this explanation is inadequate. A pronoun functions grammatically exactly as a noun does; it may be subject, complement, modifier; in addition, it may be used as a connective. And if we are to have both nouns and pro-nouns, why not have verbs and pro-verbs, adjectives and pro-adjectives, adverbs and pro-adverbs? If a pronoun stands for a noun, as we are told, so are there words which stand for verbs, like *did* in "He learned and so did I"; words that stand for adjectives, like *the same* in "You are lazy and I am the same"; words that stand for adverbs, like *so* in "He worked quickly but she less so." All these are word-substitutes, pro-words, and they might reasonably be so named.

True, there are more noun substitutes than verb, adjective, or adverb substitutes, and this fact might seem to justify making a special pro-noun group. But then there should be good clear distinctions between nouns and pronouns, whereas few grammarians agree altogether on what a pronoun is. Nearly any common noun may be a pro-noun, as *book* may stand for *Ivanhoe* or *man* for *F. Frothingham Smith.* According to the usual definition of pronoun, the word *thing* is pronominal in practically every one of its uses, since it nearly always stands for something more specific than itself. Indeed, *something* and *anything* are commonly classified as pronouns, although they do not stand for another noun so clearly as does *thing* itself, a word always classified as a noun. Any number can be used pronominally ("*Two* were present," "I saw *hundreds*"), as can words like *dozen, pair, couple, several, few*.

All the numbers can also serve as adjectives, and any comparative or superlative adjective can be used pronominally: "I have three sons; the *youngest* is in kindergarten, and the *oldest* is at Harvard." Color words can be pronouns, as well as nouns or adjectives: He chose the *yellow*." "I bet my money on the bobtail nag; somebody bet on the *bay*." Dictionaries label *former* and *latter* as adjectives, but they usually function pronominally to stand for a noun in a preceding sentence or clause. *Here* and *there*, usually called adverbs, take the place of nouns in phrases like "from here to Denver" and "from there to Santa Fe."

And not all pronouns are substitutes for any noun. Look at *none* and *nothing*—pronouns by classification but not standing for any person or thing. And as for the pronoun *I*, you might say that in conversation the use of your individual name would be a substitute for the pronoun, rather than the other way around. For the individual speaking of himself, the use of any word but *I* and *me*, is so rare that by no show of reason can this be taken for anything but normal standard practice.

Evidently the noun-substitute test is not sufficient for pronouns. Perhaps we recognize pronouns not so much by word of textbook as by some inner light, some grammatical intuition or instinct possessed by the fortunate. These objections to the definition and delimitation of the pronoun are not new; they are well known to students of grammar. And they appear as obvious facts when we cease merely repeating grammatical rules and begin thinking about grammatical ideas.

If we try to find some real distinction that sets apart nouns and pronouns, we shall have to consider first the "case-survival" words already mentioned. Those six subjectives (*I, we, he, she, they,* and *who*) together with their objective forms (*me, us, him, her, them,* and *whom*) make up the twelve words about whose use there is more uncertainty than any others in the English language. They present special problems even to the native speaker and are seldom fully mastered by the foreign one. They must be studied and handled separately. We cannot even say with complete accuracy that the subjectives are subjects and the others complements:

> It might have been (I, me).
> I expected it to be (she, her).
> (Who, Whom) do you think he was looking for?
> (Who, Whom) do you think he was?

The traditionally correct choices are *I, her, whom,* and *who;* but such choices are likely to trick all who use English. From Shakespeare to Mark Twain to James Thurber, there are innumerable instances of reputable writers departing from conservative practice on pronoun case. Broadly speaking, there's no English-speaking person who knows absolutely how to use *who* and *whom, I* and *me, he* and *him* in rapid or unguarded speech. Apparently grammarians only make the situation worse. Studies have shown that when it comes to using pronouns more mistakes are made by students in the higher grades than in the lower ones. It seems that teachers' efforts to make their pupils conscious of grammar have largely served only to confuse the issue, causing students by overconcern to make additional errors.

Pronouns have a number of categories, but this terminology is largely irrelevant to their effective use grammatically. No speaker or writer thinks consciously, "Now I want a demonstrative pronoun"; these things come instinctively. Yet although pronoun classification is, for the most part, not a matter of communication but of terminology, you may find the labels used below helpful in discussing grammar.

¶ PERSONAL PRONOUNS

These are inflected by person, number, case, and (in the third person singular) gender. The *first person* is used for the speaker or writer (*I, my, me, we, our, us*); the *second person* is used for the person addressed (*you, your*); the *third person* is used for someone or something written or spoken about (*he, his, him, it, its, she, her, they, their, them*). In addition we have the possessive predicative forms (*mine, yours, hers, ours, theirs*) that are really adjectives and peculiar survivals of an otherwise outmoded grammar. In older English (and today in what we might term imitative King James Biblical style), *mine* and *thine* could be interchanged with the personal possessive pronoun ("Mine eyes have seen the glory of the coming of the Lord," "It is thine adversary"). By analogy to *mine* and *thine,* American frontiersmen (and some of their isolated descendants) coined *yourn, hisn, hern, ourn,* and *theirn;* but these were used only after the verb *to be* or in absolute form ("The hat is *hern,*" "My life or *hisn*") and never as an adjective before a noun ("*hern hat,*" "*hisn rifle*").

Old English had dual pronouns for *we two* (*wit, uncer, unc, uncit*) and *you two* (*git, incer, inc, incit*), and we can be thankful for their disappearance. Medieval and Elizabethan English distinguished between the second person singular and plural by using *thou, thy,* and *thee* in the singular and *ye* or *you* and *your* in the plural, but we now have no way except the context to know whether *you* is being used for one person or a group. (Accordingly Americans resort to *all of you, you all, youse,* and even *you-uns.* Sometimes Yankees use *you all* for the singular as well, but no one who has grown up with the phrase ever does so.) The only thing gained by dropping the second person singular is the removal of subjective and objective case endings. These still bother ministers who improvise prayers in ersatz Elizabethan. If you expect to conduct prayer meetings, you should know that God is addressed in the subjective case as *thou* (with *art* or with verb forms ending in *-st* or *-est*—"thou dost," "thou goest") and in the objective as *thee* ("We supplicate thee").

There is no reason why God cannot be addressed as *you;* it certainly carries no disrespect. Actually, during the Elizabethan period English used both *thou* and *you* in the second person singular, as French uses *vous,* Spanish *Usted,* and German *Sie* for either singular or plural, the choice being dependent not only on number but also upon one's relationship to the person addressed. When we had *thou* as a second person singular, it was used to address either inferiors or intimates and loved ones; in the latter sense, it is used for the Deity. In Shakespeare's *Richard III,* Richard wooing Princess Anne first addresses her courteously as *you,* while she spurns him contemptuously with *thou.* By the end of the scene, Richard has so far won her that she speaks to him respectfully as *you,* and he calls her intimately *thou* and *thee.* Shakespeare was not always so careful nor are many historical novelists. Even in *Quentin Durward,* Scott has the Duke of Burgundy tell Durward, "But if you falter or double in your answers, I will have thee hung alive in an iron chain from the steeple of the market-house, where thou shalt wish for death for many an hour ere he come to you." The Quakers insisted on using only the second person singular, as a symbol of universal equality, just as they refused to remove their hats before monarchs and judges. Thus there is a joke that a Quaker mother, angered at her troublesome child, said, "Oh, thou little *you,* thee." George Fox, founder of the Quakers, wrote:

Do not they speak false English, false Latine, false Greek . . . and false to the other Tongues, . . . that doth not speak *thou* to *one,* what ever he be, Father, Mother, King, or Judge is he not a Novice and Unmannerly, and an Ideot and a Fool, that speaks *You* to *one,* which is not to be spoken to a *singular,* but to many? O Vulgar Professors and Teachers, that speaks Plural when they should Singular.

But O, George Fox, that uses a singular verb (*doth* and *speaks*) with plural subjects (*they, Professors and Teachers*). Eventually the Quakers discarded *thou* and used the objective *thee* for the wrong case and with the wrong verb; "*Thee are* (or *is*) a good whaler." The proper cases appear in "And some mishap befell thee and thou lost thy apparel." [1] In Europe young men do not address girls with *tu* or *du* until they are on kissing terms. Such distinctions are social, rather than grammatical, but they can be useful.

Some personal pronouns are confused with their homonyms; thus people mistakenly interchange *its* with *it's, their* with *there* and *they're,* and *your* with *you're. It's* is a contraction of *it is; there* is an adverb or an expletive; *they're* is a contraction of *they are;* and *you're* is a contraction of *you are.* Confusion is a sign either of carelessness or bad habit; careful proofreading should eliminate sentences like "The beetles were brought in from Kansas, where there use in cleaning skeletons for the museum was discovered by accident."

In isolated backwoods communities, you sometimes encounter the plural pronoun followed by *-uns* (*we-uns, us-uns, you-uns, they-uns*). This is probably a slurring of *ones* rather than a carry over of the German *uns* (*us*). At any rate, *-uns* is a dialect form that is best discarded from standard usage. *Hit* (for *it*) lingers in the Southern Appalachians as a vestigial survivor of standard Chaucerian speech.

¶ DEMONSTRATIVE PRONOUNS

This and *that,* with their plurals *these* and *those* are called demonstrative pronouns when they are used to indicate or point out something close at hand. ("*This* is my toy; *those* are yours.") Actually they function more often as adjectives ("*These* men have scurvy," "The rats are leaving *this* ship"). The main error is that

57

nonstandard English speech often uses the personal pronoun *them* instead of the plural demonstrative. ("Can I have another of *them* brochures on the tropical fish?" "Where do I find *them* ice caves?") This nonstandard use of *them* often appears in folk songs ("I've been in the Bend/ With *them* rough and rowdy men") and in fiction dialogue, but in other contexts it should be avoided. The error is doubled when *them* is used for the subjective case (*Them* is graceful birds in the water. *Them* chigger bites itches), and it is tripled when it is used with a singular verb ("*Them* is mighty good corn squeezings"). Perhaps "God damn them bugs" [2] is more expressive than "God damn those bugs," but it lacks the proper credentials.

Another common error is using *this* and *these* to refer to something that is vague and unfamiliar to the reader or listener: "There was *this* girl," "I sat on *this* bench," "*This* bird sat on my hat." What girl, what bench, what bird? In these cases, what should be used is simply the indefinite article *a*: "*a girl*," "*a bench*," "*a bird*." Suppose Thomas Wolfe had written "This stone, this leaf, this door"? The reader wouldn't know what he meant. J. D. Salinger's Holden Caulfield is addicted to the vague use of demonstratives. It is a hallmark of teen-age jargon. ("There was *this* mother in the zoo standing before *this* hippopotamus and telling *this* kid not to stick his hand in too far because he should remember what happened when *this* monkey got hold of him.")

¶ RELATIVE PRONOUNS

Who, whose, whom, which, what, and *that,* with their compounds *whoever, whosoever, whomever, whichever, whatever,* and *whatsoever,* are termed relative pronouns when they are used to connect, or relate, a subordinate clause to the rest of the sentence ("Moby Dick was the whale *that* took off Ahab's leg"). In this capacity they act as a subordinate connective, but they also still function as a subject or object:

> Lohengrin is the knight *who came* in the swan boat.
> Polyphemus is the Cyclops *whom* Odysseus *blinded.*
> This is the house *that* Jack *built.*

Actually it is their function of relating the dependent clause to the main clause that distinguishes relative pronouns. The italicized words are not relative pronouns at all in the following sentences:

Let's have no nonsense *whatsoever.*
Whoever cooked the soup should be drowned in it.
I'll eat *whatever* is on the menu.
Whosoever finds Mycenean relics must turn them over to the
Greek government.

¶ INTERROGATIVE PRONOUNS

Most relative pronouns *(who, which, what,* and their compounds)
double as interrogative pronouns, which are used to begin direct or
indirect questions. More significant is the fact that every interrogative pronoun is always a subject ("Who is it?"), a complement
("What do you mean?"), or a modifier ("Which book did you
buy?" "Where did he go?").

¶ REFLEXIVE PRONOUNS

In such sentences as "I celebrate myself," "He cut himself," "You
will make yourself ridiculous," "They fell over themselves," the
words *myself, himself, yourself, themselves* are termed reflexive
pronouns, because they reflect back the action of the verb upon
the subject:

	SINGULAR	PLURAL
1ST PERSON	myself	ourselves
2ND PERSON	yourself	yourselves
3RD PERSON	himself, herself, itself	themselves

In nonstandard speech you sometimes hear *hisself, theirself, their-
selfs* and *theirselves,* by analogy to the possessive form in *myself,
ourselves,* and *yourself.* Having used a plural pronoun in faulty
agreement with a singular subject, Holden Caulfield once com-
promised with a reflexive *themself,* half singular and half plural,
as in "a guy that's crazy about themself." Medieval and Elizabethan
English often used the personal pronoun reflexively in forms that
are now obsolete: "It likes me" (meaning "I liked"), *"I doubt me
whether . . . ," "I think me."* The latter lingers in the archaic form
methinks.

¶ INTENSIVE PRONOUNS

These are the same in form as reflexive pronouns and are used to
emphasize or intensify the antecedent ("I'll do it *myself.*" "Give it

to the king *himself*." "Penelope *herself* failed to recognize Odysseus."). In Irish dialect, one sometimes finds the intensive pronoun used alone, as subject or object: "*Myself* will give you a whipping." "Pass *himself* the whiskey." The same nonstandard forms used for reflexives turn up again as intensives (e.g., Huckleberry Finn's "There set Pap, his own self!").

¶ INDEFINITE PRONOUNS

All, any, both, each, every, few, many, much, no one, one other, several, and *some* act as modifiers before a noun ("Is there *any* peanut butter?") but function as pronouns when they appear alone as subjects or complements (*All* is ready). Since they have no specific antecedent, they are called indefinite. These pronouns include *none* and compound forms with *body, one,* and *thing—anybody, anyone, anything. One* can take a plural form ("one of the good *ones*"). For practical purposes, *they* has also become an indefinite plural ("*They* don't build houses the way *they* used to").

It is not important to remember the categories of pronouns so long as you know how to use them. Some of the problems connected with their use are dealt with in the next two chapters.

5 √ Who's on First? Riddles of Reference

"If you've been chigger-bit, you ought to put nail polish on them." This is good advice, but it is ambiguous, since the pronoun *them* does not refer clearly to any other word in the sentence. What you ought to do, of course, is to put nail polish on the chigger bites. If you hear someone saying, "I hardly ever drink myself, but I keep some on hand for visitors," you assume that *some* refers to liquor, but there is no clear grammatical reference. Sometimes such faulty reference is no problem; sometimes, it is awkward; and occasionally it is downright confusing, as in "The driver of the 45-foot tank truck nonchalantly lighted a big cigar and expertly maneuvered it through Boston traffic, en route to central Massachusetts." [1] Here *it* seems to refer to the cigar, creating an intriguing but inaccurate mental picture. When you encounter the ad, "Ann Landers will be glad to help you with your parents. Send them to her in care of this newspaper enclosing a stamped self-addressed envelope," you might wonder what the postage will be and whether Miss Landers knows what she's doing. At least, you might consider marking the envelope "Fragile" and sending it "Special Handling."

Harassed by such statements as "T. S. Eliot's poems are full of bald-headed men who worry about it," English teachers sometimes declare that every pronoun must have a clear and definite antecedent. However, it is not true that a pronoun always must, should, or even can, have an antecedent. A good proportion of such words —*what, whoever, anyone, none, they, I,* even *who* and *he*—may be used correctly without any antecedent whatever. What is the antecedent of *He* in "He who hesitates is lost," or of *Who* in "Who strives succeeds"? What is the antecedent of *I* in any of its uses?

And furthermore, it is often just as important for a noun to have an antecedent as for a pronoun to have one; the absence of the antecedent leads to ambiguity just as surely. Take, for example, the sentence "On the table lay *David Copperfield, Macbeth,* and *Rob Roy;* I picked up the book and began to read." The meaning is ambiguous because we don't know the antecedent of the noun *book.* If the sentence stated that the titles were *David Copperfield, Macbeth,* and *A Golden Trashery of Mad* and that I picked up the non-book, then there would be no question.

I, of course, does not need a direct antecedent; the speaker or writer is understood. But, since the repetition of *I* may become immodest and overly intrusive, some writers bend over backwards to avoid using it at all, especially in impersonal, technical, or other specialized professional fields. Likewise, the language of business and bureaucracy prefers to efface the individual in favor of the corporate or departmental image. The result is an excessive and cumbersome use of the passive voice, which gives sentence structure the motion of two steps forward to one step back. Unless you are writing a first-person narrative, you should not bother the reader with chatty first-person observations or reactions; many students spoil the interest inherent in any objective opinion by saying more about themselves than about their topic. ("When I first read *Walden,* I thought Thoreau was some kind of a kook, but then I thought the matter over, and I decided that maybe he had something to say to me. I don't dig a lot of Thoreau, but I think I know what I should get out of his ideas.") But you should not be afraid of using *I* or *me* when they are appropriate, when for instance you are expressing a personal judgment, wish, or opinion. "I think" and "I hope" are infinitely preferable to "It is the opinion of the author that . . ." and "It is hoped that . . ."; "I am grateful to . . ." is more gracious than "Gratitude is due to . . ."

The clinical or editorial *we* can be both irritating and ludicrous. When a nurse says, "Now it's time for us to take our nap," the patient may either invite her to join him or tell her to go and take her own nap—depending on the state of the patient's recovery and the attractiveness of the nurse. If she says, "Let's take our medicine like a good boy," the patient is justified in demanding that she take her half of the prescribed dose. The editorial *we* is an annoying mannerism, especially if the reader disagrees with the editor. Perhaps editors use it to surround themselves with imaginary collaborators lest a frail editorial *I* seem exposed too naked to the world. But unless you (as the author) and the reader are mutually involved, you should avoid the editorial *we* and stand by your own guns. The only *we* acceptable in the singular is the royal *we* ("We [*King Henry*] do hereby decree . . ."), theoretically because the king speaks for the kingdom but actually because he can command, "Off with his head," if someone challenges him—at least, he could in the old days.

As an indefinite pronoun, *one* is academic and stuffy ("One often finds one's conventional views challenged in college"). It is best to minimize such constructions. If one insists on using *one*, one can at least improve the example by replacing the second *one* with *his*, can't you? This garbled sentence illustrates another point: once you have used a pronoun, be consistent in maintaining it in the same person throughout, and do not switch from *I* to *you* to *one* or vice versa. (E.g., "One doesn't enjoy movies when people are talking behind *you*," "Football is no fun for *me* when *you* have to sit in the rain." Besides, the use of different pronouns makes the meaning of the last sentence unclear; perhaps the speaker doesn't mind the rain himself but is concerned only for his companion.)

You is more relaxed and less abstract than *one* and seems to speak more intimately and directly to the reader. But beware of using either pronoun in inappropriate or ludicrous situations. Analyzing the work of J. D. Salinger, one student felt so much empathy for the characters that he wrote, "One wants to get in the tub with Zooey." The student can speak for himself, but the reader may not wish to share this sudsy experience. Keep your audience in mind. When coeds write themes telling you how you iron your lingerie or put your hair in curlers, a male reader may reply, "Who, me?" Hemingway writes what it's like when you shoot a kudu, or when you kill a man for the first time, or when you order absinthe, or when you have the moment of truth in the bull ring, as if the reader has done these things or should have done them if he's to belong to the club. Bad imitators of Hemingway write things like, "When you want to smash somebody's teeth in, you should use brass knuckles so you don't cut your hand."

In the case of *they*, grammarians can be too rigid in insisting on an antecedent. Technically, English has no plural indefinite pronoun, but *they* has pretty much come to fill this function. For example in the sentence, "In London they have lots of fog," it is pedantic to insist that *they* is unclear and that the sentence should be revised. The French use *on* and the Germans *man* to mean *they*, *you*, *people* (*on dit* and *man sagt*, "people say"); and there is no reason why English cannot use *they* in the same way, as long as

63

there is no ambiguity. Certainly Thurber's "I wandered into Stoeger's famous gun house in Fifth Avenue the other morning to see if they could repair my derringer" poses no difficulty, whereas any revision, e.g., "to see if the employees could repair," would be clumsy without any gain in clarity.[2]

It is only when *they* is used as a nameless pressure to conformity that you had better be on guard. Thoreau complained:

When I ask for a garment of a particular form, my tailoress tells me gravely, "They do not make them so now," not emphasizing the "They" at all, as if she quoted an authority as impersonal as the Fates, and I find it difficult to get made what I want, simply because she cannot believe that I mean what I say, that I am so rash. When I hear this oracular sentence, I am for a moment absorbed in thought, emphasizing to myself each word separately that I may come at the meaning of it, that I may find out by what degree of consanguinity *They* are related to *me,* and what authority they may have in an affair which affects me so nearly; and, finally, I am inclined to answer her with equal mystery, and without any more emphasis of the "they,"—"It is true, they did not make them so recently, but they do now."

That is one way to beat the system. *They* is more difficult to put down when it is the voice of rumor: "They say that so-and-so is up to such-and-such unsavory activity." If you ask, Who says so? you are apt to be told, "They all do," one advantage of this sort of vague reply being that it begs the question of responsibility and reliable evidence. In political purges, *they* can be sinister in its shapelessness: *they* accuse you; *they* say that you are guilty; *they* condemn you; and you never learn who *they* are that you must answer and oppose.

When *they* or *them* does have an antecedent, the reference must be clear. In the movie *Them,* when scientists in the New Mexico desert find a child in a state of shock screaming "Them!" over and over, they have to discover what "Them" refers to; "them," or rather *they,* are in fact, giant predatory ants caused by atomic mutation. In the sentence, "If Proctor had really been a witch, they would have given him their forgiveness and his life," it is not clear who "they" are. The sentence, "Bundles of wood were placed about the witch's feet, and a torch ignited them," is equally open to question. What was ignited, the feet or the bundles? There is even more confusion in an ad for "Playskool Puzzles": "After each of the individual puzzles has been accomplished—or if yours is an exceptional child—it is recommended that they be mixed to offer a more difficult challenge of a 12-piece puzzle." Here the interjected comment makes it appear that children, rather than puzzles, should be mixed. Students are frequently guilty of using a construction in which *they* refers to some idea or *ism,* rather than to its followers: "These are a few basic principles of deism. By reason they felt they could better understand God and their role in life." Here the noun must be substituted: "By reason, deists felt . . ." Sometimes it is clear enough what the pronoun stands for, yet the reference is grammatically unbalanced, as in "Annixter professes that he is a woman hater. The real problem is that he doesn't know how to act in their presence." *Their* referring to *women,* not to *woman hater,* the first sentence needs to be rewritten. Truman Capote writes, "Within the next quarter-hour a stag party had taken over the apartment, several of them in uniform." [3] Here *them* stands for party-goers, not for party; but the meaning is clear enough and perhaps conciseness and style excuse the grammar, since a revision (e.g., ". . . a stag party had taken over the apartment; several of its members in uniform") would be longer and more formal.

Whenever a pronoun's meaning depends upon reference to a particular noun or another pronoun, the antecedent should be specific. Another common and clumsy construction in student writing is, "In Griffin's book he states a problem of which I was unaware." Here, once again, the third-person pronoun has no clear antecedent, though the reader probably assumes that *he* stands for Griffin. But *he* could refer to someone else contributing to Griffin's book, in which case the meaning should be made clear. The solution is, "In his book Griffin states a problem of which I was unaware." Sometimes when there are two names to which a pronoun could refer, you have to include explanatory nouns in apposition: e.g., "Captain Flume had obtained this idea from Chief White Halfoat himself, who did tiptoe up to his cot one night as he was dozing off, to hiss portentously that one night when he, Captain Flume, was sound asleep, he, Chief White Halfoat, was going to slit his throat open from ear to ear." [4] If the pronoun seems to refer to the wrong noun (usually one closer to it than the actual antecedent) or to no noun at all, the meaning may be confused or nonsensical. (E.g., "Many times the cars and trucks would break down, and with the little money saved they bought spare parts at an exorbitant price.") Such errors occur particularly often in the use of the *it:* "He was very sick and died of it." Of what? "In Franklin, God should be worshiped because he deserved it." This should be revised to read,

"Franklin believed God deserved to be worshiped." In the sentence, "I wasn't being very entertaining, but I didn't feel up to it," *it* doesn't sum up the previous clause but implies a contradictory idea. Sometimes dialogue (as, for example, Holden Caulfield's in *The Catcher in the Rye*) is deliberately nonstandard (Holden explains that he is quite illiterate but reads a lot); but sometimes in informal conversation *it, that, this,* or *which* can refer to the idea of an entire preceding clause, though such vague reference is avoided in a formal style:

INFORMAL. The penguins were diving into the water, which was an amusing sight.

FORMAL. It was amusing to see the penguins diving into the water.

INFORMAL. The St. Bernard wasn't satisfied with dog biscuits for supper and made no bones about it.

FORMAL. The dean was not satisfied with tenure policy and was quite specific in his criticism.

But even careful stylists sometimes use vague pronominal reference. Mark Twain wrote, "I never was so scared before and survived it," and James Thurber wrote of Harold Ross, "He was a horse player, completely addicted to it, and a steady loser." [5] If Thurber's grammar were smoothed to "He was completely addicted to horse playing and was a steady loser," the sentence would lose flavor and stress. On the other hand, Alfred Duggan's "All summer the fleet remained at Sandwich, which was very expensive" gives the reader a double take.[6] Rather than rules, the careful writer should consider clarity and style. There is some grammatical awkwardness in the sentence "Proctor is essentially a strong-willed man, which is shown in his actions with the court," but the revision "Proctor is essentially a strong-willed man, a fact which is shown . . ." is even worse; the proper formal style would be "The fact that Proctor is a strong-willed man is shown . . ." "Although it is not a common practice to frost pound cake, it can make a pleasant convenience for autumn and winter dining," is unclear. Does *it* refer to practice, to the act of frosting, or to the pound cake itself? Particularly objectionable in both grammar and style are constructions like "Just because society says something is evil, this doesn't mean that it is evil." "The fact that society says something is evil doesn't necessarily make it so" is clearer and more concise.

Despite the various grammatical hazards involved, you shouldn't be afraid to use pronouns. Often they are necessary to avoid repetition and create more fluid transitions:

66

Before he went to Hollywood, Errol Flynn had a number of exotic adventures in the South Pacific. Errol Flynn was a sailor, a plantation boss, and a sheep-gelder. Errol Flynn was even a slave trader. Once Errol Flynn bought a cargo of slaves and paid for them in San Francisco exposition tokens, which Errol Flynn told the chief were more valuable than money. Later the chief vowed he would kill Errol Flynn if he could ever get his hands on Errol Flynn.

This paragraph has the jerky movement of a car driven for the first time by a learner who can't handle the clutch. The substitution of *he* and *him* for most of the repetitions of the name *Errol Flynn* would unify the paragraph and connect the sentences more smoothly.

Any useless pronoun should be cut. A frequent and annoying construction is "In the Bible it says . . . ," "In *Hamlet* it says . . . ," "In algebra it says . . ." *It* is nothing but dead wood; "The Bible says . . ." is sufficient. Many students are addicted to "In such and such it says," and careless writers use this construction automatically. One *Life* editorial used it twice in successive sentences: "It says in the U. N. Universal Declaration of Human Rights that 'Everyone has the right to leave any country, including his own . . .' But it says in the U. S. State Department rulebook that the U. S. disapproves of the principle of asylum." [7] *Commonsense Grammar and Style* says *it* would never be missed.

Exercise 2: Correct any errors in unclear pronoun reference.

1. Many times the cars and trucks would break down, and with the little money saved they bought spare parts at an exorbitant price.
2. In gun-running they pay off handsomely.
3. We tried to inflate the air mattresses without a pump, which was an exhausting procedure.
4. John Carradine killed Tyrone Power in *Jesse James,* and he was killed in *Stagecoach, The Grapes of Wrath, The House of Frankenstein, Mary of Scotland,* and *Captain Fury.*
5. Sociologists observe that a person often votes for the same party your family voted for.
6. During his experiences at sea, Melville observed a great deal of man's inhumanity to man; and this made him skeptical of the Transcendentalist concept that there is really no evil.
7. One park visitor pushed a bear into the front seat of his car next to

his wife to photograph them together, which was an incredibly foolish thing to do.

8. In New York they wouldn't even pay attention if an octopus reached out of the sewer to drag down a pedestrian.
9. On the sign at the park entrance it says that feeding the bears is unlawful.
10. When the Lone Ranger jumped off the roof, he missed his horse, which made him fall flat on his face.
11. Many of the Cherokees were quite civilized in the 1820's, which made President Monroe suggest that they should be made citizens.
12. But in the late 1820's, gold was discovered on Cherokee land in North Georgia, and this made the squatters and speculators try to dispossess the Indians.
13. The eleven white missionaries to the Cherokees were sentenced to four years apiece at hard labor for speaking in the Indians' defence, which Chief Justice John Marshall said was unconstitutional.
14. It does not say in the Preamble to the Constitution that all men are created equal; it says so in the Declaration of Independence.
15. Porkypine's Uncle Baldwin kissed Miss Hepzibah, which made her blush.
16. On the night before exams, it is better to go to the movies and not worry about it than to stay up all night studying.
17. I don't enjoy drive-in movies when you have to run the windshield wiper.
18. In trial by ordeal, a person accused of witchcraft might be tied and thrown into a river. If he sank, he was innocent (but drowned); but if he floated, he was guilty, and they put him to death.
19. In Mark Twain's later writings, he often discussed "the damned human race."
20. Puritans believed that most men would be damned because they deserved it.
21. Just because a state passes a law, this doesn't mean the law is legitimate.
22. During the Fourth of July weekend, there was a great deal of vandalism, many of them adults who should have known better.
23. In Walt Kelly's *Pogo* he deliberately writes in nonstandard grammar for humorous effect.
24. Ruth pointed out Martin Eden's nonstandard grammar, which embarrassed him and made him try to improve himself.
25. Some people call reactionaries conservatives, but they don't really want to conserve anything.

6 √ Pronoun - Antecedent Agreement

"A person in there looks just like they did in life, only with a nice tan, like you have right now," said the coffin salesman.[1] Here death's sting is in the forked tongue of the salesman. This unctiously commercial pitch is dubious in taste, misleading in theology, false in comfort, and wretched in grammar. The coffin is also expensive; but then the salesman can justify the cost by saying that it's large enough for two—at least, it had better be if "they" are to look right in it. Is this a case of "When a body meets a body?" Or has the salesman had too much rye? Or is this the first recorded case of posthumous schizophrenia? Obviously, there is only one body, and it should have a singular pronoun.

A pronoun must agree with its antecedent in person, gender, and number—but not in case. The case of a pronoun depends upon its use in its own clause. Thus if you are to use pronouns correctly you must be aware of grammatical construction and the relationship of words. First find the pronoun; then see if it has an antecedent. If it does not, or if the antecedent is unclear, you have an error in reference, unless the pronoun can stand alone. When you have found the antecedent, see what its person, gender, and number are. Then look at the person, gender, and number of the pronoun. Are they the same? If not, there is an error in agreement; and you must change either the pronoun or the antecedent to make their person, gender, and number the same. This sounds like a painstaking process, but you need to follow it only if you are addicted to error in this area. Most experienced writers don't have to think twice about agreement but handle it by conditioned reflex. Unfortunately, many people habitually use the wrong pronoun, so their grammatical reflexes need reconditioning by practice in conscious sentence analysis.

EXAMPLE	EXPLANATION
I comb *my* hair with greasy kid stuff.	*My* is first person singular to agree with *I*.
The *girl* had *her* purse stolen.	*Her* is feminine third person singular to agree with *girl*.
The *gnu* scratched *its* nose.	*Its* is neuter third person singular to agree with *gnu*.
The *tigers* sharpened *their* teeth.	*Their* is third person plural to agree with *tigers*.

¶ PERSON

Disagreements in person occur almost exclusively with vague or impersonal pronouns. The sentence "One should watch your step" has a second-person pronoun, *your,* and a third-person antecedent, *one.* It is necessary to be consistent and to avoid errors, such as, "In Zenith one was forced to conform to conservative politics and live your life the way the group wanted you to." A particularly choice example occurred in an article entitled "Blowing Rock, N.C.": "Years ago they could tell a stranger was 'an outsider by the cut of your pants.' But education and business has seeped up from the big cities and universities to the hills, and they have changed somewhat the cut of their own pants."[2] Here we have a third-person singular antecedent *stranger* mismatched with a second-person singular pronoun *your*—an error in both number and person. The second sentence is a real hodgepodge: *education and business* require a plural verb. It is not clear whether *they* refers to *education and business, hills,* or something else. And if the hills change the cut of their pants, then the metaphor is ludicrous.

Another amusing shift in person appears in a young actress's statement, "*My* figure's all right—*I* don't mind it. Sometimes it gets a little out of hand after *you've* had a three months' vacation when *you* just sit around the pool getting tan and fat . . . then *I* have to go on a crash diet. . . . *I* have such an investment in a whole lot of stretch pants and they all fit within an eighth of an inch and if *you* gain more than a half ounce *you've* had it. *You* can't wear them." (Italics mine.) This becomes doubly deranged if the reader imagines that *you* refers to himself.

¶ GENDER

The gender of a pronoun should be the same as that of its antecedent. This seems obvious, and the reader is not likely to make

70

errors like "Mr. Lummox got tired of commuting every morning with twenty-five pounds of bread in *her* lap." Most errors occur with relative pronouns. *Who* should be used to refer to persons; *which,* to refer to things; and *that,* to refer to persons, animals, or things. In an assignment on *The Grapes of Wrath,* students wrote of "the tractors who," "the farmers which," "the turtle who," "the ant who," "the car who," "the migrants which." In each of these the gender is wrong; *who* is masculine or feminine, *which* is neuter, and *that* can be used without regard to gender. Sometimes the choice should depend on euphony: *the sandwich that* is obviously preferable to *the sandwich which.* In the possessive, *whose,* though masculine or feminine, is sometimes used for things as well as persons, to avoid the awkward *of which.* "The ship whose side was rammed" is better than "The ship the side of which was rammed." Thus abstract rules have to surrender to concrete problems of style.

Because English uses natural gender, there is little problem with personal pronoun reference; most nouns take *it.* Even an animal with a specific sex, like cow, bull, and sow, can be referred to as *it.* Usually we reserve specific gender for persons. But in casual practice we assign *it* to many things. All ships are feminine, even *The Great Harry* or *The General Hahn.* Melville wrote of *The Pequod,* "She was a ship of the old school, rather small if anything; with an old fashioned claw-footed look about her." But often when the specific word *ship* is used as an antecedent, the pronoun that follows is *it*: "The ship changed its course." Cars are customarily feminine, so much so that Faulkner wrote in *Intruder in the Dust* that "the automobile has become our national sex symbol." Yet Faulkner referred to the car as *it.* Most people say, "She needs a grease job," "Fill her up," or "She has only 35,000 miles." A very few may say, "Fill it up," but you never hear, "Fill him up." Axles, bushings, brakes, and other parts of the car are usually neuter, though almost any machine or tool can be feminine: "Hand her here," "She has a good cutting edge," "She has a lot of power," "Set her down carefully." Even weapons are often referred to as feminine, from the huge Scottish cannon Maun's Meg to the Old Betsy. "What's her range?" an artilleryman might ask. Despite Burt Lancaster in the movie *From Here to Eternity,* instructors for the .30 caliber machine gun warn, "Never hold the barrel in your bare hand if you fire from the hip; she gets red hot, and she'll roast your hand."

Except for mares, cows, and dogs that have just become mothers, the gender of most animals, when not referred to as *it* is masculine. Whitman wrote, "The spotted hawk swoops by and accuses me; he complains of my gab and my loitering." In *The Old Man and the Sea,* Santiago's giant marlin and the sharks that devour him are spoken of as masculine, though, in fact, they could equally well be feminine. The first man to have seen bacteria is reported to have said, "I can't make out his shape. But he is alive!"

Finally, semantic change has altered the gender of some words. *Harlot* was once masculine and meant simply "young fellow," as in Chaucer's description of the Summoner as "a gentil harlot and a kynde." And *girl* once meant a young person of either sex and could take a masculine pronoun.

After an antecedent of mixed or indeterminate gender, the masculine pronoun is conventionally used:

> *Every child* should put away *his* toys.
> *Everyone* is to bring *his* own camping equipment.

The men and women were told that *everybody* must contribute *his* share. "Everybody must contribute his or her share" is long-winded and pedantic. When the antecedent is specifically feminine, then it is followed by a feminine pronoun: "The ladies' bridge club decided *everyone* should bring *her* own cards."

¶ NUMBER

Most errors in agreement occur in number, usually because a singular antecedent is erroneously followed by a plural pronoun. There are several constructions that may create difficulties.

1. The pronoun should be plural when it has two or more antecedents connected by *and*:

> My wife and I took *our* vacation in Grundy Center.
> Fitzgerald and Hemingway had some rifts in *their* friendship.
> Brutus and Cassius killed *themselves*.

2. When a collective noun is considered as a unit, it takes a singular pronoun:

> *Congress* adjourned *its* eighty-first session.
> The *congregation* supported *its* minister.
> The Slippery Rock football *team* had *its* forty-fourth consecutive undefeated season.
> The *enemy* issued *its* ultimatum.

72

3. When a collective noun is considered as a number of separate individuals, it takes a plural pronoun. Thus you would write, "The audience applauded *its* speaker," but "The audience *were* cheering, hissing, and booing *their* speaker"; "The jury followed *its* instructions," but "The jury were divided in *their* verdict."

Wildlife are at *their* best in backcountry.
Congress are divided on *their* views of foreign aid.
The *congregation* were sufficiently divided about *their*
    minister to drive Jonathan Edwards from his parish.
The Slippery Rock *team* got permission to postpone *their* exams.
The *enemy* were both resisting and running away from *their* attackers.

Sometimes an unexpected word appears as a collective plural noun. Thus, Thomas Hutchinson wrote in the eighteenth century, "New Hampshire, by *their* convenient situation were induced to become *their* own importers." *Importers* is the key word here that makes New Hampshire plural.

Other errors occur when a collective noun followed by a plural pronoun is given a singular verb:

"The public only *thinks they* are saving money." [3]
Apparently the Student Government mimeograph service *has* been
    derelict in performing *their* duties.
In *The Grapes of Wrath* the bank *moves* in with *their* tractors.
"I wonder if the Army's generous with *their* peanut butter"
    [italics mine]—Truman Capote, *Breakfast at Tiffany's* [4]

The first two examples require a plural verb: *think* and *have*. The last two should keep the verb singular and change the pronoun: "*its* tractors," "*its* peanut butter." Actually the last example being part of the dialogue in a novel is in the original entirely appropriate in character.

4. Traditionally the possessive personal pronoun is put in the singular when its antecedent is *each, either,* or *neither,* even if it is followed by a plural object:

> *Each* of the queens lost *her* head.
> *Either* of the candidates could alienate *his* followers
>   by an unpopular stand.
> *Neither* of the magicians would reveal *his* tricks.

Often colloquial speech uses a plural verb and pronoun: "Neither of them were willing to stop their quarrel." But in the preceding examples, logic and grammar combined require the singular pro-

73

noun. Sometimes, however, logic is on the other side, especially if the plural modifier precedes *each, either,* or *neither*: "The three little pigs each built themselves a house" is more fluent than "The three little pigs each built himself a house." An ad for glue says of its ingredients, "*Each . . . has his* contribution ready. But E-Pox-E Glue sticks to iron, steel, brass, copper, bronze and bonds *them* to *each* other." Here *each* is singular as a subject but plural as an object following *them*. In "The principal stands behind each of his students when they accept a job," common sense requires the plural; "when he accepts a job" would seem both illogical and vague in reference.

5. Conservative grammar requires the use of a singular pronoun when there is a numerically indefinite antecedent, such as *anyone, anybody, each, either, every, everybody, everyone, neither, no one,* and *nobody*:

> "What if *everyone* in the whole world suddenly decided to run away from his problems?"[5]
> "Let *everyone* carry out *his* own corpse," Jim Fisk told the investigators.
> "You mean *anyone* can have a giant in *her* washing machine?"—detergent ad.

But in general practice, these indefinite antecedents are often followed by a plural pronoun: "Everybody has their lunch," "Nobody got their dessert." This is a particularly sore spot with many grammarians. The controversy is caused by the difference between a formal and a colloquial style of grammar. Formal, conservative grammar requires that the number of a pronoun be governed by its form, regardless of meaning, whereas colloquial usage is usually concerned solely with conveying meaning. Each of these numerically indefinite antecedents has a plural meaning but a singular form; and since meaning generally carries the day, the formalists are losing ground. In Thurber's "The Interview," an irascible writer tells a reporter: "Everybody replies to my questions the way they think I want them to reply. You can say that I say 'everybody-they'; I hate 'everybody-he.' 'Has everybody brought his or her slate?' a teacher of mine, a great goat of a woman, used to ask us. There is no other tongue in the world as clumsy as ours is—with its back to certain corners." [6]

Certainly many able writers sometimes agree in practice with Thurber's author. Hemingway, Steinbeck, Mary McCarthy, Edmund Wilson, John P. Marquand are a few of them. ". . . everybody no

74

matter what superficial annoyance they might show, liked to be recognized and noticed." [7] Norman Mailer regularly uses such constructions:

"Nobody minds if they read in the papers that they were thrown in a swimming pool when in fact they did not go near a glass of water." [8]

". . . everybody else in the book is connected by their skin to another character who is connected to still another." [9]

On the political scene we find Governor Scranton of Pennsylvania saying, "I feel very strongly that one of the mistakes that we have made in the past is to try to tell everybody how they should vote at a national convention." [10] And General LeMay has stated, ". . . no one is going to start a war unless they think they are going to win." [11]

Of course, politicians are not necessarily dependable guides in grammar; some are quite the reverse. But there are situations where *everybody* and the other indefinite antecedents require a plural pronoun if a sentence is to make any sense; e.g., "He talks to everyone as if they matter." "He talks to everyone as if he matters" completely reverses the meaning. "Practically everybody in Congress would like to get the budget down; sometimes they form up in assault squads to do it." [12] If "he forms up in assault squads," he is certainly fragmenting his personality. "Had *everyone* felt and acted as Proctor did, or had *they* been free to do so, the mass hysteria of the witch trials never could have controlled Salem," requires *they* for the plural meaning. So does Edmund Wilson's observation, "And, as seems to have been natural in the nineteenth century so much more than it is in our own, *everybody* speaks in character in such a way that one can often almost hear *their* voices." [13] (Italics mine.) In "*Neither* driver knew *he* was leading until *they* reached the Morogoro checkpoint," clarity requires that the first pronoun be singular and the second plural. "Everybody was very courteous; they gave me hay to sit on," requires *they* for meaning, though the situation remains curious.

On the other hand, meaning as well as form often requires a singular pronoun. "Everybody thinks their own child is remarkable" is awkward. Does everybody have the same child, and how many parents does the child have? "Everyone calls everyone Richard or whatever their name is, if they don't call them darling," is a double dose of grammatical schizophrenia. [14] Common sense says that specific situations, rather than abstract rules, should determine whether an antecedent like *everybody* takes a singular or plural pronoun. As the parents sing in *The Fantasticks,* "No one can hear with beans in their ears." *"Every* wine has *its* proper glass—it's imperative to know *them* all" has faulty agreement in form but makes sense in context, while "Everybody is writing their autobiography" is confused, mainly because a plural possessive pronoun is coupled with a singular object.

Another reason for confusion, and one that more legitimately bothers formalists, is that *anyone, everyone, no one,* etc., always take a singular verb, whether or not they are followed by a plural pronoun. You never hear, "Everybody are coming home," "No one were raking their leaves," or similar constructions. Presumably, if words like *everybody* have a plural meaning, they could take a plural verb, but the *-body* and *-one* endings make a singular verb habitual. Accordingly, unless the meaning requires a plural pronoun, it is better to stick to the traditional form and use the singular. There is no reason for defending "Nobody brushes their teeth in the bathtub." In conversation it is usually not necessary to worry about pronoun-antecedent agreement, but any lack of agreement, such as in "Anyone in good physical condition can climb Mount Rainier if they have the desire," needs to be revised for careful writing. How, then, do you know when the rule is flexible? "Every daisy in the dell seems to know but they won't tell—Mary Ann." You have to use your own judgment. Look at the following examples and see if you would revise them or let them stand:

If you make a quality product, you can't make enough of them.

The Cuban crisis really shook everyone up in their fear of an all-out nuclear war.

"You ask anybody from around Chun King. They'll tell you Aunt Jenny's the best cook in town."

He sees everyone sitting around town waiting for Friday night so that they might start their parties.

Of course, not all sentences can be taken out of context. "Everyone helped when they hatched aboard ship in the Arctic" sounds like science fiction, but the meaning becomes clear when it is preceded by "His Excellency took a great interest in my butterflies." [15]

Unfortunately, many people—perhaps proceeding by analogy with *everybody* . . . *they*—use *they* with any third person singular antecedent. *Anyone . . . they* can sometimes make sense, but *a person . . . they* does not. "Can they be a nurse?" asks an ad. They can't if they're schizophrenic, but maybe they can if they're Siamese twins. This indiscriminate use of *they* has become so widespread that some people seem to have forgotten the use of *he, she,* or *it.* One minister used *they* so regularly ("One should get on their knees and ask God to forgive them") that he barely avoided saying *God . . . they.* "Whoever. invented radiators should have their head examined." Yes, and his grammar revised. "The minimum time any *clerk* can work in this Hi-Fi department is 3 days! After that, we send *them* to a boiler factory for a week, to relax *their* nerves!" we read in *Mad.*[16] (italics mine). The pronoun-antecedent agreement is mad, too. Sometimes it is the antecedent that should be changed, rather than the pronoun: in "Mark Twain was impressed with the Negro and regarded them as fellow human beings," *them* is the right pronoun, but the antecedent should be *Negroes.* Conceivably *Negro* might be considered a collective noun that could take a plural, as in Norman Mailer's ". . . and the Negro had already demonstrated to the collective psyche of America that they had the greatest potential for violence of any political body in our American world; now, on this afternoon, they chose to show that they also possessed the finest capacity for order and discipline in the nation." [17] But Mailer is too obviously violating agreement when he writes, "Once inserted into politics a lady betrays the difference between a person and their project." [18] Or are *they, their,* and *them* to replace the third-person singular, as *you* did *thou?* This may come to pass, but in the meantime, you should use a singular pronoun with a singular antecedent and avoid such careless prose as Stony Burke's "It's too bad somebody can't make themselves a few bucks helping me," or "If there was a real-life prototype of a part she was about to portray, Ingrid hunted them out, examined and absorbed their uniqueness." [19] Miss Bergman did play in *Dr. Jekyll and Mr. Hyde,* but it was Spencer Tracy who portrayed the double character.

"In Puritan New England, breaking the law would show disfavor in the eyes of God, since they were set up by those considered under His divine influence." The faulty agreement here creates ambiguity; unless *law* is changed to *laws, they* seems to refer to "the eyes of God." Again, the antecedent rather than the pronoun needs changing in "From the Calvinist point of view, *man* is so wretched that the only true justice would be everlasting fire for all of *them.*"

Finally, when a subordinate clause comes first, the pronoun may be the antecedent for the noun, with occasionally such attendant confusion as, "Through his preoccupation with his work, teachers often neglect their families." Some teachers even write grammar books.

Exercise 3: Select from the words in parentheses those that will agree with their antecedents.

1. Once more the soldier saw the gnome, (which, whom) he had quite forgotten.
2. Thoreau disliked seeing everybody hurry around wasting (their, his) lives.
3. Mississippi has (its, their) top unit in there right now.
4. Professor Dibdin received his M.A. and Ph.D. degrees from Southeastern University and has been a professor in (its, their) English Department since 1938.
5. Nobody's ever told that joke (has he, have they)?
6. When a person grows up in the city, (one, you, he) goes wild over trees.
7. Doesn't everybody have a TV set in (his, their) Rolls-Royce?
8. You and every other American own Cape Hatteras National Seashore, as (you, he, they) should know.
9. One should not go shopping with curlers in (their, your, his, her) hair.
10. If someone in your neighborhood has seen this movie, don't let (them, him, one) tell you the ending in which the butler is revealed as the killer.
11. One can always identify a logger by the way (you, they, he) (stir, stirs) coffee with (your, their, his) thumb.
12. The actor (which, that) has been seen by the largest audience is Charlton Heston.
13. The cast (was, were) celebrating (their, its) one hundredth performance of *Mr. Limberlost, or The Kind Keeper.*
14. Does the Prohibitionist Party really think (their, its, it's) candidate has a chance?
15. How many officers use Top Brass to condition (one's, your, their, there) hair?
16. The audience appalled Henry James by (its, their) vulgarity at the opening of *Guy Domville.*
17. The Army is penny-wise with (its, their) pencils and paper and pound-foolish with expenses for (its, their) top brass.
18. Only two of Henry VIII's wives lost (her, their) (head, heads).
19. Ruritania thinks (their, its) king is Rudolph V, but Rudolph Rassendyl of England was crowned at Strelsau in (its, their) cathedral.

78

20. Neither Henry James nor H. G. Wells would patch up (his, their) friendship.
21. Pythagoras discovered the relationship between the length of a string and (their, its) pitch.
22. Neither John Carter nor Thuvan Dihn know where (he, they) were until (he, they) reached the Carrion Caves.
23. Everybody was very considerate; (he, they) let me sit next to the fire.
24. Whoever invented daylight saving should have (his, their) head examined.
25. Shakespeare often borrowed a plot from some previous author but transformed (it, them) into an original work of art.

Exercise 4: Some of the pronouns in the following sentences fail to agree with their antecedents in person, number, or gender. If the pronoun does not agree, underline the wrong word and put the correct one in the blank.

1. If the student returns to you the next term for enrollment, they must first come to me for their folder. . . . .
2. The United States has a government who represents the people. . . . .
3. Everybody in the bakery looked like they had a big question mark over their heads. . . . .
4. When we wanted to reward someone, we would give them five or six cartridges. . . . .
5. When a person is climbing mountains, one should watch your step. . . . .
6. At the Jinja golf course, any player may lift their ball out of a hippopotamus footprint without penalty. . . . .
7. If nobody has a toy elephant, I can give them one. . . . .
8. One man which was bitten by a rattlesnake used the snake for a tourniquet. . . . .
9. The book is written in plain language by a University of Michigan scientist which really knows his mushrooms. . . . .
10. Somebody who would take their mother-in-law for a drive in a small foreign car is asking for trouble. . . . .
11. We need a candidate what can speak for the people. . . . .
12. Does anybody want a banana on their cereal? . . . .
13. Often a person working overseas cannot adjust to unfamiliar ways that cause him culture shock. . . . .
14. Bats vary to a degree what hardly seems possible. . . . .
15. The Scruff family is holding their annual reunion at Huggins Hell. . . . .
16. Nobody in their right mind wants a python for a house pet. . . . .
17. Amaryllis and she won first prize for her rhododendrons. . . . .

18. When you take polaroid pictures, one should be careful to throw their negatives in a proper receptacle and not on the ground.   . . . .
19. The big dog which followed father home belongs to Mr. Schildkraut and their boys.   . . . .
20. The way you tell a black widow spider is that they have a red spot on their underneath.   . . . .

7 √ Case and Its Curiosities

EVANS.	What is your genitive case plural, William?
WILLIAM.	Genitive—horum, harum, horum.
QUICKLY.	Vengeance of Jenny's case! Fie on her! Never name her, child, if she be a whore.
EVANS.	For shame, 'oman.
QUICKLY.	You do ill to teach the child such words: he teaches him to hick and to hack—which they'll do fast enough of themselves, and to call "horum"; fie upon you!
EVANS.	'Oman, art thu lunatics? Hast thou no understanding of thy cases, and the number of the genders?

WILLIAM SHAKESPEARE, The Merry Wives of Windsor

Finno-Ugrian has sixteen cases. This is of no concern to anyone except philologists and Finno-Ugrians. For the latter, it is quite a headache. Modern English has only three cases; it is on this score one of the simplest languages in the world, yet the case of our nouns and pronouns causes a great many difficulties and controversies. Arguments over *who* and *whom, I* or *me, we* or *us* have ruined marriages, made children rebel from their parents, and caused grammarians to denounce each other as prissy schoolmarms or dangerous subversives.

Actually, case in English was once a great deal more complicated than it is at present; the language has become increasingly streamlined, and the issue at hand is (partly) whether it should be simplified further. In a highly synthetic language like Latin or German, case is indicated by inflection (that is, by changing the ending), and students must suffer the ordeal of learning various laborious declensions. In Latin there are five main cases with forms in the singular and plural, and the problem is further confounded by artificial gender. Thus the Latin word for *farmer* (*agricola*), belongs to the first declension and is feminine in gender:

81

	SINGULAR	PLURAL
NOMINATIVE	agricola	agricolae
GENITIVE	agricolae	agricolārum
DATIVE	agricolae	agricolīs
ACCUSATIVE	agricolam	agricolās
ABLATIVE	agricolā	agricolīs

And there are four other declensions in Latin, each with characteristically different endings, making a total of fifty possible case endings, though some of these duplicate each other. This should be evidence enough that English does not have Latin grammar and is infinitely better off without it. In German not only the nouns, pronouns, and adjectives but also the articles (*the, a, an*) must be inflected according to number, gender, and case. Old English was similarly complex; it had four cases (nominative, genitive, dative, accusative, and sometimes a fifth—the instrumental), each with different endings in the singular and plural. There were five major declensions, four minor ones, and variations on all of them. The adjective had a strong and weak declension and had to agree in case, number, and gender with the noun it modified. As in German, the definite article was fully inflected.

But in modern English one can forget all this. Our articles and adjectives do not inflect at all (except for the comparative and superlative forms), and our nouns do so only for the plural or in the possessive case. The only problems with nouns are some irregular plurals, the use of the apostrophe (not really a grammatical issue), and the use of the possessive case for nouns modifying gerunds. The three cases used in modern English are the subjective, possessive, and objective. Sometimes these are given the Latinate names nominative, genitive, and accusative; but we shall use the English terms. Latinist grammarians used to insist that English had five cases, but instead of dative and ablative inflections, we use word order or prepositions. Case endings are essential in Latin to indicate a noun's function; instead we rely upon word order to distinguish subject from object. Thus "Nero interfecit Agrippinam" and "Agrippinam interfecit Nero" both make Nero the murderer and Agrippina the corpse, but there is considerable difference in English between "Booth killed Lincoln" and "Lincoln killed Booth."

Only the personal and relative pronouns are still inflected in English, and it is with them that most problems arise:

PERSONAL PRONOUNS

	SUBJECTIVE CASE	POSSESSIVE CASE	OBJECTIVE CASE
		Singular	
1ST PERSON	I	my, mine	me
2ND PERSON	you	your, yours	you
3RD PERSON	he, she, it	his, her, hers, its	him, her, it
		Plural	
1ST PERSON	we	our, ours	us
2ND PERSON	you	your, yours	you
3RD PERSON	they	their, theirs	them

RELATIVE

Singular and Plural

who	whose	whom

A pronoun's case depends upon its use in its own clause and not upon the case of its antecedent. Formal grammar employs the following conventions:

1. The subjective case is used for pronouns that are
   (a) Subjects of verbs ("*He told* her *he loved* her, but oh, how *he lied*").
   (b) Pronouns in apposition to subjects ("Three winners—Susy, Ermentrude, and *I*—shared the prize").
   (c) Complements of the verb *to be* ("The accused confessed it was *he* who operated the still").
2. The objective case is used for pronouns that are
   (a) Objects of verbs ("The moose frightened *us*").
   (b) Objects of prepositions ("The moose charged at *us*").
   (c) Pronouns in apposition to objects ("The moose chased *us* —Edgar and *me*—into the lake").
   (d) Subjects or objects of infinitives ("I told *him* to drop dead." "I pretended to be *him*").
3. The possessive case is used for pronouns that
   (a) Modify a noun or another pronoun ("The vampire climbed into *his* coffin." "These are *my jewels*").
   (b) Modify a gerund ("She scolded the toucan; she disapproved of *its* eating her African violets." "*His seeing* the abominable snowman was the most exciting part of the trip").

83

There are several situations in which these conventions are changing. Though formal grammar requires the subjective case for the complement of the verb *to be,* colloquial usage usually takes the objective. Some die-hard purists protest, but nowadays practically no one says "It is I," or "It was she."

    " 'You don't have to talk as though you were addressing a meeting any longer, Willis,' Bess said. 'It's only me.'

    " 'Only I, Bess,' Willis said, 'only I.'

    " 'Oh, my God,' Bess said, 'I bet you clipped a coupon and bought one of those courses in proper speech.' "[1]

Bess's "It's me" is perfectly acceptable; she does not say "you was addressing" or "them courses," which would have made her English substandard. Very much on the make, Willis is a social climber and a snob, and his self-conscious grammar here reflects his phoniness. As Ensign Pulver says nervously in *Mr. Roberts,* "Captain, it's me. It is I, Ensign Pulver."

For most people, "It's me" is habitual and needs no apology. The French have always said, *"C'est moi."* "It's me" has been used by distinguished writers from Shakespeare to Hemingway and has been generally colloquial since Elizabethan times. Teachers who insist dogmatically upon "It is I" usually succeed only in causing their students to write, "Between you and I . . ." or, "Serve the pizza to Irving and I." "It's him," "It's her," "It's them," "It's us" are likewise common colloquial forms and are so recognized by the *Oxford Dictionary.*

If a pronoun after the verb *to be* is followed by a relative pronoun introducing a clause, then both pronouns are in the subjective case ("It's I who am to be married." "It's we who are to blame"). Colloquial speech usually avoids such constructions. As an answer to such a question as "What do you say [or see or think or like]?" one ordinarily says, "Who, me?" or "Who, us?" though the rule calls for *I* or *we* along with the subjective *who*. But "Who, me?" has become idiomatic, like the French *"Qui, moi?"* Nobody ever heard a Frenchman say, *"Qui, je?"* Yet for some reason (perhaps from hearing too many Indians in Hollywood movies say, "Me gottum firewater"), many people unconsciously feel that *I* is more aristocratic than *me,* regardless of its grammatical function. Notice the different connotations of *The King and I* and *Me and the Colonel.*

Nobody but little children and aborigines in the movies ever uses *me* in a subject ("Me want play outside." "Me want Dorothy La-mour"). Nor does *us* ever appear directly preceding the verb ("Us are playing poker"). But a frequent nonstandard practice is to use *us* for the subject if there is an appositive intervening between it and the verb. Thus Huckleberry Hound says, "Us jungle boys are real swinging types," though not even Huck would say, "Us are real swinging types." Apparently the intervening noun causes confusion. This seems to be equally true of a compound subject, where the error is often doubled by using a singular verb): "Me and her was at the dance," "Him and me is hungry." But no one would say "me was," "her was," "him is," or "me is." Grammarians have complained of the cigarette ad, "Us Tareyton smokers would rather fight than switch." The admen replied that "We Tareyton smokers" would sound sissified to the working stiffs at whom the ad was aimed.

Similarly a compound object often seems to cause confusion and result in the wrong case being used: "I once went dancing with she and Princess Margaret" and "Thangbrand took Phil and I to see John Gielgud in *King Lear*." But one would never say, "I once went dancing with she" or "Thangbrand took I." You shouldn't let compounds disconcert you, for doubling the subject or object doesn't change the case of the pronoun. "Show it to Sally and I" or "He loves both you and I" are not only nonstandard; they are particularly annoying to careful grammarians.

¶ PRONOUNS AFTER THAN, AS, LIKE

Than and *as* are conjunctions used in comparison, and formal English grammar requires a pronoun following them to be in the same case as the noun to which it is compared.

> Subjective: John Carradine is thinner than *I*.
> She is as good a fencer as *they*.
> Objective: The dinosaur impressed them no less than *me*.
> The code puzzled us as well as *him*.

The first two constructions are clumsy and appear mostly in grammar textbooks. In casual speech many literate people now say, "John Carradine is thinner than me"—unless they are thinner than John Carradine. Conventionally, *than* is supposed to connect two clauses, with the pronoun following as the subject of a verb understood ("John Carradine is thinner than I am"), but many people think of *than* as a preposition that should be followed by an object. There is no innate reason why *than* cannot be a preposition; it is for usage to decide; and the reader can be cautious or relaxed, suiting his grammar to the occasion.

Traditionally, *like* is a preposition and not a conjunction. Today it often appears as the latter ("Let's all sing like the birdies sing"); but when it is more correctly used as a preposition, it is followed by the objective case. ("He doesn't look a bit like me.") Here an obsession with grammatical correctness often leads the half-educated to confuse *like* with the conjunction *as* and say, "He looks like I," which merely sounds affected:

> So be like I,
> Hold your head up high,
> You will find the bluebird of happiness.

All you really find is an awkward rhyme.

¶ TO WHOM IT MAY CONCERN

In a Washington phone booth, under the sign, "Who Shall I call First?" someone wrote, "An English teacher." Traditional grammar calls for *whom* as the object of the verb, but this tradition is rapidly breaking down. When an interrogative pronoun appears as the opening word of a question, *who* has become the customary form to use except in formal occasions. Not even the most fastidious grammarian, if his daughter shouted that she saw a weird face peering in the kitchen window, would answer, "Whom did you see?" Bergen Evans claims there is a basic vulgarity to "Whom are you talking about?" In such a situation *whom* sounds too calculated and betrays an affected snobbishness, like the false elegance in a modest backyard of cast-iron dogs and flamingos. The semi-literate snob is apt to think that *whom* is invariably preferable and to use it indiscriminately or when he wishes to make an impression. "So I gave him a haughty look and I said, 'Whom do you think you are, anyways?' " [2] This sort of speech is about as aristocratic as Mamie Mullins in the comic strip. As James Thurber wrote satirically, " 'Whom' should be used in the nominative case only when a note of dignity or austerity is desired. . . . To address a person one knows by a 'Whom are you?' is a mark either of incredible lapse of memory or inexcusable arrogance." [3]

Who has become practically universal as an interrogative pronoun, even when it is the object of a verb or preposition. Thus if someone said, "We're going to stake the vampires next," his companion might ask, "The who?" "The whom?" sounds comically affected. When someone asks, "Tell who off?" the pronoun seems the right choice. "So who do they get to be the baby sitter? Me, that's who." In this colloquial context *whom* would be so unnatural as to call attention to itself. Henry James's "whom the deuce I did know" is incongruous, with the grammatically fastidious *"whom"* being followed by the slang *"the deuce."*

In common usage, then, *whom* is weakening except after prepositions ("He is the man *to whom* I was talking." "Stanley, a brown, black, and white basset hound, is the mascot of the Betas, *with whom* he has resided for the past two and a half years"). In conversation one is likely to avoid such constructions. ("He is the man I was talking to.") Even after *to, whom* is barely holding its own. In *Catch-22,* when Yossarian explained that he gave away all the fruit juice and dried fruit he got from the mess hall, " 'To who?' cried Milo, in a voice cracking with dismay." [4] Elizabethan English was rather freewheeling in its use of *who* and *whom.* Shakespeare could write "To who?"; and the translators of the King James Bible have Jesus say, "Whom say ye that I am?" Today the English language shows some disposition to get rid of *whom* altogether, and unquestionably it would be a better language without it. French has gotten along for centuries with *qui* for both cases (*Qui va là? A qui avez-vous donné le chat noir?*).

As it is, *whom* causes only confusion. Norman Mailer has fun with it when he writes: "But there is a tool of investigation for political mysteries. It is Lenin's formula: 'Whom?' Whom does this benefit? Who prospers from a particular act? Well, whom? . . . Whom? asked Lenin, who benefits?" [5] You sometimes hear someone say, "What are the choices for dessert, and what would whom like?" You read in the paper, "Major Gagarin, whom the Soviets say has orbited the globe safely, is shown with his wife." But in both of these examples *whom* should be changed to *who,* for it is the subject of a verb; and though *who* is becoming acceptable for *whom,* the reverse is not true.

"Whom should he meet but Mr. MacGregor," sounds neatly old-fashioned; and when you see Charlton Heston as El Cid, battered and bloody after hand-to-hand combat, gasping, "To whom does the city belong now?" you know you are hearing the stilted dialogue of a Hollywood epic. "Who's shooting who?" Thurber asked in one of his final stories.[6] "Who do you love, I hope?" sings Annie

Oakley in *Annie Get Your Gun*. "Who would you vote for?" asks a UPI wire. "Hayley Mills is very particular about who she goes out with," one reads. "Who do you call at General Tel?" asks an ad. "Amateur genealogist wonders who he'll find in his family tree," appears in *Life*.[7] "Historically, in the West, who has taken advantage of who?" asks Glendon Swarthout.[8] "Tracking would be easier if the Comrade General would explain exactly who he is after," says a character in Mark Rascovich's *The Flight of the Dancing Bear*. *Mad* prints a "What to Buy Who" questionnaire. Television programs are called *Who Do You Trust?* and *Who Do You Kill?* One might protest that these are not very literary examples, but they indicate widespread usage. Besides, grammar isn't everything. If someone asks, "Who do you kill?" you have other things to worry about than the case of the pronoun.

If a person deliberates too much about which pronoun to use in conversation, he sounds bookish and formal. In a relaxed atmosphere it is better not to worry whether a grammatical slip is showing. But for carefully written prose, you should know the established practice; you can then decide whether or not to use it as the context requires.

Most *who* and *whom* errors occur with infinitives or in parenthetical constructions, where it is not immediately clear if the pronoun is used as subject or object. There is no difficulty with "That is the doctor *who* made the monster." If a parenthetical clause like "they claim" is added, the pronoun is still the subject of the verb: "That is the man *who*, they claim, made the monster." Such parenthetical clauses do not affect the function of the pronoun, but a careless or uncertain writer is apt to become confused and alter *who* to *whom*.

WRONG CASE	EXPLANATION	CORRECTION
The man *whom* I hear is an excellent pianist also plays the flugelhorn.	Pronoun is the subject of *is* and requires the subjective case.	The man *who*, I hear, is an excellent pianist also plays the flugelhorn.
He is the teacher *whom* the students say gives the roughest exams.	Pronoun is the subject of *gives* and requires the subjective case.	He is the teacher *who*, the students say, gives the roughest exams.
Give the shakuhachi to the one *whom* you think plays it best.	Pronoun is the subject of *plays* and requires the subjective case.	Give the shakuhachi to the one *who* you think plays it best.

Whoever and *whomever* follow the same rule as *who* and *whom* but are often confused when they follow a preposition or a transitive verb and seem to be objects. In "Give it to whomever you will," the objective case is needed; but in "Read it to whoever will listen," the pronoun functions as the subject of *will listen,* rather than as the object of *to*; the complement of the preposition is the entire clause, "whoever will listen."

WRONG CASE	EXPLANATION	CORRECTION
Move *whomever* is in the way.	Pronoun is the subject of *is*; entire clause is object of *move*.	Move *whoever* is in the way.
The sergeant gives KP to *whomever* finishes last.	Pronoun is the subject of *finishes*; entire clause is object of *to*.	The sergeant gives KP to *whoever* finishes last.

Overconcern about *who* and *whom* can lead people to use *whom* when they shouldn't. This is not sanctioned by contemporary usage and is simply a grammatical flaw. Though Wilson Follett is sometimes unsound in his denunciation of *Webster's Third New International Dictionary,* he objects legitimately to its apparent approval of *whom* and *whomever* as subjects: " (a . . . recruit whom he hoped would prove to be a crack salesman) (people . . . whom you never thought would sympathize) . . . (I go out to talk to whomever it is) . . . (he attacked whomever disagreed with him)." Usage could make these forms standard; but it has not yet done so, and they remain errors to be avoided.

¶ POSSESSIVE CASE

The possessive, or genitive, case is used to indicate possession ("The wombat burrowed under *Bligh's* floor." "He put greasy kid stuff on *his* hair") and modification ("all in the *day's* work," "a *month's* rent"). The best solution would be to abolish the apostrophe altogether; but as long as it's still in operation, one should know how to use it:

A singular noun forms the possessive by adding an apostrophe and -*s*: *aardvark, aardvark's habitat.*

EXCEPTION: If a noun of more than one syllable already ends in -*s*, one may add an apostrophe only: *fortress, fortress' gate.*

WARNING: If a noun ends in *-s,* put the apostrophe after the *-s,* not before it. Correct: Henry *Adams'* (or *Adams's*) house. Incorrect: Henry *Adam's* house.

A plural noun ending in *-s* forms the possessive by adding an apostrophe only: *bears, bears'* den.

A plural noun not ending in *-s* adds an apostrophe and *-s: women, women's* hats.

These rules could be simplified into one; if a noun, singular or plural, ends in *-s,* then add an apostrophe only to form the possessive; if it does not end in *-s,* then add an apostrophe and *-s.* If possession is indicated by the preposition *of* (a periphrastic possessive —"*The Bride of Frankenstein,*" "a reunion of the Coopers"), the objective rather than the possessive case is used. (Wrong: "a reunion of the Coopers' "; Even more wrong: "a reunion of the Cooper's.")

Personal and relative pronouns do not use an apostrophe in the possessive case; thus *our's, her's, their's, your's, you're, it's,* and *who's* are wrong. The first four do not properly exist; *you're, it's,* and *who's* are contractions for *you are, it is,* and *who is.* Sometimes small children form faulty possessives by analogy: "Yours is the green towel, and mines is the pink one." There are also the semiliterate variants of possessive pronouns—*his'n, ourn, hisself*—and Southerners have a problem with the possessive for *you all,* which is rendered variously as *you all's, your all, your all's* ("I forgot to bring your all's desserts"). Here the solution is to drop the *all* and change "Your all's eggs are ready" to "Your eggs are ready," although if one insists on using *you all, your all's* is probably the correct possessive.

The only difficult rule is the one that requires the use of the possessive case for a noun or pronoun modifying a gerund. (A gerund is a present participle used as a noun.) Thus, "She didn't like *him* being late," calls for the possessive case. She may have liked him quite well; what she objected to was the being late. Whose being late? *His* being late. If, however, the participle is used to modify the noun or pronoun, then the latter takes the objective case.

PARTICIPLE AS A MODIFIER	PARTICIPLE AS A GERUND
Strether found Chad having tea.	Strether was disturbed by Chad's refusing to come home.
I'm glad to see you doing your homework.	I admired your speaking up.

90

In such instances colloquial usage is more and more gaining ascendency and usually abandons this rule, putting the modifier in the objective case. ("I don't like you working at night.") Thus Truman Capote writes, "You can love somebody without it being like that." [9] Both the possessive case before a gerund and the subjective *who* are neatly illustrated in the following sentence (italics mine): "The colonel was insecure about Milo because other colonels were trying to lure him away and Colonel Cathcart still had that lousy Big Chief White Halfoat in his group *who* that lousy, lazy, Captain Black claimed was the one really responsible for the bomb *line's* being moved during the Big Siege of Bologna."[v 10]

Sometimes an author may deliberately violate standard usage to create a desired effect, as in the reverse snobbery of the Tareyton ad. A better example appears in John Osborne's *Luther*:

MARTIN: Father, why do you hate me being here?
HANS: Eh? What do you mean? I don't hate you being here.[11]

The father is an uneducated man who has sent his son to the university at great sacrifice and resents his becoming a monk. Here Osborne uses the objective case with the gerund, to have Martin and his father speak colloquially as they would at home. In addition, Martin really feels his father may hate *him* (for) being in the monastery; and the father's answer also includes this double meaning. This example is rather far removed from the Tareyton ad but shows the difference between a commercially contrived solecism and the careful use of a nonstandard form for artistic purposes.

Occasionally an awkward situation arises, such as "The president of the university's son's wife's dog just dug up our petunias. What shall I do?" The only way out of this jumble is to rephrase the entire sentence, preferably forgetting about academic connections, or more simply to take the dog home and replant the petunias. Another puzzler occurred when a critic wanted to explain the title of Fellini's movie "8½." It couldn't have been Fellini's eight and a halfth film, so it must have been his eighth and a half.

¶ FALSE POSSESSIVES

Sometimes modifiers, especially proper names ending in *-s*, are mistaken for possessives and adorned with needless apostrophes:

Hjalmar Hjalmarson was naturalized a United States' citizen.
Lester Cholmondeley is a distinguished General Motors' executive.
A Henry Adams' scholar.
A Scribner Modern Standard Authors' book.

None of these examples have any idea of personal possession, and the apostrophe should be dropped. *United States, General Motors, Adams, Authors* are used as adjectives, like *news* in *news item* or *mathematics* in *mathematics professor*. Likewise there is no apostrophe needed in *Highways Department* or *Public Works Administration*; and the apostrophe is often omitted from *Lions, Odd Fellows,* and *Elks Club.*

¶ POSSESSIVES WITH TITLES

Certain royal and ecclesiastical titles are preceded by a possessive pronoun. Kings and queens are addressed as *your majesty* or *your highness,* dukes and duchesses as *your grace,* bishops and archbishops, as *your excellency,* cardinals as *your eminence,* patriarchs as *your beatitude,* the pope as *your holiness.* In the third person, they are referred to as *his highness, his holiness,* and so forth. When in 1876 the Republican politicians, through bribery and forgery, changed twelve electoral votes to give the Presidency to Rutherford B. Hayes, the Democrats referred to Hayes as "His Fraudulency."

¶ PARALLEL POSSESSIVES

"You or your family's hands cast in glowing pewter—a decorative and personal gift." A unique gift indeed; the only question is where to store you, but perhaps the delighted recipient can place you at the door as a pewter footman. To avoid such awkwardness, put both parts of the parallel construction in the same case (Your hands or your family's cast in glowing pewter . . .). Otherwise, you might end up as the missing *corpus delicti* in the perfect crime.

Exercise 5: Put in the blank the correct substitute for any error in the case of a noun or pronoun.

1. One circus performer had a friend whom, he said, could flap his arms and fly off like an eagle.   . . . .

2. The rabbit wasn't hers; it was her brother. . . . .
3. At the door, the princess saw the frog, whom she had quite forgotten. . . . .
4. "Whom did it?" Snoop asked Blabber. . . . .
5. That evening Dad took Mom and I to see *Frankenstein Meets the Wolf Man*. . . . .
6. The girls who were making accusations as to whom the witches were, did so to escape being accused themselves. . . . .
7. It seemed as if his fate were controlled by he himself. . . . .
8. Martin states that certain traits show whom is a barbarian. . . . .
9. They invited his wife and him to the beach party. . . . .
10. This turtle may be symbolic of the Joad family, around who Steinbeck centers his story. . . . .
11. What will you do in the event of Arnold leaving? . . . .
12. We are set back, but have no fear that us will rally. . . . .
13. I hope you don't mind me interrupting. . . . .
14. Us Star Plug chewers would rather bite than spit. . . . .
15. May and she went to the Museum of Natural History. . . . .
16. "Quick," hissed the hunchback; "run the current through it's electrodes." . . . .
17. A large bat fluttered by Helen and I. . . . .
18. Jean Valjean was sentenced to five years imprisonment for stealing a loaf of bread. . . . .
19. As a prisoner, Jean Valjean spent nineteen years in the galley's. . . . .
20. Two members—Eugene and me—were initiated into the Abner Bibberman fan club. . . . .
21. Whose playing a transistor radio during the concert? . . . .
22. Fenimore took an instructors position in the Arizona Veterinary College. . . . .
23. The ranger didn't like them cutting the rhododendrons. . . . .
24. Kathy admires Julian Breams adaptation of Ravels "Pavane for a Dead Princess." . . . .
25. Presley has more old volume's of *National Geographic* than most doctors offices do. . . . .

Exercise 6: In the following sentences, choose the appropriate pronoun case.

1. One of the most important things in schools is the opportunity to talk to those who know more than (I, me). . . . .
2. You don't have perforating fingernails like (I, me). . . . .
3. The dispossessed farmers wanted to fight somebody, but (who, whom) could they fight?

93

4. "Junior, (who, whom) are you playing with in there?" said the mother kangaroo. . . . .
5. He was seen with a girl (who, whom) he said was his cousin. . . . . .
6. I like music according to (whom, who) is performing. . . . .
7. Bring your friend, (whoever, whomever) she is. . . . .
8. I like to know (who, whom) I'm talking to. . . . .
9. We observe the failure of individual initiative in the face of (he, him) who is bigger. . . . .
10. Ivan the Terrible, (who, whom) everybody thought was dying, rose wrathfully from his bed. Moral: Never think dead of the ill. . . . .
11. The person who picked the rattlesnake orchids should be ashamed, (whosoever, whomsoever) he may be. . . . .
12. I want to make certain of (who, whom) I'm dating. . . . .
13. Here are two perfectly good cups of coffee for (whoever, whomever) wants them. . . . .
14. This is a perfect day for Don and (I, me) to climb Mt. LeConte. . . . .
15. After H. G. Wells's attack, there was no chance for a reconciliation between Henry James and (he, him). . . . .
16. The personnel director ruled that all seasonal employees except (we, us) experienced ones must be available from June 1 to Labor Day. . . . .
17. (Who, whom) do you think was killed in more movies—John Carradine or Basil Rathbone? . . . .
18. Does it come in anything except pressurized cans? I get nervous about (them, their) exploding. . . . .
19. Was it (they, them) (who, whom) the skunk had sprayed? . . . .
20. The buffet was prepared by two members—Mrs. Cooper and (I, me). . . . .
21. Do you know (who, whom) invented the Franklin stove? . . . .
22. Julie gives a kiss to (whoever, whomever) buys a bond. . . . .
23. The boat needs caulking, and (it's, its) bottom should be scraped. . . . .
24. The doctor told Boris and (I, me) to meet him at the deserted mill. . . . .
25. The burgomeister told (we, us) men to take torches and search the woods. . . . .

8 √ The Wayward Verb

No other part of speech causes so many mistakes, misunderstandings, mutterings, and such general mayhem as the verb. Even pronouns are tame by comparison. Nouns are simple; adjectives and adverbs, even simpler; but verbs, though slightly streamlined since Anglo-Saxon days, still have the most complex forms of any words. Functionally, verbs indicate the central action or essential being of their subject; they state what the subject does ("Cats *chase* rats") or what its condition is ("Achilles *is* dead." "Things *are* not what they *seem*"). They also indicate tense, person, number, mood, and voice. All of these functions have their own forms, either by inflectional endings or changed vowel stems. These various forms of a verb are called its *conjugation*. Thus innumerable errors are possible with verbs, and most of them are as widespread and stubborn as the common cold. To shift the metaphor, in an age of zippers, verbs are like the old snap fasteners or hook and eye; many of them are apt to be missed or to come undone when you are in a hurry. Of all the parts of speech, verbs are the most academic; yet English, as she is spoke in the vernacular, is a very unacademic language, governed by habit and not by learning. Habit operates with a minimum of conscious effort. With the verb there are so many variations to keep in mind, so many formalities to observe and choices to make that some people, instead of taking deliberate aim, give up altogether and fire at random: "If I would of knew verbs was so hard, I might could have give them more attention."

¶ PRESENT TENSE

Let us first look at the verb in its simplest form. The dictionary entry is the infinitive, which is usually the stem for the present tense; it may appear with or without *to*: *to laugh* or *laugh*. The

95

present tense (except for the verb *to be*) uses the infinitive without inflection except for the third person singular. (*I laugh, you laugh, he laughs, we laugh, they laugh.*) The third person singular adds an *-s* to the stem, except for the verbs *to be* and *to have*; *haves* is awkward and *has* serves instead. There are two problems in spelling. Verbs ending in *-o* add *-es* (*go—goes*), and those ending in *-y* change the *y* to *i* and add *-es* (*cry—cries, deny—denies*). Verbs *never* form the third person singular by using an apostrophe and *-s*. Wrong: *comply, comply's*.

Older English used different endings for the second and the third person singular; the second person ended in *-st* or *-est* ("thou laughest," "thou hast") and the third person in *-th* or *-eth* ("he hath," "he knoweth"). In Middle English, the first person singular ended in *-e,* and the plurals in *-e* (*n*), but the latter forms had disappeared by the Elizabethan period. During the later Middle Ages, *- (e)s* began to occasionally replace the *-eth* ending in the third person singular. In the English Midlands, *-eth* remained dominant, while *- (e)s* developed in the northern shires. By Shakespeare's time *-eth* or *- (e)s* could be used interchangeably, even in the same sentence. As *Hamlet* opens, Marcellus asks, "Who *hath* reliev'd you? What, *has* this thing appear'd again tonight?" (Italics mine.) At the same time, *you* began to replace *thou* for the second person singular; as it did so, the *- (e)st* ending vanished. Today, *- (e)st* and *-eth* appear only as deliberate archaisms; ministers, seeking to imitate the prose of the King James Bible, often use them though one finds in the King James Bible the more modern forms as well. The present tense causes problems in agreement, but not in form, except for occasional errors in spelling.

¶ TENSION OVER TENSES

It is with the less uniform forms of the other tenses that the difficulties come. In the past tense (or preterit) English has both weak (regular) and strong (irregular) verbs. Most are weak, and form the past tense by adding *-d* or *-ed* to the infinitive (*blame, blamed, want, wanted*). The past tense of weak verbs also serves as the past participle. But many of our most common verbs are strong and form the past tense and past participle by changing the root vowel (*blow, blew, blown; ring, rang, rung*). There are some recurrent patterns in strong verbs; e.g., the *-ow, -ew, -own* forms (*grow, grew, grown; know, knew, known; throw, threw, thrown*) and *-ing, -ang,*

96

-ung; but there are a great many variants and inconsistencies. Some verbs change both vowel and consonant (*seek, sought*; *think, thought*; *will, would*). Some strong verbs are identical in their past tense and past participle (*sit, sat, sat*); others have a different form. A few are called defective, or preterit-present, verbs because they use the same form for both present and past tenses (*ought, must, can, shall, may*). The past of the latter three (*could, should, might*) are used for the conditional present. *Durst*, the older preterit-present of *dare* is now considered nonstandard: "You durst not do it." A few verbs have both strong and weak conjugation.

Obviously there are innumerable possibilities for confusion. It is impossible to rely upon analogy as a foolproof guide to the principal parts of verbs. If we have *lie, lay, lain,* why not *try, tray, train*? If the past of *bring* is *brought,* why shouldn't the past of *ring* be *rought*? In fact, some people reverse this and use *brang* as the past of *bring.* Here are a few more possible but nonexistent analogical forms: *slay, slew, slain—play, plew, plain* ("I plew lacrosse yesterday"); *stand, stood—land, lood* ("I lood the plane safely"); *sit, sat —knit, knat* ("She knat a shawl")—*flit, flat* ("A bug flat against the window")—*quit, quat* ("Herman quat his job"); *strike, struck —like, luck* ("He always luck to have a beer on the way home"); *wind, wound—blind, blound* ("The sun blound him"); *stick, stuck —nick, nuck* ("The bullet *nuck* him")—*prick, pruck* ("The needle pruck her"); *sink, sank, sunk—think, thank, thunk—wink, wank, wunk* ("I wunk at her"); *eat, ate, eaten—beat, bate, beaten* ("He bate her with a broom"); *draw, drew, drawn—saw, sew, sawn* ("I sew a cord of lumber"); *take, took, taken—make, mook, maken* ("She mook a doll")—*bake, book, baken* ("Grandma book a cake"), and so on. These errors are purely imaginary, but show the danger of analogy. People often make strong verbs weak by analogy ("I fell and hurted my knee," "The bug bites bleeded," "The no-see-ums bited me"), but rarely make weak verbs strong. Little children are particularly prone to weaken strong verbs: "My elephant drinked her snurf medicine," "I hanged onto the tree while the bear eated my food." In the Smokies you sometimes encounter a weak verb made strong. A few of these may be archaic holdovers from Elizabethan days, since language tends to make strong verbs weak (e.g., *shined* instead of *shone, dived* instead of *dove*). One North Carolina author claims that "If I'd a-knowed it was you, I'd a-flang out my arm and wove at you" sounds like Chaucer.[1] It sounds more like Snuffy Smith. There is no longer any pure Chau-

cerian or Elizabethan speech remaining in the hills, and this specimen of freewheeling grammar demonstrates the fact.

¶ PRINCIPAL PARTS

Here are the principal parts of the most common irregular verbs:

INFINITIVE AND PRESENT	PAST	PAST PARTICIPLE
be, am, is, are	was, were	been
bear	bore	borne
beat	beat	beaten
begin	began	begun
bite	bit	bitten
bleed	bled	bled
blow	blew	blown
break	broke	broken
bring	brought	brought
build	built	built
burst	burst	burst
cast	cast	cast
catch	caught	caught
choose	chose	chosen
come, become	came, became	come, become
deal	dealt	dealt
dig	dug	dug
dive	dove, dived	dove, dived
do	did	done
drink	drank	drunk
drive	drove	driven
eat	ate	eaten
fall	fell	fallen
find	found	found
flee	fled	fled
fly	flew	flown
forget	forgot	forgotten
forsake	forsook	forsaken
freeze	froze	frozen
get	got	got, gotten
give	gave	given
go	went	gone
grow	grew	grown
hang (suspend)	hung	hung
hang (execute)	hanged	hanged

98

INFINITIVE AND PRESENT	PAST	PAST PARTICIPLE
have	had	had
hear	heard	heard
hold, behold	held, beheld	held, beheld
know	knew	known
lay	laid	laid
lead	led	led
lend	lent	lent
let	let	let
lie	lay	lain
light	lighted, lit	lighted, lit
lose	lost	lost
prove	proved	proved, proven
ride	rode	ridden
ring	rang	rung
rise, arise	rose, arose	risen, arisen
run	ran	run
see	saw	seen
set	set	set
shake	shook	shaken
shine	shone, shined	shone, shined
show	showed	showed, shown
shrink	shrank, shrunk	shrunk
sing	sang	sung
sink	sank, sunk	sunk
sit	sat	sat
slay	slew	slain
slide	slid	slid
slink	slunk	slunk
speak	spoke	spoken
spin	spun	spun
spit	spit, spat	spit, spat
spring	sprang, sprung	sprung
stand	stood	stood
steal	stole	stolen
stink	stank, stunk	stunk
strive	strove, strived	striven, **strived**
swear	swore	sworn
swim	swam	swum
take	took	taken
teach	taught	taught
tear	tore	torn
throw	threw	thrown
tread	trod	trodden, trod

INFINITIVE AND PRESENT	PAST	PAST PARTICIPLE
wake	waked, woke	waked
wear	wore	worn
weave	wove	woven, wove
win	won	won
wind	wound	wound
wring	wrung	wrung
write	wrote	written

¶ EXCEPTIONS AND ERRORS

Though there are several recurrent patterns here, there are so many exceptions that no rules hold. Each set of principal parts must be learned separately, until they become habitual. The trouble is that many people have already formed habits—the wrong ones—that are all the more difficult to change because they are unconscious. No one can stop to weigh each word; if we did, conversation would be as slow as bricklaying. Errors in selecting the right principal part are among the most common and obvious yet most ineradicable examples of nonstandard usage. Perhaps for that reason, grammatical purists or those who use speech as a social measuring rod find them particularly objectionable. The use of *seen* for *saw,* or *throwed* for *threw,* for example, creates no barrier to understanding or any imprecision in meaning. These and other nonstandard inflections may well become standard in time, without in any way corrupting the language. As it is, those who use them could say (if they ever thought about the matter) that they simply have a different set of rules that are valid for them, because standard, in their environment. In the appropriate cultural context, nonstandard verb forms are perfectly acceptable. But this is not so in the world of higher education and business, or of any communication in writing more official than family correspondence or notes to the milkman. Of course, if you are writing fictional dialogue, you should use whatever grammar is appropriate for the speaker. Actually some nonstandard forms have so much character that it is a pity to amend them. Their use accounts for much of the richness of language in *Huckleberry Finn, The Grapes of Wrath,* Faulkner's fiction, and other great works of American literature. Accordingly, let us examine some representative nonstandard practices, so that you can know how to use them or avoid them, as the case may be.

One of the simple errors with the verb *give* is the use of the present for the past tense: "I give him the money yesterday." *Come* is also misused this way ("Uncle Silas come around last Monday"), but this is more likely a result of confusing the past participle with the past tense.

As we have already seen, children and many adults tend to make strong verbs weak by using -*ed* for the past tense and past participle:

> I've teached [taught] everybody how to fight fires.
> My toenails haven't been cutted [cut] for a long time.
> He blowed [blew] his horn both loud and shrill.
> The monkey drawed [drew] my picture so it didn't look like me.
> I seed [saw] a moose a-coming down the road a little piece away.

Sometimes children add a double -*ed* to a weak verb: "I washeded my hands," "The kitten drowneded." Sometimes the strong form of the verb appears with an -*ed* tacked on, making it doubly past: "I founded the map," "I was borned and raised in Cataloochee," "Last week in the course of two hours it blewed and snowed and friz." And occasionally you encounter a weak verb used with -*ed* but with the root vowel changed: "That horse trompled [trampled] me," "It holped [helped] a man not to be beholden to nobody." And the standard instruction for weaving patterns is the archaic "Tromp as writ," instead of "Tramp as written." Though the tendency of linguistic change is to make irregular verbs regular, there are a few strong verbs that once had weak endings. Seventeenth-century authors could write, "We had builded our houses," and *The Book of Common Prayer* speaks of "language understanded of the people." One ancient form, though labeled dialect, is persistent: Articles purchased from a store (usually clothes) are always "store-boughten," never—or almost never—store-bought.

It is less common for a weak verb to be treated like a strong one, but it sometimes happens in error or in jest; e.g., "He clumb [climbed] on his horse," "It holpt [helped] to keep the varmints out," "Cal clen [cleaned] the stable," "I should have stood [stayed] in bed," and "Who thunk [thought] the skunk stunk?"

One of the most common and noticeable errors is the use of the past participle for the past tense of strong verbs. Most frequently substituted are the past participles *been, seen, done, come, gone* for the past tenses *was, saw, did, came,* and *went.* Since these verbs are five of our most necessary words, habitual errors in the use of their principal parts occur with damning regularity: Thus it is considered semiliterate to say, "I never seen nothing in these here hug dances," "The girls in our family done all the grinding," "They done it themselves," "I been sick," "The preacher come yesterday." Perhaps the speakers meant to use the present perfect tense and simply omitted the auxiliary—"I've been sick"—but in any event the grammar needs revising. *Whodunit,* frequently used as a slang noun for mystery novels, owes its popularity to the conscious humor of its gumshoe grammar.

Again, people sometimes mistakenly use the past tense for the past participle, particularly with the verb *go.* You hear in jest, "My get-up-and-go has got up and went" (never *gone,* the required past participle), but similar statements occur in nonstandard speech; e.g., "We should of went across that bridge," "I was shook up when I found a tarantula in my boot," "It might have fell out," "If I would of knew it was so far, I would of stayed home." Apart from other errors—especially the use of *of* for *have*—these sentences need *gone, shaken, fallen,* and *known.* Occasionally someone plays it safe (and is doubly wrong) by using both the past tense and past participle, instead of a perfect tense construction: "That crow's done gone and went." Often the final *-n* of a strong past participle is dropped in nonstandard speech: "Beef cut and froze" or the memorable "The dam has broke!" from James Thurber's *My Life and Hard Times.*

One verb has caused international friction. In American English, *get* has two past participles, *got* and *gotten,* whereas during the eighteenth century the English dropped *gotten* and have since used *got* almost exclusively, though *gotten* has occasionally reared its ugly head through the influence of American books and films. Neither side is right or wrong; each country's usage is perfectly valid at home. But temperamental and inaccurate British writers insisted for a long time that Americans never say *got,* that to use *gotten* exclusively is an identifying mark of the Yankee. Thus some British fiction writers made their American characters speak quite absurdly and inaccurately. Though we have both past participles, they are not interchangeable, even if there are no definite rules governing the choice of one over the other. The distinction is partly idiomatic and partly a matter of emphasis and rhythm. *Got* has dozens of different meanings in England; when it appears in the sense of *become,* we tend to prefer *gotten:* "I've gotten sick every January for the past ten years." When it means *have* or is used to intensify *have,* we prefer *got:* "I've got a cold," "Have you got the

102

answer?" Thus, the American in British fiction who says, "I've gotten an idea," sounds fake.

¶ PERFECT TENSES AND IMPERFECT AUXILIARIES

The past participle is combined with the appropriate form of the auxiliary verb *have* to form the perfect tenses. The present perfect indicates an action or condition completed past action ("I have done the deed") or past action extending into the present time ("I have forgotten"). The past perfect indicates action or condition completed or existing before the time stated or implied in the sentence ("He had swallowed the drink before he realized it was poison"). The future perfect indicates an action or condition that will have been completed in relation to some time in the future ("We shall have traveled 10,000 miles by the end of summer"). The auxiliaries used are *has* and *have* for the present perfect tense, *had* for the past perfect, and *shall have* for the future perfect. This seems simple enough, yet confusion reigns, resulting in much nonstandard practice. Because *have* is often contracted to *'ve,* pronounced *uv* with conditional verbs ("I might've," "they could've"), many people mistakenly use *of* for the auxiliary verb. In slurred speech it is difficult to tell whether *have* or *of* is used, but the error is obvious when *of* is written for the verb in student themes. Fiction writers like Mark Twain or John Steinbeck deliberately use *of* as an auxiliary in dialogue to show illiteracy. (Sometimes they prefer *a:* "You'd a thought so.") In more conventional writing, "I might of gone," "He should of read the assignment," "I wish you would of danced with me" stand out like flies in the soup. A cure might be to make students guilty of this practice write a hundred times, "I *of* eaten my spinach," and "I *of* gone."

The genuine semiliterate wastes none of his opportunities but combines as many errors as possible in any one sentence. Thus he will use *of* as a verb with the wrong principal part ("We could of went to the Whipsnade Zoo, but we seen the Tate Gallery instead"). Another favorite illiteracy is the use of several auxiliaries together, most of them wrong. A popular error is the use of *done* for *have,* as in the folk song "Another Man Done Gone." Again, *done* and *did* appear erroneously to reinforce *have* (or the substandard *of*) in such constructions as, "We've done left Grandpappy to be et by the wolves" and "The boys have done finished the work." Here *done* is useless and should be cut. *Is,* likewise, does not qualify as an acceptable auxiliary when it is used as part of the perfect tense. In the passive voice, *is* functions with the past participle to form the present tense ("He is hurt"), but *is* must be replaced by *have* in "My arches is fallen" and by *has* in "This is got to be my last game." Colloquial English sometimes uses *got* as a passive auxiliary ("I got bug-bit," "Walt got hit by a car"), but *was* or *has been* are preferable in informal and formal style alike. *Got* is superfluous, but may be defended if it makes the auxiliary emphatic.

In conditional perfect constructions, redundancies abound. *Might could* and *might would* are idiomatic in some regions: "I might could make some molasses." It seems that *might could* means *maybe I could,* as in "I thought she might could cry." In this instance, the only valid objection is that the phrase is a limited regionalism. But there are numerous other cases where multiple auxiliaries are sheer dead wood, like *had* in "You had ought to mend the fence." "You didn't ought to have let that fire out," says Piggy in William Golding's *Lord of the Flies*; the standard form is *ought not.* "They shouldn't had ought not to of done it" is riddled with errors, including redundancy; "They shouldn't have done it" is accurate and concise. Sometimes the whole construction needs to be changed: "I used to could touch my toes" requires the infinitive, "I used to be able to touch my toes." The first has a commendable brevity, but is nonstandard.

Conditional constructions seem particularly troublesome in introductory subordinate clauses. "Did I of known, I would of said something" not only misuses *of* but has an extra word; "Had I known, I would have said something" is correct. Sometimes *did* is misused for an introductory *if,* as in "Did I could, I would take the car." These examples are somewhat exaggerated but a common error in student writing is the use of *would have been* instead of the concise *had been*: "If these actions would have been [had been] done, we could have succeeded." "If I would have known [had known] it was so far, I would have stayed home." In short, be precise and never use a useless auxiliary verb.

¶ FUTURE TENSE

Most people, if asked how English expresses future time, would say that it uses the future tense, combining the appropriate form of

104

shall and *will* as an auxiliary with the infinitive: *I shall be late*; *The time will come.* Actually there are many other ways to indicate futurity. Some languages, like Latin and French, have a whole set of special verb endings for the future tense. English dispenses with these and relies upon a variety of expressions. Often we use the present tense, modified by an adverbial phrase, to show habitual action or future condition:

> I go to Washington next Monday.
> The ship sails next week.
> Christmas comes on Friday this year.

We also use the progressive present:

> I am going to propose to Sophie.
> We are vacationing in the Caribbean next summer.
> Jethro is coming next week.
> Are you going to the Hallowe'en party?

The infinitive can be used to express the future: "There is to be a church picnic." And we can even use the past tense to express futurity: "It's time we *went* home."

Many teachers ignore these devices and concentrate on *shall* and *will*. Generations of schoolchildren have puzzled over the distinction between them and have been browbeaten into believing the rule that in declarative sentences, to express simple futurity *shall* is used in the first person and *will* in the second and third persons, and to express determination these auxiliaries are reversed, with *will* used in the first person and *shall* in the second and third persons. But few people, including grammarians, follow this edict with any consistency. It is ironic that perhaps the best-known grammar rules are the three least important or valid ones: *shall* vs. *will*, and the prohibitions against splitting an infinitive and against ending a sentence with a preposition. The half-educated pedant who knows no other grammar expounds these as dogma. To him they are the hallmarks that distinguish the "cultured" person from the peasant. Actually this discrimination is moribund and was never really alive to begin with. Like the Frankenstein monster, it is an artificial creation. In Elizabethan English there was no inflexible difference, though *shall* was more common for the first person and was sometimes used for determination, as in Horatio's urging Hamlet, "You shall not go, my lord." *Will* appears indiscriminately in sixteenth-

and early seventeenth-century writing. But in 1653, the British mathematician John Wallis, who wrote in Latin under the name Johannis Wallis, formulated in *Grammatica Linguae Anglicanae* the quite arbitrary edict about the use of *shall* and *will*. It was not based upon actual usage; it became a rule only because Wallis so proclaimed it. Eighteenth-century grammarians, devoted to authority, hardened this decree into dogma; and subsequent teachers and editors did their best to enforce it. The few realistic linguists, such as Joseph Priestley, who criticized Wallis's unrealistic ruling were dismissed as eccentrics. Priestley was a religious heretic anyhow, so his challenge to grammatical authority was simply a further indication of his unregenerate state. Thus argued the academicians, though they failed to follow the so-called "rule" themselves.

There is an old, apocryphal, and oft-repeated story of a Scot, thrashing around in a mill pond, who cried, "I will drown, and nobody shall save me." Because of his future auxiliaries, bystanders thought he was determined to drown and so made no attempt to rescue him. Had he said, "I shall drown, and nobody will save me," someone might have thrown him a lifeline. This is an overly subtle distinction, unjustified by actual usage. Benjamin Franklin wrote in one proverb, "He that lieth down with dogs, shall rise up with fleas"; in another, "He that falls in love with himself, will have no rivals." Today *shall* is rarely used in declarative sentences; it sounds artificial and self-conscious except when it is used for a first-person question: "Shall we dance?" "Shall I see who's at the door?" "Shall I pick you up at eight?" *Will* here would be out of place, though either *will* or *shall* can sometimes be used in first-person questions: "Will I see you tomorrow?" In general speech, *will* is used without regard to person; it sounds affected to say, "I shall take the clothes to the cleaners." *Shall* still occurs with some frequency after *we* to avoid the repetitive *w* of *we will* if the stress is on the subject: "We shall see." If the auxiliary verb is stressed, *will* is more common: " 'Be on time.' 'We *will*.' " Usually people use the contraction *'ll* ("*I'll do it*," "*He'll give it to you*"), making it impossible to tell if the verb is *shall* or *will*. *Shall* is appropriate for the fastidious Prufrock's "I shall wear white flannel trousers and walk upon the beach," but most people say, "I'll be down to getcha in a taxi, honey." Legal statements still require *shall*: "The author shall receive ten percent." As for the negative contraction *shan't,* it sounds overfastidious and outdated as if it belonged to a day when boys had their hair in ringlets and wore Lord Fauntleroy suits.

106

There is nothing wrong with *shan't* as a word, but it has the wrong connotations.

The conditional future is expressed by combining the auxiliary verb *should* or *would* with the infinitive: "I would like to visit Tahiti." Fastidious writers and speakers are fond of using *should* with the first person and of choosing the conditional tense, instead of the present, as a sign of courtesy. We might call this practice the polite oblique; instead of saying, "I want a drop of sherry," one says, "I should like a drop of sherry." It is possible to be too oblique. "Will you marry me?" is preferable to "I should like to inquire whether you should find that you can marry me." Though this is an extreme example, too many *shoulds* hedge a statement, making it sound hesitant and a bit slithery. In general speech, *should* is weakening except in the sense of *ought to*: "We should get the TV set repaired."

After this lengthy discussion, you may suddenly start to wonder whether you use *shall* and *will, should* and *would* correctly. For all practical purposes there is no reason for you to be concerned. The few real distinctions are idiomatic and come naturally; any others are artificial and nonessential.

¶ TENSE SEQUENCE

It is necessary to be consistent in using tenses; never use a different tense to express the same time. Students writing papers about some past-tense narrative often shift back and forth from the past to the historical present: "When Goodman Brown *goes* into the forest, he *met* varius figures who *reveal* to him the hypocrisy of his society. The climax *came* when Brown *realizes* that his wife Faith *is* at the witches' sabbath. He *urged* her to resist the devil, whereupon the scene *disappears*. Brown *was* so thoroughly disillusioned that he *becomes* an embittered misanthrope and *condemned* all mankind as corrupt." This shifting of tenses is quite disconcerting; either the past or the historical present might have been used successfully, but there must be no vacillation between the two.

Often a sentence requires the use of more than one tense. In the sentence, "Alfred *forgot* that the earth *is* the third planet from the sun," the second verb must be put in the present tense, *is*, to show that its subject is in a continuing or present state of existence; *was* makes it seem as if the earth were no longer the third planet from the sun. Thus whatever is true at the time of writing calls for the present tense, no matter what other tenses may be used in the sentence: e.g., "Horpington *wondered* why the ninth month *is* [not *was*] called September."

Conditional constructions require a use of the conditional tense consistent with sense. "Eisenhower *said* he *will* go to Korea to end the war" is wrong. What Eisenhower said was, "I will go to Korea." The indirect statement should be "Eisenhower *said* that he *would* go. . . ."

Finally, use common sense. "We hope the New Year *will be* as kind to you as it *has been* to us" is nonsensical. Last year may have been kind, but the New Year has just begun for both you and us.

¶ THE MOODY SUBJUNCTIVE

Besides person, number, and tense, verbs have mood and voice. Verbs are most frequently used in the indicative mood: this mood indicates what occurs or take place factually. The imperative mood is used for commands ("Nay, answer me," "Stand and unfold yourself"), instructions ("Go, bid the soldiers shoot"), and requests ("Get thee to a nunnery"). In form, it is the infinitive without *to* (e.g., "Hurry! Please hurry and help him!" and may be used with or without a subject ("You come right here!" "Come here!"). It is often considered that it is used only in the second person present tense, but it can be used with the first person plural as well ("Well, sit we down, And let us hear Bernardo speak of this"). There are no grammatical difficulties connected with the imperative, so don't worry about it.

The subjunctive mood, on the other hand, does pose difficulties, partly because most people have never heard of it. Accordingly, the subjunctive is disappearing, though certain uses linger in our speech. Latin has an elaborate subjunctive—a complete conjugation that matches each tense of the indicative. Old English also had an involved subjunctive, and we are well rid of it. Today the subjunctive forms of the verb *to be* are used for all numbers and persons: *be* for the present (*I be*) and *were* for the other tenses (*he were*). The subjunctive is still used to express possibility (*"if it be true"*), hypothesis (*"if Pogo were President"*), wish (*"if only El Kabong were there"*), improbability (*"if Marjorie Main were playing Hamlet"*), and condition contrary to fact (*"if the earth were flat"*). As you see, it is often introduced by *if* (or *though* or some other conditional word). Some liberal grammarians say that it is being too

108

fastidious to bother with the subjunctive—that it is as obsolete as the farthingale or moustache cups—and it does sound strained in the following translation given in a German auto manual: "Should trouble occur and there *be* no Borgward workshop, care must be taken when carrying out adjustments." (Fortunately the Borgward runs better than this sentence, which has also an awkward use of the passive voice and a dangling modifier.) But it is still non-standard to say "If I was king," instead of the subjunctive "If I were king." (Incidentally, this famous line, the most famous of the French poet François Villon, was not written by Villon at all but by Justin McCarthy in the melodramatic novel that was thus entitled.) Try to imagine Ronald Colman declaiming, "If I was king, ah, love, if I was king," and you get a line as bad as Tony Curtis's "Yonder lies duh castle of duh caliph, my fadduh."

The subjunctive also survives in some idiomatic expressions ("Be that as it may," "Be it ever so humble, there's no place like home"). It is even enshrined in the national anthem: "Thus *be* it ever when freemen shall stand . . ."

Finally, the subjunctive is still used in *that* clauses after verbs like *demand, require, insist, recommend, suggest,* or the phrase *it is necessary that.* ("I demand that *he resign* immediately." "I suggest that *she take* a nap." "It is necessary that *he go* to London.") Informal style would probably turn the latter into "It is necessary for him to go to London." Often we avoid the subjunctive either by using the infinitive (thus "It is impossible that he come" becomes "It is impossible for him to come") or a verbal phrase with *can, may, should,* and *ought* ("If it were to happen" becomes "If it should happen"). But formal parliamentary procedure still requires the subjunctive: "Fogbound moved that Dogpatch be reapportioned," "It was moved and seconded that the bill be sent to committee." You will encounter the subjunctive far more often in the works of older writers than of contemporary ones. Shakespeare's dialogue is full of it:

> If music be the food of love, play on.

> If it be now, 'tis not to come; if it be not to come, it will be now; if it be not now, yet it will come: the readiness is all.

> If Hamlet give the first or second hit,
> Or quit in answer of the third exchange,
> Let all the battlements their ordnance fire. . . .

I'll cross it, though it blast me.
No spirit dare stir abroad. . . .

If this be error and upon me proved,
I never writ, nor no man ever loved.

Samuel Johnson is supposed to have said, when offered refresh-
ment, "If this be coffee, give me tea; if this be tea, give me coffee."
Imitating Shakespeare, scriptwriters for Hollywood epics often
favor a use of the subjunctive, but the result is usually stilted
bombast instead of eloquence. A British critic found the film *Cleopatra* "lavish in subjunctives." James Thurber observed that the
subjunctive "lends itself most easily to ranting and posturing"; but
instead of the affairs of Cleopatra, he wrote a definitive analysis of
the subjunctive as used by a jealous husband and a defensive wife,
who employs such constructions as "Far be it from me" for indignation and hauteur. Rhetorical vacillations from the subjunctive to
the indicative and back again create dangerous misunderstandings.
"Husbands have come to know that a wife's 'if . . . were' usually
means that what she is presenting as purely hypothetical is, in reality, a matter of fact. Thus, if a wife begins, one evening after an
excellent dinner, 'Dear, what would you do, if I were the sort of
woman who had, etc.,' her husband knows full well that it is going
to turn out that she is the sort of woman who has. Husbands are
suspicious of all subjunctives. Wives should avoid them." [2]
Today we find the indicative in many situations that formerly
used the subjunctive. "If he go, I shall perish" sounds archaic; we
would say, "If he goes, I shall perish," or, more likely, something
less melodramatic. In practice, you need not worry about *be*; probably you use *be* habitually in idiomatic phrases; and in others, it is
not essential. The main problem is whether to use *was* or *were* in
conditional clauses. When the sentence states a real condition,
rather than a hypothetical one that is improbable or contrary to
fact, the indicative is called for: "If he was there, he was guilty."
Consider the ad for the movie *The Playgirls and the Vampire:* "She
knew . . . when she felt his lips on her, that there was no other
man for her . . . *if this was a man!*" This is all right because
there is a real alternative, instead of a wish or condition contrary
to fact. In this case, grammar is not the primary concern; the girl
needs a crucifix, holy water, wolfbane, or a stake more than a subjunctive verb.

110

¶ REFLEXIVES WITHOUT REFLEXES

French and German have a number of so-called reflexive verbs—verbs that are conjugated with a reflexive pronoun as direct or indirect object, where we would use none. Whereas we say "go away," the French say *"allez-vous en"*—"go you away." Other similar French reflexive verbs are *se lever* (to get up), *se promener* (to take a walk), *se tromper* (to make a mistake). Contemporary English is fortunately free of this encumbrance, but medieval and Elizabethan English sometimes employed it, as in "Get you gone," "Get thee to a nunnery," and "It likes me well" (meaning "I like it"). Today it still lingers as an archaism in some Southern Appalachian speech, particularly with the verb *happen*:

Hit didn't happen me that I wushed to contrary the revenoors . . .

Hit happens me I don't wush any more bussin' from you.

Pap uster say when the North jumped on the South, his paw just blowed up an' yelled: "Hell is a-hootin' now, an' hit happens me I'm a-jinin' up with the Confedricsy."

In very colloquial usage, we all use a reflexive occasionally, as in "I got me a bargain," or "I got me out of there."

¶ THE PERILOUS PASSIVE

Transitive verbs can be used in either the active or the passive voice. In the active voice, the subject does the action ("The painter dropped a bucket"); in the passive voice the subject is on the receiving end ("Irving was hit by the bucket"). The passive voice is formed by combining the appropriate form of the verb *to be* with the past participle of the transitive verb:

PRESENT	I am hit	PRESENT PERFECT	I have been hit
PAST	I was hit	PAST PERFECT	I had been hit
FUTURE	I shall (or will) be hit	FUTURE PERFECT	I shall have been hit.

Future Perfect Conditional: "After all this, I should have been hospitalized." The passive voice can also be used with infinitives of the verb *to be:* " 'tis a consummation devoutly to be wish'd."

When newspaper headlines, in their clipped style, omit the auxiliary verb in passive constructions ("Six Senators Accused"), you cannot always tell whether the verb is active or passive. Are the senators accusing or being accused? Headliners are so addicted to this practice that they make even active verbs suspect: "George Romney Crowned Webberville Firemen's Oxroast Queen"—as a headline, this causes a double take.

The passive voice is axiomatically less forceful than the active voice and therefore should be used sparingly. The last sentence illustrates an appropriate use; when the verb refers to a general rule or procedure, when the action has an indefinite rather than a specific actor, then the passive voice is suitable. For example, "It's a club rule . . . that any ball swallowed by a goat can be replaced without loss of stroke or distance." [3] The passive voice makes the object of the action into the subject; thus it can be used effectively when the object is to be emphasized at the beginning or when the action is to be emphasized at the end of the sentence. "My appendix is to be removed" is more emphatic than the active "The doctor is going to remove my appendix." "Civil liberties must be defended" is more forceful than "We must defend civil liberties," unless *we* is the word that is intentionally to be stressed. Probably the most familiar passive construction occurs in the sentence, "Dinner is served." Thus when the performer is less important than the performance, the passive may be preferable; e.g., "Let justice be done."

But the passive has a number of potential dangers. Since it reverses the direction of the action, its use in narrative makes sentences crawl backward like the crab. Thus there is a stylistic ricochet in "The rifle was aimed by the marksman who was hidden behind the fence; the trigger was squeezed; the bullet was fired; and the victim was struck in the chest and knocked from his saddle." This sort of thing is less common than the overworked use of the passive in technical and professional writing. In an attempt at objectivity, some engineers, scientists, and businessmen go to absurd lengths to avoid first-person comments; instead of writing *I* or *we,* they resort to passive constructions which often hobble them. "It was decided," "It was discovered," "It is believed," "It has been confirmed," "It is observed," and similar forms have become lifeless stock phrases. Such self-effacement is not only clumsy; it can be evasive, hiding individual thought and responsibility. In fact some of the better scientific magazines have broken the taboo against the first person and now use it when it is appropriate. Scholars in the humanities are less prone to bog their prose down with passives, but they have been frequently guilty, also.

112

A solitary passive now and then causes little deceleration of prose movement, but piled-up passives can be ponderous. The historian C. Vann Woodward uses passives appropriately, but barely manages to escape entanglement in a series of them: "The new Southern system was regarded as the 'final settlement,' the 'return to sanity,' the 'permanent system.' Few stopped to reflect that previous systems had also been regarded as final, sane, and permanent by their supporters. The illusion of permanency was encouraged by the complacency of a long-critical North, the propaganda of reconciliation, and the resigned compliance of the Negro. The illusion was strengthened . . ."[4]

Sometimes the passive voice with its reverse movement, creates needless obscurity: "Care should be taken in assembling the parts that the wires are not left uninsulated and that the screws are all tightened so that no loose connections are left by which malfunctioning can be caused to occur and danger of shock is permitted." Is it not clearer to write, "Insulate the wires and tighten all the screws to prevent malfunctioning or possible shock."

Another danger of the passive is the dangling modifier. "When using it to fight fires, a Pulaski should be kept sharp." In such constructions, the subject (whoever is using the Pulaski) is omitted; the object (the Pulaski) is turned into the subject, and there is no one for the participial modifier (using) to modify. Again, the passive encourages the use of bumbling prepositional phrases—"by the board of directors," "by the administration," "through the proper authorities," "by the driver"—that are better avoided.

Finally, there is sometimes simply a confusion in voice: "The pioneers were abhorred by the Indian way of fighting." An educated Indian, like the Cherokee writer Elias Boudinot, would have abhorred the paleface's prose.

¶ INTRANSITIVES IN TRANSIT

Verbs are classified as transitive or intransitive. Transitive verbs can take a direct object. ("The cook made moose-meat pie.") Intransitive verbs cannot take a direct object, though they may have an indirect one or a modifier as complement. ("The lady vanished." "Don't look at the Gorgon." "I feel bilious.") Obviously, some verbs can function either transitively or intransitively. ("Lord Randall tasted the broth [transitive]; the broth tasted like eels [intransi-

113

tive]." "When Isaac felt his son [transitive], Esau felt hairy" [intransitive].) Verbs like *sing, think, feel, speak* can be either transitive or intransitive. Most verbs can be used without an object, particularly in the progressive form ("I am writing"), but a few require an object, e.g., *carry, bring, lug* ("I'll lug the guts into the neighbor room"). Verbs like *travel, swim, arrive, disagree, succeed, look, complain, grumble, fall* ("The sky is falling!") are always intransitive, as are the various linking verbs. If you want a test for whether a verb is transitive, try to turn it into a passive construction, in which the object becomes the subject. If there is no object, obviously you can't do this. "I clobbered him" can become "He was clobbered," but "Tarzan was swimming" cannot become "It was swum by Tarzan."

Most people couldn't care less whether a verb is transitive or intransitive, and most grammars devote little space to the distinction, except to stress the difference between *lie* and *lay, sit* and *set. Lie* (in either meaning) and *sit* are intransitive and never take an object, while *lay* and *set* are usually transitive, except in a construction like "The sun is setting." Though these pairs are frequently confused, the wrong choice is still considered nonstandard, and they are not interchangeable. *Lay* means to put or set down, and *lie* to recline. Thus you *lay* your cards on the table, but you *lie* on the bed for a nap. One idiomatic exception is with snow; snow may lie on the ground, but you frequently hear "Is the snow laying on the ground?" not "Is the snow lying?" Perhaps the confusion stems in part from the older use of *lay,* with a personal pronoun in the objective case, as in "Now I lay me down to sleep." Without the pronoun, this is unacceptable, as in the sloppy ad for a movie called *The Head:* "It just won't lay down and stay dead!" *Sit* means, in the inimitable words of *Webster's New Collegiate Dictionary,* "1. To rest upon the haunches; to occupy a seat. 2. To perch or roost with the body drawn up close, as birds. . . ." *Set* means primarily to place or to cause to sit. You *set* the chairs in place and then you *sit* on them. A setting hen sits while she sets. This is elementary stuff, but habits are hard to break. Besides the related meaning and similar sound, the words in each pair are further confused by their principal parts.

PRESENT	lie	lay	sit	set
PAST	lay	laid	sat	set
PAST PARTICIPLE	lain	laid	sat	set

114

The present of *lay* is the same as the past of *lie,* and people also confuse the past participles. Actually, although the forms of *lie* are rarely if ever used for *lay,* all forms of *lay* are frequently and mistakenly used to replace *lie.* Once when the editor of a military manual designed to teach English to Germans changed "He laid in bed" to "He lay in bed," the commander ordered him to restore the faulty original, on the grounds that ninety percent of the GI's spoke that way. If these statistics are accurate, *lay* may come to replace *lie;* meanwhile, GI language is not always the best model.

Thanks largely to advertising, there is an increasing use of intransitive verbs in transitive situations. Thought up by some Madison Avenue man with an unbuttoned button-down mind, these are not justified by actual usage; but ubiquitous commercials may brainwash us with their language as well as make us buy Big Brother's detergents and deodorants. Thus we learn that "Pall Mall travels the smoke further," though the smoke does the traveling. Hoover's portable vacuum cleaner "looks and carries like luggage"; apparently, luggage is now its own porter. "The flavor [of Calvert Extra] is rich and full—yet it swallows easy." So beware, lest the drink you are about to swallow gulps you down instead; it has already turned the adverb into an adjective. Maybe you should switch to Nestle's Quick, which "tastes best and fixes easiest." What could be easier than a drink that fixes itself? Perhaps Doom Flakes, which "tastes and eats like a cereal should." Here is one way to avoid indigestion. But then some things "cook smelly and eat good." One ad asks, "Does the bread chew as hard as it tears?" Not if it has good teeth. James Thurber was irritated by this sort of confusion between transitive and intransitive verbs, whereby cars handle and ride well, instead of being handled and ridden. Actually most of these ads use the intransitive to avoid the passive voice. Vacuum cleaners are carried; Calvert is swallowed; Nestle's is fixed; cereal is eaten; things are cooked; bread is chewed; but try converting the admen, and they answer with a masking tape that "sticks immediately, holds securely, and removes cleanly." Thurber wrote sarcastically that his radio "listens fine, and travels and limpids the sound," and that he expected to encounter, "We can sleep twenty people in this house in a pinch, but we can only eat twelve." In fact, the Pennsylvania Dutch say, "Come eat yourself, Henry; Ma's at the table, and Pa's half et." So perhaps there is some precedent. A Southern Appalachian highlander might say, "Hit grumbled the old woman some." When we read that pens load with a cartridge, instead of being loaded, we can find a precedent in muzzle-loaders and breechloaders. Yet you might wonder about a vinyl that "cuts like cloth, looks like leather . . ." Do your vinyl and cloth have a dull blade these days? Perhaps they are like the can that doesn't pour well. Then there is the garment that "walks like a culotte but sits like a skirt." You don't even have to wear it. And why waste time sleeping when you can have "the 'Play-jama' that sleeps like a little girl"? You might also try "soft sleeping foam rollers," since verbals as well as verbs can be confused. As for foam rollers, "Hair that combs is a must."

If you drive through the malodorous town of Canton, North Carolina, you might conclude that Champion Paper cooks smelly and writes good—just the thing for the student who has difficulty with assignments. Of course, the topic counts, but Bob Considine claims that "San Francisco writes pretty easy, whether you're writing about its bridges—Golden Gate and Harry—or its ball club and joints." Photographs may help; Ed Sullivan's pitchgirl Julia Meade says that "Pictures remember but words forget." The only trouble is that you may not remember where you put the pictures. Elephants are better. As for literature, it is good to learn that Joyce Cary is reprinting. Presumably his books are being reprinted too. We need some stimulating literature, since "Textbooks all look and read alike." Perhaps the textbooks are afraid of being censored and of losing their positions. If you feel by now that you're losing your mind, blame it on the advertising copy men who "swarm an idea." If "Friskies chops up easily," so do verbs. The ad that the '63 Chevrolet "rides like a limousine" may remind us of Emerson's complaint, "Things are in the saddle and ride mankind." Let the buyer beware and the writer keep his transitive and intransitive verbs in their proper compartments.

Even among transitive verbs, the correct verb choice is sometimes controversial. *Teach* and *learn* are a case in point. Here the distinction is in meaning; the instructor teaches, and the student learns. Nobody ever uses *teach* for *learn,* but *learn* often replaces *teach* in nonstandard English: "I'll learn you to keep quiet," or the fake rustic, "I'll learn ye, dern ye." Shakespeare used *learn* in this fashion; Hamlet says:

> Our indiscretion sometimes serves us well,
> When our deep plots do pall; and that should learn us
> There's a divinity that shapes our ends,
> Rough-hew them how we will—

116

In time, *learn* will probably become a synonym for *teach,* but at present its misuse is unacceptable in standard practice.

Another pair of verbs often confused are *leave* and *let.* Expressions like "Leave us go home" and "Leave us not be hasty" are all right for cartoon characters but not for standard speech. Such errors occur mostly when *leave* usurps *let's* meaning "allow" or "permit," in constructions with the infinitive. These require *let* in standard English: "Let us be." The ad "Between parties—just let it standing in the center of the dining table—you need no other centerpiece!" needs revision either to "leave it standing" or to "let it stand."

Slang often uses *bust* instead of *burst.* Purists do not consider *bust* a legitimate verb, yet there are two uses where it is not only permissible but necessary. Trusts and broncos are always *busted,* never *burst.* A purist who tried *bronco-bursting* or *trust-bursting* would doubtless get clobbered in either activity.

¶ VERBS VERSUS VERBALS: INFINITIVES

Not all forms of the verb actually function as verbs. Participles and infinitives are incomplete by themselves; they cannot be combined with a subject to make an independent clause. Thus some grammarians call them verbals, or verbids, instead of verbs. It is important to recognize the distinction; students who do not, often write fragmentary sentences under the illusion that they have a verb when all they have is a verbal. "The dog barking outside" is not a sentence; "barking" is a present participle modifying "dog"; it cannot serve as a verb. We shall return to this issue in more detail when we consider sentence structure. Meanwhile, let us consider infinitives and participles. As we have seen, the infinitive is the form given in the dictionary entry. Used with or without *to*— *to sing* or *sing*—it can serve as modifier and as subject or complement of a verb. Modifier: "She felt an urge to scream." Subject: "To err is human; to forgive, divine." Complement: "Captain Vere persuaded the court to convict and sentence Billy Budd." In the last example, the first infinitive (*to convict*) is preceded by *to,* which is not repeated for the second (*sentence*). Pronoun subjects of the infinitive take the objective case: "The commander ordered *them to cease* firing."

There is little chance for error here unless you get the wrong word, such as confusing *sit* for *set* or *light* for *lighten.* Occasionally

117

a whopper turns up. One Southern mountaineer said, "The last time me and Hounddog went we only got us one coot, and hit was so pore we sot hit on a limb and let hit went." [5] *Sot* (for *set*) is pretty good, but *let hit went* (for *go*) is a masterpiece matched only by the Democratic slogan of 1844: "Times ain't now as they used to was."

Sometimes infinitives are used ambiguously. The infinitive of purpose is a troublemaker. "I do not intend to run" is clear enough; but "He hurried as much as possible only to get home late for supper" suggests that he hurried in order to be late, whereas the real meaning is that he was late in spite of hurrying. Again, "Christopher Columbus defied the skeptics to discover America" should give you pause. It sounds as if Columbus said, "Skeptics, I defy you to discover America," or that he defied the skeptics for the purpose of discovering America. The meaning, of course, is that he defied the skeptics and then went on to discover America. "Food prices have risen to frustrate the housewife" suggests purpose rather than result. Heaven knows, the housewife is frustrated enough without having food prices deliberately decide to raise themselves in order to irritate her. For a final misleading infinitive of purpose, consider "Elizabeth Barrett defied her father to marry Robert Browning." The only solution for such sentences is to rephrase them and avoid the awkward infinitive.

Sometimes infinitives suggest future action: "The convention is to be held next week." But be careful not to use such a construction unless you intend to imply futurity. "It was the most successful Tupperware convention to be held in Logan" suggests that it was the most successful one that will ever be held there. Simply omit the infinitive and the difficulty vanishes. Likewise, "This is one of three dormitories to be coed" should be changed to read, "This is one of three coed dormitories." *To be* is dead wood in "This was one of the worst droughts ever to be recorded"; "ever recorded" is enough. To avoid the implication of futurity, use a relative clause instead of the infinitive. "This is the only team to have an undefeated season" should be "Slippery Rock is the only team that has had an undefeated season." For the future, *shall* or *will* is preferable to *are to*. "I am to meet you at Waterloo Bridge" suggests passive obligation; "I shall meet you" is better. Headlines often use the infinitive for brevity: "Atomic scientists to announce startling discovery"; but "will announce" is only two letters longer.

118

¶ SEX AND THE SPLIT INFINITIVE

Purists insist that the infinitive must never be split by the insertion of an adverb after the *to*: "to rapidly eat." Actually this is not a problem worth worrying about. Many competent writers split the infinitive (Arthur Miller wrote "to forever guard against his own complicity with Cain. . ."), and most all of us do so in casual conversation. If the stress is on the adverb, you may want it before the verb: "To accurately portray Melville's ideas in motion-picture dialogue is exceedingly difficult." The adverb can always be placed before the *to* (cf., Shakespeare's "gently to hear, kindly to judge our play"), but this formation may seem archaic ("Accurately to portray"), and in conversation most people are not that precise. Usually there is no good reason to split the infinitive, but your only concern should be to avoid awkwardness, such as, "The self-reliant viewpoint seems to not recognize that we are partially dependent on the resources of other nations." "The thoughts in Thoreau's writings were almost impossible to practically apply" is both clumsy and ambiguous. Obviously "I like to not got home" is substandard but on other counts than the split infinitive. Arguing against overpunctitious proofreaders, Raymond Chandler stated, "When I split an infinitive, damn it, I split it so it will stay split. . . ."

Some infinitives cannot be split because they are used without *to,* in such constructions as "We must *go*," "You'd better *hurry*," "I can't *hear* you," "I don't *know*," for example.

The infinitive we have so far been discussing is the simple present infinitive, usually termed simply the infinitive. There are also the present progressive infinitive (*to be singing*), the present passive infinitive (*to be loved*), the perfect infinitive (*to have written*), the progressive perfect (*to have been working*), and the perfect passive (*to have been kissed*).

¶ VERBS VERSUS VERBALS: PARTICIPLES

Like the infinitive, participles are verbals, or verbids, that cannot serve as the verb in a main clause. The present participle is the infinitive or present stem plus *-ing* (*know, knowing*). When the stem ends in *-e,* the *-e* is dropped before *-ing* (*come, coming*). The past participle we have already examined as one of the principal parts; it is used with auxiliary verbs to form the perfect tenses and the passive voice. Both participles can be combined: *having suf-*

119

fered, being invited, having been insulted. The present participle
is used with various tenses of the verb *to be* to form the progressive
tenses indicating continuing action: *I am drinking, he was drinking,
we shall be drinking, she has been drinking, they had been drinking, everybody shall have been stinking.*

Present participles can function as nouns, as subjects or objects
of verbs and prepositions; when they do so, they are called *gerunds,*
though this term is artificial and is therefore rejected by some
grammarians. Subject: "Swimming is excellent exercise." Object:
"Lester dislikes hunting." Object of preposition: "I'm tired of
arguing."

Participles frequently function as modifiers, and, as verbals, they
can in turn be modified by adverbs: "Breathing heavily, he stag-
gered down the stairs." Sometimes it is difficult to tell whether a
past participle is used as a modifier or as part of a passive construction. "The driver was uninjured" could be either; in "The driver
was uninjured but nervous" the participle is more clearly a modifier.
Confusion comes when it is not clear what the participle modifies;
if it dangles or is misplaced, the result is such a sentence as "The
librarian ordered books appealing to children with big print" or
"Drinking martinis, life seemed tolerable again." We shall return
to this problem in a later chapter.

¶ TRANSPOSING

As we have seen with nouns and pronouns, there are many words
that cannot be pinned down and limited to a single part of speech.
Often the same stem can function as several parts of speech, though
when it is, its form sometimes changes to take on the endings
(for case, number, person, tense) required by that function. Many
nouns and adjectives and even some prepositions ("Up the volume,"
"Outen the light") can be used as verbs. The noun is particularly
adept at this double role; such unlikely candidates as *Fulbright,
ammunition, telephone pole, billboard, gooseflesh, porpoise, rainbow, steamroller, pancake, orator, subway, ash can, hemorrhage,*
and *bellyache* have appeared as verbs, and H. L. Mencken has
noted that the Gideons have spoken of "Bibling a hotel." Some new
verbs are back-formations, the result of a removal of the ending
of a noun or adjective: *enthuse* (from *enthusiastic*), *resurrect* (from
resurrection), *sculpt* (from *sculptor*), *chiropract* (from *chiropractor*),

and *frivol* (from *frivolous*). Others are formed by adding suffixes to nouns; probably the most common and controversial is *-ize,* to which few object in *glamorize, lionize, popularize, publicize,* or many similar constructions, but which draws howls of outrag, d protest in *finalize.* Another device is the addition of prefixes, often negative ones, to make verbs from nouns or even new verbs from old ones (e.g., *to deglamorize*). But usually the unattended noun doubles as a verb (except for person, tense, or participle endings); as Snooper says, "It's some handsome, devil-may-care guy imposturing me."

The interchange of nouns and verbs is ancient and honorable, yet some cases remain controversial. Though it is gradually becoming respectable, probably the biggest shibboleth is still the use of the noun *loan* as a verb: "Loan me five bucks." Among purists, this usage is substandard, though it is widely heard and perfectly clear. The only objection (not a very valid one) is that we already have the established verb *lend* and there is therefore no need for another one. Actually, the criticism of *loan* is merely a lingering though moribund bit of linguistic snobbery.

The Southern Appalachian highlanders often show a fluent ingenuity in transposing verbs, adjectives, and nouns; the result may be grammatically nonstandard but colorful. If *fish* can be a verb, why not *squirrel,* as in "Jethro is a-fixin' to go squirrelin' "? "I don't *confidence* them dogs," said one mountain man, as he *buttocked* down in his chair; his son didn't *contrary* him none. And many a mountaineer has seen *hants* (*haunts*) in the hills.

¶ THEME ME DEADLY

In modern usage, parts of speech are becoming increasingly interchangeable. On the credit side, this gives the language an increasing flexibility, but sometimes it entangles it in jargon. In the Southern Appalachians this transposition is part of a freewheeling grammar; there is no calculation behind it. But advertisers and journalists often make a fetish of coy or contrived diction. The mountain man will make you a *run* of corn liquor; magazines inform you that you can *julep* Bourbon or you can *highball* it. And "When you go *supermarketing,* look for plump broiler-fryers . . . for they are the buy-wise choices." *Vogue* advertises "a slouchy new polo shirt that cowls as it hoods" and informs the reader that

121

"The mystique of this dress is made up of equal parts of shift and slink." These examples are harmless enough. Poets and novelists often interchange parts of speech for literary effect; Robinson Jeffers even used *sarcophagus* as a verb. But artists use the language creatively, while journalists sometimes get trapped in cliché. Thus it is practically obligatory for gossip columnists to write that somebody *guested, hosted,* or *gifted* someone ("Elvis Presley gifted Ann-Margret with a huge circular bed for her new home") or is *romancing* someone. Parties are *themed* with exotic decorations. The *Christian Science Monitor* complained that nouns are being made into verbs at a madly accelerated rate. Books are no longer written; now they are *authored*. Music critics so often use *guest, solo,* and *duet* as verbs that the *Monitor* wonders if Isaac Stern will soon have symphonied Brahms's *Double Concerto*. The *Toronto Globe and Mail* glumly observed, "So now that we have Christmased and New Yeared, we shall Leap Year while faithing that however we language ourselves we have already been outsolecismed." The point is not whether English can make new verbs or nouns; obviously it can, and usage can make them acceptable. It is that the majority of these words become so routine a jargon that they numb the language instead of giving it new life. Thus the language spoken in the Smokies or by Faulkner's characters, nonstandard though it is, is often preferable to that of Madison Avenue. The first is living; the latter, synthetic.

Exercise 7: Correct any errors in verb form or function in the following:

1. The reason I put salt on it is that it were a radish.
2. If those bug bites is chiggers, you had ought to put nail polish on them.
3. Grandma used to could do a cancan kick.
4. I could of went to Portland, but I ended up in Kennebunkport.
5. Ben Gunn founded the treasure of old Captain Flint.
6. We was brung up here in the cove.
7. The minister's been setting up with the sick.
8. The women in our house done all the churning.
9. It is inefficient for cereal boxes to be shook at the factory to make them appear full upon arrival.
10. Walking in public or talking in groups of two or three was forbidded in Puritan Boston.
11. If Thoreau would have been born today, he would have gone out of his mind.
12. I axed him to fotch me my rifle.
13. I thought a little bit further ahead than you may think I have thunk.

14. I drawed a monster for Papa to color.
15. The tobacco made his breath a bit strong, but he chewn a feenamint.
16. Would stout Cortez have been thinner if he would have taken Metrecal?
17. We should of went to Ft. Lauderdale spring vacation.
18. Did you ever took a picture of a fish being fitted with contact lenses?
19. These are claw marks that bears have did.
20. Schroeder plew the piano with amazing virtuosity.
21. Where was you fotch up that you don't know about bears?
22. When I brung up marrying, I weren't thinking of myself.
23. This German book is writ in some foreign language.
24. We was thinking that we ought to of brung a spare tire.
25. Homer brang the mustard, and Ajax fotched the pickles.

Exercise 8: Correct any errors in subject-verb agreement and put the appropriate form in the blank.

1. They was not sure whether it were a wildebeest or a harte-beest.   . . . .
2. Melvin don't like paprika in his deviled eggs.
3. I have backslid in my time, but it seem sin don't rise so strong in me now.   . . . .
4. The people wasn't even there when the bear went through their tent.   . . . .
5. Even if the couple is married, they have to walk outside their home in a discreet manner.   . . . .
6. *The Seven Pillars of Wisdom* are just out in paperback.   . . . .
7. Is the grownups ready for coffee?   . . . .
8. If you get chigger-bit, take a bath in warm soda; it will draw the chiggers before they gets set.   . . . .
9. The directions for the do-it-yourself Frankenstein is on the box.   . . . .
10. There is people in the cities that has never seen a cow.   . . . .
11. Some lumber companies and mining firms has opposed the establishment of various national parks.   . . . .
12. There is hogs so stubborn that they'll cross hell on a rotten rail to steal a camper's dinner.   . . . .
13. There are many kinds of mountain crafts that has been revived.   . . . .
14. The most vivid and affectionate accounts of mules was written by William Faulkner.   . . . .
15. The Joad family is not religious, but they certainly are a God-fearing family.   . . . .
16. Thomas Jefferson were denounced as a dangerous radical when he ran for President.   . . . .

17. Ivory, apes, and peacocks was brought by the Queen of Sheba. . . . .
18. If I lets go of the roof, I'll fall on my head bone. . . . .
19. Some twins looks so much alike that they forgets who they are. . . . .
20. Women should marry people that understands them. . . . .

Exercise 9: In the following sentences the passive voice is sometimes used effectively and sometimes not. Turn any clumsy passive constructions into the active voice.

1. Although inelegant, the pickup truck was driven by us to the country club.
2. It has been confirmed that the porcupine was the first animal to have its own short-wave radio call letters.
3. The five monkeys were seen by the guests climbing up the lace curtains.
4. It is recommended that ammonia and chlorine cleansers not be used in combination.
5. When using it for medicinal purposes, vodka should be taken in small doses.
6. In attaching the buttonholer to the machine, care must be taken that the throat plate be covered with the metal shield indicated in diagram A and that the buttonholer be securely attached to the presser bar B by tightening firmly screw C.
7. Bread is made by dissolving yeast in a warm liquid and then by mixing the liquid with flour, and by subsequent kneading, rising, and baking.
8. When the grime was removed from Eliza Doolittle, a pretty girl was seen.
9. A gazebo was built by her in the backyard into which she retired to write long novels.
10. It was decided that the filing system in the library should be changed from the Dewey decimal to the Library of Congress catalogue system.
11. It is observed that while American publications render Alfred, Lord Tennyson as Alfred Tennyson, British publications list F. Scott Fitzgerald as Scott-Fitzgerald, Francis.
12. It was discovered when the freight was unpacked that several crates of cockatoos were missing.
13. Automobiles, houses, power lines, boat moorings, and farms were obliterated by the hurricane.
14. The elephants are attacked with spears until they are succumbed through loss of blood.
15. The guitar strings are numbered by counting the smallest as the first.
16. In combining the strokes of the thumb with those of the fingers, care should be taken to play the notes one after the other from the lowest to the highest.

17. In using the third finger, the little finger must be lifted from the face of the guitar.
18. When notes of the same pitch are joined by a slur, the first note only is played, prolonging its duration for tied notes to be made.
19. The Small Bar is made with two fingers on the middle strings.
20. It was decided by the committee that a holiday should be declared.

9 √ "Is You Is or Is You Ain't My Baby?" Subject - Verb Agreement

Verbs should agree with their subjects in number and person. When the subject is singular, the verb should be in the singular form; when the subject is plural, the verb should be in the plural form. A first-, second-, or third-person subject requires a verb with first-, second-, or third-person inflectional endings.

"I is ready" is an example of faulty agreement in person; *I,* the first-person singular pronoun, requires *am,* the first-person singular verb. "We is coming" uses a first-person plural pronoun with a third-person singular verb; the verb should be changed to *are.* "He sure am lazy" has a third-person singular pronoun with a first-person singular verb; the verb should be changed to *is.* "They was going to the steak house" has a third-person plural subject with a third-person singular verb; the verb should be changed to *were.* Except for the verb *to be,* all errors in agreement occur in the formation of the present tense, since other verbs have only one form in the past tense, no matter what the number and person (e.g., *I worked, you worked, he worked, we worked, you worked, they worked*). Only in the past tense of the verb *to be* are the first and third person singular *(was)* distinguished from the second person singular and the first, second, and third persons plural *(were).* There can, of course, be faulty agreement in the present perfect tense, but only in the use of the present tense of the auxiliary verb *have.* As more errors occur with the verbs *to be* and *to have* than with any others, their present tenses follow:

126

	SINGULAR	PLURAL	SINGULAR	PLURAL
FIRST PERSON	I am	we are	I have	we have
SECOND PERSON	you are	you are	you have	you have
THIRD PERSON	he, she, it is	they are	he, she, it has	they have

One of the most obvious and widespread errors is the persistent use of *was* with *we, you,* and *they: were* is required by standard grammar. "Was you there yesterday? They said they was there, and we was coming, but the car broke down" is almost a hallmark of some regions, but it is also anathema in educated circles. Until the late eighteenth century, *you was* appeared frequently in literature for the second person singular, and Webster defended *was* for the singular and *were* for the plural, though he was overruled by Joseph Priestley and other linguists. Since the early seventeenth century, the lack of any distinction between the second person singular and plural has been a nuisance in English; and we try to get around it by using *you all, youse, yousuns,* and other forms to indicate more than one *you* to compensate for the older distinction between *thou* and *ye* (at first the subjective but later replaced by the older objective *you*). In Webster's day, it might therefore have been logical to say *you* (singular) *was* and *you* (plural) *were,* although the same reasoning could be applied to retaining *art* for the second person singular present of the verb *to be.* With this sort of logic, those who say *you was* should say *you all were*; but instead, from the ambiguous *you* that can be singular or plural, *was* has been extended to cover all the plurals; and *were* has ceased to exist as a verb for many people. In some areas, even the better-educated invariably use *was.* Any logic behind this has undoubtedly been forgotten generations ago, and today those using *was* indiscriminately speak from habit, as we all do.

A less common error but one that appears to have been characteristic of the Southern Appalachians is the use of *were* (often pronounced *war* and so spelled in dialogue) instead of *was* with the first and third person singular.

He war a moonshiner.

Hit war further to the still than I thought hit war.

"Grandpappy war plumb delighted. . . . Thar war considerable confusion."[1]

"Kaze he war all drooped-up with the milk pizen, I lick-splitted hit t'the blockader's still, which war appearantly a-bein' run successful-like aspite the revenoors, an' fotch him a jair of brandy." [2]

But this practice is inconsistent, even in the same paragraph. One Civil War veteran was quoted as saying, "I were with Ransom, in ole Virginia. . . . I were shot purty nigh the last. Hit wuz when we wuz tryin' to git out'n Petersburg afore the Yankee line lapped round us." [3] You also encounter *you was:* "We didn't know you was coming, and we look a fright."

Nonstandard English speech in the Old (sometimes the New) South and in the backwoods, as can be seen in the dialogue of Mark Twain and William Faulkner, frequently uses a singular verb with a plural subject: "Them is mighty good corn squeezings," "Since they dredged out that new baptizing hole, they gets more conversions down in the valley," "Thar's two eyes a-shinin' out of the cave," "There's raccoons up there, isn't there," Huck Finn's "all kings is mostly rapscallions," and the King's "your eyes is lookin' at this very moment on the pore disappeared Dauphin, Looy the Seventeen, son of Looy the Sixteen and Marry Antonette."*Huckleberry Finn* has hundreds of such examples. These errors in number are often combined with faulty past tenses and participles ("When we fell in the creek, our britches was froze solid").

Conversely, another error widespread throughout the country is the use in the third person singular of the plural *don't* for *doesn't* ("He don't like pepper in his buttermilk"). You also find *doesn't* used, instead of *don't,* with the first person singular ("I doesn't take kindly to having my ears scrubbed"). This indicates another characteristic of nonstandard speech: the use of the third-person singular verb with *I,* as in *I is, I likes, I thinks, I says* or as in the mountain woman's explanation, "I plants cucumbers afore sunup so's the bugs won't eat 'em soon's they bust the dirt." [4] This error in person is compounded by one in number when the subject is the first-person plural pronoun *we: we is, we likes, we thinks, we says,* etc. Another error in number is the use of the plural *are* (sometimes spelled *air* in dialect) with the first or third person singular, as in "Only Babalooey knows who El Kabong really are" or the Appalachian "They look mighty peaceful like off yander, but you ought to git tangled up in them laurel slicks onct an' you'd change your mind 'bout how purty an' friendly Old Smoky air." [5]

These errors are either a matter of habit or of total grammatical unconsciousness. The problem, then, is to break such habits, to consider the relationship of the words in a sentence, and to form new habits by conscious effort. It would seem simple enough. All

128

you have to do is find the verb, locate its subject, and ask yourself the number and person of both subject and verb. If they are not the same, make them so. In practice it is not always so easy. There are a number of constructions that may cause difficulty.

1. Two or more singular subjects connected by *and* require a plural verb:

Frankenstein's monster and the Wolf Man *are* wrecking the laboratory.
Frankie and Johnnie *were* sweethearts.
"The Walrus and the Carpenter *were* walking close at hand."
Both Knossos and Mycenae *have* been excavated.

There are three exceptions to this practice. If the multiple subjects are preceded by *each* or *every,* they are considered as acting individually and are followed by a singular verb:

Every bear and woodchuck *is* hibernating.
Each camper and picnicker *cleans* up his own area.

If two singular subjects joined by *and* refer to a unit, to the same thing or person, then they take a singular verb:

His Lord and Saviour *is* Jesus Christ.
Her pride and joy *was* the cherry orchard.
Liver and spinach *has* been the most unpopular meal in the Army.

Addition or multiplication calculations may use a singular or a plural verb:

Four times five *is* twenty.   Four times five *are* twenty.
Two and two *is* four.   Two and two *are* not five.

But in subtraction, "ten minus three *is* [not *are*] seven."

In the actual practice of their craft, many famous authors have used a singular verb with several subjects joined by *and.* Shakespeare, Joseph Addison, Thomas Carlyle, Thomas Wolfe, George Orwell, Evelyn Waugh, Aldous Huxley, J. P. Marquand, Eleanor Roosevelt, not to mention various scholars are among those who have done so. Clarence Darrow wrote, "Ignorance and fanaticism is ever busy and needs feeding." The King James Bible states, "Out of the same mouth proceedeth blessing and cursing." Hamlet says, "Your fat king and your lean beggar is but variable service." In *Othello,* Brabantio asks, "Is there not charms/ By which the property of youth and maidenhood/ May be abus'd?" And Sir Laurence Olivier says of Shakespeare, "There's too much tears and bloody sweat in it." In *Catch-22*, Joseph Heller writes, "There were too many dangers for Yossarian to keep track of. There was Hitler, Mussolini, and Tojo, for example, and they were all out to kill him. . . . There was Appleby, Havermeyer, Black and Korn. There was Nurse Cramer and Nurse Duckett. . . . There were bartenders, bricklayers and bus conductors all over the world who wanted him dead . . ." [6] In this example, one might defend Heller's use of verbs in the singular by saying that the subjects appear to be people considered as a unit; but what counts is that the writing is effective, even if the mathematics fails to add up.

2. Two or more singular subjects connected by *but, or,* or *nor* take a singular verb:

> Not Hamlet but Claudius *was* chosen king.
> Not only Bette Davis but also Flora Robson *was* cast as Queen Elizabeth.
> Dickens or Thackeray *is* to be taught in seminar.
> Neither *Tarzan* nor *The Scarlet Letter* is allowed free circulation in the Plunkville Library.

3. If a singular and a plural subject are connected by *but, or,* or *nor,* the verb agrees with the nearer one:

> Neither Polonius nor Rosencranz and Guildenstern *were* able to deceive Hamlet.
> Not only Lon Chaney but also Charles Laughton and Anthony Quinn *have* played Quasimodo, the hunchback of Notre Dame.
> Either Dickens or Tennyson and Browning *are* to be taught in seminar.
> Either the Brontës or George Eliot *is* to be taught in seminar.

4. If two subjects connected by *or* or *nor* are different in person, the verb agrees with the nearer one:

> Either you or I *am* to die.
> Either you or Melvin *has* committed the crime.
> Neither Irving nor you *are* to come home late.

Such constructions may be clumsy and require rewriting for clarity and style. "She or you are keeping a stray dog in the cellar" is better rephrased as, "Either she is keeping a stray dog in the cellar, or you are."

5. A subject in the singular followed by a plural modifier takes a singular verb:

One of the ships at anchor *has* broken its mooring.
The *photographer* of the mob scenes *keeps* forgetting to remove
the lens cover.
The *response* of the critics *was* gratifying.
A *volume* of Civil War photographs *is* in the reading room.

Casual speech might use *are* in the last example, but there is no justification for it in careful prose.

6. If a subject in the singular is followed by some such construction as *along with, as well as, in addition to, including,* or *together with,* the number of the verb remains singular:

The captain, along with his supporters, was set adrift in the
longboat.
The whole party, including the rangers, was caught in the down-
pour.
A mother bear, together with three cubs, lives near the Big
Locust Trail.

7. Used as pronouns, *any* and *none* can take either a singular or a plural verb. Conservative usage prefers the singular, but general usage is indifferent, though sometimes a plural modifier after the pronoun requires the verb to be plural. Thus we say, "Any of the books on the list is [or are] appropriate," but we need the plural in "Are any of you ready for dessert?" There is no real problem here; common sense and clarity select the appropriate verb.

Do any of the campgrounds have a vacancy?
Does any of the campgrounds have a vacancy?
Any of the planes *is* able to make the flight in three hours.
None of us *is* [or *are*] able to shoe a horse.
None of the officers *were* [or *was*] sober.
None of you *is* going to squeal on Rocco.

8. The indefinite pronouns *anybody, anyone, each, either, everybody, everyone, neither, nobody, no one, somebody,* and *someone* usually take a singular verb:

Each of the vampires *has* his own coffin.
Neither of the clowns *was* funny.
Somebody has been eating my porridge.
Has anybody here seen Kelly?

Since *each, either,* and *neither* are often followed by a plural modifier, they are often used with a plural verb in casual conversation: "*Neither* of them *are* of legal age," "*Each* of them *have* swatted me with a fraternity paddle." Formal style still requires the singular, but this convention is breaking down. The suffix makes us habitually use a singular verb with pronouns ending in -*body* or -*one*; nobody ever says "*Everyone are* finks," though if other words come between the subject and the verb, you may hear "*Every one* of them *are* sick." Despite the singular verb, the subject is obviously plural in "Everybody is either insulting or nuts." [7] The main trouble is that careless speakers or writers follow -*body* and -*one* words with a singular verb but then refer to them with plural pronouns: "*Everybody* is kicking up *their* heels." The reason is that words like *everyone* are singular in form but collective in meaning; form governs the verb, but meaning is apt to make us use a plural pronoun. (Cf. p. 76.) This is also true of a singular subject preceded by *any, each,* and *every*: "Every *Republican thinks they* can run for President" needs the personal pronoun changed to the singular, *he*. Though the meaning is clear enough in "*Everyone is* cleaning *their* rooms," there is an inconsistency in agreement. Such constructions are nonstandard but harmless enough; they usually pass unnoticed in casual conversation. Careful style requires more precision and would use a singular pronoun to match subject and verb: "*Everyone is* capable of letting *his* ideas become intolerant." Yet many distinguished writers have used a singular verb and plural pronoun after *everybody,* and sometimes sense requires such formal inconsistencies. (Cf. p. 78.) Clarity is preferable to dogma.

9. When a collective noun is considered as a unit, it takes a singular verb. When its component parts are each considered individually, it takes a plural verb. This practice includes words like *half, number, part, percent, rest,* and *remainder.*

SINGULAR	PLURAL
"The people is a great beast."— Alexander Hamilton	The people are divided in their reaction to the plan.
The rest of the fish and chips is yours.	The rest of the penguins are eating fish.

"The rest of the penguins is disturbed" is ambiguous; out of context, there is no way to tell whether the word *rest* means "repose" or "remainder." If the penguins are taking a nap and a helicopter lands near them, then their rest *is* disturbed; whereas if some penguins have gone for a waddle, then the rest *are* sliding and swimming. As a collective noun, "The rest is silence." An ad informs us that "Forty percent of the American population possesses hair of a lifeless color"; but since each person has his own—not his or her own, for pity's sake—hair in various lifeless colors, the plural verb *possess* should be used. "The United States have one of the best national park services" is wrong: one nation and not fifty individual states is (note the use of *is*, to go with the singular *nation*) concerned, so "The United States" *takes* a singular verb. Emerson has a curious example of a collective noun with a plural verb where most authors would use the singular: "The private poor man . . . goes to the post-office, and the *human race run* on his errands; to the book-shop, and the *human race read and write* of all that happens, for him. . . ." (Italics mine.) Yet the plural can be justified on the grounds that *human race* here consists of acting individuals, rather than an abstract collection. Another unusual plural occurs in Lawrence of Arabia's statement, "The Navy were already collecting," where "collecting" implies a plural activity.

People often use a singular verb and a plural pronoun with collective nouns and thus cause an inconsistent and erroneous disagreement in number. "Is the family satisfied with their condition?" requires either a plural verb or a singular pronoun, preferably the former. "Schumans *keeps* ten horses in *their* stables" needs a singular pronoun, since "Schumans" is a single hostelry. "The opposition feels that they can stop all the trouble by killing the leader" needs a plural verb: "The opposition feel that they . . ." The leader needs either some bodyguards or political asylum.

10. Titles of books, stories, poems, songs, magazines, newspapers, plays, and movies take a singular verb. This applies even when the main noun of the title is plural. *Mad* ridiculed the grammar of Alfred Hitchcock's movie, *"The Birds* Is Coming!" but Hitchcock was quite right. On the other hand, if a character in the film had run around saying, "Help, the birds is coming," he would have deserved to be bonked on the head by a sea gull. Varying titles with plural and collective nouns, we can make the following rundown:

> *The Birds* is coming!
> The wildlife is coming.
> *The Frogs* is coming.
> *The Alligator People* is coming!
> The enemy is [or are] coming.
> *The Misfits* is coming.
> *Them* is coming!
> The ants are coming.

> *Leinigen versus the Ants* is coming.
> *The Little Foxes* is coming.
> *The Four Horsemen of the Apocalypse* is coming.
> Look out! the giant squid is coming.
> Look out! the giant squid are coming.
> *(Irregular plural, like deer)*

And I'm getting out of here.

11. Nouns that are plural in form but singular in meaning (e.g., *economics, mathematics, news, physics, politics,* and the names of some products) customarily take a singular verb. Thus we hear that "Rollaids consumes 47 times its weight in excess stomach acids." Huckleberry Hound says "Kellogg's Sugar Stars is new and improved oat cereal." These statements are correct but annoying; the subject seems plural yet functions as a singular ("Friskies doesn't stick to the spoon"). We are used to hearing that the *news is* bad or that *blues is* one of the oldest forms of folk music, but we do a double take when we hear, "New Burgerbits gives your dog everything he needs at every age." When a subject is plural in both form and meaning, it cannot be used with a singular verb; the emcee who asked "Is there any other bingos?" did not have a winning verb.

12. When a relative pronoun is the subject of a verb, the verb should agree in number and person with the pronoun's antecedent. Thus "There are the carding machines that combs the wool" has faulty agreement; the antecedent, *machines,* is plural and requires a plural verb.

> This is one of the *rangers who supervise* the campground.
> This is the *mouse that smokes* cigarettes.

Difficulties often arise in "one of the . . ." constructions, where the singular pronoun *one,* is followed by a plural noun. Usually each is the subject of a separate verb, so you need a singular and a plural verb to match the respective subjects:

> One of the men who work at the factory was injured.

One is the subject of *was,* while the subject *who* refers not to *one* but to *men.* Parentheses may clarify the agreement:

> One (of the men who work at the factory) was injured.

Another problem occurs if the antecedent of the relative pronoun is a word, such as *either* or *neither,* that traditionally takes a singular verb, though colloquial usage is increasingly using a plural one:

134

Neither of the movements being discussed (have, has) been conducted without violence.

Movements is plural, but *neither* still requires the singular verb *has*.

Some curious examples occur in John Osborne's play *Luther,* where the third-person relative pronoun, rather than its antecedent, determines the person of the verb:

> "Deign to listen to me, most holy father, to me who is like a child."[8]

> "Or was it just you who was made free, you and the princes you've taken up with, and the rich burghers and—" [9]

Customarily, we would say "to me who am," though it too is awkward; and certainly "you who were" is the form required by standard usage, but the speaker here is Luther's father, an unlearned man, who would probably say "you was" if the language he spoke were English.

13. If a sentence begins with *There* or *Here,* the verb agrees with the subject following:

> There *is* an *elephant* in my back yard.
> There *are* the *daggers.*
> *Are* there any *ladies* present?
> *Is* there a *doctor* in the house?
> Here *is* a bad *case* of dandruff.
> Here *are* three *kittens.*

14. Complements of the verb *to be* do not alter the number of the verb, which always agrees with its subject:

> Ship *models* are his favorite hobby.
> His favorite *hobby is* ship models.
> One *thing* I can't stand *is* noisy neighbors.
> Noisy *neighbors* are one thing I can't stand.

It is tempting to make the verb match the number of the complement; but when tempted, you should not yield. If a sentence is too clumsy, rewrite it altogether. "The irritating thing about daytime television programs is aggressive masters of ceremonies, inane giveaway shows, and treacly soap operas, all played at top volume." This is grammatically accurate but stylistically awkward, and should be revised to something approximating, "For heaven's sake, turn off the idiot box."

Exercise 10: Underline the verb that agrees with its subject in person and number.

1. *The Flintstones* (is, are) my favorite TV program.
2. These scissors (is, are) dull.
3. Both Tarzan and T. S. Eliot (was, were) born in 1888.
4. There (is, are) only three months until our projectile departs from planet earth.
5. Is that all the animal crackers there (is, are) ?
6. I hope none of the boys (gets, get) hurt.
7. One or four (cost, costs) no more.
8. Alabama (takes, take) over on their six-yard line.
9. The remains of Noah's ark (is, are) awaiting discovery on Mt. Ararat, according to some theories.
10. There is a dramatic pause when the last note of the arpeggios (is, are) struck.
11. The shelves (is, are) as bare as last year's mouse nest.
12. The audience (stands, stand) up for the Hallelujah Chorus.
13. The Philippines (is, are) a chief producer of copra.
14. The Bill of Rights (is, are) the first ten amendments.
15. Wufflebeepers (klong, klongs) scurfly in the norp.
16. Can you name three works of English literature that (has, have) someone's arm torn out of the socket?
17. Friskies (has, have) some of the best commercials on television.
18. Crispy Critters (is, are) made from oat flour, brown sugar, precooked corn flour and wheat starch, salt, calcium carbonate, U.S. certified color, niacin, and vitamin B1.
19. It is too bad you (were not, was not) there for the festivities.
20. Lots of people (takes, take) to marriage.
21. The Smokies (has, have) about 300 bears and 3,000,000 bugs.
22. Poe is one of the few authors that (improves, improve) in translation.
23. The music of many neglected composers of sixteenth and seventeenth century England (has, have) been revived since the advent of the LP record.
24. *The Anatomy Lesson of Dr. Nicholas Tulp* is one of those paintings that you admire but that (do, does) not go well over the dining room table.
25. The New York edition of the works of Henry James (has, have) been reprinted recently.

Exercise 11: Underline the subject in the following sentences:

1. Wandering over hills and dales, through villages and towns, striding about the city by night, alone was I.
2. It is recommended that an optimum amount of fertilizer be used on the African violets.

136

3. "Who's afraid of the big bad wolf?"
4. "After many a summer dies the swan."
5. Pink, puce, chartreuse, magenta, and olive drab are not a very happy choice for a color scheme in the new apartment.
6. Here's King Kong now.
7. To listen further was beyond his patience.
8. From Lagos to Nairobi is as far as from Seattle to New York.
9. What people will think has been a recurrent anxiety.
10. About three o'clock is the best time for the meeting.
11. Whence came the giant sea serpent?
12. What makes you tick is a mystery to me.
13. To go to the theatre in New York is too expensive for many people.
14. That Thoreau refused to pay his taxes bothers some businessmen, even though they try to find various tax dodges.
15. To see a unicorn eating a rose in one's garden is a rare and remarkable experience.
16. That the elephant's trunk weighs about 300 pounds is a little-known fact.
17. "Where are the songs of Spring? Ay, where are they?"
18. "Had we but world enough, and time,
    This coyness, Lady, were no crime."
19.   "Darkened so, yet shone
    Above them all the Archangel. . . ."
20. "Ten thousand saw I at a glance,
    Tossing their heads in sprightly dance."

10 √ Adjectives and Adverbs

Adjectives are not really and truly interesting.
GERTRUDE STEIN

Adjectives and adverbs are words that function as modifiers; that is, they limit, qualify, or describe some other word or group of words in a sentence. According to the traditional definition, adjectives modify nouns and pronouns; and adverbs modify verbs, adjectives, and other adverbs. Actually, adjectives can also be used to modify other adjectives. Adjectives have several different classifications. The commonest type is descriptive: "a *hot* potato," "the *rainy* season," "a *Grecian* urn," "the *American* experience," "*Fearless* Fosdick," "the *laughing* man," "a *broken* promise." As in the last two examples, present and past participles are often used as adjectives. Adjectives can also limit or specify the element they modify: "*your* hat," "*her* gloves," "*this* time," "*that* place," "*another* country," "*The Second Mrs. Tanqueray*." They can also specify and qualify number: "*one* meatball," "*both* brothers," "*many* moons." Some adjectives, both descriptive and limiting, are made from proper nouns: "*Jacksonian* democracy," "*Spenserian* stanzas," "a *Byronic* hero," "the *Napoleonic* Wars," "*Italian* art."

Sometimes an adjective modifies a compound governing element, that is, two or more words at once: "good bread and butter," "white shoes and stockings." And sometimes two or more adjectives are joined together by words such as *and, or, but*: "a poor but honest cobbler," "red or white roses."

Very often a whole clause or group of words is used to modify a noun. In "Bring the tana leaves that the mummy needs," the words *that the mummy needs* provide the answer to the unspoken question, which leaves? and therefore serve as an adjective. Similar groups of words are *who work now and then* in "Students who work now and then don't progress very fast" and *we need* in "This is the

138

sort of program we need." Such descriptive groups of words functioning as adjectives are called clause adjectives or adjective clauses.

Another form of a group of words used as an adjective modifier appears in "That is a mule of great stubbornness," where *of great stubbornness* tells what the kind of mule is. This is known as a prepositional adjective phrase; other instances are "the edition *of 1945*," "the cat *on the table*," "ships *at sea*," "children *at play*," "pictures *on the wall*."

Predicate adjectives are used as both complement and modifier. Usually they come after a linking verb: "That camel is *dignified*," "This toast is *burned*," "I feel *fine*." For emphasis (usually in poetry) the predicate adjective may come first: "Black is the color of my true love's hair." However, except for the predicate adjective, the adjective modifier is usually placed next to its governing word. If it is a word, it normally comes before the word it modifies; if it is a phrase or clause, it may come after. Occasionally this rule does not hold. We say "bread enough," "life everlasting," "the house beautiful." In poetry especially, adjectives often follow their governing words.

Parts of speech, as we have seen, are often inadequate labels; some words that function as adjectives serve elsewhere as nouns, pronouns, verbs, or adverbs. There are some distinguishing adjective suffixes:

-able (debatable)	*-ese* (Japanese)	*-ive* (constructive)
-al (trivial)	*-esque* (picturesque)	*-less* (hopeless)
-an (Martian)	*-ful* (hopeful)	*-like* (doglike)
-ant (hesitant)	*-ian* (Grecian)	*-ly* (lively)
-ar (circular)	*-ible* (digestible)	*-ory* (sensory)
-ary (documentary)	*-ic* (impolitic)	*-ose* (verbose)
-ate (passionate)	*-ile* (infantile)	*-ous* (jealous)
-en (golden)	*-ish* (British)	*-some* (quarrelsome)
-ent (persistent)	*-ite* (finite)	*-y* (tricky)

But even these are not exclusive, and we can find words with some of these endings serving as other parts of speech. *Martian* and *criminal,* for instance, can be used either as adjective or noun.

Many other nouns can double as adjectives: *monster* rally, *wolf* man, *cargo* ship, *tramp* steamer, *brick* wall, *turtle* wrapping, *Christmas* present, *Thurber* dog, *Napoleon* complex. Budd Schulberg even wrote of Hollywood actresses's "little brigittebardot bottoms." In a sense, all personal first names are adjectives, for they describe and

139

specify each member of a family, so that you can tell *Jack* from *Robert* Frost and *Ernest* from *Leicester* Hemingway. Oscar Wilde wrote a whole play about the importance of being named Ernest. Likewise, all possessive-case nouns and pronouns function as adjectives, for they describe to whom or what something belongs. All ordinal numbers (*first, second, third,* etc.) are adjectives, and so are the cardinal numbers (*one, two, three,* etc.) when they are used with nouns: "five miles," "three ships," "a hundred years." All colors can serve as both nouns and adjectives. Sometimes the use of a noun as an adjective becomes a bit strained, as in "Calvert Extra is as whiskey a whiskey as any whiskey you can buy." The current fad of *fun* as an adjective has become a pseudo-sophisticated mannerism ("a fun time," "a fun party," "a fun movie"): "Don't you find *The Scarlet Letter* a fun book to teach?" And the grammar is rudely wrenched in the ad, "It's a better kind of *different*."

Likewise, some words that are customarily adjectives can function as nouns, as when we speak of "making the *sick* well," sing of "the land of the *free* and the home of the *brave*," or refer to *the uprooted, the underprivileged, the innocent,* and *the guilty.* We watch a *Western* at the movies; in India, moviegoers see *mythologicals.* And, of course, television offers an occasional *special* or *spectacular.* Some country people use *smart* as a noun: "I have a right *smart* of mint in the herb-garden." And, at some time or other, you have probably been asked, "Do you want some *hot* in your coffee?"

In the Southern Appalachians, adjectives and verbs were often interchanged. Adjectives appear as verbs in "He was biggin' and biggin' the story. . . . I didn't do nary a thing to contrary her; hit benasties a man's mind. . . . He weren't no good at politing people around." Verbs turn into adjectives in "the travelin'est hosses; the talkin'est woman, the nothin' doin'dest day." [1] A word like *film* can be either a noun ("Put in the film") or a verb ("Did you film the action?").

Some words are customarily nouns or adjectives and are only rarely encountered in more than one capacity; but others serve just as well in either role. Clearly, *political* is exclusively an adjective in *political convention*; whereas *motion picture* is equally a compound noun and an adjective: *motion-picture festival.* Many words, as we have already stressed, cannot be labeled as primarily an adjective or a noun: the part of speech depends upon the context, and form follows function. When a word that can be a noun (e.g., that can

140

serve as the subject of a verb) functions as an adjective, it can in turn be modified by an adjective. Take, for example, the phrase "a grammar textbook." Here the noun *grammar* is an adjective modifying *textbook*. Yet *grammar* may be modified by an adjective, as in the phrase "an English grammar textbook," and we can even add an adjective to modify *English* as in "an Old English grammar textbook." In the same way we may say ⸀a newspaper story" or "a Boston newspaper story." In these examples the words *old, English, grammar, Boston,* and *newspaper* are all adjectives; but *English, grammar,* and *newspaper,* being naming words as well, can be fitted with adjectives.

Adjectives answer the question of *which, whose,* or *what kind.* Thus we can add adjectives to adjectives: when *blue* modifies *dress,* we can ask what kind of blue and get *a deep blue dress.* Though it is usually not advisable, we can pile up adjectives in this way to make a phrase: "The sick old merchant's three very beautiful tall blonde daughters." What kind of daughters?—blonde. What kind of blonde daughters?—tall. What kind of tall blonde daughters?—beautiful; and so on, backwards.

Perhaps to avoid stacking adjectives in this way, or possibly because adolescent writers striving for effect depend too heavily upon adjectives, some editors and instructors advise the use of as few adjectives as possible. According to one manual of instruction, "The work of skilled writers shows that verbs and nouns contribute more than adjectives in giving a reader a vivid and real impression." Yet in this very statement, the key words are *skilled, vivid,* and *real*—all adjectives. Mark Twain wrote, "As to the Adjective: when in doubt, strike it out." Literary historians tell how the young Hemingway took his manuscripts to Ezra Pound, who crossed out most of the modifiers. Yet there are seven adjectives in the first two sentences of *A Farewell to Arms.* This denunciation of the adjective can bear examination.

Literary analysts have proved by weary counting that Walter Pater, Henry James, Edith Wharton, and their kind favor the adjective more than do Rudyard Kipling, Jack London, Robert Louis Stevenson, and their kind. The work of Kipling and his ilk presents a sense of swift action; the school of Pater does not. But the present age is an age of action. Ergo, the conclusion is clear: the adjective must go! This, in thoughts of one syllable, seems to be the line of reasoning taken by the statistical analysts of literary style.

141

It is true that adjectives can be overworked; often the precise choice of a noun or descriptive verb can eliminate the need for modifiers. But does the adjective really have a "subordinate" function? Let us begin innocently enough by asking someone, "Which house is Bob Fawcett's?" The answer is, "It's the house painted white with green shutters, the house just beyond the bank." The sentence is easy to analyze: subject, *it*; verb, *is*; complement, *house, house*. But try saying, "It is house, house." The words do not tell us the information we require. That information, the heart of the answer to our question, inheres in the adjective elements: "painted white with green shutters, just beyond the bank." Indeed, if our informant were in a great hurry, he might gasp out those adjective phrases as his full reply, and we should understand him readily. In literature, the carefully aimed adjective can be highly effective, as in the following description from Joseph Heller's *Catch-22*: "General Dreedle, the wing commander, was a blunt, chunky, barrel-chested man in his early fifties. His nose was squat and red, and he had lumpy white, bunched-up eyelids circling his small gray eyes like haloes of bacon fat." [2]

Take almost any literary passage at random and rewrite it, omitting the modifiers and see what you have left. Try, for instance, taking the adjectives out of Friar Laurence's lines in *Romeo and Juliet*, Act II, scene 3:

> The grey-eyed morn smiles on the frowning night,
> Chequering the eastern clouds with streaks of light;
> And flecked darkness like a drunkard reels
> From forth day's path and Titan's fiery wheels.

You will find that the essence of the lines resides precisely in the arresting adjectives. Or take this stanza from Coleridge's "The Rime of the Ancient Mariner":

> The fair breeze blew, the white foam flew,
> The furrow followed free;
> We were the first that ever burst
> Into that silent sea.

If this were reduced to "The breeze blew, the foam flew, the furrow followed; we were the first that ever burst into the sea," the spell is gone. Keats's "magic casements" cease to be magic when they are just plain casements.

Who would agree to read another two lines—from *Macbeth* this

142

time—as, "Out, out candle; life's but a shadow, a player . . ." Without the adjectives *brief, walking,* and *poor,* not only all poetry but almost all intelligibility vanishes.

It may reasonably be held that the adjective is normally as important a speech element as its governing noun, in that it is the function of the adjective to define or give point and sharpness to what would otherwise be a vague, general term. We may say *books* without any vivid image, but *old books, rare books,* are phrases to conjure with. By itself the word *school* does not convey very much; we want to know if it is a *grade school, art school, music school, graduate school, high school.*

But imprecise speakers and writers often use adjectives that are so vague as to be useless. A great many "utility words"—so-called because they can be used without much critical thought—are weak, anemic adjectives like *neat, swell, great, terrific, interesting,* and *nice.* Imagine the following dialogue between a housewife packing to go overseas and the moving man:

> MOVING MAN: How large is the bed?
> HOUSEWIFE: Oh, it's pretty big, but not too big.
> MOVING MAN: What does the refrigerator weigh?
> HOUSEWIFE: Well, it's kinda heavy.
> MOVING MAN: How many appliances do you have?
> HOUSEWIFE: Several.

When the actual packing is done, the moving man may conclude: "I hate to tell you, lady, but your sea freight is overweight."

Once there was a substitute park naturalist who knew very little about flora and fauna. When asked, "What kind of tree is that?" he would answer, "That's a big tree." To the question "What is that flower?" he would reply, "That's a pretty purple flower." Such descriptions are not very informative. On the other hand, you should be careful not to strain too hard for effect, as in "The fanged white cuspidors of dawn." (In this last example, the modifiers are also metaphors.) A number of readers claim to have taken up arms against James Joyce's "the snot-green sea."

Though the adjective does not deserve an automatic bluepenciling, it is advisable not to pile up too many modifiers, lest your prose develop a paunch: "Be a Much-in-Demand Highly-Paid Invisible Reweaver at Home . . . in Your Spare Time!" There is too much weight in front in "The handsome young frog's rich booming vibrato bass voice charmed the princess." Henry James's description of Harriet Beecher Stowe is more dizzying than dazzling when he wrote of "her extraordinary little, vaguely observant, slightly wool-gathering, letting her eyes wander all over the place, kind of little way." Piling up too many adjectives is a favorite device of journalists, who intend to make their prose compact but actually make it far too ponderous, smothering the noun and blocking the movement of the verb; e.g., "Former President of the Home for Aged Oxcart Drivers' Association Elmo Fink was arrested for drunken driving." Journalists are much too fond of putting a string of titles before a name: "Among the victims was Acting Punxatawny Wildlife Museum Director Homer Hartebeest." The titles are better put as a modifying phrase after the name of the titleholder: "The victims included Homer Hartebeest, Acting Director of the Punxatawny Wildlife Museum." Excessive use of compound adjectives reverses the movement of the sentence and brings the reader up against a blank wall, so that he has to go back and figure out what he has just read, as in, "The catalogue called for a 1:00 P.M. Wednesday afternoon November 27 Thanksgiving holiday commencement." This reads better as, "The catalogue states that the Thanksgiving holiday begins at 1:00 P.M. on Wednesday, November 27." Piling up adjectives separates the object from its verb or the object of a preposition from its preposition or the subject from its verb, as in "Difficulties in study-room scheduling at Erickson Hall exist." This reads better as, "There is difficulty in scheduling the study rooms at Erickson Hall." The massed modifiers are ambiguous in "Fire destroyed the 617 South Succotash Street home of Abraham Enloe early this morning." This implies that Enloe has other homes elsewhere; it should be changed to read ". . . the home of Abraham Enloe at 617 South Succotash Street."

Some modifiers are simply dead wood and should be removed. But sometimes piled-up adjectives can have an impressive cumulative effect. Hamlet denounces his uncle: "Bloody, bawdy villain!/ Remorseless, treacherous, lecherous, kindless villain!" The metaphors are memorable in Shakespeare's "mad mustachio, purple-hued malt worm." What reaction do you have to the New York *Herald Tribune*'s description of *Catch-22* as "A wild, moving, shocking, hilarious, raging, exhilarating, giant roller-coaster of a book?" Is this effective, or is it too much like Hollywood's technique of stacking up superlatives?

Sometimes the correct choice between alternative adjectives is

144

controversial. One is the fast-disappearing distinction between *few* and *little, fewer* and *less.* The precise grammarian uses *little* and *less* with a single unit or substance; *few* and *fewer,* with several units: "They had few rifles and little powder," "Waldo has less hair but fewer cavities than his brother." But one of the more ubiquitous ads promotes toothpaste that results in 37 percent "less cavities." This usage is growing but it is not yet accepted by careful stylists.

Adjectives ending in the suffix *-ish* often have a derogatory sense (*doltish, sluggish, foolish*); they should not be used inappropriately. *Manly* and *womanly* are complimentary in tone whereas *mannish* and *womanish* refer respectively to overly masculine women and effeminate men. *Large* is more positive than *largish,* which has the qualified meaning of "rather large."

A major mistake, already referred to in the discussion of pronouns, is the substitution of the objective third-person pronoun *them* for the demonstrative adjectives *these* and *those.* This is a particularly strong shibboleth, so you should avoid statements like "Them big brown eyes get me" or "Bring them books over here," both of which call for *those.*

Another frequent error is the omission of the terminal *-d* or *-ed* from past participles used as adjectives (*prejudiced, supposed*) or adjectives in similar form (*pigeon-livered*). This is more noticeable in writing than in speech and is in fact due to the slurring of the suffix in imprecise enunciation. Thus people mistakenly write of "a bias person," "a prejudice viewpoint," "an unaccustom procedure," "one-arm driving." All of these require a *-d* or *-ed* ending, as does *size* in, "One stroke of Mennen Speed Stick is so man-size, it protects almost 3 times the area of a narrow roll-on track."

Finally, an irritation to many clergymen is the use of the title *reverend* as a solitary noun: "Reverend, will you speak next Wednesday to the Thursday Club?" Even worse is, "Hey, Rev., how's everything?" The proper forms of address are "The Reverend Mr. Morgan," "The Reverend Jack Morgan," "Father Morgan," or "Mr. Morgan," but not "Reverend Morgan."

When several adjectives in a series all modify the same noun, there should be a comma between them but not between the last adjective and the noun: "There was a tall, thin, stoop-shouldered man at the door." But when the last adjective forms a unit with the noun or the first adjective modifies the second one, then there

145

should be no comma: "the big bad wolf," "a fuzzy purple worm," "the deep blue sea." "Greasy, kid stuff" is wrong; *greasy* doesn't modify *kid,* but *kid stuff.*

If by now you think English adjectives far from easy, Latin and German ones are even more difficult. We are fortunate that the modern English adjective is totally uninflected. By contrast, adjectives in Latin, German, and Old English are required to agree with their nouns in case, number, and gender. Latin adjectives have three different declensions and are inflected in both the singular and plural for five cases and three genders. Here is the breakdown for *bonus* ("good").

Singular

	MASCULINE	FEMININE	NEUTER
NOM.	bonus	bona	bonum
GEN.	bonī	bonae	bonī
DAT.	bonō	bonae	bonō
ACC.	bonum	bonam	bonum
ABL.	bonō	bonā	bonō

Plural

NOM.	bonī	bonae	bona
GEN.	bonorum	bonārum	bonorum
DAT.	bonīs	bonīs	bonīs
ACC.	bonōs	bonās	bona
ABL.	bonīs	bonīs	bonīs

Latin comparative and superlative adjectives also have full declensions. German adjectives have a strong and weak declension with three genders and four cases in the singular; all genders have the same four case-endings in the plural. Thus there are thirty-two possibilities, though some of the endings coincide. French adjectives are much simpler, but even they have two genders and a plural form. You can immediately forget all this and be thankful for the admirable simplicity of the uninflected English adjective. This simplicity includes the articles, which are a form of limiting adjective.

In modern English the simplest parts of speech are the definite article (*the*) and the indefinite articles (*a, an*). This was not true of

146

Old English, where articles were fully inflected, taking endings for case, number, and gender to match the noun they modify.

Modern English, fortunately, is not bothered with these problems; as Gertrude Stein might have put it: *"The is a the is a the is a the."* Still, there are some questions of usage connected with the article, and one is the distinction between *a* and *an*. Most people never have to think about this—at least, not in speaking—for it is generally used correctly as a matter of habit; but occasionally, in writing, the wrong article is used. *A* is used before words beginning with a voiced consonant (*"a kangaroo"*) or with *eu* or *u* when pronounced *y* (*"a* European education," *"a* euphemism," *"a* university," *"a* unicorn," *"a* unique proposal"). A double consonant would cause a stuttering sound (*"an nitwit"*), but to have something to get our teeth into and to avoid grunting over two vowels (*a aardvark*), we use *an* before words beginning with a vowel (*"an apricot," "an orang-utang"*) or with a silent *h* (*"an heir," "an honor," "an hour"*). It is acceptable but archaic to use *an* before *historical, habitual, university,* perhaps because these suggest a Cockney accent (*"an 'istorical hepisode"*). *An* rather than *a* should be used before initials and figures that begin with a vowel sound (*"an RKO movie," "an RCA record," "an $18,000 house"*).

Repetition of the definite or the indefinite article before each noun in a pair or series places a rhythmic stress on the individual words (*"The Power and the Glory," "A Stone, a Leaf, a Door"*). If you don't want this stress, one article will do for all (*"The Army and Navy forever. . ."*).

A frequent nuisance in student writing is the omission of the initial article from a title; thus one encounters "Frank Norris' the *Octopus," "Norris' Octopus," "In Grapes of Wrath,* Steinbeck . . . ," "Tennessee Williams' *Streetcar Named Desire.*" On the other hand, there is no article before *Adventures of Huckleberry Finn,* although some publishers mistakenly insert one. If titles of different works overlap, an omitted or inserted article might lead to confusion, as when a student wrote of Faulkner's *Hamlet* (*The Hamlet*). Another student, confused by *The,* thought *The Fountainhead* was a character (like the Batman) as well as the title of Ayn Rand's novel, and wrote: "In *The Fountainhead,* the Fountainhead was an architect who would not compromise his principles. The Fountainhead said . . ." This way lies madness. When the title of a publication is used as a modifier, the article is sometimes dropped; "a *New Yorker* story" or "a *Saturday Evening Post* cartoon" is used to avoid the

147

double article in "a *The New Yorker* story" or "a *The Saturday Evening Post* cartoon."

Claiming that articles have no meaning and so are expendable, newspapers often omit them in order to achieve a telegraphic conciseness ("Senate Investigating Committee expresses belief that main agency of narcotics smuggling is Mafia"). But omitting articles does not really speed reading; it is likelier to make the reader pause and fill in the gaps. If articles were really useless, we doubtless would have gotten rid of them long ago, but *the* particularizes its noun, while *a* and *an* indicate one of a class. When some historical novelists attempt to give an archaic flavor to their prose by leaving out articles, they succeed only in writing stilted sentences like, "Bellegarde clapped hand to hilt, drew sword from scabbard, and pinked opponent in shoulder." Though the omission of articles can be awkward, their excessive or careless use can cause confusion. "Hector Heathcliff, the professor of English at Harvard University" implies that Harvard has only one professor of English. "Rousseau the French primitive painter" is proper because he is well enough known and because the modifier distinguishes him from Rousseau the philosopher. But sometimes *the* bestows a distinction that is unjustified. "Mañana Iguana the painter" may frustrate the reader with the feeling that he should recognize the name, whereas in this case the painter has a well-deserved obscurity.

There are a few special uses for the definite article. The proper form of address for ministers is "The Reverend Mr. Jones" rather than "Reverend Jones." Heads of Scottish and Irish families sometimes take *the* as in Robert the Bruce. And the official name of certain institutions, such as The John Hopkins University (vs. Duke University), requires the use of *the* in the title, sometimes even retaining it when the form is shortened (The Hopkins).

A and *an* are dead wood in such constructions as "kind of a dog," "sort of an impression." Though these forms are used fairly often by competent writers, it is better to use *kind of* and *sort of* without the article, on the principle that unless necessary in dialogue, any useless word is better omitted.

¶ ADVERBS

Whereas the adjective tells *which* or *what kind of* and describes single words (nouns, pronouns, and adjectives), the adverb modifies verbs, adjectives, other adverbs; and it may accompany both single

148

words and entire phrases and clauses. It answers such questions as *how, when, where, why,* and *in what direction*; but the term *adverb* is misleading, for adverbs are used not only with verbs.

Here are some examples of adverbs. *Carefully* tells how the nitroglycerine is to be carried in "Carry the nitroglycerine carefully." *Very* describes how *carefully* it is to be carried in "Carry the nitroglycerine very carefully." *Finally* answers the question of when with *turned* in "Mr. Hyde finally turned into Dr. Jekyll." *East* tells in what direction to turn in "Turn east." The adverbs are italicized in the following: "Do *not* make mistakes," "*Always* be careful," "Raccoons live *here now*," "*Never* mind," "Practice *often*," "Come *in*," "Be *off*," "Sit *down*," and "We sail *tomorrow*." And, of course, *how, when, where,* and *why* are themselves used as adverbs.

Sometimes a phrase or clause functions adverbially. In "At last Mighty Mouse arrived," *at last* answers *when*. So does *when he tried* in "When he tried, he succeeded in becoming a teen-age Frankenstein." In "Take off hell-for-leather," *hell-for-leather* explains how. *Because he forgot to watch the fire* explains why in "Because he forgot to watch the fire, Alfred burned the cakes."

Whereas the adjective generally precedes its governing word, the adverb may come almost anywhere in the sentence. Take for example "The monster began to revive" and see where the adverb *slowly* will fit. It may occur in any of four positions: "*Slowly* the monster began to revive," "The monster began to revive *slowly*," "The monster *slowly* began to revive," and "The monster began *slowly* to revive."

Sometimes a noun functions as an adverb, for example, the italicized words in the following examples: "We went shopping *yesterday*," "She died last *Wednesday*," (tells when) "Jennie walked *miles*," (tells how far) "Hawthorne and Melville talked *hours*," (tells how long), "The idol weighed *tons*" (tells how much). Compare "The idol weighed tons" with "The explorers weighed the idol." In the first, *tons* is an adverb giving the answer to how much; in the second, *idol* is a direct object telling what was weighed. When a noun serves as an adverb, it can still have an adjective modifier like *twenty* in "Wakefield returned twenty years later," or *last* in "She disappeared last Wednesday." In Southern Appalachian speech, adverbs occasionally double as nouns: "A man has a rather about what he'll drink."

One of the most frequent specimens of nonstandard grammar is the use of an adjective where an adverb is required. Yet it is often difficult to distinguish between the two. Often the same word is an adverb in one sentence and not in another. For instance, *very* is an adverb in "Fight very fiercely" but an adjective in "That's the very ingredient he needs." Conventionally *good* is an adjective and *well* an adverb: "Betsy is a good cook who cooks well." But *well* is also an adjective meaning *healthy*. "Smithers didn't feel *good,* but the doctors insisted that he was *well.*" Naturally this situation results in confusion, with the wrong word being used for an adjective, as in the ad: "A big delicious glass of orange juice (with ice in it) goes good with almost anything, or all by itself." Often, but by no means always, adverbs end in *-ly: surely, repeatedly, softly, hurriedly, commonly, gladly.* But adjectives may also end in *-ly;* we speak of "a timely book," "a kingly bearing," "a manly act," "a fatherly kiss," "a princely present." Some words ending in *-ly* are both adjective and adverb, like *early* and *leisurely.* We can take a *leisurely* drive and view the mountains *leisurely.* To confuse matters further, we have pairs of words, one with and one without *-ly,* in which both are adjectives: a *dead* king, a *deadly* poison; a *kind* queen, a *kindly* dwarf; a *low* branch, a *lowly* peasant; a *live* wire, a *lively* dance; a *sick* basset, a *sickly* invalid; *world* affairs and *worldly* possessions.

Usually when the same base appears with and without *-ly,* the plainer form is the adjective, and the *-ly* one the adverb; *light* vs. *lightly, bright* vs. *brightly, safe* vs. *safely, near* vs. *nearly.* But this is not always the case. *Hard* is an adjective, but the adverbial form is also *hard; hardly* has another meaning. You say, "The trunk closes hard; please slam it," not "The trunk closes hardly." Likewise, *lately,* though an adverb, is not the adverbial equivalent of *late* but instead means *recently.* Scott wrote "The gallant came late," not "The gallant came lately." Similarly, the meaning is different in "Travel light" and "Travel lightly" or "I like to drive cool" and "I like to drive coolly." In informal usage, some adverbs drop an *-ly* that might appear in more formal prose: both *loud* and *loudly, slow* and *slowly, quick* and *quickly, quiet* and *quietly* appear as adverbs, though formal usage prefers the latter of each pair. By overcompensation, some people add an *-ly* where there should be none and so create illegitimate words like *thusly, muchly,* and *firstly;* the only acceptable forms are *thus, much,* and *first.*

Sometimes it is impossible to distinguish adjectives from adverbs. Take, for example, the sentences, "True seeing is seeing charitably" and "Charitable seeing is seeing truly," where the same word *seeing* takes adjective and adverb indiscriminately. Is *seeing* a noun or a verb? Functionally, of course, it is a noun; yet as a gerund, it is the present participle of a verb and takes an adjective. Yet how can a noun be associated with an adverb? Then there is *precisely* in "Precisely what I wanted lay there." Now *precisely* is the adverb form, by contrast to the adjective *precise*; yet *precisely* modifies the clause "what I wanted," which functions as the noun subject of the verb *lay*. Here again, then, we have what seems to be an adverb modifying a noun, in the teeth of every rule of grammar.

Observe the first word in "Comparatively few came." In form it is an adverb; in function, an adjective. Take "They are all equally complete, all equally sentences." Try this on your grammarian. First give him the sentence with the three last words omitted, and ask him what *equally* is, and what it modifies. He will reply that *equally* is an adverb modifying the adjective *complete*. Now spring the second *equally* on him and ask him what it is if not an adverb and what it modifies if not the noun *sentences*.

Nowadays the adverb seems to be losing its tail; -*ly* forms are dropped and the adjective form doubles with an adverbial function in much current usage. Telephone companies advertise, "Dial direct with us." (Contrast *dial directly* with *direct dialing*.) Stretch-weave diapers "pin on easier, smoother, snugger." An ad for want ads quotes a student as saying, "I am very happy that I sold the banjo so quick." Aeroxon Fly Ribbons advertise "Catch flies safe & sanitary," making it appear that *safe & sanitary* are adjectives modifying *flies*, though of course they are used adverbially to modify *catch*. (The traditional adverbial forms are *safely* and *sanitarily*, or you could say "in a safe & sanitary way.") If you use Sea & Ski lotion, "You sure will tan, sure won't burn." Elvis Presley's first movie was *Love Me Tender*, and the title song goes on to urge that the lover "love me true." Sidney Bechet wrote an autobiography called *Treat It Gentle*. You are urged to "Shop early . . . shop easy for your personalized Hallmark Christmas cards." If you buy Christmas presents, get a mechanical dog: "Gaylord looks kind of crazy, moves kind of lazy." And the *Vogue Pattern Book* explains, "Frogs are made easiest if you work on a flat surface and pin loops." [3] In these examples, conservative usage would employ the adverbial forms: *directly, more easily, more smoothly, more snugly, quickly, safely, sanitarily, surely, tenderly, truly, gently, easily, lazily,* and *most easily*.

Thus many people say "awful slow," "Homer is hurt bad," "real good" when an adverb (*awfully, badly, very*) is required. At the same time, they use adverbs when adjectives are needed; one questionnaire found that three fifths of the students interviewed said "I feel well" rather than "I feel good," and two fifths said "I feel badly." This brings us back again to the question of predicate adjectives. Besides *to be* there are other linking verbs (*feel, become, act, seem, taste, grow, look, sound, turn, fall,* and others) that, in addition to having regular meanings of their own, can connect a modifier to its subject. In such cases, the modifiers are predicate adjectives: "He fell *silent,*" "The beanstalk grew *tall,*" "Prufrock became *old,*" "She died *young,*" "Natasha acted *odd,*" "Boris seemed *uneasy,*" "The slumgullion tastes *good,*" "Fosdick looked *sick,*" "The cider turned *sour.*" Many people mistakenly use an adverb instead of the predicate adjective. But there is a difference between "Natasha acted odd" and "Elvis acted oddly." In the first, *odd* describes Natasha; in the second, *oddly* describes Elvis's acting. Thus it is nonstandard to say "Aunt Bossy is feeling poorly" (which seems to describe her ability to feel rather than the state of her health), "I hope your folks are all gaily," or "He acts toughly."

Sometimes it is a borderline case whether a word should be an adverb or a predicate adjective. In "Take it easy," does *easy* serve as an adverb modifying *take* (the usual adverb form is *easily*), or is it an adjective modifying *you* understood? In "Sin rises strong," does *strong* modify *rises* (should it therefore be *strongly*) or *sin*? In "He dresses *shabby,*" should *shabby* be *shabbily* to modify *dresses,* or does it modify *he*? When a Southern restaurant advertised "Eat segregated in comfort," *segregated* does not modify *eat* but *you all* understood.

A great many advertisements use this sort of borderline adjective. We are urged to "Live modern—smoke an L&M," to "Shop smart," to buy Smirnoff Vodka and "Think tall." Here *modern, smart,* and *tall* could conceivably modify *you* understood, rather than the respective verbs. But what do you make of the grammar in "Go *Rambler,*" "They eat *cute* in California," "Think *big,* raise elephants," "Think *pink,*" "Think *crisp* with round Kix," "Go *jet-smooth* in a '63 Chevrolet," or "Think *young*"? Clearly the italicized words are adverbs, rather than objects of verbs, yet they are very oblique adverbs. Yet "Go Ramblerly," "Think pinkly," "Think crisply," "Go jet-smoothly" would never do. Perhaps we have here a new elliptical dimension.

Other ads combine the adjective used adverbially with a confusion between transitive and intransitive verbs. Thus we get the

152

curious dimension of "Nestlé's Quik tastes best and fixes easiest," "The flavor [of Calvert Extra] is rich and full—yet it swallows easy," "Plastic rolling pin rolls light and easy . . . wipes clean," "Shampoo pours rich," "White Owl cigars taste so good, smoke so mild," and "The instruments looked strange, but they listened good." Here we approach a sort of dehumanization in which things fix, swallow, wipe, pour, smoke, and listen to themselves while devouring the adverb in the process.

If adverbial forms are widely neglected today, the language may not be degenerating so much as regressing to an earlier phase. In the sixteenth and seventeenth centuries, Englishmen often preferred the adjective form for adverbial function. Hamlet speaks of theatrical performances "come tardy off" and describes himself as "indifferent honest." In *Richard III,* Lord Hastings speaks of "the crown so foul misplaced." We would say *tardily, indifferently,* and *foully* but Shakespeare often dropped the -*ly,* "and sure he is an honorable man," as Antony said of Brutus. *Sure* was used regularly instead of *surely* in Elizabethan English. In the early seventeenth century, *scarce* was common instead of *scarcely* as an adverb; William Bradford wrote that in Plymouth, "of 100 and odd persons, scarce 50 remained." An English folksong over four hundred years old has a farmer blow his horn "both loud and shrill." And throughout English and American literature, we find adjective forms used adverbially. In the following examples, the italics are mine.

> Through care of my parents I was taught to read *near* as soon as I was capable of it. . . .
>> —JOHN WOOLMAN

> He that drinks fast, pays *slow.*
>> —BENJAMIN FRANKLIN

> If one can think at all, in serious difficulties, one thinks *quick.*
>> —WILKIE COLLINS, *The Woman in White*

> It is not necessary that a man should earn his living by the sweat of his brow, unless he sweats *easier* than I do.
>> —HENRY DAVID THOREAU, *Walden*

> Every atom belonging to me as *good* belongs to you.
>> —WALT WHITMAN

> . . . the Day/Turned and departed *silent.*
>> —RALPH WALDO EMERSON

A bird with an angelic gift
Was singing in it *sweet* and *swift*.—ROBERT FROST

Do not go *gentle* into that good night.—DYLAN THOMAS

In conversation with Lillian Ross, Hemingway usually employed adjective forms adverbially: he shoots good, eats good, writes wonderful, moves pure, hits solid. On the other hand, he said, ". . . in war they talk profane, although I always try to talk gently." [4] Norman Mailer wrote that "James Jones can write as good as anyone who writes a book review." [5] Another reviewer claimed that David Stacton "writes quick and dry and funny. . . ." [6] And "A good way to end a story is, 'The prince and the princess lived happy ever after and the mice lived happy ever after too.' " [7]

Certainly it is too fastidious to insist that *quickly* rather than *fast* or *quick* must always be the adverb. "Get rich quick" has become a cliché. Many adverbs can appear either with or without *-ly*. *Loud, slow, quick* are all right after verbs but not before them. We can say "Drive slow," "Think quick," "He plays rough," "Talk louder," but not "Loud she sings in church," "Slow he eats dinner," or "Quick he slammed the door." We can say "He talks slow," but we must say "He talks slowly when he is thinking carefully." Sometimes sound requires that *-ly* not be added, especially if it will make a word end in *-lily*. In *Julius Caesar*, Brutus says, "How ill that taper burns." The line becomes ludicrous as "How illy that taper burns." So does "View the mountains leisurelily," "Juliet dances lovelily," "Step livelily," and so forth.

Despite Madison Avenue and other sources, it is not yet advisable to use adjectives indiscriminately as adverbs. There is still a difference between "Some kids can't speak English plainly" and "Some kids can't speak plain English." Two misused utility words are the adjectives *powerful* and *plenty* employed as adverbs in such constructions as "powerful lazy and powerful slow," "If you're hungry for flavor, Tareyton's got plenty—and it's plenty good," and "Marlboro cigarettes are plenty rich, yet plenty mild." Here the modifiers filter out the linguistic flavor. Likewise, you must be careful not to use adverbs indiscriminately: certainly the choice is askew in "Bulldozers *rapinely* crush tiny glades."

The adverb can be overworked until it becomes a mannerism. Henry James employed them somewhat noticeably in his late prose. For example, in "The Jolly Corner" we find, "But, quite beautifully, she had too much tact to dot so monstrous an *i*, and it

154

was precisely an illustration of the way she didn't rattle"; and " 'You came to yourself,' she beautifully smiled." As James himself put it of one of his characters, "He importantly qualified." In James, the adverbs are usually not too obtrusive, but they become markedly so in the Tom Swift books popular at the turn of the century. Whenever Tom uttered some dramatic (or even dull) statement, the author modified it adverbially. In 1963, this inspired a book and a game, "Tom Swifties," in which the idea is to make the adverb a pun on the main idea. For example, " 'I'm not so sure about the recipe for the spice cake,' she said gingerly," or " 'I barely avoided a collision,' said Tom recklessly." Joseph Heller's *Catch-22* is full of Tom Swift-type adverbs that contribute to the book's sardonic humor:

> "Did the dead man in my tent have a share?" Yossarian demanded caustically.
> "Of course he did," Milo assured him lavishly.[8]
>
> "I did try," admitted Milo gloomily. . . .
> "It's the end," Milo agreed despondently. . . .
> "Why don't you sell your cotton to the government?" Yossarian suggested casually. . . .
> Milo vetoed the idea brusquely. "It's a matter of principle,"
> he explained firmly.[9]

Here the adverbs are part of the satire, but ordinarily it is advisable to use them with restraint.

In an essay, "Theory and Practice of Editing *New Yorker* Articles," Wolcott Gibbs wrote: "Writers always use too damn many adverbs. On one page recently I found eleven modifying the verb 'said.' 'He said morosely, violently, eloquently, so on.' Editorial theory should probably be that a writer who can't make his context indicate the way his character is talking ought to be in another line of work." [10]

¶ COMPARATIVES AND SUPERLATIVES

In their ordinary form, adjectives and adverbs are in the positive degree. The comparative degree indicates a contrast between two elements: the superlative degree, among three or more elements. To form these degrees, words of one or two syllables usually inflect by adding the suffixes -*er* for the comparative and -*est* for the superlative. Longer words usually keep the positive form, preceded by *more* for the comparative and *most* for the superlative. If the comparison is a diminished one, the positive form is used preceded by *less* for the comparative and *least* for the superlative. The use of the positive preceded by the modifiers (or function words) is sometimes called periphrastic comparison. A few words change their stem for the comparative and superlative degree: *good, better, best*; *bad, worse, worst*; *many, more, most*; and *little, less, least*.

Throughout the history of the language, people have used the superlative to give increased emphasis when the comparison is limited to two members; even such a careful stylist as Dr. Johnson did so. But conservative contemporary usage disapproves and calls for a careful discrimination. Thus you would write, "Who was stronger, King Kong or Godzilla?" and "Who is the stupidest of the Three Stooges?" Venus is *closer* to the sun than the earth is, but Mercury is the *closest* planet of all.

	POSITIVE	COMPARATIVE	SUPERLATIVE
ADJECTIVE	ugly	uglier	ugliest
	green	greener	greenest
	lovely	lovelier	loveliest
	lonely	lonelier	loneliest
	squeamish	more squeamish	most squeamish
	comfortable	more comfortable	most comfortable
ADVERB	late	later	latest
	hard	harder	hardest

If both the adjective and adverb end in *-ly,* the comparative and superlative can be formed by adding a suffix (*early, earlier, earliest*); but if the adverb already ends in *-ly,* it cannot add another suffix and so must be preceded by *more, most, less,* or *least.* No one ever uses *quicklier, wildliest, hopefulliest.* In other cases, the question of whether the alteration is made by adding a suffix or an auxiliary modifier does not depend absolutely on the number of syllables, but is partly a matter of idiom. Theoretically, a two-syllable word could use either method, but you'd never use *squeamisher* or *squalidest.* Most three-syllable words use periphrastic comparison; but there are exceptions; you'd never use *glamorouser* or *beautifulest,* but you could use *slipperiest.* Both *most unlikely* and *unlikeliest* are acceptable. The inflected form gives slightly more stress to the root and the quality it indicates (dear′ est), and the periphrastic *more* or *most* gives more emphasis to the degree. Thus, while one-

156

syllable words usually inflect, we use *most* in speaking of "every thing we hold most dear." Hamlet says, "This is most brave," " 'tis most sweet," and speaks of his father's "most dear life," where ordinarily the form would be *bravest, sweetest,* and *dearest.*

Often the comparative form is used without the second term of the comparison ever appearing; we hope for *better things,* speak of *lesser evils* and *baser metal,* support *higher education.* The periphastic superlative also is often used emphatically, with *most* being used for intensity without any specific comparison being indicated: "You are *most generous,*" "Orson is *most intelligent,*" "Caesar was *most ambitious*"; Hamlet frequently uses "most vile" in this way.

Theoretically, words that represent an absolute cannot be compared. Such words as *perfect, round, alive, dead, final, straight, pure, excellent, impossible, unique, black, white, complete* logically have no further degree of meaning. Yet we often modify them ("By gad, it's absolutely perfect"), and in practice they are often compared. There are, in fact, degrees of black and white; if these were absolutes, we wouldn't need such metaphorical clichés as "jet black," "black as pitch," "black as the ace of spades," "white as snow." Thus Shakespeare has Othello say of Desdemona that he "would not mar that whiter skin of hers than snow/And smooth as monumental alabaster." Shakespeare also used "most excellent." Though *pure* should be 100 percent, Thomas Gray wrote, "Full many a gem of purest ray serene,/The dark unfathomed caves of ocean bear. . . ." And our own Constitution begins with the intent "to form a more perfect Union." Often we admit a degree of comparison without actually using the comparative or superlative form of an absolute word itself; we speak of something as "more nearly perfect," "most nearly impossible," and so on. When used metaphorically, absolutes are often less than absolute and can be compared: "You look even deader than I do." *Unique* is often used informally to mean *rare* or *unusual,* rather than *one and only,* yet a critic for *Newsweek* called Arthur Miller's description of Marilyn Monroe as "most unique" a "barbarous locution." But there is, nevertheless, plenty of precedent, and Miller is certainly more a master of language than members of the *Newsweek* staff.

Modern grammatical convention forbids the use of both modifier and suffix to make a double comparative or superlative; e.g. "*The Attack of the 50-Foot Woman* is the most funniest movie I've ever seen." Shakespeare, on the other hand, often used a double comparative or superlative: Mark Anthony calls the wound Brutus gave Caesar "the most unkindest cut of all"; in *Richard II,* John of Gaunt speaks of "the envy of less happier lands"; in *Othello,* Cassio says, "The worser that you give me the addition"; and Othello says, "she comes more nearer earth than she was wont . . ." These are clear and emphatic, and there is no reason why the double degree could not make a comeback, but at present such usage is considered nonstandard. For a century, people have been amused by the grammar in Nathan Bedford Forrest's statement of getting there "firstest with the mostest men."

¶ PSYCHOSEMANTICS

Sometimes vague, inappropriate, and misleading modifiers appear in sentences where they confuse or even reverse accurate meaning. *Semantics* is the study of the meaning of words; and some words are used in ways that are muddled, befuddled, psychotic, or downright sinister. Beginning with a harmless example, we encounter, "It was a literal picture-postcard of a day, and we lived every minute of it." *Literal* and *literally* are often used when the speaker really means *figurative* or *metaphorically*; but the careless speaker strives so hard for emphasis that he reverses the meaning and sometimes becomes ludicrous, as in "I literally blew my top." Then there is "Could we have about four folders, please?" Why *about*? Does the speaker really want three or five folders? If he wants exactly four, he should say so with no *abouts*; and if he is really trying to finagle half a dozen, he should ask for six. It is advisable to minimize and, whenever possible, eliminate timid qualifiers like *rather, somewhat, a bit,* and *little.* "Rather tasty," "somewhat attractive" are too uncommitted. The teacher who is grading a poor theme may pull his punches by noting, "This is a bit vague," or "This is rather routine." Likewise, intensive adverbs intended to serve as strengtheners,—such as *so, such,* and *very*—often weaken the force of sentences in which they appear. Consider, for example, "Sara sank into the nearest chair; she had had such a hard day, and she was so tired"; omit *such* and *so,* and you will find a distinct improvement. Schoolgirl style is sprinkled with such gushy emphasis that it only makes the prose soggy. In "Beneath her snow-white veil, the bride looked almost virginal," the intended effect of awe is ironically undercut by the qualifying adverb. And in "Scott said the Russian and probably American intelligence agencies undoubtedly knew where the Red Chinese would produce nuclear weapons," the ad-verbs (*probably* and *undoubtedly*) contradict and cancel each other. Then there are modifiers that mislead by not being what they seem. Merchandisers advertise, "Send 25 cents and a box top for your *free* thingamabob." Radio stations announce, "After this commercial we resume our program of *uninterrupted music.*" Many motion-picture theaters advertising "art" films do not show genuine art films by such directors as Ingmar Bergman, Federico Fellini, Sergei Eisenstein, Satyajit Ray, Akira Kurosawa, Stanley Kubrick, and Tony Richardson, but specialize in cheap striptease and nudist pictures. When a motion picture or television program lists someone as "guest" star, the matter is not one of hospitality but of calculated business transaction, whereby someone else gets top billing but the "guest" retains status by being a guest instead of a supporting or bit player. As for TV "immortals," they are lucky to last three seasons. How accurate is the word *average* in the sentence, "The average American sees 10,000 TV commercials a year?" To avoid making loose and faulty generalizations, you should omit words like *average, typical, all, every, always, most, never,* and *none* unless you possess reliable statistics, for all too often the sweeping *always* or *never* turns out to have a good many exceptions.

Voluntary is of questionable accuracy when you read in the newspaper, "Local action group wants to require voluntary school prayer" or "Stalin sent agents to capture a scientist and bring him back in a voluntary-compulsory manner." *Democratic* is certainly inaccurate when the Communist powers call themselves "democratic." In fact, practically all political adjectives—e.g., *liberal, conservative, realistic, austere, forward-looking, constructive, economical*—should be scrutinized, in the context in which they appear, for accuracy. Even *patriotic* becomes debatable in meaning when extremist groups calling themselves "patriotic" or "superpatriotic" accuse the Chief Justice and President of the United States of treason and indulge in abusive and seditious methods to brand as unpatriotic anyone who favors fluoridation, civil rights, academic freedom, the United Nations, public school integration, or social security. Should such slander be dignified by the word *patriotic?*

Often we use negative adjectives and adverbs in a favorable sense. "She's a mean cook" and "She slings the nastiest ankle in the dance hall" are meant to be admiring. People speak of being "dreadfully happy," "terribly fond of someone," and use words like *terribly, insanely, frightfully, horribly* as adverbs with *beautiful, desirable,* and

159

being in love. James Thurber found such semantics sinister in the modern age of anxiety and stated, "I think we must learn to brighten the human idiom, as well as make it communicable." [11] Both adjectives and adverbs can contribute to jargon. Pseudo-sophisticated ads recommend items that are *verve-y, un-huge, un-skintight,* or *loose-ish.* Observe in the "Negatives" chapter how the Newspeak of George Orwell's *1984* totalitarian society eliminates contrasting adjectives and different shades among near-synonyms by using, for example, *ungood, plusgood,* and *doubleplusgood* to replace *bad, better, excellent, splendid,* and other words that require exact critical judgment. To make adjectives in Newspeak, one adds the suffix *-ful* to nouns or verbs; and to make adverbs, one adds *-wise.* Thus *angry* would be *angerful,* and *angrily* would be *angerwise.* Without any governmental pressure, we already seem to be moving somewhat in that direction. In some modern jargon, *proud* becomes *prideful, healthy* becomes *healthful,* and *fierce* adds a dead-wood suffix to become *fierceful.* The suffix *-wise* is far more prominent and has even become a joke on some occasions. Certainly the speaker who says, "Beethovenwise, you'll hear the Emperor Concerto," has a gray-flannel-suit mind. Shakespeare's "a muddy knave" would sound like a denizen of Madison Avenue if he were described as "a knave mudwise." What would happen to the poetry if the wise guys were to turn Macbeth's meditation into:

> Tomorrow creeps tomorrowwise and tomorrowwise
>   pettypacewise from day to day
> To the last syllable recorded timewise;
> And all our yesterdays have lighted fools
> Dustydeathwise. Out, out brief candle;
> Life's but a shadow walkingwise; a poor player
> That struts and frets hourwise, stagewise,
> And then is heard no more; it is a tale told
> Idiotwise, soundwise, furywise,
> Nonsignifyingwise.

'Tis devoutly not to be wished, consummationwise.

Exercise 12: In the following passages, underline the adjectives with a single line and the adverbs with a double line.

1. A brownish-colored Java python, with a row of large, irregularly-shaped black blotches down the back, is approximately ten feet long and measures up to five inches in diameter.

160

2. "The snow-white Northern Gannets, *Morus bassanus,* are strong, goose-sized sea birds with heavy, streamlined bodies."
—Back cover of *Zoonooz,* May, 1964.

3. "On the first day of Christmas my true love sent to me
A partridge in a pear tree."

4. "Inebriate of air am I
And debauchee of dew,
Reeling through endless summer days
From inns of molten blue."

5. The barred owl has a more emphatic hoot than that of the great horned owl, but his eight accented hoots are less deep.

6. "The morn in russet mantle clad
Walks o'er the dew of yon high eastward hill."

7. The ear tufts of the horned owl are larger and more spread apart than those of the long-eared owl.

8. Clad in pajamas, the deformed monster lumbered clumsily out of the smashed laboratory, carrying the doctor's daughter.

9. "The ram was fat behind, sir,
The ram was fat before.
He measured ten yards round, sir,
I think it was no more."

10. Some woodpeckers have white bars on their back or white rumps, but the hairy woodpecker is white backed.

11. "Last night you slept on a goose-feather bed,
With the sheet turned down so bravely O!
Tonight you'll sleep in a cold, open field,
Along with the wraggle-taggle Gypsies O!"

12. The olive-sided flycatcher appears to have a dark jacket unbuttoned down the front.

13. "If you will come along with me
Under yonder flowering tree
I might catch you a small bird or two."

14. "Oh bring on your rubber-tired hearses,
Bring on your rubber-tired hacks.
They're taking Johnny to the buryin' ground
And they won't bring a bit of him back."

15. Blank verse is unrhymed iambic pentameter.

Exercise 13: Correct any faulty adjectives or adverbs in the following:

1. All us cats is high-strung, but I'm high-strungder than most.
2. Hegel was far-yonderer than Kant on some points.
3. A milch goat gives more richer milk than a mountain cow.
4. The Cherokees used seven different kind of woods to make ceremonial fires.

5. The Kuikuru are not offended if you refuse their food as long as you do it tactful.
6. General Forrest came instanter than General McClellan.
7. If the bear den is not uninhabited, we must run quick.
8. The one advantage of a pitch pipe over a piano is that it fits into your guitar case easier.
9. In southern Ohio, "You lackum wrapper" and "You like them riper" sound similarly.
10. The horse is afeard to jump across the chasm.
11. If the wind gets any worser, this cabin will blow off the mountain.
12. You'll be sorrow if you miss Dogpatch.
13. The hurrier I go, the behinder I get.
14. Bib-overalls are great for leisure living.
15. The pioneers had little rations left when they were finally rescued.
16. I hate them mice to pieces.
17. We were suppose to pick up our tickets before 8:00 P.M.
18. Henry VIII was a very mannish monarch.
19. We had 57 percent less mosquito bites after spraying with "Phew!"
20. The harpsichord was made from a eighty-five-year-old cherry tree.
21. Will you please put them pots in the sink?
22. The campers were unaccustom to dealing with an elephant in a state of must.
23. Clancy is the goodest left fielder since Casey was at the bat.
24. Rainy days are no time to have a active child around the house.
25. Bruno Bumpergarde, the physics professor at M.I.T., was mugged on an holiday to New York.

Exercise 14: Replace any adjectives with conventional adverb forms when the adverb is required in the following:

1. Cowboys weren't near as glamorous on the job as many people think.
2. The bears live peaceable if not provoked.
3. W. C. Fields was a juggler previous.
4. Zack can use a whip so accurate that he can pick flies off a mule's back.
5. The crocodile came out of the water prompt and hurried towards the cook beating the dinner gong.
6. I hate to see you give up so easy when you are almost finished.
7. The door shut very soft and quietly.
8. The huckleberries aren't doing so good this year.
9. The potato salad was made different tonight.
10. You can live cheaper in a warmer climate except for insect repellent.
11. The Hollywood system does not allow artists enough freedom in which to direct uninhibited.

162

12. I'm saving Confederate money in case the war's refought and comes out different.
13. Iced tea goes good with pizzas.
14. The bear looked suspicious at the artichoke.
15. Snakes have to be handled very careful.
16. If you tune your guitar too high, you may break a string.
17. You didn't divide up the gooseberry fool fair.
18. Play the snaredrums gentle or you'll wake up the poodles.
19. He's handy as a three-legged stool.
20. A sheik walks different from ordinary people.
21. The retreat was quick becoming a rout.
22. The old Moulmein pagoda looks lazy at the sea.
23. You have to quick shut the door to keep out the bugs.
24. Cades Cove eroded very gradual whereas some Western canyons show more spectacular erosion.
25. Auda ate slow without his false teeth.

Exercise 15: Underline the proper form of the comparative and superlative modifiers.

1. Going down the Colorado River by boat was the (excitingest, most exciting) vacation I've ever had.
2. Which Invisible Man was the (invisiblest, invisibler, most invisible, more invisible) —Claude Rains, Vincent Price, or Jon Hall?
3. Which version of *The Prisoner of Zenda* did you like (better, best) — the Ronald Colman or the Stewart Granger one?
4. Clark Gable's *Mogambo* was a remake of *Red Dust* but was (most successful, more successful, successfuller).
5. The Clark Gable-Charles Laughton version of *Mutiny on the Bounty* was (more, most) dramatically effective, but the Marlon Brando version was the (more, most) colorful.
6. Which was the (funnier, funniest, more funny, most funny) Marx Brothers movie—*Duck Soup, Animal Crackers,* or *A Night at the Opera?*
7. My uncle preferred Hardy to Laurel, but my father thinks Laurel is (more, most) talented.
8. Of the actors who portrayed Napoleon in the movies, Charles Boyer was the (more, most) sympathetic, Marlon Brando was the (more, most) dynamic, and Herbert Lom was the (sinisterer, sinisterest, more sinister, most sinister).
9. In *Duel in the Sun,* Gregory Peck was supposed to gun down Charles Bickford; but Bickford had acted in so many Westerns that he was (quicker, quickest) and kept beating Peck to the draw.
10. This is the (fast-risingest, fastest rising) dough I've ever seen.

163

Exercise 16: Put the proper modifier in the blank.

1. Jane appears in (less, fewer) than half the Tarzan books. . . . .
2. I don't know why you are still (bias, biased) against oatmeal. . . . .
3. Can I have another of (those, them) travel folders on East Africa? . . . .
4. Pork skins are (wonderful, wonderfully) crisp. . . . .
5. "The Frog Galliard" is one of the (greatest, most great) pieces of music ever written, even though it is (comparative, comparatively) obscure. . . . .
6. West Branch, Iowa, was the (less, least) exciting of the historical landmarks we visited last summer. . . . .
7. This box of crayons has (much, many) different colors. . . . .
8. Have you become (accustomed, accustom) to the noise? . . . .
9. Joe Blfstk (?) is the (most unique, uniquest, most nearly unique) character I know of. . . . .
10. Boccherini's "Quintet in E for Guitar and Strings" is a (more masterful, masterfuller) composition than Tschaikovsky's symphonies. . . . .
11. How (much, many) more exercises do you have to do? . . . .
12. Pink is my (best, bestest) color. . . . .
13. *Thuvia, Maid of Mars* has a picture of Thuvia and a banth on (its, it's) cover. . . . .
14. The sky was (redder, more red) at dawn today than at sunset. . . . .
15. Stewart had (much more, many more) gray hairs after returning from the Amazon. . . . .
16. It is no longer respectable to be (prejudiced, prejudice) against minority groups. . . . .
17. Was Elmo Lincoln, Johnny Weismuller, Bruce Bennett, Gordon Scott, or Jock Mahoney (better, best) at giving Tarzan's cry of the bull ape? . . . .
18. Because of sprawling suburbia, there are (less and less, fewer and fewer) places where one can be alone in the woods. . . . .
19. The riders saddled (their, they're, there) mounts. . . . .
20. I have (less, fewer) wrinkles after using Murphy's Mud. . . . .

Exercise 17: Replace any incorrect modifiers with the proper form.

1. One-arm driving is dangerous.
2. You are suppose to report at 8:15.
3. He looks differently after the party.
4. Jaggars is a muchly disturbed lawyer.
5. Don't feel too badly about the philodendron.
6. They don't dare attack Mike direct, so they attack his friends.
7. There is a much ancient monastery at Mt. Sinai.

8. Herman is bad off after the hunting accident.
9. We were alarmed by his criminalistic behavior.
10. It was near impossible to prove his guilt.
11. Butch acts toughly, but he's really quite gentle.
12. Many fanatics are real sincere, but they'll kill you all the same.
13. The girl hippopotamus dances beautiful to "The Dance of the Hours."
14. *Ulysses* is muchly more difficult than *The Winning of Barbara Worth*.
15. It evident doesn't matter which route you take to Cudjo's Cave.
16. Firstly, we must have your credentials.
17. Edgar sudden heard a knocking at the lattice.
18. Dawn came quite earlily, before the cock crowed.
19. Natural, we need candles for a birthday cake.
20. Waldo became a full fledge eagle scout.
21. Albert felt quite sadly when his candidate lost the election.
22. Pepe reads English as good as he reads French.
23. Pogo once ran off to be a orphan like the girl in the funny papers.
24. You will probable feel better after a good night's sleep.
25. If it rains, let's have the picnic anyways.

11 √ Ambiguous Modifiers

E. M. Forster, discussing motion pictures, wrote in *Abinger Harvest,* "American women shoot the hippopotamus with eyebrows made of platinum." Reading the book, James Thurber was brought up short at that point. "I have given that remarkable sentence a great deal of study," he commented, "but I still do not know whether Mr. Forster means that American women have platinum eyebrows or that the hippopotamus has platinum eyebrows or that American women shoot platinum eyebrows into the hippopotamus." [1]

Probably the most amusing grammatical errors—many downright ridiculous—occur because of ambiguous modifiers. There are two main causes for such ambiguity: dangling modifiers and misplaced ones. In "That bust looks like Beethoven with my glasses off," the modifier is dangling; "with my glasses off" should be describing the speaker, but seems instead to be describing Beethoven. Modifiers dangle when there is no word in the sentence for them to modify; when this occurs some part of the sentence must be rewritten to supply the missing noun or pronoun. Nothing needs to be added for most misplaced modifiers; they simply have to be moved next to whatever they modify. Occasionally a modifier can be both dangling and misplaced. "Did you ever eat chicken with false teeth?" Tasty, wasn't it? But "Did you ever, with false teeth, eat chicken?" is clumsy; the modifier has malocclusion. The solution seems to be, "Did you ever eat chicken when you were wearing false teeth?"

There are several ways for modifiers to dangle. In "He returned from the war with one leg, which he had lost," the modifier not only dangles but goes with the amputated leg, not the one that came home. A more common sort of error is, "Now ninety-two years old, his marriage has remained a happy one." This, obviously, is not the golden-wedding anniversary but a petrified one. Obviously it is the husband and not the marriage that is ninety-two

166

years old. In the sentence, "The first Bourbon king of France, his mistresses were many," how can the feminine plural *mistresses* be modifying the Bourbon king of France? "In his underwear, the tent was suddenly cold." Any self-respecting tent should be not only cold but downright embarrassed to be seen wearing only his underwear. "As a career wife, occasionally the apartment isn't immaculate." Maybe the apartment should get a divorce and marry the tent in the preceding sentence. "Before coming to Hollywood, Hector Troy's real name was Woffington Van Pelt III." But it was Troy, not his name, that came to Hollywood. In these examples, the modifier is an opening phrase followed by a shift of attention from what should have been the subject to the object, with the result that the original subject is omitted altogether and the object becomes the new subject. The solution is to make the thing modified the subject of the main clause.

> Now ninety-two years old, he has continued to have a happy marriage.
>
> The first Bourbon king of France had many mistresses.
>
> In his underwear, he found the tent suddenly cold.
>
> As a career wife, Phyllis occasionally fails to keep the apartment immaculate.
>
> Before coming to Hollywood, Hector Troy was known only by his real name of Woffington Van Pelt III.

On the other hand, the attention shifts from object to subject when Huckleberry Hound says, "As my prisoner, I have to see that you're comfortable." This is saner if it is changed to read, "Since you are my prisoner, I have to see that you're comfortable."

Many dangling modifiers are participial phrases that cause confusion by seeming to modify the subject of the clause that follows. "Dead in the moment of victory, few would not mourn for Wolfe." But it was Wolfe, not *few*, who was dead. In an even grimmer example, we find Anthony Nutting writing, "Being of only a very light weight, the boy's death-struggles were unusually prolonged." [2] But it was the boy himself, not his death struggles, that was light of weight. Mark Raskovitch wrote, "Being the embassy of Her Britannic Majesty, Queen Elizabeth II, there was no fear that proceedings would become boisterous." [3] Here we have an entire embassy dangling. "In turning the wheel, the truck went out of control and crashed into the fence." So did this sentence, for trucks are unable to turn their own wheels. Neither do police arrest themselves, though the campus police saw fit to report, "When apprehended in their apartment, we found that the drapes had been cut with a razor blade so that they would fit the windows." As before, the remedy in each of these instances is to turn the phrase into a subordinate clause: "Because he was only a very light weight . . . ," "Since it was the embassy . . . ," "When he was turning the wheel . . . ," "When we apprehended them . . . ." The first example is trickier because of the word order. It can be clarified as "Few would not mourn for Wolfe dead in the moment of victory," but the drama is lost. A better solution would be, "Dead in the moment of victory, Wolfe would be mourned by many."

Many modifiers dangle because the verb is put in the passive voice; and the original subject, which would have been modified, is therefore omitted. "With a family of five children, floor lamps are constantly being knocked over." A pity; Mama and Papa lamps should be treated with more respect. A manual for a foreign car advises, "When refilling the cooling system, the heating system should be bled by adopting the following procedure." Both present participles dangle here; certainly the heating system does not refill the cooling system. "While speaking of the sheriff, the deputy must not be overlooked." The remedy is to put the sentences in the active voice, restoring the original subject:

> Since the Gooches have a family of five children, they are constantly knocking over floor lamps.

> When refilling the cooling system, you should bleed the heating system by adopting the following procedure.

> While speaking of the sheriff, you must not overlook the deputy.

Yet even professionals sometimes stumble into the pitfall of the passive. Irving Stone wrote, "After passing six years in the district school his first pair of long trousers was given to him . . . ." [4] Did the pants spend six years in school before they were given to him? Stewart Holbrook wrote, "Acting through Donald Smith, one of the Bay Company's big men, and George Steven, head of the Bank of Montreal, six million dollars was raised." [5] But no amount of money, not even in millions, can act through anybody. Norman Mailer wrote, "This way, failing to conquer Cuba, the road was left open for Khrushchev to commit a blunder as large as Kennedy's . . . ." [6] According to one newspaper, "The minister said his friendship with a Negro was 'treated as a subversive plot to integrate the college' by members of the administration." Certainly we can't have administrators integrated with faculty. Again, the active voice clarifies the grammar, even if it doesn't enlighten the administration:

> After passing six years in the district school, Darrow received . . .
>
> Acting through . . . Bank of Montreal, they raised six million dollars.
>
> This way, failing to conquer Cuba, we left the road open . . .
>
> The minister said members of the administration treated his friendship with a Negro as a subversive plot to integrate the college.

In signs and advertisements, ellipsis often makes modifiers dangle, as in "Stop ahead when flashing" or "Not responsible if left over 60 days." "Amazing new easy way puts on pounds and inches of firm, solid flesh without overeating." It's gratifying that it is the way, rather than yourself, that puts on the flesh; apparently it also avoids overeating, whereas you might work up an appetite by watching it.

Sometimes, there are dangling infinitives, as in the following examples: "Life goes too fast to waste it," "To inspect the battery cells, a naked flame should never be used," "The pioneer is dressed in buckskins because civilization is too far away to get other clothing." Usually you can easily correct these by inserting a subject (in the objective case) for the infinitive: "too fast for us to waste it," "too far away for him to get other clothing." If there is a verb in the passive voice, make it active: "To inspect the battery cells, you should never use a naked flame."

Finally, a modifier may not dangle as much as be badly aimed: "As a result of the preceding paragraph, the hunter missed the duck." Experienced hunters should know better than to have paragraphs cluttering their line of fire.

"Did you ever drive a car with tired blood?" "Look at that fellow holding a submarine sandwich with a green sweater." The church bulletin announces, "Sermon: The Importance of Babies delivered by the Rev. Waldo Ralph Dimmesdale." These sentences are ridiculous because of misplaced modifiers. Modifiers naturally tend to modify the possibility nearest to them. Ordinarily correction is simple; merely move the modifier next to the word or phrase it modifies: "that fellow with a green sweater," "Sermon delivered by the Rev. Waldo Ralph Dimmesdale: The Importance of Babies." "Did you ever, with tired blood, drive a car?" is clumsy and requires

169

rewriting: "Did you ever drive a car when you had tired blood?" If you did, you should see your doctor and learn what is wrong, since "tired blood" is not medically accurate. If your car doesn't have tired blood, did you ever hit a jack-rabbit doing eighty? If the rabbit was doing eighty, how fast were you driving? Here again a subordinate clause is needed: "when you were doing eighty."

Some misplaced modifiers, like "A man in a brown suit named Jones came into the room," are merely amusing. Others, less obvious, may twist the meaning, sometimes reversing what the writer intended to say. Thus a letter to the editors of the *Lansing State Journal* complained, "Already the government is in the electric power business with both feet, competing with investor-owned electric utilities with unlimited government money." If investor-owned utilities have unlimited government money, we'd better have an investigation. According to *Life,* "Project water is expected to increase greatly the alfalfa crop of Colorado, which already has about a million acres of alfalfa in the soil bank that no one is allowed to cut." [7] What can't be cut—the acres, the alfalfa, or the soil bank? Returning to the *Lansing State Journal,* we find an editorial stating, "The present harmonious tune of 'We're All for Lyndon' may strike some discordant notes, with the peaceful and illogical union under his banner of Northern big-city liberals and Southern conservatives falling apart at the seams." [8] The modifier was meant to go with *union,* but some Southern conservatives may indeed be falling apart at the seams. There is a patent contradiction in "Deists conceived of God as being good and not an angry God who had created things for delight." A journalism student wrote, "The death of Elijah P. Lovejoy at 35 by a mob, November 7, 1837, in defense of his fourth printing press presents today's newspapermen with a challenge to remain free." But the antiabolitionist mob did not murder Lovejoy in order to defend his press. After the defeat of the Confederacy, Thaddeus Stevens said vengefully, "We have conquered them, and as a conquered enemy we can give them laws . . ." The prose makes "as a conquered enemy" seem to modify "we," though nobody encountering Stevens in person would make such a mistake. Defending the amiable and harmless bloodhound, James Thurber ridiculed the misplaced modifier by quoting a sentence from an unscholarly article reviling the animal: "Terrible to look at and terrible to encounter, man has raised him [the bloodhound] up to hunt down his fellowman." Thurber was delighted that careless grammatical construction made man terrible to look at and terrible to encounter.

170

Other misplaced modifiers create marvelous implausibilities. The *Lansing State Journal* announced, "Bruce Gorsline, 14, views the totem pole of Sakau'Wan he carved shortly after it was raised Tuesday at Carl G. Fenner Arboretum." It's easier to carve totem poles before they are raised, but maybe this craftsman preferred to do things the hard way. When you read, "He had deep blue eyes and a beautiful plaid necktie that quivered with anticipation," you may conclude that he has a nervous Adam's apple. Though Emily Dickinson never married and spent all of her life in Amherst, Massachusetts, she seems to be going West to enter a *menage à trois* when a student writes, "The most serious of Emily Dickinson's loves, the Rev. Charles Wadsworth, was married when she met him and moved not long after to the Pacific Coast." According to the New Testament, Herod Antipas lusted after Salome, but according to the student who wrote the following sentence, he seems to have been a Sodomite: "He is referring to the niece of the king who tried to seduce John the Baptist." Moving the modifier will not cure this sentence: "He is referring to the niece who tried to seduce John the Baptist of the king." The remedy is to turn the partitive genitive (of the king) into an ordinary possessive: "the king's niece who tried to seduce John the Baptist."

Some misplaced modifiers cause a double take. According to one student paper on *The Octopus*, "Annixter had to fight against the exhaustion produced by a losing battle to save his home and a nervous stomach!" He did, in fact, eat prunes to cure a nervous stomach, but the student meant to write of "exhaustion produced by a nervous stomach and a losing battle." In *Catch-22*, Joseph Heller writes, "She would have been perfect for Yossarian, a debauched, coarse, vulgar, amoral, appetizing slattern whom he had longed for and idolized for months."[9] Because of their position, the modifiers seem to describe Yossarian, but of course they belong to *she*. "Though nineteenth century in origin, she's fond of a tall mahogany cubby-hole desk which she dates around 1820." Unless she is a great-grandmother, she is probably twentieth century in origin; the opening phrase needs to be turned into a subordinate clause: "Though it is nineteenth century . . ." Then there is the provocative statement, "I've got to buy some thread for my dress that I'm running out of." Evolution seems to be called into question in, "The wind blew down a branch that hit a man that had something to do with horses on the head." ". . . hit a man on the head that had something to do with horses" is still ambiguous;

". . . a branch that hit on the head a man who had something to do with horses" is awkward, but, at least, clear.

Sometimes the position of just one word is essential. "Yogi Bear is cordial to even strangers" should be corrected to read, ". . . even to strangers." A common but nonstandard colloquialism is the use of *anymore* at the beginning of a sentence, as in "Anymore the Cherokee don't play stickball as rough as they used to." The best solution here is to omit *anymore* altogether. Doubly nonstandard is the use of *anymore* for *nowadays,* as in "Anymore I mop the floor at night because the children are in the way" or "It's hard to tell boys from girls these days. Anymore they all have short hair and long pants." In these latter examples it is the meaning rather than the placement of "anymore" that is objectionable. To be logically precise, you should generally put "only" immediately after, and not before, the word it modifies; thus "Only apply to smooth, flat surfaces" would become "Apply only to smooth, flat surfaces." "I only like to go out on Saturday night" could be misleading, because the speaker doubtless likes to do other things as well, but he likes to go out only on Saturday night—never on Sunday. In practice, such concern about the placement of *only* is hairsplitting. Distinguished authors from Dryden to T. S. Eliot have placed *only* earlier in the sentence than the word it modifies. Cyrus Day of the University of Delaware cites examples from Joseph Addison, John Henry Newman, Thomas H. Huxley, Matthew Arnold, A. E. Housman, Havelock Ellis, George Moore, Somerset Maugham, Edna St. Vincent Millay, Robert Frost, Eugene O'Neill, Bertrand Russell, and Harry Levin, among others. Today it is almost a standard idiom for *only* to come before the verb rather than later. As *Vogue* described the MG sports car, "It'll only carry two people, but it carries them in utter glory."

The placement of *not* is more important, "All are not" seems to be replacing "not all are" in common usage. In casual conversation the issue is not very important, but carefully written prose should avoid the illogic of such a statement as, "All anthologies are not books." Some of them are books. "All the busy executives aren't in offices." Where are they then? The adjective, rather than the verb, should carry the negation: "Not all the busy executives are in offices." Occasionally "all are not" leads to amusing oddities, such as "Being in show business, Barnum was regularly exposed to the charms of other women, and all of them were not freaks."[10]

172

Occasionally one encounters a combination of misplaced and dangling modifier. In Robert Lewis Taylor's *A Journey to Matecumbe,* a character says, "They were my father's squirrel rifles, that got killed in the war." It was, of course, the father and not the rifles that was killed. One of the best former oboe players in the nation announced, "This is Mitch Miller inviting you to help us open our Christmas mail, next in color, on NBC." Mitch's mail may come in color, but most people get theirs in white envelopes. "Next in color, on NBC" could modify Mitch, but it actually refers to the program.

Sometimes a preposition can make a modifier ambiguous: "The princess and the frog got into the coach with eight horses" sounds a bit crowded; "A coach pulled by eight horses" is clearer. Discussing the Salem witch trials, a student wrote, "The girls were dancing nude in the woods with a boiling pot containing a frog nearby." Were they dancing with a boiling pot, and did the pot contain a frog that was nearby it? "The girls were dancing nude in the woods, and a boiling pot containing a frog was nearby" is less intriguing but also less ambiguous. The Pennsylvania Dutch say, "Throw the horse over the fence some hay." Do you throw the horse over the fence? Does "over the fence" modify "throw" or "hay?" Probably the clearest version is, "Throw some hay over the fence to the horse." According to Peter Bart, "Miller was able also to win a significant tax saving . . . for one client who had purchased an expensive house only to have its pipes freeze soon after moving in." [11] Here the adverb modifying the infinitive suggests that the client's only purpose in buying the house was to have its pipes freeze. And sometimes punctuation is necessary to make a modifier unambiguous. "Give us Barrabas, live, on the Hallmark Hall of Fame" is a demand that seems to require some conjury. "*Give Us Barrabas,* live, on the Hallmark Hall of Fame" returns us to sanity, though the ratings may be lower. Finally, a double meaning can make a modifying phrase ambiguous even when it does not dangle, as in "Easter Matinee. Every child laying an egg in the usher's hand will be admitted free."

Sometimes a modifier may be amusingly incongruous. In a paper on *The Octopus,* a student wrote, "Suddenly, from the depths of an indignant rage against the railroad, Annixter notices Hilma Tree's white arms." You wonder how they stay white when you read, "Mingled among all the bloodshed, graft, starvation, and exploitation of the story is found Hilma Tree." Here she sounds more mangled than mingled. Finally some modifiers are not so much ambiguous as downright nonsensical:

At the end of "The Outcasts of Poker Flat," the bodies are very much purified, serene, and unable to tell which one had sinned the moast [sic] throughout her life.

After she dies, Miss Watson does reconsider Jim's case and grant him his freedom.

R.I.P.

Exercise 18: Correct any dangling and misplaced modifiers.

1. George Gundersdorf erected the statute in the museum which he carved.
2. Weighing 500 pounds and over 100 years old, Chadwick was impressed with the Galapagos tortoise.
3. Did you ever walk a dog in a plaid bathrobe?
4. Having been born in captivity, the zookeeper provides special care for animals neglected by their mothers.
5. When tending the desk, a volume of James Bond was read.
6. The Galapagos tortoises were taken to the San Diego Zoo, facing the threat of extinction.
7. Sleeping in the rain, a case of rheumatism was developed.
8. With horns 36 inches long, hunters prize the bongo of the African forest.
9. Growling hungrily, the keeper gave the Bengal tigers their noon meal.
10. The largest of all white rhinos, the hunter captured them in Rhodesia.
11. With her floppy ears cocked, the dowager frowned at the spaniel.
12. Sleeping in foxholes, trench foot sometimes breaks out.
13. Long thought to be extinct in their native habitat, the New Yorkers admired Przewalski's wild horses at the game farm.
14. Losing interest in mating, the zoo director explained that captive cheetahs become slack and indolent.
15. Grandmother used the fish in making the chowder we caught yesterday.
16. While walking by a stone fence, a snake struck at me and ignited the matches in my pocket.
17. The patrolman brought the wallet to the desk that he had found in the parking lot.
18. After spending a night at Camp Muir, a side trip is made to the Cowlitz Glacier in the morning.
19. A rarity in zoological collections, Dilsingham admired the marbled cat's white-patched ears and bicolored whiskers.

20. By providing the mother polar bear with privacy, she can have her cubs undisturbed.

Exercise 19: Correct any dangling and misplaced modifiers.

1. Breakfasting on acacia leaves at sunrise, Howard photographed the typical feeding posture of the gerenuk.
2. Formerly thought to run from 70 to 90 miles an hour, zoologists now find that few cheetahs can do more than 56 miles per hour.
3. An adult pair of Sclater's Crowned Pigeons, hatched in the rain forest of New Guinea, are shown with their month-old chick.
4. Having disappeared in Asia, maharajahs now import cheetahs to hunt from Africa.
5. Exploring the cave, a large deposit of bat guano was discovered.
6. We hardly saw any of the park bears.
7. The developer bought the property from a farmer that he later sold for an immense profit.
8. Walking along the beach, a strange footprint was encountered.
9. While going down to the cellar, a loose board made me stumble.
10. The landlord gave the old clothes to a Salvation Army worker that had been stored in the attic.
11. While climbing over a barbed-wire fence, the farmer's dog bit me.
12. Being only a sophomore, my advisor would not let me take graduate courses.
13. "The Greenland Fisheries" should be sung with a strong rhythm, paying careful attention to the dramatic details of the story.
14. Driving over Bear Mountain Bridge, the New York skyline can be seen.
15. Hiking the Appalachian Trail, shelter cabins are found every seven or ten miles.
16. Stacy brought the snake to the museum, which he later put on display.
17. Looking out of the bus window, a mother moose and young were seen grazing in the park meadow.
18. Exercising every day, thirty pounds were lost.
19. A bright orange specimen, Lothar carefully photographed the flame azalea.
20. Looking into the aquarium, a bottle-nosed dolphin was seen.

12 √ Confused Conjunctions and Prepositional Puzzles

Both conjunctions and prepositions are connectives, used in joining a word, phrase, or clause to the rest of the sentence. But whereas prepositions always form part of a phrase, conjunctions stand before or between grammatical units (clauses, phrases, words), which they connect or contrast. Conjunctions are essential to the balance, rhythm, and structure of sentences; the wrong choice can shift the weight, alter the tempo, splatter the punctuation, fragment the meaning, joggle the transition, and sink the sentence or give it a seasick lurch. The careful stylist must select conjunctions to give the exact shade he wants of coordination, subordination, pause, contrast, or other relationship. He must make certain his conjunctions carry appropriate weight—not too much or too little. Effective use of conjunctions is one of the more discriminating tests of style. The nonstylist uses them like buckshot, but the professional takes careful aim. Even use of the simple word *and* can become a matter of literary art. Ernest Hemingway told Lillian Ross, "In the first paragraphs of 'Farewell' [*A Farewell to Arms*] I used the word *and* over and over the way Mr. Johann Sebastian Bach used a note in music when he was emitting counterpoint." [1]

We shall consider conjunctions more thoroughly later in the chapter on sentence structure. Meanwhile, some classification may be helpful. Most people know of nouns, verbs, and adjectives (though one student, when asked to give an example of a verb said "sweater," and when asked what its past tense would be, replied "sweaters"), but cannot distinguish relative pronouns and the various kinds of conjunctions. Except in a classroom, if you should ask someone whether he can describe a subordinating conjunction, the chances are he'll decide you're a suspicious character—a lawyer or a spy. These classifications are not matters of common knowledge.

176

Teachers cannot count on their students' being familiar with them, as the students would be with a championship bout or the latest automobiles. Yet the distinction is not mere pedantry but is essential in constructing effective sentences.

¶ COORDINATING CONJUNCTIONS

Coordinating conjunctions (*and, but, for, or, nor, yet*) connect words or groups of words that are equal in grammatical form or rank. They can join two or more main clauses in a compound sentence. When they do so, they are preceded by a comma ("Johann Strauss wrote *Die Fledermaus,* and Richard Strauss wrote *Der Rosenkavalier*") but not when they connect two words ("Mutt and Jeff") or phrases ("Little John hit Robin Hood with a quarterstaff and knocked him into the stream"). When a coordinating conjunction is omitted between main clauses, it should be replaced with a semicolon, not a comma.

Some teachers have a taboo against beginning sentences with a coordinating conjunction. Competent professional writers have no such scruples and do not hesitate to start sentences with *and, but,* or other conjunctions. Dr. Herman Struck of Michigan State University found that such diverse writers as E. B. White and Loren Eiseley begin one tenth of their sentences with coordinate conjunctions and this is also true of one fifth of the sentences in F. L. Lucas's *Style,* whereas the timid style of doctoral dissertations shun opening coordinates as a breach of decorum. But obviously any decision about usage should be based, not on propriety, but on style and sense. If an initial coordinating conjunction coordinates effectively, use it; if it creates a false transition, use something else.

Some uses of *and* are too colloquial for expository prose. "Be sure and go there" should be changed to "Be sure to go there." *Good and* is emphatic ("good and hot," "good and mad") in casual conversation, but inappropriate for more formal style. *Took and is* even more so: "He took and fixed the huge machine."

¶ SUBORDINATING CONJUNCTIONS

Subordinating conjunctions are more difficult because there are more of them and because the function of connecting a subordinate, or dependent, clause is more subtle than coupling equal elements. As we have seen, the relative pronouns (*who, whose, whom, which,*

177

what, that) have two grammatical functions, one of these being to double as subordinating conjunctions. Other subordinating conjunctions are:

after	before	so (so that)	where (wherever)
although	how	unless	whether
as (as if)	if	until	while
because	since	when (whenever)	why

Besides serving as connectives, conjunctions are often used to indicate contrast, comparison, result, or condition; some subordinating ones also have adverbial functions and may indicate time, direction, causal relationship, and interrogation. The subordinate clause that such conjunctions introduce may appear before, after, or within the main clauses, depending upon the relationship and rhythm:

Clark Kent ran to the phone booth *when* he heard the cry for Superman.

Li'l Abner refused to get married *until* his idol, Fearless Fosdick, supposedly married Prudence Pimpleton.

Unless the turnip termites are driven away, Dogpatch will perish.

I don't know *why* the Lone Ranger insists on wearing a mask *when* he has no alter ego to conceal.

Whenever Richard Cory went down town,
We people on the pavement looked at him: . . .

The legislators want to know *who* is responsible for the beer parties.

There are several specific problems with subordinating conjunctions. *While* should usually be used only in its sense of "at the same time"; if it is used for *although, and,* or *but,* it may cause confusion, as in "Boris Karloff played the monster in *Frankenstein* (1932), while Bela Lugosi played it in *Frankenstein Meets the Wolf Man* (1943)"; or in "I was born in Hackensack, while my father was born in Punxatawny."

After the verb *to be* it is best to avoid using a clause introduced by *when:* otherwise, you will find yourself stating that some noun is "when." All too often students produce such a sentence: "An eclipse is when the moon is between the sun and the earth," or "An example is when the Puritans persecuted the Quakers." "The reason is because . . ." is similarly awkward.

That is often omitted when necessary and inserted when unnec-

178

essary. It can be omitted in constructions like "She said that her hands were cold" or "He said that he would destroy the world." But sometimes common sense requires *that,* as in "The soothsayer said on March fifteenth Caesar would be murdered." He didn't say it on March fifteenth: " . . . said that on March fifteenth . . ." is the correct form for such statements. Again the missing *that* creates ambiguity in "He added the bill could be charged to the expense account." He did not add the bill; rather, he was talking and added that the bill could be charged. If you have two subordinate clauses, you may need two *thats* to keep the second clause from seeming coordinate, e.g., "The zookeeper said that the hippopotamus is expecting, and attendance is going up." Without a second *that,* you can't tell if the last clause is the writer's comment or part of the zookeeper's statement.

But that is awkwardly formal and should be avoided. In "I do not doubt but that students could read more than they do," *but* can be cut. To use *but what* with *doubt* is nonstandard, as in "We don't doubt but what the water level has risen." The use of *being as* for *because* or *since* is also nonstandard: "Being as Tarzan couldn't remember his parents, he thought his mother was an ape."

Than and *as* are used as conjunctions with comparisons in which something is smaller or greater than something else:

Henry V's army was much smaller than that of the French.

Despite popular legends to the contrary, Richard the Lion-Hearted was probably a worse ruler than his brother John.

As in these examples, *than* or *as* is usually followed by an elliptical clause in which the verb has been dropped. This can cause difficulty in using the proper case when a pronoun is the subject of a verb understood:

Dr. Horstwessel is madder than he (not *him*).
Herman is not as musical as she (not *her*).

¶ CONJUNCTIVE ADVERBS

Conjunctive adverbs (sometimes called transitional conjunctions) are used to connect two sentences or two main clauses requiring a heavier transition in meaning than coordinating conjunctions provide. As adverbs, they modify their entire clause. The main ones are:

accordingly	besides	indeed	still
also	consequently	likewise	that is
again	furthermore	moreover	that is to say
anyhow	hence	nevertheless	therefore
at the same time	however	on the contrary	thus

When used as conjunctions, they are preceded by a semicolon, and the more weighty ones are often followed by a comma. Sometimes a conjunctive adverb appears in the middle of a clause, rather than at the beginning: "Despite the death of Banquo, Macbeth felt uneasy upon the throne; he went, *therefore,* to consult the witches once more."

CONJUNCTIVE ADVERB: The giraffe's kick is strong enough to damage an automobile; *consequently,* the giraffe has the right-of-way on all highways.

ADVERB: Any physical exercise, *however* slight, is too much for Butch.

It is best to minimize the use of the heavier conjunctive adverbs. Too many weighty *howevers, neverthelesses,* and *moreovers* can sandbag your style. The prose is as heavy-footed as a hippo in "When Friday evening arrived, I was pooped; moreover, I had a headache; furthermore, my stomach was unsettled; nevertheless, I had to go bowling; however, I recovered sufficiently; indeed, I found that I had won the trophy; consequently, I was glad I had not gone straight to bed."

As an adverb, *too* can be synonymous for *also,* but it should not be used as a conjunctive adverb. At the beginning of clauses, *too* is an annoying affectation: "Too, she was wearing a mink stole." Most professionals find this as mannered as false eyelashes or *forsooth.*

¶ CORRELATIVE CONJUNCTIONS

These are sometimes called preconnectives because they signal that a connective is approaching and mark off the limits of the first connecting part. They include *as . . . as, both . . . and, either . . . or, neither . . . nor, not so . . . as, not only . . . but also,* and *whether . . . or.* Some grammarians find it illogical to use *both . . . and, either . . . or,* and *neither . . . nor* for more than two things. This would brand as incorrect the sentence, "He liked neither grammar, French, nor algebra." They also tell us not to

180

use *nor* as a correlative with anything but *neither*; not to say, for example, "He never shirked nor complained." Yet competent writers often disregard these warnings, both of which are broken in "Learning to spell is not a matter of intelligence, industry, nor logic so much as of memory." More useful is the advice to place correlatives in strictly parallel form. "It is neither the result of luck nor of wisdom" should be corrected so that neither is placed after *result*. Faulty parallelism sometimes results in ambiguity, as in "The authors both wrote sincerely and eloquently."

As . . . as can be awkward, with an *as* too many or 'two few. "T. S. Eliot is as influential as a critic as as a poet" stutters hopelessly. Yet in this sentence the third *as* completes the comparison, and the fourth is needed as a preposition with *poet* to balance the *as* with *critic*. The only solution is to rephrase the sentence: "as influential as a critic as he is as a poet" or "as influential in criticism as in poetry." Conversely, "Uncle Fudge says *Son of the Blob* is as good or better than *The Alligator People*" should be changed to "as good as or better than."

Sometimes *hardly . . . than* and *scarcely . . . than* turn up as correlatives. Wilson Follett calls these "intolerable"; whether they are so to you depends upon your degree of tolerance. Formal usage replaces *than* with *when* or prefers *no sooner . . . than*.

We shall return to coordination and subordination when we consider sentence structure. Meanwhile, we can proceed to another kind of connective.

¶ PREPOSITIONS

Then comes the thing that can of all things be most mistaken and they are prepositions. . . . I like prepositions the best of all. . . .
—GERTRUDE STEIN

For the person learning English as a second language, prepositions pose one of the greatest difficulties. Even native speakers find them a frequent headache. Formally, prepositions are quite simple; except for unusual constructions, such as "The week before's laundry came back this week," prepositions are never involved with inflectional endings. The difficulties come in the choice and function of prepositions and in the fact that many of these are idiomatic and illogical.

English uses prepositions to introduce a prepositional phrase and relate it to another part of the sentence. A highly inflected language like Latin minimizes prepositions, using instead the inflected case endings of the genitive, dative, and ablative case. English is simpler, using prepositions for this function with uninflected nouns. Prepositions always have an object and show direction or relation between the object and the word or words it modifies:

He went home *for* lunch. (noun to noun)

Waldo was hungry *for* learning. (noun to adjective)

Irving dropped the watermelon *on* his foot. (noun to both noun and verb)

If we start with a boy standing at the door of his house, he may go *down* the walk, *up* the drive, *across* the street, *to* the school, *around* the block, *over* the bridge, *away* from home, *through* the door, *toward* a policeman. In all these phrases, the italicized word shows the direction of his going. Or imagine two people talking. They may talk *of* the weather, *in* low tones, *about* their friends, *for* an hour, *with* much enjoyment. Here the italicized prepositions do not show direction but indicate the relationship between the talking and *weather, tones, friends, hour,* and *enjoyment.*

The term *preposition* is misleading, for it suggests something placed *before,* whereas a preposition may, and often does, follow its object. Like a conjunction, it connects two or more parts of an expression. But unlike the weak conjunction, it not only joins but shows the nature of the relationship, and holds more individual meaning. In "go to the bank" and "go away from the bank," the words *to* and *from* are alike in showing the connection between going and the bank, but they indicate opposite directions. Grammatically the object in a prepositional phrase takes the objective case. This is no problem with nouns, but occasionally causes difficulty with pronouns. The distinction is clearly indicated in Hamlet's question, "What's Hecuba to him or he to Hecuba?" A common and irritating error, probably caused by overanxiety about standards of grammar, is "between you and I," or "Give it to Carolyn and I." In conversation, the objective case is more and more disappearing in instances like "Who did you give it to?", the grammatically approved form being, "To whom did you give it?" *Whom* is unlikely to vanish altogether, being preserved in literature—*For Whom the Bell Tolls* is probably the best known example.

Many words that function as prepositions can also serve in other capacities. Some double as adverbs, as conjunctions, or as both. A few can even be nouns ("an *in* with the boss," "an *out* in case of in-

182

vestigation"). *Aboard* is a preposition in "Aboard the ship, mutiny was brewing," but it is an adverb in "Queeg went aboard."

PREPOSITION: Quick Draw McGraw went *after* the rustlers.
ADVERB: Jill came tumbling *after.*
CONJUNCTION: *After* the hurricane was over, the islanders began to rebuild.
PREPOSITION: The boat was tied *alongside* the pier.
ADVERB: The car pulled *alongside.*

Likewise, prepositional phrases can be adjectival modifiers ("the man *at the wheel*," "dinner *at eight*"), adverbial modifiers ("go *to school*," "jump *in the lake*"), or complements ("Arnold thought *of going to the movies*"). The last example has two prepositional phrases in a row. Usually prepositional phrases follow the nouns they modify: the lady *in the lake*," "ships *at sea*," "a time *to weep*." For some reason authors seem to favor using prepositional phrases for titles: *Of Time and the River, Of Human Bondage, Of Mice and Men, In Dubious Battle, In the Cage, To the Lighthouse, On the Road, By Love Possessed.* Many other titles contain prepositional phrases: *Life on the Mississippi, Portrait of a Lady, The Wings of the Dove, Intruder in the Dust, The Grapes of Wrath, This Side of Paradise.*

Prepositions can themselves be phrases (usually containing another prepositional phrase), as well as single words: "Jason sailed *in search of* the golden fleece." Stylistically it is best to minimize the use of long prepositions (*in accordance with, in relation to, by means of, in connection with, on the part of, in order to, in regard to*); they can usually be replaced with shorter ones. Some prepositions are composed of two words; *because of, instead of, next to, across from, down below.*

The idiomatic use of prepositions in English presents one of the great stumbling blocks to those who are not native born to the tongue, because this usage is neither rational nor predictable. We say not only *full of* but also *filled with, a victim of circumstances* but also *a victim to greed, by this means* but also *in this way* and *after this fashion.* One is guilty *of* a crime, and one also pleads guilty *to* it. If you beat somebody *up,* you may knock him *down.* The British say a building is *in* the street, when we say it is *on* the street. (Actually it is next to the street.) A house can *burn up* or *burn down.* You can drink something *up* or drink it *down,* but when you drink it *down,* it is all drunk *up.* But it always clouds *up,*

183

never *down.* And if you *live it up* too much, you may not be able to *live it down.*

Some prepositions are logical; *knock down and drag out* makes sense. But some combinations of verb and preposition have several quite different meanings. *Carry out* does not mean the same thing in "carry out the garbage" as it does in "carry out orders." When you get up in the morning, you put on some clothes and then put on some coffee. There may be no turn involved when something unexpected turns up. You look up to see an airplane, but you also look up someone in the phone book or look him up when you are in his neighborhood. And if things are looking up, they are improving. The warning "Look out!" is different from looking out the window. When you look over somebody's work, you look at it and through it but not over it. When you look after someone, you take care of him and do not stare after him. When you go through with a project, you may not go anywhere or with anyone. *Go about* can mean "to be occupied with"; *go along,* "to agree with"; *go by,* "to be known as"; *go in for,* "to have a liking for"; *go off,* "to happen"; *go out,* "to be extinguished, to become outdated, to sympathize, and to go on strike"; *go through,* "to suffer, to get approval, to spend"; and the number of similar idioms is legion. As the instructions advise on washroom paper towels, "Pull down and pull up to pull out."

Prepositions can also be combined with verbs to make nouns (*sellout, turnout, blowout, showdown, tossup, holdover, outlook, withdrawal, holdup, handout, sit-in, cookout, layout, layaway, layoff, hideout, hideaway*), with nouns to make nouns (*sundown, sunup, insight, inmate, outlaw, outboard, overhead*), with nouns or verbs to make adjectives (*overdue, outgrown, overland, outspread, underdone*), or with nouns and verbs to make new verbs (*outlaw, overlook, outrun, update*). When a preposition is tacked onto the end of a verb, the verb rather than the preposition is inflected, though one child recovering from the flu said, "Hey, I'm not throw-upping anymore."

Since prepositions occur on the average of one to a sentence, the possibilities for error are formidable. In one set of twenty-three high school papers, twenty-four errors in the use of prepositions appeared, including "It is to [in] my opinion correct," "Take the train till [to] Times Square," "Doesn't he resemble with his father?", "The contrast of [between] Portia and Calpurnia," and "Strike three times to [at] him."

184

Prepositions in English are the more difficult because the language itself sometimes shifts. *Averse,* coming from two Latin words meaning *from* and *turn,* should not logically have *to* following it, yet we say "He is not averse to studying," instead of the older "He is not averse from studying." *Oblivious* is just as remote from *to;* in Latin and less current English it was followed by *of,* yet we say "He was oblivious to his surroundings." *Of* used to function in the sense of *by,* as in "He was despised and rejected of men." People still die *of,* not *from,* something: "She died of a fever/With no one to save her,/And that was the end of sweet Mollie Malone."

The choice of prepositions is particularly controversial in several situations. *Different than* is forbidden by pedants, who demand *different from.* This is a hair-splitting distinction that is often justifiedly ignored. Margaret Nicholson has pointed out that Thomas Fuller in the seventeenth century; Addison, Steele, Defoe, Richardson, Goldsmith, and Fanny Burney in the eighteenth; and Coleridge, Southey, De Quincey, Carlyle, Thackeray, Newman, and others in the nineteenth used *different than* on occasion, and so do many competent writers today. Unquestionably *from* is the more grammatically precise preposition; but the conjunction *than* could be considered as introducing a subordinate clause with the verb understood: "different from me" or "different than I [am]." Of course, what you find is "different than me." The overfastidious therefore have a point in their denunciation of *different than me,* and if you want to be discriminating, you should stick with *different from.*

Another distinction is made in the use of *between* and *among.* Conventionally, *between* is used with two items ("between you and me," "between heaven and hell") and *among* with three or more ("life among the Polynesians"). There is no challenge when *among* is used in the sense of "in the midst of," but it is being threatened by *between* when a choice or comparison is involved. Thus Alexander Bumstead says, "The malt shop has 25 flavors, and it is difficult to choose between them," and *Vogue* describes a party that "will swirl between three different hotels." The careful grammarian would choose *among* in these situations.

There is frequent confusion in the use of *in, into,* and *in to,* for these are not interchangeable. You live *in* a house but go *into* it. If you go out, you might drive *in to* the city and go *into* a restaurant. If "Snideley Whiplash turned himself into the nearest Mountie station," he performed a remarkable magic trick; the preposition

185

should be *in to*. But sometimes there is unavoidable ambiguity, as in "The truck turned into the nearest garage." Usually, context and common sense make the meaning clear. *In* is stationary ("Fish live in the water"), *into* indicates movement from the outside to the inside ("Tarzan dived into the water"), and *in to* has a separate stress on each preposition. Logically, each of these prepositions is correct in "Put it [in, into] the box," but *in* is preferable because the inert enclosure, rather than the movement inward, is stressed.

As of is jargon and it is not an acceptable substitute for *at* or *on*. *On* is better in "As of Wednesday the store was still closed," and *at* is preferable in "As of six o'clock supper was not ready." *As of now* means simply *now*. *As per* is another bit of jargon in "Your assistance in proctoring the Natural Science Final Examination, as per [according to] the above schedule, will be appreciated."

With causes some awkward constructions as an adverbial preposition. "Horpington was the most popular member of his class with Fosdick in second place" calls for a double take. To keep from suggesting that he was popular with Fosdick, change *with* to *and*: "and Fosdick was in second place." "The second car crashed into the first one with the third going into a ditch" is ambiguous; "and the third went into a ditch" is clearer. How would you remove the confusion in the following?

> Schmertz fed the wombat with the koala bear waiting for his turn.
>
> She bit him on the ear with her cigarette burning his lapel.

Like the omnivorous *-ness* suffix, *on* seems to be gradually eliminating all other prepositions. The appropriate choices are in brackets in the following examples:

The administration questioned Horpington on [about] his drinking.

The public can be satisfied on [as to] my candidate's honesty.

The cast was disappointed on [at] the poor attendance.

The city council is waiting on [for] medical testimony about fluoridation.

Some success has been made on [in] cancer research.

Security controls have been lifted on [from] the new aircraft.

We are educating underdeveloped nations on [in] better methods of agriculture.

Whenever you are in doubt as to the proper choice of a preposition, it is advisable not to guess but to consult your dictionary.

Another point of contention is *due to* versus *because of*. In conservative grammar, *due* is an adjective followed by the preposition *to*; thus *due* can modify only nouns and pronouns, not verbs. Yet *due to* as an adverbial preposition has become so widespread that it must be recognized (if not accepted) as standard. Porter G. Perrin's *Writer's Guide and Index to English* cites Professor John S. Kenyon who in 1930 conceded, albeit reluctantly, that much as he personally disliked the prepositional *due to,* it was established in the work of reputable writers. Perrin also cites Margaret M. Bryant's report, based on a survey of thousands of books and periodicals, that *due to* appeared as a preposition in 56 percent of the cases, *because of* in 25 percent, and *owing to* in 19 percent. Even so, the more conservative grammarians condemn the prepositional *due to.* It is illogical to be indignant against it, but if you want to avoid their criticism, you should use *because of* in constructions similar to "We arrived late due to an error in the program announcement." The following examples illustrate the contrast in traditional practice:

The demonstrations were *due to* disagreement over the census count. (Adj.)
The game was called *because of* darkness. (Prep.)
The ship ran aground *because* the captain was drunk. (Prep. Not "due to the captain's drunkenness.")
Professor Crabshaw's reputation was *due to* his study of Richard III. (Adj.)
Because of bad weather, the picnic is postponed. (Prepositional adv.)
The postponement is *due to* bad weather. (Adj.)

¶ AS YOU LIKE IT

One of the hottest conflicts between prescriptive and descriptive grammarians is over the use of *like, as,* or *as if* in a metaphor or comparison. The prescriptive position is that *as* and *as if* are subordinate conjunctions used between clauses, whereas *like* is a preposition that can be used only to introduce a prepositional phrase and never to introduce a clause. The issue is complicated because *as* is also used as a preposition in some comparisons: "black as pitch," "hot as blazes," "cool as a cucumber." By and large, *as* causes no trouble; the cries of alarm and anguish come when *like* usurps the role of conjunction. Purists protested bitterly, particularly denouncing the cigarette slogan "Winstons taste good like a cigarette should" as a symbol of linguistic decay. The Winston people respond by having the Flintstones sing the jingle, thus giving it unquestioned antiquity.

187

Actually if we look back, we find the Elizabethans combining all the rivals in *like as if, like as, like to,* and *like unto.* Thus Shakespeare's Richard III complains of looking "like to a chaos or an unlicked bearwhelp." One of Edmund Spenser's sonnets begins "Like as a ship that through the ocean wide," and another, "Like as a huntsman after weary chase . . ." The King James Bible is thoroughly inconsistent. In The Song of Solomon we read, "Thy neck is as a tower of ivory; thine eyes like the fishpools in Heshbon, by the gate of Bath-rabbim: thy nose is as the tower of Lebanon which looketh toward Damascus," and again, "His head is as the most fine gold . . . His cheeks are as a bed of spices, as sweet flowers: his lips like lilies, dropping sweet smelling myrrh." And "This thy stature is like to a palm tree . . ." Today we would use *like* in all of these comparisons, and the Revised Standard Version does so. In St. Matthew we read, "The kingdom of heaven is like to a grain of mustard seed. . . . like unto treasure hid in a field. . . . like unto a merchantman" but also "The kingdom of heaven is as a man traveling into a far country." Again, the Revised Standard Version replaces all of these with *like.*

Today we seldom see *as* misused for *like* ("She looks as her mother," "He looks as King Kong"). Most complaints come when *like* is used for *as* and *as if.* Yet authors from Shakespeare to Keats to John F. Kennedy have used *like* in this way, and they are hardly vulgarians. As long ago as 1923, James Thurber observed that Joseph Conrad and Henry James used *like* for *as,* but that he didn't care because he admired their style and content. Certainly the use of *like* as a conjunction antedates the Winston ad. "Let's All Sing Like the Birdies Sing" and "If You Knew Susie Like I Know Susie" are earlier.

Tyrone Guthrie was careful to make the traditional distinction when he wrote of an actor: "He can coo like a dove, roar like a lion, shriek like a banshee, rattle like a machine gun, sing like an angel and curse like—well, as only Australians can." [2] So was the translator in ". . . he behaved like a king, and as if the young sovereign were merely his heir." [3]

On the other hand, Lawrence Durrell violated the prescriptive rule when he wrote, "He had, in fact, been nailed to this tree by bullets for all the world like the body of a jay is nailed to a barn door, as a warning." [4] John Dos Passos also did so several times in *Midcentury.* Sir Laurence Olivier said that Othello must "stand like a strong man stands, with that sort of ease, probably straight-

188

backed, straight-necked." Princeton historian Eric Goldman wrote in *The New York Times* of "a novel which sounds like it should be light reading." And President Kennedy said of Khrushchev, "I would suspect he has his good months and his bad months like we all do."

Clearly it is not proof that you are vulgar or illiterate if you use *like* in place of *as*. A descriptive grammarian would say that conservative usage opposes the use of *like* as a conjunction; that if you want to play it safe, you should follow conservative practice; but that many educated people do use *like* for *as* and that this is no sign of degeneracy or cause for alarm. Perhaps the choice is one more of diction than of grammar. Certainly *like* is inappropriate when at the climax of the movie *Phaedra,* Anthony Perkins (in a role analogous to that of Hippolytus in the ancient Greek drama) says, "She loved me like they did in the good old days." Here the flat, modern colloquial style fails to sustain the mood of high tragedy the film was trying to achieve. The weakness is not alone in the grammar of *like* but equally in the diction of "they did in the good old days."

Webster III outraged purists by presenting *like* as if it were a synonym for *as*. It did not make this reversible, with *as* a synonym for *like*. In fact the two are not interchangeable. "Like an Indian, I made my way through the forest" is quite different from "As an Indian, I made my way through the forest." In the first, the narrator is walking like an Indian; in the second, he is impersonating an Indian. Notice the difference that occurs if the title of John Howard Griffin's *Black Like Me* is changed to *Black As Me*. Sometimes a wrong use of *like* or *as* can cause ambiguity and confusion. "Code 10 disappears into the blotter like it disappears into your hair" may use *like* as a conjunction, but it is at least clear, whereas "Code 10 disappears into the blotter as it disappears into your hair" suggests that it disappears into the blotter at the same time that it disappears into your hair. "I'm going to throw that typewriter out the window just like General What's-his-name" suggests that the general is going to be tossed out the window; the sentence is clearer as "I'm going to throw that typewriter out the window just as General What's-his-name did." The meaning is also ambiguous in "The State Library serves students just like any Michigan citizen." This might be interpreted as meaning that any citizen serves students the way the library does, whereas the real meaning is that the services of the library are the same for students and citi-

189

zens alike. Again, *like* makes the modifier ambiguous in "Joy'll treat your hands just like a bubble bath." In the ad for "Beatnik Wigs . . . look like they just got off the boat," the confusion is caused not by *like* but by the picture of the wigs walking through customs. In his attack on *Webster III*, Wilson Follett denounces "that darling of the advanced libertarians, *like* as a conjunction, first in the meaning of *as*, secondly (and more horribly) in that of *as if*." These uses he calls "no more than a regional colloquialism." [5] But regional colloquialisms are not nonstandard, though they may be highly inappropriate outside their own setting; and the use of *like* as a conjunction is certainly not confined to nor characteristic of any particular region. Besides, what is so horrible about the practice, even if it is a borderline case? *Like* can be a conjunction if usage so determines; and in fact Mr. Follett admits that it was used this way in the Middle Ages, but claims that this usage, once dropped, is not entitled to make a comeback. Why not? Stylistically, *as if* may be awkward and *like* more effective: "It looks like we're late" vs. "It looks as if we're late."

Looks like, though unacceptable to purists, is rapidly becoming idiomatic. Certainly in casual speech, it has a smoother sound than *looks as if*, which shifts gears an extra time: "She looked like she'd wink" comes naturally; "She looked as if she'd wink" seems grammatically self-conscious. On the back cover of *Mad* (January, 1964) we read, "Next week my company starts using a new-type can, and I'll be able to stuff those eight great tomatoes in that little bitty can without ending up looking like [more effective than as if] I've been attacked with a meat cleaver." And "It looks like the octopus got him" is far more likely to be heard than "It looks as if the octopus got him."

But to conform with formal and conservative practice, replace the use of *like* as a conjunction with *as* in the following:

"I thought I'd boil off the whale blubber, like the Eskimos do," said the museum director.

Eat the sucker when you're through
Or save it like the squirrels do.   *—Holiday Inn menu*

Like I always say, if at first you don't succeed, do something sneaky.
        —HOKEY WOLF

I wish he'd bury his bones like other dogs do.

I brought in Snideley Whiplash like I said I would.   —DUDLEY DO-RIGHT

190

Conservative usage and traditional grammar prescribe the use of *such as* in "a pan like you cook brownies in," and *as if* or (preferably) *as though* in "Seems like the whole country's gone Dial happy," or "Your hair looks like you bleached it twice." But for all practical purposes, *like* has become a conjunction, and you should not be outraged that such is the case. Depending on the situation, you may so use it yourself. If you are indignant at the Winston ad, you can switch to tea, for "Lipton's satisfies as no other tea can." The important question about Winstons is whether they really taste good.

¶ ENDING SENTENCES WITH A PREPOSITION

What would we really know the meaning of?   —RALPH WALDO EMERSON

. . . this only is reading, in a high sense, not that which lulls us as a luxury and suffers the nobler faculties to sleep the while, but what we have to stand on tip-toe to read and devote our most alert and wakeful hours to.
                                             —HENRY DAVID THOREAU

That the Bastille was attacked with an enthusiasm of heroism, such as only the highest animation of Liberty could inspire, and carried in the space of a few hours, is an event which the world is fully possessed of.
                                             —THOMÁS PAINE

The prison to which the new ministry were dooming the National Assembly, in addition to its being the high altar and castle of despotism, became the proper object to begin with.   —THOMAS PAINE

Clearly the Ipswich minister was a fighting as well as a praying parson, whom Cromwell should have delighted in.   —VERNON L. PARRINGTON

Stewards in church and state, he would have none of.
                                             —VERNON L. PARRINGTON

For whom would a poem on Spring be by?   —ROBERT FROST

Had Lincoln been born in a sweatshop he would never have been heard of.
                                             —EUGENE DEBS

> The undiscover'd country from whose bourn
> No traveller returns, puzzles the will
> And makes us rather bear those ills we have
> Than fly to others that we know not of.
>   —WILLIAM SHAKESPEARE

I am as lonesome and as happy as I can be in that town we lived in and worked and learned and grew up in, and then fought our way back into.
                                             —ERNEST HEMINGWAY, *quoted by Lillian Ross*[6]

In Shakespeare I always try to reassure the audience initially that they are not going to see some grotesque, outsized dimension of something which they can't understand or sympathize with. —SIR LAURENCE OLIVIER

It's the kind of music we love to sink our collective teeth into.

—THE BROTHERS FOUR

THOU SHALT NOT END A SENTENCE WITH A PREPOSITION!!!

This is one of the few widely known "rules" of grammar and a totally false one. If it is such an absolute command, why do so many superior writers ignore it? Because, as we discussed earlier, it was never based on actual usage. It was John Dryden, sitting in his study one day in the late seventeenth century, who decreed that English sentences must never end with a preposition, and prescriptive grammarians have preached the dogma ever since, although as a matter of actual fact, some sentences can end no other way. For example, how is it possible to end Hamlet's declaration, "My head should be struck off," without using a preposition? In *The Prince and the Pauper,* when Tom Canty is asked what he used the Great Seal of England for (not for what he used it), he answers, "To crack nuts with!" Should he have said, "With which to crack nuts?" Consider the awkward alternatives to placing the preposition at the end in the following:

On what did I step?	What did I step on?
At what are you laughing?	What are you laughing at?
I'm going up to live it.	I'm going to live it up.
For what is this?	What is this for?
We must prevent war out from breaking.	We must prevent war from breaking out.
Of what are you scared?	What are you scared of?
Ten cents is a fraction of for what it sells.	Ten cents is a fraction of what it sells for.
His sister is very particular about with whom she out goes.	His sister is very particular about whom she goes out with.
On what the hell am I sitting?	What the hell am I sitting on?

There is a well-known story that when a secretary revised one of Winston Churchill's sentences so that it would not end with a preposition, Churchill wrote a note, "This is the sort of impertinence up with which I will not put." When a writer goes out of his way to avoid ending a sentence with a preposition, his prose usually has an overstuffed Victorian sound, as in the following passages from Edgar Rice Burroughs' *Tarzan and the Lost Empire:*

192

The first few steps that von Harben took onto the grassy meadow land revealed the fact that it was a dangerous swamp from which only with the greatest difficulty were they able to extricate themselves.

They had been paddling for hours, and the heat and the monotony had become almost unbearable, when a turn in the water-lane revealed a small body of open water, across the opposite side of which stretched what appeared to be low land surmounted by an earthen rampart, along the top of which was a strong stockade.

Thus when such a careful stylist as Edmund Wilson writes, "Neither the Soviet Russians nor we were very much beloved by the peoples in upon whom they had moved," the sentence seems curiously contrived.[7]

The preposition "rule" is one that not even the most adamant purist can always follow. In *Pygmalion* (and *My Fair Lady*) Professor Higgins finally loses his temper and tells Eliza, "Marry some sentimental hog or other with lots of money, and a thick pair of lips to kiss you with and a thick pair of boots to kick you with." [8] This piles up terminal prepositions almost as much as Ehrich von Kanehl's statement that Pop art "gives the observer something he is familiar with and emotionally with to look at and identify with."

The reason that a preposition is so often placed at the end of a sentence, in spite of prescriptive grammarians' thunderings, is that we do not think of the preposition as taking an object but as being linked to the verb that immediately precedes it and forming with it a verbal unit. A preposition following a verb usually has an adverbial function as well, so that it is normal and natural to keep them together. The prepositional-adverbial relationship is disturbed in a contruction like "To whom did you talk?" Breaking the normal speech pattern, it seems too strained and contrived for easy, relaxed conversation.

Conservative grammarians also object that ending a sentence with a preposition often causes people to put what is actually the preposition's object in the subjective case: "I don't know *who* these earmuffs belong to," "*Who* did you give them to?" Usually this occurs in direct or indirect questions where, as we discussed earlier, the use of *whom* as an interrogative pronoun is already vanishing anyway.

Clearly it is nonsense to ban the use of a final preposition when leading writers from Shakespeare to Shaw have used it. Even that fastidious stylist Henry James often ended sentences with a preposition. Despite the critics of *Webster III* and other pedants, we are not being corrupted by "Music to pour Sugar Smacks by" or Quick Draw McGraw's explaining, "These packages are not to draw on; they're to eat out of." The real problem about Quick Draw is, "Where docs El Kabong hang his rope from?" When Tussy "In-a-wish" mascara advertises, "Now you can have the kind of lashes you would sell your soul for," you should worry more about the theological implications than the grammar. Again, the logic rather than the language is demented in this quotation from Joseph Heller's *Catch-22*: "The case against Clevinger was open and shut. The only thing missing was something to charge him with." [9] In the same book, General Dreedle asks, "You mean I can't shoot anyone I want to?" [10] This statement calls for a psychiatrist, not a grammarian.

Sometimes the too self-conscious person, trying to avoid ending with a preposition, fumbles and inserts an extra one from habit: "He is the man to whom I was talking to." A student wrote that sharecroppers "had not owned the farms upon which they were living and working on." In Norman Mailer's *The Naked and the Dead,* a nervous officer says, " 'You said you had been to a place to which . . . *in which* you hadn't even been within a mile of.' In the midst of his anger, [General] Cummings felt a mild contempt at the way Binner had mangled the sentence." [11]

Sometimes sentences end with two prepositions: "Something should be done away with." But it is far better not to pile up prepositions, especially at the end of a sentence, lest you stumble into some such trap as "What is that box for the birds to be fed out of inside for?" or "He would have nothing to compare the creed he is looking into with."

Though it is permissible to end sentences with a preposition, it is not always advisable to do so. "Thoreau says the individual has the right to oppose any law which he does not agree with" has a weak climax; *with* should have been placed before *which.* Likewise, the climax is destroyed in "Steinbeck reveals the unethical policies of the merchants whom the migrants are forced to deal with." By placing *with* before *whom,* you end with the proper stress on *deal.* If you have a *whom,* it is best to put *with* before it and avoid the stumblefootedness of "In the movie there is a scene in which the sailor whom Billy Budd had the fight with dies while on duty." "This turtle may be symbolic of the Joad family, who Steinbeck centers his story around" is doubly weak, both because it trails off with an unemphatic preposition and because the relative

194

pronoun is in the wrong case; *around whom* solves both problems. On the other hand, because *lived with* seems to form a verbal unit, "Flameless electric home heating is the most comfortable heat we've ever lived with" is better than ". . . with which we've ever lived." So the only standard should be clarity and grace.

For careful grammarians, one of the most objectionable non-standard habits is ending a sentence with *at* after the verb *to be:* "I don't know where the theatre is at." Actually, this construction is undesirable not because of the preposition at the end of the sentence but because *at* is redundant. A final stressed *at* is an ugly adenoidal sound. In the middle of sentences, *at* is usually slurred as a rapid *ut;* but at the end it is usually drawn out to sound like *aayht.* In "That was what I was laughing so hilariously at," *at* is not dead wood, but the sentence is more logically constructed and has more euphony if it is changed to "That was what I was laughing at so hilariously." "What are you looking at?" is perfectly acceptable; there, *at* is not dead wood and is not overstressed. But dead wood is doubly objectionable, and the *at* should be cut from such a sentence as, "Where's the vacuum cleaner at?" The trouble is that people think of *is at* as a unit, as in "He is at the chicken-pluckers' convention," and so use *at* habitually and indiscriminately after the verb *to be.* At the end of the 1960's, phrases like "Where it's at" have become faddish as a form of radical chic, but the *at* remains redundant and stylistically undesirable. Should the fad continue and become fixed, we may someday even hear, "I think, therefore I am at."

¶ DOUBLED IN DEAD WOOD

There are a great many prepositions besides *at* that can be used meaninglessly. The final word should be cut from "What have you been doing of?" "Where will it all end up?" and "Where's the opener to puncture this can with?" Dead wood can occur anywhere in a sentence, but it is not always easy to get a coroner's certificate. Clearly the second word should be pruned from the following pairs: *inside of, parallels with, despite of, near to, revert back, off of.* It is sufficient to cancel; you need not cancel *out.* Following orders is enough; you need not follow them *out. Up* is useless in "up until three years ago." You don't need *about* in "studying about chemistry." You don't crave *for* something; you simply crave it. A criminal confesses his guilt instead of confessing *to* it. It is enough to

195

meet and to marry; you are overdoing it to *meet up with* or *marry up with* someone. If something is *over* (finished), why make it *over with*? *Up and* is pointless in "He up and died," especially if he died in bed. Some prepositions can be shortened: *because* is better than *on account of* and *behind* than *in back of*. The interrogative *why* is better than *what for* in "What did you do it for?"

Yet many redundant prepositions are borderline cases. *Over* may seem dead wood in "He lives over in Deadwood"; you wouldn't say, "The President lives over in Washington." Yet *over* may be legitimate if it suggests some geographical barrier—"over [the mountains, the river, the hills and far away] in [name of place]." Shakespeare's Coriolanus speaks of "what we have compounded on," though *on* is not needed. We are particularly prone to add *up* to verbs where the preposition is not strictly necessary: *hurry up, lock up, fatten up, chain up, clean up, fill up, open up, eat up, check up on, divide up, fix up, foul up,* and *end up*. It is enough to hurry, lock the gate, fatten the pigs, chain the bear, clean the stables, fill the tank, open the door, eat the steak, divide the loot, fix the machinery, foul the works, and end without doing all these things *up*. Yet *up* adds intensity and underscores the idea of completion or thoroughness, as in the difference between doing something and really doing it up. "Drink it up" is more emphatic than "Drink it." If you eat something, you may not finish it; but if you eat it up, there's none left. You rarely if ever hear someone tell a gas station attendant, "Fill her," instead of "Fill her up." There is a genuine difference between cutting something and cutting it up. *Follow* means to go after or pursue, whereas *follow up* means to follow closely and persistently or to continue with even more of the same; *follow out* means to carry out fully; and *follow through* means to continue and complete.

When you have unequivocal dead wood, remove it. *From* is wrong in "A crowd of from fifty to sixty thousand was expected," "Receipts of from two to three hundred dollars were received." Meteorologists seem addicted to needless prepositions: "Logan, Utah, received [from] four to six inches of rain last night," "High winds [of] between forty and seventy miles an hour are predicted." *At about* should be simply *at* in "I'll call for you at about eight." *Rather* is wrong in "Deism seems to be more of a philosophy rather than a religion." *Of* is unnecessary in "good of an idea" or "that small of a child." Yet even great authors are not immune to this sort of failing; Hemingway wrote Lillian Ross, "Time is the least

196

thing we have of." [12] Imagine Robert Penn Warren's novel retitled
All of the King's Men.

On the other hand, unstressed prepositions are sometimes
dropped in casual speech, whereas a well-formed style requires
them:

> A couple [of] hamburgers.
> What type [of] music do you like?
> Play the record [at] its right speed.
> What size [of] shoe do you wear?
> There is plenty [of] homework for tomorrow.

It is all right to omit the preposition in constructions such as
"Write [to] me," "Give me," "Show me," but less acceptable to do
so in "Give it [to] me" and "Show it [to] me."

You need not repeat a preposition when two verbs or nouns both
use it ("Give it to Min and Bill"); but when a sentence has two
words that require different prepositions, both are necessary:

> The life of Prufrock's drawing-room and teacup society is too
> far *removed [from* not needed] and *sheltered from*
> the vital questions of existence.

> Abner is *interested in* and *addicted to* movies.

> Naturalists are *concerned for* and *fascinated by* wildlife.

The accurate use of prepositions contributes considerably to effective style and is sometimes crucial for clarity. But quarrels over
like, as, and *as if*; *different from* and *different than*; *between* and
among; *due to* and *because of*; and the issue of ending a sentence
with a preposition are too often mere quibbles. It is advisable to be
as precise as possible, but sniping at *different than* is not going to
save the English language because *different than* is not the real
danger. The genuine threat to clarity and style is jargon, dead
wood, bumblery, circumlocutions, verbosity, vague and slovenly
diction, and other impediments to logical thought and clear communication. Critics should not waste their ammunition on trivia
but go after the main target.

Exercise 20: Identify and underline the subordinating conjunctions in
the following sentences:

1. When you study speech, the subject you begin with is phonetics or
   sounds.

197

2. It is the column of air that enters or leaves the lungs that forms the basis for sounds.

3. Proving this air current escapes unobstructed, it forms the sound which we write as *h*.

4. What obstructs the air current is some one of the speech organs.

5. The lips, teeth, tongue, nose, palate, and vocal cords are called speech organs because they help produce sound.

6. After the air leaves the lungs, it passes through the larynx, where the vocal cords are located.

7. If these vibrate, the sound which results is called a voiced sound; *h*, on the other hand, is a breath sound.

8. The simplest voiced sound is *ah*, as it is made with open unobstructed throat.

9. That is why doctors tell you to say *ah* when they want to see your throat.

10. If you want to know how voiced and breath sounds differ, compare *p* and *b*.

11. Whenever the bell was rung, Pavlov's dogs salivated.

12. If you want to know whether mushrooms are edible or poisonous, eat some and see how you feel the next day.

13. The lancers found that the telegraph wires had been cut.

14. I don't understand how people who love animals can also enjoy hunting.

15. I did but see her passing by, yet will I love her till I die.

16. There is a message from Count Alucard, who wants to know when we can deliver the coffins to the old abbey.

17. The reinforcements never saw the bugler again after he climbed the walls of Fort Zinderneuf.

18. Mark Twain said that he would rather be damned to John Bunyan's heaven than have to read a novel by Jane Austen.

19. Henry James criticized *War and Peace* because he thought it was too sprawling and formless.

20. The wolf man becomes Laurence Talbot until the next full moon transforms him again.

Exercise 21: Eliminate unnecessary prepositions from the following:

1. The austerity program should cut expenses by from 50 to 100 thousand dollars.

2. Hercules had to clean up the Augean stables.

3. Have you finished all of the kickapoo joy juice?

4. The freeway should shorten driving time by from two to three hours.

5. Quasimodo was chosen as king of the Carnival of Fools.

6. The smugglers' hideout was near to the cliffs.

198

7. Ever since Sputnik, Americans have been aware of the need for trained scientists.
8. The Barebones Parliament was named for a Puritan member named of Praise-God Barebones.
9. Movies were silent up until 1927.
10. Placing of the area under quarantine was necessary.
11. Fearless Fosdick knocked the robot off of the bridge.
12. Nobody saw King Kong enter into the cave, carrying Fay Wray.
13. It is evident that, if everything goes along as planned, that the project will be a huge success.
14. The grass doesn't need mowing for a couple of more days.
15. Look out of the window; a bear has knocked over the garbage can.
16. Where is the grapefruit native to?
17. There is a cow up on the ridge over across the valley.
18. Tyrone Power sliced through the candle in *The Mark of Zorro* without knocking it off of the candlestick.
19. Basil Rathbone, who did the candle bit with Tyrone Power, repeated it over in a burlesque scene with Danny Kaye in *The Court Jester*.
20. There were approximately about ten percent more visitors this year.

Exercise 22: Replace any inappropriate prepositions or conjunctions in the following sentences.

1. He won't come in without you ask him.
2. Will you join me in a slice of watermelon?
3. In *The Son of Frankenstein*, Lionel Atwill stuck darts into his wooden arm while waiting on his turn to throw.
4. We bought some fruit jar whiskey of a moonshiner.
5. Emma Bovary died from arsenic poisoning.
6. What is Admiral Bilgewater protesting for?
7. Africans and Europeans had different ideas of what slavery consisted in.
8. When you're in the Great Smokies, be sure and visit Cades Cove.
9. This rifle belonged of my great uncle Thad.
10. You can't have pearls without you find oysters.
11. Ramon Navarro played Ben Hur in the 1925 movie while Charlton Heston played him in the 1959 remake.
12. Being as we shall be out late tonight, you must take a nap.
13. We don't know but what the murderer is in this room.
14. Beowulf tore off Grendel's arm. Too, he pursued Grendel's mother and killed her.
15. Neither poor eyesight or faulty memory seems to faze Mr. McGoo.
16. We had scarcely begun the picnic than a bear turned over our ice chest.
17. Follow the Appalachian Trail til the turn off to Mt. LeConte.
18. The contrast of the white rhinoceros and the black rhinoceros is provocative.

19. Concentrating on his work, Handel was oblivious of his household.
20. The apostles divided the loaves and fishes between the five hundred.

Exercise 23: Put the appropriate traditional preposition or conjunction in the blank.

1. The Indian elephant's ears are different (than, from) the African elephant's. . . . .
2. Crispy Critters already have sugar (like, as) Froot Loops do. . . . . .
3. There were so many new records that Jethro couldn't choose (between, among) them. . . . .
4. The Brysons divide their vacation (between, among) the mountains and the beach. . . . .
5. (As of, On) Labor Day, most seasonal park rangers go home. . . . .
6. Inspector Bucket was discouraged (on, by) the lack of evidence. . . . .
7. The Round Bottom caravan was canceled (due to, because of) high water at Straight Fork. . . . .
8. Pogo tried to disguise himself (like, as) Little Orphan Annie. . . . .
9. (Owing to, Because of) storm and shipwreck, many ships of the Armada never reached Spain. . . . .
10. Neither Simpatico del Sarto's (or, nor) Mañana Iguana's style approach the simple symmetry of Pasquatanx's. . . . .
11. The victory at Crecy was (due to, because of) the English archers. . . . .
12. As the mad monk in *Rasputin and the Empress,* Lionel Barrymore looked (like, as if) he had crawled out of the woodwork. . . . .
13. (Being as, Since) they hardly ever make them anymore, Jethro wrote his latest lyrics in Spenserian stanzas. . . . .
14. Francis X. Bushman played Messala (while, and) Charlton Heston played Ben Hur. . . . .
15. I wish we could have an air-conditioned lawn mower (like, as, such as) all the other kids have. . . . .
16. I don't know (but what, whether) "The Three Ravens" is prettier than "Whoops, Do Me No Harm, Good Man." . . . .
17. John Keats died (from, of) tuberculosis and not (of, due to) harsh literary criticism. . . . .
18. In the Renaissance, most painters had to look (at, to) wealthy patrons for support. . . . .
19. Grace thought the giraffe was (as good, as good as) or better than the twelve-string guitar. . . . .
20. Luther wrote that man is justified (on, by) faith alone. . . . .

13 √ Negative Negatives

One of the most frequent and obvious signs of nonstandard English is the double or multiple negative. When H. L. Mencken translated the opening of the Declaration of Independence into burlesque vulgar usage, he multiplied every possible negative: "without asking no permission from nobody . . . not trying to put nothing over on nobody . . . nobody ain't got no right to take away none of our rights . . . nobody else ought to have no say in the matter." Actually, Mencken overdid it; even speakers of nonstandard English don't go that far. But the use of the double negative serves as a powerful shibboleth; statements like "I don't want no supper," brand a person as a clod or a clown, and it is certainly better to avoid them.

The songwriters of "You Ain't Nothing but a Hound Dog" and "I Don't Want No Ricochet Romance" self-consciously use the double negative for contrived folksiness. A less obviously planned double negative often occurs with the words *hardly* and *scarcely*, for these adverbs being indirectly negative require a positive verb. Thus "I couldn't scarcely eat a thing," "There wasn't hardly any furniture in the house," and "She can't scarcely see ten feet" should be corrected to read "could scarcely," "was hardly," and "can scarcely."

But prescriptive grammarians often give illogical reasons for commanding, "Thou shalt not use the double negative." Certainly there is no sensible reason for an absolute injunction against it. The French have always doubled the negative with *ne . . . pas, ne . . . jamis,* and *ne . . . rien.* Old and Middle English regularly used a multiple negative, and Shakespeare employed it on occasion: "I never writ, nor no man ever loved." Today custom frowns on it, but it could make a comeback if usage so determined. The only commonsense argument against double negatives is that they are superfluous—a sort of dead wood. On the other hand, it can be argued that multiple negatives, though nonstandard, increase a

201

statement's emphasis and intensity, as in these examples from the Great Smokies: "I hain't got nary none," "That boy never done nothin' nohow," "I can't get no rest nohow," and "It holped a man not to be beholden to nobody." The Appalachian "Hit don't make no nevermind" has the wrong verb form as well, but is certainly more vivid than "It doesn't matter."

The argument that two negatives make a positive is a faulty analogy from mathematics. Meaning is not mathematics; and when a person says, "He doesn't read no books," he does not mean he does read *some* books, no matter what purists may argue.

Standard English does sometimes use a double negative but for an evasive rather than an emphatic effect, as in "There is no one who does not sometimes make mistakes." It is clearer and more direct to write, "Everyone sometimes makes mistakes." But jargon often prefers evasion and likes to weaken statements by the non-committal negative, particularly the *not un-* formation, where two negatives do not quite make a positive but rather a diminished affirmative. "I'm not certain that it is honest" is less forceful than "I think that is dishonest." *Not infrequent* is less forthright than *frequent*; *was not faithful* is less blunt than *betrayed*; *not very worthwhile* is less emphatic than *practically worthless*; and *not very attractive* is less damning than *ugly*.

Apparently many people today hesitate to commit themselves. In "Politics and the English Language," George Orwell cites as a horrible example the following sentence from Professor Harold Laski's *Freedom of Expression*: "I am not, indeed, sure whether it is not true to say that the Milton who once seemed not unlike a seventeenth-century Shelley had not become, out of an experience ever more bitter in each year, more alien [*sic*] to the founder of that Jesuit sect which nothing could induce him to tolerate." This is a poor example of unfettered literary expression, for Laski gets so tangled in negatives that he conveys the wrong meaning, using the negative *alien* when he means *akin*. This sort of style erects a series of barriers, like the false turns in a labyrinth, and a reader may never find the exit. The *not un-* is a hesitant construction and may thus, as Orwell suggests, give banal statements an appearance of profundity. A reader should not be taken in by it and should avoid it in his own work. As a cure, Orwell recommended memorizing, "A not unblack dog was chasing a not unsmall rabbit across a not ungreen field."

Besides the tangle of jargon, negative implications are difficult to remove; sometimes they raise needless doubts that then have to be removed. The Department of Agriculture urges its writers to think positively and not to drag in negative suggestions that must later be canceled. Thus, "We cannot fail to be impressed" should be changed to "We are greatly impressed."

Negative affixes are sometimes a problem. Sometimes they do not actually negate. The undead are not exactly alive; vampires and zombis are hardly living dolls. (When in the film *White Zombi,* some tourists in Haiti see zombis slaving in a grist mill—zombis usually seem to slave in grist mills—and ask their coachman about these strange people, he replies, "Them's not people; them's dead *bah*-ties [bodies].") A nonbook is still a book; and currently, e.g., in such terms as *nonperson, nonmusic, nonbook, nonsentence,* the prefix *non* means "illegitimate" or "debased" or "deficient," rather than "not." Neither does the negative with an adjective necessarily indicate the opposite. *Not right* doesn't have to mean "absolutely wrong"; *not my friend* doesn't mean "my enemy"; *not full* doesn't have to mean "empty." There are degrees of shading and contrast for subtleties of distinction.

Since subtleties require thought, the totalitarian thought controllers of George Orwell's *1984* manipulate language and enormously reduce vocabulary to purge the diction of critical thinking and make unorthodoxy impossible. One way is to eliminate positive opposites (and hence choice) by replacing them with the prefix *un-.* "Given, for instance, the word *good,* there was no need for such a word as *bad,* since the required meaning was equally well—indeed better—expressed by *ungood.* All that was necessary, in any case where two words formed a natural pair of opposites, was to decide which of them to suppress. *Dark,* for example, could be replaced by *unlight,* or *light* by *undark,* according to preference." [1] By this method and others, language is impoverished until only the rigid jargon of Newspeak remains, in which dehumanized people express the dogmas of the Party.

Both prefixes and suffixes can be used to negate a word, but you should not use both on the same root. *Irregardless* is undesirable not mainly because it is considered vulgar but because the suffix is sufficient; *regardless* is proper; the prefix, worthless and irritating. There are many negative prefixes: *a-, anti-, contra-, contre-, counter-, de-, di-, dis-, dys-, ig-, il-, im-, in-, ir-, mal-, mis-, non-,* and *un-.* These cannot be used interchangeably, but custom is the only rule governing their use, so you have to learn each word individually.

Thus we have *achromatic, antithesis, disarrange, ignoble, illiterate, immature, incomplete, irreverent, misbehave, nonrestrictive, unscientific.* Some words with a negative prefix have no positive counterpart; there is no *mune, effable, cessant, delible, ane, nominy, ert,* or *dignant,* for *immune, ineffable, incessant, indelible, inane, ignominy, inert,* and *indignant.* Some negative prefixes have other meanings as well, and occasional confusion results. *Inflammable* means that the substance can catch fire, but some people seeing the sign on trucks thought that the prefix meant *not,* so *inflammable* has been replaced by *flammable,* which means the same thing.

Many contractions are negatives with an auxiliary verb: *can't, couldn't, won't, wouldn't, doesn't, don't, didn't,* the practically obsolete *shan't, shouldn't,* and the notorious *ain't.* A frequent error here is the omission or misplacement of the apostrophe, which should be between the *n* and *t* to replace the *o* in *not.* Often careless writers misplace the apostrophe, and even the novelist John W. De Forest wrote, "It wo'nt burn!" Not all contractions duplicate in shortened form the original word; *won't* is not literally a combination of *will* and *not* but strictly speaking, a new word used to express the idea. The actual contraction, which one four-year-old girl coined by analogy, is *willn't.* Sometimes small children confuse the negative contraction with the infinitive and precede it with the positive verb. The aforementioned four-year-old asked questions like, "Why could he couldn't play?", "Why did she didn't go to nursery school?", "Why did they didn't say hello?", "Why would they wouldn't fall off the mountain?", and once stated, "I'm going on the back porch where the hornets are aren't."

Though the bête noire of purists, *ain't* is quite as logical as *won't;* it simply isn't sanctioned. *Ain't* replaces *am not* ("I ain't"), *is not* or *isn't* ("he ain't"), and *are not* ("they ain't"). *Isn't* is a slithery word, and *ain't* may be more euphonious. In questions, *ain't* is used for *are not* (*ain't I* vs. *aren't I*). *Aren't I* is technically ungrammatical though approved; the logical but unpronounceable form is *amn't I,* and formal English would use *am I not.* *Ain't got no* and *ain't got none* are triply unsanctioned. Besides the double negative, *ain't* here is a contraction of *has not* or *have not.* Hence the contraction is illogical, with no audible relation to the actual verb. Perhaps the soundest argument against *ain't* is that it could easily become an indiscriminate catch-all contraction.

Possibly more common than *ain't* in nonstandard English is the erroneous use of *don't* for *doesn't* in the third person singular ("he don't"). Another fallacy with contractions is the use of *didn't ought* or *hadn't ought.* Since *did* and *had* are meaningless here, the proper form is *ought not,* which you sometimes hear (but seldom see written) in the contracted form of *oughtn't.*

Do with a negative often loses all meaning and becomes purely functional, with the infinitive carrying the full sense, as in "I do not think so," "I don't know," "He doesn't want any." Older English might omit *do* and instead use the form, "I think not so," "I know not," "He wants none," with the negative following the verb.

Sometimes people confuse the negative by simply omitting it when sense and meaning require it. A particularly prevalent version of this error is the statement, "I could care less," when the speaker means, "I could *not* care less." Such carelessness gives the opposite meaning from the one intended. Perhaps the insistence that when a person says, for instance, "I could care less about religion," he really means that he does care about it corresponds to claiming that a double negative makes a positive; nevertheless, the "could care less" habit is indeed careless and betrays a slovenliness of thought.

Exercise 24: Correct any multiple or unacceptable negatives in the following:

1. It doesn't cost only thirty cents.
2. Fish aren't biting nohow in this rain.
3. Father's not working none; he's just trafficking around.
4. With a not inconsiderable number of supporters, Ringo Starr made a not unmemorable campaign for President.
5. Lon Chaney looked horrifying as the Phantom of the Opera, but Claude Rains wasn't hardly scary even without his mask.
6. In the coldest weather some New Englanders don't wear no coat.
7. Errol Flynn was a not insensitive actor when he had a script that was not unworthy of his intelligence.
8. In the mountains you won't find nary a person that says a good word for the revenuers.
9. James Thurber couldn't hardly picture Henry James confronting Brigitte Bardot.
10. Allen insists on going without no reservations.
11. Not even the chains couldn't hold King Kong when the flashbulbs went off.
12. It didn't take scarcely a moment for Quasimodo to swing down from the scaffold and whisk Esmeralda to safety.

13. It is a not unreasonable claim that *The Carpetbaggers* is a not unlikely candidate for the worst novel ever written.
14. There wasn't no black bean soup in stock at Shaheen's supermarket.
15. A not unsooty raven was making a not uncacaphonous caw in a not un-apple tree in the not unmowed field at Oconaluftee.
16. There is not, according to literary scholars, no reliable evidence to show that Shakespeare did not write his own plays.
17. To say that Bacon wrote Shakespeare is not scarcely different from claiming that Darwin wrote *Vanity Fair*.
18. Ben Gunn was disappointed that Jim Hawkins did not have no cheese in his pocket.
19. After the disastrous opening night of *Guy Domville,* Henry James did not want no more active connection with the theater.
20. After losing money on foolish speculations, Mark Twain became cautious and did not buy no stock in the new Bell Telephone Company.

14 √ Sentence Structure

Knowing how to use the parts of speech is not very helpful if you cannot use them to construct effective sentences. It is quite possible to use correct grammar and have a totally undistinguished style. H. L. Mencken wrote that President Warren G. Harding's prose reminded him "of a string of wet sponges." Harding enjoyed making speeches ("I like to go out into the country and bloviate," he said), but few people enjoyed listening to them. Instead of "bloviating," you need to organize your thoughts logically and then express them in a clear and orderly fashion. If your paragraphs and pages are to be persuasive, you must not rely on sheer bulk of argument or narrative, but must construct each sentence carefully. For a few writers, the sentence rather than larger units, holds the essence of their art. Emerson and Thoreau often ramble in their wording, seeming to neglect logical development and transition, but their individual sentences are polished like gems. *Walden* is largely a mosaic of brilliant sentences, which Thoreau had written years before he placed them in a larger organization.

Unfortunately, many people are unsure when they have written a sentence. It is as necessary for the writer to know the structure of a sentence as for a mechanic to know that of his machines. First we must differentiate between phrases and clauses. A phrase is a group of words combined as a unit without a subject and a verb. It may form all or part of the subject or all or part of the predicate, but both are needed for a clause. In the following examples, the phrases indicated by the italicized words function in each sentence in a different way grammatically:

The magic word "Shazaam" turned Billy Batson into Captain Marvel.
    (Phrase is subject.)
Snoopy is *Charlie Brown's dog.* (Phrase is complement of the verb.)
Superman emerged *from the phone booth.* (Phrase modifies verb.)

207

Without his mask, the Lone Ranger might have better eyesight.
(Phrase modifies subject.)
L'il Abner's hair is parted on whatever side *faces the reader.*
(Phrase is a predicate.)
Alice the Goon *has not appeared* lately in the "Popeye" comic
strip. (Phrase is a verb.)

Each of these sentences has several other phrases beside the ones italicized. Sometimes there are phrases within phrases. In "Mighty Mouse rescued Pearl Pureheart *from the clutches of Oilcan Harry,*" the over-all phrase modifies the verb *rescued,* and *of Oilcan Harry* modifies *clutches.*

¶ MAIN CLAUSES AND SIMPLE SENTENCES

There are two types of clauses: main (or independent) and subordinate (or dependent). Both must have a subject and a verb. But a main clause is self-contained and does not function as a subject, modifier, or complement. It can be an independent simple sentence, consisting of just a subject and a verb: "She sells." To this we can add an object ("She sells seashells") and assorted modifiers ("She sells overpriced seashells by the seashore"). A main clause can have two subjects ("Jack and Jill went up the hill") or two verbs ("Jack fell down and broke his crown") or two subjects for the same two verbs ("Frankie and Johnnie went to the bar and had a few drinks"). Two or more main clauses can be combined to make compound sentences:

Art is long. (One main clause as a simple sentence.)
Art is long, but *time is fleeting.* (Two main clauses joined as a compound sentence.)
Mark Twain was a realist and *so was Henry James,* but *they didn't like each other's work.* (Three main clauses joined as a compound sentence.)

A main clause can have a number of qualifying phrases and still the whole will be an independent simple sentence: "Our hearts, though stout and brave, still, like muffled drums, are beating funeral marches to the grave." This has only one subject (*hearts*) and one verb (*are beating*). In a compound sentence, the main clauses must be connected either by a coordinating conjunction (*and, but, for, or, nor, yet*) preceded by a comma or by a semicolon with no conjunction. Use of a comma alone constitutes a comma splice, a serious

208

flaw in punctuation. If the clauses are simply run together with no conjunction or punctuation, then there is a run-on sentence; this is rightly considered an even more serious flaw.

¶ SUBORDINATE CLAUSES

A subordinate (or dependent) clause has its own subject and verb, but it cannot stand alone. Usually introduced by a relative pronoun or a subordinating conjunction, it depends upon the main clause and functions as subject, modifier, or complement:

John Wayne is the only actor *who killed two giant squids.* (Clause modifies *actor.*)

As soon as the fire alarm rang, Smokey Stover was on the job. (Clause modifies *was.*)

I don't understand *why Prudence Pimpleton puts up with Fearless Fosdick.* (Clause is complement of verb *understand.*)

Why Beetle Bailey isn't promoted or discharged is a mystery. (Clause is subject of *is.*)

Orphan Annie is the girl *whose eyes are blunked out.* (Clause modifies *girl.*)

Occasionally, the connective is omitted ("Lois Lane is the girl *Clark Kent loves*"). A sentence may contain several subordinate clauses: "*When Ming was ruler of Mongo,* he ordered *that all men must be bald.*" Sometimes the subordinate clause is elliptical, with the verb understood: in the sentence, "Blackstone gave away more rabbits *than any other magician,*" the verb *did* is understood.

Subordinate clauses introduced by conjunctions can have various positions in a sentence, whereas those introduced by an interrogative or relative pronoun usually cannot. "I don't understand *how Popeye eats spinach through his pipe*" has fixed word order, as does "Jack Jawbreaker is the man *who robbed the bank.*" "Only the Shadow knows *what evil lurks* in the heart of man," is the normal word order, though this could conceivably be phrased, "*What evil lurks in the heart of man,* only the Shadow knows." "When I go to a ball game, I don't like to sit in the rain" could just as well be "I don't like to sit in the rain when I go to a ball game." Notice that a subordinate clause is followed by a comma when it precedes the main clause, unless it is the subject of that clause, but is not set off by a comma if it comes after the main clause.

Sentences with one subordinate clause and one main clause are called complex sentences. Those with two main clauses and one or more subordinate clauses are compound-complex sentences, like Thoreau's "One value even of the smallest well is, that when you look into it, you see that earth is not continent but insular."

Though subordinate clauses can serve as a verb's subject, object, or complement, they are not always used this way effectively. According to *Time*, ". . . President Kennedy told his press conference that just because some merchant has Polish ham in his shop does not brand him as unpatriotic."[1] In this complex sentence, "just because some merchant has Polish ham in his shop" is not grammatically adequate as the subject of the verb, *does*. Similarly, "Just because Babbitt rebels" is not an adequate subject in "Just because Babbitt rebels does not mean that he becomes genuinely liberal." As complement, a subordinate clause can be equally clumsy, as in "A baby is so you could be the boss" and "Marriage is so your brothers and sisters should grow up and get married and then you could be the only child,"[2] though not always with such comic effect. The clumsiness of "One thing no good about a big brother is when you hit him he hits you right back"[3] can be cured by additional subordination—the insertion of *that* between *is* and *when*. But then the sentence isn't as much fun.

¶ VARIETY IN SENTENCE STRUCTURE

Books for beginning readers are usually written in a sequence of simple sentences, and elementary writers often follow suit: "Once upon a time there was a hippopotamus. His name was Harry. Harry ate too much one night. He ate 275 cabbages. He ate 312 bananas. He ate 25 bags of potato chips." Or they connect a series of short main clauses by *and* with monotonous regularity: "Harry ate 46 hamburgers, and he ate 79 pounds of peanuts, and he ate 13 cantaloupes, and he drank 32 bottles of root beer, and he ate 115 pizzas, and for dessert he had seven gallons of fudgi-wudgi ice cream. Then Harry felt sick, and he went to the wise old owl, and the wise old owl told him to go to the magic spring and drink some water from it. Harry asked where the spring was. The wise old owl told him it was three mountain ranges away. Harry felt too sick to go there, so the wise old owl told him to get some help." This is not quite as deadly as "See Spot run. Run, run, run. Run, Spot, run," but it has little variety. Grammatically such prose is correct, but stylistically it is flat unless it is done by Hemingway, who achieved considerable subtlety with deceptively simple grammatical repetition. Possibly the best example of terse statement packed with what now seems comic implication is the climax of the pot-boiler novel *The Sheik*: " 'I haven't!' 'You aren't!' She was." Some students go to the other extreme and get lost in a tangle of involved verbosity. Clarity is essential, but so is a degree of variety—though a writer should never strain to achieve it. Paragraphs in which most sentences have the same length and structure plod along with the monotony of an ambling nag:

> Thoreau's *Walden* is partly an autobiographical narrative. It tells about the two years and two months and two days that Thoreau spent in the woods. He went to the woods to simplify his life. He also wanted to prove that men could live adequately without a lot of money. He borrowed the land from Emerson and bought a railroad shanty. He worked little so that he could read and study nature. Thoreau did not urge everybody to do as he did. He wanted each man to find his own solution. According to Thoreau, most men lead lives of quiet desperation.

If Thoreau had written no better than that, no one would read him today. On the other hand, too much variety may seem like tutti frutti as in this example from Edgar Rice Burroughs: "Those who could fled, until at last there were no more to pay the penalty for a deed, which, while not beyond them, they were, nevertheless, not guilty of." [4] This involved, stumbling construction seems punctuated with panting pauses so that writer and reader can catch their breath. If Burroughs' sentences were so clumsily complicated consistently, his readers would have soon lost patience. Though their sensibilities were worlds apart, the mandarin prose of Henry James's late period sometimes resembles this specimen from Burroughs. In "The Altar of the Dead," James wrote, "He had found little change indeed, he had brought the little change back; it was the little change that stood there and that, do what he would he couldn't, while he showed those high front teeth of his, look other than a conscious ass about." In his later writing, James inserted a great many hesitant parenthetical qualifications that sometimes made his style so involuted that it became asthmatic.

Sometimes subordination and combination can help give variety and improve transition:

> It was the beginning of February, 1821. Two ships of imperial Russia, the *Vostok* and the *Mirnyi,* rounded Cape Horn. They cruised South into the ice-choked Weddell Sea. They were searching for uncharted land. The Russians hoped this might prove the existence of the legendary Antarctic

continent. Captain Thaddeus von Bellingshausen commanded this small squadron. Twelve months before it had explored the islands east of the Cape. Now it was a year and a half out of Kronstadt. It was completing a circumnavigation of the world in the south polar latitudes.

Here is the beginning of an interesting story botched by a bumpy style. Notice the improvement in the following:

At the beginning of February, 1821, two ships of imperial Russia, the *Vostok* and the *Mirnyi,* rounded Cape Horn and cruised south into the ice-choked Weddell Sea searching for uncharted land that might prove the existence of the legendary Antarctic continent. This small squadron, under command of Captain Thaddeus von Bellingshausen, had twelve months before explored the islands east of the Cape and was now, a year and a half out of Kronstadt, completing a circumnavigation of the world in the south polar latitudes.

Here the first sentence of version one is turned into a phrase; the subject in sentence two picks up the verb in sentence three and cuts the repeated subject; sentence four becomes a participial modifying phrase; and sentence five becomes a subordinate clause. What changes are made to combine the remaining sentences?

Sometimes making a clause subordinate is undesirable. "There's a whole lost city that nobody knows where it is" is grammatically off the track. The sentence should be coordinated to "There's a whole lost city, and nobody knows where it is." Subordinate clauses, especially those beginning with *which,* can be dangerous in that they tend to proliferate out of control: "He took his daughter to see the penguins in the Vancouver Zoo, which was located across the isthmus which bridged Stanley Park, which had been set aside by the city and which included twelve miles which have both beaches and almost virgin forests which are penetrated only by a few paths which are always well tended." *Which* clauses not only sprawl but often pile up passive voice constructions: "It was an obsolete car, for the repair of which a diligent search for spare parts was required and for which a mechanic occasionally had to make a new part." James Thurber writes that "Trying to cross a paragraph by leaping from 'which' to 'which' is like Eliza crossing the ice. The danger is in missing a 'which' and falling in." [5] In "Rufus went to the zoo, which was in the park, which had his favorite rhinoceros which he liked to feed and calmed his nerves," the twittering "whicher" dropped the last *which* before *calmed.* Sup-

212

pose you write, "It is a program which we must adopt or go bankrupt." Something is wrong here, so you plunge in and try, "It is a program which we must adopt or which will go bankrupt." You run your fingers through your hair and try, "It is a program which we must adopt or by which we will go bankrupt." Foiled again, you shake your head grimly and write, "It is a program which we must adopt or which, if we do not adopt, will bankrupt us," and so on. By the time you get the sentence straightened out ("We must adopt this program or go bankrupt"), you may have gone bankrupt yourself.

¶ PERIODIC SENTENCES

When an introductory subordinate clause, a long introductory phrase, or a group of modifiers comes before the main clause, we have a periodic sentence. Depending on their content, periodic sentences can be simple, compound, complex, or compound-complex. Such sentences are often effective in opening with an emphasis and building to a climax: "From the time Tarzan left the tribe of great anthropoids in which he had been raised, it was torn by continual strife and discord. . . . As Terkoz reached the group, five huge, hairy beasts sprang upon him." [6] One of the most spectacular examples of a periodic sentence occurs in Whitman's "Song of Myself," where we find one sentence eighty lines long, with the subject and verb in the last line preceded by a series of modifiers modified by other modifiers. By all rules this should not work, but it succeeds as one of Whitman's finest pieces of poetry:

By the city's quadrangular houses—in log huts, camping with lumbermen,
Along the ruts of the turnpike, along the dry gulch and rivulet bed,
Weeding my onion patch or hoeing rows of carrots and parsnips, crossing
    savannas, trailing in forests,
Prospecting, gold-digging, girdling the trees of a new purchase,
Scorch'd ankle-deep by the hot sand, hauling my boat down the shallow
    river,
Where the panther walks to and fro on a limb overhead, where the buck
    turns furiously at the hunter,
Where the rattlesnake suns his flabby length on a rock, where the otter is
    feeding on fish,
Where the alligator in his tough pimples sleeps by the bayou,
Where the black bear is searching for roots or honey, where the beaver pats
    the mud with his paddle-shaped tail;

Over the growing sugar, over the yellow-flower'd cotton plant, over the rice in its low moist field,

Over the sharp-peak'd farm house, with its scallop'd scum and slender shoots from the gutters,

Over the west persimmon, over the long-leav'd corn, over the delicate blue-flower flax,

Over the white and brown buckwheat, a hummer and buzzer there with the rest,

Over the dusky green of the rye as it ripples and shades in the breeze;

Scaling mountains, pulling myself cautiously up, holding on by low scragged limbs,

Walking the path worn in the grass and beat through the leaves of the brush,

Where the quail is whistling betwixt the woods and the wheat-lot,

Where the bat flies in the Seventh-month eve, where the great gold-bug drops through the dark,

Where the brook puts out of the roots of the old trees and flows to the meadow,

Where cattle stand and shake away flies with the tremulous shuddering of their hides,

Where the cheese-cloth hangs in the kitchen, where andirons straddle the hearth-slab, where cobwebs fall in festoons from the rafters;

Where trip-hammers crash, where the press is whirling its cylinders,

Wherever the human heart beats with terrible throes under its ribs,

Where the pear-shaped balloon is floating aloft, (floating in it myself and looking composedly down,)

Where the life-car is drawn on the slip-noose, where the heat hatches pale-green eggs in the dented sand,

Where the she-whale swims with her calf and never forsakes it,

Where the steam-ship trails hind-ways its long pennant of smoke,

Where the fin of the shark cuts like a black chip out of the water,

Where the half-burn'd brig is riding on unknown currents,

Where shells grow to her slimy deck, where the dead are corrupting below;

Where the dense-starr'd flag is borne at the head of the regiments,

Approaching Manhattan up by the long-stretched island,

Under Niagara, the cataract falling like a veil over my countenance,

Upon a door-step, upon the horse-block of hard wood outside,

Upon the race-course, or enjoying picnics or jugs or a good game of base-ball,

At he-festivals, with blackguard gibes, ironical license, bull-dances, drinking, laughter,

At the cider-mill tasting the sweets of the brown mash, sucking the juice through a straw,

At apple-peelings wanting kisses for all the red fruit I find,
At musters, beach-parties, friendly bees, huskings, house-raisings;
Where the mocking-bird sounds his delicious gurgles, cackles, screams, weeps,
Where the hay-rick stands in the barn yard, where the dry-stalks are scatter'd, where the brood-cow waits in the hovel,
Where the bull advances to do his masculine work, where the stud to the mare, where the cock is treading the hen,
Where the heifers browse, where geese nip their food with short jerks,
Where the sun-down shadows lengthen over the limitless and lonesome prairie,
Where herds of buffalo make a crawling spread of the square miles far and near,
Where the humming-bird shimmers, where the neck of the long-lived swan is curving and winding,
Where the laughing-gull scoots by the shore, where she laughs her near-human laugh,
Where the bee-hives range on a gray bench in the garden half hid by the high weeds,
Where band-neck'd partridges roost in a ring on the ground with their heads out,
Where burial coaches enter the arch'd gates of a cemetery,
Where winter wolves bark amid wastes of snow and icicled trees,
Where the yellow-crown'd heron comes to the edge of the marsh at night and feeds upon small crabs,
Where the splash of swimmers and divers cools the warm noon,
Where the katy-did works her chromatic reed on the walnut-tree over the well,
Through patches of citrons and cucumbers with silver-wired leaves,
Through the salt-lick or orange glade, or under conical firs,
Through the gymnasium, through the curtain'd saloon, through the office or public hall;
Pleas'd with the native and pleas'd with the foreign, pleas'd with the new and old,
Pleas'd with the homely woman as well as the handsome,
Pleas'd with the quakeress as she puts off her bonnet and talks melodiously,
Pleas'd with the tune of the choir of the whitewash'd church,
Pleas'd with the earnest words of the sweating Methodist preacher, impress'd seriously at the camp-meeting;
Looking in at the shop-windows of Broadway the whole forenoon, flatting the flesh of my nose on the thick plate glass,
Wandering the same afternoon with my face turn'd up to the clouds, or down a lane or along the beach,

My right and left arms round the sides of two friends, and I in the middle;
Coming home with the silent and dark-cheek'd bush-boy, (behind me he
    rides at the drape of the day,)
Far from the settlements studying the print of animals' feet, or the moccasin
    print,
By the cot in the hospital reaching lemonade to a feverish patient,
Nigh the coffin'd corpse when all is still, examining with a candle;
Voyaging to every port to dicker and adventure,
Hurrying with the modern crowd as eager and fickle as any,
Hot toward one I hate, ready in my madness to knife him,
Solitary at midnight in my back yard, my thoughts gone from me a long
    while,
Walking the old hills of Judaea with the beautiful gentle God by my side,
Speeding through space, speeding through heaven and the stars,
Speeding amid the seven satellites and the broad ring, and the diameter of
    eighty thousand miles,
Speeding with tail'd meteors, throwing fire-balls like the rest,
Carrying the crescent child that carries its own full mother in its belly,
Storming, enjoying, planning, loving, cautioning,
Backing and filling, appearing and disappearing,
I tread day and night such roads.

Not until the last line are the subject *I* and the predicate apparent. All of the preceding lines tell where and how Whitman
treads—by the houses, in huts, camping, along the ruts, weeding,
prospecting, scorch'd, hauling; then comes a series of subordinate
clauses modifying *hauling*: where the panther, the buck, the rattlesnake, the otter, the alligator, and the bear live; then follow another series of modifiers of *I*—over this and that, scaling, walking
(followed by dozens of lines modifying where he walks)—followed
by another series telling how he walks, pleased with this and that,
looking, wandering, coming home, etc., and so on down to the nine
present participles in the second and third lines from the end.

The periodic sentence is sometimes necessary for climax. "We
won the game after having ten penalties and fumbling the ball
twelve times" leaves the impression of penalties and fumbles rather
than victory. "After having ten penalties and fumbling the ball
twelve times, we won the game," gives the necessary chronological
explanation, contrast, and culmination. Again, the subordinate
clause is an ambiguously placed modifier in "Adam and Eve did not
have to go out into the cruel world and work until they had sinned."
Sinning was not the result of too much work, so the word order
should be, "Until they had sinned, Adam and Eve did not have to

216

go out into the cruel world and work." Periodic sentences are often stately and sometimes static. Since they weigh down the structure so heavily before reaching the sentence's subject and predicate, they may impede the forward movement of narrative action. And after too much of a build-up, the action may seem too trivial. How effective is the following? "Unversed in jungle craft, overwhelmed by the enormity of the catastrophe that had engulfed him, his reasoning faculties numbed by terror, Wilbur Stimbol slunk through the jungle, the fleeing quarry of every terror that imagination could conjure." [7] Perhaps the verb *slunk* is insufficient to carry so much weight. At any rate, be careful not to make your sentences top-heavy.

¶ INVERSION AND WORD ORDER

Since emphasis and stress normally fall at the beginning and end of the English sentence, a skillful writer often inverts normal word order to place what he wishes to have emphasized at the sentence's beginning or end. This is particularly common in poetry. "Divine am I inside and out," wrote Whitman, more dramatically than if he had written, "I am divine inside and out." "Exploitation there was . . ." wrote C. Vann Woodward about the Jim Crow laws. Emerson's "In self-trust all the virtues are comprehended" is more emphatic than, "All the virtues are comprehended in self-trust." By omitting an auxiliary verb, inversion can make a line of poetry more dramatic and concise: Macbeth's "Saw you the weird sisters? Came they not by you?" has more urgency than "Did you see the weird sisters?" "Infected be the air whereon they ride," he curses. On the other hand, sometimes inversion is used to delay the climactic word until the end, as in Richard III's "Than my Lord Hastings no man might be bolder."

Milton was particularly prone to use inversions in both his poetry and his prose. As a result, his work is sometimes more stately than vigorous. Critics have observed that Homer has the *Iliad* well under way but Milton is still invoking his inverted muse after a dozen lines. Sometimes, poetic inversion forces the reader to straighten out the lines in order to clarify the meaning. The Puritan poet Edward Taylor wrote:

> This thing
> Souls are but petty things it to admire.
> Ye angels, help! This fill would to the brim
> Heaven's whelmed-down crystal meal bowl . . .

217

Prose would say, "Souls are but petty things to admire this thing. . . . This would fill Heaven's whelmed-down meal bowl to the brim." How would you straighten out the following lines from Chaucer?

> Of his complexioun he was sangwyn. . . .
> An housholdere, and that a greet [great], was he;
> Seint Julian he was in his contree [country]. . . .
> With-out bake mete [meat pie] was never his hous,
> Of fish and flesh, and that so plenteous
> It snewed [snowed] in his hous of mete and drink.

Word order is one of the subtlest and most important problems of style. There are no rules or reliable guidelines; the best way to learn how best to order a sentence is to read widely among skilled writers and educate your ear to possible rhythms. Sometimes word order involves logic, as with misplaced modifiers. "Lowell's essay on Thoreau suffers from lack of argument and wandering purpose" is clearer as "Lowell's essay on Thoreau suffers from wandering purpose and lack of argument." Otherwise, lack of wandering purpose may seem to be what the essay suffers from. But usually the issue is more one of style than sense. "Life, Liberty and the pursuit of Happiness" has exactly the right order. The meaning is as clear, but something is lost in "Life, the pursuit of Happiness, and Liberty," "Liberty, Life, and the pursuit of Happiness," or "The pursuit of Happiness, Life, and Liberty." ". . . we mutually pledge to each other our Lives, our Fortunes and our sacred Honor" again has the inevitability of the right word order. Had Jefferson written, "our Lives, our sacred Honor, and our Fortunes," the proper culmination would be missing. Again, contrast "Man does not live by bread alone" with "Man doesn't live only on bread." Not only the style but even the connotative meaning is subtly altered. Effective word order is as much a matter of intuition as rationale. Why is Shakespeare's "Something wicked this way comes" better than "Something wicked comes this way?" Perhaps a slight shift in the normal word order creates dramatic tension. Ordinarily a modifier should be placed next to the word it modifies, but notice how delaying the key word until the end gives it an explosive power when James Baldwin writes, "Yes, it does indeed mean something— something unspeakable—to be born, in a white country, an Anglo-Teutonic, anti-sexual country, black." [8]

Some problems of word order are dealt with in other chapters in this book, particularly in the sections on jargon, circumlocution, and dead wood. Sometimes people talking too rapidly, carelessly, or fumblingly toss off sentences with staggering structure or use redundancies, such as "All I did was, I did . . ." or "So what I decided to do, I decided . . ." Or they start a subordinate clause with *that,* fail to follow up the subject with a verb, and get side-tracked into some other clause: "He was playing the kind of pool that you knew he was a professional." Holden Caulfield often uses such constructions in *The Catcher in the Rye,* but they are appropriate only when creating ficitional dialogue. In "All we did, we just went to see the walrus," the first clause should be eliminated, as it should in "What I did was, I pulled his hat over his ears."

Some grammarians warn against piling up adjectives or nouns, but at times these can be effective. The nouns are weirdly formidable in the ad for Chrysler's marsh screw amphibian: "For water, mud, marsh, sludge, slosh, slough, bog, fen, morass, quagmire, snow, slush, sand, silt, muck and mire." This is not a complete sentence, but doubtless the author was unable to slog along any farther. More artistically, John Donne piled up nouns like a series of hammer blows in:

> Thou'rt slave to Fate, chance, kings, and desperate men,
> And dost with poison, war, and sickness dwell . . .

Ultimately the arrangement of words is an artistic rather than a strictly grammatical matter. Styles vary from the stark sentences of early Hemingway to the full diapason of Faulkner, whose open-stopped sentences sometimes go on for as long as six pages, full of subordination upon subordination, participle upon participle, and parentheses within parentheses. Most writers settle somewhere between these two extremes.

¶ PARALLELISM

Parallel constructions contain two or a series of units identical in form grammatically, balancing ideas of equal weight. When these parallel elements are not in similar grammatical form, the balance is upset and the syntactical logic weakened. Thus, "The polar bear likes eating, sleeping, and to swim" has as the combined object of *like* two present participles and an infinitive. This faulty parallelism can be corrected by using either three participles ("eating, sleeping, and swimming") or three infinitives ("to eat, to sleep, and to swim"). The parallel structure may be clearer if printed:

| African wildlife is endangered by | the growth of agriculture and industry, the activity of poachers, the callousness of trophy hunters, | and the resultant destruction of the balance of nature. |

Here the verb *is endangered* has four nouns as objects: *growth, activity, callousness,* and *destruction*. If any of them were changed to another part of speech, the balance would be destroyed, e.g., "endangered by the growth of agriculture and industry, the activity of poachers, to satisfy trophy hunters, and the resultant destruction of the balance of nature."

"To err is human, to forgive divine." In this line by Alexander Pope, we have a parallel construction of two infinitives, followed by *is* (the second understood) and a predicate adjective. If the line were altered to read, "To err is human, to forgive being divine," the sense remains unchanged, but the style is sabotaged. Rhythmical measure and balance in both poetry and prose is often the direct result of effectively using parallel structure. Emerson wrote, "There is a time in every man's education when he arrives at the conviction that envy is ignorance; that imitation is suicide; that he must take himself for better for worse as his portion; that though the wide universe is full of good, no kernel of nourishing corn can come to him but through his toil bestowed on that plot of ground which is given to him to till." Here the succession of parallel subordinate clauses beginning with *that* holds the sentence together in stately procession. "There is a time in every man's education when he arrives at the conviction that envy is ignorance and it is suicide to be imitative because he must take himself for better or even worse as his portion . . ." destroys the parallelism and makes Emerson's muse a crippled pedestrian. Again, Emerson wrote, "What we are, that only can we see. All that Adam had, all that Caesar could, you have and can do." How much less effective this is as, "We are only what we can see. You can have all that Adam had and can do what Caesar could do." The paraphrase is still in parallel structure, but the ordered, cumulative rhythm of the original is ruined.

Lacking Emerson's style, a student wrote, "Thoreau says to live free and uncommitted and that a farm can imprison a man." Here *says* has two complements joined by *and*—an infinitive and a subordinate clause. For proper parallelism they must be in the same grammatical form: "Thoreau says that a man should live free and uncommitted and that a farm can imprison him." This is still not a brilliant sentence, but it holds together. According to another student, "Reading Thoreau and of *Walden,* we become aware of another world around us." Here the opening participle has a direct object parallel to a prepositional phrase. There are various remedies: "Reading Thoreau, we become aware . . . ," "Reading *Walden,* we become aware . . . ," "Reading Thoreau's *Walden,* we become aware . . . ," or "Reading of Thoreau's life at Walden, we become aware . . ."

Even worse are lumpy series without parallelism, such as "Three things prevail. These are man's inhumanity to man, worth of things is not determined by dollars and cents, and the migrants' condition was uncontrollable by them." This combines a noun (*inhumanity*) and two coordinate independent clauses in a senseless hodgepodge. One girl described her boy friend: "Jerry is six feet tall, brown eyes, black unruly hair, and weighs about one hundred and sixty pounds." Lest it seem that Jerry is eyes and hair, this series needs an inserted *has* before *brown eyes,* so that there will be three verbs (*is, has, weighs*) in parallel construction. "Everyone in *Babbitt* has the same type of homes, dress very similar, must give the same type of parties, ect.," is triply botched. The singular subject needs singular verbs, but the sentence shifts from *has* to the plural *dress* to *must.* Perhaps the student was thinking backward from *must give* to *must dress* but skipped the first *must.* Finally, *ect.* is both misspelled and unnecessary. Too often *et cetera* or *etc.* is used when the writer can think of no further examples and wishes the reader to think for him. "The tenant farmers' futile attempts at shooting bulldozers, etc., were ineffective" is ineffective; certainly it takes more than one example to make a series.

Infinitives, present participles, and subordinate clauses often get tangled in faulty parallel constructions. "Casy wasn't satisfied telling them that sometime they would have a better life and just to suffer until then" links the subordinate "that . . . they would have" with the infinitive "to suffer." The sentence needs two subordinate clauses, instead. "Franklin made many contributions in the field of science and by forming such things as a postal system, a library, and a college" joins a noun (*contributions*) to a participle (*forming*). Actually, this sentence should not be parallel; the cure is simply to cut *and.* "Franklin believed virtue was something to be

221

developed through conscientious effort and which in the end would be rewarding" combines a passive infinitive (*to be developed*) with a relative subordinate clause (*which . . . would be*). The remedy is to turn the first into a subordinate clause ("something which could be developed").

Finally, the omission of a necessary past participle often mars parallel constructions: "Americans have [fallen] and will continue to fall short of this idealism" and "The perfect naturalistic novel has not [been] and never will be written."

When the reader encounters a parallel construction, he expects the writer to continue it. If incongruous elements intrude, both the sound and the sense are jarred. So if you begin using nouns, adjectives, infinitives, present participles, or relative clauses in a grammatical series, continue with nouns, adjectives, infinitives, participles, or relative clauses until you reach the end. When you use a coordinating conjunction (*and, but, for, or, nor, yet*), make sure the elements it joins are coordinate. In conversation it is sometimes difficult to keep track of parallel units, but you should be able to do so in your writing, by revising it if necessary.

¶ FRAGMENTARY SENTENCES

To be grammatically complete, a sentence must contain a main clause capable of standing independently. It is too vague to say that a sentence must contain a complete thought. Actually, sentences may contain several complete thoughts, and a fragmentary sentence may have a complete thought and yet be grammatically incomplete. "As the giant sloths were about to attack him, Mandrake gestured hypnotically." Here, "Mandrake gestured hypnotically" is a main clause that could be a separate sentence, whereas "As the giant sloths were about to attack him" is subordinate to or dependent upon the main clause and cannot stand alone. Occasionally one encounters what seems to be a main clause that cannot stand alone; e.g., "One value even of the smallest well is" in "One value even of the smallest well is, that when you look into it, you see that earth is not continent but insular." Here the problem is that the three clauses making up the rest of the sentence are really complements of *is* and thus are part of the main clause. Such a pattern of concentric clauses is the exception.

There are many situations in which fragmentary sentences are perfectly acceptable. Some are simply interjections or exclamations:

222

"Great gobs of goose grease!" "Donner and Blitzen!" "Great Caesar's ghost!" Some are questions or answers to questions: "One lump or two?" "Two, please." "About ten o'clock." Others are balanced expressions like "Better late than never," "First come, first served," or Robert Frost's "No surprise for the writer, no surprise for the reader." Conversation and informal writing often use fragmentary sentences with perfect legitimacy. So does advertising, which often consists of a series of phrases like "*Secret Fighting Arts of the World* by John F. Gilby. Suppressed for generations! Twenty of the world's most secretly guarded fighting techniques vividly described in one volume: the Oriental delayed death touch; the destruction wrought by the fingertips of an obscure Mexican; the shout of doom; the lightning-like destruction inflicted by a Peoria bookworm—and many more vicious fighting tricks."

Certainly there should be no absolute injunction against fragmentary sentences, or minor sentences as they are sometimes called. Most modern authors use them at times, and they are often necessary in dialogue. But they are acceptable only when they work stylistically. The professional writer, when he uses fragments, does so intentionally to achieve a desired effect. Most unacceptable fragments occur when the writer simply fails to understand what constitutes a sentence. Usually he severs a subordinate clause, verbal, phrase, or participial phrase from the rest of the sentence to which it belongs. In the following examples, the italicized passages are faulty fragments.

SENTENCE FRAGMENT	INTERPRETATION	CORRECTION
I was raised with a gun in hand and am a fairly good shot. *My best score being 91 out of a possible 100.*	Italicized passage is a participial phrase modifying the main clause.	I was raised with a gun in hand and am a fairly good shot, my best score being 91 out of a possible 100.
In the early hours of the morning, the city is like a graveyard. *The buildings resembling huge tombstones and monuments and the barren streets paths between the graves.*	Again, we have a participial phrase modifying the main clause.	In the early hours of the morning, the city is like a graveyard, the buildings resembling huge tombstones and monuments and the barren streets paths between the graves.

223

SENTENCE FRAGMENTS	INTERPRETATION	CORRECTION
Fearless Fosdick dived into the garbage can. *When the machine guns opened fire.*	Italicized passage is a subordinate clause modifying *dived.*	Fearless Fosdick dived into the garbage can when the machine guns opened fire.
The Human Torch never burns up. *Although he often throws part of himself as fireballs against criminals.*	The italicized clause is subordinate and cannot stand alone.	The Human Torch never burns up, although he often throws part of himself as fireballs against criminals.

In all of these examples, the writer used a period when he should have used a comma. These period faults are easy to correct. But some fragments require a bit of rewriting. For instance, "Popeye could not decide. Rescuing Olive Oyl or salvaging his spinach," needs to be changed to "Popeye could not decide whether to rescue Olive Oyl or to salvage his spinach." "It was a dreadful ordeal for the climbers. Surviving a blizzard, suffering frostbite, and driving off the abominable snowman." Here the fragment consists of a series of gerunds that should be turned into verbs or used as modifiers: "In a dreadful ordeal, the climbers survived a blizzard, suffered frostbite, and drove off the abominable snowman" or "The climbers had a dreadful ordeal, surviving a blizzard, suffering frostbite, and driving off the abominable snowman." "What she wants to know is. Will a silver bullet kill a teen-age werewolf?" This should be an indirect question: "She wants to know whether a silver bullet will kill a teen-age werewolf."

Sentence structure brings us to the matter of structural linguistics, which are alternately praised and denounced in current grammatical controversies. There is a difference between descriptive grammarians and structural linguists. The latter are descriptive rather than prescriptive, but they often go a step further and discard traditional grammatical terms and methods. Structural linguistics is related to anthropology and was developed from the study of Oriental, African, and American Indian languages, which are structurally quite different from Indo-European ones. Some of these exotic tongues use no verbs, and many depend upon tone and pitch for word meanings. Applying to English the scientific method used in examining these diverse and often unwritten languages, structural linguists stress form more than function and generally reduce questions of meaning to "same" or "different." According to W. Nelson Francis, "Meaning is such a subjective quality that it is usually omitted entirely from scientific description." Structural linguists like to use jabberwocky sentences to illustrate form independent of meaning; e.g., "Blindfolded garages burp violently." This is nonsense, yet the formal relation of the words is clear. Of course there must be some meaning, or there can be no structural pattern, even though the meaning may be absurd. In "Blagenbogen grizzafapple bynapoz veeblefetzer," there is no grammar. Structural linguists separate words into "form-classes" that can fit function slots. Thus the slot in "The . . . is brilliant" can be filled with such forms (formerly labeled nouns) as *painting, ballet, drama, novel,* and *sunlight* but not with *erroneous, tangential, consequently,* or *yawned.*

Lincoln Barnett claims that structural linguists are incapacitating school children and making them incapable of clear writing. Many students are indeed incapable of clear writing, but structural linguistics is not to blame, for the simple reason that it is not being taught in elementary and secondary schools, except in a few avant-garde situations. The overwhelming majority of English teachers have studied and continue to teach traditional grammar. Probably the real villain is not the sort of grammar but the fact that over-worked teachers with overcrowded classes sometimes lack sufficient training in language and almost always lack time to teach writing adequately. The sheer burden of grading weekly themes for hundreds of students is murderous. And to be really effective, the English teacher must give his students a good deal of individual attention, having them revise, correct, revise again, and examine every sentence and paragraph for the best diction, rhythm, organization, and lucidity—in short, he must teach not merely grammar but logic and style. In most teaching arrangements today, this is impossible. Ultimately the effective writer teaches himself.

Exercise 25: Identify the italicized elements as (1) phrase, (2) main clause, or (3) subordinate clause.

1. Wonder Woman deflected the bullets *with her bracelets.*   .   .   .   .
2. Some Asians think *that the rhino's horn is magic.*   .   .   .   .
3. Sergeant McChesney *arrested Sergeant Archibald Cutter* for insubordination.
4. With a rifle butt, *Auda smashed his Turkish false teeth.*

5. "I was armed to the teeth with a pitiful little Smith & Wesson's seven shooter, *which carried a ball like a homeopathic pill,* and it took the whole seven to make a dose for an adult."
—Mark Twain . . . .

6. Turhan Bey fed the mummy boiling tana leaves *in order to keep it alive.* . . . .

7. *Sergeants McChesney and Cutter put elephant elixir in the punch* in order to remove Higginbotham from the expedition. . . . .

8. When the first World War broke out, Lawrence was in the Near East *working with an archaeological team.* . . . .

9. When Marco Polo returned to Venice, *he told of cheetahs at the court of Kublai Khan.* . . . .

10. *Winslow Homer made some of the best drawings* of the Civil War. . . . .

Exercise 26: Underline the subordinate clauses in the following:

1. They knew that Mighty Mouse would save the day.
2. When Dick Tracy was a prisoner of Mrs. Pruneface, she fed him two forkfuls of water a day.
3. Though the Mullins family have entered the affluent society, Kayo still sleeps in a bureau drawer.
4. I'm glad to hear that the Green Hornet is back on the radio.
5. Only the Shadow knows what evil lurks in the heart of man.
6. Why did it have to rain when the Human Torch was about to throw his forearm at the criminals?
7. Ranger Smith said that if Yogi Bear once more broke regulations, he would be sent to the St. Louis Zoo.
8. The train ride from Asheville to New York is still essentially as Thomas Wolfe described it.
9. Before McChesney could stop him, the guru jumped into the cobra pit.
10. At first Annie collapsed after she took the elephant elixir.

Exercise 27: Correct any comma splices and run-on sentences in the following:

1. Paul Gauguin deserted his family to become a painter eventually he left France for the South Seas where he died.
2. Melville and his friend Toby deserted the whaling ship *Acushnet* at Nukuheva, then they were captured by the Typees.
3. For revolutionary activities Dostoevsky was condemned to death, a mock execution was held before the victims were told their sentences were commuted to Siberian imprisonment.

4. Vincent Van Gogh was a fine writer as well as a painter, his letters to his brother Theo are literary masterpieces.

5. Stephen Crane's style has been called prose impressionism because he used bold color effects like, "The red sun was pasted against the sky like a wafer."

6. Henry James never managed to write a successful play ironically his novels and stories adapted for the stage, movies, and television have been very well received.

7. Copernicus worked many years on his magnum opus, *The Book of the Revolutions of the Heavenly Spheres,* not published until after his death, it was one of the worst-sellers of all times.

8. Some hunters make sound shots they can't see anything but they shoot at any sound and sometimes kill their companion.

9. My wife is a great admirer of the poems of Matthew Arnold she likes best "The Forsaken Merman," "Thyrsis," and "Rugby Chapel."

10. Ernest Dowson fell off a bar stool and died he was courting a twelve-year-old girl named Adelaide at the time.

11. Akaba is fast becoming the Acapulco of the Near East it doesn't seem so long since Lawrence of Arabia captured it.

12. Jonathan Edwards was driven from his pulpit at Northampton, where he had been the minister for a quarter of a century.

13. Boccherini spent some years at the Spanish court he later wrote for the guitar.

14. Ralph Vaughan Williams' skill as an essayist is not as well known as his music but it is quite impressive.

15. Sinclair Lewis turned down the Pulitzer Prize for *Arrowsmith* in 1925, he should have received it for *Babbitt* but the judges were overruled.

16. When Nathaniel Hawthorne was dismissed from his job at the Salem Customs House, his wife gave him the money she had saved from housekeeping and said now he could write his novel.

Exercise 28: Rewrite any fragmentary sentences to make them grammatically complete.

1. The American Pronghorn being the only animal that is as fast as or faster than the cheetah.

2. Baby clouded leopards not to be confused with the marbled cat.

3. We must insist that our customers list the articles in their bundle. Otherwise our count will be taken as correct.

4. The Detroit zoo the most successful at raising polar bear cubs.

5. A pursuit that also leads to finer products, new ways to serve you better.

6. Zookeepers failed to realize. That rhinos may be mating when they batter each other.

7. We found the Volkswagen was right at home in the Alps. And would recommend a similar trip to anyone.
8. Her father having a large record collection of frog calls.
9. Fitsi fitsi a kind of bush spirit.
10. The revenuers used to ride their horses up the streams, and when the horses would no longer drink, because the stream contained fermented slops from a still.
11. Never having heard a transistor radio before. The Eskimo thought it was an instrument of torture.
12. Tree kangaroos and birds of paradise dwelling in the San Diego zoo.
13. Deposits of bat guano fifty feet deep located in Carlsbad Caverns.
14. Death rates are being lowered. Because of improved medical care and sanitation.
15. Zoos establishing special survival centers for animals in danger of extinction.
16. Did you see the pygmy hippo? Resting in its bathing pool?
17. Some mountain people used Victorian euphemisms well into the twentieth century. It was startling to hear one hunter say. That his rifle wouldn't stay roostered.
18. Most people these days. Seem to think that privacy is very bad form.
19. White rhinos requiring undisturbed privacy in mating season.
20. The cars were backed up half a mile. At the point where the bear was holding up traffic.

Exercise 29: Revise the following sentences to correct any errors in parallelism.

1. Aunt Minnie likes shops full of things and to putter.
2. There is an instrument for each member of the family and to accompany Mother on the piano.
3. The idea of the hero as good looking and smooth dialect prevails in TV Westerns.
4. Hilma Tree's appearance, attitudes, and personality are all perfect, daughter on the farm, earthy characteristics.
5. At the low wages that were being paid, a man could not get enough money to feed his family, much less putting it to work to earn more money for himself.
6. We are taught to believe in truth as an absolute and that things are either always true or not true at all.
7. Americans have and will use pragmatism many times without realizing it.
8. His opponents said that such things as a lack of occupation, a vagrant to civil duty, or never attending church were characteristic of Thoreau.
9. Guilt by association is unfair, dangerous, and threatens civil liberties.

10. The chairman said that we would discuss the supplementary readings at the next staff meeting and to study the list carefully before then.

11. Eugene said that movies are often stupid and ridiculous and he was addicted to them.

12. It is absolutely untrue that bloodhounds are vicious, terrifying, and attack people fiercely.

13. King Kong showed his ability to wrestle dinosaurs, strangle pterodactyls, rescue Fay Wray, and how to climb the Empire State Building.

14. For the sake of your health, your nerves, and in the interests of your sanity, don't translate *Finnegan's Wake* into Arabic.

15. Poe gives no moral such as occurs in many of Hawthorne's stories, but rather how art can be its own justification.

16. Hippopotamuses are awkward on land but often leaping gracefully over underwater barriers.

17. Mrs. Warren told the laundryman she wanted either two new sheets or her own sheets being returned.

18. Reading widely has contributed to my becoming a more liberal person and to help me think more logically.

19. *Moby Dick* gives a documentary account of whaling and how a mad captain destroys his crew for the sake of egotistical monomania.

20. Henry James admired Hawthorne's fiction and how he made use of moral allegory.

15 √ The Pitfalls and Pratfalls of Punctuation

Everybody agrees that a sentence must end with a period, question mark, or exclamation point. That is almost the only form of punctuation about which there is unanimity. Various instruction manuals dictate rules for punctuation, but practice differs widely, from manual to manual and office to office. What is standard operating procedure in business correspondence may be heresy in military reports. Some organizations require a rigid conformity to their particular punctuation policy; if you work for such an outfit, you had better learn its rules and follow them. In creative writing, individualism is rampant; authors, editors, and publishers differ widely on details of punctuation. Though many composition teachers used to uphold an inflexible set of punctuation rules (doubtless some still do), it should be self-evident that there can be no absolutism here. Nor is punctuation in any way connected with effective use of spoken language. And language is essentially spoken; writing is merely a symbolic representation of our thoughts or speech. Punctuation is visual, a set of printer's artificial marks to indicate the pauses and vocal stresses of our speech. In written English, we need signs to break up the otherwise uninterrupted flow of words. Even the space between words is a sort of punctuation. Anglo-Saxon manuscripts have no punctuation, sometimes not even a clear break between words; the translator therefore has to decipher before he can translate. Chaucerian punctuation is minimal, and Elizabethan is extremely haphazard, so editors sometimes substitute modern punctuation for clarity. In fiction, if a character's mind is unclear and his subconscious thoughts run together by free association, the author may eliminate punctuation for paragraphs or even pages, as in

230

the Quentin Compson section of Faulkner's *The Sound and the Fury*. In an attempt at greater realism, Faulkner makes the reader follow the erratic flow and abrupt shifts of Quentin's stream of consciousness. This makes difficult reading, but its very confusion brings ultimately a greater understanding.

E. E. Cummings, who was a painter as well as a poet, novelist, and essayist, used the visual quality of punctuation and typography to illustrate his verbal imagery. For the word *look,* why not give it eyes bracketed by cupped hands?: *l (oo) k!* Cummings developed this technique in elaborate and witty forms. Of course, the visual quality is lost when the poems are read aloud, and some have their words so rearranged that they can only be appreciated when seen, not heard.

Punctuation, therefore, is flexible, but only to a degree. Some consistency is needed for clear communication and common sense. Effective punctuation enables the reader to read faster and with better comprehension, whereas missing or misplaced punctuation slows him up, makes him retrace his ground to be sure he has the sense of the passage. Thus punctuation may be compared to the center line and the speed, curve, hill, and warning signs on a highway that help the driver to proceed with greater assurance and accuracy.

When speaking, we indicate our meaning by vocal inflection as well as by diction and grammar. In written English, the meaning can be ambiguous without punctuation. When the playwright Richard Brinsley Sheridan was serving in Parliament, he was once required to apologize to a fellow member of Commons. Sheridan rose and replied, "Mr. Speaker I said the honorable member was a liar it is true and I am sorry for it," adding that the honorable member could place the punctuation marks where he pleased. If the fellow member had a grain of wit, he would have realized that the insult had been repeated. Once a college class was given the following sentence to punctuate: "Woman without her man is a savage." There was a revealing difference between the interpretation by boys and girls. Most of the former wrote, "Woman, without her man, is a savage," while the girls wrote, "Woman! Without her, man is a savage."

Certainly, punctuation must be precise in love letters. In the old sixteenth-century play *Roister Doister,* the oafish hero bungles his wooing of Dame Custance by sending her the following love letter. (I have modernized the spelling.)

Sweet mistress whereas I love you nothing at all
Regarding your substance and riches chief of all,
For your personage, beauty, demeanor and wit,
I commend me unto you never a whit.
Sorry to hear report of your good welfare.
For (as I hear say) such your conditions are,
That ye be worthy favor of no living man,
To be abhorred of every honest man.
To be taken for a woman inclined to vice.
Nothing at all to Virtue giving her due price.
Wherefore concerning marriage, ye are thought
Such a fine paragon, as ne'er honest man bought.
And now by these presents I do you advertise
That I am minded to marry you in no wise.
For your goods and substance, I could be content
To take you as ye are. If ye mind to be my wife,
Ye shall be assured for the time of my life,
I will keep ye right well, from good raiment and fare,
Ye shall not be kept but in sorrow and care.
Ye shall in no wise live at your own liberty,
Do and say what ye lust [desire], ye shall never please me,
But when ye are merry, I will be all sad,
When ye are sorry, I will be very glad.
When ye seek your heart's ease, I will be unkind,
At no time, in me shall ye much gentleness find.
But all things contrary to your will and mind,
Shall be done: otherwise I will not be behind
To speak. And as for all them that would do you wrong
I will so help and maintain, ye shall not live long.
Nor any foolish dolt shall cumber you but I.
I, who ere say nay, will stick by you till I die.
Thus good mistress Custance, the lord you save and keep,
From me Roister Doister, whether I wake or sleep.

When Dame Custance charges him with writing her an arrogant, nasty, and insulting note, poor Roister Doister denies he wrote the letter. He had, in fact, paid a scrivener to write it for him; and the scrivener points out that Roister Doister must have copied it wrong, fouling up the phrasing and punctuation. The letter should have read:

Sweet mistress, whereas I love you, nothing at all
Regarding your riches and substance: chief of all
For your personage, beauty, demeanor and wit
I commend me unto you: Never a whit

232

Sorry to hear report of your good welfare.
For (as I hear say) such your conditions are,
That ye be worthy favor: Of no living man
To be abhorred: of every honest man
To be taken for a woman inclined to vice
Nothing at all: to virtue giving her due price.
Wherefore concerning marriage, ye are thought
Such a fine paragon, as ne'er honest man bought.
And now by these presents I do you advertise,
That I am minded to marry you: In no wise
For your goods and substance: I can be content
To take you as your are: if ye will be my wife,
Ye shall be assured for the time of my life,
I will keep you right well: from good raiment and fare,
Ye shall not be kept: but in sorrow and care
Ye shall in no wise live: at your own liberty,
Do and say what ye lust: ye shall never please me
But when ye are merry: I will be all sad
When ye are sorry: I will be very glad
When ye seek your heart's ease: I will be unkind
At no time: in me shall ye much gentleness find.
But all things contrary to your will and mind
Shall be done otherwise: I will not be behind
To speak: And as for all they that would do you wrong,
(I will so help and maintain ye) shall not live long.
Nor any foolish dolt shall cumber you; but I,
I who ere say nay, will stick by you till I die.
Thus good mistress Custance, the lord you save and keep.
From me Roister Doister, whether I wake or sleep.

Thus punctuation can be a lover's undoing. Even the simple "Will you marry me?" can be altered to the imperative "Will, you marry me!" We use punctuation marks both to separate ideas and to group together the related words that express an idea. We also use them to indicate pause and emphasis. Thus punctuation is like a measure of music, with symbols to indicate cleft, key, tempo, tune, time, staccato, legato, volume. Because punctuation is an aid to interpretation, it is closely allied to grammar. Before you can end a sentence with a period, you have to know when you have written a sentence. If you cannot recognize sentences, clauses, appositives, serial and parallel constructions, restrictive and nonrestrictive modifiers, parenthetical insertions, or distinguish direct from indirect questions and quotations, you cannot punctuate properly. Even to use the apostrophe correctly, you need to know the detailed workings of nouns and verbs. However, even effective grammarians and stylists are sometimes unreliable in punctuation, especially if they write rapidly. The hurried writer may know when he needs punctuation, but he will not take time to consider the kind of punctuation, and he is apt to use commas and dashes indiscriminately or to omit punctuation altogether except to stab in a period at the end of a sentence.

¶ THE PERIOD

1. The main use of the period is to mark the end of a declarative sentence. If you fail to use a period, your sentences will be what is known as fused or run-on. If you use a period before the sentence is completed, you have written a sentence fragment. ("When I bit down on the roll. I lost my filling.") Both errors are annoying and indicate that the writer's thoughts are not clearly organized. Many amateur writers love to use exclamation points for mildly emphatic statements, but a simple period is usually preferable, just as a plain suit carries more authority than a screaming sport shirt. Sometimes students confuse declarative with interrogatory sentences and fail to distinguish between the use of a period and a question mark. An indirect question takes a period:

> I asked her if she liked Beethoven.

WRONG: I asked her if she liked Beethoven?

CONFUSED: When Huck Finn considered that Jim was a runaway slave, he wondered why was Tom Sawyer helping Jim escape?

The last example is a mixture of a declarative and interrogative sentence, and it is better not to mix the two. The solution is to make the question indirect and end the whole with a period:

> When Huck Finn considered that Jim was a runaway slave, he wondered why Tom Sawyer was helping Jim escape.

2. A period is used with certain abbreviations. Practice varies here; the military does not use a period (Ft Knox), and some abbreviations (CIO) do not customarily have periods. It is best to check your dictionary or the policy of your employers. Conventionally a period is used after abbreviated titles (*Dr., Rev., Mr., Mrs., Capt.*), names (*Edward G. Robinson, George C. Scott, Francis X. Bushman, E. B. White*), months (*Jan., Sept., Dec.*), states (*Cal., S. Dak.*). A title used alone without a proper name, should not be

234

abbreviated; students are wrong who write that the *Dr.* performed the operation. In such cases the word should be spelled out and put in lower case.

3. A period is used between dollars and cents ($2.99) and before a decimal (".07 of his income," "a .30 caliber machine gun").

4. Three spaced periods (. . .) called ellipses are used to indicate the omission of words in a quotation. If the omission comes at the end of a sentence, a fourth point—the period for the sentence—is added. Some students indiscriminately use ellipsis points instead of dashes and semicolons, and/or use dashes, hyphens, or half a dozen (instead of three) ellipsis periods to indicate omission. You should avoid this sort of splatter punctuation. Ellipsis points can also be used to indicate a pause ("Does she . . . or doesn't she?"). Schoolgirl style favors a peppering of gushy ellipses, but the careful stylist shudders at saccharine paragraphs like: "When all the little children are abed . . . scrubbed nestling cherubs clutching teddy bears and rabbits . . . when quiet house and warm hearth fire make a haven . . . when, sitting peacefully in a rocking chair, mending little garments, you muse over the small happenings of the day . . . then you know that no career . . . no glamorous job . . . could ever be as satisfying . . . as . . . MOTHERHOOD."

5. Most experienced writers in this country place a period at the end of a quotation inside the quotation marks whether it is part of the quotation or not:

Mad printed a burlesque of Melville, called "Morbid Dick."

¶ EXCLAMATION AND QUESTION MARKS

1. The exclamation mark (!) is used after strongly emphatic words or sentences and after particularly emphatic imperative commands:

> "Tiger! Tiger! burning bright"
> "Poets to come! orators, singers, musicians to come!"
> " 'Courage!' he said, and pointed toward the land"

Amateur writers tend to overuse the exclamation point to the extent that it loses its emphasis, like the boy who cried wolf. The real emphasis must be conveyed by the wording itself; if the language is inadequate, punctuation will not help. Ads like "Remove unwanted body hair!" fail to create a sense of urgency. Poetry and fic-

235

tion use exclamation points more freely than does expository prose, where they are rarely called for. And even great poets overwork the exclamation point. It is needless after a line like Browning's "Notice Neptune, though,/Taming a sea-horse, thought a rarity,/Which Claus of Innsbruck cast in bronze for me!" A university student used(¡), reversing the exclamation point, to show that he couldn't care less.

2. (a) The question, or interrogation, mark (?) is used at the end of every direct question:

Didst thou not fall out with a tailor for wearing his new doublet before Easter?

Tybalt, you ratcatcher, will you walk?

(b) When a request is put in the form of a question, it may be followed by a question mark in a formal statement, but the question mark is not necessary generally:

FORMAL: Will you please present your credentials to the secretary?
GENERAL: Will you please be seated.

(c) The question mark is not used after an indirect question.

RIGHT: Sir Palamedes asked the churl if he had seen the Questing Beast.
WRONG: Hamlet asked Polonius if he had a daughter?

(d) It is awkward to combine a declarative statement and a question in a single sentence, although this practice is becoming more and more common.

Emerson is an inspirational writer, but how long does the inspiration last?

Tom Tryon, a cowboy type without the light of thought, spirituality or emotion in his square-jawed pan, is a hero that must make everyone in the theatre feel if he can make it, why not me?   —DWIGHT MACDONALD

(e) The question mark in parentheses is used after questionable statements and uncertain dates: Ben Jonson 1573 (?)–1637. It is sometimes used in this manner as an ironic commentary but is a feeble form of sarcasm:

Your courtesy (?) is greatly appreciated.

We enjoy the soup (?) very much.

(f) The question mark is placed inside the quotation marks when it is part of a quotation but is placed outside if it is not part of the quotation:

236

Juliet asked, "Art thou not Romeo, and a Montague?"

Have you read "The Snows of Kilimanjaro"?

Only one question mark should be used after a double question:

Did Alfred E. Neuman really ask, "What, me worry?"

¶ THE SEMICOLON

The semicolon (;) is not interchangeable with the colon or the comma. It has several special uses of its own. If you learn these, you are reasonably safe in using the comma for those other situations where you might be tempted to use the semicolon.

1. The main use of the semicolon is to separate two main or independent clauses that are not joined by a coordinating conjunction (*and, but, for, or, nor, yet*).

Nobody but teen-agers could see the monsters from outer space; the adults refused to believe they existed.

The monsters from outer space were all eyeball; nothing could destroy them but the headlights from teen-agers' hot rods.

The drive-in theatre is getting another science-fiction film next week; it's a new one called *Teen-agers from Outer Space*.

A comma is not strong enough to mark the break between two independent clauses; a semicolon or period is needed to indicate break, so that the reader does not run one clause over into the other. If there were no punctuation at all, we would have run-on sentences. When there is only a comma, we have a comma splice. In very short sentences comma splices are all right ("Take your umbrella, it's raining"), and some established authors (e.g., Alan Moorehead in *The Blue Nile*) use them fairly regularly, but as a general rule, they are better avoided.

2. A semicolon is used before a conjunctive adverb bridging two main clauses. These connectives are too weak to take only a comma. The most common of them are *accordingly, also, anyhow, besides, consequently, furthermore, hence, however, in addition, indeed, likewise, moreover, nevertheless, still, then,* and *therefore*. The heavier of them take a comma after them:

Huck Finn had been taught that slavery was proper; consequently, he tried to turn Jim in.

Henry James revised some of his early works in his later style; however, not all critics think this is an improvement.

Theodore Dreiser's brother Paul was a popular song writer; indeed, for a time Paul was the better known of the two.

Ben Jonson killed an actor in a duel; hence he was branded on the thumb.

When these conjunctive adverbs are used parenthetically, they are enclosed by commas and not preceded by a semicolon:

Jonson, however, escaped hanging because he could read like a clerk.

3. A semicolon may be used before a coordinating conjunction joining two main clauses if (a) there is internal punctuation between the clauses or (b) the sentence is unusually long. Otherwise, a comma is used before a coordinating conjunction.

4. A semicolon should be used to separate the items in a series that contains internal punctuation:

Mark Twain traveled to St. Joseph, Missouri; Salt Lake City, Utah; Carson City, Nevada; Virginia City, Nevada; and finally to San Francisco.

The runaway camel knocked over Mr. Koontz, the milkman; Dr. Ijams, the dentist; P. E. Funk, deliveryman for the Capital Laundry; and Alfred E. Neuman, representative from Ballantine Books.

If commas were used instead of semicolons, it might seem that Mark Twain went to St. Joseph *and* to Missouri *and* to Salt Lake City *and* to Utah, and so forth, or that the camel knocked over Mr. Koontz *and* the milkman *and* Dr. Ijams *and* the dentist and so on.

If none of these four situations exist, do not use a semicolon. It should not be used after an introductory subordinate phrase or clause, between a main clause and a following subordinate phrase or clause, or to replace the colon before a formal quotation or a long list or series. Gertrude Stein claimed that semicolons "really have within them deeply within them fundamentally within them the comma nature"; but if so, it is better to go against nature.

¶ COMMAS

The comma is the most common and the most frustrating of all punctuation marks. Its omission where it is necessary is an obstacle to clear, rapid reading, and so is its inclusion where it is not necessary or where some other mark of punctuation is required. Too many students punctuate with the comma intuitively, instead of

238

rationally. When asked why they used a comma in some particular case, they answer, "I don't know; I just felt I should put something there." This guesswork approach is like splatter painting; successful results are largely accidental. You should avoid this method and know when and why to use the comma. When there is no reason for it, don't use one. According to Gertrude Stein, "Commas are servile and they have no life of their own. . . ." This is true in spoken language, where we use vocal inflections and pauses instead; but in writing, there are specific uses for the comma together with some optional ones.

1. The comma is used before a coordinating conjunction (*and, but, for, or, nor, yet*) connecting two main clauses. Some writers omit a comma here, and it is better dropped in very short sentences, but its omission is usually a nuisance and can sometimes cause confusion:

Bartleby at first does an immense amount of copying, but he soon refuses to do small jobs around the office and then announces that he has given up copying altogether.

Notice that there is a comma before *but* but not before *and*; a comma is not needed between two verbs with the same subject:

WRONG: I think I shall lie down, and take a nap.

In "A sniper's bullet killed a Negro woman and three men were wounded by gunfire Monday night in Jacksonville," a comma before *and* is needed for clarity, as well as for separating the clauses; otherwise it seems at first glance that the bullet killed a woman and three men. A similar confusion occurs in "Scabs were fighting strikers and little children were throwing bottles at trucks." A comma is needed to show that scabs were not fighting little children. A reader can make out the meaning of these sentences without a comma, but he has to read them twice to do so.

Many people mistakenly put a comma both before and after a coordinating conjunction (*,but,*); but there should never be one after such a conjunction unless some parenthetical insertion requires it. Also there should be no comma with a coordinating conjunction that connects words or phrases, rather than main clauses:

WRONG: Jack, and the beanstalk.

2. A comma is used after an introductory subordinate clause or a long phrase preceding the main clause:

When Mark Twain's brother went to Nevada, he took a six-pound un-abridged dictionary with him.

If you get there first, save me a place in line.

Having eaten 425 cabbages, Harry the Hippopotamus felt sick.

After several generations of neglect, Melville's work was rediscovered by modern literary critics.

A comma is not necessary if the introductory matter is quite short and/or closely related to the main verb:

UNNECCESSARY: For supper, we are having grits and grunts.

3. In a compound-complex sentence where there is a main clause followed by a subordinate clause that encloses another subordinate clause, a comma is used at the end of the enclosed subordinate clause. Obviously you have to be able to recognize clauses to punctuate effectively.

Mark Twain observed that when Brigham Young was given a whistle for one of his children, he had to buy a hundred and ten whistles to make his other children happy.

Brigham Young told Mark Twain, "And if ever another man gives a whistle to a child of mine and I get my hands on him, I will hang him higher than Haman!" (Here the *if* subordinates both the *man gives* and *I get* clauses.)

4. When a subordinate clause or phrase follows a main clause, a comma may precede it if the clauses are not smoothly related or essential to the sentence's principal meaning.

Melville deserted on his first whaling voyage, jumping ship in the Marquesas.

Melville could not support his family by literature, though his first books had been popular.

Finally Melville settled into obscure security when he got a job as customs inspector. (No comma needed.)

Don't tell me you were late because you missed the bus. (No comma needed.)

5. Commas are used to enclose nonrestrictive clauses but not to enclose restrictive clauses. A restrictive clause is one that is essential to specify or identify the word it modifies. In the sentence "Henry V was the king *who won the battle of Agincourt,*" the italicized modifying clause is restrictive because it is needed to indicate a specific fact that identifies the king. If there is only one king

and no question as to his identity, then we would have a nonre-strictive modifier: "Take this pie to the king, who is sitting in his countinghouse." The modifier is clearly restrictive in "It is neces-sary for a democratic government to have laws [no comma] that will give men justice."

RESTRICTIVE	NONRESTRICTIVE
Michigan is one of many states that have abolished the death penalty.	There are a great many lakes in Michigan, which calls itself the "Water Wonderland."
Utah is the only state that has executions by firing squad.	The Mormons were the first settlers in Utah, which they called Deseret.
People who are afraid of heights should not try parachute jumping.	Parachutists, who have careful train-ing, have a low accident rate. (This might be considered restrictive, de-pending upon the weight given the modifier.)

Usually a nonrestrictive modifier can be left out of a sentence with-out making it meaningless, whereas the omission of a restrictive modifier mangles the sense. There is a crucial difference between "Soldiers who give information to the enemy are traitors" and "Sol-diers . . . are traitors" or between "Everybody who goes to Af-rica must have yellow fever shots" and "Everybody . . . must have yellow fever shots."

Unless it occurs at the end of a sentence, a nonrestrictive modi-fier must be set off by two commas, one before and one after it. If the second comma is missing, the results may be confusing, as in "A path meanders from the house across Wapsinonoc Creek, where Hoover paddled as a boy to the new Herbert Hoover Library, re-pository for many of the former President's official papers." With-out a comma after *boy*, it seems that Hoover paddled to the new library when he was a boy.

6. Commas are used to enclose parenthetical or appositive con-structions not sufficiently pronounced to require parentheses or dashes:

The lettuce, you will no doubt admit, is not improved by boiling.
The mother bear, understandably enough, was annoyed at the tourists.

241

Next weekend, with luck, we shall finish tunneling through the walls.

The elephant, she says, is eating cabbages.

If the commas are omitted, there can be a confusion in meaning:

Hemingway did not like Ambrose Bierce disappear over the border.

Unless there are commas around *like Ambrose Bierce,* it seems at first glance that Hemingway did not like Ambrose Bierce. Such an error occurred in a Michigan newspaper, which printed, "Bartlett says Hatch demonstrates a lack of understanding," reversing the actual statement, "Bartlett, says Hatch, demonstrates a lack of understanding."

Conjunctive adverbs are often set off by commas when they are parenthetical or introduce a sentence:

The pirates, however, were pursued by giant land crabs.

Furthermore, the pirates forgot where they had buried the treasure.

7. Commas are used to enclose appositives. Appositives are identifying phrases equivalent to the noun or pronoun they explain:

William James, *brother of Henry James,* was a distinguished pragmatist.

Some students confused William James with Will James, *author of cowboy novels.*

Julia A. Moore, *the Sweet Singer of Michigan,* was a model for Mark Twain's Emmaline Grangerford.

Similarly, commas set off a title following someone's name: Sir Walter Scott, Bart.; Geoffrey Crayon, Gent.; H. M. Pulham, Esq.; Felix Flutz, Ph.D.; Sam Spade, Private Eye.

Do not confuse appositive phrases with restrictive or nonrestrictive modifiers, which are usually relative clauses. When an appositive is obvious and unstressed, it should not be set off by commas. No comma is needed in *my uncle Jules* or *his brother James.* Commas are needed for the first appositive but not the second in "Tarzan, lord of the jungle, made friends with Tantor the elephant."

8. Commas are used to set off names and other nouns directly addressed, whether they occur at the beginning, middle, or end of a sentence:

I had a dream, dear.

Go down, Moses, way down in Egypt's land.

Madam, I protest that you misunderstood me.

That is not, sir, an adequate explanation.

All right, you clods, stop yodeling in the halls.

I think, Dr. Frankenstein, that you have gone too far.

Apparently direct address is implied in the title *Rabbit, Run.* A misplaced comma can change the meaning radically. Notice the difference between *Call Me Madam* and *Call Me, Madam*; between *I Remember Mama* and *I Remember, Mama*; and between "That's North Carolina honey" and "That's North Carolina, honey."

9. Commas are used to separate items in a series:

The recipe for Kickapoo Joy Juice calls for formaldehyde, alarm clocks, skunk oil, white lightning, and anything else you care to throw in.

The survivors were a Peruvian policeman, an unemployed zoo-keeper, an Eskimo craftsman, two juvenile delinquents, a missionary to the Tuckapoo Indians, and an ex-bullfighter who would eat only frijoles.

Philip Guedalla divided the works of Henry James into three periods— James I, James II, and the Old Pretender.

If a comma is omitted, there may be ambiguity, as in the difference between *James Joyce and Proust* and *James, Joyce, and Proust.* Again, a program for *The Duchess of Malfi* listed among the cast; "Attendants, servants, madmen executioners." There are no *madmen executioners,* but there are madmen *and* executioners, so a comma is needed between the last two items. When there is an *and* before the last item in a series, a comma before it is optional; *Farrar, Straus and Cudahy*; *Holt, Rinehart and Winston*; or *bacon, beans, and beer.* If there are conjunctions between each of the items in the series, commas should not be used: "Ham and eggs and onions make a tasty omelet." If the items contain internal commas, semicolons should be used to seperate the units.

10. When adjectives are used in a series, a comma should be inserted between them:

There was a drooling, fanged, hunchbacked monster at the window.

You niddering, dunderheaded, thimble-brained, invertebrate imbecile!

In the first example, each adjective modifies *window*; in the second, each modifies *imbecile.*

Missing punctuation creates confusion; for example, in "Dinosaurs became extinct and smaller, less massive creatures took their place," it might at first glance seem that dinosaurs became extinct and smaller, and that less massive creatures then took over. This is illogical; the proper punctuation should be, "Dinosaurs became extinct, and smaller, less massive creatures took their place."

11. A comma is placed before a negative appositive element:

Mañana Iguana is a painter, not a sculptor.

Evidence reveals that it was a werewolf, not a wolf.

Call the Southern highlanders "mountain people," not "hillbillies."

A comma is not used for a *not this but that* construction: "Mañana Iguana is not a painter but an imposter."

12. Commas are inserted between the various elements in place names, addresses, dates, and numbers:

Mozart lived in Salzburg, Austria. (Comma between city and nation or state)

Los Angeles, California, may soon be the largest city in the world. (Comma between city and state and after state)

Sherlock Holmes lived at 21B Baker Street, London. (Comma between street and city)

Both Shakespeare and Cervantes died on April 23, 1616. (Comma between day and year)

How much money does Daddy Warbucks have—$1,345,798, $999,999,001, or $2.00 Confederate? (Comma between each three figures)

13. A comma is used after an introductory *yes, no, oh,* or exclamation:

Yes, I was in Macao in January, 1932.

Oh, no, the soldier ants are coming!

Curses, it's that muscle-bound mouse.

What, me worry?

14. Commas are used to set off direct quotations from the rest of a sentence:

Emerson wrote, "A foolish consistency is the hobgloblin of little minds."

"And now," said Snagglepuss, "I shall exit stage left."

"Nuts and berries—yeech," grumbled Yogi Bear.

Neither commas nor quotation marks are used with indirect quotations.

Hemingway said that *Huckleberry Finn* is the best American novel.

244

See the discussion of quotation marks for a fuller treatment of punctuation with quotations.

15. A comma may be used wherever necessary for clarity. Missing punctuation has caused confusion in several songs. Many people think the Christmas carol goes "God rest you, merry gentlemen," whereas it should be phrased "God rest you merry, gentlemen" with *merry* modifying *rest*. And there is no *Alice Ben Bolt*; the song asks, "Oh! don't you remember sweet Alice, Ben Bolt?" Probably Ben Bolt has forgotten her. In the sentences, "Through this spiritual Negro laborers expressed their oppression," there should be a comma after *spiritual,* lest it seem that *spiritual* modifies *Negro laborers.* Occasionally a comma is needed to keep separate elements from running together. In "It is necessary to recognize clauses. Students who do not often write fragmentary sentences," a comma is necessary after *not* to make clear that *not* modifies *do* rather than *often.*

The above cases involve a modifier that could belong to two different words. Other parts of speech might have two possible functions. A noun subject might be mistaken for the object of a preceding verb: "When the burglar left, the house was stripped of all valuables." (Not "When the burglar left the house. . . .") "After the storm struck, the water rose rapidly." (Not "After the storm struck the water. . . .") Conjunctions and prepositions too can cause confusion: "She cried out, for an elephant was standing on her foot." (Not "She cried out for an elephant. . . .") And finally a comma is customarily used between a word that occurs twice together: "What the boss's wife does, does not interest Betty." Then there are idiosyncratic errors. A book list alphabetized by authors listed:

Macaulay, *History of England*

Mill, *On Liberty*

Mill, *On the Floss*.

16. The comma should not be misused. Perhaps the most common misuse is the already discussed comma splice. Some students carelessly place a useless comma between subject and verb:

At present, some government agencies, retain patent rights on research and development discoveries.

Another reason to criticize the validity of the trials, stems from the handling of evidence.

There is no point to the commas inserted after *agencies* and *trials*. Again, there is no need for a comma between the indirect and direct object in "Bruce Catton gives the Southern troops and their leader, the credit due them." In "Still, the scientific observer, Hale tries to find evidence either way," the comma after *still* interrupts what should be a unit modifying *Hale*. There should be no comma in "William Faulkner's novel, *The Sound and the Fury*," because Faulkner wrote many novels; and *The Sound and the Fury* is a restrictive appositive. The commas are even more ridiculous in "Steinbeck's, *The Grapes of Wrath*, is filled with religious symbolism." Here the title is the subject, and *Steinbeck's* modifies it.

The tendency today is to minimize punctuation and to omit it if there is an option. Victorian writers often punctuated to excess, just as they favored ornamental excess in architecture and interior decoration. Though modern students are more apt to omit even necessary punctuation, some punctuate with flamboyant garishness. James Thurber complained of *The New Yorker's* overuse of commas. A professor of English once asked Thurber why there was a comma in "After dinner, the men went into the living room." Thurber answered that it "was Ross's way of giving the men time to push back their chairs and stand up." [1] As an example of excess, try this added punctuation for Shakespeare's lines:

> If, it were done, when, 'tis done, then, 'twere well
> It were done, quickly. . . .

¶ THE COLON

The colon (:) is not interchangeable with the semicolon, but has several specific uses of its own.

1. The colon is used after the salutation in a formal letter, whereas a comma is generally used in an informal one:

Dear Sir: Dear Dr. Karloff: Gentlemen: Dear Madame: Dear Mrs. Schultz: (as opposed to the casual *Dear Pete, Dear Herbie,* and *Hiya, Honeybun*).

2. The colon is used before a relatively long list of appositives or a formal series:

Here is the reading list for the oral examination: *The Odyssey, Oedipus Rex, Troilus and Criseyde, King Lear, The Duchess of Malfi, Paradise Lost, An Essay on Man, Tom Jones, Don Juan, Bleak House, Walden,*

246

Leaves of Grass, Moby Dick, Huckleberry Finn, The Return of the Native, The Waste Land, and *A Farewell to Arms.*

Do not use a colon before a brief, casual series. Wrong: "The sports I like best are: skiing, fencing, and girl watching." Here there should be no punctuation after *are.*

3. The colon can be used before a long or formal quotation:

Thoreau explained his purpose in going to Walden: "I went to the woods because I wished to live deliberately, to front only the essential facts of life, and see if I could not learn what it had to teach, and not, when I came to die, discover that I had not lived."

4. A colon can be used before a clause that is a restatement, illustration, or explanation of a preceding one:

Fitzgerald once quarreled with Hemingway: the latter had made a disparaging reference to him in "The Snows of Kilimanjaro."

Thurber tried to be demoted at *The New Yorker*: he had been hired as an editor but wanted to be a writer.

Naturalistic writers denied that man has a soul or free will: they claimed that the same laws govern the stones of the roadway and the mind of man.

In summary, the colon is used to set off material that explains or sums up something anticipated in the preceding expression. It creates a telegraphic brevity and conciseness (for which reason some news magazines favor it); but when it is used excessively, it becomes a mannerism.

¶ THE DASH

Some casual students use the dash indiscriminately whenever they wish to indicate a pause, clause, or stop. But this is merely slapdash. Both Queen Victoria and Jack Kerouac used dashes instead of commas and periods; this is all they had in common, and Kerouac's editors changed his punctuation. Unlike the tight colon, with which it is often confused, the dash creates a loose prose that too easily becomes limp. The dash has several specific purposes and is otherwise best kept under restraint.

1. A pair of dashes are used to set off interpolations that are both logically and grammatically interruptions:

Abner Bieberman—he once played Young Toad Face in *Gunga Din*—now directs some programs for *The Twilight Zone.*

247

What could D'Arnot do against Sabor—or if Bolgani, the gorilla should come upon him—or Numa, the lion, or cruel Sheeta? [2]

—EDGAR RICE BURROUGHS

Being an American, it was impossible you should remain what you were born, and being born poor—do I understand it?—it was therefore inevitable that you should become rich.[3]   —HENRY JAMES

Such constructions sometimes take parentheses instead of dashes, but parentheses make the interruption even more pronounced. When the interpolation comes at the end of a sentence, only one dash is needed.

It is not money, it is not even brains—though no doubt yours are excellent.[4]   —HENRY JAMES

2. A dash is used to set off a final explanatory or summarizing word or statement:

What's it made of—hammered gold?

To abolish slavery, John Brown committed another crime—murder.

Valentin de Bellegarde lived in the basement of an old house in the Rue d'Anjou St. Honoré, and his small apartment lay between the court of the house and an old garden which spread itself behind it—one of those large, sunless, humid gardens into which you look unexpectingly in Paris from back windows, wondering how among the grudging habitations they find their space.[5]

3. A dash is used to indicate an unfinished or interrupted statement:

"I'm sorry," she said, "but the lettuce—"
"The lettuce seems to have been washed in detergent," he remarked dryly.
"Yes, er—yes—that is—" and she rushed from the table.
"Why, I wanted the *adventure* of it; and I'd a waded neck deep in blood to—goodness alive, AUNT POLLY!"

Sometimes a double dash is used to indicate an interruption at the end of a speech. Ellipsis points can also be used for this sort of construction.

4. After a quotation, a dash can be used to set off the source.

I loafe and invite my soul,
I lean and loafe at my ease observing a spear of summer grass.

—WALT WHITMAN

248

Sagebrush is free. Stuff some in your trunk.
—FEARLESS FERRIS

Commas cannot substitute for dashes in an appositive interruption.

I have lived in various states, [should be dash] Ohio, Indiana, and Florida, [should be dash] and I have spent vacations on the east coast; but never have I encountered the demoralizing, disagreeable weather offered by the state of Michigan.

In typing, two hyphens (--) make a dash.

¶ PARENTHESES

Parentheses ( ) are used in pairs to enclose interruptions, asides, explanations, illustrations, and cross references:

South-eastward from the Cape, off the distant Crozetts, a good cruising ground for Right Whalemen, a sail loomed ahead, the Goney (Albatross) by name. —HERMAN MELVILLE, *Moby Dick*

Look at his hump, which would be as fine eating as the buffalo's (which is esteemed a rare dish), were it not such a solid pyramid of fat. *—Ibid.*

Only one of Henry VIII's wives (Katharine Parr) outlived him.

(*Cf.* p. 897)   (See Appendix B)   (Consult *The Dictionary of American Slang*)

Amalgamated Chicken Wire sells for seventy-five dollars ($75.00) a share.

When a parenthetical insertion occurs at the point where a comma is needed, the comma goes after the second parenthesis:

When the first man brought the first dog to his cave (no doubt over and above his wife's protests), there began an association by which Man has enormously profited.[6] —JAMES THURBER

Either dashes or parentheses can be used to set off a distinct interruption, but usually that with dashes is sharper. Sometimes both occur in the same sentence. As Thurber wrote about a mother dog with her pups,

For six weeks—but only six weeks—she looks after them religiously, feeds them (they come clothed), washes their ears, fights off cats. . . .[7]

Brackets are used for parentheses within parentheses, but parentheses are used for insertions in a passage set off by dashes.

My mother had never liked the congressman—she said the signs of his horoscope showed he couldn't be trusted (he was Saturn with the moon in Virgo) —but she sent him a box of candy that Christmas.[8]

It is possible to overwork parentheses. William Faulkner has parenthetical passages that run for several pages, with parentheses within parentheses within parentheses. Faulkner is a master of narrative by indirection, but even he sometimes stumbles, and the ordinary writer should keep parentheses within reasonable limits.

¶ BRACKETS

Brackets [ ] are used mainly to enclose writer's or editor's inserted commentary or explanation within a quotation. Sometimes when a quotation is taken out of context, an explanatory word or phrase is necessary.

An early exponent of pragmatism was [William] James.

To Bobby [Kennedy] the world is black and white.—Gore Vidal

When Henry James published his first novel, *The American* [actually, it was his second], he was already a master of the form.

When a reproduced text has unclear, incomplete, or omitted words or punctuation, the editors may add material within brackets to give an explanation or fill in the omission.

In his Majesty['s] service—in this ship indeed—there are Englishmen forced to fight for the King against their will.   —HERMAN MELVILLE, *Billy Budd*

If a quoted passage contains an error, you can place *sic* in brackets immediately after the word to indicate that the error is not yours but is in the original: "Cooper's *The Bathfinder* [*sic*] is the fourth novel he wrote in the Leatherstocking Series."

Brackets are also used to indicate parentheses within parentheses.

Most typewriters do not have bracket keys, but you can make brackets by using the diagonal with an underscore above and below, thus: ⌈ ⌋

¶ THE DIAGONAL

The diagonal is used to indicate alternative or fusion in situations like either/or, both/and, and/or. "A program for a modern-dress version of *The Duchess of Malfi* indicated the time as 1504/contemporary." The diagonal is also used to separate lines of poetry when they are run together in a text: "The patent of a lord/And the bangle of a bandit/Make argument/Which God solves/Only after lighting more candles."—Stephen Crane.

¶ THE HYPHEN

Like the hydra, the hyphen is many-headed and full of deviltry. It has so many and such varied uses that one can go mad trying to catalogue them all. Mostly it is copy editors who go mad, since the hyphen is more their problem than the writer's. For writers who do their own copy editing, an explanation of the more common uses may help. Basically, the hyphen is used to join two or more words into a compound and to divide an overlong word at the end of a line. In printing, hyphenation is sometimes unavoidable to make the right margin even, but in manuscript or typescript, you should try to avoid line-end hyphenations; it is better to crowd the margin or carry the entire word to the next line. If you must break a word, do so between syllables. Never hyphenate a one-syllable word nor a short two-syllable one. Students sometimes make errors similar to the following:

ta-	lo-	ea-	lo-	lau-	gas-	re-
ke	ve	t	oked	gh	p	ad

These are even worse when the first half is at the extreme right margin and the second at the extreme left. If you must hyphenate, try whenever possible to do so between prefix and root or root and suffix.

manu-	dis-	bio-	phil-	marriage-
script	locate	chemistry	harmonic	able

Avoid separating merely the first letter from the rest of a word.

WRONG:	A-	u-	F-
	merican	niqueness	rench

Never separate a suffix of less than three letters from the rest of the word. It is all right to separate -ing, but not -ed, -al, -le, -ly.

CORRECT: construct-	WRONG: perpetu-	construct-	complain-	usual-	princip-
ing	al	ed	ed	ly	le

If you hyphenate compound words, keep each part of the compound intact.

251

motor- boat	sun- shine	moon- light	lawn- mower	bath- room

When you are uncertain where to divide a word, consult your dictionary.

The greatest difficulty with hyphens is the problem of compound words. There are three ways of writing compounds: as two separate words (*freight train*), as one word (*playboy*), or hyphenated (*teenager*). Sometimes the same word can be written any of the three ways. There is an increasing tendency to write compounds as one word, especially if each half has one syllable (*mailman*), but there is sufficient variety so that the only reliable guide is a current dictionary. A few generalizations may be helpful.

1. A hyphen is sometimes used in fractions and always in compound numbers beginning with *twenty-one*: *one hundred forty-four, five-eighths, seven-tenths, one sixty-fourth.*

2. A hyphen is used when a prefix is joined to a proper noun or adjective: *anti-McCarthy, pro-Churchill, un-American, pre-Roosevelt, pre-Shakespearean.*

3. A hyphen is used between *ex-* ("former") and a noun: *ex-governor, ex-husband, ex-convict.*

4. A hyphen is used with *in-law* family relationships: *mother-in-law, sister-in-law.*

5. Most compounds beginning with *self* are hyphenated: *self-love, self-esteem, self-serving, self-control, self-sufficient,* but not *selfless, selfsame,* or *selfhood.*

6. Sometimes a hyphen must be inserted to avoid confusion with a similar word: *re-signed* vs. *resigned, re-claim* vs. *reclaim, re-act* vs. *react, re-cover* vs. *recover.*

7. A hyphen may be used in joining a prefix ending in a vowel to a word beginning with the same vowel: *re-enlist, re-elect, re-enter, re-enact, pre-empt, co-ordinate.*

8. The most common use of the hyphen is in compound modifiers before a noun. These include compound numbers.

a bug-eyed monster	a ninety-seven pound weakling	a high-pitched scream
English-speaking peoples		
a run-on sentence	a seven-room house	a muscle-bound brute
a poverty-stricken family	a worn-out shirt	a burnt-out case
	a feeble-minded clod	a beat-up bum

Sometimes you may wonder whether you need a comma between two or more adjectives preceding a noun, or a hyphen with a compound modifier. The answer depends on your meaning. Note the difference between *dark-rimmed glasses* and *dark, rimmed glasses*; the rims are dark in the first and the lenses in the second. The focus is off in *a high, pitched scream,* which makes the modifier separate adjectives rather than a unified compound. Occasionally a hyphen is needed for clarity in otherwise ambiguous modifiers. A *new home-owner* is new at owning a home; a *new-home* owner may have owned many old homes before buying a modern one. In *a deep blue pool, deep* modifies *pool*; whereas it modifies the color in *a deep-blue pool,* which might be shallow.

When a compound modifier follows a noun, it usually is not hyphenated.

She wore a seventeenth-century costume.
The costume is seventeenth century.
There was a horrible-looking fiend.
The fiend was horrible looking.

Longer compounds are usually hyphenated, no matter where they occur: *up-to-date, face-to-face, tête-à-tête, never-to-be-forgotten, twenty-one-year-old, pay-as-you-go.*

9. Arabic numerals before modifiers and letters before nouns are hyphenated: *L-shaped room, 8-hour day, 40-hour week, A-bomb, U-boat, 5-string banjo.*

10. A hyphen is not interchangeable with a dash. Students often make this error in typing because there is no actual dash on the typewriter. To type a dash, you need two hyphens--otherwise you lack a sufficient break.

Except to clarify ambiguity, the hyphen is a purely mechanical device that has no relation to the writing of effective English. It is far more essential in mathematics. A hyphen omitted from an equation could cause the destruction of an $18,000,000 rocket designed to probe Venus. Fortunately editors are free from this sort of red ink.

¶ QUOTATION MARKS

There are two sorts of quotation marks: double (" ") and single (' '). Double quotation marks are more common in the United

States; single ones, in Great Britain. Both are equally valid; and single quotes, which are neater, are gradually gaining acceptance in the United States.

1. (*a*) Quotation marks are used to indicate the actual words of a speaker or writer:

According to Emerson, "For nonconformity the world whips you with its displeasure."

What novel opens with the line, "Call me Ishmael"?

The Queen of Hearts shouted, "Off with her head!"

"So," he sneered, "you thought to betray us."

Quotation marks are also used to enclose words attributed to a speaker, though he did not say them.

Since Patrick Henry's speech to the Virginia delegates is a reconstruction by William Wirt, Henry probably did not say, "Give me liberty, or give me death."

If a quotation is interrupted by *he said, they exclaimed,* etc., two sets of quotation marks are necessary. Some modern fiction writers do not use quotation marks for dialogue. This is sometimes an annoying obstacle to the reader.

When you are quoting a real statement, rather than writing fiction, you must be careful to quote verbatim, including the original punctuation and spelling. An approximate quotation will not do when the authentic one is available. If all you have is an approximation, you should indicate this. Inaccurate quotation is unscholarly. In politics it can be dangerous. Unscrupulous demagogues make a practice of distorting quotations, wrenching them unfairly out of context, or even inventing fictitious quotations and attributing them to their enemies. The fact that the late Senator Joseph McCarthy did all these things was one reason he was censured by the Senate for conduct bringing disgrace on that body.

Likewise, if you use the words of another author, you must enclose them in quotation marks and acknowledge your source. Otherwise you are guilty of plagiarism. Some students—either through ignorance or through unwillingness to do their own work—take paragraphs from other writers, change a few words here and there, and consider that they have made an acceptable paraphrase. But something like "Fourscore and seven years ago our ancestors [fathers] brought forth on this continent a new country [nation],

254

conceived in freedom [liberty], and dedicated to the concept [proposition] that all men are born [created] equal" is still in every essential, despite the replacement of some words by synonyms, the work of Abraham Lincoln. This is a blatant example, but such inadequate paraphrasing often occurs with less obvious material. If you quote three or more consecutive words from another's writing, you should enclose them in quotation marks. If you paraphrase, do so completely.

(*b*) Quotation marks are never used in a paraphrase or for indirect discourse and quotation:

DIRECT QUOTATION: Huck Finn said, "All right, then, I'll go to hell."
INDIRECT QUOTATION: Huck Finn said that he would go to hell.
WRONG: He said "that he would be late for the game."

(*c*) If a quotation continues for several paragraphs, opening quotation marks should be placed at the beginning of each paragraph (to indicate that the quote is continuing), but closing quote marks are used only at the end of the last paragraph, where the quotation itself ends. Usually in dialogue a separate paragraph is devoted to each speaker. On the other hand, an appropriate quotation may be placed in the body of a sentence without any form of break.

(*d*) You may indicate a lengthy quotation from a piece of writing by indenting it, centering it on the page, and single-spacing it. In print, such quotations are generally put in smaller type. When you single-space and center a quotation, you do not need to use quotation marks. For example:

Why should we be in such desperate haste to succeed and in such desperate enterprises? If a man does not keep pace with his companions, perhaps it is because he hears a different drummer. Let him step to the music which he hears, however measured or far away.   —HENRY DAVID THOREAU, *Walden*

2. To indicate a quotation within a quotation, use the alternate form of double or single quotation marks than those in the outer quotation. In other words, if your outer quotation marks are double, use single quotes in marking the inner quotation, and vice versa.

3. Quotation marks are often used to show that a word is being considered as a word, to be defined, or explained:

"Animism" is the word given to primitive man's belief in ghosts and spirits in natural objects.

What does "potrezebie" mean in *Mad*?

The English dog, after centuries of pure breeding, does not have a powerful constitution and is subject to certain virus infections and a destructive stomach ailment called "bloat." [9]   —JAMES THURBER, *Thurber's Dogs*

Bloodhounds are frequently handicapped by what is technically known as the "fouling" of a trail by sightseers and other careless humans.[10]—*Ibid*

Notice the difference between "There is scholarship in the dictionary" and "There is 'scholarship' in the dictionary." In print, instead of quotation marks italics can be used to designate words specified as words.

4. When a word is called into question or is particularly ironic, it may be enclosed in quotation marks:

Immigrants were given "free" transportation to America, but their fare was deducted from their wages, so that they were immediately plunged into debt.

Sometimes slang words and phrases or familiar figures of speech are put in quotation marks. This is an annoying mannerism. If the words are inappropriate, do not use them. If they are appropriate, use them straight. Some students protest that their teachers told them to put all mild colloquialisms in quotation marks. The result is that they enclose every third word in quotes and produce pages resembling a swarm of gnats. Movie ads are becoming addicted to putting the names of characters in quotes: Tony Curtis as "Antoninus," Peter O'Toole as "Lawrence." This is a feckless device, even when the character is fictitious. Certainly Lawrence of Arabia did not sign his name T. E. "Lawrence." In the old days, Charles Laughton simply played Henry VIII, not "Henry VIII." One of the fussy mannerisms of Henry James's later prose is the setting apart of ordinary words by quotation marks "He had come —putting the thing pompously—to look at his 'property'. . . . He was the owner of another, not quite so 'good'. . . . He could live in 'Europe' as he had been in the habit of living. . . ."—"The Jolly Corner"

5. Quotation marks are used to enclose the titles of articles, short stories, chapters, short poems, and songs. Titles of books and periodicals are underlined or italicized. Never mark a title by both quotation marks and italics, or underlining.

WRONG: Arthur Miller's *"The Crucible."*

256

"Baker's Blue-Jay Yarn" first appeared in Mark Twain's *A Tramp Abroad.*

"The Rime of the Ancient Mariner" was in the 1798 *Lyrical Ballads.*

"Old Man River" is a Jerome Kern song from *Showboat.*

In footnotes and bibliographies, the titles of chapters and of the sections or divisions in a published book or periodical are put in quotation marks. The first example following is for a footnote; the second, for a bibliography:

James Thurber, "The Secret Life of Walter Mitty," *My World—and Welcome to It* (Harcourt, Brace and Company, New York, 1942), p. 73.

Fujimura, Thomas Y., "The Appeal of Dryden's Heroic Plays," *PMLA,* Vol. 75, March 1960, pp. 37-45.

6. You should avoid loose, indiscriminate use of quotation marks. An Iowa City mortuary displayed an ad urging "Mark every grave." The sign was not quoting anyone but the signmaker, so there was no point to the punctuation. "Mark every grave."— George Washington. This might lend some authority but could lead to charges of inaccuracy. "Mark—every grave" has a dramatic pause, and "Mark every grave!" might arouse some urgency, but perhaps the most appropriate punctuation is "Mark every . . . grave?"

¶ QUOTATION MARKS WITH OTHER PUNCTUATION

Practice varies somewhat on the position of other punctuation marks in conjunction with quotes. The following advice is safe.

1. Put the period or comma at the end of a quotation inside the closing quotation marks, whether or not it is part of the quotation. Other punctuation marks go inside the closing quotes only when they are part of the quotation:

"It appears," said the Rajah, "that you have forgotten about the cobras."

Maury Maverick coined the word "gobbledygook."

Note that there are not two periods at the end.

2. When the quotation is a direct question, the question mark is placed inside the closing quotes; in other cases, it is placed outside:

"Am I a coward?" asked Hamlet.

What play contains the line, "My kingdom for a horse!"?

Have you read Faulkner's "Dry September"?

On bended knee, Horpington tenderly asked Patricia, "What's for lunch?"

(There is no need for a period after the question mark.)

Hardly a man takes a half-hour's nap after dinner, but when he wakes he holds up his head and asks, "What's the news?" as if the rest of mankind had stood his sentinels. —HENRY DAVID THOREAU, *Walden*

3. The same practice holds for exclamation marks as for question marks:

Hamlet cried, "O, horrible! O, horrible! most horrible!"

"O, I am fortune's fool!" said Romeo.

Don't call me a "fink"!

4. Semicolons and colons always go after end quotes.

"That is right," he said; "I do come from the Carpathian Alps."

Ronald Colman said, "It is a far, far better thing I do than I have ever done"; then the camera moved up past the guillotine.

Note that in the first example, the semicolon between the two main clauses is placed after *he said* rather than inside the first end quote.

5. Ellipsis points at the beginning or end of a quotation are placed inside the quotation marks:

Thoreau wrote, ". . . I would have each one be very careful to find out and pursue *his own* way, and not his father's or his mother's or his neighbor's instead."

If a fourth point is added to indicate the end of the sentence after an ellipsis, it is also placed inside the quotation marks.

Thoreau explained, "My purpose in going to Walden Pond was not to live cheaply nor to live dearly there, but to transact some private business with the fewest obstacles. . . ."

6. When a quotation is broken off by a dash, the dash is placed inside the quotation marks, and it is not followed by a period even if it ends the sentence.

"It's perfectly clear, my good man, but—Good heavens—"

258

¶ UNDERLINING AND ITALICS

In handwritten and typed copy, underline words that would be *italicized* in print.

1. Underline complete titles of books, periodicals, plays, motion pictures, and the names of ships, planes, and trains. Titles of songs and short poems are put generally in quotation marks, rather than italicized. Titles of chapters, articles, and short stories are also put in quotation marks:

Fitzgerald's "Babylon Revisited" was published in *Taps at Reveille*.
Melville's "Bartleby" is one of the *Piazza Tales*.
Many of Faulkner's stories first appeared in *The Saturday Evening Post*.
"Passage to India" is one of the major poems in Whitman's *Leaves of Grass*.
A Passage to India is a novel by E. M. Forster.
Many novels of intrigue take place on the *Orient Express*.
The mutiny aboard H. M. S. *Bounty* occurred in 1789.
Will Rogers was killed in the crash of the *Winnie Mae*.

If the title of an article includes the title of a book, underline the book and enclose the whole title in quotation marks: "A Study of James's *The Ambassadors*." Be careful to underline all the words in a title and no words that are not in the title.

WRONG: *The Autobiography* of Mark Twain or *The Autobiography* of Mark Twain
RIGHT: *The Autobiography of Mark Twain*
WRONG: *The Maritime History* of Massachusetts
RIGHT: *The Maritime History of Massachusetts*

Students frequently fail to underline the article in a title and so commit such errors as "Cooper's the *Deerslayer*," "Norris's *The Octopus*," "Hemingway's a *Farewell to Arms*." Again, students sometimes take the heading used in an anthology for the book's actual title, writing such absurdities as, "In Thoreau's *From Walden* . . . ," "In Paine's *From Common Sense* . . . ," or "*Billy Budd and the Critics* is Melville's final novel."

2. Underlining or italics may be used to emphasize a word or phrase.

"$12.95—for a *magazine?*"
"Well, what *did* you say, then?"
". . . ef you en Huck fetches a rattlesnake in heah for me to tame, I's gwyne to *leave*, dat's *shore*."

Mark Twain used this device effectively, but it can easily be over-worked by less skillful writers.

3. Words and phrases still considered foreign (consult your dictionary) are underlined or italicized: Gemütlichkeit, coup de grâce, Zeitgeist, memento mori.

4. Words and phrases considered specifically as words can be underlined or italicized. They may, alternatively, be put in quotation marks, a practice more common in writing or typing than in printing:

Curfew comes from the French couvre feu ("cover the fire").

To coöperate in the highest as well as the lowest sense, means to get our living together. —THOREAU, Walden

¶ CAPITALIZATION

There are many words that require a capital, or upper-case, letter. Editorial practice varies, but most uses follow well-established conventions. If you are writing for an organization with special rules of style, you should consult its manual (e.g., the *Government Printing Office Style Manual*); otherwise, the following instructions are generally held acceptable.

1. The first word of a sentence is capitalized. When a complete sentence is enclosed in parentheses, the first word is capitalized if the sentence in parentheses stands outside the preceding sentence; but if the parenthetical matter is inserted to stand within a sentence, the first word starts with a small letter.

Mt. Rainier is not the highest mountain in the continental United States (it is 14,410 feet high), but it has the most spectacular rise from sea level.

The first word of a quoted sentence is capitalized, but if the sentence is broken into during the course of the sentence, the continuation does not begin with a capital letter until another complete sentence.

Thoreau wrote, "The mass of men lead lives of quiet desperation."

"I think," he said casually, "that all hell is about to break loose."

"Come, Goodman Brown," cried his fellow-traveller, "this is a dull place for the beginning of a journey."

"You jest," he exclaimed, recoiling a few paces. "But let us proceed to the Amontillado."

260

When a phrase, not of dialogue, is quoted, it does not usually begin with a capital letter.

Christopher Cranch drew a cartoon of Emerson as "a transparent eyeball."

If the beginning of a quotation is omitted (sometimes it is replaced by ellipses), the quotation is not capitalized unless it begins with a proper noun.

According to Thoreau, ". . . a man is rich in proportion to the number of things which he can afford to let alone."

2. Proper names are capitalized. These include the names of people (Alfred E. Neuman); races, nationalities, and tribes (Mexican, Indian, Cherokee, Eskimo); places (New Zealand); languages (German, Yoruba); months; days of the week; holidays (Groundhog Day, the Fourth of July, St. Agnes' Eve); historical events and periods (the Boxer Rebellion, the Battle of the Bulge, the Reformation, the Enlightenment, Reconstruction, the New Deal); documents (the Ten Commandments, the New Testament, the Bill of Rights, the Monroe Doctrine); names of ships (*The Golden Hind*); religious denominations ("Methodists, beware Mormon crickets"); organizations and institutions (Loyal Order of Moose, Prudential Insurance, State University of Iowa).

Adjectives from proper nouns are capitalized unless they have become too common: *Elizabethan, Shakespearean, Darwinian, Platonic, Thomistic, Restoration drama, Petrarchan sonnets, German philology, Jacobean drama.* Some proper nouns and their adjectives have become common nouns and are no longer capitalized: *boycott, bologna, bourbon whiskey, brussels sprouts, chinaware, cordovan leather, french dressing, lynch, maverick, mercurial, portland cement, sandwich,* and many others.

German simplifies matters by capitalizing all nouns, but in English, common nouns are generally written with a small letter. Sometimes the distinction is difficult. Seasons of the year are not capitalized, though the months are. Compass directions are not capitalized unless they designate a region of the country (and this distinction is weakening).

To find the Moose Hall, turn north two blocks, and then go east a mile.

There was sectional antagonism between the industrial North and the agrarian South.

Many words are uncapitalized common nouns unless they are used in a title; common among them are *school, college, university, church, hospital, hotel, street, park, fort, city, mountain, river,* and *island:*

Lyndon Johnson once taught school.

Thomas H. Johnson teaches at the Lawrence School.

Most colleges and universities are expanding.

Michigan State University has 27,000 students.

After the battle at the fort, the casualties were taken across the river into the city; there they were lodged in hospitals, churches, hotels, and some in the streets and parks.

The inspectors visited Fort McHenry, Patterson Park, Charles Street, the Johns Hopkins Hospital, the Patapsco River, Old St. Paul's Church, and the Lord Baltimore Hotel. Then they flew to Salt Lake City.

Sometimes, capitalizing a noun will change its meaning or make it more specific. Uncapitalized, *depression* is a common noun; capitalized, it refers to the decade following the crash of 1929. Similarly, *red* is a color, whereas *Red* is a political designation. There have been lots of armadas, but the *Armada* is the one that sailed from Spain in 1588. Many things have been restored; the *Restoration* denotes the return of the Stuart monarchy to England in 1660. Notice the difference between *friend* and *Friend, genesis* and *Genesis, virgin* and *Virgin, advent* and *Advent, catholic* and *Catholic. Army, navy, marines, air force* are not capitalized unless they refer to a specific organization:

Tarzan saw an army winding its way over the mountains.

Most navies had abolished flogging by 1850.

Senator Joe McCarthy was revealed as a demagogue in his attack on the Army.

3. Professional and official titles are capitalized when followed by a proper name or when used to stand for a specific person. When used as a general term, they are left in lower case. *Sir, Lady, Mr., Mrs., Miss, Master,* and *Mistress* are capitalized before a proper name:

Is there a doctor in the house?

There's a phone call for Dr. Sawbones.

Some professors have to publish or perish.

The dean told Professor Crabshaw to publish or perish.

A colonel and several generals were drunk.
Aunt Agatha sent a billet-doux to Admiral Bilgewater.
"As I live and breathe, it's the Major," said Snagglepuss.
Nell Gwynn was Charles II's mistress.
Falstaff liked to sponge off Mistress Quickly.

When referring to the United States government leaders, *President* and *Vice-President* are always capitalized:

When Franklin Pierce was President, he made Hawthorne consul to Liverpool.
The First Lady entertained the delegation from Opar.

4. Names of relatives are not capitalized unless they are followed by the relative's name or clearly stand for a specific individual. *Mother, father, mom, pop, uncle, aunt, brother, sister*, etc., without the name are not capitalized if preceded by a modifier (usually a possessive noun or pronoun) but are capitalized when used alone as proper names. Sometimes an author departs from this practice. *We Escape from Madrid* contains the sentence, "Stewed cat cost mother and me a dollar a plate in Madrid."

The princess's twelve brothers were turned into ravens.
Sir Joseph Porter had sisters, aunts, and cousins by the dozens.
Tom Sawyer often bamboozled Aunt Polly.
Mrs. Day was shocked at Father's language.
Thomas Wolfe's letters to his mother have been published.
"Just before the battle, Mother . . ."
Most fathers aren't excited by the P.T.A.
"Come up from the fields, Father."
Oscar Homolka played Uncle Chris in *I Remember Mama*.

When used as slang, *brother* and *sister* are not capitalized:

Listen, brother, you better pay protection money, or else.
Just remember, sister, don't get smart with Rocco, see.

5. Titles of books, stories, articles, songs, and organizations customarily have the first and last words capitalized, and generally all others except articles, conjunctions, and short prepositions.

The Sound and the Fury	*The Ides of Mad*
Much Ado about Nothing	The Fraternal Order of Eagles
The Last of the Mohicans	*A View from the Bridge*
The Portrait of a Lady	*Once upon a Mattress*
"Smoke Gets in Your Eyes"	*The Middle-Aged Man on the Flying Trapeze*

In business correspondence each letter in a title may be capitalized, so that the typist won't have to stop to underline: HOW TO IMPROVE YOUR VERBAL SKILLS. Sometimes an author, like e. e. cummings, does not want any of his title's words capitalized; and, of course, titles and all other words in books written by a cockroach who can't hit the shift key of his typewriter must be in small letters.

Titles of school courses are capitalized (History 204), but except for languages, school subjects in general are not; "Lumpington was studying history, math, physics, French, Russian, and psychology; he was carrying too many hours."

6. The pronoun *I* is capitalized; otherwise, it might easily be lost among the words with more letters (e.g., "They wondered why i insisted upon skiing"). The French *je* has an additional letter for support and so is not capitalized. Likewise the English vocative *O* is capitalized, though *oh* usually is not.

7. Nouns standing for the name of the Deity are capitalized; usage is divided on pronouns. This practice has no necessary connection with a writer's religious beliefs, though a militant nonbeliever might make a point of using a small letter. When used in a general sense, *god* should not be capitalized: "The ancient world believed in many gods." Otherwise, *God, Christ, Jehovah, Allah,* and the like are treated as proper nouns. So are words like *Saviour, Redeemer, Messiah,* the *Lamb,* the *Trinity, Father, Son,* and *Holy Ghost* that refer to the Christian Trinity. Unitarians probably would not capitalize pronouns referring to Jesus; Trinitarians often do, though the Gospels do not. Deists used to capitalize *Reason,* and some humanists capitalize *Man* and *Mankind.* Pantheists might capitalize nature; Frank Lloyd Wright said, "I put a capital *N* on nature and go there." But pronouns referring to *Reason, Man,* and *Nature* or to mythical deities are left uncapitalized.

The Almighty will protect us by His Providence.
Christ told His Apostles that He would be with them always.
The Lord does not always reveal His will.
I know that my Redeemer liveth.
Saturn devoured his children.
Athena carries the head of the Gorgon on her shield.

8. Abstract nouns are often capitalized if they are personifications or if they denote institutions or ideals.

Where then shall Hope and Fear their objects find?
Must dull Suspense corrupt the stagnant mind?
　　　—SAMUEL JOHNSON, "The Vanity of Human Wishes"

With close-lipped Patience for our only friend,
Sad Patience, too near neighbor to Despair:
　　　　　—MATTHEW ARNOLD, "The Scholar Gipsy"

Can Honor's voice provoke the silent dust,
Or Flattery soothe the dull cold ear of Death?
　　　—THOMAS GRAY, "Elegy Written in a Country Churchyard"

The Constitution requires the separation of Church and State.

By the same token, nouns standing for a nation's flag are capitalized: *Old Glory, the Stars and Stripes, the Stars and Bars, the Tricolor, the Oriflamme, the Union Jack.*

9. Customarily the first letter in each line of verse is capitalized, though poets are free to follow any practice that they wish. Sometimes the entire first word is capitalized:

MUCH madness is divinest sense
To a discerning eye;
Much sense the starkest madness.
'Tis the majority
In this, as all, prevails.
Assent, and you are sane;
Demur,—you're straightway dangerous,
And handled with a chain.—EMILY DICKINSON

10. Solitary letters followed by a hyphen to form a compound are capitalized: *A-bomb, H-bomb, L-shaped, T-square, X-ray, U-boat.* So are Roman numerals except for prefatory page numbers, which are printed in small numerals.

11. Authors can, at their discretion, capitalize words for emphasis or stylistic effect:

If all these companies have their way, and it looks as if they will, our country will have the sweetest-smelling people in the world, If they don't turn green first.

¶ A FINAL WORD

This chapter does not attempt to cover all the possibilities in punctuation. Many situations are too specialized and may require you to consult a manual of professional or business style or to use your own initiative. This chapter has been rather prescriptive in setting forth rules. In practice, not all of them are hard and fast. Some offices and some editors may be rigid, but practice varies among them. In creative writing you should feel free to experiment and suit punctuation to your style and subject. Clarity is ultimately the only test.

A few final words of advice may be in order. You should never begin a new line of typing, or writing, with any punctuation except quotation marks. Some confused students begin a new line with a comma or semicolon that belongs with the words on the previous line. One, unable to finish his paragraph at the end of a line, wrote as his last line:

. . . ."

Neither should you end a line with the quotation marks belonging to the words on the next line:

WRONG: Hemingway said, "
        Morals are what you feel good after."

Exercise 30: Correct any errors in capitalization.

1. Last hallowe'en, uncle Hermie took mom and pop to a Witches' sabbath.
2. Last year Horpington studied Geology, History, American Literature, and Chicken Plucking.
3. Cardinal Newman's brother translated *Hiawatha* into Latin and Arabic.
4. In parts of the American west there are still fewer than ten people per square mile.
5. In High School, Lumpington excelled at cafeteria attendance.
6. In *The Plumed Serpent,* D. H. Lawrence's characters try to revive the aztec Religion.
7. All presidents of the United States except Jackson and Franklin Roosevelt have been Baptized after death in the mormon church.
8. Don't write "According to Webster." Webster has been dead for over a century, so indicate what Dictionary you are using: e.g., Webster's new collegiate dictionary.
9. Don Marquis is the author of *the lives and times of archy and mehitabel.*
10. Grandmother does not know Brigitte Bardot is french.
11. Rölvaag wrote *Giants In the Earth* in norwegian.
12. In some Schools, Freshmen still wear beanies.

266

13. The United States has thirty-one National Parks.
14. Rita Hayworth, as Salome, tried to save John the baptist and ended listening to the sermon on the mount.
15. The Johns Hopkins University band used to wear ROTC uniforms dyed black and blue and sam browne belts.
16. Bernard winterset, Art Critic, leaned back in his chair and surveyed with distaste the Bearded creature before him.
17. Thangbrand O'connel saw the siamese cat stalking him and said tentatively, "Here, Kitty, Kitty."
18. His name is wu the Inscrutable; don't call him "kitty"—he doesn't know he's a cat.
19. Edgar Rice Burroughs wrote twenty-four Tarzan Novels, eleven Mars books, and three books about the Land that Time forgot.
20. Henry the eighth had six wives, but Charles the second had innumerable Mistresses and tried hard to be the Father of his Country.

16 √ The Antic 's

The one advantage German has over English is the lack of apostrophes. There was no apostrophe in Old or Middle English. It appeared during the Renaissance along with printing, and it has plagued us ever since. Basically, the apostrophe is a printer's mark rather than part of the language proper. It is never used in speech except by Victor Borge, yet no one ever has any trouble distinguishing meaning without it. In written English it is more of a nuisance than a help. Its rules are inconsistent and full of exceptions; and students, advertisers, and journalists often use it incorrectly, omitting it when required and inserting it when it is not called for. It would be better to have no apostrophe at all than to have it so misused, and George Bernard Shaw did try to get rid of it. You might welcome its early demise; but as long as it is still required, you should know how to use it properly.

1. The apostrophe is used to indicate the possessive case in nouns. A singular or plural noun not ending in s adds an apostrophe and s to form the possessive ("man's hat," "women's hats"). A singular or plural noun already ending in s or an s sound adds the apostrophe only (Essex' execution, Leibnitz' philosophy, Jesus' parables, Apostles' Creed), though it is also acceptable to add an apostrophe and s to singular nouns even when they already end in s (either "Charles' head" or "Charles's head").

This seems simple enough, yet it is often confused by people who don't look carefully at the original noun. If it already ends in s, the careless reader is apt to put the apostrophe before the s and so make a bungled back formation. Thus students mistakenly write of "Henry James's fiction," "Yeat's poems," "Robert Grave's criticism," and "Jonathan Edward's theology." One student even wrote of "John Dos Passo's U.S.A." Some usage is relative, but these errors are always and absolutely wrong, and display sheer carelessness or

268

an inability to read clearly. Of course, there is no Jame, Yeat, Grave, Edward, or Dos Passo; the proper possessive is *James', Yeats', Graves', Edwards',* and *Dos Passos'* (or alternatively, *James's, Yeats's, Graves's, Edwards's, and Dos Passos's*). Again, people write the wrong form by adding a nonexistent *s* to a singular noun and then using the apostrophe. Thus Theodore Dreiser is transformed to Dreisers when a student writes of "Dreisers' *Sister Carrie.*" Students are not the only ones at fault; several learned correspondents, including a Harvard professor and Pulitzer Prize winner, wrote to *The New York Times Book Review* to comment on a history by Will and Ariel Durant, which they indicated as *the Durants's* book. But the singular is *Durant;* the plural, *Durants;* and the possessive plural, *Durants'.*

Elizabethan English sometimes avoided the apostrophe by pronoun constructions, such as "the king his army." This may serve as a clue to modern usage; in "the cat his pajamas," the word *cat* has no *s* and so needs both it and an apostrophe when written in our possessive form, whereas in *the cats their pajamas, cats* already has the *s* and needs only the apostrophe.

2. In compound nouns, the *'s* is added to the element nearest the object it modifies ("mother-in-law's house," "attorney general's action," "Jason Robards, Jr.'s performance").

3. Joint possession or possession in a series usually takes the possessive case only in the last item ("Simon and Schuster's office"; "Harcourt, Brace & World's new dictionary"; "Montgomery Ward's catalogue"), but for individual or alternate possession, each item should be in the possessive case:

Do you prefer Cecil B. deMille's or Ingmar Bergman's movies?
The wombat's and the koala's feeding habits are significantly different.
St. Bartholomew's Men's Club is having Ladies' Night.
Have you read Hemingway's and Faulkner's fiction?

4. For titles, geographic names, and names of organizations, follow the official form, whatever it may be. Often these are contradictory. Thus we find *St. John's College* but *St. Elizabeths Hospital, King's College* and *Queens College,* the *Teamsters Union* but the *International Ladies' Garment Workers' Union.* Sometimes there is no apostrophe even though possession is implied, as in *Peoples Church, Painters Supplies, Investors Mutual.* There are no apostrophes in *Rutgers* or in *Johns Hopkins University,* since *Johns*

was Hopkins' first name and *Hopkins* modifies *University* just as [John] *Harvard* does. Thus *John's, Hopkin's,* and *Hopkins'* are all wrong. Increasingly the apostrophe is being dropped from official names, where it is simply a bother. The U.S. Geographic Board has ruled it out of places with a possessive proper name: e.g., *Harpers Ferry, Devils Courthouse, Pikes Peak, Hells Canyon, Huggins Hell, Silers Bald,* and *Charlies Bunion.* As yet there is no evidence that anyone has lost his way because of the missing punctuation.

5. As a general rule, no apostrophe is used in words more descriptive than possessive that end in *s*:

Massachusetts law (vs. Gresham's law)	United Nations Assembly
teachers college	United Auto Workers Local
Actors Studio	White Citizens Councils
Home Owners Policy	Hotels-Restaurant Employees & Bartenders International Union

An exception is *Veterans' Administration,* because the apostrophe is in the enabling statute. There are some other exceptions, including *rogues' gallery* (which is plural as opposed to *rogue's march*). If the modifier is a personal name ending in *s,* people sometimes confuse it with a possessive; thus the *Michigan State News* turned *Olds Hall* into *Old's Hall.* There should be no possessive in *United States Constitution,* but it is sometimes written as *United States' Constitution,* or worse, *United State's Constitution.*

6. Possessive personal pronouns (*ours, yours, hers, its, theirs*) never take an apostrophe, but impersonal ones require it.

anybody's game	everybody's choice	nobody's business
anyone's guess	everyone's dismay	someone's child
each other's families	one's self I sing	*but* someone else's mistake

7. The apostrophe is used in such general phrases as:

author's royalties	lamb's wool	sailor's hornpipe
baker's dozen	pitcher's elbow	shepherd's pie
confectioner's sugar	printer's devil	traveler's checks

8. An apostrophe is used to indicate the omission of letters or figures and the plural of letters, numbers, and symbols.

270

a '59 Thunderbird	p's and q's	wouldn't
a '22 Stutz Bearcat	6's and 7's	you're
the spirit of '76	MP's	won't
the 49'ers	VIP's	it's (it is)
'em (them)	¶'s	ne'er

The apostrophe is not used in spelled-out words 'or numbers (*twos and threes, ifs and buts*) unless it is needed for clarity (*do's and don'ts*). In some abbreviations and contractions the apostrophe is now omitted: *til, Frisco, Halloween*. Many people no longer realize that the latter, spelled alternatively *Hallowe'en*, is a contraction, for All Hallow Even meaning the evening before All Hallow (All Saints') Day; and the apostrophe has vanished along with the religious connotation. As for contractions, when we are talking, we no longer think of them as a combination of two words, but use them habitually as independent words (even the pronunciation of *don't* is different from *do not*), so there is no reason except custom for retaining the apostrophe. As it is, some people confuse any final *nt* with a contraction and so create absurdities like *mean't* and *len't*.

9. The apostrophe is never, never, never, never used to form the subjective and objective plural of nouns or the third person present singular of verbs. Yet many people, indiscriminately associating a terminal *s* with the possessive, mangle plurals and verbs grotesquely. Inadequately sophisticated suburbanites label their houses as "The Morrison's," "The Glub's," or send invitations for a party at "the Jone's." The errors here are doubly dyed, being wrong in number as well as case; there is no *Jone,* and no one uses *the* with the singular in referring to a family's name. Morrison, Glub, and Jones want the subjective or objective plural, which is *Morrisons, Glubs,* and *Joneses*. This confusion of the plural with the possessive is increasingly common in slipshod advertising and journalism, as well as in student writing. Thus one reads of "Roy Acuff Exhibit's" in Gatlinburg, and sees ads for "Bagel's Toasted and Buttered," "Poncho's for Sale," "Hat's on Sale Reduced," or "Save $100 or more on piano's." Students write "The early Puritan's considered the Indian's to be servants of Satan," and "The Joad's could not afford adequate food and clothing." *Redbook* advertises "Christmas with the Kennedy's and Queen Elizabeth," and journalists write that "Reporters covering receptions may only watch the guests arrive and ask the Kennedy's to pose for pictures." Though ex-

271

tremely common, these faulty plurals remain illogical and unacceptable. Often they are combined with fuzzy thinking, as in two statements from the reactionary Cinema Educational Guild, Inc.: "In 1918, Woodrow Wilson, the first of their [i.e., "Communist traitors" like J. P. Morgan, John D. Rockefeller, and Bernard Baruch] Benedict *Arnold's* was elected President," and "[President Kennedy and] the INVISIBLE COMMUNIST GOVERNMENT OF OUR COUNTRY forbid the Cuban *refugee's* to organize an invasion Army to try to regain their country." (Italics mine.)

Sometimes the error is compounded when the plural is spelled differently from the singular. *Negro, hero, banjo* and similar words add an *es* to form the plural. So when one advertises "banjoe's weighing up to fifty pounds" or writes, "During Reconstruction, most Negroe's endured great hardship," he has a misspelled singular possessive instead of the desired subjective plural.

When a noun ending in *s* is to be used in the possessive plural, many students are totally dumbfounded, since they don't even know how to form the noun's plural. Thus, for *the Phelpses' farm* in *Huckleberry Finn,* students wrote *Phelp's farm, Phelps' farm, Phelps farm, Phelpes' farm, Phelpeses' farm,* and *Phelpeses farm.* But the case is simple enough: singular—*Phelps,* plural—*Phelpses,* possessive plural—*Phelpses'.*

Similar to the confusion over the plural is the mistaken use of the apostrophe and *s* to form the third person present singular of verbs. The proper procedure is simply to add an *s* to the infinitive (*eat—he eats*) unless the verb ends in *y,* in which case you turn the *y* into an *i* and add *es* (*carry—he carries*). But again, some people cannot resist using an apostrophe with any final *s,* and so they write "he try's," "she sing's," "it rumble's." (In a Roadrunner cartoon, Wile E. Coyote ordered a weapon labeled "Acme boomerang return's to owner.") Another difficulty is that some simple verbs are confused with contractions. Since *let us* is contracted to *let's,* one student wrote by faulty analogy, "The landlord let's us cook in our room." Later this same student omitted a necessary apostrophe from a contraction, writing "Lets go to the circus."

The apostrophe is so extremely idiosyncratic in practice that one sign even transformed *cafe* into *caf'e.* This way lies schizophrenia, and we would do well to follow German and get rid of the apostrophe altogether. Where we write "brother's hat," the Germans write "Bruders hut." In spoken English we don't need the apostrophe; and in writing as well, context would make the meaning clear so that one could tell *my brothers term paper* from *a Marx Brothers* script and both from *The Brothers Karamazov.*

Exercise 31: In the following sentences some words lack a necessary apostrophe and others have apostrophes incorrectly used. If there is an error, enter the proper form in the blanks.

1. When Huck first arrived at the Grangerford's, he found them hospitable. . . . .
2. Horpington is studying Henry Adam's *Mont-Saint-Michel and Chartres'.* . . . .
3. Dwight Macdonald claimed that the last good Hollywood movie was Orson Welles's *The Magnificent Amberson's.* . . . .
4. The Indian's sold enormous tracts of land for trinkets. . . . .
5. E. E. Cumming's *The Enormous Room* is one of the best World War I novels. . . . .
6. My wife made me watch *The Mummy's Curse* on the Late Late Show. . . . .
7. You're one of the lucky one's. . . . .
8. Spencer Tracy won his first Academy Award for *Captains' Courageous.* . . . .
9. Many critics think *Howards End* is E. M. Forster's finest novel. . . . .
10. *Thurbers Dog's* is now out in paperback. . . . .
11. Theres no use arguing; I won't lend you my copy of *Mad.* . . . .
12. You cant borrow *The Brothers Mad,* either. . . . .
13. Spencer Tracy won his second Academy Award the next year for *Boy's Town.* . . . .
14. This pfeffernuss is made with Mrs. Evan's cookie recipe. . . . .
15. Horpington couldn't understand the vocabulary in James Gould Cozzen's *By Love Possessed.* . . . .
16. James Baldwin is an eloquent spokesman for Negroe's rights. . . . .
17. Don't confuse Dos Passos' *Three Soldiers* with Kipling's *Soldier's Three.* . . . .
18. Can you sing "St. Jame's Infirmary"? . . . .
19. I refuse to watch *My Brother Talk's to Horses* on the Late Late Show. . . . .
20. Nobody knows how many member's there are in the Mafia. . . . .
21. Critics admired Douglas Fairbanks's, Jr., performance in *The Prisoner of Zenda.* . . . .
22. "Help," cried Una O'Connor; "the monsters coming! Look at it's horrible face." . . . .
23. Spencer Tracy played Robert Rogers in the movie of Kenneth Roberts' *Northwest Passage.* . . . .

273

24. Theres no use arguing; you can't keep an aardvark in the cellar. . . . .
25. "Fill er up," Horpington told the attendant, as he parked his 33' Duesenberg. . . . .
26. Several students collapsed with writers' cramp. . . . .
27. Funk's and Wagnall's company is well known for its dictionaries and encyclopedias. . . . .
28. The syllabus seemed confused; the course required *The Doctors Dilemma, Roget's International Thesaurus, All the King's Men, Pigeon Feather's, Lysistrata,* Holme's "The Chambered Nautilus," and Howells *A Modern Instance.* . . . .
29. Spencer Tracy murder's Ingrid Bergman in *Dr. Jekyll and Mr. Hyde.* . . . .
30. The flame azaleas in the Great Smokies are at their best on Gregorys Bald. . . . .

Exercise 32: In the following sentences, correct any grammatically inaccurate words or constructions.

1. Them cattle is speckled, spotted, and ringstraked.
2. You hadn't ought to tell a good dream until it has come true.
3. Is you finished washing of your hands?
4. I thought I had losted my plastic bottles.
5. Groundhogs is the same as them woodchucks whom some people call whistle pigs.
6. You got to be having a visa to enter Egypt.
7. Mother Hubbard's dog was eaten her outen house and home.
8. Why come is the buzzards waiting here?
9. I resembles my brother William—Bill, us calls him.
10. They is a lot of work to do before supper.
11. I isn't made up my mind which way to vote.
12. Them sudden stops can make a fellow seasick.
13. Carter is got some very peculiar tastes.
14. I already seen *The Three Stooges Meet Hercules.*
15. Them's not moth holes; them's bullet holes.
16. The Cherokees, which was the most civilized Indians, wouldn't hardly write no sentences as this one.
17. They was seventeen cattle friz solid in a stack.
18. Skinks is different than skunks.
19. Is the campground got any vacancies?
20. You should not of lost your temper that way.
21. I don't believe the bloodhound is ran away.
22. Give me back my glasses so's I can see you.
23. I never knowed you were so fond of liver mush.

274

24. Us has got the same color hair but different color eyeballs.
25. Claude talks like he must of run for Congress.

Exercise 33: Add any necessary punctuation and remove any unnecessary punctuation from the following:

1. Since it is the desire of every woman in Africa to get children if she doesn't get a husband it will make her unhappy.
2. In vain did all the rain doctors of the locality, engage in the formidable task of controlling the weather.
3. The first son of the late chief, brought the cow, immediately afterwards.
4. Then the oldest woman, advised the seven wives of the late chief, to give account of themselves, since they lost their husband by death, a couple of years ago.
5. The first wife, walked to the cenotaph and said "You know that I have carried out all the necessary formalities according to custom. If I did not may today, be, my last day on earth.
6. In this solemn and thought provoking way, the remaining six women, gave account of themselves.
7. Everybody was in great suspense, as to what would be the outcome, of this historic ceremony.
8. As the animals were trying to escape the people pursued them and killed them, with hatchets.
9. The villagers argue that if the juju fails to operate the result will be bloodshed.
10. Courage he said and pointed toward the land
    This mounting wave will roll us shoreward soon.
11. Anybody, with any experience in the ways of the West, would have known better than to stop in the Sierras with a storm brewing.
12. I did not like the strange behavior of the begonia trees said the matriarch.
13. Do you want to go to the Birunga, gorilla sanctuary
14. But it amused us to hear a Kuikuru at some unexpected moment muttering under his breath chick chick quack quack oink oink.
15. Bob Hawk will pay you as he hollers Yes you're a Lemac now.
16. I do not like your aunt want to look at all the shops in Fleagle street.
17. Dejah Thoris was captured by Matai Shang the Holy Hekkador of the Sacred Therns.
18. I have just come from the doctors mother and he says my baby is due in six weeks.
19. Susy Clemens said mama loves morals and papa loves cats.
20. Orphan Annie says Gee Willikens Sandy and Little Annie Rooney says Gloriosky Zero.

21. William Walton one of Englands leading contemporary composers wrote the musical scores for Laurence Oliviers films of Henry V, Hamlet, and Richard III.
22. Do you remember the scene in The *invisible Man* when Claude Rains ran down the street in his underwear singing Here we go gathering nuts in may.
23. Samuel Johnson liked pussycats, but disliked Whigs and Scots.
24. The boys, who sprayed paint on the Blue Ridge Parkway bridges, were fined and ordered to remove the damage.
25. Errol flynn ran basil rathbone through in captain Blood and the Adventures of robin hood tyrone power ran rathbone through in The mark of zorro a french peasant stabbed him in a tale of two cities richmond's troops killed him in *The Tower of london* gary cooper threw him into a tiger pit in the adventures of marco polo and joan fontaine crushed him with a suit of armor in frenchman's creek but he escaped the frankenstein monster and killed the hound of the baskervilles.

17 √ Grammar Is Not Enough: A Digression on Diction

Language is the source of all misunderstanding.
ANTOINE DE ST. EXUPERY

Having finally polished her grammar, Eliza Doolittle is ready to make her appearance in society. Picture, then, a group of supremely nonchalant, elegantly dressed spectators at the Ascot races. With the aristocrat's disdain for vulgar emotion, they languidly observe the horses coming in for the finish. Then, from among the superbly stylish ladies, Eliza cries out, "Come on, Dover!!! Move your bloomin' arse!!!" [1] The grammar is perfectly acceptable, but the diction is hilariously inappropriate to the setting.

Diction as well as grammar reveals a good deal about one's background—geographically, occupationally, educationally, and socially. Though we share a common language, there are hundreds of differences in British and American speech and vocabulary. For a long time, the British looked down upon Americanisms, while Americans tended to consider the British affected. But there is no real linguistic advantage gained whether you use the British *lorry, petrol, spanner, bonnet,* and *windscreen* or the American *truck, gasoline, wrench, hood,* and *windshield.* You can play the same record on a *gramophone* or a *phonograph* and see the same picture at the *cinema* or the *movies.* There are many regionalisms within both Britain and the United States, and considerable differences in diction between Australia and South Africa. Various occupations have their own terminology and jargon, and a habitual use of substandard slang or of precise diction can place you on the social scale. There is no magic value in words themselves, though many primitive peoples believe there is and use them for charms,

277

curses, and incantations. The only moral or social value in a word is the way in which we have been conditioned to respond.

But there are different levels of diction, and they should be used appropriately. Kenneth Roberts complained of a British novelist who had a wealthy Detroit manufacturer on a safari say, "Wa-al, I reckon I guess we ain't fur from the lion-huntin'!" The author claimed that he was using regional dialect for local color, though such fake folksiness is more like Dogpatch than Detroit. Roberts retaliated by writing a scene wherein a British lord and his son discuss an American professor:

> The earl bit savagely at the end of a moist, black cigar. "Coo!" he said bitterly. " 'Ere's a ruddy nuisance! 'Oo's goin' to look after this blighter if 'e comes bargin' abaht?"
>
> The Hon. Vivyan smiled affectionately at his father. " 'Old your 'osses, guv'nor!" he said. "Don't get your blinkin' wind up over this Yank! 'E's nuffin to worry abaht, not 'alf!"

This is certainly not the speech of English aristocrats. Again, Roberts imagined a Cotswold shepherd and his wife complaining of the imminent sale of their cottage.

> "Blimey!" he says in his rough, shepherd's voice, "blimey, but it's cruel 'ard to be chucked out of one's digs wivout a blarsted word! Eighty-two years come Michaelmas Oi'm lived in these 'ere digs, by Cripes, an' now 'ere Oi be, throwed out like a bloomin' old straw 'at!"[2]

This burlesque Cockney speech is ludicrous in the mouth of an ancient Cotswold peasant. It would be equally ridiculous to have a London clergyman talk in the dialect of "Waltzing Matilda" or a Boston professor of 1964 sound like a Nevada miner in the days of the Comstock Lode.

Thus style and diction are as important as grammar—perhaps ultimately more so. Correcting grammar is a mechanical process, whereas style and diction require a degree of literary art. Great writers may violate grammatical conventions, while many a hack has ground out reams of grammatically proper but totally undistinguished prose. Often students write sentences that are grammatically correct but hopelessly awkward. Many themes are wordy and witless, with fumbling language betraying fuzzy thoughts. The careless writer chokes his prose with mumbled meanderings and uses any approximate word, rather than find one most suitable for sound and sense. The prolific British novelist John Creasey says that the most devastating criticism he has ever encountered was Dorothy Sayers' evaluation of his mystery novels: that if the author "cannot think of the right word, anything vaguely approximating it in sound will serve." [3] The literary artist does not rely upon hackneyed diction nor employ the first word that comes to hand, but makes a conscious, deliberate choice, for as Dr. Johnson stated, "What is written without effort is in general read without pleasure."

¶ LEVELS OF DICTION

Standard English has several levels of diction. *Popular words* are those that we all know and use regularly without having to think twice about them. In fact several linguists claim that nine words comprise 25 percent of our speech, though they disagree as to which are the nine. G. H. McKnight votes for *and, be, have, it, of, the, to, will, you*; Godfrey Dewey claims *a, and, in, is, it, of, that, the, to*; and the Bell Telephone Company tabulates *a, I, is, it, on, that, the, to, you*. McKnight claims that thirty-four more words (including the competitors for his nine) make up another 25 percent, so that forty-three words make up 50 percent of our speech. Most people have a vocabulary of from ten to twenty thousand words but actively use only a small fraction of these, the others being recognition or recall vocabulary. If all words were popular, there would be little need for dictionaries except for foreigners, but other words are less commonly known, though well-educated people use many of them in conversation. Others, largely literary, are used mostly in writing, while others are so specialized that they send even scholars to the dictionary. The last three groups are learned words having increasing degrees of unfamiliarity. The length of a word is no measure of its learnedness (*ventilation* is popular, whereas *laud* is learned), but many learned words are coined or borrowed from Greek or Latin:

POPULAR	LEARNED	POPULAR	LEARNED
fire	conflagration	letter	epistle
imprison	incarcerate	show	evince
chew	masticate	sixty-fourth note	hemidemisemiquaver
house	domicile	wordy	verbose
will	volition	very long words	sesquipedalia
neglect	dereliction	brave	intrepid
lash	scourge	agree	acquiesce

279

POPULAR	LEARNED	POPULAR	LEARNED
surrender	capitulate	rashness	temerity
think	cogitate	boast	gasconade
stolen	purloined	improve	ameliorate
elephant	pachyderm	self-denial	abnegation
childish	puerile	hard to understand	abstruse, recondite

If you use learned words to unlearned people, you are apt to be resented as a snob. A stock comic figure is the hobo professor, patent medicine peddler, or seedy Thespian who likes to display his elaborately extensive vocabulary. Some of William Faulkner's Southern aristocrats use a grandiose vocabulary with recurrent immolations, commiserations, relinquishments, abrogations, suzerainty, intransigency, recalcitrance, effluviums, sentience, apotheoses, avatars, and things circumambient; but even Faulkner's full-blown style consists mainly of popular words; the grand manner is more in the rhythm than the diction. Also in the South, some characters in *Pogo* use a mad mixture of grandiloquent rhetoric and swampy slang.

Words or phrases that are used mainly in casual conversation are termed colloquialisms. These are perfectly acceptable in standard English. There is nothing vulgar about them, though some may be inappropriate for more formal levels of usage. Some are clipped words (*prof* for *professor, exam* for *examination, home ec* for *home economics, psych* for *psychology*); others have the breezy character of:

okay	swell	tough (difficult)
pal	sure enough	jam (difficulty)
buddy	you bet	nifty
buy	nope	hold on (wait)
scram	corny	hot dog (food and enthusiasm)
beat it (leave)	uh, uh	awfully (very)
done with (finished)	yep	kids (children)
doggone it	nix	kidding (joking)
flunk	lousy	pooch

Some colloquialisms are actually slang; others have more status.

¶ SLANG

Slang has long been controversial and is sometimes considered the sign of linguistic disreputability. As defined by Ambrose Bierce,

"Slang is the speech of him who robs the literary garbage-carts on their way to the dumps." Walt Whitman, trying to break the barriers of Victorian gentility, was sometimes deliberately and aggressively slangy in the poetry that he called his "barbaric yawp." In very unslangy language, he described slang as "the wholesome fermentation or eructation of those processes eternally active in language, by which the froth and specks are thrown up, mostly to pass away, though occasionally to settle and permanently crystallize." But Whitman was attacked by the same prudes who condemned the language of *Huckleberry Finn*. *The London Critic* (1856) wrote, "Walt Whitman gives us slang in the place of melody, and rowdyism in the place of regularity. . . . Walt Whitman libels the highest type of humanity, and calls his free speech the true utterance of a man; we, who may have been misdirected by civilization, call it the expression of a beast." Such criticism was directed partly at Whitman's ideas but also at his language. Even in *The Oxford English Dictionary* slang is defined in part as "the special vocabulary used by any set of persons of low or disreputable character."

This is a sweeping generalization and only partially accurate. According to Sir William S. Craigie, co-editor of the *OED,* "The nation's best textbook of slang is the Congressional Record . . . ." [4] In fact everyone uses slang, and a good deal of it is perfectly respectable, though perhaps not appropriate for formal occasions. Stuart Flexner, one of the lexicographers of the *Dictionary of American Slang,* estimates that the vocabulary of the average American includes about two thousand slang words, or approximately 10 percent. When the term *slang* originated in the eighteenth century, (slang, without a label, is as old as civilization), it referred to the special cant of criminals, rogues, and beggars—a sort of code known only to the initiate. Today various subgroups have their special vocabulary and idioms, partly for shoptalk but partly as passwords for a clique, separating the initiated from the outsiders. Prominent among these subgroups, Stuart Flexner lists hobos, immigrants, the army, navy, and merchant marine, the underworld, narcotic addicts, jazz musicians and fans, financial-district employees, college students, high school students and teen-agers, railroad workers, baseball players and fans, show business people. Slang is the more widely used speech of these subgroups. Obviously some of them are more legitimate than others. Many slang phrases include obscenities; some are grammatically nonstandard; but many are perfectly proper in a casual context. In fact, as we saw above, it is not always possible to distinguish between slang terms and colloquialisms. Some slang terms become standard; others continue for centuries without social recognition. But most slang is ephemeral and is lucky to last a decade. Nothing dates dialogue in fiction more clearly than its slang, much of which has gone the way of "twenty-three skiddoo."

The drawbacks of slang are two. First, it is a communication barrier to the uninitiate. The British edition of *Babbitt* had to have a special glossary explaining Sinclair Lewis's slang terms. "Waltzing Matilda" has to be decoded for non-Australians. When an American GI asked an Austrian tavern owner if there was a one-armed bandit (slot machine) in the joint, she said indignantly that she ran a reputable establishment with no thieves on the premises. See how comprehensible is W. E. Henley's rendition of François Villon's ballade of medieval Parisian criminal cant into the slang of the London underworld:

VILLON'S STRAIGHT TIP TO ALL CROSS COVES

Suppose you screeve? or go cheap-jack?
   Or fake the broads? or fig a nag?
Or thimble-rig? or knap a yack?
   Or pitch a snide? or smash a rag?
   Suppose you duff? or nose and lag?
Or get the straight, and land your pot?
   How do you melt the multy swag?
Booze and the blowens cop the lot.

Fiddle, or fence, or mace, or mack,
   Or moskeneer, or flash the drag;
Dead-lurk a crib, or do a crack,
   Pad with a slang, or chuck a fag;
   Bonnett, or tout, or mump and gag;
Rattle the tats, or mark the spot;
   You cannot bag a single stag—
Booze and the blowens cop the lot.

Suppose you try a different tack,
   And on the square you flash your flag?
At penny-a-lining make your whack,
   Or with the mummers mump and gag?
   For nix, for nix the dibs you bag!
At any graft, no matter what,
   Your merry goblins soon stravag—
Booze and the blowens cop the lot.

It's up the spout and Charley Wag
With wipes and tickers and what not;
Until the squeezer nips your scrag,
Booze and the blowens cop the lot.

Unlike learned jargon, which signifies an in-group all its own, most slang is short and sassy. It favors one-syllable words rather than elaborate gobbledygook, preferring to voom than to locomote itself. But like jargon, slang becomes a collection of clichés—handy phrases to fill a linguistic gap without bothering to find more precise words. This is drawback number two, for too much reliance on slang dilutes clear thinking. Some slang is deliberately vague, avoiding the need for precise logic or evaluation. Things are *cool, hep, crazy, skizzy, dullsville, square,* or *weird,* with no reasons given. A *kook* or a *weirdie* can be anything from a mongoloid idiot to a nuclear physicist; what makes him weird is some sort of nonconformity, the fact that he differs from whatever group is deriding him. And by rejecting others with automatic thoughtlessness, the slang-slinger affirms his intuitive rapport with his group of cool cats. Thus a great many teen-age slang words are vague terms of praise and condemnation.

Mr. Flexner observes that "Slang . . . always tends toward degradation rather than elevation" and that with reverse morality, "much of our slang purposely expresses amorality, cynicism, and 'toughness.'" [5] Perhaps for this reason or because much slang is occupational rather than domestic, more men than women make and use slang.

On the credit side, many slang terms are attempts at colorful and unconventional speech. Some are humorous hyperboles and comic metaphors; e.g., moonshine whiskey is rattlesnake juice, white mule, corpse reviver, white lightning, and a person who has too much liquor can be jug-bitten, pie-eyed, loaded, half-seas over, listing to starboard, three sheets in the wind, tanked up, or high as a kite. These too easily become trite, though the French *"Mes yeux ne sont pas en face des trous"* ("My eyes aren't opposite the holes") has not yet gone stale.

The issue is not if you should use slang but if you can use it effectively. Dwight Macdonald observes that *jalopy* is more concise and vivid than *dilapidated automobile,* but often slang is more feeble than fresh. Of course, *bug, crazy, cool, drag, drip, neat, heap, pad, tiger, rumble, octopus,* and others are old words that become slang only in an idiomatic context, whereas *jalopy* was a new word. Anyhow, if you want to be ginchy instead of a goopus, get with it, dad; be an abominable snowman and all that jazz, but play it cool and know when to knock it off, so you'll be in orbit and not out to lunch.

Learned words, popular words, colloquialisms, and some slang are all valid in the speech and writing of educated people, but they may not be equally valid at all times and in all situations. Just as there are several levels of style for clothing, so are there for language. Some occasions require formality; others are more casual. Formal style is more often literary than spoken, though it is used at certain ceremonial events. Highly rhetorical, it is characterized by long, stately sentences (often in an inverted word order), introductory participial phrases and subordinate clauses, conservative grammar, learned words, and the avoidance of colloquialisms and contractions. It is the language of the Declaration of Independence, the Gettysburg Address, and other dignified documents. Its danger is that it may become pompous and ponderous. John Milton, Samuel Johnson, Edward Gibbon, and many classic prosodists regularly used a highly formal style. In such masterful hands, it functions like a Rolls-Royce; but for most writers, it is unmaneuverable, poor on mileage, and subject to frequent breakdowns.

Colloquial style has a casual manner, favoring the use of popular words, relaxed grammar, contractions, a liberal helping of colloquialisms and slang, and frequent incomplete sentences. It is used in writing for light humor, friendly correspondence, appropriate dialogue, and palsy-walsy advertising, such as:

And for the Morning After—Executive Eye-Opener. When you've had a little too much of some things, or a lot too little of others, let pure USP Oxygen take up the slack, make up the lack.

Or

Should you wear paisley underwear with a beret? Certainly. But never to the opera. For such an occasion we suggest Carter's knit boxers in Persian Squares: lively but not aggressive. . . . Best friend a well-dressed knit-picker ever had.

Or to be really colloquial,

Look, chum, why don't you skadoodle over to Moe's and really live it up with a mug of Mumblebrau—the brew that's true for you. Just ask Moe—he's a gasser.

284

In between these two extremes is informal—the style most commonly used. A highly formal style is disappearing, along with the top hat and tails; scientific and bureaucratic jargon is replacing it with the stylistic equivalent of the space suit; but if you don't wish to be a jargonaut, you will find that informal style is appropriate for most occasions. It is the prose of most novels, magazine articles, and untechnical essays that want to avoid the extremes of stately formality and chummy colloquialism.

The answer to which style is best depends upon the occasion. You do not wear blue jeans to a ball nor a tuxedo to a picnic, and a scuba and skin-diving suit is highly specialized. Even more incongruous is mixing levels of style. Imagine getting dressed with indiscriminate articles of apparel. You might combine Bermuda shorts with a tuxedo shirt, a cowboy bandana, ski socks, a frogman flipper on one foot and a sandal on the other, a motorcycle jacket, and a deep-sea diving helmet. You would be dressed but hardly ready to go anywhere except out of your mind. Yet the inattentive writer sometimes mixes levels of style almost as ludicrously. Once you decide what style suits your purpose, you should stick to it and avoid inconsistencies such as appear in the following:

When Napoleon invaded Russia in 1812, he was seemingly at the height of his power. He anticipated little resistance from the Russians, whom he considered a *bunch of freaps*. Personally leading the Grand Armée, he struck at Smolensk and then *booted* the Russians back to Moscow. Engaging the forces of General Kutuzov at Borodino, *Boney* expected to *clobber* his opponents with little difficulty. The battle was bloody but indecisive. The French held the field but lost so many men that they could not sustain their victory. With the threat of winter and increased Russian resistance, Napoleon decided to *take it on the lam*. In the light of burning Moscow, set aflame by incendiaries, the French began to *vavoom out of there*. The retreat became a disaster. Winter caught the ill-prepared *Frogs*, and Russian guerrillas harassed *Boney's boys*, turning the ordeal into a nightmare. The haggard survivors were a mere ghost of the invincible *dogfaces* that had set out so confidently.

This is admittedly an extreme example, but students write scrambled statements like "Jonathan Edwards was gung-ho on religion," "Walt Whitman was more gung-ho American than T. S. Eliot," or "Emerson and John Winthrop would have had quite a rhubarb had they lived during the same time." It is not appropriate to write chummily of Henry James, "In 'Madame de Mauves,' Henry tells of a rich young girl that is tricked into marriage to a slob." (Despite our American folksiness, it is crude to address or write of celebrities or political dignitaries by their first name or a nickname—Ike, Winnie, Eleanor, Jackie, Lyndon, Liz, or even Nikita.) One student wrote, "Emerson was a real weirdy in some of his beliefs." According to another, "Whitman believed in pantheism and the oversoul and all that stuff," and yet another explained, "J. Alfred Prufrock can't cut the mustard."

Ministers sometimes mix Biblical quotes and archaic seventeenth-century phraseology with current colloquialisms. Mark Twain complained of James Fenimore Cooper's tendency to "divide each sentence into two equal parts: one part critically grammatical, refined, and choice of language, and the other part just such an attempt to talk like a hunter or a mountaineer, as a Broadway clerk might make after eating an edition of Emerson Bennett's works and studying frontier life at the Bowery Theatre a couple of weeks." According to Mark Twain, the rules of literary art "require that when a personage talks like an illustrated, gilt-edged, tree-clad, hand-tooled, seven-dollar Friendship's Offering in the beginning of a paragraph, he shall not talk like a negro minstrel in the end of it."

It is often essential to suit your style to the level of your audience. This does not mean adopting nonstandard grammar and diction for the sake of conformity. But it is obviously ineffective to talk over or under the heads of your audience. Instructions for the assembly or operation of equipment are worthless if they are not clear. It is hardly appropriate to lecture an elementary Sunday school class in the language of Paul Tillich or to teach primer lessons to seminarians. A highly formal style is too pretentious for friendly correspondence, and a slangy style too frivolous for scholarly publications. Style indicates something of one's attitude toward his subject. Contrast "Gimme a little kiss, willya, huh?" with this speech by Cyrano de Bergerac:

> And what is a kiss, when all is done?
> A promise given under seal—a vow
> Taken before the shrine of memory—
> A signature acknowledged—a rosy dot
> Over the i of Loving—a secret whispered
> To listening lips apart—

and so on. Cyrano is undoubtedly too florid for modern girls, but clearly his style makes both the kiss and the bestower of it more important than does the slack-jawed, gum-chomping style of the first request.

Some statements seem to be acceptable in formal prose that would be objectionable on another stylistic level. There is a story ("That's a joke, son") about a boy who saw some bow-legged men and said to his mother, "Mama, mama, look at the bow-legged men." She smacked him on the hand and told him not to say such things, but the next week he saw them again and once more shouted, "Look at the bow-legged men." This time his mother made him study Shakespeare for a month to teach him more dignified language. The next time he saw the men, he remarked, "Lo, what manner of men are these/That walk with their legs in parentheses!"

¶ JARGON

The formal style of Dr. Johnson and other neoclassic men of letters may have been heavy but it was not clumsy. It was usually as graceful as an intricate dance pattern and could be eloquent or ironic. Though it was sometimes slow, it was always clear and often quotable.

Is not a Patron, My Lord, one who looks with unconcern on a Man struggling for Life in the water and when he has reached ground encumbers him with help? The notice which you have been pleased to take of my Labours, had it been early, had it been kind; but it has been delayed till I am indifferent and cannot enjoy it, till I am solitary and cannot impart it, till I am known, and do not want it.

This excerpt from Johnson's letter to Lord Chesterfield slowly but powerfully gathers force until the total effect is devastating.

By contrast, much modern formal prose is frozen into jargon— ugly, unrhythmic, unmelodious chunks of verbiage that go together as gracefully as two freight cars coupling. A species of pretentious bumblery, it is long-winded, unnecessarily difficult, and sick with what James Thurber called carcinonomenclature. Thus *food* becomes *units of nutritional intake, baby sitters* become *custodial supervisors of juvenile activities and recreation,* and Donald Duck's Dubble Fudgi-Frost is identified on the wrapper as "a quiescent frozen product."

Some jargon is legitimate within limits: the technical terminology of various sciences, trades, and professions. Presumably such termi-

287

nology is clear and necessary in its proper context. But too often people borrow or imitate it for prestige in other areas. In some schools, bureaus, and publications, it seems more important to know the orthodox jargon than to show any critical and original thought. In fact, once you learn the jargon, it almost does your thinking for you. Decide to use Freudian, Marxian, or any other esoteric terminology, and your criticism automatically falls into place. Moreover, you will be a member of that particular in-group and can feel superior to the uninitiated. In literary and artistic criticism, the jargon addict may show considerable ingenuity in finding verbal and symbolic devices to fit his subject into the pattern, but the pattern is standardized. Thus Richard Chase writes, "The psycho-analyst might say that Billy Budd has avoided the Oedipus struggle by forming an attachment to the mother at the prephallic level of 'oral eroticism' and has allayed his fears of castration by symbolically castrating himself (by being consciously submissive) and by re-pressing his rage and hostility against the father in order to placate him." [6] Sometimes such ritualized dialectic creates distortion; for example, in one criticism of Hemingway, Sam the cook in "The Killers" becomes "the wooing mother-surrogate," "the dark hermaph-roditic mother-guide." On the other hand, some invent their own jargon that seems to have no pattern at all in such pretentious nonsense as: "The latest painting by Trudwick Zerch reveals the subliminal thrust of the tender tendrils of resurrection against a bleak background suggestive of a Bach toccata played by an Eskimo band before the northern lights as the Plutonian antipodal winter is about to engulf the Proserpine equinox."

Some literary critics subject their subject to excessive analysis— more weight than the traffic can bear. H. L. Mencken called Thor-stein Veblen's prose "a cent's worth of information wrapped in a bale of polysyllables." Too many scholars turn prose and poetry into pedantry. Graduate students and even established scholars have claimed that they were required to rewrite material because their style was too clear and their arguments too lucid. Apparently it is felt that if the material is too accessible, the scholar loses status; the veil of the temple is rent and the sacred mysteries revealed. Thus the jargon of Academia is sometimes more incantation than communication. Many matters are indeed so complex that they cannot be reduced to the popular level; but obscurity or devious elaboration is not desirable for its own sake, and some writing is unjustifiably difficult.

288

And dull. There are different species of jargon, and a lot of it is not learned or profound but merely long-winded. It creates obscurity when there is nothing obscure. To conceal a lack of ideas, the experienced bumbler beats around the proverbial bush, turning verbs into phrases, snarling his syntax, preferring polysyllabic and learned words to short and direct ones and abstract words to concrete ones. Thus we find the following sorts of inflation, given to the right of their simpler equivalents:

if	in the eventuality that
this refers to	this is in reference to
useless	devoid of usefulness
imprecise	reveals a lack of preciseness
I think that	My trend of thought leads me to the conclusion that
I feel	I have a feeling that
I conclude	It is my conclusion that
many	a not inconsiderable number of (or a substantial number of)
repair	restore to operational condition
failed	did not succeed in achieving its objective
prefer	demonstrate a preference for
dislike	manifest an antipathy towards
supports	is supportive to

To the unsophisticated, such jargon may suggest scientific detachment, an attempt to avoid subjective interpretation and hasty conclusions. Actually it is a lot of blah, a species of circumlocution and dead wood, expansive and elaborately vacuous. If your mind is empty or your thoughts not clearly organized, it is helpful to have a handy collection of jargon, cliché terms and phrases; they are a falsely impressive and more elaborate way of saying "and . . . uh . . . er . . ."—of clearing your throat while groping for what next to say.

Such gobbledygook bloats the language with a verbal elephantiasis that destroys its grace and impairs its vigor. It can be dangerous, for as George Orwell wrote in "Politics and the English Language": "the slovenliness of our language makes it easier for us to have foolish thoughts. . . . The great enemy of clear language is insincerity." In politics, jargon can be a way of avoiding direct statements, or it can be a means of channeling thought. Its pseudo-scientific terminology tends to turn people into abstractions or statistics and reduce the individual to a member of the mass. As a sort of bureaucratic slang, it can have the same effect in avoiding the need for precise logic or evaluation and in causing people or concepts to be accepted or rejected by a more elaborate name-calling. Whether that of the Communists or that of the ultraconservatives, political jargon offers a set of stock phrases that can evoke the desired response with a minimum of intellectual effort.

Some jargon employs euphemisms to make things more attractive or more impressive than they really are. Thus hydrogen bombs have been called "thermo-nuclear deterrents" as if they are a defense against hydrogen bombs. The cold war powers are also working on "clean" bombs, which can kill millions of people with one blast but leave no dirty fallout. Leonard R. N. Ashley calls these "the Ultimate Detergent." A Mauldin cartoon about the American invasion of Laos has an officer tell a noncom, "No, Hanson, you didn't find a box of bullets and two bags of rice. You captured an ammo dump and a supply depot." Military reporters in Vietnam have been instructed never to write of napalm but to call it "selective ordnance," to call mercenaries "civilian irregular-defense group volunteers," to rename "search and destroy" operations as "search and clear." Art Buchwald suggested that bombing Cambodia with B-52s might more euphemistically be called "interdicting enemy supply routes from the north," making a defensive ordnance drop on fixed enemy positions," or "neutralizing a free-fire area." Even "the free world" is partially euphemistic jargon, since it includes South Africa, Franco's Spain, Haiti, and various right-wing dictatorships around the world. They are free only by token of not belonging to the Communist bloc. At home, various reactionary hate groups call themselves by various patriotic names, though by "patriotism" they mean censoring textbooks, attacking the Supreme Court, denouncing the United Nations, condemning civil rights, opposing public education, and slandering as subversive anyone who favors fluoridation, mental health, environmental ecology, academic freedom, the Bill of Rights, or democracy.

This distortion of meaning is as new as *1984* and as old as history. In the fifth century B.C., Thucydides wrote that under demagogues, "The meaning of words had no longer the same relation to things but was changed by them as they thought proper. Reckless daring was held to be courage; prudent delay was the excuse of a coward; moderation was the disguise of unmanly weakness; to know everything was to do nothing. Frantic energy was the true quality of a man. . . . He who succeeded in a plot was deemed knowing, but a still greater master in craft was he who detected one."

290

A good deal of jargon is a by-product of bureaucracy, in both government and corporations. Secretary of Agriculture Orville Freeman told his staff, "The fright of verbs is one of the most dismaying, but most characteristic attributes of the language of big bureaucracies. Why? Maybe because the language is originated by people who feel far removed from decision and action, and therefore, who subconsciously shrink from such bold, plain, and clear expressions as 'We think' or 'We will tell you' and retreat behind some form of the static and listless verb 'to be' coupled with a prepositional phrase denoting a condition ('of the view that . . .') in place of owning up to the active decision which is the actual fact that should be communicated." Thus "We are of the view that . . ." should be "We think . . . ," and "Request is hereby made to establish . . ." should be "Please establish . . ." "You may be assured that careful consideration will be given to all the facts" should be changed from the passive to the active, "We will consider carefully all the facts."

One pitfall of jargon is the overused passive. The passive voice is by definition less active than the active voice, and too many passive constructions create a negative movement like the Army definition of marching in place: "You's going, but you ain't going no *where*." When the subject really is the passive recipient of action, when the actor is indefinite rather than specific, or when the verb indicates a general procedure, the passive voice is appropriate. (Cf. p. 112.) But too much scientific and sociological writing and bureaucratese deliberately prefers the passive even when an active verb is more effective. The rationale is that active verbs in the first person ("I did," "I think," "We propose") lack the required flavor of scientific objectivity and organizational impersonality. The jargonaut considers the passive more clinical even though it may be clumsy and obscure. Despite this self-effacing manner, things are not done by themselves; people do them, and in some instances it is hypocritical to hide behind the passive. The passive eliminates the actor and leaves only the act; there is nobody to get the credit or the blame. Scientific objectivity is commendable, but scientism (as in Aldous Huxley's *Brave New World*) can reduce the individual to a cipher; and in bureaucracies, where the office is more important than the official, the excessive passive voice is an additional harness on the organization man. Hannah Arendt, in her study of Adolph Eichmann, found him merely an extreme example of the bureaucrat who disclaims responsibility and seeks refuge in passivity: "I was ordered, I was instructed, I was required to obey." The passive is also a tool of the informer and inquisitor in a police state. "It is charged, it is reported, it is known . . ." You are accused, but there is no visible accuser. In such cases it may be necessary to distinguish between the active and passive. In *A Man for All Seasons,* Sir Thomas More, persecuted for refusing to approve Henry VIII's marriage and the Act of Supremacy, says to the King's prosecutor, "So I am brought here at last."

CROMWELL: Brought? You brought yourself to where you stand now.
MORE: Yes—Still, in another sense—I was brought.[7]

Some government agencies are finally recognizing the inefficiency of jargon and are trying, like Secretary Freeman, to eliminate it. The State Department is giving its officers courses in elementary composition so that they will be able to understand each other's communications. The Postmaster's office no longer approves calling post offices "major mail-handling facilities" or garages "postal lubritoriums" and criticizes such gobbledygook as, "Space will be available for balloons for accommodation distribution, and creepers will be installed to assist personnel in the cannibalization of bums."

Still, jargon continues like a creeping fungus. Pentagonese flourishes with words like *deprojectmanagerize.* When the Army bought portable showers for workers to wash off spilled rocket fuel, it called the showers "rocket propellant personnel neutralizers." Merchandising gets into the act with instructions (for Replicap Bottle Resealer) like: "The inner carbonation retention structure for this successful resealer is such that application should be from the back of the bottle mouth—forward—using the heel or palm of hand to ease cap into resealing position." Sociologists are said to call orgies "sexual educational group dynamics." (Washington University has begun a $135,000 a year project to turn sociological jargon into plain English.) Educationists—as distinct from teachers—are often addicted to a ponderous prose that James D. Koerner (in *The Miseducation of American Teachers*) calls "Educanto." In a search for pseudoscientific status, teachers become "instructional personnel"; the classroom is "the teaching situation"; bright students are "fortunate deviates"; collecting information becomes "assemblizing imponderables"; and the teacher (or rather "director of experience") gets ahead by using ritual words such as "insightfulness" and progressing to formidable phrases like "the progressive familial subcultural mental retardation," "the normative generalization reference cue," or "the extrinsic dualistic organization of coordinate administration." Mr. Koerner observes that such jargon "masks a lack of thought, and in fact makes thought of any important kind extraordinarily difficult." [8] This is true of jargon in general; it becomes a sort of mechanical litany like the brainwashed chanting of party slogans. Most jargon is more muddled than sinister, but it is second-hand—and handy, so that when you fumble for a thought, you can draw an automatic phrase from the stockpile of jargon. Even if the terminology is technical rather than bumbled, it can be constricting. Thus Norman Mailer writes, "Psychoanalysis. An artist must not explore into himself with language given by another. A vocabulary of experts is a vocabulary greased out and sweated in committee and so is inimical to a private eye." [9]

Even religion is not immune from jargon. For some ministers and seminarians, *kerygma* and *didache* are more prestigious than *preaching and teaching. Koinonia* is more imposing than *fellowship,* though it sounds less inviting. German sounds more learned than English, so *angst, Wissenschaft, Kirchliche Dogmatik,* and *Heilsgeschichte* replace *anxiety, knowledge, church dogma,* and *salvation history.* Academia generally is fond of *Zeitgeist, Weltanschauung, Weltschmertz,* and other German jawbreakers. Some terms, though syllabically segmented as a centipede, are a shorthand; *redaktionsgeschichte* is briefer than "the historical study of how the written gospels were edited from the oral teaching of the early church." [10]

To avoid jargon, cut all unnecessary words, eliminate *not-un* constructions, minimize the passive voice, replace vague verbal and prepositional phrases with active verbs, cut or replace colorless adjectives, do not pile up nouns, and whenever possible use short English words instead of long, foreign, and pretentiously scientific ones.

¶ PSEUDOLITERARY LANGUAGE

Some amateurs, trying too hard to be literary, come up with strained metaphors and overly ornate diction. On the one hand they become turgid, like the *Time* movie reviews cited by Dwight Macdonald: "Like a giant caldron the screen boils with life, and Kurosawa's telescopic lenses, spooning deep, lift the depths to the surface and hurl the whole mess in the spectator's face"; or "The Bergman who made this picture still had akvavit in his veins. Intellect, that glittering and treacherous Snow Queen, had not yet struck her icy sliver into his heart." [11]

Or they lace their language with archaisms, affected allusions, learned insipidities, and feckless effusions. Certainly "It stinks" is more authentic than "A fragrance like to that of the celebrated Augean stables arises in our vicinity and, wafted by gentle zephyrs, permeates the dewy air and penetrates my proboscis, thus offending my olfactory senses." This is a deliberately grotesque example; but one sometimes encounters a simpering style "With many holiday and lady terms" (as Hotspur put it). In *Hamlet,* the foppish Osric speaks thus, and Hamlet parodies him: "Sir, his definement suffers no perdition in you; though, I know, to divide him inventorially would dozy th'arithmetic of memory, and yet but yaw neither in respect of his quick sail. But, in the verity of extolment, I take him to be a soul of great article, and his infusion of such dearth and rareness as, to make true diction of him, his semblable is his mirror, and who else would trace him, his umbrage, nothing more." Such phony elaboration is obviously pseudoliterary. While avoiding such blatant extremes, some writers create more sound than sense with strained pseudoliterary clichés, such as: "Chicago mothers all peoples, rich or poor, famous or unknown. In the shadows of towering, austere skyscrapers are huddled crowded masses of humanity. Yet this city of steel, din, and confusion envelopes her people with a stubborn and protecting love. Buffeted by the tormented Lake Michigan waters and swept by the Iowa prairie winds, Chicago stands firm and unyielding." Perhaps, but such trite and overemphatic prose falls on its face.

There is no special language for literature, though it may draw upon a larger vocabulary than ordinary conversation. It is most effective when it uses contemporary idiom. Even a poetic drama like T. S. Eliot's *Murder in the Cathedral,* about the twelfth-century tragedy of Thomas à Becket, avoids conscious archaisms and uses modern diction. But eighteenth- and nineteenth-century writers did often employ a special literary language consisting largely of imitation Shakespearean and Biblical grammar and vocabulary. The Bible was a profound stylistic influence and was the only book many people ever read. Even Thomas Paine wrote of Deism in the cadences of the King James translators: "The Creation speaketh an universal language . . . ." Much eighteenth-century style has a commendable clarity and directness, but some authors wrote elaborately ponderous prose full of polysyllabic Latinate words; and some became so addicted to false elegance that they favored such circumlocutions as calling fish "the finny folk" and birds "our little feathered friends." Wordsworth called for a new poetry written in the language of the people, though he did not always follow his own advice. The popularity of historical novels from Sir Walter Scott on gave new life to archaisms, and the genteel tradition encouraged them as a sign of elevated purity. The result was often ludicrous and provoked the ridicule of Mark Twain, Artemus Ward, and other satirists. When "middle-aged female No. 2" asked Artemus Ward's landlord, "Dost never go into the green fields to cull the beautiful flowers?" he replied, "I not only never dost, but I'll bet you five pound you can't bring a man as dares say I durst." In another episode, Ward describes encountering an evangelist for women's rights:

"I hope, marm," sez I, starting back, "that your intensions is honorable! I'm a lone man hear in a strange place. Besides, I've a wife to hum."

"Yes," cried the female, "& she's a slave! Doth she never dream of freedom—doth she never think of throwin off the yoke of tyrinny & thinkin & votin for herself?—Doth she never think of these here things?"

"Not bein a natral born fool," sed I, by this time a little riled, "I kin safely say that she dothunt."

In modern literature, realistic dialogue prevails, even while poets and novelists have found new and surprising resources in the language. If they sometimes wrench the language violently, they do so with originality, whereas a special literary diction and grammar is a sort of jargon. Deliberate archaisms still appear in historical fiction and are sometimes burlesqued; Snagglepuss as Robin Hood declaimed, "I robbeth from the richeth and giveth to the pooreth." Ersatz Biblical language also fossilizes some legal documents:

Memorandum of Agreement made this 31st day of February, 1972, between Herbert Homefreeze, party of the first part (hereinafter called the "Author"), and party of the second part (hereinafter called the "Publisher"), Witnesseth: that whereas the said Author desires that a work be published and put on the market by the said Publisher: Now, therefore, in consideration of the premises and of one dollar to each in hand paid by the other, the receipt whereof is hereby acknowledged, the parties hereto do covenant and agree as follows.

The language of Hollywood Biblical epics usually sounds as musty as Samson's jawbone of an ass. Yet priests and ministers still favor

Jacobean jargon. Perhaps they do so to be consistent with Biblical readings in the services. Still it sounds strange to have prayers for the President of the United States couched in the phraseology of the Tudor and Stuart monarchs. The Rev. Dr. Krister Stendahl, professor of Biblical studies at Harvard, urges Protestants to dispense with archaic *thees* and *thous* and verb endings (*Thou speakest, he goeth,* etc.). He observes that Jesus favored plain language and taught that God is a father rather than an inaccessible deity who can be addressed only in a special sacred language. As literature, the King James translation surpasses any modern ones, but for "language understanded of the people" there are several excellent versions in contemporary diction and style. Among some religious extremists these later translations have been denounced and even burned as infidel and subversive, though the original testaments were written in Hebrew and Greek, not in seventeenth-century English. On the other hand, a version of the gospels in modern teen-age slang fell completely flat and reduced to absurdity the majesty of the original. Still, a special ecclesiastical style can lead to exchanges like "Wilt thou take this woman to be thy lawful wedded wife?" "I wilt."

¶ DEAD WOOD

Not all dead wood is jargon; a lot of it is just clumsiness or the unwillingness to find more exact language. In J. D. Salinger's *The Catcher in the Rye,* Holden Caulfield lets his sentences dangle with "and all," "and everything," or "or something" when it's too much strain to be more precise. These loose phrases are quite legitimate for Salinger's realistic dialogue, but they serve no purpose aside from characterizing Holden. How informative are "measles and all," "Hallowe'en and all," "my Sunday school teacher and all," "Errol Flynn and all," "September and all," "bathtub ring and all," "an intellectual and all," "geology and all," "nervous and all," "science fiction and all," "a doctor or something," "homework and all that stuff," "Utah and everything," "asleep or something," "soup or something," "a porpoise or something," and "without a hat on or anything?" Sometimes such phrases are even more ludicrous, as when a student wrote about a literary character, "She was illegitimate or something like that." What is something like that?

A particularly pernicious habit ·is the pointless and repetitive use of "you know" to clutter up a statement. Usually the listener does not know; in any case, he does not need to be told dozens of times that he does. The "you know" virus, which has reached epidemic proportions, is a verbal equivalent of scratching oneself, you know. If, you know, people use the phrase all the time, you know, then, you know, they don't know what they're saying, you know. Even if, you know, someone points out to them, you know, that they are hooked, you know, on this mindless repetition, you know, they don't realize, you know, that they're doing it, you know what I mean? So far, "you know" is as bad as the common cold; no one has discovered a cure for it.

Much dead wood is mere redundancy, like "this modern-day world of ours in which we live," which should be shortened to "this modern world." "Visitors gaze in awe at the magnificent panorama before their eyes." Where else, if they gaze? So cut "before their eyes." Since celebrities are by definition famous, *famous* should be cut in "In the Via Veneto, famous celebrities are hounded by reporters." "To the present day" is obvious and hence unnecessary in "since the beginning of time to the present day." Again, the last phrase should be cut from "Our vocabularies have been broadened through the introduction of new words with which to communicate." What else do we do with words? In the following examples, consider why the dead wood (enclosed in brackets) is unnecessary:

National parks offer many recreational activities [for anyone interested in participating in them.]

Some students don't want to work as waiters [as far as a job is concerned].

Horpington has trouble writing [verbally].

Society is becoming more complex. As a result [of this situation], people are becoming frustrated.

The reason for this situation is [due to] the fact that neither side understands the other.

Despite advertising, people usually buy the brand [of product] they like [the] best.

Most people read for enjoyment or to gain knowledge [on a certain subject].

An example is [that of] automation.

Thoreau was opposed to living [life] in a hurry.

It has been said that a lot of litter is not literature. As a general rule, never use superfluous words. Whenever possible, replace rambling phrases with single words. "Healthy" is better than "in a state of health." "A socialistic form of government" can be reduced to "socialism." "Many desire" is preferable to "It is the desire of many." "Many years ago" is briefer than "many years prior to this day." 'Except for a few exceptions" can be "with a few exceptions." "Defined" is better than "expressed a definition of." "Frost's writings in the form of poetry" means simply "Frost's poems." "The quote of Jefferson's relating that those who labor in the earth are the actual chosen people of God is a statement that needs consideration" should be condensed to "Jefferson's statement that those who labor in the earth are the actual chosen people of God needs consideration." Besides, Jefferson was not quoting anyone. Note how cutting dead wood (in brackets) can tighten the following: "The quote [should be "Jefferson's statement"] 'The legitimate powers of government extend to such acts only as are injurious to others,' [by Thomas Jefferson] is somewhat [of a] misleading [statement] when taken out of context [from Jefferson's writings]."

The following example of student writing (about a poem of Edward Taylor's) is so wordy that the writer stumbles over his own dead wood.

The imagery of the second stanza is of a very effective nature. The stanza contains what is called a word paradox. It is of such a manner that the use of the paradox and metaphorical type imagery was an effective method describing the everlasting love of God conjoined in an embodiment of man to form Christ.

This can be greatly condensed and clarified:

The second stanza makes effective use of paradox and metaphor to describe the everlasting love of God conjoined and embodied for man in Christ.

"Bret Harte's characters are mining and gambling individuals" is better as "miners and gamblers." A particular nuisance is the bracketed dead wood in "Professor Crabshaw stated [this following quote] in his book, [quote], 'Richard III was unjustifiably maligned by Tudor historians.' [Unquote.]" Another is "In Martin's *Civilizing Ourselves,* he describes the modern barbarian," which is better as "In *Civilizing Ourselves,* Martin . . ." And sometimes there is simple repetition: "Overpopulation is one of the greatest problems in the world. It is a problem that is of great importance everywhere."

298

The dead-wood addict, whether jargonaut or simple bumbler, particularly likes to change verbs into nouns and then add weak and needless verbal phrases:

There was a difference in their criticisms.

There was is the grammatical subject, but it is meaningless; the significant word is *criticisms,* and the idea is both strengthened and shortened as "Their criticisms differed." *There is, there are,* and similar constructions can often be dropped:

There is something in your attitude that bothers me.
vs.
Something in your attitude bothers me.

There were several people who walked out of the meeting.
vs.
Several people walked out of the meeting.

There is a probability that the bill will be passed.
vs.
Probably the bill will be passed.

There was a dislike of Mark Twain for Henry James's novels.
vs.
Mark Twain disliked Henry James's novels.

Whenever possible, turn nouns back into verbs:

The discussion in the committee was about parking fees.
vs.
The committee discussed parking fees.

The statement of the faculty is that salaries should be increased.
vs.
The faculty state that salaries should be increased.

The proposal of the engineers is that they should dam the canyon.
vs.
The engineers propose to dam the canyon.

Besides the weak verb *to be,* the past participle of other weak verbs can turn the real verb into a noun. Such feeble constructions include:

accomplish	bring about	give	provide	show
achieve	cause	make	result	take place
affect	exist	occur	serve	transpire

These are so general that they are often interchangeable:

Elimination of inefficiency has been accomplished.
Elimination of inefficiency has been achieved.
Elimination of inefficiency has been brought about.
Elimination of inefficiency has occurred.
Elimination of inefficiency has taken place.

To really eliminate inefficiency, turn the noun back to a verb:

"Inefficiency has been eliminated."

A frequent type of dead wood is the use of *the . . . of . . . the* with gerund phrases. Perhaps influenced by *The Taming of the Shrew* or by the lines of the Christmas carol, "The rising of the sun/And the running of the deer,/The playing of the merry organ,/Sweet singing in the choir," people write clumsy constructions like "She is responsible for the washing of the dishes," or "The Constitution called for a setting up of a Supreme Court." Again, clauses or phrases can sometimes be condensed by an infinitive: "Al Capp proposed psychological tests for the screening of candidates for the Senate" rambles with its two awkward *fors*; "tests to screen candidates" is better. "Opportunity for the betterment of himself" is better as "to better himself."

But yet, but nevertheless, and etc., revert back, return back, and *where is it at* are redundant. So are many prepositions, which are all right in colloquial speech but should be pruned for a concise effective style: e.g., fix *up,* flatten *out,* parallels *with,* crushed *down,* follow *out* orders, hurry *up,* and so on. *I have got* can be shortened to *I have,* though *got* may be more emphatic (cf., "I've got rhythm" and "I have rhythm"). Since *impossibility* is an absolute, there is no need for the adjective in "a complete impossibility." Savages are by definition uncivilized, so "an uncivilized savage" is as redundant as "a vegetarian who doesn't eat meat." Finally we have dead wood in a circular argument: "Booster Club meetings in *Babbitt* show how childish grown men can really be because they carry on in a most childish manner." But occasionally dead wood is all right for inverted emphasis, as in Doggy Daddy's saying, "If there is one thing I can't stand, it's a lamp that says *Yowtch!*" Otherwise the best thing to do with dead wood is to cut it out.

¶ THE PRECISE WORD

The ability to think in abstractions is a sign of intellectual maturity, but abstractions must be based on and related to specific details if they are to have any vitality or validity. Too much academic prose consists almost entirely of abstract words, which create a lifeless style that seems to divorce the content from reality. John Dewey was an extremely influential figure in modern philosophy and education, yet even his admirers find his prose almost unreadable because of its abstract diction. The ideas may be provocative, but they are presented in a style largely impenetrable.

On a less scholarly level, students often water their writing with vague words like *nice, great, swell, interesting, different, unusual, strange* that offer only the feeblest concrete evaluation. "How was the play?" "Oh, it was terrific" (or *tremendous* or *great* or *not bad* or *fair* or *lousy*), which is not very enlightening. Such modifiers have been called *utility words,* because you can use them with no intellectual effort. Usually a general quality or action can be made more specific. Note how many related words *Roget's International Thesaurus* gives for each general one. The verb *walk* might variously be more accurate as *stride, shuffle, limp, amble, strut, pace, tread, stroll, march, saunter, shamble, flounce, swagger, scuttle* depending upon the occasion. *Sword* can be subdivided into *saber, rapier, broadsword, cutlass, smallsword, claymore, scimitar, falchion, hanger.* Of course these are not all interchangeable. In dialogue, *he said* and *she said* can be monotonous and might be varied by more descriptive verbs: *suggested, replied, snorted, snarled, chuckled,* etc. However, such diction can be overworked until it calls attention to itself and the reader again longs for a plain *he said.*

Words have degrees of specificity; *dog* is more specific than *animal* but less so than *dachshund.* From left to right the following examples become increasingly specific, like the guessing game "animal, vegetable, mineral" that requires players by an ever-narrowing of category to hit upon the exact object that one person has chosen:

structure	house	igloo
America	North America	Mexico
breakfast food	cereal	Froot Loops
TV program	cartoon show	Yogi Bear
plant	vegetable	spinach

The situation determines how precise a word you need. If someone invited you over to his fraternity house to see the new pet, you might like to know in advance whether you are to see a terrier or a tarantula. When you ask, "What's for supper?" you may find "food" an inadequate answer. It might turn out to be filet of fenny snake, eels in eel broth, or haggis.

To be effective, writing must often present precise detail in an exact vocabulary. The amateur sometimes hits well off target, failing to select the exact word among near synonyms or missing the right word altogether: *willfully* is not interchangeable with *willingly*. In "Ring Lardner accomplished in giving vivid realism to the characters of his story," the verb should be *succeeded*. *Perceptively* should be *perceptibly* in "The daily routine of the average American home slows perceptively after dinner." *Gradually* makes no sense in "If a person accused of witchcraft did not confess, he would gradually be hanged." *Notorious* should be *notable* in "John Dewey was affiliated with four notorious universities." Jack Frost Confectionery Sugar XXXX intended to use *induced,* not *influenced,* in "The velvety smoothness of the frosting is influenced by sufficient beating." The emphatic *wallop* is absurdly weak in such journalism as "50-megaton bomb delivers wallop," and so is *punch* in "New missile has sufficient punch to destroy 50-mile area." And the adjective is altogether unsuitable in "Billy Budd went to his death with a boisterous prayer."

Some people distort words by mangling or inflating them, bloating *virtue* into *virtuousness, unconventional* into *unconventionalized, excess* into *excessiveness, mediocre* into *mediocratic, savage* into *savagerous, criminal* into *criminalistic, loyal* into *loyalistic, confidence* into *confidentiality, potential* into *potentiality, analysis* into *analyzation, orient* into *orientate, bias* into *biasness,* and *excess* into *excessiveness. Disobedience* gets warped into *disobeyance, chrysanthemum* into *chryseantheum,* and *defeatist* is blurred into *defeatus* ("a defeatus attitude"). Jargon gets into the act with such pseudo-sophisticated modifiers as *verve-y, un-huge, un-skin-tight, loose-ish,* and *Beethovenwise.*

Then there are ludicrously mixed metaphors: "a sweeping statement that will not hold water," "a deep-seated hatred of long standing," "floods sparked by the hurricane," "uranium rolling out of our ears," "scrubbing the floor with a fine tooth comb," or "industrialism suddenly snowballed." One student wrote, "To really over-balance the apple cart, Poe placed much emphasis on morbidity, and to add the topping to the pudding, he allowed a ship containing dead people to overtake the ship and pass it." Students are not alone in this. In a passage of *The Octopus,* Frank Norris describes the railroad as a galloping monster with iron hoofs, bellowing hoarsely, with a Cyclopean eye, "the leviathan with tentacles of steel," "the monster, the Colossus, the Octopus." Someone wrote that "Socrates died from an overdose of wedlock, but before he went he had the crowned heads shaking in their shoes." This combines mixed metaphor with malapropism, as does "We are living on the edge of an abbess that stands ready to crush us."

¶ **MALAPROPISMS**

A malapropism is a ridiculous confusion of words, usually an unintential pun, in which a word with a similar sound but entirely the wrong meaning is used instead of the precise word. The name comes from Mrs. Malaprop, a character in Sheridan's eighteenth-century comedy *The Rivals,* who blundered into such phrases as "an allegory [alligator] on the banks of the Nile." Such confusion is still with us today when writers have a tin ear, can't spell, or fail to proofread. Thus we are told that an octopus is a person who hopes for the best and that the big dogs that rescue people in the Alps are called Sarah Bernhardts. Students write that Arabs wear turbines on their heads and that the Christian custom that allows a man to have only one wife is called monotony. In a movie review, the *Michigan State News* (January 21, 1963) printed: "Melina Mercouri as Phaedra is superb, but she is surpassed by Raf Vallone who spays [plays] her husband, a wealthy Greek shipowner, sacrificed in Phaedra's fire." *The Lansing State Journal* wrote of Euripides' *Media (Medea)*—mass media, no doubt. The Greeks took another beating when a student wrote of the Four Horsemen of the Acropolis. Another thought that euthanasia (mercy killing) was Youth in Asia. As for religion, we read of gregarious chants in honor of the Lord's annotated. One student wrote of the Quakers, "The Quackers were called Quackers because they quacked when they received the Holy Spurt [Spirit]." (Another wrote of the San Francisco earthquack.) As for the Puritans, "They thought every event was significant since it was a massage from God." But some Puritan colonists became ill or starved and "parished in the wilderness." Other pioneers went west and eventually crossed the Appellations. Some Puritans believed that "the rich are virtuous and the poor are viscous. But as man can only attain true happiness through virtuosity, God wishes a virtuous human race." On the other hand, "Thomas Paine believed it was an absolute waist of time to go to church. Paine says if you want to know God, go out

303

and imbrace a tree or bush, ect." What does *etc.* mean here, let alone *ect.?* Perhaps the student meant to write *eccch.*

Continuing with malaprop American history, we read of "ragged individualism" and learn that "John Marshall knew that if the Constitution of the United States was to last through the years it must be interrupted liberally." We find that "Poe was kicked out of West Point for gamboling." He wrote "tales of the supper natural" and at one point "had a romance with Mrs. Stanard that was purely plutonic." His contemporary Emerson wrote that "A foolish consistency is the hemoglobin [hobgoblin] of little minds." One student explained that Whitman was influenced by Emerson and wrote, "I was simpering, simpering [simmering] and Emerson brought me to a broil [boil]." According to another, "Whitman used much illiteration and compacked verse. He often wrote long and rumbling [rambling] lines." And so we could continue to mangle American literature clear down to *The Christian Science Minotaur.*

In concussion we might attribute some of these faults to spelling, others to careless listening, and some simply to ignorance. Taking notes, one student wrote Karl Marx as Carl Marks. Dimmesdale becomes Doomsdale, Hurstwood becomes Hearsewood, and everything ends in a state of chassis (chaos). Some people slur their speech and so write *another words* for *in other words, next store* for *next door, apart* for *a part* and confuse *pastime* with *past time.* Sometimes a person responds to standard pronunciation with, "Oh, you mean flars [flowers]," "Oh, you mean a bray [beret]," or "Oh, you mean a pome [poem]," Chicago has a Goethe street, but if you ask a taxi driver for it, he's apt to say, "Huh? Oh, you mean Go-eethy Street [or Gertz or Gooth or Goath Street]." So in diction, you can't take pronunciation for granite.

Proofreading is important. The misstriking of one letter on the typewriter can turn *interior* to *inferior, internal* to *infernal, bigger* to *bitter, daughter* to *laughter, ping pong* into *king kong,* while reversing two letters can change *alter* into *later.*

¶ TRANSLATIONS

The problem of finding the right word or idiom is particularly evident in translation. The difficulty is increased because the translator must not only find the denotative equivalent of the original but must also find the right level of diction and avoid wrong connotations. Homonyms and near synonyms increase the translator's headache, and unintentional puns turn it into a nightmare. We often hear of a literary work that it loses in translation. This is particularly true of poetry or of fiction where dialect and slang are involved. *Huckleberry Finn* must seem strange in German. The French are particularly fond of William Faulkner's fiction, but his Mississippi dialect must be odd with a Gallic flavor. James Thurber owned a collection of Western dime novels in French, in which the Redskins were *les Peaux-Rouges,* several of whom taunted a captured scout with the comment, *"Vous vous promenez très tard ce soir, mon vieux!"* In Germany, all Hollywood movies have dubbed dialogue. It seems incongruous to hear Gary Cooper or Errol Flynn speaking fluent German, but it is even more startling to see Randolph Scott gallop up to a Sioux chief, say "How!", and have the Sioux answer, "Wie gehts?" It is really enlightening to see *King Kong* in German as *König Kong, der Herr des Urwalds* and to hear exotic savages crying, *"Ach, hilfe! Kommt der Kong!"* Besides creating the wrong atmosphere, the dialogue is often inexact in dubbed translations. In French versions of Westerns, *redeye* is *vin rouge,* while in Japan, the *OK Corral* is the *Yes Corral.* There is nothing new about this; the late seventeenth-century play *Love's Last Shift* was translated into French as *La Dernière Chemise.*

Americans are equally guilty of inept translation. The French sometimes call De Gaulle "le grand Charles," which *Life* vulgarized into "Big Charlie." Again, someone translated Albert Einstein's *"Raffiniert ist der Herr Gott, aber boshaft ist er nicht"* as "God's tricky, but he ain't mean," which is an inappropriate level of both grammar and diction. One English version of the *Iliad* turns Achilles' manly breast into his shaggy bosom, transforms the ashes of Anchises into cinders, and says of Apollo that "his arrows jiggled as he jogged along." Often a literal translation will not do: the English equivalent of the French *haut peuple étranges* ("strange noblemen") is not *high strange people.*

Grammar as well as diction can be inept in translation, especially if the translator has not mastered the language into which he is translating. The German who translated the instruction book for a German automobile made many dangling modifiers and clumsy passive voices. Dutch translators came up with some amusing sentences when they rendered into English some Amsterdam and Rotterdam criticisms of a visiting American pianist: "In his phrasing he made light rubato's and a little reservation before each heavy chord gives to the melody a friendly heave, which makes the whole movable and also moved and a sensitivity that is originally musical. . . . It is only a few pianists given to play the Mephisto Wals the way the young American pianist . . . did. The temperament both of this work and it's interpretor covered each other entirely and the exorbitant technical difficulties were conquered by . . . overcourage and bravoure. . . . Throughout, he gave evidence of his tender toucher. It is seldom that an audience greets a performing artist with feettrample."

Probably a machine could do as well as this translator. In fact there are electronic translators now converting Russian into English at the rate of about 2,400 words a minute. Its operator needs no knowledge of Russian, and the machine can turn out in half a minute a page that it would take a person forty-five minutes to translate. Considering the vast bulk of scientific and political material that needs to be translated, such machines are invaluable. But they have no sense of style and no ability to distinguish subtleties of diction. One machine turned "The spirit is willing but the flesh is weak" into "The wine is available but the meat is poor." Jargon makes language itself too mechanical. In an essay on Boris Pasternak as a translator, George Reavey wrote: "The babel of modern civilization, the unprecedented and appalling eructation of ambiguous verbiage, and the apparent superfluity of means at man's disposal, have perhaps so inflated his [man's] disordered ego as to lead to some unreflecting contempt for a traditional labor of love."[12]

Samuel Johnson wrote that "No book was ever turned from one language into another, without imparting something of its native idiom," but it is more likely that the native idiom will be lost and replaced by mechanical substitutions or inappropriate connotations. Sometimes these can be unintentionally insulting or ludicrous. In the Nigerian novel *Things Fall Apart,* a missionary to the Ibos keeps mistranslating the word *myself* as *my buttocks,* to the derisive amusement of the Africans. There is no word for *virgin* in the Algonquian language, so the Puritan John Eliot who translated the Bible into Algonquian had to render the wise and foolish virgins as young men.

Some phrases cannot be meaningfully translated. James Baldwin observes in *Giovanni's Room* that "find yourself" is not in any other language and that the phrase reveals something crucial about the American way of life.

306

Circumlocution is related to jargon in that they are ways of evading a direct statement by talking around a subject. Some politicians are such masters of circumlocution that they can give an impression of integrity and profundity when they have actually said nothing but only emitted a blast of hot air. The technique is to discourse in pompous platitudes that are totally vague or else to bumble over a sequence of polysyllabic, pretentious, and preferably abstract words. The listener may not discover any sense in them, but he is apt to be stunned into awed admiration.

In *Roughing It,* Mark Twain had fun bringing together a slangy Nevada miner with a circumlocutory minister fresh from an Eastern seminary. Scotty Briggs, delegated to find someone to bury Buck Fanshaw, asks the minister, "Are you the duck that runs the gospel-mill next door?" When the clergyman is perplexed, Scotty asks again if he is "the head clerk of the doxology-works next door?"

"I am the shepherd in charge of the flock whose fold is next door."

"The which?"

"The spiritual adviser of the little company of believers whose sanctuary adjoins these premises."

After Scotty has proceeded to explain that Buck Fanshaw has "passed in his checks" and that his friends need "to roust out somebody to jerk a little chin-music for us and waltz him through handsome," the minister, increasingly bewildered, pleads, "Would it not expedite matters if you restricted yourself to categorical statements of fact unencumbered with obstructing accumulations of metaphor and allegory?" Scotty replies with more slang from card-playing; he'll have to pass, because he "cant neither trump nor follow suit." Finally he explains that Buck Fanshaw has "gone up the flume," "throwed up the sponge," "kicked the bucket—"

"Ah—has departed to that mysterious country from whose bourne no traveler ever returns."

"Return! I reckon not. Why pard, he's *dead!*"

So getting to business, Scotty asks "if we can get you to help plant him—"

"Preach the funeral discourse? Assist at the obsequies?"

After more explanation, the minister asks, "Had deceased any religious convictions? That is to say, did he feel a dependence upon, or acknowledge allegiance to a higher power? . . . Well, to simplify it somewhat, was he, or rather had he ever been connected with any organization sequestered from secular concerns and devoted to self-sacrifice in the interests of morality?"

"All down but nine—set 'em up on the other alley, pard."

Despite the minister's display of learning, Scotty's language is more vital; and when he eventually becomes a Sunday school teacher and tells Biblical stories in slang to the Nevada small fry, he is immensely successful.

A stock-in-trade comic figure is the long-winded professor addicted to painfully learned and circumlocutory prose. In *Tarzan of the Apes* we find Jane's father, Professor Porter, and his companion Mr. Philander lost in the jungle. The latter breaks into Porter's conversation to inform him that they are being pursued by a lion, but the professor is more annoyed than alarmed:

> "And now I find you guilty of a most flagrant breach of courtesy in interrupting my learned discourse to call attention to a mere quadruped of the genus *Felis*. As I was saying, Mr.—"
>
> "Heavens, Professor, a lion?" cried Mr. Philander, straining his weak eyes toward the dim figure outlined against the dark tropical underbrush.
>
> "Yes, yes, Mr. Philander, if you insist upon employing slang in your discourse, a 'lion.' But as I was saying—"[13]

Obviously, *lion* is not slang, and the jungle is no place for the professor's jargon. Henry James, in his later fiction, tried to make his characters and prose so refined in subtlety that his paragraphs are often monuments of circumlocution. Edith Wharton recalled James's trying to ask an old man the directions to the King's Road at Windsor:

> "My good man, if you'll be good enough to come here, please; a little nearer—so," and as the old man came up: "My friend, to put it to you in two words, this lady and I have just arrived here from *Slough*; that is to say, to be more strictly accurate, we have recently *passed through* Slough on our way here, having actually motored to Windsor from Rye, which was our point of departure; and the darkness having overtaken us, we should be much obliged if you would tell us where we now are in relation, say, to the High Street, which, as you of course know, leads to the Castle after leaving on the left hand the turn down to the railroad station."

Receiving a dazed look, James went on:

> "In short, in short, my good man, what I want to put to you in a word is this: supposing we have already (as I have reason to think we have) driven

past the turn down to the railway station (which in that case, by the way, would probably not have been on our left hand, but on our right), where are we now in relation to . . ."

"Oh, please," I interrupted, feeling myself utterly unable to sit through another parenthesis, "do ask him where the King's Road is."

"Ah—? The King's Road? Just so! Quite right! Can you, as a matter of fact, my good man, tell us where, in relation to our present position, the King's Road exactly *is*?"

"Ye're in it," said the aged face at the window.[14]

This episode is harmlessly amusing, but some readers find Henry James's late prose frustrating and flawed by strained and needless circumlocution. James, however, revised much of his early work to make it conform to his late style, and the results are sometimes unfortunate. In the 1877 edition of *The American,* the hero "was clean-shaved"; in the 1907 revision, "he spoke, as to cheek and chin, of the joy of the matutinal steel." There is no gain in refinement, merely a loss of strength.

¶ EUPHEMISM

Related to circumlocution is euphemism—the avoidance of a direct word or phrase by the substitution of a more genteel, fastidious, prestigious, abstract, or indirect one. Usually a euphemism is intended to make something blunt, ugly, or unpleasant seem more attractive or less offensive. In Melville's *Billy Budd,* we find euphemism and circumlocution combined, when the villainous Claggart says, " '. . . the man in question, had entered His Majesty's service under another form than enlistment.' At this point Captain Vere with some impatience, interrupted him: 'Be direct, man; say impressed men.' "

In a science-fiction story where babies are illegal because of surplus population, a Congressman tells the Director of the Population Planning Agency he has heard that "a bounty has been offered for infants born after the grace period."

"That is false," the director said. "Absolutely incorrect. It is true that remuneration has been offered for information leading to the recovery of illegal infants, but this is in no sense a bounty."

"To many people," the chairman said, "it might appear to be a distinction without a difference."[15]

Some sinister political euphemisms have become so familiar that they have lost their innocent connotations. *Purge* and *liquidation* no longer have any associations other than the blood baths they actually are. Others do not attempt to fool anyone but are used as a matter of discretion, such as calling someone a *prevaricator* instead of a *liar*. John T. McNaughton, the Defense Department's counsel, told a colleague, "Never, under any circumstances whatsoever, use the word 'lie.' Don't use it negatively; don't use it positively. If you have to tell the committee you want to lie down, say 'recline.'" (*The Reader's Digest*, LXXXIII, August, 1963, p. 40.) Elizabethan duellists made a fine art of giving the lie; there were ingenious evasions, but if one wished to send a formal challenge, an expert advised, "In this writing it also behooveth to use all plainness of words and phrases, leaving aside eloquence and ambiguity of speech."

Other euphemisms are not so deadly but can be hypocritical, like the military's speaking of *planned withdrawal* when a retreat takes place or like television's disguising censorship by the term *continuity acceptance* and calling its censors *editors*. Many jobs get euphemistic titles, to avoid unfavorable connotations and gain prestige. Whenever possible, the addition of *engineer, expert, technician,* or *scientist* is helpful. Thus *undertaking* becomes *mortuary science, embalming* is *restorative art, cemetary salesmen* are *memorial counselors, cemetary operators* are *cemetarians,* and the whole death business becomes *grief therapy.* (Of course, *death* and *corpses* are never mentioned on pain of . . . of being launched into eternity.) The Purina Pet Care Center discovered a stupefying variety of euphemistic titles for dog-catcher: *Dog Officer; Dog Constable; Supervisor of Dog Control; Dog Law Enforcement Officer; Stray-Dog Supervisor; Dog Pound Superintendent; Poundkeeper; Canine Controller; Pet Rehabilitation Officer; Chief Humane Officer; Mongrel Administrator; Supervisor, Missing Dog's Bureau; Chief, Dog-Depot Section;* and *Director of the Animal Regulation Division of the Department of Public Health. Garbage men* became *sanitary engineers, pawn brokers* became *loan experts,* and we may find *window washers* becoming *transparent wall engineers.* You might be tempted to say *bull* to all this, but in Puritan communities you'd better not. Victorian society was so outwardly prudish that it refused to mention directly anything physical, lest it seem vulgar or even suggest s-e-x. Obviously, then, *bull* must be a taboo word, and in some places it still is. In America, New Englanders called it a *critter, sire, toro,* or *top cow*; Midlanders referred to it as an *ox, sire,* or *mule cow*; and Southerners termed it a *steer, male cow, beast,* or *brute.* On the prairies, pioneers often built fires with bison manure, made more attractive by the term *buffalo chips.*

Motivational researchers in advertising are particularly practised at using euphemisms to avoid unpleasant financial or physical connotations and have a genius for making bad breath, body odor, gluttony, nausea, constipation, false teeth, pimples, obesity, general pathology and creeping debility seem glamorous or at least palatable. Certainly *halitosis, overindulgence, gastric distress, nature's tardiness, dentures, blemishes* sound more respectable. If you do not survive, at least the aforementioned grief therapists will see you off with extreme unction. No one will call you a stiff. But we do find books in semi-stiff (e.g. paperback) bindings; and if the trend continues, we may find orators giving speeches not from soap boxes but detergent packaging. Euphemisms have become so much a way of thinking that they appear even when there is no point to them. Thus submarines no longer sink; they have *negative buoyancy.*

The opposite of euphemism is the more infrequent dysphemism: for example, naming a restaurant *Sloppy Joe's* or *The Greasy Spoon,* calling butter *axle grease,* drinking *bug juice,* driving a *tin Lizzie,* referring to one's father as *my old man* or to one's wife as *my old lady.*

¶ WORDS AND CENSORSHIP

Sometimes squeamishness leads to demands for censorship. The self-styled pure in heart (apparently not so secure in their purity) challenge the right of authors to use realistic dialogue and description. There are unscrupulous peddlers of pornography who should be prosecuted, but too many censors lack critical discrimination. Some, when questioned, have admitted that they rarely read, have seldom if ever seen a play, have no interest in the arts, but still insist that they are qualified to be arbiters of what should be available to the public. Often, on the basis of book lists or because of the cover or title, they condemn books that they have not read. If they have read the books, they usually select words, phrases, and scenes out of context and use them to show that the entire work is contaminated. But most significant literature, from the Bible to Shakespeare to the latest Nobel Prize winner, has words or passages that may be objectionable by themselves but in the context of the entire work are justified as part of a realistic portrayal of people and conditions. Any work intended to arouse moral indignation at some injustice or inhumanity will have to portray scenes that can create that indignation. Thus they may include the horrors of war, starvation, murder, sexual degradation, bigotry, slums, in order to make the reader fully aware of what is wrong with these things. The issue, therefore, is not whether a book contains certain words and scenes but what the purpose and the effect of these are upon the normal adult reader. Obviously many books are unsuitable for children, but this does not necessarily justify making them unavailable to responsible adults. If an adult has lewd or psychopathic reactions to reading Chaucer, Shakespeare, Hemingway, or Salinger, then he had better consult a psychiatrist rather than clamor for a censor. Practically no one is so sheltered that he has escaped hearing profane or obscene words, and encountering them in a passage of literary realism is not going to make him profane or obscene unless he is so already.

Actually, no word is good or bad in itself. Words are simply sounds to which we have attached meanings. Thus a Yugoslavian immigrant just learning English asked a teacher which words were improper, for she wanted to avoid them but couldn't tell them just from listening or from the dictionary. Most of the taboo words are four-letter monosyllabic ones of Anglo-Saxon origin. The same excremental acts that they name are expressed by other terms that are perfectly acceptable, though they may not be appropriate for dinner-table conversation. It is therefore not the natural acts themselves but simply the mental associations we have evolved that make some words forbidden and their synonyms acceptable. Still, the mental associations are there, so it is advisable not to shock people by offensive language. But in literature such language may be necessary for realistic portrayal. This is not necessarily "strong language"; some people of limited vocabulary and impoverished imagination rely so heavily upon a few favorite four-letter words that their speech is insufferably stale.

Often the genteel tradition is ridiculous, as when the Victorians draped the legs (or rather "limbs") of their pianos lest they arouse lascivious thoughts. Such prudery is really dirty-minded, seeing dirt where a wholesome mind would find none. Certainly anyone who responded lecherously to piano legs was in a bad way. The absurd delicacy of nineteenth-century Puritanism appears in Edward Ellis's *The Hunter's Cabin*. In a perilous moment, Annie, the genteel heroine, is trapped with the heroic hunter Ferrington in a cabin besieged by Indians. Seeing some movement in the bush, Ferrington utters the uncouth statement:

"It is a devilish Indian contrivance—"

" 'Sh, George; do not speak thus," she interrupted, noticing the expression, in spite of the tumultuous feelings that reigned in her breast.

"I beg pardon. It is an Indian contrivance, and there are Shawnees hid behind that same bush."

When Whitman and Mark Twain broke some of the taboos, to use a more realistic language of the people, their works were denounced for using vile obscenities. *Huckleberry Finn* was banned in some communities for containing such impure words as *dern* and *sweat*. In *Pygmalion,* George Bernard Shaw had fun with the proper Edwardians' squeamish shibboleth against *bloody.* Henry Higgins' housekeeper tells him:

. . . there is a certain word I must ask you not to use. The girl has just used it herself because the bath was too hot. It begins with the same letter as bath. She knows no better; she learnt it at her mother's knee. But she must not hear it from your lips.

Today, when the ban against *Tropic of Cancer* and *Lady Chatterly's Lover* has been lifted, it seems as if almost any language can be allowed, provided the author has a serious purpose and is not merely trying to give his readers a cheap excitement. Usually there is no need for an author to indulge in ubiquitous obscenities. Yet some censorship groups and even some teachers try to prohibit writing which contains even the mildest profanity. It is a truism that beauty and vileness are in the mind of the beholder. In John Steinbeck's *The Grapes of Wrath,* Casy says "Maybe you wonder about me using bad words. Well, they ain't bad to me no more. They're jus' words folks use, an' they don't mean nothing bad with 'em." [16] Certainly *hell* and *damn,* as used colloquially, have lost any theological meaning and are merely expletives and intensifiers, as when something is called "damned good," "damned fine," "important as hell," "colorful as hell," "sleepy as hell," or "a helluva great guy." When you read that "All hell broke loose," you are not likely to be converted to diabolism.

One of the books most often attacked by would-be censors is J. D. Salinger's *The Catcher in the Rye.* At the climax, the protagonist encounters the most notorious of all four-letter words scrawled on a school wall. He is revolted and tries to erase the word, which he sees symbolising the modern loss of innocence. In context, the word makes the empathic reader share Holden's and Salinger's moral indignation, whereas the would-be censors are mistakenly indignant at Salinger. The rest of the book is sprinkled with *hells* and *damns* used in a purely harmless fashion. These passages do not make Holden corrupt, nor will they corrupt any reader in his right mind. The lesson to be learned here is not that the book should be censored, but that Holden has, as he admits, a lousy vocabulary.

Hell and *damn* have become trite utility words that the careful stylist should avoid unless they are appropriate in dialogue. As for well-meant profanity, *The New Yorker*'s editor Harold Ross once told John McNulty, "Well, God bless you, McNulty, goddam it," and James Thurber observed that Ross had two deities, one upper and one lower case.[17] Conversely, an Australian clergyman denied that bullocks cannot be driven without blasphemy. To prove his point, he cracked the whip and roared, "You rapturous archangels! You sublimated cherubim! You sanctified innocents! Get ye up and hence!" And they did.[18] Which shows that profanity is more in the mind and the manner than in the words themselves. As the Virginian says, "When you call me that, smile."

The controversy in California over the *Dictionary of American Slang* can best illustrate the inverted thinking of some censors. The dictionary, a scholarly reference work, includes among its more than 20,000 definitions about 200 that contain obscene words. Since these are part of American English, the compilers had no choice but to include them. A person consulting the dictionary might run across them, but they are not in a context that would give a normal person any erotic or antisocial ideas. Yet in the spring of 1963, a student using an assumed name checked out of the Sacramento library a copy of the dictionary and turned the stolen volume over to a state assemblyman. The California State Superintendent of Public Instruction denounced the book as "a practicing handbook of sexual perversion," and recommended that schools censor the dictionary on the grounds that it is unfit for children. Stuart Flexner, one of the authors, replied that many books are not written for children, e.g., *Advanced Geometry, Gone with the Wind, How to Prepare Your Income Tax*.[19] And American courts have ruled it unconstitutional to ban books for adults because they are not suitable for children. Most librarians protested the pressure for censorship, and the book's defenders pointed out that any dictionary contains the word *sin* and defines most of the individual sins without in any way tempting readers to commit them. Yet some of the would-be censors, when challenged, said that they could not control themselves when they encountered a suggestive word in print. Who then, has the dirty mind? Some would-be censors refused to look at the book, but others carefully excerpted all the taboo words and compiled lists of them. Various ultraconservative organizations and hate groups joined the fray, denouncing as immoral and probably subversive the politicians, teachers, and librarians who defended the book. Some self-appointed custodians of public morals wanted to discharge the entire state school board. No one ever tried to condemn the book under the state penal code against obscenity, because they knew they did not have a legitimate case; instead they tried to ban the book and its defenders without due process of law. Censorship groups urged others to reproduce their lists of "dirty words" and circulated them widely throughout the state, distributing them indiscriminately on street corners and in housing units, stores, and parking areas. Many fell into the hands of children, but one censor insisted, "I don't care if every teen-ager in California reads the filthy excerpts we're showing. What we're trying to do is protect unborn generations." [20] One distributor of the lists said he hoped to cover the state with 100,000 copies, to make sure that nobody missed reading the "dirty words." A mother wrote Mr. Flexner that she had never heard of any of the taboo words and that his dictionary defined them all wrong. Another correspondent "suggested the Constitution be rewritten on 'sound principles' to eliminate freedom of speech and guarantee 'each one a wholesome . . . life' instead." [21] Ultimately the furor died down; all it succeeded in doing was to provide an outlet for various social and political frustrations and to give the self-righteous would-be censors a chance to make certain that everybody learned the words that they wanted concealed from everybody. When a woman congratulated Dr. Johnson for omitting indecent words from his dictionary, he replied, "So you have been looking for them, Madam?"

Exercise 34: There are 320 words in the following passage from James Fenimore Cooper's *The Deerslayer*. By cutting all surplus diction and lifeless detail, Mark Twain reduced the passage to 220 words; and the omission of 100 words tightened the episode and made it more dramatic.

Without changing any of Cooper's words, underline those that can be omitted, and see if you can do as well as Mark Twain.

In a minute he was once more fastened to the tree, a helpless object of any insult or wrong that might be offered. So eagerly did every one now act, that nothing was said. The fire was immediately lighted in the pile, and the end of all was anxiously expected.

It was not the intention of the Hurons absolutely to destroy the life of their victim by means of fire. They designed merely to put his physical fortitude to the severest proofs it could endure, short of that extremity. In the end, they fully intended to carry his scalp into their village, but it was their wish first to break down his resolution, and to reduce him to the level of a complaining sufferer. With this view, the pile of brush and branches had been placed at a proper distance, or one at which it was thought the heat would soon become intolerable, though it might not be immediately dangerous. As often happened, however, on these occasions, this distance had been miscalculated, and the flames began to wave their forked tongues in a proximity to the face of the victim that would have proved fatal in another instant had not Hetty rushed through the crowd, armed with a stick, and scattered the blazing pile in a dozen directions. More than one hand was raised to strike the presumptious intruder to the earth; but the chiefs prevented the blows by reminding their irritated followers of the state of her mind. Hetty, herself, was insensible to the risk she ran; but, as soon as she had performed this bold act, she stood looking about her in frowning resentment, as if to rebuke the crowd of attentive savages for their cruelty.

"God bless you, dearest sister, for that brave and ready act," murmured Judith, herself unnerved so much as to be incapable of exertion; "Heaven itself has sent you on its holy errand."

Exercise 35: Condense or revise the following sentences to make them as concise as possible. For example, "The wealth of industry is market creating" can be reduced to "Industrial wealth creates markets."

1. The basis of the purpose of the novel *Babbitt* is to expose vulgarity and intolerance.
2. The test of the poet is to use simplicity and precision in his usage of words.
3. Conwell's first statement concerning the attainment of wealth states that a man can attain it at home.

4. George Stevens budgeted for the spending of $15 million for *The Greatest Story Ever Told*.
5. When a person entertains today, it seems imperative that he must have liquor on hand.
6. Today there are many countries that practice a democratic form of government.
7. Many years prior to this day, Richard III was killed at Bosworth.
8. The hope is in some of our minds that we can finish ahead of the schedule that we have.
9. If people try to express views other than what the group feels to be right, they are ostracized and a great dislike for these individuals arises.
10. This is symbolic of how God's love is of an evil crushing quality.
11. Without any pause for the sanitation of showering, he went directly to the pool.
12. Wolfert stood apart by himself alone, observing the scene with an indifferent eye.
13. The Batman descended down from the roof by means of a rope.
14. The chestnut blight killed the life of all the mature trees.
15. Ebenezer secretly thought to himself that the weather seemed ominous.
16. Margarine is cheaper than the seventy-cent spread, and it doesn't cost as much.
17. The hardened jargonaut never uses one word when he is able to make employment in addition of several other words besides.
18. It is advised and cautioned that endemic ursine creatures not be offered digestible sustenance within the confines of the park.
19. The electric coffee pot is something that I wonder how I got along without before I had it.
20. If one should chance to partake of an illicit beverage that is the product of domestic distillation, he may endanger his ocular faculties to the point of blindness or may even render himself a member of those who are not of the living, if the beverage under consideration was vaporized and condensed not in a copper cooking utensil and curvilinear tube but was produced in those containing the malleable metal symbolized as Pb, the chemical sign for lead.

Exercise 36: Underline the dead wood that should be cut from the following:

1. In my opinion I consider Billy Budd to be a tragic hero.
2. A Deistic belief was that of the concept of God as a prime mover.
3. Not everyone approved of the placing of the defeated territory under military rule.
4. In contrast to frontier life, life today seems to be of a more pessimistic nature.

317

5. A battered house greets the family the day as they move in.
6. One of the main characters in *The Octopus* is that of Buck Annixter.
7. Gatsby does nearly everything with the idea in his mind of winning Daisy again.
8. Huck is from a family quite dissimilar to that of Tom's.
9. There has been tyranny in nearly all the governments that man has created during his existence.
10. In *Walden* Thoreau wrote the results of the experience of the living in a state close to that of nature.
11. I came back to my room and was shocked by all the bags, clothes, and boxes that were piled high in my room.
12. Since the beginning of time to the present day, man has been afraid of crocodiles.
13. Godzilla felt the same towards King Kong also.
14. Freezing foods has become one of the most popular methods of food preservation.
15. Every time I walk past Bessey Hall, I imagine in my mind seeing about ten students in each room wearing striped uniforms, scraping tin cups across the windows.
16. Because of her very nature of foundation, society must fight individuality.
17. Another unjustifiable rule is the rule that prohibits freshmen from having cars on campus.
18. For the past couple of three weeks we have been studying about anatomy.
19. That's too good of an idea.
20. Sharecroppers did not own the farms upon which they were working and living on.
21. We met a fellow named of Gonzales Pilkington O'Toole the Fourth.
22. The accused did not reply back when the prosecutor asked him to confess to his guilt.
23. The doctors never saw that small of a child.
24. This type of thump keg is a good type of thump keg because it takes the impurities out of the whiskey.
25. That is the way in which Americans would like to be in the modern society of today.

Exercise 37: Replace the malapropisms on page 303 with the right words.

Exercise 38: Replace any faulty diction or typographical errors in the following sentences:

1. Lincoln waited until 1863 to issue his Emaciation Proclamation.

318

2. Scott Fitzgerald's stories are full of long, blonde women, beautiful and sofasticated.
3. In Faulkner's *The Bear*, Isaac McCaslin learns of his grandfather's miscegenation and discovers the tinted line of his ancestors.
4. Many of Hawthorne's stories are moral allergies.
5. Blanche DuBois became notarized in her town for her loose morals.
6. It was all many a pioneer could do to eek out an existence.
7. The Rev. Mr. Hale became dissolutioned with the Salem withcraft trials.
8. Professor Crabshaw felt that the murder of the princes could not be contributed to Richard III.
9. In *The Grapes of Rath,* the Joads were depraved of almost everything.
10. In Faulkner's "Dry September," Miss Minnie Cooper went down town wearing a shear dress that was a reveling garment.
11. Holden Caulfield was hesitant about excepting adult responsibilities.
12. The P. and S. W. Railroad charged exuberant freight rates.
13. Horpington felt that the lack of electives narrowly circumsized the curriculum.
14. The Arias disbelieved in the Christian trinity.
15. School droopouts contribute to juvenile deliquency.
16. After a long, hot day, the cook was in a state of nervous prostitution.
17. Poe's poetry intensifies the aurora of mystery.
18. The A & P was full of costumers the day before Thanksgiving.
19. Zachary went to business school to learn bookeeping.
20. The bubonic plaque devastated England in 1349.
21. The Puritans would not tolerate any religious hearsay.
22. The villian tried to destroy the newlyweds' martial bliss.
23. We now have freeways where formally there were farms.
24. The Jerrybuilders are creating a housing development next store to the high school.
25. A swarm of gnats inflitrated the campground.

Exercise 39: Underline the dead wood that should be cut from the following:

1. Social workers have been working for years in trying to find a remedy to this problem.
2. In Stephen Crane's "The Open Boat" the story is written in an impressionistic manner.
3. Smurdly is too kind of a man to take advantage of anyone.
4. Grendel took and swallowed the thane.
5. Babbitt and his friends urged for conservative politics.
6. I made matching muu-muus for the whole entire family, but Grandma she wouldn't even try hers on.

7. Has it ever occurred to you that chicken soup with rice it should be chicken with rice soup?
8. The Greenland whale was a-twitching of his tail.
9. Martin Eden realized that he did not have a big enough of a vocabulary.
10. "I wonder who it is at the door," she said, clutching the monkey's paw in her hand.
11. This here man is to have apartment B1B1.
12. Built in 1901, the Oconaluftee pioneer farmhouse is not so old of a building.
13. Here comes the Good Humor man coming up the road.
14. There wasn't nobody noticed the hidden secret passage through the fireplace.
15. You've eaten an entire whole package of Necco candies.
16. That there speck on Mt. Rushmore it is James Mason chasing Cary Grant up around on George Washington's nose.
17. In *The Lost Weekend*, Ray Milland hung whiskey bottles out of the window and hid them secretly up in the chandeliers.
18. What sort of a coffin contains sacred earth in it?
19. Hawkeye went and followed the trail of the treacherous Huron.
20. What is the unknown secret ingredient put in the salad?

18 √ The Future of Grammar

What, it is often asked, is the language coming to? Are we making progress in communication and literacy, or were the critics right who saw in *Webster III* the opening blast of some linguistic Armageddon? Can we arrive at a universal language that can overcome the barriers of tribalism, provincialism, and nationalism and thus promote the cause of international understanding and cooperation? Will we become strangled in the red tape of jargon or be brainwashed by some totalitarian Newspeak? If we develop an international tongue, will local ones become dead and forgotten? Should we, and can we, streamline and simplify grammar and spelling by regulation rather than by linguistic evolution?

From the Middle Ages until almost modern times, Latin served as the international language of Western scholarship and diplomacy, but its knowledge was confined to scholars and diplomats. During the eighteenth century, on the continent, French largely replaced it as the language not only of diplomacy but of the cultured aristocracy. At the time of Napoleon's invasion of Russia, many Russian nobles, living in the artificial, sheltered world of court and privilege, spoke only French, then suddenly the language of the enemy. Nevertheless, obviously, national barriers had not been overcome.

So why not have a new language altogether? As early as 1887, Dr. L. L. Zamenhof invented Esperanto (hope), a synthetic language for international use, based on a streamlined combination of various Romance languages. Esperanto did not come into general use; and when the United Nations was founded and the need for communication acute, technology and simultaneous translation provided a solution to the problem. Michael Fraym in *The Manchester Guardian* parodied the Esperanto approach in his proposed anthem for the Common Market, which concludes:

321

Wir werken ensemble kos wir laik es dass Weh,
Nous sommes ein gemütlich and schnug Familie-Grupp—
Spaghetti pour Breakfaast und Schnitzel pour Tee—
So Gott geb lang vita au grand Kommun Krupp!

We are unlikely to have such a spoken smorgasbord, but there
have been linguistic simplifications. Turkish and Japanese introduced the Roman alphabet, and Russian and Arabic (in some
areas) were simplified. German has dropped the old Teutonic type
and is streamlining its script. The Communist Chinese government
decided in 1956 to simplify some of its complicated brush-stroke
characters, but the program backfired when people all over the
country started inventing their own abbreviated characters, creating illegible inconsistency. One newspaper complained of the resultant breakdown in the postal service and sighed, "Who would
have thought that the reliability, which was unshaken by civil
wars, would succumb to the vagaries of writing reform." The Chinese claim that they plan ultimately to replace their ideographic
characters with the Roman alphabet.

On the other hand, there have been twentieth-century movements to re-establish an older national tongue, such as Gaelic in
Ireland and Hebrew in Israel. (Because of Nazi nationalism, Hitler
closed the six hundred schools of Esperanto in the Third Reich.)
But these "reforms" seem to lack urgency for the ordinary people,
who do not give up their habitual vernacular and embrace some
unfamiliar tongue just because of government pressure and propaganda, any more than Americans could become fluent in Algonquian if politicians decided that its revival would promote national
pride.

Instead, the trend is to the more widely used languages, to the
extent that some local ones may be completely lost except to scholars; and in some cases, with no written form and no recordings,
may be entirely lost. Cherokee, the only American Indian language
with a written form devised by one of its own members, is a case in
point. Sequoyah's Cherokee syllabary, with a character for each
syllable (eighty-six) rather than each phoneme in the language,
may well be a more efficient system than our own alphabet. Now
the Cherokees are almost all English-speaking; and if another language is to be taught in their schools, they are interested in learning one of the major European ones to broaden their education.
Those who still speak Cherokee learn it only at home. In its writ-

322

ten form, it may be one of the few Indian tongues that will escape oblivion, but the spoken form is dying out.

A similar situation exists in India and parts of Africa, where English, from the days of the British Empire, has been taught in the schools and is the language of the civil service and of the governmental and diplomatic elite. It also serves as a means of communication between dialects and tribes. Except for Communist China, English is increasingly used in Asia to conduct business, banking, transportation, science, and politics. First the British and now the Americans have exerted tremendous political and economic pressure in the Orient, with the result that despite emergent nationalism, English has become a status symbol. In Hong Kong it is the official language as well as the elite tongue of the upper classes. Since World War II, the Japanese and the Koreans have made English compulsory in the public schools. Despite former Dutch colonization, the Indonesians use English in advanced university courses. In Malaysia, English rivals Malay as one of the two legal languages. Tagalog is the official language of the Philippines, but in practice, English breaches dialectal barriers and is the language of the law, newspapers, the schools, politics, and business. In India, it was the legal language, and the thirteen million who can use it are the dominant power. When in 1965, Hindi replaced English as the official language, a series of bloody riots ensued in which a railway station was burned and over seventy people were killed. The rioters were not inspired by a love of English but by a resentment that Hindi, the language of northern India, was superimposed over their regional tongues. English is no longer official in Pakistan, but it is required in the schools and is necessary for communication between Bengali in the East and Urdu in the West. In Africa, English is the official language of Nigeria (which has over 250 regional languages or dialects), Ghana, Sierra Leone, and Gambia, and is widely used from Capetown to Cairo. Even in Latin America, English is competing with Spanish as the language of commerce. And in Europe, many schoolchildren elect or are required to study English for some years, especially in Germany, Scandinavia, and Russia.

English may receive a profound impact by its use as a lingua franca in countries which are now ready to develop industrially and participate fully in international affairs. Perhaps it will be modified by the native tongues of those who use it around the world. Pidgin English has been in use in Africa and in the Orient for some time. This is basically English words (altered by local pronunciation) grafted onto the local syntax, or sometimes used with no apparent syntax at all, with tense, number, case, and gender all jettisoned. It can be much more elaborate than "no tickee, no shirtee." A sailor might be "him fella allatime belong boat," and an often quoted specimen is the Chinese servant's explanation that his master's sow had produced a litter: "Him cow pig have kittens." In Edgar Rice Burroughs' *The Monster Men,* the Chinese servant warns the heroine, "No talkee so strong, walle have ear all same labbit." Since pidgin was used to conduct trade, the word is a slurring of *business* into *bidgin* into *pidgin.*

Pidgin is completely unacademic, but even when Orientals have studied English, they sometimes produce a strange amalgam. Here is an essay submitted by an Indian for a civil-service examination in 1961 and reprinted by Evelyn Wood in *Thought,* published in Delhi, January 20, 1962:

The cow is one wonderful animal, also he is quadruped and because he is female he gives milk, but he will do so only when he is got child. He is same like God sacred to Hindu and useful to man. But he has got four legs to-gather. Two are forward and two are afterwards.

His whole body can be utilized for use. More so the milk. What it can do? Various ghee, butter, cream, curds, whey, kova, and the condensed milk and so forth. Also he is useful to cobbler, watermans and mankind generally.

His motion is slow only. That is because he is of amplitudinous species and also his other motion is much useful to trees, plants as well as making flat cakes in hand and drying in sun.

He is the only animal that extricates his feeding after eating. Then afterwards he eats with his teeth whom are situated in the inside of his mouth. He is incessantly in the meadows on the grass.

His only attacking and defending weapons are his horns especially so when he has got a child. This is done by bowing his head whereby he causes the weapons to be parallel to the ground of the earth and instantly proceed with great velocity forwards.

He has got tail also, but not like other similar animals. It has hair on the other end of the other side. This is done to frighten away the flies which alight on his whole body and chastises him unceasingly whereupon he gives hit with it.

The palms of his feet are so soft unto the touch, so that the grasses he eats would not get crushed. At night time he reposes by going down on the ground and then he shuts his eyes like his relatives the horse which does not do so.

This is the Cow! [1]

This has a weird eloquence, unlike the examples of supposedly elegant English seriously offered in J. da Fonseca's and P. Carolino's *The New Guide of the Conversation, in Portuguese and English* that seems to have been inspired by a drunken nightmare in Hong Kong:

"It delay me to eat some wal nutskernels: take care not leave to pass the season."

"Be tranquil, i shall throw you any nuts during the shell is green yet."

"The artichoks grow its?"

"I have a particular care of its, because i know you like the bottoms."

Only Chinese rivals English in the number of people speaking it. It seems that many Westerners consider Chinese an incredibly difficult and inefficient language, but this is far from the case. In the twentieth century, there has been a profound linguistic revolution in China. Long before the Christian era the written language of China had become archaic. It had stood still while the spoken language was changing through the centuries; and gradually the rulers realized that governmental ordinances, philosophical writings, legal statutes, and classical literature were all unintelligible to the ordinary person. Said the Prime Minister Kung Sun Hung, about 120 B.C., "The imperial edicts and laws . . . are not generally understood by the poorly educated public officials, who are incapable of explaining them to the people." Here was a major administrative problem, yet conservatism smothered common sense. One emperor, Shih Huang Ti (200 B.C.) saw the need for modernization, but in trying to bring it about he ordered a complete holocaust of Chinese books and so outraged the scholars that they cordially detested him for the next two thousand years.

There evolved in China a civil service system in which the scholar was supreme. Fitness for administrative service was determined by the candidate's knowledge of the difficult, dead literary language and the philosophy written in it. Accordingly there grew up a scholastic class or hierarchy, which passed the precious learning from hand to hand, often from father to son. Ostensibly democratic, the system became very nearly hereditary. Imagine a country far more populous than the United States, where every candidate for public office, whether judge, tax assessor, policeman, or dog catcher, had as the sole test of fitness to pass an examination on *Beowulf* in the original Anglo-Saxon ("Hwaet we gar-dena in geardagum. . . ."), using Anglo-Saxon himself in his examination paper. Imagine, moreover, not a fairly simple *Beowulf* in alphabetic symbols, but a rebus *Beowulf* expressed in pictures, each word having its individual picture, and each picture a complicated arrangement of lines having small observable relation to the idea expressed. Imagine further a *Beowulf* which is not a story but an exposition of the most abstruse philosophical ideas which the candidate is expected not only to remember but to understand.

There you have the system which ruled China, with some interruptions, for several millennia. Under it the mandarin class continued to rule until 1905, when the Manchu Empress agreed to abolish the examinations, together with the many abuses which had grown up around them.

Quite apart from this elaborate literary-political-philosophical system were the various vernaculars of the common man—of the Cantonese in the south and the northerner in Peking. No one bothered about this vulgar speech, yet little by little it developed a literature. It appeared first in the early centuries of the Christian era, in anonymous popular songs and ballads. In the ninth century, vernacular prose began to appear, to flower magnificently in the great anonymous novels of the sixteenth century. Yet at the beginning of the twentieth century, this living language and literature were ignored by classical scholars except for entertainment.

The breakdown of the traditional civil-service examinations was followed by the revolution of 1911, after which the vernacular came into its own. For the first time, the actual speech of the people was officially recognized. The new national language was the northern dialect, which was simpler and more mature than the southern and which was intelligible to nine out of ten Chinese. It was not the same as the tongue of the old novels and ballads, for the Chinese vernacular had changed just as Middle English developed into Modern English. According to Hu Shih, professor of philosophy at Peking before the Communists took over, the new idiom is "the most highly developed language in the world." If so, and because of its numerical rivalry to English, it deserves a comparison with English. In alphabet and orthography, English is infinitely superior to the Chinese pictographic characters. It is in grammar that Chinese may be better developed. It is an inflectionless language that uses form words instead of changed endings to express tense, number, case, and so on. Modern English is developing in the same direction, using the form words *has, have,* and *had* instead of inflections to indicate the perfect tenses of the verb. In certain constructions, *do, it, there,* and *to* have lost all definiteness of meaning to become merely formal units. Instead of the termination *-ess,* the feminine gender is often indicated by the formal use of *she, girl,* or *woman* (*a she-wolf, a girl bandit, a woman lawyer*), and other constructions are comparable (*a child prodigy, the child-buyer, a hound-dog man, the god-seeker*). Chinese is a monosyllabic language, with a sentence order much like English (usually subject-verb-object).

Perhaps the most significant likeness between Chinese and English is functional shift, by which a word can function as various parts of speech, being a modifier in one sentence, a noun in another, a verb in a third, and so on. Thus *round* may be a noun in "a round of golf," a verb in "to round the cape," an adjective in "a round ball," a preposition in "round the house," and an adverb in "to walk round." Functional shift is one of the distinctive features that gives modern English its flexibility. Chinese has gone even further in this direction; there are no distinctive parts of speech but just words whose function determines their classification. English has not yet attained this ideal state, but it is heading that way. In the cold war, the two languages are not apt to influence each other, and it is ironic that they have so much in common.

It is notable that the efficient simplicity of Chinese came about because it developed for twenty centuries unimpeded and uninterfered with by the literary class. As a result of this complete freedom, the language underwent a revision more logical and more thorough than any other in the world. This could not have happened so completely without scholarly neglect. Scholarly attention would have tried to arrest the process of growth, and the good fortune of Chinese was its complete freedom to change.

Today the Communists seem to be tampering with the language, developing political jargon and propagandistic juggling. Meanwhile, in English there is an increasing gap between the terminology of science and the language of literature and between the jargon of bureaucracy and everyday speech. The linguistic gap between the advanced scientist and the man in the street is almost as wide as it was when Latin was the language of scholarship. (In fact many scientific terms are borrowed or coined from Latin.) We have, in

327

addition, a pseudo-scientific approach, perhaps comparable to the medieval astrologer or alchemist, used in various businesses and particularly in advertising. While the scientist and the sociologist are busy trying to strip words of connotations and arrive at "operational definitions," Madison Avenue makes words fairly reek with connotative meaning. And with the proliferation of new drugs, fabrics, and cosmetics (legend has it that all possible syllables are dumped into a computer which obediently grinds out all the possible combinations for names) and new products by more conventional coinages (from *rayon* and *nylon* we now have a suffix *-on* or *-lon,* as in *Ban-lon, Herculon, Corlon, Fabulon,* and even *Silk-a-lon*), scientific and advertising activity produces a linguistic fallout which is sifting into the vernacular.

Can we predict at all the future of the language? We have noted several patterns of development: the spoken language is written down, the writings become "scripture," the "scriptures" become the language of scholarship and a new vernacular develops, sometimes by peaceful evolution and sometimes by conquest. The pattern of language and the main linguistic problem is in the balance of freedom and authority. Arthur Miller writes, "I will listen to anything that leads toward lucidity, to nothing that only simplifies." [2] Can you, should you regulate a living language without fossilizing it? Language has a way of regulating itself, and it is unlikely that we shall ever have complete anarchy. If we have another separation of the "scriptures" from the vernacular, it will probably be specialized jargon—administrative, military, scholarly, sociological—from the main current of English. This is not necessarily sinister, but George Orwell in *1984* eloquently described the dangers of Newspeak.

And then there's Mars. Two favorite devices of science-fiction writers are: either the people in outer space are beings of superior intelligence who know all about us already or who learn English with phenomenal ease, or they use telepathy, or both. We in turn may have developed ESP, LSD, and subliminal advertising on Telestar to work out an Esperanto for outer space. Let us hope so if we do find intelligent life there. We have enough linguistic problems on our own planet.

To solve them, grammarians have been devising new approaches to English. *Commonsense Grammar and Style* is a descriptive grammar in historical perspective, following the principle that usage governs linguistic change, but it employs traditional terminology for the sake of the general reader. The new grammars are competing to a degree among themselves; and some methods that discard the old terminology provide so many new terms that they require an extensive glossary. A brief sketch may introduce the main schools to the reader, who can pursue them in more depth if he wishes.

The main methods of describing English grammar are traditional, structural, transformational-generative, and tagmemic. To invent classifications for the structure of language, linguists have devised various systems. Linguists may be anthropologists, psychologists, philosophers, literary critics, and scientists of various disciplines as well as grammarians.

Structural linguistics is as much a branch of anthropology as of grammar. Concerned with describing verbal behavior rather than with verbal skills and literature, it considers language as a set of observable data that can be catalogued rather like botanical and zoological specimens. The first prominent structural linguist in America was Leonard Bloomfield, whose book *Language* (first published in 1914 and revised in 1933) became the seminal volume in the discipline. Basically, structural linguistics grew out of the study of American Indian and other "primitive" languages that did not follow an Indo-European model. Linguists approaching such languages with no preconceived ideas about their structure found that none are really primitive, that all are complex and sophisticated on their own terms. One of Bloomfield's disciples, Benjamin Lee Whorf, did extensive study of the language of the Hopi Indians and concluded that the structure of a person's language reflects and influences the way in which he understands his environment.

With scientific detachment, the structured linguist makes no value judgments and does not assume the superiority of languages descended from Latin and/or German. His technique is to find an informant (a native speaker willing to work with him; Charles Carpenter Fries tape-recorded 50 hours of telephone conversations with his acquaintances in Ann Arbor) and to record his language, using the International Phonetic Alphabet (IPA), since our 26-letter one does not cover all phonemes—the minimal units of sound. English has from 40 to 45 phonemes (linguists disagree on the number) with a variety of pitch, stress, and juncture, or silent pause. These are arranged into morphemes—the minimal units of meaning. The structural linguist prefers the term "morpheme" to "word" because the latter is vague and often a matter of opinion; *never-*

theless may be considered one or three words, but it is indisputably three morphemes. Structural linguists try to identify all morphemes in a language and then classify them into base morphemes, affixal morphemes (prefixes and suffixes), and intonational morphemes. In regular English verbs, past tense endings and third person present singular -*s* endings are also morphemes. Pitch sequences indicate questions or emphasis through rising and falling intonations, and stress morphemes indicate such differences as that between *líght córd* (for turning on a lamp) and *líght córd* (a cord that is lightweight). On paper we can see such distinctions through context or punctuation; in the spoken language, which is what concerns structural linguistics, they are indicated by intonation. Thus, in addition to grammar, structural linguists study phonology, morphology, and syntax.

Structural linguistics became prominent in the 1930's and 1940's. In the 1950's, Charles Carpenter Fries, James Sledd, W. Nelson Thomas, and others tried to apply it to teaching. Fries developed a structural system for identifying parts of speech by a new classification, using four structural classes, and for describing the structural elements of the sentence by fifteen function groups (A through O). But Fries and Sledd were methodists, not theoreticians. Most linguists consider theirs a pure rather than an applied science and maintain that linguistics ceases to be structural when it is applied. By this time structural linguistics was on the decline; and towards the end of the decade, transformational-generative grammar, as advocated by Noam Chomsky, Robert Lees, and Owen Thomas, began to supplant it.

The transformational, generative, or transformational-generative grammarians retain respect for traditional grammar and use its terminology together with refinements of their own. They claim that the structuralists merely describe different kinds of sentences and that this is not enough; in addition, the linguist must explain how all the possible sentences are made. Accordingly, transformational-generative grammarians seek to theorize a grammar that will generate only grammatically valid sentences and eliminate invalid ones—that will generate, for instance, "The boy rides a bike" and prevent "The boy bikes the ride" or "The store were divide four section." This is the generative part. The transformational part is concerned with showing how an infinite number of sentences can be made from a limited number of basic structures. The basic

330

sentence patterns are "kernel structures," and all others are "transforms" or variations of the kernels. Transformational-generative linguists try to see how the kernels generate all possible sentences within a language, especially by analyzing the way in which a statement can be transformed from the active to the passive voice, from a declarative sentence to a question, from an independent to a subordinate construction. Then transformational-generative grammar adds phonology (the study of a language's sound system), distinguishing four categories: words that are acceptable and do occur (*sing*), words that are acceptable and do not occur (*fing*), words that are unacceptable but do occur (*psychology*, with its silent *p*), and words that are unacceptable and do not occur (*blfstyk*). The second is conceivable though nonexistent in English; the fourth is anomalous and could not be an English word.

Combining the syntactic with the phonetic description of a sentence, transformational-generative grammar leads to a semantic interpretation—the sentence's meaning. Here a problem is to distinguish between possible alternative and ambiguous meanings (e.g. "He shot the bolt on the door" could mean that he locked it or that he shot it with a firearm) and to rule out anomalous sentences like "The bricks drank the giraffe."

Yet another school of linguistics is the tagmemic one, headed by Kenneth Pike, which tries to go beyond the sentence and to include consideration of artistic, social, and connotative responses to language. Pike asserts that "Beyond the linguist lives the artist" and that "when the linguist is through with his fun and his mechanisms, the important problems of value permanence, esthetic impact, and social relevance must then be tackled by the literary critic."

This explanation of the new linguistic approaches to grammar is quite streamlined; the actual details become highly complex. There is no short and simple account of the various linguistic theories and methods. Nowadays, some administrators are requiring English teachers to have competence in linguistics rather than in literature, apparently in the expectation that linguistics will solve students' problems with reading, writing, and speech. In fact, linguistics is a highly theoretical "pure" science. Linguists do not concern themselves with utilitarian application of their concepts and do not wish high school students or college freshmen to study structural or transformational-generative grammar. Many linguistic texts are

331

written in mathematically expressed formulas and theories on such a high level of abstraction that they are incomprehensible to all but professionals.

If the linguists themselves do not intend their work to lead to pedagogical application, what value does it have for the regular teacher of English and for his students? Linguistics is the application of the scientific method to language. The facts of a language may change, but the method remains. Linguistics stresses the need for detached objectivity, for a rejection of authoritarianism, dogma, received opinion, and unexamined assumptions and for an avoidance of value judgments. The scientific linguist urges the need for adaptability and the elimination of preconceptions if they do not concur with the examined facts. Using inductive reasoning, he tries to collect impartial observations and to describe a language rather than prescribe rules for it. Terms like "good" and "bad," "right" and "wrong," "correct" and "incorrect" offend him when they are applied to language because their value judgments imply prejudiced attitudes. Likewise he rejects the imposition of Latin over English grammar and such arbitrary rules as the rigid distinction between "shall" and "will" and the prohibition against ending a sentence with a preposition. In these ways the current dictionaries show the influence of linguistics, and so does *Commonsense Grammar and Style*.

Linguists are concerned with much more than grammar, though it may be one of their most active fields. They study also phonology, morphology, syntax, the history of a language, dialect geography, usage, semantics, lexicography, even the relationship of our speech and our nervous system (neurolinguistics) and the psychology of language. For some, linguistics is a branch of philosophy.

Books attempting to popularize one of the new grammars and promote it as a "revolution in teaching" do not really get down to details of classroom practice. Certainly neither structural nor transformational-generative grammar is likely to do much to improve one's style in spoken or written standard English. Linguistics is a science, but writing is an art. What therefore the revolution in teaching is all about is an attempt through linguistics to help students think inductively rather than submit to received opinion about language. The main value of having secondary school and undergraduate college teachers aware of linguistics is to eradicate prejudices and rigid, dogmatic opinions about speech and speakers. The promoters of linguistics for English classes want to help students to become less passive and to begin asking questions about language instead of merely listening to answers by teachers. If all this sounds vague, it is because the professional linguist does not concern himself with application, and the teachers are still groping for effective ways of applying linguistic knowledge and methods to the classroom. In practice, unfortunately, some teachers trying to apply linguistics become just as doctrinaire as the old authoritarians.

Administrators may think that linguistics will be useful in remedial English, helping students with severe handicaps in their use of the language—those who are habituated to nonstandard speech or for whom English is a second language. This is not the purpose or the method of linguistics. Linguistics is useful in recording and analyzing hitherto unrecorded languages and in studying English regionalisms and dialects. In the latter capacity, linguistics may help a teacher and in turn his students to understand the dialect of inner city or ethnic minorities and so not embarrass them, ridicule them, or condescend to them. Furthermore, if a teacher understands the structure of such dialects, he may be able to recognize nonstandard embedded structures and so come to grips with the students' linguistic problems. Mainly, linguistics can help change people's attitudes. Because linguistics denies that there is any linguistic aristocracy, elitists who consider their usage intrinsically superior resent linguistics and drag anchor against it.

Teachers should not consider the language of the barrio or of inner city blacks as lazy, sloppy, or defective but should try to understand the ways in which it functions, so that they can then deal with the problems some students have in reading and speaking standard English. If the teacher and classmates have some grasp of the fairly rigid patterns of the speech of the ghetto and barrio, they can then work with it instead of dismissing it out of hand and causing the speaker embarrassment and resentment. Characteristic ghetto pronunciations, such as the omission of final consonant sounds ("roo' " for "root," "ben' " for "bend"), the omission of the -s ending for nouns ("two shoe"), the use of the masculine pronoun to refer to women as well as men, multiple negatives, and special constructions with tense and with the verb "to be" are not mere carelessness but regular and recognizable dialectical features.

Some scientific linguists go so far as to reject the idea of nonstandard English. Objecting to value judgments and finding moral attitudes about language "repulsive," they are interested in speech

333

communities without rating or evaluating them; their only concern is whether the members are intelligible to each other. Combining linguistics with sociology and politics, they maintain that standard English is a form of racism and that it is psychologically damaging and socially undesirable for schools and society to criticize the variant language of ethnic minorities, especially in black and Chicano inner city communities. Particularly, some socio-linguists object to the "deficit notion" of "black English" and to the "eradication movement" in schools to replace it with standard English. On the one hand, they are skeptical of the social and psychological desirability of assimilation, saying that it may cause crises of identity, that it is culturally chauvinistic, and that a pluralistic society is preferable. One professor calls for "benign neglect" of standard English for black students.

Furthermore, some phrases characteristic of ghettoese, notably "Where it's at," are in vogue to the extent that they have already become clichéd jargon. Sandra Haggerty, herself black, observes that "black rhetoric is one of the most commercial items on the market today. . . . Some black educators feel that it should be totally discarded in favor of proper English. Others think it should totally transplant proper English." Her own conclusion is that "Since most business is executed in the United States with the English language as the medium of communication, it is patently advantageous for us (and our children) to speak proper English. Ideally, we should be verbally ambidextrous."

This ambidexterity is what linguists call bi-dialecticalism—the idea that blacks would speak their own dialect at home but learn standard English when it is necessary for a career. James Sledd has called this a version of white supremacy, and some linguists have in fact urged the rest of the nation to accept black English rather than require or expect blacks to learn standard English.

Certainly there is no "proper" English, which implies a linguistic etiquette or even mortality. But one might also ask whether there is really a "black English." Certainly not all blacks reside in a ghetto and use ghettoese. A great many naturally use standard English, which is certainly not the monopoly of whites. The term "black English" unfortunately suggests a polarization in which standard English is "white English," which (if this were true) blacks might have some reason to resent. But language has no pigmentation. It would be both artificial and unworkable to require those blacks who do not speak it to learn the argot of the

334

ghetto as a hallmark of race. At the most, ghettoese is a recognizable dialect (just as there are various white dialects); but linguists have found a remarkable consistency in it, to the degree that some consider it a valid language that (in the words of black columnist William Raspberry, who disagrees with the idea) "should have equal acceptance with standard English in schools attended by slum children." Curiously, it is white linguists who have been promoting the "separate and equal" theory of "black English," whereas outspoken black writers have rejected it. Roy Wilkins complains that "it may not be long before the language of the ghetto becomes the first language and that of Shakespeare, Disraeli, Winston Churchill and Henry James the second language in skin-color-happy America." One might add the language of such eloquent black writers as Frederick Douglass, Richard Wright, Ralph Ellison, James Baldwin, Robert Hayden, and others, none of whom writes in ghettoese. Wilkins objects to the idea that if black students have trouble with standard English, they should not be held to its standards but should be allowed or even encouraged to use "black English" instead. He considers the general waiving of standards for blacks to be condescending and observes that, "Some old-fashioned black people may see this language bit as, well, 'racist.' They may feel it is a fancy way of saying their children are inferior and, perhaps, incapable of learning even the language of the American mainstream." Wilkins objects to the statement by Thomas Kochman, an Illinois linguist, that social mobility is an "improper motivation" and remarks that Kochman's motto is probably "Stay where you are!"

William Raspberry likewise rejects the "He-be-sick" school of linguists and quotes Dr. Kenneth B. Clark, New York psychologist and teacher, who is also black, and who told the Council for Basic Education, "I believe that the purpose of school is to teach the standards of a society in language, arithmetic, social studies. I do not believe that you can make the deviations and the variants the standards. . . . it serves no useful purpose to elevate subcultures to the point where they are given the same value as the standard. . . ." Dr. Clark also labels such permissiveness an "insidious, racist approach" and charges that the "He-be-sick linguists" are attempting to "institutionalize the very inequities and manifestations of inequities that a democratic society and a democratic education should attempt to neutralize." Clark concludes that while the ghetto norms may have some exotic interest, they "are not salable" in general society and that linguists who would present ghettoese to black students as the norm are dooming them to a separate and unequal station in life.

Certainly the issue, whether or not a racist one, is at least a racial one. No one is urging that the nonstandard speech or writing of whites should be accepted without question. As for Chicanos, Spanish is one of the world's great languages with a major literature, but clearly Chicanos need fluent English for the purely pragmatic aim of getting and holding jobs in an overwhelmingly English-speaking nation. Conversely, Butch Cassidy and the Sundance Kid found it an exasperating handicap to try to rob Bolivian banks when they could not speak Spanish and had to read or memorize their holdup dialogue.

Whether it is just or not, it remains a fact that social and economic mobility still require standard English; and to argue that the urban blacks should not be expected to learn it but should retain or acquire the language of the ghetto is to say in effect that they should stay in the slums. At least it is to say that they should limit themselves to jobs as laborers, since most of the professions require competence in standard written and spoken English. Thus the argument for "black English" is a curious reversion to the "Uncle Tom" argument of Booker T. Washington in his Atlanta Exposition Address (1895) to the black to "Cast down your bucket where you are," not aspire above the level of a laborer, and be content with an inferior lot. W. E. B. DuBois eloquently attacked this position and stressed the need for education to provide opportunity for blacks.

Thus, notes William Raspberry, when Dr. Joan C. Baratz of the Education Study Center attempted to give texts in nonstandard English to slow readers among black students attending Catholic schools in Washington, D.C., the parents wanted no part of the program and found it offensive, complaining that their children were being used for dubious experiments.

"Black English" is not so very different in grammar from standard English. The dialect differs in the omission of the word "is," in special uses of the verb "to be," in multiple negatives, in plurals, and in some special vocabulary. The main difference is in pronunciation, which can be so far from printed English as to pose a major obstacle to reading and spelling; the written word has little connection with the sounds the inner city black hears and speaks. If he says "Wha'," "Whe' da'," "de'," "ten'," "muvvah," and so forth, he is not likely to connect them with the printed "What," "Where is that," "there," "tend," and "mother." If "word" and "were" sound the same to him, he cannot read "word," when for him it has no *d*. He does not understand the *t* in "let's" or the *d* in "cold," and so he may be unable to read words that do not correspond to the sounds of his speech. His speech may be perfectly comprehensible to his family and friends, and it may be linguistically valid, but it handicaps him severely.

One should not object to black pronunciation anymore than to a Bostonian's speaking of "Ameriker," to a resident of Baltimore, Maryland's saying that he lives in "Balamer, Mairlun," to a Texas politician's addressing his "fellow Murcans," or to a Brooklyn or Appalachian accent. None of us pronounces words precisely as they are spelled. In *Our Southern Highlanders* Horace Kephart tells of a Kentucky mountain man who objected to the dialect in the fiction of John Fox, Jr.: " 'Why, that feller *don't know how to spell!*' Gravely I explained that dialect must be spelled as it is pronounced, so far as possible, or the life and savor of it would be lost. But it was of no use. My friend was outraged. 'That tale-teller then is jest makin' fun of the mountain people by misspellin' our talk. You educated folks don't spell your own words the way you say them.' . . . To the mountaineers themselves their speech is natural and proper. . . ." This is equally true of the blacks.

Yet it remains a fact that if a person cannot make the connection between his speech and written standard English, he is in trouble. The problem is not primarily in grammar but in literacy. For this, one might recommend extensive work in language labs equipped with individual taping and listening booths.

Perhaps bi-dialecticalism is a partial solution for some: one dialect at home and in the neighboring community and another for appropriate academic, social, and professional situations. This has been the situation for generations in England, where some speakers of thick regional dialects may use a more comprehensible general Londonese when occasion demands. In Senegal, the Ivory Coast, and officially French-speaking nations of Africa and the Caribbean, the educated blacks use one language at home and another for education, business, and literature. In Nigeria and other African and Asian nations where English is the official tongue, educated people are multilingual. The characters in Chinua Achebe's Nigerian novels speak variously in Ibo, pidgin, and English, depending upon the circumstances; and Achebe himself and his

337

fellow Nigerian writers of various tribes and indigenous languages all write in extremely effective English.

To some extent the linguistic dismissal of standard English is a version of encouraging people nowadays to "do their thing." John Hurt Fisher, editor of *Publications of the Modern Language Society of America (PMLA)*, has said that standard English is merely a class dialect, in effect a device of the Establishment caste system. But if those in legitimate rebellion against some abuses by the Establishment also oppose standard English, they are finding it guiltier by association than it is. For standard English is not just a class dialect; there are valid reasons why it is the language of educated people. Its conventions have become established because they specify the relationships of words in a sentence and help provide clear and accurate communication. It is possible to be eloquent in nonstandard speech (Huck Finn and the Joads are good literary examples), but nonstandard speech is also apt to be limited in vocabulary and to depend heavily on stock-response slang. Pidgin English, for instance, lacks the terminology and the resources to handle complex ideas. In a multilingual society like Nigeria, educated people are generally able to converse in pidgin and sometimes do so even among themselves; but for conversations of any subtlety, they switch either to standard English or to an indigenous Nigerian tongue. Likewise, the more extreme dialects of inner city idiom and of ethnic minorities are perfectly workable for the daily business of life but limit and handicap the speakers outside their own group and in more complex communication.

The "do your own thing" buffs not only accept minority dialects, which are legitimate within their limits, but reject the discipline of standard English even for those who use it naturally but sometimes faultily. They consider it autocratic and inhibiting to call attention in class to errors in spelling, grammar, punctuation, and diction. Rebelling against verbal discipline, they also ignore style. Yet self-discipline is not servitude but self-control; it can bring freedom from formlessness, flab, and indirection. We expect an actor or an athlete to keep in training; we would not tolerate imprecision in mathematics, medicine, or engineering; but we seem to think that accuracy in language is an unreasonable requirement that stifles self-expression. Which self are we going to express? A healthy self-expression does not come from slovenliness, and a slovenly style is no more to be commended than slovenly housing and sanitation.

338

Standard English is not and cannot be fixed. A living language must change; but while it is doing so, it needs clarity and coherence. The alternatives in language, as in politics, are not anarchy versus repression (that is the either-or fallacy) but slovenliness versus style. Critics of the semantic environment who find it polluted by the language of bureaucracy, politics, racism, academic criticism, scientism, advertising, and revolution are not purists but stylists.

The abstract jargon of academia and bureaucracy is as limited as ghettoese. Bureaucratic bumblery, vague but dogmatic political slogans, and high-level academic abstraction depending heavily upon the orthodox terminology of some -*ism* all impair communication. It may be that those English professors and linguists who practice academese while endorsing ghettoese are killing off communication from either end. The language of in- or out-groups is exclusive; standard English, on the other hand, is democratic. A person may have to learn it, and nothing prevents him from continuing to use the language of the tribe within the tribe, but broad communication is the reason why standard English is standard. Both jargon and argot, as badges of a self-conscious group, become a retreat or a weapon against those who do not belong. Arguments in jargon, whether ethnic or academic, automatically exclude an opposing view and force the dogma of the speaker, whereas in standard English any number can play. To restrict oneself linguistically to one group is to restrict oneself intellectually to that group, whereas the essence of democracy is communication, reason, and the removal of barriers around encased groups. If stripped of the jargon or the slogans behind which he hides, a person must use plain standard English and accordingly think through what he has to say.

Too many people do not. Instead of logic, they rely upon emotion, invective, labelling and react to sound rather than sense. Maynard Mack, in the May, 1971, issue of *PMLA,* urges that we "put away language that inflames and divides and cleave to language that reaches out and unites—'language designed,' to borrow a phrase of Ashley Montagu's that I particularly like, 'to put man *into touch* with his fellow man.' " This is the age of shouted slogans rather than rational debate, of consensus and groupthink rather than of the democratic and voluntary cooperation of individuals. Slogans almost invariably oversimplify and provoke an adrenal rather than a rational response. Style has been defined as the unmistakable voice of an individual.

Exercise 40: Here is your chance to play editor. In the following sentences, identify the errors and put the appropriate symbol in the blank: Frag = sentence fragment; Paral = faulty parallelism; Case = error in case; PA = error in pronoun-antecedent agreement; SV = error in subject-verb agreement; REF = faulty pronoun reference; DM = dangling modifier MisM = misplaced modifier; RO = run-on sentences; CS = comma splice; Dead = dead wood; Verb = faulty form of the verb; OK = no error.

1. Each homestead was located near cool spring water which provided them refrigeration as well as drink. . . . .
2. There are crayon stomped into the kitchen floor. . . . .
3. A parent does not want to drug their children to keep them quiet. . . . .
4. Mrs. Garth wants more women in politics and to run things. . . . . .
5. Blackstone was mastered by the time he was twenty-two. . . . .
6. The cat's in the cream jar painted blue. . . . .
7. Hounds has better noses than curs, but they won't tree a bear. . . . .
8. The men from North American weighed the cartons on our scales here before they took them away, and it came to about 270 pounds. . . . .
9. A cave on the far side of the peninsula in which were found two mummified bodies. . . . .
10. Iago counted upon Othello being gullible about Desdemona's alleged faithlessness. . . . .
11. The road-runner is a cuckoo called geococcyx californianus. . . . . .
12. Whenever Wile E. Coyote orders Acme equipment to catch the roadrunner, they always misfunction. . . . .
13. You may, while frozen, brush the crab cakes thoroughly with butter and heat in the oven. . . . .
14. When the white rhino advances, their mouth works like a lawn mower. . . . .
15. The white rhino being an exceptionally harmless and docile animal. . . . .
16. T. E. Lawrence is the last person who one would have thought to be a military genius. . . . .
17. Most soils in Africa is poor in humus and leaches easily. . . . .
18. Being a large bear, the ranger approached it cautiously. . . . .
19. Mother said we'd have dinner and to save something for Uncle Gus. . . . .
20. The new part of the Blue Ridge Parkway is graded, it's going to go through the Biltmore forest.

340

21. Sleeping in church, the verger nudged Lothar with a candle snuffer. . . . .
22. African family and kinship groups are much more tightly bound than those in Western society in some ways the Africans have more security. . . . .
23. The three weird sisters are the extra cook whom we think will spoil the broth. . . . .
24. It is impossible to tell what prehistoric man really looked like. Or what skin color he had. . . . .
25. The management of the laundry is not responsible for fastness of colors, jewelry left in clothing, or in case of fire. . . . .

Exercise 41: Using the symbols from the preceding exercise, identify the errors in the following sentences.

1. Undisturbed since 1636, vandals recently mutilated the tree. . . . .
2. In Thomas Wolfe's *Look Homeward, Angel,* he wrote about his youth in Asheville, North Carolina. . . . .
3. Lots of trees has been tossed and broken to kindling by the storm. . . . .
4. "Everybody should keep their promises," said the frog to the princess. . . . .
5. Being a large child, the teacher put Sam at the end of the row. . . . .
6. The story was clear, dramatic, and variety. . . . .
7. Dr. Bruse and me brought back a collection of African bronzes. . . . .
8. The British in Africa has tried to establish courts and written law. . . . .
9. Frederick Remington wrote about the West at some length. As well as his paintings. . . . .
10. The horned lark breeds from the Arctic to Texas, and they sometimes frequent golf courses. . . . .
11. How does Orphan Annie and Sandy see with blanked eyeballs? . . . .
12. Riding a mule down the trail, three big-horned sheep were seen. . . . .
13. Most people do not know about Timbuctu having an important university in the Middle Ages. . . . .
14. Hurricane Ysolde came as a surprise, the weather men were not prepared for it. . . . .
15. Was you ever in the Yukon when it was 65 degrees below zero? . . . .

16. Who was the Baltimore lady who wrote detective stories with a man's name? . . . .
17. Mrs. Browning dabbled in spiritualism, which caused some friction with her husband. . . . .
18. A rattleless rattlesnake? Never heard of, you say, but found in Isla Santa Catalina. . . . .
19. Baudelaire was an ardent admirer of Poe's stories and poems and even suggested that he was a reincarnation of him. . . . .
20. Passing along a corridor of the Louvre, the Mona Lisa suddenly was seen. . . . .
21. Is it true that bears is all left-handed? . . . .
22. The tropics do not have winter and summer instead they have a rainy and a dry season. . . . .
23. Being overweight, the doctor ordered me to diet and exercise . . . .
24. Did you ever ride a horse in striped pants? . . . .
25. Honey was obtained by keeping bees in a hollow black gum log. . . . .

Exercise 42: Identify the errors in the following sentences as Frag, Paral, Case, PA, SV, REF, DM, MisM, RO, CS, Dead, or Verb.

1. The archaeologists recovering the sunken Greek ship kept a rabbit in the darkroom to whom they fed watermelon rinds. . . . .
2. It don't pay to talk politics to some people. . . . .
3. To make his mash ferment more quickly, the blockader added Red Devil Lye, threw in a dead cat, using horse manure, but claimed these ingredients would distill out. . . . .
4. Romanticism was a revolt against neo-classicism, which they felt was too logical and unemotional. . . . .
5. Dr. and Mrs. Leakey found in Tanganyika a skull whom they thought was 600,000 years old but whom potassium-argon tests showed to be at least one and a half million years old. . . . .
6. There was a special training session for we new men going into the field. . . . .
7. While picking blackberries, a dozen chiggers bit me. . . . .
8. In France they admired Poe's work long before they did so in America. . . . .
9. Bongos needing room to run and breed. . . . .
10. Undiscovered for thousands of years, the rangers admired the petroglyphs. . . . .
11. The farmers protested at the railroad's refusal to ship goats. . . . .
12. Greta Garbo denied she was swimming topless-bikined in the Mediterranean in a letter reported by TV producer Bill Frye. . . . .

13. Baroque art degenerated into Rococo, which they often made vulgarly ornate. . . . .

14. Neuschwanstein looks like a medieval castle, actually it was built in the late nineteenth century. . . . .

15. All information will be sent to you free and without obligation by just completing and mailing this postage-free card. . . . .

16. After Melville escaped from the Typees. He was involved in a mutiny and was put in the calaboose at Tahiti. . . . .

17. Grandmother wore a scarf around her head and a long white shawl with tasseled ends that reached almost to the ground on her shoulders. . . . .

18. Euphemisms were so habitual in the late nineteenth century that they even spoke of roostering a rifle. . . . .

19. Following the mistake of Leo Africanus in the early sixteenth century, the river was widely believed to flow from east to west. . . . .

20. Audubon was another American painter who also wrote down his observations. Not necessarily about flora and fauna. . . . .

21. Alfred E. Neuman is the candidate whom pollsters say is most likely to win. . . . .

22. Approximately about ten percent of the voters favor Ringo Starr. . . . .

23. Even with a tight lid a bear can knock over a garbage can and open it. . . . .

24. The night was spent addressing letters to Bedouin chiefs. . . . .

25. "Each step of our road to join the British was possible most; of them easy."—Lawrence of Arabia . . . .

Exercise 43: Using the symbols from the preceding three exercises, identify the errors in the following sentences.

1. Isabella of Aragon gave her daughter an excellent education for a woman of that time. Even for a princess who later became Queen of England. . . . .

2. I'm phoning from a phone booth about to go on the highway. . . . .

3. In most parts of the United States, malaria have been eliminated. . . . .

4. When you were in Rhodesia, did you see the Kariba Dam's being built across the Zambesi? . . . .

5. In colonialism there is always two conflicting attitudes. . . . .

6. Harry is a writer, and it nearly breaks his heart. . . . .

7. The bear ripped off the top of the convertible, insatiable in its search for food; it found a pound of bacon inside. . . . .

8. Names and letters three feet high were painted on the parapet of a new bridge, using a can of spray paint.　. . . .

9. Because of Wolfe's unflattering portrait of Asheville, they resented him bitterly for a long time.　. . . .

10. It is such elections as these that makes one wonder whether some communities really have democracy.　. . . .

11. Many cars brake instead of using a lower gear going down mountains, which sometimes burns out or crystallizes the brakes.　. . . .

12. Will you pick up the other library books that's at home?　. . . .

13. A kola nut was broken and passed to Livingstone and I.　. . .

14. Although the LP record was expensive when it first came out, they are one of the few items that has gone down in price.　. . . .

15. When Segovia was playing at Miami University. One of his guitar strings broke.　. . . .

16. Oedipus's killing his father and marrying his mother are the theme of the play.　. . . .

17. We may meet the bear coming back from the garage.　. . . .

18. Marcello Maistroianni is the Italian actor who is the most popular today.　. . . .

19. I saw a Sinclair dinosaur driving through town.　. . . .

20. Even though Sinclair Lewis gave a scathing portrait of Sauk Center in *Main Street,* they renamed their main street Main Street.　. . . .

21. We watched TV riding through the desert.　. . . .

22. Because Thomas Paine was a Deist. He became anathema to the orthodox Americans whom he had helped win the Revolution.　. . . .

23. The short-winded young man or the awkward young woman do not usually take up long distance running.　. . . .

24. In Texas they drink warm deer blood.　. . . .

25. Melville wrote that Washington Irving imitated English writers too much, according to Melville we did not need an American Goldsmith.　. . . .

Exercise 44:　In the following sentences correct any grammatically inaccurate words and constructions.

1. Though William Faulkner is Mississippi's greatest writer, they often denounce his books there.

2. Drivers often blow their horns in tunnels, which disconcerts me.

3. You should not of lost your temper that way.

4. You don't got to talk too long on the phone.

5. Hickory nuts be very difficult to process.

6. This rain is the worstest toad-strangler I ever seen.
7. *The Grapes of Wrath* were made into an Academy Award-winning movie.
8. It looks like millionaires can marry just about whoever they wish.
9. How are the dishes scrubbing theirselves in the cartoon?
10. I could of swum the English Channel while you were taking your bath.
11. Them pizzas looks differently tonight.
12. Hold the lid when you shake the salad dressing, so's you won't spill none.
13. There were three ravens sat up in a tree.
14. There is not so great a gulf between the *B Minor Mass* and *The Gospel Boogie* as you may think there is.
15. "I get awfully sick of sitting down here at the end of the table and having whomever wants to interrupt in the middle of a sentence."—Senator Joseph McCarthy.
16. They probable packed a picnic lunch.
17. The movie condenses the story of Lawrence and the Arab revolt considerable.
18. *Like* as a conjunction is not confined nor particularly characteristic of any region.
19. Be sure and go get the rifle Paw took and threw in the branch.
20. If you think one wife can nag, you should imagine what three polygamous wives can do together in unison.
21. African tribesmen were and are not deprived.
22. Edward G. Robinson acted toughly in *Little Caesar*.
23. Though he was hurt fatal at the battle of Zutphen, Sir Philip Sydney asked that others be taken care of first.
24. It doesn't look as if this rain will never stop.
25. Legend says that when Shakespeare first went to London he held horses, he was an Elizabethan parking lot attendant.

Answers to Exercises

Exercise 1

1. scholarship
2. beauty
3. savagery
4. anger
5. futility
6. vandalism
7. hostility
8. curiosity
9. honesty
10. aggression
11. spectacle
12. femininity
13. expense
14. suppression
15. cowardice
16. courage
17. confusion
18. misery
19. euphony
20. illiteracy

Exercise 2

Replace unclear phrases with the following. Acceptable sentences are labelled correct.

1. the owners bought
2. Gun-running pays off handsomely.
3. We found it an exhausting procedure to try to inflate . . . .
4. and Carradine was killed
5. his family
6. Melville's observation of a great deal of man's inhumanity to man during his experiences at sea made him skeptical . . . .
7. Correct in an informal way. To be more precise, try, "The park visitor who pushed a bear . . . together did an incredibly foolish thing."
8. In New York, people . . . .
9. The sign at the park entrance says . . . .
10. he missed his horse and fell flat
11. The fact that many . . . made President Monroe . . . . or Because many . . . 1820's, President Monroe suggested . . . .
12. But in the late 1820's, the discovery of gold . . . made the squatters . . . .
13. defence, a ruling which
14. The Preamble to the Constitution does not say . . . ; that statement is in the Declaration of Independence.
15. kissed Miss Hepzibah and made her blush.
16. and not worry than to stay up . . . .
17. Correct
18. was guilty and was put to death.

346

19. In his later writings, Mark Twain . . . .
20. Puritans believed that most men would receive damnation because they deserved it.
21. The fact that . . . law . . . doesn't mean . . . .
22. vandalism, much of it committed by adults who
23. In *Pogo,* Walt Kelly . . . .
24. Ruth's pointing out . . . embarrassed him . . . .
25. Correct

Exercise 3

1. whom	6. he	11. he stirs his	16. their	21. its
2. their	7. his	12. that	17. its, its	22. they, they
3. its	8. you	13. were, their	18. their head	23. they
4. its	9. her	14. its	19. its, its	24. his
5. have they	10. him	15. their	20. their	25. it

Note: 5 and 25 cannot agree logically.

Exercise 4

1. he	5. he, his	9. who	13. Correct	17. their
2. that	6. his	10. his	14. that	18. you, your
3. he, his	7. him	11. who, that	15. its	19. that, his
4. him	8. who	12. his	16. his	20. it, its

Exercise 5

1. who	6. who	11. Arnold's	16. its	21. who's
2. brother's	7. him	12. we	17. me	22. instructor's
3. Correct	8. who	13. my	18. years	23. their
4. Who	9. Correct	14. We	19. galleys	24. Bream's, Ravel's
5. me	10. whom	15. Correct	20. I	25. volumes

Exercise 6

Any options are indicated; otherwise there is only one answer.

1. I (formal), me (informal)
2. me
3. whom (formal), who (informal)
4. whom (formal), who (informal)
5. who
6. who
7. whoever
8. whom (formal), who (informal)
9. he
10. who

11. whosoever
12. whom (formal), who (informal)
13. whoever
14. me
15. him
16. us
17. Whom (formal), Who (informal)
18. their
19. they whom (formal), they who (informal)
20. me
21. who
22. whoever
23. its
24. me
25. us

Exercise 7

1. was
2. are, you ought
3. could once do
4. could have gone
5. found
6. were brought
7. sitting
8. did
9. shaken
10. forbidden
11. had been born
12. asked, fetch
13. I have thought
14. drew
15. chewed
16. if he had taken
17. should have gone
18. take
19. that the bears did (or made)
20. played
21. were you fetched
22. brought up, wasn't
23. written
24. were thinking, should have brought
25. brought, fetched

Exercise 8

1. they were, it was
2. Melvin doesn't
3. it seems sin doesn't
4. people weren't
5. couple are
6. is
7. Are the grownups
8. bitten, they get
9. directions . . . are
10. there are, people . . . have
11. have
12. there are
13. crafts that have
14. accounts of mules were written
15. family are
16. Jefferson was
17. peacocks were
18. I let
19. twins look, they forget
20. people that understand

Exercise 9

1. Although the pickup truck was inelegant, we drove it to the country club.

348

2. Correct
3. The guests saw the five monkeys climbing up the lace curtains.
4. Correct.
5. When one is using vodka for medicinal purposes, he should take it in small doses.
6. In attaching the buttonholer to the machine, take care that you cover the throat plate with the metal shield indicated in diagram A and that you securely attach the buttonholer to the presser bar B by tightening firmly screw C.
7. You make bread by dissolving yeast in a warm liquid and then mixing the liquid with flour and subsequently kneading the mixture, letting it rise, and baking it.
8. When the grime was removed from Eliza Doolittle, she appeared as a pretty girl.
9. She built in the backyard a gazebo into which she retired to write long novels.
10. Correct
11. Cut "It is observed."
12. Correct
13. Correct
14. The elephants are attacked with spears until they succumb through loss of blood.
15. You number the guitar strings by counting the smallest as the first.
16. In combining the strokes of the thumb with those of the fingers, you should take care to play the notes one after the other from the lowest to the highest.
17. In using the third finger, you must lift the little finger from the face of the guitar.
18. When notes of the same pitch are joined by a slur, you play only the first note, prolonging its duration to make tied notes.
19. You make the Small Bar with two fingers on the middle strings.
20. The committee decided to declare a holiday.

Exercise 10

1. is	6. gets	11. are	16. have	21. have
2. are	7. cost	12. stands	17. has	22. improve
3. were	8. takes	13. is	18. is	23. has
4. are	9. are	14. is	19. were not	24. do
5. are	10. is	15. klong	20. take	25. has

Exercise 11

1. I
2. amount
3. who
4. swan
5. pink, puce, chartreuse, magenta, and olive drab
6. King Kong
7. To listen further
8. From Lagos to Nairobi
9. what people will think
10. About three o'clock
11. serpent
12. what makes you tick
13. To go to the theatre in New York
14. That Thoreau refused to pay his taxes
15. To see a unicorn eating a rose in one's garden
16. That the elephant's trunk weighs about 300 pounds
17. sings, they
18. we, coyness
19. Archangel
20. I

Exercise 12

1. Adj.: colored, Java, large, shaped, black, ten feet, five
   Adv.: brownish, irregularly
2. Adj.: white, Northern, bassanus, strong, goose-sized, sea, heavy, streamlined
   Adv.: snow, goose
3. Adj.: first, true, pear
4. Adj.: inebriate, debauchee, endless, summer, molten
5. Adj.: barred, emphatic, great, eight, accented, deep
   Adv.: less
6. Adj.: russet, clad, yon, high, eastward
7. Adj.: ear, horned, larger, apart, long-eared
   Adv.: more
8. Adj.: clad, deformed, smashed, doctor's
   Adv.: clumsily
9. Adj.: fat, fat, ten, no
   Adv.: behind, before, round
10. Adj.: some, white, their, white, hairy, white-backed
11. Adj.: last, goose-feather, turned, cold, open, wraggle-taggle
    Adv.: night, down so bravely, tonight
12. Adj.: olive-sided, dark, unbuttoned
    Adv.: down the front
13. Adj.: yonder, flowering, small
14. Adj.: your rubber-tired, your rubber-tired, buryin', of him
    Adv.: back
15. Adj.: blank, unrhymed, iambic

Exercise 13

1. we cats are, more high strung
2. further out
3. richer milk
4. kinds of wood
5. tactfully
6. more instantly
7. quickly
8. more easily
9. similar
10. afraid
11. worse
12. worry
13. more hurriedly, more behind
14. leisurely
15. few rations
16. those mice
17. supposed
18. manly
19. fewer
20. an eighty-five
21. those pots
22. unaccustomed
23. best left fielder
24. an active child
25. a holiday

Exercise 14

1. nearly
2. peaceably
3. previously
4. accurately
5. promptly
6. easily
7. softly
8. so well
9. differently
10. more cheaply
11. uninhibitedly
12. differently
13. goes well
14. suspiciously
15. carefully
16. correct
17. fairly
18. gently
19. correct
20. differently
21. quickly
22. lazily
23. quickly
24. gradually
25. slowly

Exercise 15

1. most exciting
2. most invisible
3. better
4. more successful
5. more, more
6. funniest
7. more
8. most, most, most sinister
9. quicker
10. fastest rising

Exercise 16

1. fewer
2. biased
3. those
4. wonderfully
5. greatest, comparatively
6. least
7. many
8. accustomed
9. most unique
10. more masterful
11. many
12. best
13. its
14. redder
15. many more
16. prejudiced
17. best
18. fewer and fewer
19. their
20. fewer

Exercise 17

1. armed
2. supposed
3. different
4. much
5. bad
6. directly
7. very ancient
8. badly
9. criminal
10. nearly
11. tough
12. very sincere
13. beautifully
14. much more difficult
15. evidently
16. first
17. suddenly
18. early
19. naturally
20. fledged
21. sad
22. as well as
23. an orphan
24. probably
25. anyway

Exercise 18

1. George Gundersdorf erected in the museum the statue which he carved.
2. Chadwick was impressed with the Galapagos tortoise weighing 500 pounds and over 100 years old.
3. Did you ever walk a dog when you were wearing a plaid bathrobe?
4. Because they were born in captivity, the zookeeper provides special care for animals neglected by their mothers.
5. When he was tending the desk, he read a volume of James Bond.
6. The Galapagos tortoises facing the threat of extinction were taken to the San Diego Zoo.
7. Sleeping in the rain, he developed a case of rheumatism.
8. Hunters prize the bongo of the African forest, with its horns 36 inches long.
9. The keeper gave their noon meal to the Bengal tigers, which were growling hungrily.
10. The hunter captured in Rhodesia the largest of all white rhinos.
11. The dowager frowned at the spaniel, whose floppy ears were cocked.
12. Sleeping in foxholes, soldiers sometimes get trench foot.
13. At the game farm, the New Yorkers admired Przewalski's wild horses, long thought to be extinct in their native habitat.
14. The zoo director explained that captive cheetahs become slack and indolent and lose interest in mating.
15. Grandmother used the fish we caught yesterday in making the chowder.
16. While I was walking by a stone fence, a snake struck at me and ignited the matches in my pocket.
17. The patrolman brought to the desk the wallet that he had found in the parking lot.
18. After you spend a night at Camp Muir, you make a side trip to the Cowlitz Glacier in the morning.
19. Dilsingham admired the white-patched ears and bicolored whiskers of the marbled cat, a rarity in zoological collections.

20. When the mother bear is provided with privacy, she can have her cubs undisturbed.

Exercise 19

1. Howard photographed the typical feeding posture of the gerenuk, breakfasting on acacia leaves at sunrise.
2. Though cheetahs formerly were thought to run from 70 to 90 miles an hour, zoologists now find that few can do more than 56 miles per hour.
3. An adult pair of Sclarer's Crowned Pigeons are shown with their month-old chick, hatched in the rain forest of New Guinea.
4. Since cheetahs have disappeared in Asia, maharajahs now import them from Africa to hunt.
5. Exploring the cave, they discovered a large deposit of bat guano.
6. We saw hardly any of the park bears.
7. The developer bought from a farmer the property that he later sold for an immense profit.
8. Walking along the beach, he encountered a strange footprint.
9. While I was going down to the cellar, a loose board made me stumble.
10. The landlord gave the old clothes that had been stored in the attic to a Salvation Army worker.
11. While I was climbing over a barbed-wire fence, the farmer's dog bit me.
12. As I was only a sophomore, my advisor would not let me take graduate courses.
13. "The Greenland Fisheries" should be sung with a strong rhythm with careful attention to the dramatic details of the story.
14. Driving over Bear Mountain Bridge, you can see the New York skyline.
15. Shelter cabins are found every seven or ten miles on the Appalachian Trail.
16. Stacy brought to the museum the snake which he later put on display.
17. Looking out of the bus window, they saw a mother moose and young grazing in the park meadow.
18. Exercising every day, he lost thirty pounds.
19. Lothar carefully photographed the flame azalea, a bright orange specimen.
20. Looking into the aquarium, they saw a bottle-nosed dolphin.

Exercise 20

1. when	4. what	7. if, which	10. if, how
2. that, that	5. because	8. as	11. whenever
3. which	6. after, where	9. that, why, when	12. if, whether, how

| 13. that | 15. who, till | 17. after | 19. because |
| 14. how | 16. who, when | 18. that, than | 20. until |

Exercise 21

Eliminate the following words.

1. from	6. to	11. of	16. to
2. up	7. Ever	12. into	17. up, over
3. of	8. of	13. that	18. of
4. from	9. up	14. more	19. over
5. as	10. of	15. of	20. about

Exercise 22

1. Change "without" to "unless."
2. Change "in" to "with."
3. Change "waiting on" to "waiting for."
4. Change "of" to "from."
5. Change "from" to "of."
6. Eliminate "for."
7. Change "consisted in" to "consisted of."
8. Change "be sure and" to "be sure to."
9. Change "belonged of" to "belonged to."
10. Change "without" to "unless."
11. Change "while" to "and."
12. Change "being as" to "because."
13. Change "but what" to "whether."
14. Change "too" to "also."
15. Change "or" to "nor."
16. Change "than" to "when."
17. Change "til" to "until."
18. Change "contrast of" to "contrast between."
19. Change "oblivious of" to "oblivious to."
20. Change "between" to "among."

Exercise 23

1. from	6. by	11. due to	16. whether
2. as	7. because of	12. as if	17. of, of
3. among	8. as	13. since	18. to
4. between	9. because of	14. and	19. as good as
5. on	10. nor	15. such as	20. by

Exercise 24

1. "It costs only . . . ."
2. Eliminate "nohow."
3. Eliminate "none."
4. "a considerable," "a memorable"
5. "was hardly"
6. "dont wear a coat"
7. "a sensitive actor," "that was worthy"
8. "find a person"
9. "could hardly"
10. "without reservations"
11. "could hold"
12. "took scarcely"
13. "a reasonable claim," "a likely candidate"
14. "was no"
15. "a sooty raven," "a cacaphonous caw," "an apple tree," "the mowed field"
16. "There is, according to literary scholars, no reliable evidence . . . ."
17. "scarcely different"
18. "had no cheese"
19. "wanted no more"
20. "did not buy"

Exercise 25

1. *1*   2. *3*   3. *1*   4. *2*   5. *3*   6. *1*   7. *2*   8. *1*   9. *2*   10. *2*

Exercise 26

Underline the following.
1. that Mighty Mouse would save the day.
2. When Dick Tracy was a prisoner of Mrs. Pruneface
3. Though the Mullins family have entered the affluent society
4. that the Green Hornet is back on the radio
5. what evil lurks in the heart of man
6. when the Human Torch was about to throw his forearm at the criminals.
7. that if Yogi Bear once more broke regulations, he would be sent to the St. Louis Zoo
8. as Thomas Wolfe described it
9. Before McChesney could stop him
10. after she took the elephant elixir

Exercise 27

Put a period or semicolon after the following.

1. painter	5. Correct	9. Arnold	13. court
2. Nukuheva	6. play	10. died	14. Correct
3. death	7. *Spheres* or death	11. East	15. 1925
4. painter	8. shots	12. Correct	16. Correct

Exercise 28

The following clauses need to be rewritten in this fashion.
1. The American Pronghorn is the only animal . . . .
2. Baby clouded leopards are not . . . .
3. Correct
4. The Detroit zoo is the most successful . . . .
5. This is a pursuit that also leads . . . .
6. Combine both clauses into one sentence.
7. Combine both clauses into one sentence.
8. Her father has . . . .
9. Fitsi fitsi is a kind of bush spirit.
10. The revenuers . . . streams until the horses would no longer drink . . . .
11. Combine both clauses into one sentence.
12. Tree kangaroos and birds of paradise dwell . . . .
13. Deposits of bat guano fifty feet deep are located . . . .
14. Combine both clauses into one sentence.
15. Zoos are establishing . . . .
16. Combine both halves into one sentence.
17. Combine the last two clauses into one sentence.
18. Combine both halves into one sentence.
19. White rhinos require . . . .
20. Combine both clauses into one sentence.

Exercise 29

1. and puttering
2. family to accompany
3. as being good looking and speaking a smooth dialect
4. are all the perfect, earthy characteristics of a daughter on the farm
5. much less put it to work
6. that truth is an absolute
7. have used and will use

356

8. a lack of occupation, vagrancy to civil duty, and failure to attend church
9. is unfair, dangerous, and threatening to
10. and that we should
11. and that he was addicted
12. vicious and terrifying and attack
13. and climb
14. your health, your nerves, and your sanity
15. but rather shows how art
16. but often leap
17. or her own sheets returned
18. and to helping
19. and tells how
20. fiction and his use of moral allegory

Exercise 30

1. Hallowe'en, Uncle, Mom, Pop, witches'
2. geology, history, American literature, and chicken plucking
3. Correct
4. West
5. high school
6. Aztec religion
7. baptized, Mormon
8. dictionary, Webster's New Collegiate Dictionary
9. This is correct because the author does not capitalize the title.
10. French
11. Norwegian
12. schools, freshmen
13. national parks
14. Baptist, Sermon on the Mount
15. Sam Browne
16. Winterset, art critic, bearded
17. Siamese
18. Wu, Kitty
19. novels, Forgot
20. Eighth, Second, mistresses, father, country

Exercise 31

1. Grangerfords'
2. Adams' or Adams's, Chartres
3. Ambersons
4. Indians

5. Cummings' or Cummings's
6. Correct
7. ones
8. Captains
9. Correct
10. Thurber's Dogs
11. There's
12. can't
13. Correct
14. Evans' or Evans's
15. Cozzens' or Cozzens's
16. Negroes'
17. Soldiers Three
18. James' or James's
19. Talks
20. members
21. Fairbanks, Jr.'s
22. monster's, its
23. Correct
24. There's
25. 'er, '33
26. writer's
27. Funk and Wagnall's
28. Doctor's, Feathers, Holmes' or Holmes's, Howells' or Howells's
29. murders
30. Correct

Exercise 32

1. Those cattle are . . . .
2. You ought not to . . . .
3. Are you finished washing your hands?
4. lost
5. are the same as those woodchucks, which
6. You must have . . . .
7. out of
8. Why are the buzzards waiting here?
9. I resemble my brother William—Bill, we call him.
10. There is . . . .
11. I haven't . . . .
12. Those sudden stops . . . .
13. has some
14. I have already seen . . . .
15. Those are not moth holes; they are bullet holes.
16. The Cherokees, who were the most civilized Indians, would hardly write sentences like this one.
17. There were seventeen cattle frozen solid in a stack.
18. Skinks are different from skunks.
19. Does the campground have any vacancies?
20. You should not have lost . . . .
21. has run
22. so I
23. I never knew . . . .

24. We have the same color of hair but different colored eyeballs.
25. as if he must have run

Exercise 33

1. children, husband,
2. locality engage
3. Remove all commas.
4. Remove all commas.
5. Remove comma after "wife"; add comma after "said," "not,"; remove comma after "today," "be"; end sentence with quotation marks.
6. thought-provoking   women gave
7. Remove all commas.
8. escape,   them with hatchets
9. operate,
10. "Courage," he said, and pointed toward the land,
    "This mounting wave will roll us shoreward soon."
11. Remove all commas.
12. "I did not like the strange behavior of the begonia trees," said the matriarch.
13. Birunga gorilla sanctuary?
14. , "chick, chick, quack, quack, oink, oink."
15. hollers, "Yes, you're a Lemac now."
16. I do not, like your aunt, want to look at all the shops in Fleagle Street.
17. Shang, the Holy Hekkador
18. doctor's, Mother,
19. said, "Mama loves morals and Papa loves cats."
20. Orphan Annie says, "Gee Willikens, Sandy"; and Little Annie Rooney says, "Gloriosky, Zero."
21. William Walton, one of England's leading contemporary composers, wrote the musical scores for Laurence Olivier's films of *Henry V, Hamlet,* and *Richard III.*
22. *The Invisible Man*   singing, "Here we go gathering nuts in May"?
23. Remove comma.
24. Remove all commas.
25. Errol Flynn ran Basil Rathbone through in *Captain Blood* and *The Adventures of Robin Hood;* Tyrone Power ran Rathbone through in *The Mark of Zorro;* a French peasant stabbed him in *A Tale of Two Cities;* Richmond's troops killed him in *The Tower of London;* Gary Cooper threw him into a tiger pit in *The Adventures of Marco Polo;* and Joan Fontaine crushed him with a suit of armor in *Frenchman's Creek;* but he escaped the Frankenstein monster and killed the hound of the Baskervilles.

Exercise 34

Mark Twain cut the following words.
a helpless object of any insult or wrong that might be offered. So eagerly
did every one now act, that nothing was said. . . . in the pile, and the
end of all was anxiously expected. . . . absolutely . . . life . . . means
of . . . . physical . . . . the level of . . . . and branches . . . proper . . .
or one . . . it might not be . . . . As often happened, however, on these
occasions . . . began to wave their forked tongues in a proximity to the
fact of the victim that . . . in a dozen directions. . . . presumptuous . . .
irritated . . . . as soon as she had performed this bold act . . . crowd of
attentive . . . . dearest sister . . . herself unnerved so much as to be incapable of exertion . . . .

Exercise 35

1. The purpose of *Babbitt* is to expose vulgarity and intolerance.
2. The test of the poet is his simple and precise use of words.
3. Conwell's first statement is that a man can attain wealth at home.
4. George Stevens budgeted $15 million for *The Greatest Story Ever Told*.
5. When a person entertains today, it seems that he must have liquor on hand.
6. Today, many countries have a democratic government.
7. Many years ago, Richard III was killed at Bosworth.
8. We hope that we can finish ahead of schedule.
9. If people try to express views other than what the group feels to be right, they are disliked and ostracized.
10. This is symbolic of how God's love crushes evil.
11. Without pausing to shower, he went directly to the pool.
12. Wolfert stood apart, observing the scene with an indifferent eye.
13. The Batman descended from the roof by a rope.
14. The chestnut blight killed all the mature trees.
15. Ebenezer secretly thought that the weather seemed ominous.
16. Margarine is cheaper than butter and costs less.
17. The hardened jargonaut never uses one word when he can use several.
18. Don't feed bears in the park.
19. I wonder how I got along without the electric coffee pot.
20. If one drinks moonshine whiskey, he may become blind or even die if the whiskey was not made in a copper rather than a lead still.

Exercise 36

1. I consider Billy Budd to be a tragic hero.
2. Deists believed that God was a prime mover.
3. Not everyone approved of placing the defeated territory under military rule.
4. Life seems to be more pessimistic today than on the frontier.
5. A battered house greets the family the day they move in.
6. One of the main characters in *The Octopus* is Buck Annixter.
7. Gatsby does nearly everything with the idea of winning Daisy again.
8. Huck is from a family quite dissimilar to Tom's.
9. There has been tyranny in nearly all governments.
10. In *Walden,* Thoreau wrote the results of living close to nature.
11. I came back to my room and was shocked by all the bags, clothes, and boxes that were piled high in it.
12. Since the beginning of time, man has been afraid of crocodiles.
13. Godzilla felt the same towards King Kong.
14. Freezing has become one of the most popular methods of food preservation.
15. Every time I walk past Bessey Hall, I imagine ten students . . . .
16. Because of her very nature, society must fight individuality.
17. Another unjustifiable rule prohibits freshmen from having cars on campus.
18. For the past three weeks we have been studying anatomy.
19. That's too good an idea.
20. Sharecroppers did not own the farms they were working and living on.
21. We met a fellow named Gonzales Pilkington O'Toole the Fourth.
22. The accused did not reply when the prosecutor asked him to confess.
23. The doctors never saw that small a child.
24. This is a good type of thump keg because it takes the impurities out of the whiskey.
25. That is the way Americans would like to be today.

Exercise 37

alligator, optimist, St. Bernards, turbans, monogamy, plays, Medea, Apocalypse, Gregorian, anointed, quaked, spirit, earthquake, message, perished, Appalachians, vicious, virtue, waste, embrace, rugged, interpreted, gambling, supernatural, Platonic, hobgoblin, simmering, boil, alliteration, compact, rambling, Monitor, conclusion

Exercise 38

1. Emancipation
2. sophisticated
3. tainted
4. allegories
5. notorious
6. eke
7. disillusioned
8. attributed
9. Wrath, deprived
10. sheer, revealing
11. accepting
12. exorbitant
13. circumscribed
14. Arians
15. dropouts, delinquency
16. prostration
17. aura
18. customers
19. bookkeeping
20. plague
21. Puritans, heresy
22. villain, marital
23. formerly
24. next door
25. infiltrated

Exercise 39

Underline the following.
1. in trying
2. in, the story
3. of
4. took and
5. for
6. she
7. it
8. a-, of
9. of a
10. it, in her hand
11. here
12. of
13. coming
14. There wasn't, hidden
15. whole
16. there, up around
17. of, secretly up
18. of, in it
19. went and
20. unknown, put

Exercise 40

1. OK
2. SV, Verb
3. PA
4. Paral
5. REF
6. DM
7. SV
8. REF
9. Frag
10. Case
11. OK
12. PA
13. MisM
14. PA
15. Frag
16. Case
17. SV
18. MisM
19. Paral
20. CS
21. MisM
22. RO
23. Case
24. Frag
25. Paral

Exercise 41

1. MisM
2. Ref
3. SV
4. PA
5. DM
6. Paral
7. Case
8. SV
9. Frag
10. PA
11. SV
12. DM
13. Case
14. CS
15. SV
16. DM
17. Ref
18. Frag
19. Ref
20. DM
21. SV
22. RO
23. DM
24. MisM
25. DM

Exercise 42

1. MisM
2. SV
3. Paral
4. REF
5. PA
6. Case
7. DM
8. REF
9. Frag
10. MisM
11. Dead
12. MisM
13. REF
14. CS
15. DM

16. Frag	18. REF	20. Frag	22. Dead	24. DM
17. MisM	19. DM	21. Case	23. MisM	25. PA

Exercise 43

1. Frag	6. REF	11. REF	16. SV	21. MisM
2. DM	7. MisM	12. SV	17. DM	22. Frag
3. SV	8. DM	13. Case	18. Dead	23. SV
4. Case	9. REF	14. RA	19. MisM	24. REF
5. SV	10. SV	15. Frag	20. REF	25. CS

Exercise 44

1. Though William Faulkner is Mississippi's greatest writer, his books are often denounced there.
2. It disconcerts me when drivers often blow their horns in tunnels.
3. You should not have lost your temper that way.
4. You don't have to talk too long on the phone.
5. Hickory nuts are very difficult to process.
6. This rain is the worst toad-strangler I ever saw.
7. *The Grapes of Wrath* was made into an Academy Award-winning movie.
8. It looks as if millionaires can marry just about whomever ["anyone" is preferable] they wish.
9. How are the dishes scrubbing themselves in the cartoon?
10. I could have swum the English Channel while you were taking your bath.
11. Those pizzas look different tonight.
12. Hold the lid when you shake the salad dressing, so you won't spill any.
13. Three ravens sat in a tree.
14. There is not so great a gulf between the *B Minor Mass* and "The Gospel Boogie" as you may think.
15. "I get awfully sick of sitting down here at the end of the table and having whoever wants to, interrupt in the middle of a sentence."
16. They probably packed a picnic lunch.
17. The movie considerably condenses the story of Lawrence and the Arab revolt.
18. "Like" as a conjunction is not confined to nor particularly characteristic of any region.
19. Be sure to get the rifle Paw threw in the branch.
20. If you think one wife can nag, you should imagine what three polygamous wives can do in unison.

21. African tribesmen were not and are not deprived.
22. Edward G. Robinson actéd tough in *Little Caesar*.
23. Though he was hurt fatally at the battle of Zutphen, Sir Philip Sydney asked that others be taken care of first.
24. It doesn't look as if this rain will ever stop.
25. Legend says that when Shakespeare first went to London, he held horses. He was an Elizabethan parking lot attendant.

Notes

1. COMMON SENSE AND THE PSYCHOLOGY OF GRAMMAR

1. ALAN JAY LERNER, *My Fair Lady; A Musical Play in Two Acts,* adaptation and lyrics by [the author], music by Frederick Loewe (Coward-McCann, Inc., New York, 1957), p. 28.
2. CHARLES M. SCHULZ, "Peanuts," February 28, 1964.
3. HENRY NASH SMITH, *Virgin Land: The American West as Symbol and Myth* (Harvard University Press, Cambridge, 1956), p. 98.
4. EDGAR RICE BURROUGHS, *Tarzan, Lord of the Jungle* (Ballantine Books, New York, 1963), pp. 66–67.
5. HORTON COOPER, *The State,* North Carolina, March 21, 1959, p. 10.
6. JOHN STEINBECK, *In Dubious Battle* (Modern Library, New York, 1936), p. 142.
7. BERGEN EVANS, "Grammar for Today," *The Atlantic Monthly,* CCV, March, 1960.
8. LIONEL TRILLING, "Introduction," *The Adventures of Huckleberry Finn* (Rinehart Editions, New York, 1948), p. xvi.
9. T. E. LAWRENCE, *Seven Pillars of Wisdom* (London, 1955), p. 63.
10. HARPER LEE, *To Kill a Mockingbird* (J. B. Lippincott Company, Philadelphia, 1960), p. 118.
11. ALAN JAY LERNER, *op. cit.,* p. 78.
12. JAMES THURBER, *The Years with Ross* (Little, Brown and Company, Boston, 1959), p. 271.
13. LOUIS B. SALOMON, *Bulletin of the American Association of University Professors,* Vol. 38, Autumn, 1952, p. 449.
14. ERNEST HEMINGWAY, *The Fifth Column and the First Forty-nine Stories* (Charles Scribner's Sons, New York, 1938), p. 368.

3. YOU NAME IT

1. *Esquire,* Vol. 60, December, 1963, p. 16.
2. GEORGE ORWELL, *1984* (Harcourt, Brace and Company, New York, 1949), p. 310.
3. ROBERT E. MORSBERGER, *How to Improve Your Verbal Skills* (Thomas Y. Crowell Company, New York, 1962), pp. 98–100.
4. *Vogue,* Vol. 141, June, 1963, p. 18.

5. RODERICK PEATTIE, ed., *The Great Smokies and the Blue Ridge* (The Vanguard Press, New York, 1953), pp. 147–148.

4. THE PERPLEXING PRONOUN

1. EDGAR RICE BURROUGHS, *Tarzan, Lord of the Jungle* (Ballatine Books, New York, 1963), p. 85.
2. JOHN P. MARQUAND, *Sincerely, Willis Wayde* (Little, Brown and Company, Boston, 1955), p. 36.

5. WHO'S ON FIRST? RIDDLES OF REFERENCE

1. AP News, December 7, 1962.
2. JAMES THURBER, *Let Your Mind Alone!* (Harper & Brothers, New York, 1937), p. 172.
3. TRUMAN CAPOTE, *Breakfast at Tiffany's* (Random House, New York, 1958), p. 35.
4. JOSEPH HELLER, *Catch-22* (Simon and Schuster, New York, 1962), p. 56.
5. JAMES THURBER, *The Years with Ross* (Little, Brown and Company, Boston, 1959), p. 242.
6. ALFRED DUGGAN, *The Cunning of the Dove* (Pantheon Books, Inc., New York, 1960), p. 41.
7. *Life,* Vol. LIV, January 18, 1963, p. 4.

6. PRONOUN-ANTECEDENT AGREEMENT

1. "Outrage over the Death Business," *Life,* Vol. LV, September 20, 1963, p. 98 B.
2. RAYMOND SCHUESSLER, "Blowing Rock, N.C.," *AAA Motor News,* September, 1962, p. 33.
3. *Mad,* June, 1963, p. 44.
4. TRUMAN CAPOTE, *Breakfast at Tiffany's* (Random House, New York, 1958), p. 20.
5. CHARLES M. SCHULZ, "Peanuts," February 28, 1963.
6. JAMES THURBER, *Thurber Country* (Simon and Schuster, New York, 1953), p. 60.
7. JOHN P. MARQUAND, *Sincerely, Willis Wayde* (Little, Brown and Company, Boston, 1955), p. 282.
8. NORMAN MAILER, "Ten Thousand Words a Minute," *Esquire,* Vol. LIX, February, 1963, p. 120.

9. NORMAN MAILER, "Norman Mailer Versus Nine Writers," *Esquire,* Vol. LX, July, 1963, p. 65.

10. *Time,* Vol. LXXX, December 2, 1962, p. 22.

11. *U.S. News and World Report,* Vol. 55, September 2, 1963, p. 54.

12. "Pork Barrel," *Life,* Vol. LV, August 16, 1963, p. 26.

13. EDMUND WILSON, *Patriotic Gore* (Oxford University Press, New York, 1962), p. x.

14. ANN BRIDGE, *The Portuguese Escape* (The Macmillan Company, New York, 1958), p. 215.

15. MARGARET BOURKE-WHITE, *Portrait of Myself* (Simon and Schuster, New York, 1963), p. 158.

16. *Mad,* June, 1963, p. 45.

17. NORMAN MAILER, "The Big Bite," *Esquire,* Vol. LX, December, 1963, p. 24.

18. *Op. cit.,* November, 1963, p. 30.

19. JOSEPH HENRY STEELE, *Ingrid Bergman: An Intimate Portrait* (David McKay Company, New York, 1960), p. 39.

7. CASE AND ITS CURIOSITIES

1. JOHN P. MARQUAND, *Sincerely, Willis Wayde* (Little, Brown and Company, Boston, 1955), p. 34.

2. JAMES THURBER, *A Thurber Carnival* (Samuel French, Inc., New York, 1962), p. 10.

3. JAMES THURBER, *The Owl in the Attic* (Harper & Brothers, New York, 1931), p. 97.

4. JOSEPH HELLER, *Catch-22* (Simon and Schuster, New York, 1961), p. 61.

5. NORMAN MAILER, "The Big Bite," *Esquire,* Vol. LX, November, 1963, pp. 28–30.

6. JAMES THURBER, *Credos and Curios* (Harper & Row, New York, 1962), p. 34.

7. *Life,* Vol. LIV, January 18, 1963, p. 13.

8. GLENDON SWARTHOUT, *The Cadillac Cowboys* (Random House, New York, 1964), p. 65.

9. TRUMAN CAPOTE, *Breakfast at Tiffany's* (Random House, New York, 1958).

10. JOSEPH HELLER, *op. cit.,* pp. 210–211.

11. JOHN OSBORNE, *Luther* (Criterion Books, New York, 1962), p. 38.

8. THE WAYWARD VERB

1. WILLIAM T. POLK, "Folkways and Folklore," *The North Carolina Guide* (ed., Blackwell P. Robinson, University of North Carolina Press, Chapel Hill, 1955), p. 13.

2. JAMES THURBER, *The Owl in the Attic* (Harper & Brothers, New York, 1931), pp. 132–133.
3. ANN CHAMBERLIN, "Two Cheers for the National Geographic," *Esquire*, Vol. LX, December, 1963, p. 300.
4. C. VANN WOODWARD, *The Strange Case of Jim Crow* (Galaxy edition, Oxford University Press, New York, 1957), p. 8.
5. RODERICK PEATTIE, ed., *The Great Smokies and the Blue Ridge* (The Vanguard Press, New York, 1953), pp. 109–110.

9. "IS YOU IS OR IS YOU AIN'T MY BABY?"

1. RODERICK PEATTIE, ed., *The Great Smokies and the Blue Ridge* (The Vanguard Press, New York, 1953), pp. 109–110.
2. HORTON COOPER, *The State*, North Carolina, March 21, 1959, p. 10.
3. ELIZABETH SKEGGS BOWMAN, *Land of High Horizons* (Southern Publishers, Inc., Kingsport, Tenn., 1948), p. 158.
4. *Ibid.*, p. 41.
5. *Ibid.*, p. 53.
6. JOSEPH HELLER, *Catch-22* (Simon and Schuster, New York, 1961), p. 170.
7. ERNEST HEMINGWAY, *To Have and Have Not* (Charles Scribner's Sons, New York, 1937), p. 193.
8. JOHN OSBORNE, *Luther* (Criterion Books, New York, 1962), p. 75.
9. *Ibid.*, p. 89.

10. ADJECTIVES AND ADVERBS

1. RODERICK PEATTIE, ed., *The Great Smokies and the Blue Ridge* (The Vanguard Press, New York, 1953), p. 148.
2. JOSEPH HELLER, *Catch-22* (Simon and Schuster, New York, 1961), p. 212.
3. *Vogue Pattern Book*, Vol. 38, February–March, 1964, p. 91.
4. LILLIAN ROSS, *Portrait of Hemingway* (Simon and Schuster, New York, 1962), p. 37.
5. NORMAN MAILER, "Norman Mailer Versus Nine Writers," *Esquire*, Vol. LX, July, 1963, p. 63.
6. ROBERT ADAMS, "Books," *Esquire*, Vol. LX, July, 1963, p. 63.
7. RUTH KRAUSS, *Open House for Butterflies* (Harper & Brothers, New York, 1960).
8. JOSEPH HELLER, *op. cit.*, p. 258.
9. *Ibid.*, pp. 259–260.
10. JAMES THURBER, *The Years with Ross* (Little, Brown and Company, Boston, 1959), pp. 129–130.

11. JAMES THURBER, *Credos and Curios* (Harper & Row, New York, 1962), p. 92.

11. AMBIGUOUS MODIFIERS

1. JAMES THURBER, *Let Your Mind Alone!* (Harper & Brothers, New York, 1937), p. 185.
2. ANTHONY NUTTING, *Lawrence of Arabia* (Signet Books, New York, 1962), p. 15.
3. MARK RASCOVITCH, *The Flight of the Dancing Bear* (Popular Library, New York, 1962), p. 15.
4. IRVING STONE, *Clarence Darrow for the Defense* (Bantam Books, New York, 1958), p. 6.
5. STEWART HOLBROOK, *The Age of the Moguls* (Doubleday & Company, Inc., New York, 1953), p. 192.
6. NORMAN MAILER, "The Big Bite," *Esquire,* Vol. LX, November, 1963, p. 28.
7. "Pork Barrel," *Life,* Vol. LV, August 16, 1963, p. 56.
8. *Lansing State Journal,* January 9, 1964, p. A 10.
9. JOSEPH HELLER, *Catch-22* (Simon and Schuster, New York, 1961), p. 154.
10. IRVING WALLACE, *Fabulous Showman: The Life and Times of P. T. Barnum* (Alfred A. Knopf, Inc., New York, 1959), p. 167
11. PETER BART, "The Money Managers," *Esquire,* Vol. LX, December, 1963, p. 204.

12. CONFUSED CONJUNCTIONS AND PREPOSITIONAL PUZZLES

1. LILLIAN ROSS, *Portrait of Hemingway* (Simon and Schuster, New York, 1962), p. 60.
2. TYRONE GUTHRIE, "So Long as the Theater Can Do Miracles," *The New York Times Magazine,* April 28, 1963, p. 34.
3. MAURICE DRUON, *The Lion and the Lily,* trans. Humphrey Hare (Charles Scribner's Sons, New York, 1961), p. 137.
4. LAWRENCE DURRELL, *White Eagles over Serbia* (Criterion Books, New York, 1958), p. 94.
5. WILSON FOLLETT, "Sabotage in Springfield," *The Atlantic,* January, 1962, p. 75.
6. LILLIAN ROSS, *op. cit.,* p. 31.
7. EDMUND WILSON, *Patriotic Gore* (Oxford University Press, New York, 1962), p. xxviii.
8. GEORGE BERNARD SHAW, *Pygmalion* (Penguin Books, Inc., Baltimore), p. 206.

9. JOSEPH HELLER, *Catch-22* (Simon and Schuster, New York, 1961) , p. 70.
10. *Ibid.*, p. 219.
11. NORMAN MAILER, *The Naked and the Dead* (The Modern Library, New York, 1961) , p. 270.
12. LILLIAN ROSS, *op. cit.*, p. 24.

13. NEGATIVE NEGATIVES

1. GEORGE ORWELL, *1984* (Harcourt, Brace and Company, 1949) , p. 305.

14. SENTENCE STRUCTURE

1. *Time,* Vol. LXXX, December 21, 1962, p. 22.
2. RUTH KRAUSS, *Open House for Butterflies* (Harper & Row, New York, 1960) .
3. *Ibid.*
4. EDGAR RICE BURROUGHS, *The Son of Tarzan* (Ballantine Books, New York, 1963) , p. 124.
5. JAMES THURBER, *The Owl in the Attic* (Harper & Brothers, New York, 1931) , p. 106.
6. EDGAR RICE BURROUGHS, *Tarzan of the Apes* (Ballantine Books, New York, 1963) , p. 138.
7. EDGAR RICE BURROUGHS, *Tarzan, Lord of the Jungle* (Ballantine Books, New York, 1963) , p. 60.
8. JAMES BALDWIN, *The Fire Next Time* (Dial Press, New York, 1963) , p. 44.

15. THE PITFALLS AND PRATFALLS OF PUNCTUATION

1. JAMES THURBER, *The Years with Ross* (Little, Brown and Company, Boston, 1959) , p. 267.
2. EDGAR RICE BURROUGHS, *Tarzan of the Apes* (Ballantine Books, New York, 1963) , p. 176.
3. HENRY JAMES, *The American* (New York Edition, Charles Scribner's Sons, New York, 1907) .
4. *Ibid.*
5. *Ibid.*
6. JAMES THURBER, *Thurber's Dogs* (Simon and Schuster, New York, 1955) , p. 8.
7. *Ibid.*, p. 29.
8. *Ibid.*, p. 80.
9. *Ibid.*, p. 263.
10. *Ibid.*, p. 275.

17. GRAMMAR IS NOT ENOUGH

1. ALAN JAY LERNER, *My Fair Lady, A Musical Play in Two Acts,* adaptation and lyrics [by the author], music by Frederick Loewe (Coward-McCann, Inc., New York, 1957), p. 108.
2. KENNETH ROBERTS, *I Wanted to Write* (Doubleday & Company, Inc., New York, 1949), p. 400–402.
3. HERBERT BREAN, "The Man of More than 400 Mysteries," *Life,* Vol. LII, April 27, 1962, p. 22.
4. *The New York Times,* December 14, 1942, p. 16.
5. HAROLD WENTWORTH and STUART BERG FLEXNER, *Dictionary of American Slang* (Thomas Y. Crowell Company, New York, 1960), pp. xi–xii.
6. RICHARD CHASE, *Herman Melville: A Critical Study* (The Macmillan Company, New York, 1949), p. 270.
7. ROBERT BOLT, *A Man for All Seasons* (Random House, New York, 1962), p. 116.
8. JAMES D. KOERNER, *The Miseducation of American Teachers* (Houghton Mifflin Company, Boston, 1963), pp. 283–294.
9. NORMAN MAILER, "Norman Mailer Versus Nine Writers," *Esquire,* Vol. LX, July, 1963, p. 105.
10. "The Jargon that Jars," *Time,* Vol. LXXXII, November 8, 1963, p. 57.
11. DWIGHT MACDONALD, "Films," *Esquire,* Vol. LX, November, 1963, p. 70.
12. GEORGE REAVEY, ed. and trans., *The Poetry of Boris Pasternak* (G. P. Putnam's Sons, New York, 1959), p. 70.
13. EDGAR RICE BURROUGHS, *Tarzan of the Apes* (Ballantine Books, New York, 1963), p. 114.
14. EDITH WHARTON, *A Backward Glance* (Appleton-Century-Croft, Inc., New York, 1934), pp. 242–243.
15. RICHARD WILSON, "Friend of the Family," *Star Science Fiction Stories No. 2* (Ballantine Books, New York, 1962), p. 182.
16. JOHN STEINBECK, *The Grapes of Wrath* (The Viking Press, New York, 1939), p. 32.
17. JAMES THURBER, *The Years with Ross* (Little, Brown and Company, Boston, 1959), p. 6.
18. *The Readers Digest,* Vol. LXXXIII, August, 1963, p. 113.
19. STUART FLEXNER, "The Man Who Corrupted California," *Esquire,* Vol. LXI, March, 1964, p. 83.
20. *Ibid.,* p. 152.
21. *Ibid.,* p. 153.

18. THE FUTURE OF GRAMMAR

1. *Atlas,* Vol. III, June, 1962, p. 482.
2. ARTHUR MILLER, *Show,* Vol. IV, January, 1964, p. 98.

Index